THE **PRINCETON** REVIEW

STUDENT ACCESS
GUIDE TO

AMERICA'S
TOP 100
INTERNSHIPS

1994 Edition

THE **PRINCETON** REVIEW

STUDENT ACCESS
GUIDE TO

AMERICA'S
TOP 100
INTERNSHIPS

**Mark Oldman and
Samer Hamadeh**

Villard Books New York 1993

1994 Edition

ISBN 0-679-74960-8

Manufactured in the United States of America on paper using partially recycled fibers

9 8 7 6 5 4 3 2

First Edition

ACKNOWLEDGMENTS

We send our appreciation to the following invaluable players:

Elizabeth "Lix" Oldman, executive editor extraordinaire, whose incisive and good-humored editing gave this book a quantum leap in quality. Her literary talent and generous accessibility ("fax me in St. Maarten") are extraordinary.

Galen Smith, design consultant "on call," responsible for designing the entire interior and part of the cover of this book. He imbued the book with his unrivalled brand of retro art.

John Katzman, a man of derring-do, approachablity, and shrewdness. His encouragement and good counsel are greatly appreciated.

Jay Rosner, Meher Khandalavala, Joshua Shaub, Andrew Dunn, and Amy Harrington, who made sure everything came out just right.

The Stanford Career Planning & Placement Center, whose warm-spirited assistance helped launch this book. Mary Lynne Schoenbeck generously afforded us access to the Odyssey database and provided us with cross-continental updates and advice when we were in New York. Catherine Paul was also an indispensable consultant on internships.

Above and Beyond the Call of Duty: David Danelski, Shellye McKinney, Mandy "Harvard Escort" Silber, Jeff "Rocking 'n' Resourceful" Rabhan, Hussam Hamadeh, Bassim Hamadeh, Shauna Jackson, Andrew C. Humphrey, Jr., Lisa Herzog, Green Library Reference Desk, Billy Sagwala, Sido alu Salim, Frankie

"Postmaster" Simmons, Timur "Lebanese Taverna" Colak, Professor John Rick, Dr. William Thomas, Joshlyn D. Sand, Dixon Robin, Andrew Frutkin, Karen Mullet, Paige Wilson, Myles "Shredding Waves" Kim, Lyon J. Zabsky, Ben & Jerry's of Columbus Ave., Elizabeth Derksen, Fresno State School of Agricultural Sciences and Technology, Gloria Walker, Hamilton "Guardian of 75th Street," Adnan Issa, Enuga Reddy, Tom Bettag, Scott Widmeyer, Robert J. Saldich, Nascar C. Philips, Allison Stewart.

A final thank you goes to our families, whose support and inspiration made creating this book immeasurably happier.

TABLE OF CONTENTS

INTRODUCTION

ARE INTERNSHIPS
WORTH IT?

The practice of gaining supervised practical experience is nothing new. In fact, it's ancient: According to research by Lynda Wertheim, manager of legal assistants at White & Case, references to apprenticeships are found as early as 2100 B.C. in the Code of Hammurabi. The idea was obviously a good one, because apprenticeships—today known as internships—are virtually a rite of passage for students of the nineties. Indeed, the National Society for Experiential Education estimates that at least one third of all college students complete internships before graduation.

Why are internships so popular? For one, they are becoming increasingly valuable in these uneven economic times. In the May 17, 1993, issue of *Fortune*, campus-recruiting expert Maury Hanigan said that "internships are becoming more and more important. That's where students learn the soft skills of working in a corporate environment." A few months later, *New York Times* reporter Douglas Martin attested to the value of internships by writing a series of articles tracking the internship experiences of five students. Countless other publications have recognized the importance of internships, including *Town and Country* ("the right internship can be the key to a great job"); *The Wall Street Journal* ("[internships offer] the chance to take on real responsibilities while rubbing shoulders with seasoned professionals"); and *US Black Engineer* ("[f]rom chief executive officers to entry-level employees, everyone in the engineering industry . . . agrees that internships are definitely the key to corporate America's door").

The ability of an internship to launch a career should not be underestimated. A slew of America's movers and shakers owe their start to internships. George Stephanopoulos, the wunderkind adviser to President Clinton, began his governmental service interning for an Ohio congresswoman. Enuga Reddy, United Nations intern '48, went on to become an assistant secretary general of the United Nations. "I've been with the United Nations over thirty-five years," Reddy told us. "It all started when I was an intern in the Department of Public Information." And Henry Muller, editorial director of Time Inc., got the ball rolling when he interned at *Time*'s sister-magazine *Life*. "[The internship] hooked me on big-time reporting," Muller told us. "It solidified my interest in journalism."

But internships do more than advance a preconceived interest. With a little luck, internships may spark a new interest, a new career direction. Just ask Nigel Hamilton, an acclaimed biographer who's writing a trilogy on the Kennedys. Decades ago, Hamilton served an internship with *The Washington Post*, an experience he recently described in *The New York Times*: "It was a heady experience. I was an eighteen-year-old kid, and I was in the heart of things in Washington. My interest in American politics and particularly the Kennedys began there." Like Hamilton, students who have yet to settle on a career should use internships as a means of determining what really fires their passion. Try advertising or public relations. Sample publishing one summer, banking the next. Take off fall semester and work for "Late Show with David Letterman" or the U.S. Supreme Court or Surfrider. All too often students enter a profession without first exposing themselves to a range of experiences. Young adulthood is the time to explore your choices, not limit them.

America's Top 100 Internships is the ideal place to begin such exploration. We've spent months and months of full-time research hand-selecting programs that are uncommonly rewarding as well as accessible to young people from a wide variety of backgrounds. But we've just supplied a detailed map; students must make the trip, and do so with enthusiasm. That means being fired up in the application process, whether writing a forceful cover letter or impressing an interviewer with your sincerity and motivation. And it also means making the most of your time as an intern. Time and time again, we saw that the happiest interns are the ones unafraid to ask questions and to ask for more assignments. Rocky Balboa called it the "eye of the tiger" and Milton deemed it "th' inconquerable will"—but passion and persistence can take you a long way in an internship. This is not to say interns should forget that they are young, temporary observers; rather, they should strive to strike a delicate balance between diplomacy and fearless initiative.

It's an exciting world out there. We hope *America's Top 100 Internships* provides a bridge to that excitement.

THE BEGINNING

It was November of our junior year in college, and we wanted internships. Not just *any* internship—great internships, ones with challenging projects and prestige and excitement; ones that would give us a foot in the door and a leg up on the competition. But where to start? Some friends had "heard" of good internships, but this information was vague and often inaccurate. The only relevant books were internship directories—which proved to be bulky sourcebooks offering nothing more than statistics on a random sampling of internships. The campus career center had a bank of information, but there was no way of knowing which were truly the exceptional internships. We were lost in the dark night of internship uncertainty.

After we graduated, we knew there had to be a better way. A book on internships was the answer, but it had to be impossibly thorough—the kind of book we would have killed for during our internship search. In addition to determining the best of well-known internships, we wanted to ferret out the gems that have never been listed in any career center or book. We wanted the book to be written from a student's point of view, not some stodgy author who knows nothing about the needs and desires of young people. We wanted the book to be enjoyable, something that would teach as well as tickle the reader. We wanted *America's Top 100 Internships*.

WHAT IS A TOP INTERNSHIP?

Every internship was compared against other internships in its industry and was scrutinized according to a specific set of criteria. First of all, we asked, does the program offer interns substantive, challenging work? Do interns embark on meaningful projects or do they end up babysitting the photocopy machine? Certain industries (e.g., film, television, music, sports management) have internships that invariably require a lot of busywork. In these cases, we paid particular attention to whether the organization made extraordinary efforts to expose interns to life on the job—were there occasions when interns could break away from their daily routines and experience the action behind the scenes? Were permanent employees receptive to mentoring interns? Another factor was quality of life. We gauged the level of happiness and comfort interns experienced on the job. Do they have adequate working space, or are they shoehorned into sub-standard cubbyholes? Do they have their own phones, typewriters, and computers? Is there a decent cafeteria? A gym? A company store? Are there structured social events? How prevalent are freebies—do interns come away with free CDs or magazines or comic books or running shoes? And do seminars exist where interns gain insights about the organization and the industry?

We also scrutinized the organization itself, asking whether it was prestigious and/or known as an innovator in its field. Were respected newspapers and magazines deeming it a leading light or a sinking ship? Does it have "resumé radiance"—that is, would future employers be impressed by its inclusion on your resumé. Did it have the ring of a Lincoln Center, Supreme Court, or *The Washington Post*? Was it an industry pioneer like Apple, Robert Mondavi Winery, or Walt Disney Studios? In addition to considering prestige, we asked whether the organization was, for lack of a better word, "sexy." Would it enable you to do things young people dream about: make potato chips (Frito-Lay), work with comic books (Marvel Comics), live in paradise (National Tropical Botanical Gardens), or assist fashion models (Elite Model Management)?

Finally, we took into account whether an internship offered a salary or stipend, and how the pay (or lack thereof) compared with that of similar internships. We also factored in an organization's propensity to offer permanent employment to its interns. Organizations like Intel and Hewlett-Packard, each pushing a rehire rate of 70 percent, came through with flying colors in this respect.

In the final analysis, a top internship did not need to satisfy each factor optimally. A powerful showing in one or two areas could offset a deficiency in another. For example, the uncommon responsibility and prestige associated with *The Wall Street Journal* internship more than offset the program's lack of extracurricular programming. Similarly, the sexiness and potential for connections accompanying a "Late Show with David Letterman" internship compensated for its sky-high busywork. But "sexiness" was certainly no cure-all. For instance, we had high hopes for FAO Schwartz. Who wouldn't want to work amid its world-class toy collection? But after interviewing past interns and the program coordinator, we determined that the program didn't assign enough interesting and challenging work. Harley Davidson was another great name, but we discovered that its internship is primarily for children of employees.

OUR INITIAL RESEARCH

It was clear from the outset that we needed to consider as many internship programs as possible. We started in Stanford University's Green Library, where we tracked down virtually every article ever written on internships. Leaving no stone unturned, we scanned everything from *The New York Times*, *Time*, and *Variety* to *Physics Today*, *American Forests*, and *Technical Communications*. We then moved on to Stanford's Career Planning and Placement Center, whose generous counselors gave us access to Odyssey, an exclusive database listing the vital statistics of over 2,000 internships. Sifting through countless Odyssey files, we picked out the most promising programs.

After discovering dozens of potentially excellent internships this way, we then set out to seek opinions from college and graduate students. We put together a detailed questionnaire, which asked students about the internships they did and the terrific ones they knew of. To distribute the questionnaire, we visited campuses across the country, surveying hundreds of students from Stanford (undergraduate, law, and business schools), Berkeley, NYU, Princeton, Columbia, and Harvard. At every school, we set up a table in front of the student center and bribed students into completing the surveys with freshly baked chocolate-chip cookies.

Finally, we decided it was valuable to pick the brains of those who make internships their livelihood—career-center experts. During our campus visits, we conducted personal interviews with career-center representatives at Stanford, Princeton, and Harvard. Over the phone, we interviewed career experts at the Massachusetts Institute of Technology, the Fashion Institute of Technology, Stanford Law School, UC Davis, and NYU's Tisch School of the Arts.

All of these efforts yielded an initial list of approximately 800 internships. And this was the easy part!

After grouping each of the initial 800 internships by vocational discipline—law, journalism, banking, and so on—we were able to scrutinize similar programs and weed out those clearly inferior to the rest. We contacted the remaining 500 or so organizations, requesting information (brochures, bulletins, videotapes) on their internship, and where possible, interviewing the intern coordinator. From there, we were able to whittle the list to 150 internship programs.

With 150 top-notch programs slated for full consideration, we began a massive campaign to interview past and current interns from each internship. As it turned out, talking to these interns yielded recommendations about other wonderful internships in a particular field. Like a chain reaction, some interviews led to the discovery of two or three additional internships. For example, an intern at National Public Radio recommended Rykodisc Records, whose interns then alerted us to internships at BMG and Sony Music Entertainment (both of which made the final cut). Throughout our eight-month research phase, these "insider referrals" raised the number of programs to which we gave full consideration to approximately 200.

INTERN INTERVIEWS

Intern interviews were crucial in narrowing down the final group of internships. To ensure a variety of perspectives, we sought interns to interview from (1) an organization's intern coordinator, who faxed us a list of names and phone numbers of past and current interns, (2) the interns themselves, who referred us to other internship participants and alumni, and (3) our original campus surveys, which asked students for a phone number to enable us to contact them at this stage.

We assured all interviewees that their names would be kept confidential, so as to encourage their candor and impartiality. We wanted to hear the good and the bad about an internship without having interns worry about brownnosing a boss or burning a bridge. Even so, there were a few instances when we encountered interns who seemed inordinately biased, despite the fact they would be quoted anonymously. In these rare cases when we sensed disingenuously strong praise or criticism, we disregarded the interview and moved on to another intern.

For each of the 200 organizations, we interviewed at least four, typically six, and sometimes as many as ten past or current interns. Virtually all of the interviews were by phone, and they ranged in duration from twenty to ninety minutes, with an average call lasting about thirty minutes. At this point, we were working fourteen-hour days, calling interns around the clock and across the world, from Topeka to Tokyo. We were fast becoming New York Telephone's favorite customers.

Each intern was interviewed according to our fifteen-question intern questionnaire. The questions were designed to elicit responses about an internship's workload, quality of life, extracurricular activities, travel opportunities, office environment, and other important criteria. Details mattered—we wanted to know everything from how interns dressed to what they ate in the company cafeteria. After several interviews, a composite picture of an internship's offerings began to crystallize. Dozens of internships were clearly not up to snuff and were taken out of the running; others showed promise and made it to the next round.

COORDINATOR INTERVIEWS

If an internship seemed a potential winner, we then conducted a phone interview with its coordinator. Using our seventeen-question coordinator questionnaire, we sought information about a program's selectivity, eligibility requirements, application procedure, notable alumni, potential for permanent employment, and so forth. We also asked the coordinator to comment on the traits that help interns get the most out of their experience.

In several cases, we augmented the telephone interviews with on-site visits. As we were based in New York City, it was convenient to visit the coordinators at local organizations such as the United Nations, *Rolling Stone*, Elite Modeling, and Sotheby's. But we also made pilgrimages to Washington, D.C., where we checked out the White House, State Department, FBI, and CIA; and Seattle, where we spent two days behind the scenes at Boeing. Other times, we interviewed a program representative at a mutually convenient location. For example, we met Robert Saldich, CEO of Raychem, when he was visiting New York for a conference with Wall Street analysts.

THE END

After thousands of surveys, hundreds of interviews, several on-site visits, and countless midnight deliberations, we assembled the final list of top internships. In the end, we strove to provide a diversity of vocational fields, locations, and office environments. At the same time, we went to great lengths to ensure that every "top" internship left its participants with an extraordinary experience, one worthy of inclusion in this book. But no "top 100" list is ever complete, and we encourage readers to write to us with suggestions, criticisms, and salutations.

Mark Oldman & Samer Hamadeh
c/o America's Top 100 Internships
Ansonia Station
P.O. Box 463
New York, NY 10023

SELECTIVITY

Selectivity measures the approximate applicant pool and number of interns accepted for an internship session. When an organization offers its internship more than once during the year (e.g., summer, fall, and spring), the numbers given represent an average of all sessions. When an organization accepts interns any time (e.g., Elite Model Management Corporation), the numbers given represent the yearly total of applicants and interns.

Selectivity (i.e., percentage of interns accepted) is rated as follows:

- 🔍🔍🔍🔍🔍   0 - <5%
- 🔍🔍🔍🔍   5 - <10%
- 🔍🔍🔍   10 - <20%
- 🔍🔍   20 - <30%
- 🔍   30%

COMPENSATION

Compensation measures the payment interns receive, as well as any housing, transportation, and food allowances.

Compensation is rated as follows:

- $ $ $ $ $ >$500 per week for undergraduates
- $ $ $ $ $400-499
- $ $ $ $300-399
- $ $ $200-299
- $ None-$199

QUALITY OF LIFE

Quality of life measures the level of happiness and comfort interns experience working for the organization. Evaluates seminars, social activities, company culture, workspaces, cafeterias, fitness centers, freebies, etc. The examples in the box represent only a partial list of such factors; consult each entry's Description for further elaboration.

Quality of Life is rated as follows:

- ⚘ ⚘ ⚘ ⚘ ⚘   Paradise City — as good as it gets
- ⚘ ⚘ ⚘ ⚘   Excellent — extra efforts made to ensure interns' happiness
- ⚘ ⚘ ⚘   Fine — a standard and satisfying working environment
- ⚘ ⚘   Okay — no special opportunities for interns
- ⚘   Poor — no "Top 100" internship has a poor quality of life

LOCATION(S)

Location lists cities and/or states in which the internship is located.

FIELD

Field defines the primary vocational discipline associated with the organization. See Index for other related areas.

DURATION

Duration provides time parameters for the internship. All programs are full-time unless otherwise noted.

PRE-REQS

Pre-Reqs describes major requirements of the internship, including class level, minimum GPA, coursework, etc. Always consult Selection for details.

Class-levels are defined as follows:

"College grads of any age" — anyone with a college degree

"Grad students" — J.D., M.A., M.D., M.S., M.B.A., and Ph.D. candidates, unless otherwise noted

"Recent grads" — college grads out of school no more than 3 years, unless otherwise noted

"Undergrads" — college freshmen to seniors; "college seniors" refers to students who have completed their junior year by the start of the internship; "college juniors" refers to students who have completed their sophomore year by the start of the internship; "college sophomores" refers to students who have completed their freshman year by the start of the internship; "college freshmen" refers to students currently in their freshman year, except where incoming freshman are eligible (e.g., Frontier Nursing Service)

"High school students" — refers to students enrolled in high school during the internship

DEADLINE(S)

Deadline(s) states when to submit application materials. Because some deadlines change without notice, always confirm the dates with the organization's internship coordinator. Always consult Application Procedure for details.

THE BUSYWORK METER

The Busywork Meter measures the menial tasks (stuffing envelopes, photocopying, filing, clipping newspapers, etc.) that offer little educational reward and are typically performed for one's supervisor or other employees. The intern and coordinator interviews provided an approximation of the daily amount of busywork expected of an intern.

FOR MORE INFORMATION

The addresses given were approved by the internship coordinators as the best place to send in materials and ensure their proper review. **Moreover, if no phone number is given, the company does not wish prospective applicants to call with inquiries**.

THE **PRINCETON** REVIEW

STUDENT ACCESS
GUIDE TO

AMERICA'S
TOP 100
INTERNSHIPS

1994 Edition

ABBOTT LABORATORIES

SELECTIVITY	🔍🔍🔍🔍🔍
Approximate applicant pool: 3,500 Interns accepted: 150–200	

COMPENSATION	$ $ $ $ $
$340–$625/wk for undergrads; $460–$1,000/wk for grad students; round-trip travel; housing	

QUALITY OF LIFE	⬆⬆⬆⬆⬆
Free college housing; Well-organized seminars Lake Michigan cruise; Sunset picnics	

LOCATION(S)

Lake County, IL

FIELD

Health care products

DURATION

12 weeks
Summer

PRE-REQS

College juniors and seniors, grad students

DEADLINE(S)

March 31

On a cold, dark morning in June 1984, ten scientists hopped on a jet in Chicago and flew east to Washington, D.C. Their mission was urgent: retrieve a sample of one of the world's deadliest killers, the human immunodeficiency virus (or HIV). Black satchel in hand, they returned to their research site—Abbott Laboratories. Within eight months, they had developed the first U.S. Food and Drug Administration–licensed test to screen blood for HIV.

Founded in 1888 by an industrious doctor named Wallace Abbott, Abbott Laboratories has a long history of making pioneering medical advances—the anesthetic Pentothal in 1936, commercial penicillin production in 1941, and an automated diagnostic test for prostate cancer in 1991, to name a few. Abbott also leads the U.S. market in sales of infant formula and is a worldwide leader in sales of diagnostics. With almost 50,000 employees in 44 countries and sales of nearly $8 billion annually, Abbott produces thousands of health care products, everything from Similac infant formula, Clear Eyes eye drops, and Selsun Blue dandruff shampoo to IV equipment, antibiotics, and anesthetics.

DESCRIPTION

Since the late 1980s, Abbott Laboratories' Summer Internship Program has offered students positions at its Abbott Park, Illinois, corporate offices in all six of its operating divisions: Hospital Products, Diagnostic Products, Pharmaceutical Products, Ross Products, Chemical and Agricultural Products, and Abbott International. Within these divisions, students work in the following areas: Research and Development (R&D), Manufacturing, Computing and Information Science, Finance and Accounting, Human Resources, Engineering, and Sales, Marketing, and Telemarketing. Most of the interns are undergraduates; about twenty-five annually are M.B.A., M.S., M.D., and Ph.D. candidates.

Abbott's pharmaceutical research targets cardiovascular, neurological, infectious, and viral diseases. An intern assigned to the Pharmaceutical Products' Research and Discovery group "made scale-ups of key intermediate compounds for specific [cardiovascular] drugs." Availability of intermediates means that the company's scientists can speed up steps on the road to making potential medicines. "The methods I used were proprietary," she said. "I utilized column chromatography, HPLC [high-pressure liquid chromatography], and all kinds of reactions, from reductions to oxidations." Returning the following summer, she completed research in neuroscience medicine, an area of the company that investigates treatments of such afflictions as epilepsy, depression, and schizophrenia. "This time," she said, "I had even more responsibility and helped to develop new synthetic methods for compounds that [Abbott is] trying to turn into effective drugs."

Marketing interns are often exposed to the company's drug-making endeavors. One intern, for example, was assigned to the Pharmaceutical Products division to prepare marketing materials for a new application of Hytrin, a drug used to treat hypertension. Pending FDA approval, Hytrin is being developed as a treatment for male prostate enlargement. "I created materials that would allow us to hit markets as soon as the approval came through. This included training packets for our salespeople and a brochure that emphasized the cost benefits of using Hytrin instead of other options such as surgery or taking [competitor Merck's drug] Proscar."

Abbott also hires interns to help further the company's commitment to energy conservation and the environment. For example, an Engineering intern assigned to Environmental Services and Energy Management worked on Green Lights, a voluntary EPA project that investigates forms of energy saving. "I completed lighting surveys for all of Abbott's northern Illinois buildings and entered the data into a computer program to determine ways we could reduce our power requirements. We're now in the process of installing lower-watt bulbs . . . and replacing switches with 'occupancy sensors,' which turn off or on depending on the motion in the room."

Several interns are also in charge of accounting tasks. An Accounting intern in Corporate Risk Management prepared numbers for financial reports and analyzed Abbott's insurance policies in addition to completing an "interna-

tional asset valuation report." "I sent out a 30-page questionnaire to each of our international sites," he said. "[The questionnaire] asked for various information that later allowed me to determine the value of each site's assets." Abbott needs the values, he explained, in order to adequately insure its assets.

In the middle of the summer, interns gather for two important events—a business workshop and a conference titled "About Abbott Labs." At the former meeting, interns discuss the appropriate dresswear for corporate positions and learn how to work in teams. At the latter gathering, CEO Duane Burnham talks about "how to succeed by being an information sponge." By conferring frequently with managers, Burnham explains, interns can make a significant contribution. Because intern projects are challenging, Burnham's advice does not go unused. "[S]ome days you'll make no progress," said an intern, "but discussing the problem with your manager will encourage you to keep at it."

Located at Abbott Park, 40 miles north of downtown Chicago, the 480-acre Abbott Laboratories headquarters consists of more than thirty modern, redbrick buildings that offer pleasing views of on-site lakes, streams, and long stretches of grass; about five miles northeast is the company's smaller North Chicago manufacturing site. Interns work from their own desks in a friendly, cooperative environment imbued with a sense of team effort. "No matter what department you visit, you'll see that the employees enjoy being there," explained an intern. "I'm not saying that everyone is best friends, but coworkers help each other, including interns. Everyone strives toward the common goal of creating world-renowned products."

A model of corporate generosity, Abbott houses interns free of charge at nearby Lake Forest College. Though fully furnished, the single-occupancy dorm rooms have no kitchens or bathrooms. But not to worry—each floor contains a large centralized bathroom and a communal kitchen. As in college housing, RAs are designated to watch over the

> A model of corporate generosity, Abbott houses interns free of charge at nearby Lake Forest College.

dorms' occupants. Located ten miles southeast of Abbott Park, Lake Forest is just a few blocks from Lake Michigan, where interns may congregate for sunset picnics or Jet Skiing. During the week, a free shuttle service transports interns from their dorms to work and back again. Interns have a variety of prime resources available to them. For food, interns are welcome to purchase a campus meal plan or eat at Abbott's cafeterias, which offer enough food choices to please vegetarians, nonfat dieters, and meat eaters alike. For exercise, interns can use the mile-and-a-half track, which circles the Abbott Park facilities, as well as Lake Forest College's swimming pool, basketball courts, and tennis courts, all of which are within walking distance from the dorms. Interns may also buy a membership to one of Abbott's two fitness centers. For a one-time $50 fee, interns are allowed to use weights, StairMasters, treadmills, and Lifecycles and take advantage of specialized exercise instruction, a percent body-fat test, a blood pressure reading, and a cholesterol measurement.

The internship program offers an assortment of organized social activities, from a welcome orientation to a farewell social. Early on, the schedule calls for an intern picnic followed by an evening at Ravinia, a local outdoor theater, to listen to the Chicago Symphony Orchestra. Most memorable, perhaps, is the night of the Lake Michigan cruise, on which interns enjoy a catered dinner under tents and then board a yacht for dancing and socializing. "It's a time when you can turn off work mode and get to know the other interns on a personal level," said an intern.

Pay at Abbott depends on experience and placement within the company. Salaries range from $8.35 an hour for juniors in accounting and marketing to $15 an hour for engineering students at Abbott a second summer, to as much as $25 an hour for graduate students.

SELECTION

 Applicants should be seniors by the start of the internship, though younger applicants shouldn't be discouraged—a few "exceptional" juniors are accepted every year. Majors eligible include: science (chemistry, biology, biochemistry, pharmacology, physiology, etc.), engineering (including chemical, industrial, electrical, mechanical, and environmental), computer science, business, finance, ac-

counting, and marketing. The brochure lists "a strong academic record" and "outstanding communication skills" as essential requirements.

APPLICATION PROCEDURE

 The deadline is March 31. Abbott recruits nationwide at selected campuses. Those whose campuses aren't visited by Abbott may send a resumé that includes their GPA and a cover letter indicating their field of interest, particularly if it is one outside the areas listed in the internship brochure. All resumés are organized by discipline in a resumé book which is reviewed by managers, who grant phone interviews and/or on-site visits to top candidates.

OVERVIEW

 In early May, students already selected to be summer interns at Abbott Laboratories receive a Handbook in the mail. Containing a calendar of events, a map of northern Illinois, a description of dorm rooms, suggestions for what to bring, and reference phone numbers, the Handbook prepares interns for the vast range of experiences to be had at Abbott. By the end of the summer, a mixture of projects, lab tours, and workshops will have provided interns with a whirlwind education in health care—an industry whose products help prolong as well as save lives.

FOR MORE INFORMATION . . .

■ Abbott Laboratories
Manager of College Relations
Department 39K, Building AP6D
One Abbott Park Road
Abbott Park, IL 60064
(708) 937-7000

**ACADEMY OF
TELEVISION
ARTS & SCIENCES**

®© ATAS/NATAS

The Emmy Awards—Television's highest honor— and all of the glamor, prestige, sequined dresses, and preening thespians that go with it. What more could the millions of viewers who watch these annual pageants sponsored by the Academy of Television Arts and Sciences want?

Scratch the surface, and you'll find a bit of hard science behind the glitter. Hard science, you ask? Consider the derivation of the word *Emmy*. No, it wasn't named to be the Oscar's feminine equivalent. "Emmy," or "Immy" as it was initially called, is named after the now-obsolete image-orthicon television camera. Also take the Emmy statue itself—the sexy hood ornament–like figurine embracing what could be a hairball. Despite what hairball aficionados say, the statuette is actually a muse grasping a sphere of electrons.

Trivia aside, the Academy does important things. With a professional membership of nearly 7,000, it is the largest organization representing the U.S. television industry. The Academy maintains a television research library and an outdoor Hall of Fame Plaza ornamented with busts and life-size statues of inductees like Lucille Ball, Walter Cronkite, Carol Burnett, and Johnny Carson. In addition to distributing the Emmys, the Academy holds filmmaking contests, sponsors industry-wide meetings, publishes *Emmy* magazine, and manages the ATAS/UCLA Television Archives, which preserves thousands of television programs for future generations to enjoy.

DESCRIPTION

Back in 1968, the once-autonomous Los Angeles chapter of New York's National Academy of Television Arts and Sciences first made available to local students a nonpaying internship program. Ten years later, after

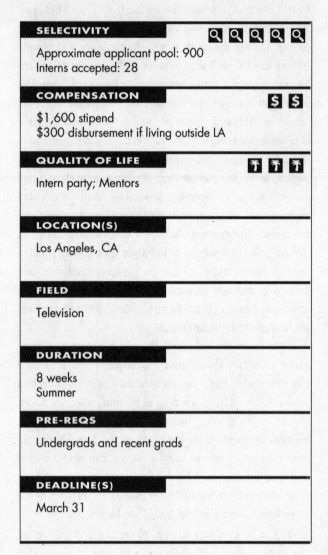

SELECTIVITY	🔍🔍🔍🔍🔍
Approximate applicant pool: 900 Interns accepted: 28	
COMPENSATION	💲💲
$1,600 stipend $300 disbursement if living outside LA	
QUALITY OF LIFE	⬆️⬆️⬆️
Intern party; Mentors	
LOCATION(S)	
Los Angeles, CA	
FIELD	
Television	
DURATION	
8 weeks Summer	
PRE-REQS	
Undergrads and recent grads	
DEADLINE(S)	
March 31	

much dispute, the Los Angeles counterpart reestablished itself as a separate organization—the Academy of Television Arts and Sciences (ATAS), which had originally been founded in 1946. In the divorce settlement, Los Angeles was entrusted with the distribution of prime-time Emmys while New York received jurisdiction over the news and sports Emmys. But ATAS retained its internship program, expanded it nationally, and modestly funded 15 interns that first year. Now, the program offers a generous stipend and internships in 24 categories: Agency, Animation, Art Direction, Business Affairs, Broadcast Promotions,

Casting, Children's Programming, Cinematography, Commercials, Daytime Programming, Development, Entertainment News, Episodic Series, Film Editing, Movies for TV, Music, Network Programming Management, Production Management, Public Relations, Sound, TV Directing (multicamera film), TV Directing (single-camera film), TV Scriptwriting, and Videotape Postproduction.

A full-time, 40-to-60-hour-a-week experience, each internship is hosted by an organization—children's shows, prime-time sitcoms, talent agencies, studios, and production companies. But unlike most Hollywood internships, the Academy's program isn't designed to solicit eight weeks of secretarial help. In fact, according to Price Hicks, the Emmy award–winning producer and program director since 1985, interns are involved in "very real-world" working situations. "We are very careful about whom we allow to host an intern," she elaborated. "We make it clear to the hosts that the internships must include very little gofer, filing, or photocopying work."

The careful selection of hosts pays off because these interns rave about their experiences. One intern in Network Programming Management worked at ABC's cartoon show "Winnie the Pooh." Playing the role of the executive, she read scripts for program development, monitored production, and provided imaginative input. "I attended creative meetings, went to the studios, and watched the voice-over recording sessions," she said. "On several occasions, an executive couldn't go to the voice-overs, and I was actually allowed to oversee the process, providing direction on how the voices should be done. One time, when I felt that the intent of a particular line had not been conveyed, I even suggested a redo."

Other interns were placed in Scriptwriting with "Star Trek: The Next Generation." They sat in on story meetings and listened to pitches for new stories. "At the meetings, we figured out the actual story progression," one said. "In the beginning, I said nothing and just put the ideas down on a big board so that everyone could follow along." But eventually, Scriptwriting interns contribute to story ideas. "I actually

wrote some of [the captain's] lines in an episode, which later appeared that fall." Interns also read speculative scripts and write synopses and opinions for each one. Exceptionally talented scriptwriting interns might even work on whole stories. Said an intern: "The show bought a pitch [i.e., a story idea from someone unaffiliated with the show], but its five-page description was flat. The executive producer didn't like it so he asked me to redo it. He loved my rewrite so much that I was hired to cowrite a script, a project that required me to stay two months past the end of the originally scheduled internship."

"[This is] the Academy Award of internships!"

Interns in Cinematography have been similarly engaged. Since 1980, they have been hosted by Dick Barlow, formerly head of the camera department at Warner Brothers' Burbank Studios and currently with Tiffen Technical Center. Under his guidance, they observe the crew in order to learn what actually happens on a set. "They don't touch the cameras," he said, "but they learn to load the film magazine and eventually become acquainted with the role of each position." Though union rules prohibit interns from working "hands-on" in these technical areas, word has it that some lucky interns in Cinematography and other equipment-intensive areas have managed to use the machines. Above all, Barlow emphasizes the importance of the observational role: "The working conditions of the professional cameraperson can't be taught in school. Students need to have professional experience—they need to learn that [camera work] means 10 to 14 hour days, and that it's a tough job."

Interns are paid $800 halfway through the program and an additional $800 upon successful completion. Those residing outside of Los Angeles County receive another $300 at the beginning of the internship to offset travel and housing expenses. "But it's very hard to live off of the stipend," said an intern. Consequently, the Academy wines and dines them; interns are invited to cocktail parties and dinner with the board of governors and to a large intern party, attended by about 250 people, who include hosts and past interns. Moreover, interns appear in the Academy's newsletter *Debut*, a biannual production of Educational

Programs and Services. The newsletter describes the Academy's programs and updates the goings-on of former interns.

Interns are paired with past interns through the Academy's mentor program. Though many find the mentor experience uplifting, others find it disappointing. "My mentor interned in a category different from mine, so he was not as helpful as he could have been when I had questions."

The internship lasts only eight weeks, and many are sad to leave Los Angeles when it's over. "We are thrust into the actual working situation of real professionals. Just when I was getting a great feel for how TV shows work, they pulled the plug, and I had to go back to school." Nevertheless, interns understand that the experience is a stepping stone to a career in television. Probably no one understands this opportunity more than Price Hicks, the program director. After administering the program for nearly a decade, she has watched a number of former interns scale the ranks in their field. "If you want to work in this business, then going through this program will dramatically improve your chances," she says. "There's no guarantee of job placement, but having been an Academy intern says something to most people in this town."

SELECTION

Applicants must be full-time students—undergraduate or graduate—seeking a degree at an American college or university. Recent college graduates are also eligible so long as they did not graduate prior to March 31 of the *previous* year. Though the program is technically open to students in all disciplines, successful candidates are typically pursuing degrees in art, theater arts, law, business, advertising, marketing, journalism, cinema, music, TV/film, and English. The internship director adds: "While applicants should have decent grades, they must also have done something besides study. Our interns are interesting, well-rounded people with a high level of maturity and often some experience in the category to which they applied."

APPLICATION PROCEDURE

Materials must be received by March 31. Applicants must submit a cover letter indicating permanent address, phone number, Social Security number, and the number and title of the category to which application is being made. Applicants must also send in a 250-word essay outlining professional and personal goals, a resumé, official college transcript(s), and three letters of recommendation. Sending additional materials is strongly discouraged. Once the deadline has passed, the category panels of eight to ten members each, read through student materials and choose three finalists per category. Several categories require additional materials for judging (e.g., scripts, portfolios, demo reels). All finalists are required to submit a videotaped interview responding to questions sent by the Academy. Note: Posters and information flyers are sent to the television departments and/or career centers at 1,000 schools nationwide. The flyer gives candidates detailed application procedures. Candidates are discouraged from calling the Academy before contacting their department or career center.

OVERVIEW

The Academy internship is special in that it places students in positions otherwise difficult, if not impossible, to obtain. "Almost every TV station, studio, or production house has some kind of internship program, most part-time and unpaid," says the program's director. "Clerical and mailroom internships are still viable entrées into the business, but the paid Academy internships provide better networking opportunities, more significant hands-on work, and they are well known." The internship is so prestigious that about 75 percent of former interns land worthwhile jobs in the television industry. Alumni include an Emmy award–winning art director for "The Bold and the Beautiful," a producer for "Northern Exposure," a story editor for "Star Trek: The Next Generation," and an assistant director for "The Simpsons." All got their start in the Academy's program, which is, for one intern, "the Academy Award of internships."

FOR MORE INFORMATION . . .

■ Academy of Television Arts & Sciences
Student Internship Program
5220 Lankershim Boulevard
North Hollywood, CA 91601
(818) 754-2830

A.C.T.

George M. Cohan is quoted in Fred J. Ringel's book, *America as Americans See It*, as saying: "When you are away from old Broadway, you are only camping out." If we are to believe Mr. Cohan, then for the past quarter century San Francisco's American Conservatory Theater has been staging one hell of a camp-out. ACT is one of the nation's largest regional companies, each year offering nine productions performed by some fifty actors. The theater's annual audience of nearly 275,000 enjoys a mix of classic drama, contemporary plays, and new work by emerging talents. Recent seasons have included such shows as *Saint Joan*, *Cyrano de Bergerac*, *The Taming of the Shrew*, *A Christmas Carol*, and *Under Milk Wood*. ACT also runs an acting conservatory of seventy full-time students and is the only American theater independent of a college to have a fully accredited conservatory.

DESCRIPTION

The ACT internship requires a serious commitment. Mirroring ACT's theater season, the internship spans a good eight months, from late summer to the following spring. Moreover, interns work long days—sometimes running over ten hours long—which precludes any other employment. But for those willing to make this kind of sacrifice, valuable training in theater arts awaits. Interns are placed in the following departments: Stage Management, Properties Construction, Stage Technician, Scenic Design, Sound Design, Lighting Design, Makeup and Wig Construction, Costume Rentals, and Costume Construction.

When the internship program began in 1976, the first department to hire interns was Stage Management. The theater's nerve center, Stage Management is charged with supervising rehearsals and procuring stage-related materials from other departments. Working alongside a head and assistant stage manager, interns are integral members of the Stage Management team. For two or three mainstage productions during the season, they carry out a range of tasks, such as making prop and costume lists, communicating messages between departments, and helping out at rehearsals. It's a superb education in the dynamics of stage management, but one that is extremely grueling. Said an intern: "Rehearsal hours varied. Some days we worked from

SELECTIVITY
Approximate applicant pool: 55
Interns accepted: 9–13

COMPENSATION
$165/week
Financial aid may be available

QUALITY OF LIFE
Theater tickets
Comfortable offices

LOCATION(S)
San Francisco, CA

FIELD
Theater production

DURATION
August/September to May
(Theater Season)

PRE-REQS
Undergrads and college grads of any age

DEADLINE(S)
May 15

10:00 AM to 7:00 PM, others from 1:00 PM to 11:00 PM. You had to be ready to deal with irregular rehearsal hours, and do so six days a week." If it's any consolation, the time Stage Management interns spend at ACT earns membership credits toward joining the Actor's Equity Union.

During the 1993–1994 season, a new dimension to the Stage Management internship was added: In addition to assisting with mainstage productions, each intern now serves as the sole stage manager for a conservatory production. Typically a Shakespeare play or a comparable piece of drama, the shows are acted out by a group of second-year conservatory students. Interns perform much of the same work for the student group that they do for mainstage shows, but "instead of being one of three stage managers, they're the ones in charge." As ACT's chief stage manager sees it, having interns manage conservatory productions serves two purposes: "It gives the interns a chance to test out what they've learned in a safe environment. And it's an opportunity for young actors to learn how to deal with a stage manager in rehearsal."

There's plenty to do at ACT besides stage management. Lighting Design interns draft designs for special effects, maintain records, attend production meetings, and, on occasion, act in the repertory designer's absence. Then there's Makeup and Wig Construction, where interns work in the repertory makeup shop on special projects under the direction of ACT's wigmaster (really, that's his title). Those with a background in drafting are eligible to work in Scenic Design, where interns sketch and make scale models of the sets and props used in ACT shows. Says a Scenic Design intern: "One of the shows I worked on was the *Imaginary Invalid*. The prop I helped design was quite complicated. I did working drawings of a piece of moving furniture that [the protagonist] used as his whole world—attached to the contraption were a toilet, medicine cabinet, and chair."

Those with a passion for costumes will be happy to know that ACT hires interns for its Costume Construction and Costume Rentals department. In Costume Construction, interns work alongside the staff, building costumes and accessory pieces for ACT's productions; they learn such costuming techniques as sewing, millinery, and leather work. Interns in Costume Rentals help maintain ACT's huge stock of costumes as well as rent outfits to corporations, other theaters, and the public. Because most of the work in this department involves renting costumes to outside parties, interns have little to do with the shows ACT is producing. It's no tragedy, though—interns have a lot of fun helping the public put outfits together. "People would call us needing clothes for a costume party. We'd work with them to find the right getup. It could be virtually any theme: a Victorian tea party, a Renaissance dinner . . . even a party spoofing "The Andy Griffith Show." Whenever business is slow, interns in Costume Rentals are encouraged to work on creating a new costume for ACT. "[The rental staff] allowed us to design and build any costume we dreamed up—so long as it was not already in stock. Using ACT materials and machines, I built a harlequin costume made out of lycra."

Until 1989, ACT operated out of San Francisco's historic, 1,400-seat Geary Theater, but the rattle and roll of the Loma Prieta earthquake left the theater badly damaged. In the best sense of "the show must go on," ACT currently performs in three rented theaters located throughout the city, while a rebuilding campaign for Geary Theater gradually gets under way. ACT headquarters is situated on the top three floors of a high-rise building in downtown San Francisco. Housing ACT's administrative offices and conservatory, headquarters is a "triumph of open-space planning," with floor-to-ceiling windows and patios that are often the site of Friday afternoon cookouts. The "shop-oriented" departments—Scenic Design, Costume Construction, and Costume Rentals—are separate from headquarters, located in the "fringe" neighborhood of Potero Hill.

Even if ACT interns were given a lot of perks, the season is so busy that there probably wouldn't be enough

> **Interns in Costume Rentals help the public put together outfits of virtually any theme: Victorian, Renaissance . . . even "Andy Griffith."**

time to enjoy them. Nevertheless, there is usually opportunity to take advantage of a few privileges. Interns receive two tickets to any ACT production, including preview and opening night performances. Tickets to the Berkeley and San Jose Repertory Theater productions are also available, as ACT has a reciprocal arrangement with these theaters. And then there's always the chance of running into William Hurt, John Turturro, Jean Stapleton, or any other of the big-name actors who grace ACT's stage.

SELECTION

 Because the ACT internship spans eight months, it is typically undertaken by undergraduates on a leave of absence from school or recent graduates. But the intern coordinator stresses that the internship is open to college graduates of any age; past interns, for example, have included a few older participants looking for a career change. Most departments require previous experience in their area of production, but an enthusiastic and sincere personality may compensate for a lack of experience in some cases. Says the chief stage manager: "My top priority in hiring Stage Management interns is finding people who are supportive and caring. Previous stage management experience is not essential—I can teach anyone to do a prop list."

APPLICATION PROCEDURE

 Applications are due May 15. The application process is nothing short of arduous, requiring one to submit (1) a personal statement (500 words or less), (2) an application form, (3) a resumé, (4) a photograph, (5) three letters of recommendation, and (6) a $10 nonrefundable application fee. Applicants seeking financial aid should write to ACT's Office of Financial Aid at the headquarters address. After the intern coordinator sorts applications based on the department preferences they list, departments select a few applicants to interview, either in person or by phone.

OVERVIEW

 This is an exciting time to be at the American Conservatory Theater. Though ACT has been known over the years for its traditional approach to theater, its new artistic director, Carey Perloff, is infusing energy into the 28-year-old regional theater. In her inaugural season as director, which *The New York Times* said "[shook] up unshockable San Francisco," she jostled the establishment by staging the Vatican farce *The Pope and the Witch* and a production of *The Duchess of Malfi*, which featured the duchess in full-frontal nudity.

ACT interns get to go along for the ride, experiencing ACT at a time of ferment and controversy, while working closely with top professionals as they design, manage, and construct the repertory production. But the experience is not for the lazy or luxury loving. Because the 1989 earthquake left ACT financially strapped and geographically scattered, interns must accept that they will be working under crisis conditions, where performances occur simultaneously at two or three different theaters around the city. Interns must also be willing to roll up their sleeves and work a rigorous schedule no different from that of permanent staff. An intern said it best: "If your interest is theater, you'd be hard pressed to find a more practical and intense experience."

FOR MORE INFORMATION . . .

■ American Conservatory Theater
Internship Program
450 Geary Street
San Francisco, CA 94102
(415) 749-2200

SELECTIVITY		
Approximate applicant pool: 200		
Interns accepted: 40–55		

COMPENSATION	$
None	

QUALITY OF LIFE	
Brown Bags	
Bradley Lecture Series; Cafeteria	

LOCATION(S)
Washington, DC

FIELD
Public policy/Think tank

DURATION
12 weeks
Summer, Fall, Spring

PRE-REQS
Undergrads, recent grads, grad students

DEADLINE(S)	
Summer .... April 30	Fall .... August 1
Spring .... January 1	

Bork. Kristol. Kirkpatrick. Perle. Cheney. Novak. D'Souza . . .

A hypothetical cast list for "Revenge of the Republicans"?

Not even close.

These are but some of the intellectual and political superstars in residence at Washington's American Enterprise Institute. Founded in 1943, AEI is a think tank committed to research on government policy, the American economy, and American politics. Although it calls itself a nonpartisan institution, few would disagree that AEI has a preponderance of conservative thinkers. From the "brilliant and bearded" Robert Bork to young gun Dinesh D'Souza (author of the bestseller *Illiberal Education*), AEI is a bastion of red-blooded conservatism. But to be fair, the institute is not without its share of centrist scholars, most notably Bill Schneider and Norman Ornstein, both telegenic purveyors of political wisdom.

DESCRIPTION

AEI interns are assigned to a "resident scholar" who is conducting research in one of three areas: economic policy, foreign and defense policy, or social and political policy. In their applications, interns may specify a preference for a particular area or scholar within that area. Positions are also available in Marketing, Public and Media Relations, Seminars and Conferences, and *The American Enterprise* magazine.

Interns working under the aegis of a scholar typically report to the scholar's research assistant for daily assignments. Responsibilities vary with each scholar, but certain tasks are common to virtually every intern. The least exciting of these is clipping newspaper articles

on subjects relevant to the scholar's research. "Every day I looked through several newspapers and cut out articles of interest to my [scholar]. It wasn't the world's most challenging work, but it made me savvy of world affairs."

The bulk of interns' time is spent carrying out research for their scholar's upcoming books and papers. Research responsibilities include canvassing the in-house library for books and journals, telephoning academics and government agencies for information, and photocopying and filing away articles for later use. Interns are also asked to arrange interviews for their

BUSYWORK METER
MEDIUM
LOW HIGH
OLDMAN & HAMADEH

scholars. An intern with Dinesh D'Souza, for example, "set up interviews with noted professors and experts. . . [I] arranged an interview with [former NAACP lawyer] Jack Greenberg and tried to arrange one with Rosa Parks." Once, when D'Souza was in New York, the intern "fielded a call from *Nightline*, who wanted to interview D'Souza that evening. . . [A]fter making a bunch of anxious phone calls, I tracked him down in New York, and he made it on *Nightline* in time."

Sometimes interns perform research requiring a good deal of synthesis or analysis. Working with research associate Jeffrey Gedmin on his book *The Hidden Hand: Gorbachev and the Collapse of East Germany*, an intern skimmed and wrote summaries of books Gedmin didn't have time to read. Another intern, this one in Judge Bork's camp, wrote summary reports on issues relevant to Bork's upcoming book on multiculturalism. "After digging up all the articles and books I could find on political correctness, I wrote a summary report describing the views of its proponents and opponents . . . [Bork] liked to have several viewpoints, so I'd give my analysis at the end of the report. Whether he used it or not is a different story."

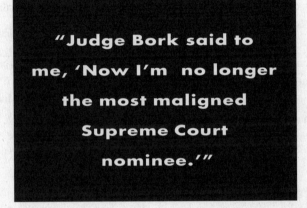

"Judge Bork said to me, 'Now I'm no longer the most maligned Supreme Court nominee.'"

When a scholar's book is near completion, interns often help with fact checking and proofreading. An intern who double-checked the footnotes on Joshua Muravchik's *Exporting Democracy* said: "It wasn't as tedious as I expected. In the process, I got to read [Muravchik's] compelling argument on why the spread of democracy should form the core of American foreign policy." Working with Robert Hahn on a paper about energy policy, another intern read over the statistics Hahn cited and made sure everything added up. "I definitely had input in the project," he said. "If something didn't make sense when I reworked the numbers, I pointed it out and [Hahn] checked it out." All this work doesn't necessarily go unacknowledged: Interns are happy to find that their efforts are occasionally credited in the finished book or paper. Said an intern whose work designing charts and graphs was acknowledged in a paper published by the *Yale Law Journal*: "It's nice to get credit for the work I did. It's tangible evidence of my tenure at AEI."

Part of the attraction of an AEI internship is the proximity it affords to renowned conservative thinkers. "If you're conservative," said an intern, "there's no better connection to the higher world of political thought." Scholars are surprisingly accessible: "All you need to do is make an appointment, and you can go in and talk to a scholar. If you're writing an honors thesis for school, this is your chance to interview a great mind on the subject." But some of the best interaction with scholars occurs at random. "No matter where you go," said an intern, "there's potential for engrossing conversations. I remember running into a scholar in the bathroom and having a great conversation on foreign policy." Even elevators are fertile ground for contact with scholars. On the first day of the Clarence Thomas–Anita Hill hearings, one intern had an elevator ride she won't soon forget. "Behind me in the elevator was Judge Bork, who said to me, 'Now I'm no longer the most maligned Supreme Court nominee.' [A]fter he exited the elevator, Jeane Kirkpatrick got on. She was talking with a friend about how to pronounce 'harassment' and turned to ask my opinion. I suggested it was pronounced 'HAIR-as-ment,' not 'her-ASS-ment.'"

If chance encounters aren't enough, there are more formal ways of tapping into scholars' wisdom. Interns are invited to attend the weekly, hour-long Friday Brown Bag Lunches, where scholars speak off-the-record about their latest research. Past luncheons have been hosted by virtually all of AEI's leading lights, including Robert Bork, who often reviews the past Supreme Court term, and Norman Ornstein, who loves to lecture on voting trends. Interns may also attend the Bradley Lecture Series, a set of evening lectures given by "non-AEI people who are influential in the world of ideas"; George Will, Alan Bloom, and Charles Krauthammer are but a few of the distinguished Bradley lecturers of recent memory.

Located across the street from the National Geographic Society and a stone's throw from the Farragut North Metro stop, AEI is in a "good business-oriented neighborhood." A "big brass AEI" adorns the outside of the organization's "modern but tacky" 12-story building. AEI occupies the building's top three floors, which are decorated with photos of the scholars and posters of AEI-published books. The library prominently displays an old campaign poster of Richard Nixon and Dwight Eisenhower, prompting one intern to quip, "You know you're not in Berkeley anymore." Interns are assigned a cubicle or "some sort of cubbyhole" within easy reach of a phone and IBM computer. The top floor boasts a subsidized cafeteria with "decent sandwiches and burgers" as well as a fancy dining room for scholars.

SELECTION

 The program is open to undergraduates of any level, recent graduates, and graduate students. Candidates from any academic background are welcome to apply, but those interested in working with economic-policy scholars should have some knowledge of economics.

APPLICATION PROCEDURE

 The deadline for the summer internship is April 30; for the fall internship, August 1; and for the spring internship, January 1. The intern coordinator says these deadlines "are not set in stone"; she often accepts applications submitted a week or two after the deadline. Required materials include a cover letter (specifying preferred program area or department), resumé, transcript, and writing sample of at least 500 words. After screening the initial applicant pool, the intern coordinator or a research assistant interviews a selection of finalists, either in person or by phone.

OVERVIEW

 Think of the AEI internship as offering students two golden keys. The first key, used by all interns, provides access to excellent research opportunities with distinguished scholars and gets students into a wealth of AEI-sponsored seminars and lectures. The other key, used only by interns with initiative and ambition, opens up other additional opportunities for research and networking. In an intern's words, "You'll never again be around such an all-star cast of great conservative thinkers. This is your chance to take the bull by the horns—knock on a few doors and get to know a few of these gurus."

FOR MORE INFORMATION . . .

■ American Enterprise Institute
Intern Coordinator
1150 Seventeenth Street NW
Washington, DC 20036
(202) 862-5800

SELECTIVITY

Approximate applicant pool: 60
Interns accepted: 4

COMPENSATION

Andelson Interns receive $2,500 stipend

QUALITY OF LIFE

Intimate office; Supportive staff;
Powerful info network

LOCATION(S)

Washington, DC

FIELD

Public policy

DURATION

10 weeks Summer

PRE-REQS

College juniors and seniors; grad students

DEADLINE(S)

February 15

You are a successful lawyer and one of the largest real estate owners in West Hollywood. You founded the Bank of Los Angeles, then served as the CEO of its holding company. The governor appoints you to the Board of Regents of the University of California.

Life is good . . . save for one detail.

You have AIDS.

Such was the fate of Sheldon Andelson. The prominent Los Angeles attorney could have fallen to pieces upon hearing the news of his affliction, but Andelson did not. A man of action, he served as a founding director of the American Foundation for AIDS Research (AmFAR), an organization established in 1985 to fight the epidemic that would take his life two years later.

Andelson's indomitable spirit lives on at AmFAR. Today, AmFAR is the nation's leading not-for-profit organization dedicated to the support of AIDS research. Since its inception, it has distributed over $61 million in support of more than 1,200 projects involving biomedical, clinical, prevention, and public policy research grants. It has also been a vigorous force in public policy, providing objective and current information on HIV/AIDS to policymakers through briefings, writings, and public testimonies.

DESCRIPTION

AmFAR considers itself a bicoastal organization with three offices: one in NY, one in LA, and one in Washington, DC The New York office reviews funding requests for clinical trials and educational programs. The Los Angeles office distributes grants for biomedical research. And the Washington, DC, office, AmFAR's newest outpost, was established in 1991 to fund public policy research and monitor federal HIV/AIDS efforts.

Interns are hired at the Washington, DC, office only. A grant from the family of Sheldon Andelson provides two "Andelson interns" each with a $2,500 stipend. The office usually hires at least two "volunteer" (unsalaried) interns. AmFAR permits volunteer interns to work part-time, so long as they put in at least twenty hours a week.

AmFAR interns monitor, research, and evaluate HIV/AIDS policy issues. One intern, for example, investigated the latest developments in AIDS vaccines. He interviewed scientists at drug companies, observed relevant hearings on Capitol Hill, and even traveled to Baltimore to spend a day with a primary-care HIV specialist. His work resulted in a report describing the latest findings on preventive and therapeutic vaccines. He added: "My research on AIDS vaccines was particularly valuable because during my internship I also worked part-time at a local AIDS clinic. . . . [I saw both] the public-policy side and the patient-based [dimension] of the epidemic."

AmFAR interns had better like writing because they do a lot of it. One intern wrote several eight-to-ten-page background papers on areas of interest to AmFAR's board of directors, such as women and AIDS, tuberculosis and the Orphan Drug Act. Another wrote a lengthy report briefing the board of directors on how health care reform will impact AIDS patients. A third intern wrote a pamphlet for adoption agencies on the importance of giving HIV-positive foster children access to cutting-edge treatment.

Interns are hooked into a powerful information network, both in the office and around Washington. They have access to the organization's extensive files of information on policy issues. They may also listen in on the weekly conference call between the NY, LA, and DC offices. "The conference call was AmFAR's way of communicating with itself. You'd hear discussions about operational issues as well as the latest controversies." Interns have a host of resources beyond the office, too. The library of the George Washington University Medical School sits a few blocks away, where interns can log on to databases—"I used MedLine for research all the time." And, of course, as Washington is the policy locus of the free world, interns are able to monitor congressional hearings, attend meetings of HIV/AIDS advocacy groups, and visit key government agencies such the Department of Health and Human Services and the National Institutes of Health.

One of the best aspects of interning at AmFAR is the accessibility to the superstars of AIDS policy-making. "If you know anything about the AIDS field, you know that a few of its leading lights are at the helm of AmFAR," said an intern. The organization's board of directors include Mervyn Silverman, M.D., AmFAR president and former health commissioner for San Francisco, and Mathilde Krim,

> **One of the best aspects of interning at AmFAR is the accessibility to the superstars of AIDS policy-making.**

chairman of the board and founding co-chair of AmFAR—both universally recognized leaders in the fight against AIDS. Although neither works out of AmFAR's D.C. office, they visit there occasionally and remain surprisingly reachable by phone. The intern who researched partner notification conferred several times with Silverman and Krim. "They were extremely helpful. They edited several drafts of my report. Dr. Silverman even wrote me a recommendation for medical school."

AmFAR owes its high-profile standing not only to policy experts but also to its affiliation with the rich and famous. AmFAR's national council includes the likes of Warren Beatty, Rosalyn Carter, David Geffen, Angela Lansbury, Jonas Salk, and Jack Valenti. And AmFAR's national chairperson is none other than "Violet Eyes" herself—Elizabeth Taylor. Taylor's busy schedule prevents her from hanging around AmFAR's D.C. office, so interns are almost never able to meet the screen legend. But one intern went with the AmFAR staff to observe the congressional hearings where Taylor testified for funding of the Ryan White CARE Act of 1990. After "being whisked into the Capitol building," the intern viewed the hearings and then attended a reception for Taylor in Senator Edward Kennedy's office. "It was exciting," she said. "I was introduced to Elizabeth Taylor. She was pleasant, though kind of aloof. Maybe it was because she had a six-foot-four bodyguard standing next to her."

Situated in an office building six blocks from the White House and a stone's throw from the Farragut North Metro stop, AmFAR is smack-dab in the middle of downtown Washington. The office is small, made up of a front room with cubicle desks, a kitchen, a conference room, and a few executive offices. Five permanent staff members work here, as do the interns. AmFAR's intimate set-up is well-regarded—"'it's conducive to informal conversations; you can easily establish a rapport with your coworkers."

SELECTION

 The internship is open to junior and senior undergraduates as well as graduate students. No previous experience or coursework is required.

APPLICATION PROCEDURE

 Applicants should apply by February 15. Required materials include a cover letter, a resumé, a list of two or three references, and a brief writing sample. Interviews are conducted in person or over the phone.

OVERVIEW

 According to AmFAR statistics, in the next three or four years as many Americans will die of AIDS as did in the 11 years since the disease was detected. While the outlook is decidedly bleak, it would be markedly worse were organizations like AmFAR not around to mobilize funds and influence policy. The AmFAR internship gets students involved in this life-or-death mission, having them research issues of urgent importance. They do so in a small office that offers unusually easy access to policy experts. In sum, the AmFAR internship exposes students to the dynamics of Washington policy-making while enabling them to make an important contribution to public health.

FOR MORE INFORMATION . . .

■ American Foundation for AIDS Research
Intern Coordinator
1828 L Street NW
Suite 802
Washington, DC 20036
(202) 331-8600

American Heart Association

SELECTIVITY	🔍
Approximate applicant pool: 700 Interns accepted: 250–300	

COMPENSATION	💲 💲
$600–$3,000/stipend (depends on class level and program)	

QUALITY OF LIFE

N/A

LOCATION(S)

Nationwide—see Description

FIELD

Cardiovascular and biomedical research

DURATION

10–12 weeks (Summer)
One-semester and one-year grants available; PT avail.

PRE-REQS

Varies with program—see Selection

DEADLINE(S)

Varies with program—see Application Procedure

What is the number-one killer in the United States? Is it AIDS? Suicide? Accidents? Cancer? Actually, it is none of these.

It's heart disease. Every year, heart attacks cause almost a half-million American deaths. Heart attacks are only one subset of a broader class of heart and blood vessel disorders called cardiovascular disease, which in total account for nearly one million deaths in the United States—over 40 percent of all U.S. deaths!

But if it were up to the American Heart Association (AHA), death from cardiovascular disease would be a problem of the past. Founded in 1924 "to reduce disability and death from cardiovascular disease and stroke," the AHA has been fighting hard to help prevent and treat heart afflictions. Though it hasn't discovered a cure, the AHA has made substantial progress in discovering and advising people on preventive measures. Community and educational programs such as Heart at Work and the Culinary Hearts Kitchen teach the public of the dangers of cigarette smoking, fatty foods, and physical inactivity. Since the AHA began to fund scientists in 1949, it has spent over a billion dollars on research—work that has led to the discovery of CPR, artificial heart valves, and bypass surgery.

DESCRIPTION

For the 1993–1994 academic year, the AHA offered student programs through 26 of its 56 affiliates as well as at the national center. According to the national center, approximately half of these were full-time summer programs, the other half part- or full-time programs for the academic year. In total, these programs allow students to conduct basic, applied, and clinical research at universities, research institutes, and medical centers throughout the country. Participating affiliates offering programs throughout their states for high school (H), undergraduate (U), graduate (G), and/or medical students (M) include: Little Rock, AR (G,M); Burlingame, CA (U,G); Wallingford, CT (H,U,M); Jamestown, ND (G,M); Newark, DE (G); St. Petersburg, FL (H,G,M); Marietta, GA (U,G,M); Springfield, IL (G,M); Indianapolis, IN (G,M); Des Moines, IA (G,M); Destrehan, LA (U,G,M); Columbia, MO (U,G,M); Omaha, NE (H,U,G,M);

BUSYWORK METER
LOW MEDIUM HIGH
N/A
OLDMAN & HAMADEH

Manchester, NH (G,M); North Brunswick, NJ (H,G,M); New York City (M); Chapel Hill, NC (H,G,M); Cleveland, OH (U,M); Columbus, OH (U); Oklahoma City, OK (U); Portland, OR (U,G,M); Camp Hill and Philadelphia, PA (G,M); Richmond, VA (M); Seattle, WA (H); Milwaukee, WI (G,M); and the National Center in Dallas, TX (M). While about half of the AHA's student programs target MD and Ph.D. students, the other half seek high school students and undergraduates. The examples given in this entry describe mostly the experiences of the latter group.

The kinds of research projects sponsored by the AHA vary significantly. Such was not the case several years ago, when past AHA interns were limited to heart-related work, such as examining possible mechanisms by which elevation of the hormone angiotensin II increases blood pressure in rabbits, investigating the role of calcium ions in triggering contraction of cardiac muscle, or determining the structure of chemically-crosslinked human hemoglobins by using x-ray crystallography. But of late, AHA affiliates have had a change of heart—many are funding projects involving all areas of biomedical research and allowing interns, for example, to help design and synthesize analogs of opioid peptides (e.g., endorphins), analyze the role of phosphorylation in regulating the enzyme phosphofructokinase, and study colposcopy, a technique that identifies cancerous areas of the cervix. "[W]e realize that at a young age, [students] will not necessarily be focused on cardiovascular research," explains the national center's program and evaluation consultant. "So we allow them to sample all areas of biomedical research … hopefully, years down the road, they'll focus on heart research."

The oldest and largest AHA student program is managed by the California affiliate. Established in 1957, California's Summer Student Research Program places nearly 80 undergraduates every summer in 60 to 70 labs throughout California. An intern from San Diego, for example, was assigned to a private research group at the

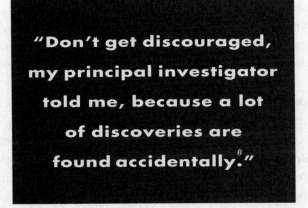

"Don't get discouraged, my principal investigator told me, because a lot of discoveries are found accidentally."

Scripps Research Institute, where he worked on a project involving cardiac gap-junction proteins. "Each protein forms a channel between two [adjacent myocardial] cells," he explained. "The channels mediate action-potential propagation, which allows the heart to expand and contract—in other words, to beat." Using an electron microscope and such lab techniques as centrifugation, gel electrophoresis, and Western Blotting, he isolated and purified gap-junction proteins from rat hearts stored in his lab's freezer. "[The lab's] long-term goal was to understand the structure and dynamics of the channels," he said, "because they're not only essential to normal heart function but also implicated in arrhythmia [i.e., irregular heartbeat]."

California affiliate undergraduate interns also work with medical schools, universities, and a few industrial corporations. One intern was placed in the University of Southern California's Department of Physiology. "I was trying to find the binding site for potassium ions in the mammalian sodium-potassium pump," she explained. "I had created some mutant [sodium-potassium] pumps using recombinant DNA [technology], but unfortunately, I didn't get a chance to test them out because the ten weeks allotted to the project ended.... That was a little frustrating." Another intern worked on a pharmacology experiment for Glycomed, Inc., a biotechnology firm in Alameda. As part of a study on how the stomach, colon, and ileum (a part of the small intestine) of rats and guinea pigs react to certain compounds, she performed animal surgeries. After putting on sterile surgeon's garb (lab coat, mask, and latex gloves) and anesthetizing the rodents, she removed their gastrointestinal tracts. Then she prepared the tissues in salt solution and injected them with various substances like histamines and prostaglandins—fatty acids that control blood pressure and smooth muscle contraction. "I learned a lot about the importance of patience and lab technique," she concluded. "That's something you can only gain with experience."

Unlike the California affiliate's undergraduate program, most AHA programs require students to propose a research project as well as a research adviser or sponsor. After finding out about the Louisiana affiliate's Undergraduate Research Program, a Louisiana Tech student interested in doing research on the retina approached a professor engaged in bio-instrumentation studies. "I went to him because I want to eventually create a retina prosthesis or develop a process for retina replacement," the ambitious senior explained. "He gave me suggestions on what to do and helped me put together a proposal." For a project in which he will study the response of rat retinas to light and electrical stimulation, the AHA awarded the undergraduate a grant for the 1993–94 academic year. "I'm very excited about the project," he said. "I can't wait to start doing eye surgeries [on rats]."

After arranging to work in the Department of Ophthalmology and Visual Sciences at Yale Medical School, a medical student in the Connecticut affiliate's program studied eye diseases linked to diabetes. "We know that a disease called diabetic retinopathy is somehow brought about by loss of oxygen to the eye because [the disease is] accompanied by extra blood vessel formation in the retina," she explained. "The extra blood vessels disrupt the structure of the eye and cause blindness." To figure out what causes these extra blood vessels to form, she grew eye cells in an oxygen-free environment, then took tissue cultures to analyze what happened. "It's still unclear," she said, with a month left to go, "but this is a good project because the research has numerous applications. For example, if we can figure out what spurs new blood vessels to grow, we can perhaps induce their formation to counteract arteriosclerosis [i.e., thickening and hardening of the arteries]."

Under the tutelage of principal investigators (PI's), interns learn proper laboratory techniques, but usually not before a few trials and tribulations. "Sometimes I screwed up, putting too many cells on an agar plate and obscuring the results," said an intern. "[B]ut don't get discouraged, my PI told me, because a lot of discoveries are found accidentally." Acting as role models, supervisors are generally praised for treating interns as competent researchers. "In the beginning, I felt like [my supervisor] really didn't need me, that the AHA had put him up to this," said an intern. "But I realized by the end of the summer that he had been training me and trying to get me to fall in love with lab research."

In every program, interns work in labs throughout the state. The physical distance separating interns means that they rarely, if ever, gather as a group for seminars or social activities. "I would've liked to talk to other students," said one intern, whose comments were echoed by several others. "I was new to research and really wanted to compare my experience with others." One AHA affiliate attempting to address this concern is California. Besides providing interns with a list of their peers' phone numbers, it designates one intern per town to act as the social coordinator for the area's interns. Meeting informally once or twice during the summer, each area's interns get together to discuss research projects or go out for dinner or movies. "Meeting the other students at our informal get-together made me feel more at ease," said an intern. "[It] also gave me a chance to become familiar with their projects."

After completing their research, interns are usually required to submit a written report. "I was required to write only three pages," said a Connecticut affiliate intern. "It was pretty easy, and it helped me to synthesize what I had learned over the previous few months." In addition to submitting a one-page summary, California affiliate undergraduate interns convene for "roundtable discussions," where they give ten-minute talks on their work, followed by a question-and-answer session. For many interns, it's their first time giving a presentation, and the dozen or more students and PI's looking on can intimidate them. "Some [interns] were nervous at first," described one participant, "but eventually, they relaxed and gave pretty insightful speeches." Public speaking jitters notwithstanding, the talks are described overall as "a great way to hear about 'hot' topics in research and learn the proper format for scientific presentations."

SELECTION

 Student programs are generally open to high school, undergraduate, graduate, and medical students, although some programs limit eligibility to certain class levels—for example, a few undergraduate programs (notably the California affiliate's) take juniors and seniors only. Usually, no research experience is required, although certain programs require applicants to have completed courses in organic chemistry, biology, and physics or calculus. In a few cases, applicants must meet a minimum GPA requirement

(Louisiana, for example, specifies a minimum 2.5 GPA). Each affiliate requires its applicants to be residents of the state in which that affiliate is located and/or students of a school in the same state as the affiliate.

APPLICATION PROCEDURE

 For academic-year awards (usually funding graduate students from July 1 to June 30), deadlines span the year (the deadline for California's graduate program, for example, is October 1 while the deadline for all of Louisiana's year-long programs is March 1). For summer programs targeted at high school students and undergraduates, deadlines vary, from January 15 for the California affiliate's undergraduate program to March 11 for the Connecticut affiliate's high school and undergraduate programs. Depending on the program, applicants must submit several, if not all, of the following: research proposal, application form, transcript, essay, one to three letters of recommendation, and resumé. Each affiliate sets up a committee which evaluates students' applications; interviews are not always a part of the application process. Students should contact the Research division of the AHA affiliate in which they wish to work for more information or the AHA national toll-free number, which automatically connects callers to the nearest AHA affiliate or division office.

OVERVIEW

 By most accounts, biomedical research is difficult but worthwhile and satisfying work. Students interested in finding out for themselves can do one of two things. They can arrange to work in a lab on their campus (sometimes for credit, other times for modest pay), or they can participate in one of the few well-paid research experiences out there—the American Heart Association's student program. "It's a way to distinguish yourself from the other students who do research at your university," one intern pointed out. Conducting research in cardiovascular or biomedical studies alongside experts, AHA interns make strides in the fight against heart disease while learning proper laboratory procedures. Concluded an intern: "I learned about the fundamental principles that research projects are built upon, the . . . task of data accumulation, even the basics of applying for those elusive grants."

FOR MORE INFORMATION . . .

■   American Heart Association
    Student Programs
    7272 Greenville Avenue
    Dallas, TX 75231
    (800) AHA-USA1

AT&T Bell Laboratories

SELECTIVITY 🔍 🔍 🔍

Approx. applicant pool: 500 (SRP)/ 2,700 (UR)
Interns accepted: 80 (SRP)/ 250 (UR)

COMPENSATION $ $ $ $

Est. $430–$520/wk for undergrads;
Est. $550–$620/wk for grad students; RT travel

QUALITY OF LIFE 🌴 🌴 🌴 🌴

Excellent mentors
Science seminars; Dorm housing

LOCATION(S)

NJ and PA—see Description

FIELD

Telecommunications research

DURATION

10–12 weeks
Summer

PRE-REQS

Varies with program—see Application Procedure

DEADLINE(S)

SRP .... December 1
UR .... February 15

"**U**.S. PATENT NO.: 4,968,542."

Pick a few numbers, slap on a "U.S. Patent No.," and you've got yourself a patent.

Not so fast. To license an invention in America, you must pay your dues. After submitting a three-page application and a $710 filing fee, there's a delay of up to two years while the Patent and Trademark Office verifies the originality of your invention. What are the chances for success? According to the Patent Office, about 65 percent of all applicants are actually awarded patents.

Amazingly enough, AT&T Bell Laboratories has become a master of this arduous process. Since its founding in 1925, nearly nine out of every ten Bell Labs applications have been approved by the Patent Office—an average of one patent every working day! It's no surprise when one considers some of the devices Bell Labs has invented: transistors, sound motion-pictures, liquid crystal displays, lasers, solar cells, touch-tone phones, transatlantic fiber-optic cables, and motion videophones.

As the research and product development arm of communications giant AT&T, Bell Labs employs over 4,000 scientists and 25,000 technicians who develop new products, systems, and services as well as conduct research in five areas to maintain AT&T's technological edge: microelectronics, software, image processing, speech processing, and photonics (technologies for generating, processing, and detecting light signals).

DESCRIPTION

In 1972, AT&T Bell Laboratories established the Summer Research Program for Minorities and Women (SRP) in order to attract minority undergraduate students to Ph.D. programs in the sciences. The laboratory's University

Relations Summer Program (UR) had already been providing structured research opportunities to college undergraduate and graduate students since 1945. Today, well over 1,200 students have gone through SRP and an even greater number through UR. While SRP students are placed exclusively in the Basic Research department and most frequently at Bell Labs' Murray Hill location, UR students work in both Product Development and Basic Research in Murray Hill, Middletown, Holmdel, Whippany, Red Hill (all NJ), and Allentown (PA).

The hundreds of laboratories at Bell Labs are known by number. The Research Materials Science Engineering & Academic Affairs division's Solid State Chemistry Research Lab is referred to more easily as Lab 11535, and the Information Sciences Research division's Mathematics of Communication and Computer Systems Lab is Lab 11211. The numbers alleviate the difficulty in trying to remember the area, division, and lab name associated with each lab. It's a good thing, too, because interns need every brain cell in their heads to understand the research going on here.

A student in Lab 11535 "detwinned" superconducting crystals—that is, he realigned the oxygen molecules (of which each crystal is partly composed) with the other molecules in the crystal. "First I had to find suitable crystals, those without cracks or jagged edges. Since the crystals are only tenths of a millimeter on each side, it's impossible to locate imperfections visually. So I X-rayed them and then read the diffraction pattern; a non-uniform pattern indicated that there was a crack." Once located, good crystals were subjected to heating at 600 to 800°C; the heating lines up the oxygen molecules. Occasionally, however, a tiny imperfection unseen by the X ray would cause the crystal to destruct upon heating. "Sometimes I'd open the oven door and discover a small pile of dust."

An intern in the Research Physics division was paired with a professor investigating "chaos theory"—the idea that apparently irregular or random systems, like the weather, exhibit some predictability. "[The professor] discovered that an array of solid-state devices called Josephson tunnel junctions exhibit chaotic behavior," he said. "[So] if we could determine how the junctions work, we'd go pretty far in understanding how chaos works." But Josephson tunnel junctions themselves are not clearly understood and are difficult to make. Consequently, while the professor performed lab experiments on the junctions, the intern programmed a computer to simulate them. "I developed a 600-line program using C (a computer language) to describe what

> "The people here love what they do; they share jokes, and they stay late . . ."

was going on mathematically. As you can imagine, it took me several weeks to write the code . . . and plot the output using a graphing program specifically designed for chaotic systems."

Interns may be found in Basic Research as well as Product Development and not all intern projects involve heavy-duty scientific research. An intern in Software Development Tools, for example, spent the summer creating a database to categorize the 100 or so computer hardware and software products that her department utilizes in its work. "I was asked to use two programs to develop the database," she said. "One was a commercial program called INFORMIX and the other was a program that [Bell Labs] had developed called GHOST. We wanted to see if GHOST worked as well as INFORMIX did in keeping track of all the items in the stock room." But because there was no manual for GHOST, she explained, she had to read the code—several hundred pages' worth. "It filled a two-inch binder and was so complicated. . . I didn't really have the background to fully understand it." On top of that, her summer ended before she could make the GHOST database. "At least I learned more about computer programming and how [INFORMIX] works."

As the last two examples would suggest, student projects are often so complex that interns find it difficult to finish by the end of the summer. It's a situation ripe for frustration, so Bell Labs assigns supervisors and mentor-scientists to whom interns may turn for assistance. Many mentors are world-renowned, such as Jim West, inventor of the modern telephone microphone, and Jim Mitchell, head of the Analytical Chemistry department. But one had better schedule meetings with his or her mentor well in advance, cautions one intern: "These people are very busy."

The summer begins with a half-day orientation over breakfast followed by an information session and a speech on the advantages of attending graduate school. The highlight of the day is a talk given by Vice President of

Research Arno Penzias, who welcomes the interns and answers their questions about the organization. Employed by AT&T Bell Labs since 1961, Penzias is no stranger to research: He shared a Nobel Prize in physics with Bell Labs' Robert Wilson in 1978 for his codiscovery of faint background radiation, proving that the universe was created by the Big Bang billions of years ago.

Several large five-story buildings sit at the center of AT&T Bell Labs' headquarters in Murray Hill, surrounded by meticulously maintained lawns and an abundance of trees. Inside, interns are impressed with the winding, maze-like corridors, enormous labs outfitted with top-of-the-line equipment, and an oversupply of old computers, many of which lie waiting to be shipped out as donations. It is no wonder that the company's researchers are eager to spend long hours here. Remarked an intern: "The people here love what they do; they share jokes, and they stay late all the time even though there's no overtime pay." This spirit certainly rubs off on the interns, who often work ten hours a day. "But no one lords over you; you can take a long lunch or leave early," said an intern.

Interns are encouraged to occasionally leave the confines of their labs and attend the workshops and weekly talks given at the Murray Hill location (shuttle service is provided from the other sites). Focusing on advances in technology and science, the discussions explore such topics as post-magnetic fields, planetary magnetospheres, and blackbody radiation as well as videophones, infrared cameras, and high-definition television. "Afterwards, if one of the discussions interests you, and you want to return for a second summer," said an intern, "you can go up to the speaker and see if he or she would be willing to take you on as a future intern."

For years, the company has arranged for student housing at nearby Rutgers University. Maintaining campuses in several cities, the university houses Bell Labs interns at its Busch campus, in Piscataway, NJ. Nearly 90 percent of all Bell Labs' interns live in these dorms, priced at $300 to $400 a month, which is deducted from interns' paychecks. Typical of dorms, carpeting is often found to be "ratty" and air-conditioning not as powerful as it could be. "At least Rutgers gym is close by and free, and we party on Friday nights," said an intern. Because the dorms are a considerable distance from the company buildings, bus transportation to and from work is provided.

At the end of the summer, interns give presentations of their work to groups of managers. Afterward, the several hundred interns gather together for the last time at the farewell picnic. One of the internship coordinators makes a few opening remarks, and then interns dive into barbecue and beverages. In between swimming, volleyball, basketball, and softball, interns exchange phone numbers and parting words. "It was a really fun day, capping off a wonderful learning experience," recalled an intern.

SELECTION

 SRP applicants must be college sophomores, juniors, or seniors. UR applicants, on the other hand, may be B.S., M.S., or Ph.D. candidates so long as they are available for permanent employment within two years after the internship. Only students with a minimum 3.0 GPA are considered. Both programs target those studying ceramic engineering, chemical engineering, chemistry, communications science, computer science/engineering, electrical engineering, information science, materials science, mathematics, mechanical engineering, operations research, physics, or statistics. Students majoring in other technical fields are considered by the UR program. Brochures cite "academic achievement . . . [and] demonstrated interest and motivation in scientific fields" as key selection criteria.

APPLICATION PROCEDURE

 The SRP deadline and UR deadline fall on December 1 and February 15, respectively. The company accepts applications as early as October 15. SRP candidates must submit an application form, official transcript, resumé, three letters of recommendation, and a personal statement answering the four questions that appear on the application form. UR candidates need only submit a resumé, cover letter, and official transcript. The best candidates are interviewed over the phone by department managers.

AT&T also administers five scholarship/fellowship programs. The Cooperative Research Fellowship Program (CRFP) and the Graduate Research Program for Women (GRPW) provide summer jobs, tuition, and living stipends to minority and female college seniors who will pursue a

Ph.D. in science or engineering. The Dual Degree Scholarship Program (DDSP) provides summer jobs, tuition, and room and board to minorities and women willing to pursue two degrees at one of nine specific East Coast schools. The Engineering Scholarship Program (ESP) provides full tuition, room and board, and summer jobs to minority and female college seniors who will pursue a B.S. degree in computers or engineering. The Ph.D. Scholarship Program (Ph.D.) provides tuition, living stipends, and research assignments to Ph.D. students nominated by their departments. Interested students should contact the appropriate program manager for further information.

OVERVIEW

 An AT&T Bell Laboratories internship is one of the most rigorous in its class. Applying their talents to any number of challenging research projects, interns are exposed to cutting-edge physics, electronics, and materials-science research inside one of the world's preeminent industrial research and development institutions. In addition to gaining knowledge from renowned scientists, interns might someday end up using a product on which they themselves did research. Over the nearly 50-year history of the internship program, hundreds of interns have helped develop the touch-tone telephone, the Telstar communications satellite, which made cable TV possible, and the cellular telephone. Now future interns have an opportunity to make an impact on voice-controlled robot arms, digital radio, and high-definition television.

FOR MORE INFORMATION . . .

- AT&T Bell Laboratories
  University Relations
  (Name of Program) Manager
  101 Crawfords Corner Road
  P.O. Box 3030
  Room 1E-231
  Holmdel, NJ 07733-3030
  (908) 949-3000

And unto Adam He said, Because thou . . . hast eaten of the tree . . . cursed is the ground for thy sake; in sorrow shalt thou eat of it all the days of thy life.
—*Genesis 3:17*

After savoring an apple, Adam and Eve were condemned to a life of sin. A Red Delicious caused their fall. The apple, at least for this fig-leafed couple, represented the ultimate seduction.

But the people at Apple Computer, Inc. believe that the apple means something else. They contend that the fleshy fruit represents something healthy and natural. When Steven Jobs and Stephen Wozniak named the company in 1976, they wanted to symbolize their venture's propensity for fresh ideas and innovation. A rainbow-colored apple fit the bill, and thus was born what would become one of today's most recognized corporate symbols in the world.

Yet the idea of an apple as seducer still fits Apple Computer. After all, the company lures consumers into buying millions of its remarkably useful Macintosh computers every year. From the Macintosh Classic to the Macintosh Powerbook, Apple has been winning over the world's personal-computer users with uncanny success. But Apple isn't stopping there. Its Newton Information Architecture technology is pioneering new avenues of information management. The first Newton product—the Newton notepad—integrates advanced handwriting recognition, communication, and data-management technologies. It's one of several new Apple products setting the standard for the digital information age.

DESCRIPTION

It's a given that the Apple Internship Program is interested in computer scientists and engineers. But liberal arts majors should not be discour-

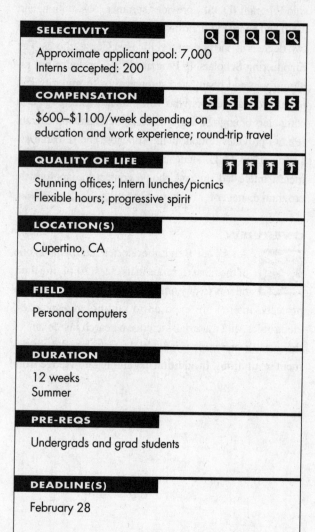

SELECTIVITY	Q Q Q Q Q
Approximate applicant pool: 7,000 Interns accepted: 200	

COMPENSATION	$ $ $ $ $
$600–$1100/week depending on education and work experience; round-trip travel	

QUALITY OF LIFE	↑ ↑ ↑ ↑
Stunning offices; Intern lunches/picnics Flexible hours; progressive spirit	

LOCATION(S)
Cupertino, CA

FIELD
Personal computers

DURATION
12 weeks Summer

PRE-REQS
Undergrads and grad students

DEADLINE(S)
February 28

aged: Opportunities exist for those interested in nontechnical areas such as marketing, finance, public relations, and art design. In either case, the departments hiring interns include the following: Apple USA (Sales), World Wide Operations (Manufacturing), Macintosh Systems, Administration, Enterprise Systems (Networking Solutions), Advanced Technology, and Personal Interactive Electronics.

One intern worked in the Macintosh Systems division for two successive summers. During the first, she was assigned to the System Integration and Compatibility Group, where she tested third-party software written for Apple's System 6.5. "I ran different educational software packages to see if they worked smoothly in the system. If I found a bug in the software, I'd report the problem to the company that designed the program. If the glitch was in the system, I'd have an Apple engineer look at it." She "stayed with the bugs" the following summer, working on an in-house bug-tracking program. "I helped write some of the code for new features, like an Apple menu option that displays the number of bugs an engineer was assigned to repair."

An intern in the Enterprise Systems Division had a completely different experience. Because she had a background in both museum studies and computer science, she was asked to help the 3-D Graphics Group create a CD-ROM showing off Apple's best graphics technologies. Called the Virtual Museum, the software takes a user on a 3-D tour of a computer-generated "museum," complete with stops at an astronomy gallery, a medicine room, and a plant gallery. The intern helped design the graphic-user interface, planning "what [the museum] looks like and how [the user] travels through it." She also helped write the HyperCard scripts that integrated the graphical artwork, video clips, and sound; the scripts were "the glue that brought all the pieces of the multimedia project together," she explained. Despite working long hours, she said the working environment was ideal: "The permanent staff respected my aesthetic sensibility and background in museums. I was given a tremendous amount of creative freedom."

Another intern in the Enterprise Systems Division spent six weeks doing a market-research study on V.I.T.A.L. (Virtually Integrated Technology Lifecycle), a strategy for connecting Apple's computers with mainframes, minicomputers, and other microcomputers. His assignment was to determine the ways in which V.I.T.A.L. is useful to corporate consumers. "I attacked the problem from several angles," he said. "I reviewed all of Apple's literature on

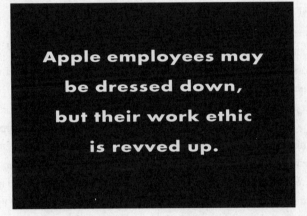

Apple employees may be dressed down, but their work ethic is revved up.

V.I.T.A.L. I then interviewed some experts, including a VP from Liberty Mutual and a researcher at Stanford." He also organized a focus group, whereby computer users were gathered together and asked questions about their hardware preferences and needs. "It was my first time running a focus group," he said. "I rented an official focus-group room in San Jose. While a moderator asked the group questions, I watched behind a one-way mirror. A camera was set up behind the mirror, capturing the event on film."

In the Apple USA division, a finance major worked on strategies for marketing Apple products to college students. He said: "I helped create back-to-school promotions and other student marketing plans. I also developed ideas for advertisements, which I reviewed after they were put together by [the creative department]. You could say I provided a student's perspective, telling the creative people 'this is how students think, this is what they want.'" Managers were so impressed with the intern's work that they had him design an Apple convention booth and go on the road to supervise the booth at conventions. "It was like a rock-and-roll show," he said. "We'd roll into town a few days before the convention. We'd do a massive setup, with stages and all sorts of props. At the event, I'd supervise the Apple booth, organizing everything from staffing to software." Apple covered all flight and hotel expenses on his trips; the "tour" took him to conventions in Atlanta, Las Vegas, Dallas, and Washington, D.C.

It's no rarity that interns have an opportunity to travel. One intern was flown to Las Vegas, where he attended the Siggraph convention for computer graphics. Another made a business trip to the Mac World convention in Boston. Others are sent to trade shows in the San Francisco Bay Area. Aware that a change of scenery can stimulate thinking, Apple encourages its employees to take "off-sites" or one-day working vacations; an intern made an off-site with his marketing team to a winery, where they spent the day engaged in productive strategy talks, while somehow finding the time to enjoy a "delicious lunch and dinner." Another intern received paid leave when she attended a Chicago meeting of the Society of Hispanic Professional Engineers; she said: "Although the trip was not work related, Apple saw the value in one of its employees representing the company at the convention."

The relaxed atmosphere of the Bay Area pervades Apple's corporate culture. Or is it a *counter*-corporate culture? Working hours are delightfully flexible; said an intern, "No one checks to see what time you come in. You set your own hours." And everyone wears casual clothes. Sweats and shorts are perfectly acceptable. Said an intern: "When the manager [from Apple] who interviewed me was wearing shorts, I knew something was up." One intern boasted of skateboarding to work in flip-flops. So accepted is informal dress that even some executives favor "regular clothes, sometimes even leather jackets" over pinstripes and suspenders.

Lest one gets the wrong impression, Apple employees may be dressed down, but their work ethic is revved up. Apple attracts the crème de la crème of the computer world, and it shows. Indeed, one intern said she had "never before worked with such a group of bright, hardworking people." But this concentration of silicon chip virtuosos, many of whom are "hellbent on proving themselves," creates an intensity that puts some interns off. "It sometimes seems like there are 14,000 geniuses running around trying to get promoted. This can make for a sink-or-swim attitude around the office. . . . [At Apple], interns can take the ball and run with it—but they've got to go out and get the ball; it won't necessarily be given to them."

The internship coordinator tries to alleviate the daily pressure by organizing an assortment of extracurricular activities. Interns are given tours of the Apple TV station (where instructional videos are produced), the library (where all of Apple's computers are on display), and a Cray computer, "one of the world's largest and fastest computers." Intramural sports are popular; everyone gets fired up for the Corporate Games, a company-wide athletic competition pitting groups of employees against each other. Three or so times a session the coordinator plans intern picnics. And the company holds a few "forum lunches" at which a high-level executive addresses the interns.

Apple's physical plant clocks in as "stunning," "sooo nice," and "delightfully modern." About an hour's drive from San Francisco, Apple's headquarters is spread throughout the Silicon Valley town of Cupertino. Many buildings have airy lobbies. One has "the coolest black-and-white tile floors." The new R&D complex has a "lovely" cafeteria with outdoor seating. Wherever one goes, stress-relieving devices abound from toy basketball hoops to super squirt-guns, and juggling pins.

As computers are Apple's lifeblood, one would expect interns to have powerful computers at their disposal. Well, they do. Most work on the Macintosh 2 FX, one of Apple's most advanced computers. A few are loaned the exalted Macintosh Quadra, the computer equivalent of a Ferrari Testarossa. Gushed an intern: "The Quadra is some piece of work. It's powered by a 33-megahertz Motorola 68040 microprocessor."

Fringe benefits at Apple are almost as prevalent as microchips. Interns whose homes are at least 50 miles from Cupertino receive reimbursement for travel to and from Apple; they are also put up in a hotel for up to a week until they find housing in the Cupertino area. Interns have full health benefits, including a free physician's visit. At the company store, interns receive a sizable discount on Apple products. Said an intern: "The store offers about a 50 percent discount when your make your first purchase. The discount becomes progressively less on each successive purchase, to discourage people from abusing the privilege."

To top it all off, interns are compensated handsomely for their efforts. Pay is based on one's level of education and years of applicable work experience. A sophomore with a nontechnical background can expect to make a hefty $600 a week. On the other end of the scale, an MBA with a few years of technical experience will pull in around $1,100 a week.

SELECTION

The internship is open to undergraduates of any level and graduate students. The majority of Apple interns are studying computer science, electrical engineering, and computer engineering, but the program welcomes applicants from all academic backgrounds.

APPLICATION PROCEDURE

 The deadline is February 28. Applicants should submit a cover letter describing their academic background and how it applies to their area of interest. A resumé is also required. After receiving these documents, Apple enters them into a special database, which is perused by the managers of various departments. The managers conduct brief phone interviews with the candidates they deem most promising. Applicants who do well at the initial interview are given an extensive phone interview a few days later. Local applicants may interview in person, but most candidates are interviewed over the phone.

OVERVIEW

 It's good to be where the action is. The action, at least in terms of personal computers, is at Apple Computer, Inc. A leader in shaping the information highway of the next century, Apple assigns its interns challenging, real-world projects. Add a progressive on-the-job climate, a fat salary, and the recreational charms of the San Francisco Bay Area, and the Apple internship seems "ripe" with opportunity.

FOR MORE INFORMATION . . .

■ Apple Computer, Inc.
Internship Program
College Relations
20525 Mariani Avenue
MS: 75-2J
Cupertino, CA 95014
(408) 996-1010

ARTHUR ANDERSEN

ARTHUR ANDERSEN & CO, SC

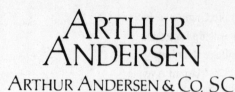

These days, accounting majors can learn the tricks of the trade from several introductory accounting textbooks, written by such big-wheel professors as Kaplan, Anthony, Weygandt, and Horngren. But back in the early 1910s, students of accounting in the U.S. were limited to only one available textbook, appropriately titled *Complete Accounting Course*. While this book represents an important accomplishment in the history of accounting, its author is less known for his writing than he is for establishing a small Midwestern accounting firm in 1913. That author's name is Arthur Andersen, and the company bearing his name—The Arthur Andersen Worldwide Organization—has since grown into a global powerhouse.

Composed of Arthur Andersen and Andersen Consulting, The Arthur Andersen Worldwide Organization is the world's largest professional services company, with 80,000 clients in every major industry, 318 offices in 72 countries, and yearly revenues of over $6 billion. Among the Big Six accounting firms — comprising Arthur Andersen, Price Waterhouse, KPMG Peat Marwick, Ernst & Young, Deloitte & Touche, and Coopers & Lybrand—Arthur Andersen is the largest in the United States.

SELECTIVITY	🔍 🔍 🔍
Approx. applicant pool: 2,200 Interns accepted: 300	

COMPENSATION	$ $ $ $ $
$500–$625/week on average	

QUALITY OF LIFE	⭮ ⭮ ⭮ ⭮
Exceptional training course Mentors; Professional atmosphere	

LOCATION(S)
Nationwide—see Description

FIELD
Public accounting and business consulting

DURATION
10–12 weeks Summer, Winter

PRE-REQS
College juniors and seniors A minimum of 12 units of accounting

DEADLINE(S)
Summer .... February 15 Winter .... October 31

DESCRIPTION

Since around 1950, the Arthur Andersen Internship Program in the U.S. has offered students entry-level positions in both Audit & Business Advisory Services and Tax & Business Advisory Services. "The office's goal . . . is to replicate the same experiences and situations that a new hire would have during their first year," says the coordinator. The following offices in total routinely hire approximately 100 interns in the winter and 200 interns in the summer: Atlanta, Boston, Charlotte, Chicago, Cincinnati, Cleveland, Columbus, Dallas, Denver, Detroit, Hartford, Houston, Indianapolis, Kansas City, Los Angeles, Memphis, Miami, Milwaukee, Minneapolis/St. Paul (the Twin Cities), Nashville, New Jersey, New Orleans, New York, Omaha, Philadelphia, Pittsburgh, St. Louis, San Francisco, Seattle, Stamford, Tampa, and Washington, D.C.

Interns in Tax help out with about a half dozen projects, from researching inquiries of the local and state tax boards to preparing corporate, partnership, and individual tax returns. Interns in tax might also work on appraisal and valuation projects, helping to price clients' tangible and intangible assets, and in corporate tax consulting, where they help improve clients' corporate structures and accounting methods in order to minimize corporate taxes. One Tax intern worked on a client's 1040—a number dreaded by most hardworking Americans. Looking over the client's broker reports, he made sure that she had reported every dividend but had not reported nontaxable items such as principal payments or interest from tax-exempt securities. "I sifted through her files and prepared the work papers for Text Processing, the department that fills out the actual return." In the course of their projects, interns often do research at Arthur Andersen's libraries. "One of our clients was being audited by the State Franchise Tax Board," explained an intern. "The board disagreed with us over the nature of the company's income, and I spent some time at the library searching for relevant legal cases." Tax interns are also involved with the creation of compensation packages. "An executive we were representing wanted to improve his cash flow so that he could pay off his mortgage. We came up with lots of options to present to his board of directors, and I created a spreadsheet that enumerated all the options' present values," recalled an intern.

During audits, Arthur Andersen reviews the books and accounts of its clients—from manufacturers and hospitals to advertising firms and professional sports teams. Assigned to audit teams off-site at clients' offices, each Audit intern examines one or more sections of the balance sheet—cash, accounts payable, stockholders' equity, etc.—to "obtain reasonable assurance about whether the financial statements are free of material misstatement," as Andersen writes in nearly every annual report it audits. Interns also work on Audit projects in operational consulting (concerned with enhancing client business practices to improve profitability), information-systems consulting, bankruptcy recovery, and litigation support. One Audit intern, assigned to a manufacturing firm, worked on inventory: "The firm had

already counted the items in its plants, so I went through Andersen's checklist to make sure the firm's book-to-physical adjustment was correct." Another Audit intern was assigned to a large cosmetics company. After setting up Andersen files according to the special procedure for labeling and indexing, he audited cash, investments, and fixed assets. "I had to do everything from interviewing employees about processing cycles to getting summaries of bank accounts," he recalled. Required to investigate the company's refrigerated warehouse in Pennsylvania, he remembers "putting on a heavy down jacket" and counting boxes of vials in a $-40°F$ cold room. "Boy was I freezing," he said.

During the winter, interns experience what the accounting industry calls the "busy" season, the three months preceding two IRS due dates: March 15 for corporate tax returns and April 15 for individual returns. "You'll definitely work on more projects during the winter," affirms an intern. "Companies are busy doing year-end inventories, and individuals are scrambling to get their returns in on time."

In between assignments, there's a bit of busywork—looking up industry statistics on CD-ROM, arranging files, photocopying, and running documents from one department to another. For most interns, these tasks are assigned during the first week or two of the program. "I got the feeling it was a test of sorts," surmised an intern. "The managers want to see if the photocopies you make and the files you put together are complete and legible. After all, clients look at these things, and if you prove that you're careful, managers will give you great assignments." Besides gaining more responsibility, interns who are happy to attend to some busywork will familiarize themselves with the office. "You may be the lowest man on the totem pole for that one week or so," said an intern, "but it's a great way to start before you're thrown in the fire. In addition to learning how to use the computers and how to create a Lotus spreadsheet, you meet your coworkers."

> Interns would be ill-equipped, were it not for Arthur Andersen's Center for Professional Education.

Since most interns have yet to experience classes in audit or advanced tax (senior-year courses), one might think that they are unprepared to tackle their assignments. "What I learned in school was helpful the first two days only," confirmed an intern. Actually, interns *would* be ill-equipped, were it not for the organization's Center for Professional Education, hidden away in St. Charles, Illinois. At this former women's college, the firm trains interns, new-hires, and employees to the tune of $340 million every year, an amount that allows Arthur Andersen to remain the world's leading employee educator. Audit interns go to the St. Charles school for two weeks. Tax interns spend a few days at the firm-wide orientation and the Tax Intern Leadership Conference. Both groups live in well-furnished dorm rooms, most without TVs, so ample time to socialize with peers is available. Instructed by experienced partners and managers, interns learn the various ins and outs of Arthur Andersen accounting procedures—balance sheets, audits, and tax returns. "Without the training," said an Audit intern, "it would have been much more difficult to grasp Arthur Andersen's standard procedures for audits. I would have had to ask my manager too many questions, distracting him from his job, and we would have had to bill the client for that extra time."

Informally known as the "campus," the Center for Professional Education comprises 151 acres on the Fox River. Though the center offers standard city conveniences such as a hair salon, a dry-cleaning shop, a cafe, and a bar, there's plenty of rusticity to balance them out: a vast woods, the Fox River, and jogging trails snaking through the forest. After the usual 12-hour day of classes, interns may release their tensions by playing basketball, tennis, volleyball, softball, or soccer. The center also offers two putting greens and a fitness center informally known as the "sweat shop." Moreover, shuttles go into St. Charles and Chicago, approximately 45 minutes away, every weekend.

Back at the office, the training continues. Interns are often assigned not a single mentor but a team of them—usually a partner, a manager, and two seniors. During and after every assignment, a member of the team sits down and evaluates the intern's work. "The first time I did 'receivables'—probably the toughest of the balance sheet items to do—my senior walked me through it," said an Audit intern. "[A]nd every time I finished a section, the senior

would look over it and make suggestions or corrections." Even when mentors take interns out to lunch (a common occurrence) or mingle among interns at office social functions, they help interns augment their education. "By talking to the bosses, I learned everything from the value of networking to the kinds of work partners and managers do," explained an intern.

With their large, oak doors and mahogany-lined walls, the offices at Andersen exude an "old and established" air. Because they work mainly in the office, Tax interns sit at their own cubicles, two to an IBM PC. Audit interns, on the other hand, are almost always off-site; they share areas of workspaces and phones with other interns. Professionalism mandates that all employees, including interns, wear suits. However, most Andersen-ites know when to shed their business attire for more casual garb; employees get together to socialize at happy hours, watch major-league baseball games, and exercise at the local gym.

Interns' salaries vary from site to site. Depending on experience, overall economy of the city in which the office is located, success of the office, and cost of living, each intern may make anywhere from $500 to $625 per week on average plus overtime pay. "A person working in New York will obviously make more than one working in Seattle," says the coordinator.

SELECTION

The internship is open to college juniors and seniors. Generally, a minimum of 12 units of accounting coursework is required for applicants. While most interns are accounting majors, students in finance and economics sometimes participate in the program.

APPLICATION PROCEDURE

The deadline is February 15 for summer and October 31 for winter. Note that the number of students applying to the summer internship is much higher than the number applying for the winter positions. Therefore, your chances might be higher if you can take part in the winter session. Working through campus placement offices, recruiters interview students throughout the country. Candidates whose campuses aren't visited by Arthur Andersen should send a resumé and cover letter to the desired office; only in the event that applicants are unable to locate a specific office's address and phone number should they contact Arthur Andersen's headquarters. Top candidates are invited to the offices for interviews; long-distance applicants are flown in.

OVERVIEW

 Since 1981, *Public Accounting Report* has polled accounting department chairs at over 100 U.S. colleges and universities. For 12 consecutive years, the professors have ranked Arthur Andersen number one overall for new graduates starting careers in public accounting. What holds true for recent graduates holds true for undergraduates. Arthur Andersen interns receive an in-depth introduction to public accounting, full exposure to partners and managers, intimate contact with clients, and an impeccable level of training. Moreover, completing the internship dramatically improves interns' chances of being offered permanent employment: approximately 80 percent of interns return to the firm.

FOR MORE INFORMATION . . .

■ Arthur Andersen
Internship Program
69 West Washington Street
Chicago, IL 60602-3002
(312) 580-0069

SELECTIVITY

Approximate applicant pool: 200
Interns accepted: 11

COMPENSATION

$100/week plus housing

QUALITY OF LIFE

Free housing; Mountain surroundings
Free nature classes, Vegetable garden

LOCATION(S)

Aspen, CO

FIELD

Environment/nature

DURATION

12–13 weeks
Summer

PRE-REQS

College juniors and seniors, recent grads,
grad students

DEADLINE(S)

March 1

What is Aspen best known for?

Is it champagne skiing, the Aspen Music Festival, or Jack Nicholson?

Yes, but it's also a place where black bears and elk live within feet of one another, a place where cedar waxwings and Steller's jays perch peacefully together in conifer trees. In fact, the city that *Snow Country* magazine rated as the second best ski resort in the United States is a natural paradise. Positioned at the edge of Hallam Lake at an elevation of 7,900 feet is the city's wildlife sanctuary, an environmentalists' mecca called the Aspen Center for Environmental Studies (ACES).

Since its founding in 1968 by Aspen resident Elizabeth Paepcke, the private, nonprofit ACES has been educating people "to be environmentally responsible." Managing the 25-acre Hallam Lake sanctuary and another 175-acre naturalist area, ACES offers hikes and nature classes to both children and adults. It also runs the Environmental Learning Center, which houses the Scott Field Laboratory, Pinewood Natural History Library, Gates Visitor Center, and a bookstore informally known as the Den.

DESCRIPTION

Interns' responsibilities include just about everything that has to do with maintaining the center: landscaping (i.e., planting trees, repairing the boardwalks around the marshy sanctuary, and tending the garden), giving talks on the Birds of Prey program, rehabilitating injured animals and birds, teaching natural-history classes to children and adults, and leading nature walks.

During the summer, the center offers nearly a dozen programs, all taught by interns, from leading a troop of adults on a sunset walk by the lake to guiding visitors through an "early birding" expedition to teaching children about the rich diversity of insects in the area. The walks and talks emphasize not only the diversity of the surrounding flora and fauna but also the fragility of wildlife. "Our overall goal is to spread environmental awareness," said an intern, "not by bombarding visitors with a bunch of facts but by encouraging them to look around and reexamine their relationship to plants and animals."

Interns describe their role in the center's environmental crusade as "challenging" and

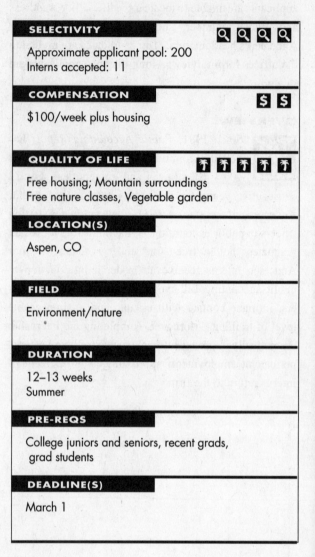

"intense." Often spending several hours a week in the center's library, they research such diverse topics as Rocky Mountain flowers, organic gardening, and black bears. Besides teaching the prescribed courses, interns may also design their own programs. Two past interns, for example, created a class that touched upon a range of subjects: tundra wildlife, animal tracking, stream life, and birds of prey. "First, we created lesson plans. Then we spent the summer teaching a four-hour course for older kids and adults, hiking into the mountains on a trail we created and pointing out specific flowers and animals."

Once a converted barn, ACES was razed in 1988 to build the Environmental Learning Center, which affords spectacular views of the lake. One room inside the new center is home to a bookstore and the information desk. Another room contains a lab, equipped with microscopes and a freshwater aquarium. The third room is used as a classroom in which some of the center's programs are held. Besides having interns staff the information desk and bookstore several hours each week, the center assigns interns to repair trails and care for the animals housed in a barn that was built alongside the main building. An intern in charge of the center's indoor exhibits took care of a collection of snakes, tarantulas, mealworms, and hissing cockroaches from Madagascar. He explained: "I fed them and administered routine health exams, looking for yeast infections under the skin of each snake, for example." ACES also maintains offices on the second floor, where interns sometimes work alongside Director Tom Cardamone, described by one intern as a particularly "easy going, approachable fellow." Open and receptive to intern ideas, Cardamone arranges for interns and the rest of the staff to meet with him once a week to discuss how things are going and to brainstorm ideas on improving the programs.

> An intern in charge of the indoor exhibits took care of the center's collection of snakes, tarantulas, mealworms, and hissing cockroaches from Madagascar.

Behind the Center is the Birds of Prey building, home to a slew of hawks, eagles, and owls. Most of the birds are injured and unreleasable to the wild—for instance, the building houses a bald eagle with a lame wing. "We had her there for teaching purposes, to show people the beauty of the eagle and to teach them to be careful, since most of the birds, like her, were shot by [errant] hunters or hit by careless drivers," said an intern. When possible, the center nurses birds back to health and sets them free. In such cases it's critical that the bird not become accustomed to human faces or else its natural instincts will diminish. For example, an intern who worked with a great-horned owl attempted to reintroduce it to the area: "I wore a cloak over my head and fed it by hand from a puppet that looks like an owl." Eventually, the owl was moved to a large cage in which it could fly. "We wanted it to get used to catching its own game. So we'd throw live mice into the cage and watch the owl pounce on them."

When Aspen residents encounter an injured bird, they know who to call—ACES. "I got a call from a fellow who said he saw a bald eagle hobbling on the side of the road. So I grabbed the jesses [short, leather straps used to secure the legs of hawks, falcons, and eagles] and the leather gloves for my arms, hopped in the truck, and was on my way." But once he got there, he found a blue grouse instead of an eagle. "They're the size of chickens so it's easy to see how the man was mistaken, especially since the blue grouse doesn't fly but instead runs about." So to illustrate the difference between a grouse and an eagle, the intern "chased the grouse around until it hid in some bushes."

One would expect a wildlife sanctuary of ACES' caliber to contain all sorts of animal and plant species, and the Hallam Lake area is definitely no disappointment. A rich diversity of plants is found along the trails and the lake.

Besides the raptors (as birds of prey are called), native to the area are waterfowl, muskrat, beaver, fox, and songbirds such as yellow warblers and lazuli buntings. Some of the animals may be routinely spotted during hiking. Others require viewing from high up and at a distance. Aspen Mountain, at 11,200 feet, is the place to go. To get there, visitors ride the gondola to Aspen Mountain's tour booth, staffed by interns and equipped with powerful telescopes which allow one to eye bighorn sheep, elk, bear, red foxes, coyotes, and eagles.

ACES' interns live on-site, lodged in two houses four blocks from one another. Down the road from the stone-pillars entrance to the center is the staff house, home to five interns. With three bedrooms, a bathroom, a kitchen, and a living room, it's described as a "tight-fitting but cozy place." The rest of the interns live in an old two-story bed-and-breakfast near Aspen Mountain, farther down the road. Slightly larger than the staff house, the bed-and-breakfast is affectionately known as the "mine dump" because of the old mining cars adjacent to it. Prior to 1993, two interns also resided in the attic of the Bird of Prey house, "right above the birds," but now the attic serves as the interns' private office, "where we can read a library book or prepare lesson plans away from tourists and ringing phones."

Interns may purchase some groceries from Clark's Market down the street, but there's plenty of food on-site as well. A garden behind the center offers interns all the vegetables they can eat, from tomatoes and lettuce to potatoes and peas. The garden even cultivates the state flower, the columbine, whose blossoms, claims an intern, are "good to eat in salads." Hallam Lake makes for "great fishing" and contains a plethora of brook trout waiting to be caught for a delicious meal. Interns often cook and eat dinners together, forming friendships that the center's "communal atmosphere" encourages.

About five minutes' walking distance from ACES is the town of Aspen, a city of endless cultural events. In the heart of downtown is a small park that hosts free summer concerts and performances. In addition, the Aspen Music Festival and Dance Aspen perform classical music and dance, respectively, every summer. Home to wealthy residents, Aspen boasts expensive restaurants and bars.

"Although they're expensive, the clubs are always filled with college-age people having a fun time," said an intern. "[A]nd there are lots of cool, inexpensive places to dance and eat, too." Aspen's gilt-edged reputation attracts a bevy of celebrities, many of whom are impassioned about the environment. "Al Gore once stopped by the Center [where signed copies of his *Earth in the Balance* are for sale]," said an intern. "Jack Nicholson's house is across Hallam Lake; Chris Evert Lloyd enrolled her two kids in our Little Naturalist program last year; and John Denver, who lives in the area, occasionally makes a visit."

As part of ACES, interns are allowed to take at least one class for free from the center's Naturalist Field School. Since one-day courses normally run from $30 to $45 and overnight courses from $80 to $390, the free classes help to compensate for interns' low pay. Teaching students to appreciate nature, the dozen or so courses that are offered render even the most ardent city-slicker more environmentally aware. Students learn how to identify, collect, and prepare wild plants as food in "Wild Edibles" or how to fish in "Fly Fishing" at the nationally-known Roaring Fork, or Frying Pan, River.

SELECTION

 College juniors and seniors as well as recent graduates and graduate students are eligible to apply, though the bulk of interns have received college degrees by the start of the internship. The center strongly prefers students who are majoring in the natural sciences (e.g., biology and chemistry), environmental studies, or related fields. While knowledge of Rocky Mountain flora and fauna is not required, First-Aid Certification is. Such certification can be obtained by taking a two-day course at a local Red Cross.

APPLICATION PROCEDURE

 The deadline is March 1. Students need only submit the center's application form; a resumé and three letters of reference are suggested but not required. After the coordinator sifts through applications, top candidates are interviewed over the phone.

OVERVIEW

 Avidly opposing the urban encroachment that has destroyed much of America's natural habitat, the private Aspen Center for Environmental Studies recruits interns to help educate the public about the environment. Living at Hallam Lake, interns are exposed to Rocky Mountain plants and animals, riparian flora and fauna, and birds of prey such as bald eagles and hawks. After spending a summer leading interpretive walks, learning animal rehabilitation, and teaching children about the environment, interns are sure to leave with a newfound appreciation of nature.

FOR MORE INFORMATION . . .

■ Aspen Center for Environmental Studies
Education Coordinator
Summer Naturalist Intern Program
P.O. Box 8777
Aspen, CO 81612
(303) 925-5756

SELECTIVITY	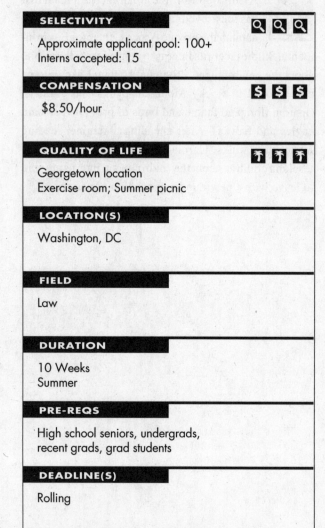
Approximate applicant pool: 100+ Interns accepted: 15	
COMPENSATION	
$8.50/hour	
QUALITY OF LIFE	
Georgetown location Exercise room; Summer picnic	
LOCATION(S)	
Washington, DC	
FIELD	
Law	
DURATION	
10 Weeks Summer	
PRE-REQS	
High school seniors, undergrads, recent grads, grad students	
DEADLINE(S)	
Rolling	

Who will protect the hemophiliacs who contract AIDS from tainted blood products? Who's going to seek redress for the people killed when a highway crew knocks a giant boulder down a mountainside? Who's going to investigate instances of nursing home maltreatment or faulty motorcycle helmets or defective breast implants? Trial lawyers, that's who.

Advancing the mission of trial lawyers is the Association of Trial Lawyers of America (ATLA), an organization dedicated to championing injury prevention and promoting justice for injured people. With a membership of 60,000, ATLA's primary interest is personal injury law, focusing on such areas as product safety, toxic releases, workers' compensation, and medical malpractice. Through the ATLA ALERT program, ATLA investigates dangerous products and reports its findings to the appropriate regulatory authorities. It also runs a full roster of educational programs for lawyers, law students, and the general public on legal issues and the legal profession.

DESCRIPTION

The ATLA internship is a mix of busywork and meaty projects. As one intern put it, "It's the type of internship where if you have an enthusiastic supervisor and prove yourself, you can end up doing challenging work." Departments taking on interns include Public Affairs, Legal Affairs, Education, State Relations, Communications, Meetings and Services, and *Trial* magazine.

Some departments give interns experience in legal research. In State Relations, for example, an intern researched the medical malpractice laws of all fifty states. "Every day

for several weeks, I went to the Library of Congress and dug up each state's malpractice statutes," he said. "I organized the information on a chart . . . for ATLA to use when members inquired about their state's laws." An intern in Education also was exposed to legal writings when he helped edit articles written for an ATLA seminar. He commented: "I proofread and checked the citations of a number of articles written by a staff attorney. But to understand their content, I needed to convert the legalese into plain language." As most interns "don't know a motion in *liminae* from an *amicus curiae*,"

ATLA sometimes has a staff member brief them on basic legal terms and research procedures. Said an intern: "A staff researcher took me to the library and showed me how to read citations and conduct basic research. . . . It made my summer a lot easier and it was great preparation for law school."

An intern in Public Affairs worked with ATLA ALERT, reviewing letters from ATLA members describing potentially harmful products, such as a bed harness that can strangle someone if attached incorrectly or a toy that is potentially toxic if pulled apart. When his supervisor thought a product merited further investigation, the intern "looked up how many accidents or deaths were caused by the product and researched the relevant product-liability statutes." After submitting a comprehensive report to his supervisor, ATLA lawyers would decide whether to take further action. "Sometimes we would write the appropriate agency—such as the Food and Drug Administration or the Consumer Products Safety Commission—and ask them to review the product," he said. "Other times we would send out a press release or hold a press conference about the product."

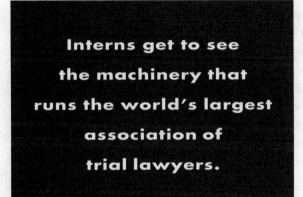

Interns get to see the machinery that runs the world's largest association of trial lawyers.

The ATLA internship isn't only for aspiring lawyers. A student "with no intention of going to law school" worked in Public Relations, where she helped publicize ATLA conferences and events. Her assignments were myriad—calling members, updating the member mailing list, stuffing envelopes for the national convention, designing posters for ATLA's evening movie series—just to name a few. She also had several opportunities to attend meetings and lectures related to public relations. Once, for example, she accompanied a few staff members to the offices of a famous media consultant, who was advising the new ATLA president on how to answer questions from reporters. Another time she went with her department to hear Attorney General Janet Reno speak at the National Press Club.

The internship kicks off with a two-day orientation program, where interns learn the ins and outs of the office— "how the phones work, where to find supplies, how to conduct research at the library, and so forth." But if orientation has a primary purpose, it is to give interns a full-scale introduction to ATLA's role in the legal community. "[Administration] does a good job of telling you everything you ever wanted to know about ATLA," said an intern. "We met with the executive director over breakfast. We heard from a panel of executives later in the day. And we saw a film on the history of ATLA."

There isn't a wealth of extracurriculars at ATLA. Interns are welcome to join the organization's softball team, which competes on the Mall against other teams. Interns may also attend the summer picnic, which in recent years has included a raffle.

ATLA is located in the heart of Georgetown, a district of Washington famous for tiny boutiques, quaint colonial houses, and a scenic harbor. Georgetown's only drawback is its inaccessibility to the Metro; commuters to the city must take a bus or make the 20-minute walk to and from the closest Metro stop. ATLA holds court in its own five-story brick building, whose interior is described by interns as "traditionally lawyerly" and "modern but not fancy." With regard to space, the office is "cramped and only the exceptional few have offices." Interns typically have their own cubicles, each with a desk and phone. Fitness fans will be happy to learn that the third floor holds an exercise room, featuring a weight machine, StairMaster, stationary bicycles, and showers. No cafeteria exists, but a selection of "yuppie cafes" and gourmet stores is just an easy walk away.

SELECTION

The internship is open to high school seniors, undergraduates of any level, recent graduates, and graduate students. Students from all academic majors are encouraged to apply, but the intern coordinator advises applicants to "demonstrate a strong interest in the law."

APPLICATION PROCEDURE

 The deadline to submit materials is rolling, but applications submitted before May 1 are given preference. Applicants should submit a cover letter (detailing why they want the internship and any particular legal interests) and a resumé. As the coordinator prefers to judge candidates on "paper value," no interviews are conducted.

OVERVIEW

 Rewarding internships for those interested in law but yet to attend law school are virtually nonexistent. One fine exception is ATLA, where interns get to see the machinery that runs the world's largest association of trial lawyers. Receiving good pay to carry out a combination of clerical and substantive work, interns have an excellent opportunity to expand their knowledge of law and decide whether they want to make law a lifelong vocation.

FOR MORE INFORMATION . . .

■ Association of Trial Lawyers of America
Intern Coordinator
1050 31st Street NW
Washington, DC 20007
(800) 424-2725

BSB

SELECTIVITY

Approximate applicant pool: 75
Interns accepted: 5–10

COMPENSATION

None
Possible bonus stipend

QUALITY OF LIFE

Chrysler building; Quality cafeteria
Two interns to an office; Intern Answer Book

LOCATION(S)

New York, NY

FIELD

Advertising

DURATION

10–12 weeks; Summer, Fall, Spring
2 to 4 days/week

PRE-REQS

College juniors and seniors; grad students
Overall GPA 3.0 or higher

DEADLINE(S)

Rolling

It seems simple enough: Distinguish a brand from its competitors and the public will buy it. But not until Backer Spielvogel Bates coined the term "Unique Selling Proposition" in the late 1970s did the idea become a hot topic in advertising agencies across the country.

As defined by BSB, a unique selling proposition (USP) is "a motivating idea, uniquely associated with a particular brand, residing in the mind of prospects." USPs have been the basis for a number of enormously successful ad campaigns, including those by BSB—"Soup is Good Food" (Campbell's Soup) and "Get Out of the Old, Get into the Cold" (Miller Genuine Draft)—as well as those by other firms—Bozell's "Something Special in the Air" (American Airlines) and N.W. Ayer's "The Right Choice" (AT&T).

Small wonder that an agency like BSB would invent an industry catchword. As the world's fifth largest advertising agency, it's no stranger to leading the pack. Headquartered in New York's Chrysler Building, BSB currently holds a roster of over 2,200 clients, including such high-profile companies as Wendy's, Magnavox, Campbell's Soup, Uncle Ben's, and Hyundai Motor America.

DESCRIPTION

All interns at BSB are placed in Strategic Planning, the department that researches consumer attitudes and trends. As BSB's director of Strategic Planning explained in the 1991 issue of *Casro Journal*, the concept of strategic planning "is based on the understanding of values, attitudes, and behavior that connect the target audience to a particular brand, company, or category. . . . [This] understanding is grounded in research that . . . goes beyond that satisfaction of needs to address hopes, aspirations, and sometimes, even dreams."

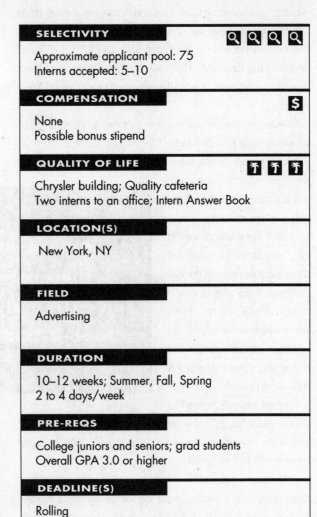

By gaining insight into what consumers really want, Strategic Planning sets the foundation upon which the rest of the agency's departments can build.

Although there's a modest amount of busywork—"occasional photocopying and faxing"—interns report that it is kept to a minimum. "I was never asked to fetch coffee or pick up laundry. It seemed like I spent most of my day thinking." Question: What do interns spend time thinking about? Answer: the challenging research projects they are assigned during the internship. One intern, for example, analyzed how "quality of life" and "consumer confidence" have changed over the years for the average American. Gathering economic and demographic data from a variety of databases and reports, he found that quality of life has steadily improved while consumer confidence in brand products has declined. His findings contributed to a report that the department eventually presented to a group of *Time* writers.

Another intern studied the increasing popularity of products with private labels. "I investigated what type of consumer buys private label products—[that is,] merchandise labeled with a particular store's name, which is typically cheaper than name brands." His research served two purposes: "Not only did this information help the department keep private labels from hurting clients' business, but it also helped the agency advise clients on when and if they should get into using private labels." He presented his conclusions in the form of a "deck," a slide presentation to the vice president and other executives, and a research paper, "which future interns will follow up on."

Some projects deal less with research on consumers and more with background information for the department. One such assignment had an intern create a report on what experts are predicting for the environment, economy, religion, and other global issues. "I've never worked so hard," she said. "I must have read or skimmed at least fifteen books. I gleaned dozens of predictions from magazines like *The Futurists* and books like *Global Outlook 2000* and *The Art of the Long View*." Another project involved compiling an index of sources from other interns' work "so future interns will know where to look when they start their projects." She found phone numbers and addresses for a wide range of arcane but useful industry associations, from the National Pet Food Association to the Cosmetic, Toiletry, and Fragrance Association.

Aiding interns in their research is an extremely powerful tool—GLOBAL SCAN. Developed and used exclu-

Aiding interns in their research is an extremely powerful tool—GLOBAL SCAN.

sively by BSB, GLOBAL SCAN is a database that stores demographic and attitudinal information on consumers from around the world. The data comes from thousands of surveys BSB administers to consumers on attitudes, interests, and product usage. With GLOBAL SCAN, one can manipulate information on consumers in innovative ways. For example, an intern used GLOBAL SCAN to track the behavior of pet owners. "From looking at consumer responses to questions like, 'Do you let your dog or cat go anywhere in the house?' I pinpointed which types of people are more apt to treat their pets like human beings. These are the kind of people who would buy a more expensive brand of pet food, and thus are ideal targets for our clients who manufacture high-end pet food."

Because they are limited to just one department, interns would benefit from opportunities exposing them to the other areas of the agency. Said an intern: "BSB is a big company. The internship keeps you pretty isolated from the other departments. I would have liked to have spent a day in Media, Creative, and Account Management." Though no such opportunity exists, interns are welcome to attend the informational presentations BSB staff sometimes holds for outside groups. They may also observe focus groups. "It's fascinating to watch the in-house moderator elicit answers from the [focus] group panels. I'd watch behind a one-way mirror and sometimes take notes that the moderator would later look at."

The best internship programs go to lengths to ensure that their interns adjust to life on the job. BSB comes through with flying colors in this respect. Interns report that the internship coordinator is an invaluable resource: "She's totally dedicated—she'd drop everything to help us." Moreover, every intern receives an official "Intern Answer Book," an 80-page spiral book detailing all aspects of the agency and the internship. Want to know BSB's newest clients? It's in there. Trouble with the fax machine? Check the "How Do I . . ." chapter. Writing problems? Consult the "Writing Hints" section.

"I work in a landmark," said an intern, and he's right. BSB occupies several floors of New York's majestic Chrysler Building, whose sleek Art Deco spire is known the world over. Decked out in gray and maroon colors, the floor where interns work is reportedly "buzzing with activity." Like most ad agencies, some offices are "littered with promotional ornaments"—such as knickknacks from Wendy's and Campbell's Soup as well as "a giant, stuffed M&M." As far as interns' accommodations go, BSB deserves kudos, for interns are only two to an office and have a stunning view of New York. And when hunger pangs strike, there's a BSB cafeteria that reportedly serves up "good meals for $5."

BSB likes to balance work with a few opportunities for play. Once a month, employees congregate after work in a large conference room, where cocktails and a "goodly amount of finger food" is had by all. Moreover, the Strategic Planning department habitually holds a catered picnic in Connecticut. Said a past picnic-goer: "It's a blast. Everyone relaxes and has fun. There was an egg toss. And, of course, there's plenty of Miller Genuine Draft to go around."

Although the program provides no salary, interns who consistently go the extra mile may be eligible for a bonus. Says the coordinator, "Interns who voluntarily arrive early and work late are sometimes given a bonus stipend of about $200. But this policy is not set in stone, and it's applied on a case by case basis."

SELECTION

 The program is designed for college juniors and seniors and graduate students. BSB seeks candidates with "exceptional writing and communications skills" and an overall GPA of 3.0 or higher.

APPLICATION PROCEDURE

 Although there are no strict deadlines, the intern coordinator advises summer applicants to apply by late May, fall applicants by late August, and spring applicants by late December. The application process is relatively painless: Simply send a resumé and a writing sample. The intern coordinator conducts interviews over the phone or in person. Interns are chosen a few weeks later.

OVERVIEW

 BSB is a biggie, no doubt about it: It's a big agency in a big skyscraper in a big city. And with challenging projects and unique research tools, BSB's internship offers big responsibility, and for most, big satisfaction. Now who says size doesn't count?

FOR MORE INFORMATION . . .

■ Backer Spielvogel Bates
Internship Program
The Chrysler Building
405 Lexington Avenue
New York, NY 10174
(212) 297-7000

BERTELSMANN MUSIC GROUP

Mention BMG to students and it brings to mind a record-of-the-month club. Why shouldn't it? Magazines like *Rolling Stone* and *TV Guide* are constantly running ads for the BMG "Eight CDs for the Price of One" offer.

But the BMG Record Club is just the tip of a very large, very successful iceberg. Owned by German entertainment empire Bertelsmann, the Bertelsmann Music Group is composed of a variety of record labels, such as Arista Records and RCA Records, as well as BMG Distribution, one of the world's most powerful record distribution systems. Generating over $2 billion in sales annually, BMG is home to international superstars (Whitney Houston, Kenny G, Annie Lennox, Lisa Stansfield), country favorites (Clint Black, Alan Jackson, Aaron Tippin), rap acts (SWV, TLC, and KRS-ONE), and alternative bands (The Charlatans, Matthew Sweet, and Rollins Band).

DESCRIPTION

Established in 1989, BMG's Alternative Marketing Program hires students to serve as regional marketing representatives; most reps promote the company's alternative (or college-market) artists, but a few are assigned to urban and R&B music. Twenty students are spread out among BMG's sales offices, located in Atlanta, Boston, Chicago, Dallas, Detroit, Los Angeles, Minneapolis, New York, San Francisco, Seattle, and Washington, D.C. The remaining students work out of their homes in one of nine "smaller but musically hot cities" such as Athens, GA; Austin, TX; Chapel Hill, NC; Denver, CO; Philadelphia, PA; Portland, OR; San Diego, CA; St. Louis, MO; and Tampa, FL. Home-based interns are loaned a fax machine and receive use of the company's phone card.

SELECTIVITY	🔍 🔍 🔍 🔍
Approximate applicant pool: 360	
Interns accepted: 30	
COMPENSATION	💲 💲
$6/hour and $220/month for field expenses	
QUALITY OF LIFE	🌴 🌴 🌴
Promotional freebies	
Meetings and conferences; possible tour work	
LOCATION(S)	
Several cities nationwide—see Description	
FIELD	
Music	
DURATION	
On-going; 6 Months to 2–1/2 Years	
20 hours/week	
PRE-REQS	
Undergrads and grad students	
DEADLINE(S)	
Rolling	

Whether based in a sales office or in their homes, interns spend much of their time in the field. Charged with tracking the sales of BMG's alternative artists, interns make frequent visits to record stores. "A big part of the job is checking up on local mom-and-pop record stores and seeing how our artists are selling. I'd find out exactly how many CDs and tapes of an artist were sold and report the numbers back to the local field-marketing manager." Interns also use these "retail visits" to spread the word about BMG bands: "Wherever I went, I handed out lots of stickers, promotional CDs, and concert tickets. I also dropped off 'point of purchase' material like posters and displays. . . . It helped build a relationship with retail stores and get them interested in BMG bands."

Because an intern's chief objective is to get alternative artists known to college audiences, they must also visit local college radio stations. As with retail stores, interns track album popularity and spread the word about new acts: "The [radio] stations knew me as the local BMG promotion guy. I'd find out which BMG artists were getting the best listener feedback. And I'd drop off loads of CDs and knickknacks." Interns are free to dream up promotions with the radio stations. Whether persuading college newspapers to do a write-up on a particular band, giving away CDs and souvenirs at a local club, or planning a special event for students (e.g., a bowling night), interns are constantly publicizing BMG bands.

Besides visiting record stores and college radio stations, interns have a number of other responsibilities. Some interns set up "listening parties," where local press, retail, and radio people meet at a club to hear a new album. At a listening party for The Church's "Priest=Aura" release, for example, an intern rented out a "cool coffeehouse" and "stocked the room with music, videos, and a live psychic." Others arrange publicity activities for a band when it comes to town. For such groups as The Charlatans, Dharma Bums, Straight Jacket Fits, and Box Car, an intern escorted band members to local record stores, where they met the public and signed CDs.

Once interns have proven themselves, they may be allowed to accompany a band on a particular leg of its tour. An intern working out of the Atlanta office got to "go on tour" with The Church, Peter Murphy, Pop Will Eat Itself, and the Hoodoo Gurus. She elaborated: "Sometimes I went to all of the gigs a band was playing in my region; other times I just saw one or two shows. I'd work backstage, making sure the right people had [backstage] passes and taking radio and retail people around to meet the band."

> **One intern said she walked away with "enough promotional posters, stickers, and T-shirts to decorate a small museum."**

Another unique facet of the BMG internship is the chance it gives interns to provide input on new acts. If they come across a promising local band, interns are encouraged to send the manager of Training and Development a demo tape and a memo detailing what makes the band special. The manager then circulates the material to the A&R (or talent scout) departments at BMG-owned labels such as Arista, RCA, and Zoo Records. Although these referrals have yet to lead to a band being signed, the process is beneficial because interns receive feedback about their recommendations. Says the coordinator: "Interns are sent a letter explaining, as is usually the case, why a particular band is not up to BMG's standards. It's a great way for interns to see what discovering talent is all about."

BMG makes a point of having interns participate in regional meetings and important music conventions. Said an intern: "I was always welcome to accompany [the marketing manager] when she hosted a dinner with local retail people. I was definitely in the loop." A few times a year, interns are flown to music conventions around the country, including Jack the Rapper in Atlanta and the New Music Seminar in New York. An intern who attended the New Music Seminar said it was a valuable experience: "During the day, I'd meet with representatives from different labels and learn about their upcoming releases. At night, the seminar showcased new bands at clubs around the city, and I went to several of these performances. It was a chance to preview the next generation of alternative bands."

Anyone in the music industry knows that the unofficial currency is free promotional items. Small wonder that interns are inundated with a slew of CDs, concert tickets, and party invitations: "There's always plenty of goodies left over after you distribute some to stores and radio stations." Another intern said she walked away from the internship with "enough promotional posters, stickers, and T-shirts to decorate a small museum."

On the whole, interns are quite pleased with BMG. An intern who had also served internships at a variety of record labels said, "Unlike the fast-moving, perform-well-or-perish ethic at many record labels, BMG is more of a solid corporate entity. BMG really wants to promote people from within. There's a sense you're being bred for bigger and better things." Another added: "I never felt insignificant or like I was being used. If anything, BMG management bent over backward to give me freedom to publicize bands as I saw fit."

SELECTION

 The program seeks undergraduates, ideally sophomores and juniors, but sometimes freshmen and seniors. Graduate students may also participate as long as they are one or two years from graduation. Students of any major are welcome to apply. As the job involves a good deal of traveling, applicants (excluding those who want to work in New York) should have access to a car. Applicants are chosen based on "creativity," "intellectual abilities," "social abilities," "passion for music," and "experience in the music business." Although the internship is geared toward alternative music, a past intern says that "applicants need not be 'Joe Alternative'—a dude with twelve earrings and a leather jacket. A solid interest in all types of music will do just fine."

APPLICATION PROCEDURE

 As openings in the Alternative Marketing Program occur sporadically, applications are accepted on a rolling basis. Applicants must submit a resumé and cover letter. When intern positions are available, the manager of Training and Development flies out to different cities around the country to interview top candidates; interviews take place at a BMG sales office or a hotel suite.

OVERVIEW

 As a Texan once said, "Breakin' into the record business is harder than eatin' Jell-O with chopsticks." While most record labels have internships, they are often unfulfilling excursions into a dungeon of disorganization, no pay, and indentured servitude. BMG's Alternative Marketing Program is the ideal antidote: structured responsibilities, decent pay, and practical experience in marketing. Importantly, BMG is committed to using the program to develop executive talent while interns are still in school—every year, at least 50 percent of interns are given full-time positions at BMG.

FOR MORE INFORMATION . . .

- Bertelsmann Music Group
  Alternative Marketing Program
  Manager of Training and Development
  1540 Broadway
  38th Floor
  New York, NY 10036
  (212) 930-4000
  Fax: (212) 930-4862

BOEING

The number 7. There's something magical about it. "Let's see a 7!" gamblers yell at the beginning of a craps round. Jazz musicians invoke it as a symbol of good luck, as in *Lucky Seven* by Malta or *Seven Years of Good Luck* by Joe Sample. And since 1958, Boeing has used the number to describe the company's series of airplanes—707, 727, 737, 747, 757, 767, and the new 777. Today, as luck would have it, Boeing is the world's largest manufacturer of commercial jets. Its airplanes are used by all the major U.S. airlines, from American to United.

Not bad for a company that produced its first plane in a boathouse. When founder and timberman William E. Boeing took the bumpy test flight of that first plane in 1916 (only 13 years after the Wright brothers' first flights), few envisioned how far the company would go. Nearly bankrupt in the early 1920s, Boeing survived and went on to operate mail routes, manufacture the first passenger airliner, and produce the B-9 bomber—all by 1931. Since then, the company has manufactured the B-29 Superfortress, which dropped hundreds of American bombs to help win World War II, and the B-52, which fought in Korea, Vietnam, and the Persian Gulf. Moreover, the nuclear-war deterring Minuteman missile, the President's palatial *Air Force One*, the B-2 Stealth bomber, and the Saturn V boosters, which sent the first men to the moon in 1969, were built by Boeing. All justify the company's 75th anniversary slogan: "Making history every day."

DESCRIPTION

 From the mid-1970s until 1985, Boeing informally brought in summer engineers to work on company projects. But in 1985, the company restructured the program, opening it up to students studying other disciplines and offering good salaries, training programs, and social activities as well. It was a good move, because in 1992 the National Society of Black Engineers selected the Boeing intern program as the number-one internship in the nation. The program recruits over 100 students each year to work in Seattle's Computer Services, Defense and Space, and Commercial Airplanes divisions. The latter places interns in such groups as Hydraulics Systems, Aerodynamics, Windtunnel, Avionics, Flight Deck, Flight Test, Mechanical and Electrical Sys-

BUSYWORK
LOW MEDIUM HIGH
OLDMAN & HAMADEH
METER

tems, and Landing Gear. Approximately 20 similar positions are available in Boeing's Philadelphia, Huntsville, and Wichita sites.

As a member of the Cargo unit of Payloads, an intern worked on caster assemblies (the manual conveyer belts inside a cargo jet). "I checked designs to make sure the assemblies would fit and to see if certain parts would be able to withstand various stresses." But reading these designs proficiently required that she study Boeing's drawing system; the newfound knowledge helped her on the next project. "Because of an FAA directive, Boeing had to modify some existing parts. So I researched old drawings to determine which airplanes had used the offending parts. Then I put together a modification kit—all the pieces plus instructions—to send out to our former clients."

Some interns are assigned to the company's 777, a wide-body twin-engine jet scheduled for delivery in 1995. Smaller than the immense 747 but larger than the 767, this new aircraft will service from 375 to 400 passengers. In addition to offering wider seats and more legroom, the 777 will contain the newest in digital entertainment and communications gizmos—optional stereo, telephone, television, and movies at each seat.

During a recent summer, the 777 Stability and Control group hosted an intern. She spent the first three weeks of her summer working on a windtunnel test of a three-foot 777 model. "We conducted the tests in a low-speed tunnel at the University of Washington," she said. "I collected data and then analyzed it on the computer to extract aerodynamic parameters like the pitching moment, the lift, and the drag." Such information helps Boeing to see if the plane can withstand powerful gusts of wind, she explained. "I spent the rest of the summer figuring out how the plane could counteract wind forces. For example, I determined how much tail movement is needed to compensate for a pitching moment [that is, when a plane starts rocking back and forth like a hobby horse]."

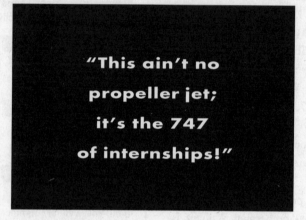

"This ain't no propeller jet; it's the 747 of internships!"

Boeing placed another intern in the 777 Hydraulics Systems group, which designs the electronics system controlling the hydraulics. Considered a full-fledged team member, the intern frequently attended planning meetings. "We'd discuss ways to reduce costs and manufacturing time, among other things," he said of the meetings. "Every two weeks, I'd make a presentation on what computer circuits the lead engineer and I were using in the hydraulic system's control box. There is no canned solution to these design problems, so I had to defend what I came up with."

During the course of the sessions, he was also encouraged to offer solutions to what he perceived as problems in other engineers' design work. "I was taken seriously whenever I had thoughts to offer," he said. "Interns are no less a part of Boeing's mission than anyone else."

But planes consist of more than their hidden circuits and sophisticated controls. Boeing engineers must also design kitchens and safety equipment. Some interns end up in less technical groups such as Galley Configurations, the department that oversees the design and layout of aircraft kitchens. "I went over designers' work to make sure Boeing's electrical and water systems were compatible with the galley designed by the suppliers," said a Galley intern. "And to make sure I knew what I was doing, I checked my work with several employees working on galley designs."

An intern in Emergency Escape Systems worked on Boeing's "emergency slides," the inflatable yellow tubing that uncurls like a New Year's party noisemaker. "We wanted data on parameters like people's time-to-door, time-to-slide-down, time-to-get-off-the-slide. And we wanted these for people of all ages. But Boeing had videotaped tests for these parameters before and didn't want to subject anyone to more tests." Because of the risk involved, she explained, the use of people in tests is discouraged. "So I reviewed the videos from previous tests and extracted data by analyzing people's reaction times in those tests," she said. She also determined slide-deployment time in subfreezing weather: "We put the slide in the cold room at −40°F for several hours, and then I timed how long it took to open up."

Boeing kicks off the summer with an orientation at which interns receive a schedule of events, including optional brown-bag luncheons, volleyball matches, and trips to Seattle Mariners baseball games. A week or two later is a reception at a waterfront seafood restaurant called Salty's. Various illustrious speakers are recruited each year to welcome the interns. In 1993, for example, Seattle Mayor Norm Rice spoke to the newcomers about the benefits of living in the Puget Sound area. Afterward, banquet attendees enjoyed salmon, grilled shrimp, cheeses, crackers, and vegetables and visited booths offering information on Boeing's bowling, parachuting, karate, and basketball clubs.

Once the summer gets under way, the company's aeronautics, mechanical, and civil engineering interns (about 30 percent of the intern class) learn how to design an airplane. Every Wednesday morning for four hours, they enjoy muffins and coffee over a design engineering class. Different managers make a presentation each week; in 1993, the first speaker offered a humorous start to the 7:30 AM meetings: "Our planes are great, big, expensive, flying Greyhound buses," he told the early risers. Afterward, interns divided into groups of ten, working for 30 to 45 minutes to solve a design problem. A hammer, a block of wood, and 25 nails were given to each group, and with only those materials, they were asked to design a tie rack. "It's only a warm-up for the more difficult airplane problems later on," remarked an intern who had worked on the tie-rack problem the previous summer, "but even designing a functional rack is harder than it sounds."

Four or five times during the summer, interns spend a day touring Boeing's facilities. Tours find interns inside airplanes, at test areas, or in the delivery center. But none of these sites gets interns lathered up like the Flight Simulator trip. Walking through the simulator building's hallways, interns sense the history of the place: hundreds of framed airline logos, many from defunct companies, hang alongside pictures of Boeing planes. At the simulators, interns see large metal boxes, each on six robotic legs, looking more like the Imperial Walkers from *Star Wars* than mock airplanes. Interns are given five minutes to test-fly these "great big video games." Said an intern: "I felt every bump and jerk.

. . . It made me so dizzy that the ground was still moving when I got out." Another intern freaked when his copilot turned off one of the engines: "I forgot that I was in a simulator and thought we were going to crash; my sweaty palms were barely able to open up the rudder to compensate for the tilt."

Seattle's proximity to Puget Sound and the Cascade Mountains makes for cool, sunny summers. Opportunities to enjoy outdoor life abound, with sailing, rock climbing, fishing, and kayaking popular among interns. In addition, each Boeing plant has a fitness center, with Nautilus weights and stationary bikes. The Everett Fitness Center, built in 1992, is probably the sleekest. With outdoor running trails, basketball, volleyball, weight machines, dozens of StairMasters, a modern locker room, and a carpeted track (*carpeted*? go figure), it rivals the facilities of most large universities. And at a fee of $15 per month, membership is a bargain.

At a company as large as Boeing, there are bound to be some choppy landings. "You're at the mercy of the system, sometimes waiting for days to get information you need because you often have to go through several channels," said an intern. Some others mention that even with all the freedom interns have to learn about the company, "there's limited time to explore—our work is demanding."

Most interns stay for 10 to 14 weeks in the summer before returning to school. Some, however, elect to work as part of the Co-op Program, augmenting their summer experience with either a spring or fall stint. But whether they spend 12 weeks or six months, most interns are incredibly satisfied: "This ain't no propeller jet; it's the 747 of internships!"

SELECTION

 Boeing seeks college juniors and seniors. Though the company does not adhere to any particular GPA cutoff, it is looking for students actively involved in extracurricular activities such as campus engineering societies. Approximately 85 percent of interns study engineering and computer science. But positions for those studying accounting, information systems, public relations, communications, marketing, and other fields also exist.

APPLICATION PROCEDURE

 The deadline is rolling. Students can begin applying as early as the fall for the co-op and summer programs but should send in materials no later than January 31. Boeing recruits at dozens of universities' career fairs, where students may make inquiries or submit resumés. The company also makes appearances at the annual meetings of the Society of Women Engineers, the National Society of Black Engineers, American Indians Science and Engineering Students, and the Society of Hispanic Professional Engineers. Applicants should send a resumé and a cover letter detailing the classes that they will complete by the start of the internship. Managers normally contact finalists by the end of May for phone interviews and offers.

OVERVIEW

 Bowing (pronounced: boh'-ing). It requires one person, one horsehaired wooden rod, and one stringed musical instrument—three pieces to create a melodious sound. But unlike musical bowing, the company Boeing needs 132,000 people, several factories, and millions of manufactured parts.

What are the odds that these elements can come together to produce world-class commercial jets, defense planes, and spacecraft? And still capture top billing in the industry? A long shot, you'd think. But Boeing reigns supreme. Why? In part because of well-trained and unusually dedicated employees, many of whom are former interns. With solid projects, weekly design classes, and an unbelievably realistic simulator at their fingertips, interns are exposed to a bevy of possibilities. Any way you spell it, Boeing is a sure bet.

FOR MORE INFORMATION . . .

■ Boeing
College Relations
P.O. Box 3707
MS 31-13
Seattle, WA 98124
(206) 393-8472

Chicago Zoological Society
Brookfield Zoo

Minutes after the Chicago Bulls second NBA championship, a sow on display at the Brookfield Zoo gave birth to 13 piglets. The staff immediately named the babies after the team's owner, manager, and Michael Jordan, Scottie Pippen, and the other players. The event made CNN.

This wasn't the first time that the Brookfield Zoo had generated press. In the summer of 1983, amidst great fanfare, Marlin Perkins of TV's *Wild Kingdom* visited the zoo to unveil a new section of the walk-through primate facility called Tropic World. In May 1991, two Moscow Zoo walruses, stricken with sinus infections, were flown to Brookfield's animal hospital. After complicated tusk surgery, the two walruses regained their health and made the Brookfield quarters their new home. The Moscow pair proved a welcome addition following the loss of Brookfield's famous walrus and most popular animal, Olga, who had lived there since 1962. And who can forget the zoo's 450-pound Aldabra Island tortoise named Peter. Every June, news cameras capture his annual quarter mile trek from Reptile House to Children's Zoo. The four-hour display of reptile ambulation is a Brookfield tradition.

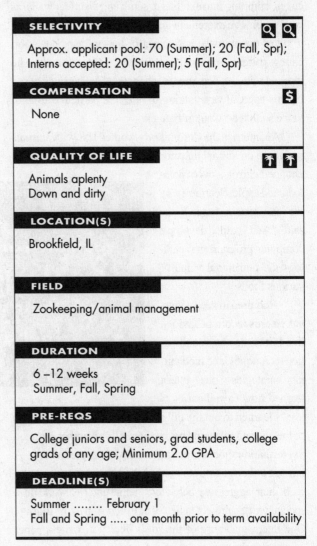

SELECTIVITY

Approx. applicant pool: 70 (Summer); 20 (Fall, Spr); Interns accepted: 20 (Summer); 5 (Fall, Spr)

COMPENSATION

None

QUALITY OF LIFE

Animals aplenty
Down and dirty

LOCATION(S)

Brookfield, IL

FIELD

Zookeeping/animal management

DURATION

6 –12 weeks
Summer, Fall, Spring

PRE-REQS

College juniors and seniors, grad students, college grads of any age; Minimum 2.0 GPA

DEADLINE(S)

Summer .... February 1
Fall and Spring ..... one month prior to term availability

DESCRIPTION

Since the late 1970s, students contemplating zoo careers have been able to intern at Brookfield Zoo. The program offers work in many departments: Small Mammal House, Seven Seas Panorama, Australia House, Animal Hospital, Children's Zoo, Conservation Biology, Birds, Hoofed Stock, Primates, Animal Commissary, or Fragile Kingdom.

Unlike most zoo internships, the Brookfield Zoo's program strives to teach the art of zookeeping—that is, maintaining ani-

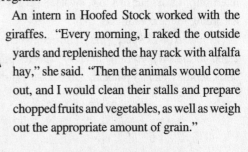

mal health and well-being. Interns also interact with visitors, directing them to exhibits and answering their questions on animals. And they assist people in finding special demonstrations or in understanding zoo services like the Parents' Program.

An intern in Hoofed Stock worked with the giraffes. "Every morning, I raked the outside yards and replenished the hay rack with alfalfa hay," she said. "Then the animals would come out, and I would clean their stalls and prepare chopped fruits and vegetables, as well as weigh out the appropriate amount of grain."

An intern in the Small Mammal House also cleaned cages, climbing into exhibits to scrub and disinfect walls, as well as remove excrement and leftover food. She also kept a log of the animals, noting out-of-the-ordinary behavior, eating patterns, or stool consistency. Occasionally, she worked with the department's bobcat. "I sometimes hosed out his cage, always talking to him in a particular tone of voice so that he wouldn't attack."

An intern in the Commissary worked less with animals and more on animal nutrition, preparing animals' diets. "I chopped carrots, sweet potatoes, and apples, learning why we use certain foods," she said. "And I helped develop a computer program that catalogs the nutritional value of various foods."

Required to keep a journal, interns record behaviors, live births, deaths, mobilization techniques, and medicating strategies, one intern learned how to veil antibiotics: "I learned to put the pill in a piece of bread or a banana so that the animal would not recognize it." Another watched a veterinarian shoot a blow dart to administer medication. A third saw the vet castrate rambunctious baboons in order to curb their aggressive behavior. Some interns work on a special written project in lieu of or in addition to the journal. One intern made use of the zoo's library to write a paper comparing the anatomies of the giraffe and its cousin the okapi. Another intern's paper explored the possibilities of "dusting" insects with mineral-enriched oils and powders in order to improve mineral intake of insect-eating animals. Moreover, interns are assigned a mentor and receive critical evaluations every six weeks. For those who arrange academic credit, there's also a grade assigned at the end of the internship. On a scale of 1 to 4, most fall between 3 and 3.8, according to the coordinator.

Situated on 215 acres, the world-renowned zoo houses 2,500 animals representing over 400 species of mammals, birds, reptiles, and amphibians and boasts realistic exhibits designed to promote animal conservation. There's Habitat Africa, offering an innovative safari featuring giraffes, zebras, African wild dogs, and exotic birds and reptiles. One can watch the dolphin shows at the 2,000-seat indoor dolphinarium or see elephant demonstrations in the (where else?) Elephant Arena. And there's Tropic World, one of the world's largest indoor zoo exhibits, equipped with a walking path for viewing monkeys, apes, and exotic birds living in simulated rainforests. If that's not enough, one can also test the flying-strength machine at the "Be A Bird" exhibit and play with computer games teaching bird anatomy.

Summer interns receive a group tour of all the animal areas, as well as the Design Department, where the zoo's signs are made. "The orientation exposes them right off the bat to the behind-the-scenes management of the zoo," explained the internship coordinator. Interns also have access to visiting specialists who give speeches to the staff. "I heard talks on animal contraception and on zoo exhibit repair," reported one intern. Other lunchtime talks have dealt with conservation techniques and tiger habitats. Moreover, all interns receive an employee pass, which allows them not only to visit the zoo during off-hours but also to park in the lots, use the zoo library, and take advantage of an employee discount on food and gifts.

But even the greatest animal lovers feel some frustration. Some are chagrined to learn that zookeeping consists of significant amounts of cage scrubbing. "Cleaning can become boring and routine," said one intern. Animal diehards, on the other hand, realize the importance of cleaning exhibits: "The longer you stay, the more you realize that cleaning allows keepers to see the animals grow and adapt." Some are disappointed in not having access to certain animals. "I wasn't allowed to work with the bats because a series of rabies shots is required," lamented one intern.

> One intern saw the vet castrate rambunctious baboons in order to curb their aggressive behavior.

SELECTION

 All applicants must have completed two years' worth of college prior to the start of the internship and must have at least a 2.0 GPA. That means that college juniors and seniors, recent college grads, grad students, and career changers are all eligible. While neither previous zoo experience nor a science background is necessary, applicants must convey an interest in animals or somehow indicate that they are contemplating animal-related careers. Many of the interns who work with animals, however, are majoring in life sciences like zoology, biology, or veterinary medicine. Insider's tip: Fall and spring terms are usually undersubscribed, and applicants for those periods often see little competition.

APPLICATION PROCEDURE

 Materials submitted for work between September 1 and May 15 must be received at least one month prior to the start of the internship. Applications to the summer internship must be received by February 1. Applicants must submit the application form (send away for this early), a resumé, an official transcript, two letters of recommendation, and a letter describing what they wish to gain from the experience and how that experience will relate to past experience and career goals. For more information on the animal as well as non-animal departments (e.g., Marketing, Public Relations, Human Resources, Education, and Graphic Arts) offering internships, request the intern program brochure. Applicants selected from the initial screening receive phone or on-site interviews.

OVERVIEW

 While many large zoos around the country offer internships in animal research, usually laboratory experiences that can lead to graduate work in genetics, immunology, or physiology, the Brookfield Zoo provides interns with a down-and-dirty introduction to zookeeping. "You're right in there from day one," says the coordinator, "working next to the keepers and contributing just like any other employee." And for those who don't want to pursue graduate studies in animal fields, the experience allows students to don a zookeeper's hat for a couple of months. "Zookeeping is one of the only animal professions where a bachelor's degree is sufficient," said one. "But you must have hands-on animal exposure in order to land those jobs, and the Brookfield Zoo—a world-class zoo, comparable in prestige to the San Diego Zoo or the National in D.C.— gives you that exposure." No wonder, then, that about 10 percent of former interns eventually become zookeepers. The internship truly is, in the words of the coordinator, "an opportunity for future zoologists to get their feet wet!" Sounds great—so long as it's not in tortoise Peter's urinal.

FOR MORE INFORMATION . . .

■ Brookfield Zoo
Intern Program Office Coordinator
3300 South Golf Road
Brookfield, IL 60513
(708) 485-0263

"**T**hink tank"—it once referred to the American military's guarded, soundproof rooms, those in which war strategies were formulated during World War II. In the 1950s, the military attached the term to its contract research organizations, such as the RAND Corporation and the Urban Institute. But by the 1960s, "think tank" was a term used by the public to describe various private research groups. It proved a fitting descriptor: Those ensconced in policy-research institutions are at once isolated and publicly displayed, like fish in a fish tank. Indeed, researchers working under the auspices of such institutions often appear on television or meet with government leaders to proffer opinions. This is certainly the case at one of America's most prestigious think tanks, the Brookings Institution.

Founded by woodenware tycoon Robert Brookings in 1916, the Brookings Institution espouses a decades-old mission—that is, "to bring knowledge to bear on the current and emerging public policy problems facing the American people" such as health care and the budget deficit. Although considered predominantly liberal in ideology, Brookings consistently publishes middle-of-the-road books such as Alice Rivlin's *Reviving the American Dream* and Thomas Mann's *Renewing Congress*, earning the institute "a reputation for scrupulous objectivity and distinguished scholarship," as *The New Republic* wrote on the organization's 75th anniversary.

DESCRIPTION

The Brookings Institution offers students formal internships in Governmental Studies, a program that researches "how—and how well— American government functions." Paired with a Senior Fellow, interns work full- or part-time, depending on Senior Fellows' needs and intern availability. Interns assist in the following research areas: the appropriations process, inner cities, international coverage in the U.S. media, courts and Congress, federalism, educational choice, race and poverty, public health hazards, social policy, U.S. energy strategy, and health care.

One former intern did statistical computer-work for a Fellow's book, entitled *The Disappearing American Voter*. The book described the decline in voter turnout over the last several decades, starting with the 1960

SELECTIVITY	
Approximate applicant pool: 75 Interns accepted: 6	

COMPENSATION	$
None	

QUALITY OF LIFE	
Intellectual environment Access to political conferences; Seminars	

LOCATION(S)	
Washington, DC	

FIELD	
Public policy/think tank	

DURATION	
12 weeks Summer, Fall, Winter/Spring; Part time available	

PRE-REQS	
College juniors and seniors, grad students	

DEADLINE(S)	
Summer ....April 15 Winter/Spring ......Dec. 15 Fall ....August 15	

presidential election. "The National Election Service sent us some computer tapes that contained voter demographic information," he said. "I wrote a program, using a statistical language that read the tapes. The program placed data from the tapes into categories such as race, age, occupation, party, and geography." The intern also searched the Brookings library for information on state voter laws. "I helped the Fellow create a database that encapsulated each state's voter laws as yes or no answers to four or five questions, such as 'can voters register by mail?'" By the end of the internship, the first few chapters of the book had been laid out. "They dispelled some of the widespread myths used to explain why people don't vote."

A few interns work for Steven Hess, described by *Mother Jones* as "a well-known scholar and longtime Republican party activist [who] logged 1,294 calls from 183 separate news organizations during 1988 alone." Hess's popularity stems from his well-known research on how the U.S. media cover foreign policy issues. As part of the effort, his former interns coded newspaper articles and surveys of foreign correspondents. "I handled *The New York Times*, reading each international news story carefully for salient points. Then I used an established list of numbers to code each article's elements: country, population, religion, and subject. I also sifted through the surveys, coding correspondents' responses to questions we asked on the countries they cover and on their thoughts about media coverage."

Because each Fellow already relies on a research assistant (RA) to complete the bulk of research, interns are often assigned clerical work. "Most of us come in bright-eyed and eager; we get a dose of reality pretty quickly." Depending on the Fellow's disposition, some interns do "bare-bones, less analytical research" while others dive into the heart of a project, doing substantial analysis. But tedious tasks such as photocopying, filing, and locating journal articles in the library need not discourage interns. "What you're photocopying often contains fascinating information," explained an intern. "If you think long and hard about that information

and then make insightful comments, the Fellow just might be impressed."

Despite their low status (they're a notch below RAs), interns find that all of Brookings' resources are open to them—such as Brookings' library, the Library of Congress, and the National Archives. Interns may even use these resources to work on their own research projects. "I was writing a political science class paper on U.S. policy toward China during the post–cold war era," said an intern, "so I interviewed Brookings' China expert Harry Harding, who gave me some articles he had written on the subject. And he explained that because China's economy is growing fast, creating good opportunities for American businesses, the U.S. should grant China most-favored-nation status."

Students sing Brookings praises "because of the incredible collegial environment, like an undergraduate department brimming with professors," said one intern. Many interns say that it's like a university and that Brookings fosters an environment of intellectual stimulation. Bimonthly Brookings-sponsored events have included conferences on such topics as NAFTA and speeches by the president of Turkey, King Hussein and Queen Noor, and the ambassador to Hong Kong. All these activities, well attended by the press and government officials, are open to fellows, staff, and interns alike.

Interns who want more of the academic or political talks are happy to learn that they may choose from among brown-bag, research-in-progress, and Friday lunches. The brown-bag lunches typically feature RAs talking about research projects; each week's sponsoring department posts flyers announcing the topic and advertising cookies to entice potential participants. (Baked on the premises in Brookings' cafeteria, these chewy morsels, chocolate-chip and oatmeal alike, draw a large following.) At the research-in-progress lunches, senior fellows or Ph.D. students on one year, paid Brookings fellowships give research status reports. "One week, we heard about the AEI [American Enterprise Institute]-Brookings joint study on the public's image of Congress," said an intern. "Contrary to popular

> On the first floor, a portrait of an exceedingly contemplative-looking Mr. Brookings hints at the mental might mustered upstairs.

belief, the scholars concluded that Congress was actually doing an adequate job." Finally, every Friday at noon senior fellows gather around a table in the cafeteria to discuss various world issues. Sometimes one or two interns are invited to join them. But the uninvited may sit on the fringes—where "it's like being at the Master's [golf tournament]: say nothing and listen carefully"—and listen to Fellows debate topics such as the Clinton energy taxes, the Mississippi River flood of 1993, and homosexuals in the military. "At times, the discussions get pretty heated," said an intern. Brookings is supposed to be nonpartisan, but fellows usually don't make much of an effort to conceal their leanings, be they conservative or liberal."

Occasionally, interns are allowed to observe luncheons the program director organizes for the media and political scientists At the spring 1993 luncheon, interns listened to Gene Sperling, the deputy assistant to the president for economic policy. A Brookings RA for Steven Hess from September 1981 to August 1982, Sperling talked about his current role in White House economic policy. Interns learned that as part of President Clinton's National Economic Council, Sperling plays a large role in formulating strategies on deficit reduction, taxes, investment, and enterprise zones. "Even though we didn't get to ask him questions, it was thrilling to hear his insights," said an intern who attended.

Brookings' eight-story, sandstone building is located on embassy-lined Massachusetts Avenue. Inside, Brookings is described by interns as "stodgy and academic" compared with the more modern American Enterprise Institute. On the first floor, a portrait of an exceedingly contemplative-looking Mr. Brookings suggests the mental might mustered upstairs. Yet scholars are surprisingly "relaxed and informal, always available to answer questions about research, graduate schools, or political issues."

SELECTION

 The Governmental Studies Program seeks college juniors, seniors, and graduate students in political science. Even so, history, public policy, and law students have been known to intern at Brookings. The brochure states that "attention to detail is essential; some research experience and library skills are helpful."

APPLICATION PROCEDURE

 The deadline to turn in materials for the Governmental Studies Program internship is April 15 for the summer term, August 15 for the fall term, and December 15 for the winter/spring term. Students must submit a resumé, cover letter, transcript plus course descriptions for all political science credits, two letters of recommendation, and a writing sample (2 to 5 pages), preferably from a political science course, to the address below. "Heavy-duty students apply here," said the coordinator. "Most have high GPAs and express an interest in a particular scholar's research, described in our brochure." After the coordinator screens resumés, senior fellows conduct phone interviews with a selection of finalists.

The Brookings Institution also offers internships in its Economic Studies and Foreign Policy Studies programs on an as-needed basis. Economic Studies internships are for the summer while Foreign Policy Studies internships, often requiring foreign language skills, are available year-round. Students interested in Economic Studies or Foreign Policy Studies internships must send a resumé to the program assistants directly at the address below. Both internships are nonpaying.

OVERVIEW

 Interns at the Brookings Institution have an "opportunity to work with the field's premier scholars—those who influence policy through careful study and analysis," as a brochure puts it. Paired with Senior Fellows, interns learn independent research techniques and leave with a heightened understanding of American government. One wouldn't expect anything less from the place the press has repeatedly deemed "the granddaddy of all think tanks."

FOR MORE INFORMATION . . .

■ The Brookings Institution
Internship Coordinator
(Name of Program)
1775 Massachusetts Avenue NW
Washington, DC 20036-2188
(202) 797-6050

BUTTERFIELD & BUTTERFIELD

Fine Art Auctioneers and Appraisers since 1865

Ever wonder where you could pick up a few Solomon Island money rolls? How about where to go for Peruvian pre-Columbian ceramics? Where does one find Native American beaded bandoleer bags, anyway? Take heart, eager collector. Butterfield & Butterfield may be your destination.

Founded in 1865 on the present site of San Francisco's Transamerica Building, Butterfield & Butterfield is the largest and oldest full-service auction house in western America. It runs a dizzying array of fine-art and antique auctions, selling everything from paintings to fine wine. It also offers a host of appraisal services, assessing single items or entire collections, for individuals or museums.

DESCRIPTION

 A range of departments accepts interns: Painting, Asian Art, Prints, Fine Photographs, Furniture and Decorative Arts, American Indian/ Ethnographic, Oriental Rugs, Rare Books, Public Relations, and Marketing. Most departments hire only one intern, although the busiest divisions, Furniture and Decorative Arts and Asian Art, usually hire two. Interns are required to work only two days a week, and thus the program allows a good deal of scheduling flexibility.

In every department, interns assist the director and other specialists in preparing for upcoming auctions. Although the program strives to keep busywork at a minimum, interns find themselves undertaking a fair amount. Be it typing letters to auction-goers, keeping track of photographs of art pieces, or photocopying auction contracts, interns spend part of their time carrying out clerical tasks. They also spend time caring for the art and antique pieces that come through their office. Duties in this area include tagging the pieces for identification

SELECTIVITY	🔍 🔍 🔍
Approximate applicant pool: 80–120 Interns accepted: 12	

COMPENSATION	💲
$10/day stipend	

QUALITY OF LIFE	🌴 🌴 🌴
Previews and appraisal clinics Free parking; Hands-on contact with objects	

LOCATION(S)	
San Francisco	

FIELD	
Auction and appraisal	

DURATION	
10 weeks Summer, Fall, Spring; At least 16 hours/week	

PRE-REQS	
See Selection	

DEADLINE(S)	
Summer .... March 15; Fall .... July 15 Spring .... October 15	

purposes, writing condition reports, and unpacking the pieces.

Interns often find that their work affords them a terrific education about a type of art or antique. Most departments have a large collection of books on a particular field, and interns are often asked to use them to determine what similar objects have sold for in the past. Interns also research the cultural histories of items that will be sold at auction, gaining insight into the historical context from which an object comes. Said an intern: "I learned so much about the pieces in my field—what

BUSYWORK
MEDIUM
LOW HIGH
OLDMAN & HAMADEH
METER

makes them valuable, why they're historically important, who owned them." In their free moments, interns are encouraged to pick their supervisor's brains and to learn as much as possible about the pieces that pass through the office.

Whereas most interns focus primarily on the art pieces particular to their departments, Public Relations and Marketing interns are steeped in the art of pre- and post-auction publicity. Duties include writing press releases, facilitating editors' requests for photos, attending press conferences as a representative of B&B, and serving as a media contact and company spokesperson. Although these interns do not gain in-depth knowledge about a particular field of art, they like working in Public Relations and Marketing because "it exposes you to all of the other departments, as opposed to working in, for example, the Painting department, where that's basically all you see."

Every Monday morning Butterfield invites the public to bring in art and antique pieces for appraisal. Interns are invited to assist at these Monday appraisal clinics, helping visitors unpack and display the objects they bring in. For many interns, the best part of appraisal clinics is simply the opportunity to sit down and observe an appraiser in action: "Watching the appraisers, you really got a sense of what's desirable in an antique. Examining firearms, for example, they would look for things like engravings, silver barrels, and gems in the handle." Interns are also encouraged to accompany appraisers and department directors on appraisal calls. Visiting all sorts of homes in the Bay Area, from modest apartments to chichi estates, interns get a sense of how art and antiques are displayed in the real world. Said one: "House calls were great. I went on about four of them. On one we inspected an entire room of African art. It was fascinating to see all those pieces laid out in a person's home."

A week or so before every auction, Butterfield runs a few preview sessions in which the public can inspect the pieces coming up for auction. Interns are often called upon to help out at these auction previews. Their main task is to display the art objects and answer questions about them. "It's not too difficult," said one intern. "You take the pieces out of their lock cases and field questions about them. If you get stumped, you can always ask an appraiser or refer to the catalog."

Clinics and previews are interesting, but in terms of sheer drama, nothing beats the main event—the auction. Expectant collectors crowd the auction room. A video screen displays each "lot" (a single item or group of items) as it comes up for sale. The auctioneer starts the bidding, usually at about one third to one half of the estimated value of the lot, as listed in the catalog. Participants hold up numbered cards when they want to bid on the lot. Tension builds until the final bid is placed, the auctioneer brings down the hammer, and the lot is "knocked down" (sold to the highest bidder).

"It sounds funny, but you get to play with wonderful objects. It's the ultimate hands-on experience for someone interested in art."

Interns enjoy being in the charged atmosphere of auctions. At the very least, auctions provide fascinating people-watching: "Depending on what was being auctioned off, you saw all types of people—timid first-timers, impassioned novices, and seasoned veterans." Interns also help out during auctions. Some are merely gofers, retrieving documents and handling pieces of art. A few do phone bidding for parties who are unable to attend the auction, although this job is usually performed by the permanent staff; interns who phone bid can't help but get caught up in the excitement of relaying a bidder's wishes: "You'd call a client from the auction room and hold up his or her numbered card when directed to. Sometimes thousands of dollars were involved. It was a big adrenaline rush."

Interns can look forward to a tiring but educational orientation day. They are sent to the main departments, spending time at Customer Service, Receiving, Art, Painting, Catalog Subscription, and the Front Desk. Every effort is made to educate them about the steps needed to produce a successful auction. At one point, interns are shown a video detailing the proper ways to handle art objects. Orientation is usually held on an auction day and culminates in the opportunity to view an auction itself.

Butterfield & Butterfield is located in an older neighborhood of San Francisco that has an abundance of galleries, showrooms, and cafes nearby. The Butterfield building is described as "clean but warehouselike." The main showroom is spacious, but, one intern sniffed, "not as plush as those at New York houses like Sotheby's and Christie's." Interns sit at cubicles in the offices upstairs. They describe the office environment as "friendly," "supportive," but "high pressured" on auction days. One warns that a few employees take their job a little more seriously than they have to.

When asked about perks, interns agree that a main benefit of being at Butterfield is the opportunity to handle and inspect all sorts of valuable antiques, the kind that are typically ensconced in glass or behind a velvet rope in a museum. "It sounds funny, but you get to play with wonderful objects. It's the ultimate hands-on experience for someone interested in art," remarked an intern. Other benefits include the occasional in-house lecture, such as a talk on jades by the director of the Asian department, and free parking, a scarce commodity in San Francisco. Interns also enjoy scoping out the celebrities who occasionally surface on auction day: "One day I saw Aaron Spelling buying some pretty fancy jewelry."

Butterfield's $10 daily stipend is no gravy train by any stretch of the imagination, but it at least covers the cost of daily transportation. Interns for whom money is no object are happy to learn that they can bid in the auctions. Said one intern: "If they want to, interns can bid on the sales. Working here, you hear insider tips about what's hot and what's not, and thus interns who have the means to bid are a step ahead of the game."

SELECTION

The program is open to junior and senior undergrads, graduate students, and college graduates of any age. Interested parties should have taken at least two semesters of art history (approximately 30 units). But, according to the intern coordinator, the program occasionally accepts candidates with no art history experience, usually for positions in less art-oriented areas like Marketing and Public Relations. Desired qualities in applicants include "a strong interest in fine arts," a "high degree of motivation," an "ability to work well with people," and "strong research skills." And, an intern added, participants "shouldn't be afraid to get dirty, because handling the various pieces of art sometimes requires you to get on your knees and brave the dust and grime."

APPLICATION PROCEDURE

Designed to coincide with academic semesters, the program has the following application deadlines: summer, March 15; fall, July 15; and spring, October 15. Students should write to the personnel director for an application. After submitting an application and resumé, highly qualified candidates are invited to the auction house for interviews with the personnel assistant and the head of the department that interests them. In "extremely rare cases," out-of-state students unable to visit will be granted phone interviews.

OVERVIEW

There are good reasons to spend a few months at Butterfield & Butterfield. Interns there receive a dual education, learning in general about the auction business and in particular about a type of art or antique. They do so at a renowned auction house, but one that is considerably more intimate than its eastern counterparts. Individuals interested in art and antiques should bear in mind the advantages of working in an auction house over a museum or a gallery. Not only does an internship with Butterfield allow you to handle pieces that would otherwise be inaccessible but it also puts you in an environment of perpetual change and variety. As one intern said: "In the art world, museums move at 10 mph. Galleries at about 60 mph. And auction houses, with their never-ending stream of events, at 250 mph."

FOR MORE INFORMATION . . .

■ Butterfield & Butterfield
Internship Program
220 San Bruno Avenue
San Francisco, CA 94103
(415) 861-7500

THE CARTER CENTER

Baseball greats become coaches. Professors become professors emeriti. Tennis stars become TV commentators. But what the heck do presidents do after their glory years? For James Earl Carter, the answer was easy. In 1982, "Jimmy" founded the Carter Center, a think tank to improve the quality of life for people around the world. Guided by Carter and staffed with distinguished professors, the Carter Center works with world leaders and dignitaries to promote democracy, resolve conflicts, protect human rights, eradicate disease, improve agriculture in developing countries, and tackle social problems in urban areas.

DESCRIPTION

In 1984, undergraduate and graduate students of international studies at Emory University participated in the Carter Center's inchoate internship program. The center was still in its infancy at that point, working strictly on Middle East issues. By 1986, however, it had attracted more fellows and programs, as well as constructed four new buildings, including the presidential library and museum. That year, the center introduced the official internship program, primarily for Emory students. A small number of students from around the country could participate as well.

Interns now work in one of the many programs in place at the center: Latin American and Caribbean Studies, African Governance, Human Rights, Global 2000 (a large scale project to improve healthcare and agriculture in developing countries), Domestic and International Health Policy, the Atlanta Project (a community-wide effort to take on social problems associated with poverty in urban areas), Task Force for Child Survival and Development, and Conflict Resolution.

SELECTIVITY

Approximate applicant pool: 60
Interns accepted: 25

COMPENSATION

None

QUALITY OF LIFE

Japanese garden
Access to high-level meetings; Intellectual atmosphere

LOCATION(S)

Atlanta, GA

FIELD

Public policy/think tank

DURATION

12 weeks; Summer, Fall, Spring
6-week Winter Break internship available

PRE-REQS

College juniors and seniors, grad students

DEADLINE(S)

Fall .... July 15   Spring .... October 15
Summer .... March 15

Positions are also available in administrative offices such as Public Information, Development, and Conferencing.

Daily activities depend on the program to which an intern is assigned, though most programs allow interns to research specific issues, monitor daily events pertaining to their program, and write articles for in-house publications. One intern in Public Information, for example, helped research mailing lists, mailed out information packets, and helped the department run press conferences. "One day I helped set up for an Atlanta Project press conference featuring a satellite appearance by Michael

Jackson," he reported. "I signed in press people, distributed packets to them, and then stayed to listen to the questions asked of President Carter." Another time, he was responsible for escorting Ted Koppel's camera crew to the interview site, making sure that they had everything needed for a *Nightline* interview of Carter.

In other departments, like the International Conflict Resolution Program, interns personally monitor the daily conditions of two to three conflicts and provide weekly updates to the ICRP team. "I would use NEXIS, newspapers, journals, books, and interviews to probe into particular countries' activities," said an intern. "I learned a lot about conflicts and became an expert on the things going on in those countries, so much so that I was able to offer ideas on how the Carter Center could become involved in the peace process."

A variety of programs contribute to the center's broad-based humanitarian agenda. Even an obscure disease such as "river blindness" is addressed. The Carter Center currently approves distributions of the drug Mectizan, which protects individuals from contracting the disease. At the Task Force for Child Survival and Development, a former intern worked on a computer program to store organizations' applications for the drug. He said: "The computer had to be up and running. The speed with which we could approve the applications hinged on that. So, in that respect, my work had the potential to make a real impact."

In addition to the special projects in which interns are involved, interns often interact with important players on the international scene. Frequently, interns are allowed to observe policy discussions. One of the largest occurs at the center's annual consultation of the International Negotiation Network, headed by President Carter. "I saw foreign dignitaries, like Javier Perez de Cuellar, the former Secretary General of the UN," said an intern. "We watched firsthand as he and other world leaders conversed; then they and Carter

"I learned a lot about conflicts and became an expert on the things going on in the countries I researched."

Center representatives dispersed into private, small groups to brainstorm resolutions to international conflicts."

On the whole, interns relish the exposure that comes with being at a policy-making organization. They might peruse draft policy-proposals or watch high-level policy discussions involving former and current world leaders. But such opportunities are not daily occurrences. "Just realize," cautioned the coordinator, "that in addition to research on countries, abuses, and conflicts, there are the day-to-day clerical tasks." By the coordinator's estimate, filing and photocopying absorb 35 percent of interns' time.

All work takes place inside five modern pod-shaped buildings, interconnected to facilitate communication among the center's diverse programs. One of these houses the center's cafe, where interns and staff members receive a 10 percent discount. To provide a respite from the fast pace indoors, the center boasts an "absolutely beautiful" Japanese garden.

The internship is unpaid. Most students receive academic credit through their schools; a few make financial arrangements through their college's financial aid office. Although the internship usually lasts for three months, interns can arrange to stay for two semesters.

SELECTION

The Carter Center is looking for students who are at least juniors with extensive coursework in their majors. It also seeks a few graduate students each term. Foreign language ability and computer literacy prove particularly helpful. Travel abroad and familiarity with history and economics are good preparation but are not required. Past interns stress the importance of having a "strong work ethic" and "an ability to quickly familiarize yourself with the background of your project."

APPLICATION PROCEDURE

 The deadline is July 15 for fall, October 15 for spring, and March 15 for summer. A six-week internship during winter break is available and should be arranged with the internship coordinator. Applicants are required to submit a short essay (150 to 200 words) explaining their interest in international studies or in a specific center program, their expectations of and objectives for the internship, and the relationship these have to career goals. A writing sample, a transcript, a resumé (if available), and two letters of recommendation must accompany the completed internship application form. The internship coordinator makes an initial screening of applications and refers them to the program directors, who make final choices.

OVERVIEW

 In the Mother Goose nursery rhyme "Tweedle-Dum and Tweedle-Dee," the two boys for whom the poem is named argue over a broken rattle. Moments before they are about to fight, a powerful crow flies overhead and dissuades them from battle. An influential force in international dispute resolution, the Carter Center is a crow of sorts, working to mediate between opposing factions and promote peace. For a young organization, the Carter Center has also been especially effective in the movements to immunize children, tackle urban problems, eliminate Guinea worm disease, and modernize farming in the developing world. An internship at the Carter Center allows students, through research projects and observation, to gain a deep understanding of a few of these problems. In the process, interns have the opportunity to learn from internationally respected thinkers and watch policymakers at work. The Carter Center internship—think of it as three months in the nest of that powerful crow of international and domestic public policy.

FOR MORE INFORMATION . . .

- The Carter Center
  Internship Program
  One Copenhill Avenue
  Atlanta, GA 30307
  (404) 420-5151

Center for Investigative Reporting, Inc.

SELECTIVITY	🔍🔍🔍🔍
Approximate applicant pool: 100 Interns accepted: 6–10	

COMPENSATION	$
$100/month	

QUALITY OF LIFE	🌴🌴🌴
Weekly seminars Meetings with journalists	

LOCATION(S)

San Francisco, CA

FIELD

Investigative journalism

DURATION

Six months; Winter/Spring, Summer/Fall
Part time available

PRE-REQS

High school students, undergrads,
grad students, college grads of any age

DEADLINE(S)

Winter/Spring .... December 1
Summer/Fall .... May 1

In 1977, freelance journalists Lowell Bergman, Dan Noyes, and David Weir founded the Center for Investigative Reporting (CIR) with the belief that the media needed a nonprofit, independent organization committed to investigative reporting. Since its founding, CIR has pursued "hidden stories . . . the hard stories, hard to assemble and hard to tell." In 1990, for example, PBS's *Frontline* aired a one-hour, CIR documentary titled "Global Dumping Ground," summarizing three years' worth of CIR stories on the international hazardous waste trade. The CIR stories had already persuaded the UN to pass a resolution restricting international transport of toxic material. But the broadcast now convinced China and other countries to ban toxic waste imports. Consequently, it's no surprise that media outlets such as *60 Minutes*, *20/20*, CNN, the *Los Angeles Times*, and *The Washington Post* have relied on CIR to produce similar stories for them. Or why the industry has honored the Center with over a dozen awards, most notably the George Polk Award for National Television Reporting, the Investigative Reporters and Editors Award, the National Magazine Award, and several Best Censored Story awards.

DESCRIPTION

CIR's brochure lists the internship's primary objective as "to teach investigative reporting skills to novice reporters." This has been the organization's credo ever since its start—back then, reporters occasionally hired an intern or two to assist in story research. Those interns learned so much about reporting that in 1983, CIR developed the present program; it gives students and nonstudents alike a chance to moonlight as journalists for a minimum of 15 hours per week for six months.

After a half-day orientation to CIR procedures and administration, interns are paired with senior reporters. Under the guidance of these senior journalists, interns gather information for stories; they make phone calls, conduct interviews, search through public records, and organize library or on-line searches as part of the research effort.

One intern worked on CIR's 1992 documentary "Your Loan Is Denied," an investigation of mortgage-lending discrimination in Chicago. The investigation discovered widespread racism at the root of a disparity in lending practices. "The vacuum created when large banks discriminate against certain clients is often filled by fraudulent mortgage lenders, who charge exorbitant interest rates," said the intern. "I researched stories on LEXIS and NEXIS and sifted through Uniform Commercial Code filings to find the names of companies who might be engaging in illegal practices." The intern stayed with CIR long enough to see his research pay off; the documentary aired on PBS's *Frontline* at the end of his internship. "It was rewarding to see the people I had tracked down being interviewed on the show."

Another intern worked on a reporter's investigation of Soviet nuclear submarine accidents. "I looked through documents, interviewed people over the phone, even drove down to Stanford to attend a conference of nuclear physicists," he said. "I interviewed several of them, including a Nobel prize winner. It was pretty heady stuff for a 21-year-old."

The list of past seminar speakers reads like a who's who in American journalism.

In addition to doing reporters' legwork, interns learn investigative techniques, ethics, and writing at weekly seminars, "the most enlightening luncheon meetings you can imagine." Some seminars teach interns how to use outside resources such as City Hall, where interns visit the tax assessor's office. "When reporters want to find out who owns a particular property or building," explained the coordinator, "they need to get their hands on the city's tax records." At another seminar, interns learn about Freedom of Information Act requests. "We learned how to expedite the filing process, how to appeal if you get a negative response, and how to use documents from several agencies to piece together information needed."

Other seminars focus on building journalism skills. At one, interns learn how to use on-line databases like LEXIS, NEXIS, and Dialog. At another, a lawyer exposes interns to legal issues in journalism. "To destroy your notes or not to destroy your notes. That is the dilemma reporters face," said an intern. "Your notes might come in handy if you need to defend yourself, but they might reveal secret sources, too." And at a third seminar, interns hear tips from a private

investigator: "He taught us how to locate missing persons and how to get information that average people cannot."

In between touring and building skills, interns interact with prominent local and national producers, reporters, and journalism instructors as well as journalists visiting from foreign countries. The list of past seminar speakers reads like a who's who in American journalism: *Rolling Stone* columnist Bill Greider, *Nation* editor Victor Navasky, muckraker Jessica Mitford, *San Francisco Examiner* reporters Steven Chen and Ricardo Sandoval, screenwriter Judy Coburn, *Mother Jones* investigative editor and CIR cofounder David Weir, *The New York Times* West Coast bureau chief Jane Gross, and UC Berkeley School of Journalism's Tom Goldstein and Ben Bagdikian. One seminar featured Mark Hertsgaard, author of *On Bended Knee*: "We sat mesmerized for an hour as [Hertsgaard] explained how the media of the '80s had caved in to the Reagan administration."

While working as assistants, interns are encouraged to research and write their own stories. The intern who worked on "Your Loan Is Denied" wrote a spin-off on San Francisco business loans: "I pitched the idea to the San Francisco radio station KQED 88.5 who aired it as a five-minute feature story." Another intern published a story in *The San Francisco Bay Guardian* on recent Rehnquist Supreme Court decisions, which he claimed were eroding press rights. "A majority of the justices construed the First Amendment in the narrowest possible terms," he wrote, "allowing contract and libel law to intrude on and even topple key precedents protecting the free press." A third intern interviewed antiwar activist Brian Willson about his involvement with the Bay Area Peace Navy. "I sat in a boat with Willson and a Nicaraguan boy named Erick and watched the Peace Navy protest war on the seas," she said. Published in *The Progressive*, her story described in poignant detail the man and boy's "special interest in peace"—Willson lost his legs in 1987 when a train ran over him during a protest at a naval weapons base; Erick was badly disfigured when bullets hit his face and shoulder during a Contra ambush in 1988.

One intern even "broke" a story—that is, made it publicly available for the first time. Fluent in Spanish, the intern came across a reference about Mexican death squads in a Mexican magazine. "I read about a purported ex-soldier hiding out in Canada and contacted his attorney. The soldier claimed to have executed between 50 and 60 people in the 1970s, and the Canadian government believed him." Certain Mexican government and army officials, whom the intern interviewed, corroborated the story. "Though there had been accusations of this sort of activity for years," he said, "no one had before brought the truth to light. My story was picked up by the Knight-Ridder wire and published in *The New York Times*."

Clearly, with publication come many benefits for the intern. Full credit and exposure is one. Financial compensation is another: those who write stories under the watchful eyes of CIR's editors take home 85 percent of what an outside news organization pays for the piece.

On the fifth floor of a nondescript building two blocks south of Market Street, CIR's headquarters sits at a scenic vantage point; from windows on the east side, one has a clear view of the Bay Bridge and what's left of the Embarcadero Freeway after 1989's Loma Prieta earthquake. Industry awards, magazine covers, and stills from documentaries adorn the walls like medals honoring journalistic battles well fought. Reporters work in over a dozen offices that surround a glass atrium. A large open area near the editorial offices houses the interns, their desks, and phones. At their fingertips is a small library and "thousands of connections."

Interns describe the working environment as "unrestricted," "calm," and "morale boosting." Because CIR is a nonprofit organization, and therefore competes for neither commercial income nor ratings, reporters take their time researching nonsensationalistic stories and writing serious, in-depth pieces. Observed an intern: "The place breeds earnest and sincere reporters who uphold the philosophy 'if we keep an eye on government and business, we can change society for the better.'"

Former interns are bent on changing the internship for the better, too. A few criticize some reporters' ineffectual mentoring. "My assigned reporter was sometimes flaky and disorganized," said one. "Occasionally, she not only kept me out of the loop on the progress of the story but also made up work to appease me." Some also point out that grunt work is compounded by interns' having to answer phones one or two hours per week. Interns also fret that the stipend is "impossible to live on." However, loyalty is strong. All acknowledge that the exposure is worth far more than any monetary compensation. And one former intern felt so indebted to the program for boosting his journalism career that he returned years later to conduct a seminar on foreign correspondents and international news.

SELECTION

 Anyone is eligible to apply, from high school seniors to college students to baby boomers thinking of career changes. CIR seeks neither a minimum GPA nor any particular major; a bioengineering major with an interest in writing was once hired to help out on a genetic engineering story. But writing ability is important. "If you're not published, just make sure you send in vivid writing samples that avoid academic or stuffy tones," said the coordinator.

APPLICATION PROCEDURE

 The deadline is December 1 for the winter/spring term and May 1 for summer/fall term. Applicants should submit a resumé, cover letter describing their interests and background, and several writing samples or published clips, though being published is not a requirement. Top candidates are asked to provide two or three personal references after a phone or on-site interview.

OVERVIEW

 Take a look at CIR's logo. It fits this nonstop investigative news agency—the ink is always flowing. Reporters have written nearly 1,000 in-depth stories since the organization's inception, thanks to significant assistance from interns. Researching important stories, interns obtain vital information— the inside scoop from people affected by the story to critical clues from places like City Hall. For tips on how to improve their reporting skills, interns attend weekly luncheons hosted by journalists. Some interns even write their own stories, the most scintillating of which are purchased by the media. For most participants, the internship launches a promising career in reporting. Former CIR interns are presently at *The Washington Post*, *Los Angeles Times*, ABC, CBS, Reuters, and CIR itself. Moreover, an intern from 1982—Katherine Ellison—shared the 1985 Pulitzer Prize for a story on the U.S. holdings of then-Philippines president Ferdinand Marcos. As one CIR intern put it: "No matter what type of reporting you do in the future, the CIR laboratory gives you a solid foundation in the investigator's art."

FOR MORE INFORMATION . . .

■ Center for Investigative Reporting
c/o Communications Director
568 Howard Street, Fifth Floor
San Francisco, CA 94105-3008
(415) 543-1200

CTY

SELECTIVITY	
Approximate applicant pool: 600–800 Interns accepted: 350	

COMPENSATION	$ $ $
RA, TA: $850/three weeks; room and board LA: $750/three weeks; room and board	

QUALITY OF LIFE	🌴 🌴 🌴 🌴
Summer-camp atmosphere College facilities; Field trips	

LOCATION(S)	
MD, CA, PA, NY, MA	

FIELD	
Education	

DURATION	
One or two 3-week sessions Summer	

PRE-REQS	
Undergrad and Grad students Overall GPA: 3.2 or higher	

DEADLINE(S)	
RA .... March 1 TA, LA .... February 1	

"*S*omebody for God's sake challenge me!"

Such are the tortured words of Daman "Math-magician" Wells, the pubescently obnoxious teenage prodigy who befriends seven-year-old Fred Tate in the movie *Little Man Tate*.

But they could be the words of any bright student who has felt limited by a fruitless educational system. Since 1980, the Center for Talented Youth (CTY) of the Johns Hopkins University has tried to fill that educational void. Committed to nurturing academic talent, CTY runs a summer school at six college campuses around the country. Preteens and adolescents who meet CTY's stringent academic standards are afforded the opportunity to study a discipline at a more advanced level than commonly available. A researcher from the Carnegie Foundation for the Advancement of Teaching called CTY "the premier program and national model for those [organizations that offer] . . . college-level courses for talented precollege age youth."

DESCRIPTION

Two kinds of CTY summer programs exist: one teaching students in grades 7 and up and the other teaching students in grades 2 to 6. The former hires five times as many staff as the latter, and as college students generally find supervising older children more challenging, the program for older students will be discussed here. Applicants interested in working at CTY are free to apply to both programs but must indicate in the application which program they prefer. They must also specify the sites at which they are most interested in working—Johns Hopkins University (Baltimore, MD), Hampshire College (Amherst, MA), Dickinson College (Carlisle, PA), Skidmore College (Saratoga Springs, NY), Franklin and Marshall College (Lancaster, PA), and Loyola Marymount University (Los Angeles, CA). Every site runs two consecutive three-week sessions, and candidates may apply to work at one or both of them.

CTY hires resident advisers (RAs), teaching assistants (TAs), and laboratory assistants (LAs). RAs live in a CTY dormitory and supervise the dozen or so students on their hall. Charged with guarding students' safety and

BUSYWORK
LOW MEDIUM HIGH
METER
OLDMAN & HAMADEH

planning their recreational activities, RAs do everything one would expect of live-in chaperons; they lay down the rules and maintain order, supervise evening study halls, visit their students' classes, and generally help them adjust to residential life. In short, RAs are responsible for their students' well-being whenever the students are not in class. As one RA concluded: "It's an intense experience. You're with your kids ten hours a day."

But CTY students aren't your run-of-the-mill "kids." Most took the Scholastic Aptitude Test (SAT) in seventh grade and scored as well as or better than college-bound seniors. "Many are bright enough at 12 to gain admission to a top college," said an RA. But among adolescents, academic talent can be inversely proportional to social adaptability, and many CTY students come from schools where they are uncomfortable and dissatisfied. Explained an RA: "Although you see a wide range of personalities, from the extremely outgoing to the introverted, students tend to be a little awkward socially. . . . [A]s RAs, we try to create an environment where they are drawn out of their shells."

RAs must be able to assume a variety of personas. First of all, they must be social facilitators. During the first week of a session, RAs sit with their students at dinner until the children feel comfortable interacting with each other. But as one RA pointed out: "It doesn't take long before the ice is broken and the kids don't need the RA hanging around their dinner table."

Another RA responsibility is akin to that of Julie McCoy from *The Love Boat*: recreation director. RAs plan and supervise activities one would find at any summer camp, such as tennis, Ultimate Frisbee, painting, improvisational drama, swimming, and so on. Watching these activities, many RAs are gratified by changes they see in their students. Remarked one RA: "You see how these kids open up in just a few weeks. One girl on my hall went from hating sports to realizing 'Hey, I'm not so bad at kickball.'"

> [One] TA tutored a student who had published a chapbook on poetry at age 16.

RAs try to strike a balance between maintaining authority and establishing friendships with their charges. "In one sense, you have to be a disciplinarian. The kids need to realize that you're in charge, that when you say, 'lights out at ten o'clock,' you mean it," explained an RA. "But you also want to gain your kids' trust. You want to be their pal and—when needed—their confidant." Achieving this equilibrium is not easy. The majority of RAs are able to exert control while remaining easygoing and affable. But a few are either "strict and humorless" or a little "too chummy." One reports that the secret to his success involved employing a few tricks, such as "putting the kids to bed early when they misbehave," "using anger sparingly, to show the students that there's a line they shouldn't cross," and "explaining calmly to students why their behavior is inappropriate, rather than punishing them without ample explanation."

Amidst the charged atmosphere generated by lively and rambunctious teenagers, RAs leave CTY with at least a few humorous memories. One RA, for example, discovered that a shy and precociously tall 12-year-old wanted desperately to ask her 22-year-old math instructor to a CTY dance. After a strong dose of encouragement from her RA, the student invited the instructor. He proved to be a good sport, and student and instructor danced the night away. Said the RA: "He made that student's summer. She was so happy just to have mustered the nerve to invite him. You could see her newfound confidence the next day. For her, it was a personal triumph." Another RA was kidnapped by his students and carried around campus, as the group sang songs to the amusement of random passersby. Perhaps the most memorable incident involved a 12-year-old who wanted to see if he could make a telephone ring using a lamp's power cord. Cutting the cord of a plugged-in lamp, the student created a power surge that shut down the power in his section of the dorm.

While RAs and their immediate supervisors, senior RAs, comprise the residential staff, TAs and LAs are known as the "instructional assistants." As the name suggests, instructional assistants help instructors carry out the work in the classroom. They perform clerical tasks (typing, photocopying, grading, etc.), tutor individual students, and proctor evening study halls. LAs also clean up after afternoon lab sessions and help the instructor plan labwork. Unlike RAs, TAs and LAs have the weekends off.

Instructional assistants are in the best position to appreciate their students' intellectual prowess and passion because they interact with students in class. "The first fact you realize is that these kids are really sharp," said a TA. "Having previously been a TA at a prep school, I was accustomed to bright kids. But CTY students were extraordinary. Virtually all of them were passionate about learning." Said another: "Being a TA is ideal if you're into teaching and if your instructor gives you responsibility. You teach kids who have an incredible desire and capacity to learn. There's no variable you could change to make the teaching environment better." Each student enrolls in one course per session, choosing from among offerings in mathematics, science, humanities, and writing. TAs can't help but be impressed by the heavy workloads their students undertake. "The amount of work these teenagers do is stunning. Some classes have their students read 40 pages of a college textbook nightly," said a TA. And every so often, a TA encounters a potential genius: "I knew of a 14-year-old who mastered a precalculus book in 12 days." Another TA tutored a student who had published a chapbook of poetry at age 16.

As CTY sites are located at college campuses around the country, staff enjoy the resources that accompany college life. A full range of college facilities at their disposal, they make use of libraries, gyms, tennis courts, and swimming pools. Cafeterias, on the whole, tend to be mediocre, but one RA praised the food at Dickinson College. Staff members live by themselves in double rooms, a few of which have private bathrooms.

Material perks are few. Every staff member receives an official CTY "Staff" shirt to be worn in front of parents on the opening and closing days of the program. Office supplies are plentiful and TAs and LAs receive free copies of the books used in their classes.

Staff members are usually so busy with their students that off-campus forays are a rarity. Even so, some TAs arrange field trips for their classes. One took his class to a local hospital; another visited an aquarium. RAs have been known to take their students to July 4th fireworks displays and the beach, although keeping track of 15 high-spirited teenagers off campus can be a "logistical nightmare."

Any program as comprehensive as CTY's is bound to receive its share of criticism. Several interns were frustrated with what they deemed "inadequate lines of communication" between the residential and instructional staffs. Said one TA: "Residential and instructional life are dependent on each other. . . . [For example], if an RA fails to enforce 'lights-out' at a decent hour, many of her students will perform below par in class the next day. The instructor and TAs will be understandably concerned. But it's difficult for them to get in touch with the RAs when each group works at a different time." Another TA warned that one's experience as a TA is shaped largely by the assigned instructor. "Although most TAs and LAs found their jobs rewarding, personality conflicts do occur. . . . A few of the instructors have chips on their shoulders and make life difficult for their teaching assistants."

SELECTION

The program is open to all undergraduate and graduate students. Although they must have a cumulative GPA of 3.2 or higher, applicants need not match the intellectual ability of CTY students. Indeed, one RA applied to CTY even though a few years back "he had not made the cut to become a student." Above all, the brochure states that candidates should be "mature, responsible, and energetic." Staff members report that the program attracts people who are "confident," "outgoing," and desirous of "intellectual stimulation."

APPLICATION PROCEDURE

The deadline for RA applications is March 1; for TA and LA positions, the deadline is February 1. In addition to a cover letter and transcripts (from all undergraduate and graduate work), applicants must arrange for three letters of recommendation to be sent directly to CTY. If an applicant has had experience directly related to CTY (i.e., as a teacher, lab assistant, resident adviser, camp counselor, or tutor), one recommendation must be from someone who supervised such work. Those who lack related experience must secure at least one recommendation from an employer. Applicants must also submit a CTY employment application. After the application deadlines have past, the CTY administration screens out the strongest candidates. Of this selected group, those with previous CTY experience are offered positions. New applicants are then interviewed by telephone, or in person if possible, to fill the remaining openings.

OVERVIEW

 College students and graduates of any academic major, here's your chance for a rewarding summer of fun with some extraordinary youngsters. Enjoy working with teenagers? Fascinated by the highly intelligent? Long for the camaraderie and warm cheer of summer camp? CTY merits consideration. The overwhelming majority of students who have worked for CTY are glad they did. Staff members tend to forge close bonds with one another; so close, in fact, that one summer brought together three couples who eventually married. Staff become so attached to the program that several elect to be "repeat offenders"; more than a few have returned for five or more summers, serving as RAs, TAs, and eventually instructors. In sum, CTY combines the charms of summer camp with the stimulation of academic achievement. For college students interesting in supervising, teaching, and learning from highly talented adolescents, it's a well-spent summer at "brain camp."

FOR MORE INFORMATION . . .

■ Center for Talented Youth
CTY Summer Programs Employment
The Johns Hopkins University
3400 North Charles Street
Baltimore, MD 21218
(410) 516-0191

"**H**ave you or any members of your family ever been employed by an agent of any foreign country?"

"No."

"Have you ever been a member of a group that is totalitarian, fascist, communist, or subversive?"

"No."

"Have you ever used marijuana?"

"Well, umm . . ."

The armband is getting a little tight. The room, a little stuffy. Your head, a little light.

But hey, if you want to intern at the CIA, you have to submit to the "black box."

The CIA has good reasons to ask internship candidates, as well as all other personnel, to take a polygraph test. As the agency charged with guarding America's national security, the CIA must take rigorous precautions. And lie-detector tests are just the beginning. CIA headquarters is surrounded by a 12-foot-high barbed-wire fence, patrolled by armed guards. An entire division of the agency, that which is involved directly in espionage and other covert activities, is shrouded in total secrecy; the in-house phone book makes no mention of the thousands of employees who work in this division. And there are offices at the CIA deemed so sensitive that they are guarded by an agency policeman in a glass cage, a turnstile, and a combination lock.

DESCRIPTION

The CIA offers two types of internships: the Minority Undergraduate Studies Program and the Graduate Studies Program. As participants of both have similar projects and share the same privileges, the following description applies to both programs, except where otherwise noted.

SELECTIVITY	
Approximate applicant pool: 500 Interns accepted: 50–60	🔍🔍🔍🔍

COMPENSATION	
$308–$375/wk (Undergrad); $375–$590/wk (Grad) Housing allowance; Round-trip travel	💲💲💲

QUALITY OF LIFE	
Tight-knit culture; Speaker series Co-op Association; Employee benefits	🌴🌴🌴🌴

LOCATION(S)

Langley, VA; Washington D.C.; and other sites

FIELD

Government

DURATION

Summer (Undergrad)
Fall, Spring, Summer (Grad)

PRE-REQS

See Selection

DEADLINE(S)

September 30 (Undergrad)
6–9 months prior to work (Grad)

Interns are assigned to one of three divisions: the Directorate of Science and Technology (DS&T), the Directorate of Intelligence (DI), and the Directorate of Administration (DA). A fourth division, the Directorate of Operations (DO), is the clandestine branch of the CIA, involved with collecting foreign intelligence through its network of "human agents" (aka spies); you guessed it: the DO is off-limits to interns.

The DS&T develops and operates the technical systems used in collecting intelligence. Video and image enhancement, chemi-

BUSYWORK METER
LOW MEDIUM HIGH
OLDMAN & HAMADEH

cal imagery, advanced antenna design, electro-optics, and satellite communications are but a few of the technologies DS&T covers. Those with backgrounds in computers, engineering, and hard sciences are the most likely candidates for DS&T work. An engineering major, for example, worked in the office of SIGNIT (signal intelligence) Operations. Although the substance of what he did is classified, in general terms he helped design equipment to collect and analyze signals. He said: "If, for instance, an operation overseas needed equipment to interpret a set of signals, we'd work with them to develop such a system."

Another DS&T office using interns is the National Photographic Interpretation Center (NPIC). After receiving training in photographic analysis, interns scrutinize photos from such sources as satellites and spy planes. Sitting at special optical contraptions (picture a heavy-duty microscope attached to a giant microfilm machine), interns scan photographs for basic intelligence data—military forces, military equipment production, natural disasters, etc. "I'd examine photographs taken at various times, looking for changes and trends," said an intern.

After information is collected, the Directorate of Intelligence (DI) gets to work analyzing it. The DI has five offices charged with observing a particular region of the world: the Office of Slavic and Eurasian Analysis, the Office of European Analysis, the Office of Near East and South Asian Analysis, the Office of East Asian Analysis, and the Office of African and Latin American Analysis. An intern in the Office of East Asian Analysis studied the political activities of China. "Using all sorts of resources, including Chinese newspapers translated by the agency, I kept tabs on the maneuverings of the Chinese government." He wrote a series of reports summarizing his research, including a paper on China's 14th Party Congress. "The bottom line," he said, "is to help the agency anticipate a government's next move." An intern in the Office of Slavic and Eurasian Analysis analyzed political crimes and military movements in the

former Soviet Union. Her analysis found its way into an in-house bulletin disseminated to members of the intelligence community on a "need-to-know basis."

In addition to regional offices, the DI has six functional offices, such as the Office of Scientific Weapons Research and the Office of Imagery Analysis. In the latter, interns examine satellite photographs and summarize their findings in written reports, some of which end up on the desks of top government officials. "Our customers are America's policy-makers," said an intern. "The analysis our office does is at the request of people like the president, vice president, and members of Congress."

The third division hiring interns, the Directorate of Administration (DA), places interns in offices carrying out the agency's daily administrative responsibilities. Drawing on students from a wide range of academic backgrounds, the DA involves interns in support areas like finance, human resources, journalism, graphic arts, and photography. An intern in the Office of Logistics, for example, helped procure office equipment for the CIA. Arranging "a slew of classified and unclassified contracts with equipment vendors," he spent the better part of his day phoning vendors and completing paperwork. Compared to the work interns do in the DS&T and DI, it's easy to see how some interns in DA find their jobs "less exciting and less uniquely CIA."

But the CIA is legendary for allowing employees to change jobs. If interns find their assignments unrewarding, chances are they will have the opportunity to switch jobs or offices. "The agency is more flexible than you'd expect," said an intern. "It will go to great lengths to make sure its employees are working at full capacity."

Working at an organization as clandestine and famous as the CIA is a mixed blessing. Interns have to get used to the fact that the nature of their work is almost always secret. Said one: "Nothing here leaves the office. Ever." But just being at the CIA is a kick. "There's a mystique here that permeates everything you do and everyone you meet," said

> **"There's a mystique here that permeates everything you do and everyone you meet."**

an intern. Interns in technical positions marvel at the advanced equipment to which they are exposed; as a brochure put it, the CIA "work(s) somewhere beyond the state of the art." Others are impressed with the steady flow of up-to-the-minute information the agency acquires: "We have access to news well before newspapers do."

The atmosphere at the CIA is like no other. Employees are fiercely loyal to the agency. Said one, "We come to work knowing that people's lives depend on what we do. There's a feeling here that we're all in this together. There's something intangible about it, but [this feeling] binds us together." Interns, too, speak well of the working environment: "The people I work with show a lot of professionalism, but they also have a lot of heart. We all depend on each other. . . . (I)t creates a tight-knit environment."

The CIA runs a summer speaker series for its interns. Held in the agency's bubble-shaped, 500-seat auditorium, the series invites various department heads to address the interns. Interns may also attend the "town meetings," which brief employees on CIA policy. Town meetings are led by a top dog of the agency, often a deputy director of one the divisions, the general counsel, or the director of the agency.

Interns work in various locations in Virginia and Washington, such as the National Photographic Interpretation Center (in Washington, D.C.), the Page Building (in Vienna, Virginia) or CIA headquarters (in Langley, Virginia). The last is the real McCoy when it comes to what one would envision the CIA compound to be. Eight miles from downtown Washington, CIA headquarters is nestled in the woods of suburban Virginia. Two fortresslike administration buildings sit at the end of a long, restricted thoroughfare. In the lobby, a huge CIA seal adorns the floor, as was depicted in a scene from the movie *Patriot Games*. Hallways inside the CIA buildings evoke a hospital-like sterility; shoes clank against the floors with austere authority. Small exhibits are interspersed throughout the buildings, including one that displays a chunk of the Berlin Wall. Bathrooms are of the typical institutional variety, except that each boasts a scale for employees to weigh themselves; "the agency wants its people in good shape," said an employee.

To further this goal of employee fitness, the CIA has a few gym facilities, each with the standard fare of Nautilus machines, StairMasters, and aerobics classes. Headquarters also has a great jogging path that snakes through the compound's woods. For the team-oriented, there's an intramural sports program (softball, flag football, men's basketball) open to all employees.

Most CIA interns elect to live in CIA-designated apartments located in Falls Church and Alexandria, Virginia. Four interns typically live in the two-bedroom apartments. The CIA provides each intern with a housing allowance of $390 per month, a sum that easily covers their rent.

As CIA brochures will attest, generosity is the operative word when it comes to employee benefits. This spirit applies to interns, too. They are reimbursed for travel to and from Washington, whether traveling by car, train, or plane. A Co-Op Association exists to help interns plan tours of Washington and other off-hours activities. Interns receive the same benefits as permanent employees, including accrual of annual and sick leave, enrollment in health and life insurance plans, participation in carpools, and use of medical services. Job-related internal training is also available to interns in such subjects as computers, foreign languages, and leadership skills.

Salaries are paid according to percentage of coursework completed. College seniors thus earn more than juniors, and so on. Students studying a hard science or engineering will receive a slightly higher salary than business or liberal-arts majors.

SELECTION

 The Minority Undergraduate Studies Program is open to minority and disabled juniors and seniors. The Graduate Studies Program is available for minority and nonminority students entering their first or second years of graduate study. Applicants must be U.S. citizens and over 17-1/2 years of age at time of application, have a minimum GPA (2.75 for undergrads, 3.0 for grads), and successfully pass medical and security screening (including a polygraph test). Although other areas of study may be applicable to the agency's needs, the CIA generally looks for students in the following majors: accounting and finance, business administration, cartography/geography, computer science, economics, engineering, hard sciences (chemistry, physics, etc.), international studies, languages (particularly non-Romance languages), mathematics, photo sciences, political science, and printing/photography.

APPLICATION PROCEDURE

 Apply E-A-R-L-Y! The deadline for minority undergraduate applicants is a startling September 30; graduate applicants should apply six to nine months prior to the desired work period. It takes the CIA at least six months to run a thorough background check on its applicants. Applicants should submit a cover letter, a resumé, and unofficial transcripts. The CIA Employment Center responds within 30 days to those judged to be the best candidates. Footing the bill for transportation and hotel expenses, the CIA invites these applicants to interview with the hiring office. Those who make it past the initial interview are asked to return to the CIA for a physical examination, psychological profile, and polygraph test.

OVERVIEW

 CIA. There are few three-letter combinations that carry more weight on a resumé. At the very least, employers know that CIA interns have passed the electronic scrutiny of the "black box." But interning at the CIA is not for everyone. Despite Hollywood's portrayal of CIA work as glamorous and dangerous, the CIA internship offers little in the way of international intrigue. Nevertheless, interns do get challenging assignments. And they receive an insider's look at what *Newsweek* has deemed the most secretive and tightly knit organization in American society. But interns must be prepared to work in a highly bureaucratic environment, one that prizes discreetness and loyalty. Many do, and every year upward of 40 percent of all interns are offered permanent jobs at the CIA.

FOR MORE INFORMATION . . .

■ Central Intelligence Agency
CIA Employment Center
P.O. Box 12727
Arlington, VA 22209-9727
(703) 351-2028

CITIBANK®

SELECTIVITY	🔍 🔍 🔍 🔍
Approximate applicant pool: 1,500	
Interns accepted: 100	

COMPENSATION	$ $ $ $ $
$500–$700/week for undergrads	
$800–$1,000/week for grads	

QUALITY OF LIFE	⚜ ⚜ ⚜ ⚜
Orientation with chairman; Entry-level responsibility	
Professional atmosphere; Good cafeterias	

LOCATION(S)
New York, NY; Chicago, IL; Los Angeles, CA; Atlanta, GA; Houston and Dallas, TX

FIELD
Banking

DURATION
10–13 weeks
Summer

PRE-REQS
College seniors, Grad students

DEADLINE(S)
April 1

You may be familiar with these innovations—ATMs which allow users to purchase shares in mutual funds . . . credit cards with their owners' photographs on the front . . . an ATM language for the visually impaired. What you may not know is that Citibank created them all. As the first bank to offer compound interest on savings accounts, checking accounts with no minimum balance requirements, negotiable certificates of deposit, and floating rate notes, Citibank has been a pioneer in modern banking since its founding in 1812.

Comprised of two divisions—Global Consumer Banking and Global Finance—Citibank has a handle on virtually every aspect of worldwide banking. Its 1,300 or so branches and offices in more than 90 countries take deposits, provide credit-card service, sell insurance, and issue home-mortgage loans. Citibank also dabbles in investment banking—interest rate and derivative products, government and corporate bonds, commercial paper, asset-backed securities, and foreign-exchange trading. Now the largest bank in America, Citibank produces over $16 billion in annual revenues.

DESCRIPTION

The Citibank Summer Associate Program dates back more than 30 years, when every summer a few college students were informally extended opportunities to explore the banking industry. Since then, Citibank's internship program has evolved into a structured experience, enabling participants to meet with the chairman at the orientation and to learn about banking through regular networking seminars. Of the 100 Citibank interns, approximately 15 to 20 are undergraduates, the rest graduate students (mostly MBA candidates). Opportunities exist in New York, Chicago, Los Angeles, Atlanta,

Houston, Dallas, and other locations which vary year to year (see recruiting literature).

Citibank's activities touch on all aspects of banking and reach all sections of the globe. Consequently, a Summer Associate (SA) can potentially work in any number of capacities and may be placed in the following business groups—Corporate Finance, Sales and Trading, Financial Institutions and Transaction Services, Consumer Banking, Corporate Audit, Corporate Financial Control, Private Banking, and Real Estate.

As part of the Consumer Banking group, an undergraduate SA immersed himself in the marketing of promotional bulletins. With minimal supervision, he wrote, designed, produced, and printed a brochure that targeted specific clients and services. "I was involved in every aspect of production, including negotiating with the publishers, layout people, and mailing team," he explained. "This was a lot of responsibility. The four-page brochure had a lot of graphics and went out to over a thousand clients." Assuming the responsibilities of an entry-level employee, he also helped write a speech for a vice president, who delivered it to the Citibank mortgage-sales team during a sales-incentive campaign. "It felt good to know that the words I had written were being used by my superior to motivate the sales force," he said.

During a summer in Corporate Finance, one graduate SA assessed what factors were critical to the success of the railroad industry. "[Citibank] had already lent a considerable amount of money to some of the railroads," she said. "[My report] helped us determine whether to issue them more loans or restructure their finances." Having spent some time in Eastern Europe, she was also called upon to write a report on the telecommunications industry in Czechoslovakia. "One of Citibank's clients wanted to do a joint venture [with the Czechoslovakian government]...the report helped them assess the viability and structuring of [this venture]."

Another Corporate Finance SA worked as a financial analyst within the Utilities Division. She examined contracts, created term sheets for the loan department, reviewed accounts, and surveyed equity investment opportunities in central Europe. "The team integrated me almost immediately," she said. "Though contracts were just one small part of what I did, I eventually examined them by myself. By the end of the summer, I had gained a firm grasp of their legal structures."

In Sales and Trading, a graduate SA assisted in the trading of short-term bonds. "I followed the roller coaster ride of the markets to gain a sense of pricing," she said. "By observing where other companies were pricing their issues, we could correctly price Citibank's paper. And by communicating with other traders, we could determine if our clients were adequately funded." She was not relegated to the role of mere observer, either. "I [did] some of the work completely on my own, though there was always someone watching over my shoulder. After all, I was handling millions of dollars in issues."

Approximately eighty of Citibank's SAs are placed throughout New York in eight offices, ranging from average office buildings a few stories in height to towering pillars of corporate extravagance. The building at One Court Square in Queens, for example, is fifty stories tall and informally known as the "Emerald Tower" for its shimmering green-glass exterior. "I worked on the forty-second floor and had a spacious cubicle, with a computer, phone, and terrific view of most of New York," explained an SA who worked there. "The location was somewhat remote, but no matter—midtown Manhattan is only a few minutes' subway ride away." As the offices for the company's senior executives and the site of one of Citibank's "model branches," the Citibank headquarters at 399 Park Avenue is a favorite workplace among SAs. "[The model branch] has tellers, securities representatives, and ATMs that communicate in five languages," described an SA, "...and there are so many ATMs there that I never had to wait in line when I needed cash." For food, SAs can partake of the fare at Citibank's cafeterias, uniformly praised for their wide variety and low prices. At One Court Square, for example, there are two cafeterias, one of which offers an all-you-can-eat daily buffet for $7. "You have to wear a coat and tie," said an SA, "but the food is excellent ... like a fine restaurant's."

Though SAs' duties vary significantly, there are many opportunities in which SAs at all levels come together to share their experiences. At the Summer Associate kickoff event, the company gathers its nearly 100 SAs from around the country into the bank's New York headquarters for a welcome and orientation with members of top management, including Chairman John Reed. "[Reed] spoke about

> **"I worked on the forty-second floor and had a spacious cubicle, with a computer, phone, and terrific view of most of New York . . ."**

the bank's financial goals and then opened up the floor for our questions," commented an SA. "We were impressed that he'd take that kind of time. . . . It certainly showed his commitment to the program."

Throughout the summer, small groups of SAs congregate for discussions with division heads. "We'd get together every week over breakfast or lunch, and managing directors would give us an overview of their areas," said an SA in Consumer Banking. An SA in Corporate Finance particularly enjoyed her informative gatherings: "we learned about securitization, equipment financing, corporate bonds, and derivatives." Since past SAs felt that their exposure to the bank's overall functions was limited—"I really didn't get to see all of the bank's divisions, so I never got a full picture of the banking process"—Citibank recently organized a mid-summer Career Fair, where vice presidents reveal the dealings of Citibank's eight business groups. "It's good, because [unlike the weekly gatherings]," explained a former SA who now works for Citibank, "the Career Fair provides an overview. . . . [I]t shows you how all the groups fit together."

As part of its commitment to the community, Citibank encourages SAs to participate in Citibank-organized public-service projects. Past SAs have volunteered their time with Special Olympics, with Prep for Prep, a group which readies disadvantaged high school students for college, and with the National Student Business League, which prepares college students to become business leaders. "Public service at Citibank is a great thing to get involved in," concluded an SA. "Besides helping out the community, it builds morale among employees . . . definitely an enjoyable part of the summer."

SELECTION

 Undergraduate candidates must have completed their junior year to be considered for the program, and graduate candidates must be one year away from graduation. While Citibank finds most of its SAs through on-campus recruiting at about 30 colleges and universities, students nationwide are welcome to apply. Students of any major are welcome, although the coordinator stresses the importance of "standing out above the crowd."

APPLICATION PROCEDURE

 The application deadline is April 1. Candidates may submit materials anytime between September and April. Since Citibank visits many college campuses, students should inquire with their schools' career centers for interview schedules. Otherwise, sending a cover letter and resumé will suffice. Due to the high volume of applications, a response may take three or four weeks. Note that although no GPA requirement exists, Citibank eventually asks potential hirees for a copy of their transcript.

OVERVIEW

 "Put not your trust in money, but your money in trust," declared the nineteenth-century author Oliver Wendell Holmes, Sr. Students who agree with Holmes and want to explore the modern equivalent of putting money in trust—that is, banking—would be wise to investigate the Citibank internship. Provided with the opportunity to influence Citibank products and services, meet Chairman John Reed, and attend several social and business events, interns sample the company's culture and gain a sense of what banking is really like.

FOR MORE INFORMATION . . .

■ Citibank
Summer Associate Programs
575 Lexington Avenue
12th Floor/Zone 3
New York, NY 10043
(212) 559-1000

SELECTIVITY	
Approximate applicant pool: 900 Interns accepted: 40–75	Q Q Q Q Q

COMPENSATION	
$390–$430/week for undergraduates $390–$580/week for graduates	$ $ $ $

QUALITY OF LIFE	
Entry-level projects; Mountain recreation Wellness Center; Intern picnic with Bill Coors	🌴 🌴 🌴

LOCATION(S)

Golden, CO

FIELD

Consumer goods (beer)

DURATION

9–12 weeks
Fall, Spring, Summer

PRE-REQS

College sophomores, juniors and seniors, grad students
Must be returning to school for at least one term

DEADLINE(S)

March 1

Bitters. Kvass. Ale. Lager. Pilsner. Mead. Stout.

Americans have been enjoying combinations of grains, water, and yeast for over 350 years, ever since the Pilgrims landed at Plymouth Rock one November day in 1620, beer on board. By then, humans had been consuming beer for over 10,000 years, hypothesize historians, who think that the concoction was discovered accidentally when some nomads' grain, coming into contact with warm water, fermented to create a primitive beer. Since its discovery, claims Washington's Beer Institute, beer has been carried onto Noah's ark, has played a role in Chinese religious rituals, and has been scrutinized for quality by the Egyptian pharaohs' royal beer inspectors. In modern times, Coors Brewing Company has also proved an influential part of beer history.

In 1868, a Prussian brewery-apprentice named Adolph Coors found his way to the United States. Arriving in Golden in 1873, he founded a brewery with a partner whom he bought out seven years later. Today, Adolph Coors is gone, but his descendants run the operation, and Adolph Coors Company ranks among the Fortune 500 of American industrial corporations. Adolph Coors' vision helped make his company the third largest brewer in the United States, next to Anheuser-Busch and Miller, and make beer as popular as it is today.

DESCRIPTION

 The Coors Corporate College Internship Program started formally in 1983 when it invited 22 students to experience life at the world's largest single-site brewery. Before that, only children of employees could secure a summer job at the beer-production company. Now, as many as 75 college students and even 30 high school students have participated in

the programs offered: Purchasing, Engineering, Sensory Analysis, Project Management, Accounting, Biology/Microbiology/Chemistry, Distributor Development, Telecommunications, Wellness Center/Recreation, and Journalism/Public Relations. However, internships in all of these departments are not available every summer. Prospective applicants should contact the college recruiting representative for further information on availability.

Coors believes staunchly that its internships must contain a strong learning component. To that end, the company established some years ago the College Recruiting Committee to set up annually substantial summer projects on which students can work. Said the coordinator: "We don't believe that the interns should have to file or simply observe a boss at work. Coors works very hard to make sure that its kids are well taken care of."

And well taken care of they are. An intern in Distributor Development, the department overseeing Coors' independent distributors and wholesalers, worked on applications submitted for purchase of distributorships. "The potential distributor would have to fill out an application and await management's approval or rejection," said the intern. "I worked on three that summer, reviewing the finances, putting the numbers into Coors' formats, and determining if the assumptions made were reasonable." She also worked on the monthlong design of an optimum distribution network, using situation analysis to examine different scenarios. Moreover, the intern was able to visit one of the Chicago distributorships for an entire week. "Coors allowed me to go on the trip so that I could gain some operational exposure," she said. "It was a real learning experience. I examined business reports, met with sales staff, even rode in the delivery truck."

Another intern, an engineer in Plant Utilities, spent the entire summer with a Coors engineer calculating a steam balance. The intern created a large Lotus spreadsheet, which summarized two binders' worth of calculations, and learned how and where the 800,000 pounds of steam generated per hour get used in the plant. "We attempted to allocate each steam load for two reasons," explained the intern. "One, we wanted to determine the in-house users, like canning, and bill them separately as customers, and two, we wanted to give the power engineers a better idea of how the system operates so that if new generators were needed, for example, the engineers would know how to balance the load."

An intern in Project Management was assigned seven projects on his first day. "I didn't know much initially," he said. "I had to sit down with the engineers and learn about all the projects. I spent a lot of time working with the different

team members." One of the projects focused on upgrading the brewing system mechanically and electrically. Given full authority as a project manager, the intern maintained the cost and the schedule of each project, observing the welding, pouring of concrete, and other minor construction. "Because I considered all phases before making a decision, I became really good at problem solving," said the intern. "Midway through the summer, employees looked to me for suggestions, and by the end, I even made the financial decisions associated with a project."

Occupying about seven square miles of space, Coors is situated between two foothills in the quaint town of Golden. Nestled against the Rocky Mountains about 30 minutes from metropolitan Denver, Golden and its environs offer exciting recreational opportunities like skiing, horseback riding, mountain climbing, and rafting. The brewery itself, whose gray concrete architecture reminds some interns of a "prison, Alcatraz style," is almost three quarters of a mile long on one side. Inside, one finds vats, a maze of piping, a red-tile floor made out of Coors Ceramics products, and plenty of brew kettles and fermenters. Surrounding the brewery are an engineering facility, a can-manufacturing warehouse, a fabrication shop, construction offices, storage rooms, and an exercise facility called the Wellness Center, which interns may use free of charge. Housed in a renovated 23,000-square-foot Safeway store at the entrance of the brewery, the Wellness Center has weights, Eagle equipment, 8 StairMasters, 25 bicycles, 10 treadmills, and a one-eighth mile running track.

Interns enjoy other perks, too. For lunch, there's the subsidized cafeteria, where interns eat for about $3. They may purchase beer at a discount from the company store, if they are twenty-one or older. Interns are afforded a 25 percent discount on all logo items, such as caps and pins. During the summer, athletically inclined interns may participate in the 40-team softball league at the recreation center or join the Ping-Pong, rodeo, and lacrosse clubs, just to name a few. Coors also assists their interns in the housing

> **Interns may purchase beer at a discount from the company store, if they are older than twenty-one.**

search. Participants work with the coordinator to find local dorm or private-family accommodations. Also available are two-bedroom apartments, deposit-free, in a spacious, well-kept apartment with which Coors has a contract. Interns don't have to pay the first month's rent until after they receive their first paycheck.

Most interns spend ten or more weeks at the brewery, during which time there are clearly many things to see and do. One of them is June's large intern picnic featuring Chairman Bill Coors and other top management. Then there are the weekly team or one-on-one meetings held by each department. Moreover, twice in the summer, interns are formally evaluated. Concluded one intern: "On a scale of one to ten, I would have to rate my experience a ten. I was a project manager from day one, doing everything, even though project managers usually have lots of previous industry experience."

SELECTION

 Generally, Coors seeks team players with excellent written and oral communication skills. Eligibility requirements, however, depend on the position sought. Students in Purchasing must be seniors with a 3.0 GPA in purchasing or a closely related major. Engineering applicants may be from any engineering discipline but must have already finished their junior year by the start of the internship and must have at least a 2.4 GPA in engineering. Students in Sensory Analysis must have completed their junior year in a food science program. Project Management applicants must be seniors or graduate students in construction management. Prospective Accounting interns must have finished their junior years in accounting or finance. Interns in Biology/Microbiology/Chemistry may be juniors or seniors in those fields. For Distributor Development and Telecommunications, only graduate students in business (with an emphasis in finance or economics) and in telecommunications, respectively, are considered. The Wellness Center and the Public Relations positions are nonpaid, credit-only (six to twelve semester units), for juniors or seniors. The Wellness Center positions are for students in wellness, recreation, or related fields. The Public Relations positions are for students (including outstanding sophomores) with strong journalism experience or coursework.

APPLICATION PROCEDURE

 The deadline for submission of required materials is March 1. Applicants must send a resumé and cover letter to the address below. Applicants to the Public Relations division must also submit a writing sample. In addition to accepting unsolicited applications, Coors conducts on-campus recruiting sessions. The career service centers at Michigan State, Arizona State, University of Texas at Austin, and the five major universities in Colorado are among the many campuses visited by the company. Coors also visits several minority job fairs. Top local-area candidates are usually invited for on-site interviews. Long-distance candidates are interviewed by phone. Those hired are required to undergo a drug test and sign a Coors Brewing Company Confidentiality Agreement.

OVERVIEW

 Of the top three beer companies in the United States, only Coors offers undergraduates a formal internship program. Thirty minutes from Denver, the company taps interns into beer processing and administration, distilling its internship philosophy to this: Talented students deserve important projects. As contributing members of the Coors team, interns present their work to a group of high-level managers or submit lengthy reports at the end of the summer. Though Coors says that it does not use the program to nip future employees, nearly 10 percent of interns receive full-time offers. The brochure's claim—"You can count on your internship being more than a summer job!"—knows what's brewing.

FOR MORE INFORMATION . . .

■ Coors Brewing Company
311 Tenth Street
Mail No. NH210
c/o College Recruiting Representative
Golden, CO 80401
(303) 279-6565

Every group has its ultimate challenge, an experience that defines those who participate as among the most talented in their field. Track-and-field enthusiasts have the decathlon. Whiz kids have the Odyssey of the Mind competition. Fitness freaks have the Iron Man Triathlon. And aspiring public servants have the Coro Fellows Program.

According to its promotional literature the 51-year-old Coro Foundation "offers the kind of hands-on experience that most graduate schools only talk about." Every year, each of the four regional Coro centers picks 12 college graduates and subjects them to a rigorous nine-month series of internships, interviews, public service projects, and seminar meetings. The Coro Fellows Program, in the words of its brochure, "provides its participants with the opportunity to step out of their schooling or careers . . . to experience new environments . . . to learn from the best . . . to discuss and analyze experiences with colleagues . . . to be challenged by demanding and changing situations."

SELECTIVITY	🔍🔍🔍
Approximate applicant pool: 300–400 Interns accepted: 48	

COMPENSATION	$
$3,500 tuition; grants, scholarships, installment plans, and tuition loans are available	

QUALITY OF LIFE	⬆⬆⬆
Variety of organizations Focus weeks; Weekly seminars	

LOCATION(S)
San Francisco, CA; Los Angeles, CA; St. Louis, MO; New York, NY

FIELD
Public Service

DURATION
9 Months September–June

PRE-REQS
College grads of any age

DEADLINE(S)
January 15

DESCRIPTION

The odyssey commences in September, when Coro Fellows begin the first of a series of five internships, each three to four weeks in duration. Some internships find Fellows carrying out a high-level project, while others are more of an observer's post, where Fellows conduct interviews with the key decision makers of an organization. By the time it's all over in June, Fellows will have interned in a government agency, a corporation, a community organization, a labor union, and a political campaign. The Fellows interviewed for this passage were affiliated with Coro's Northern California Center and thus completed internships with organizations in the San Fran-

cisco Bay Area; Fellows affiliated with the other Coro centers—Los Angeles, St. Louis, and New York—serve internships in their respective regions.

The government internship finds Fellows working in state or local government. One Fellow worked with Anna Eschoo, a city supervisor in San Mateo. In addition to "designing a program where kids from San Mateo could spend time in county departments to learn about government," she wrote a brochure that pulled together information about county services. Assigned to San Francisco's Department of Health, another

Fellow did a project coordinating the agency's services for at-risk youth; "I made recommendations on how [the department's] services can be better integrated." The highlight of one Fellow's year was interning in the office of then-mayor of San Francisco Dianne Feinstein, herself a Coro alumna. "I rotated through different areas of the office and did small projects. But the real thrill was getting to shadow her in whatever she did." Like many officials who sponsor Coro Fellows, Feinstein was unusually accessible to the Fellow: "[Feinstein] would sometimes just let me sit in her office while she carried on with her business. . . . It's so rare that a politician would give her young intern such close contact."

For their corporate internship, Fellows are placed in one of the region's larger corporations. Chevron USA was the destination of one Fellow, who spent much of her time interviewing the company's 100 employees. Another Fellow found herself at Wells Fargo Bank, where she worked with the vice president in charge of branch banking. "My main project was researching and writing a report on the potential for adding future [bank] branches in [San Francisco's] South of Market district. My recommendations were based on the growth of businesses and housing in this [formerly depressed] area." A third Fellow was sent to McKesson Associates, a "huge Fortune 500 company that acts as a distributor for things like beverages and pharmaceutical products." Working with the head of public affairs, he wrote a memo on recent legislation regulating the sale of bottled water. He also conducted several interviews with employees, including the CEO: "I got an unprecedented 45 minutes of the CEO's time. My boss later told me to consider myself lucky: the CEO had never given *him* 45 minutes of time!"

Fellows are placed in a wide range of community organizations. Assigned to an environmental advocacy group called Friends of the Earth, an intern wrote several articles for its newspaper, *Not Man Apart*. Another Fellow was sent to the San Francisco chapter of Planned Parent-

hood, where she prepared a report briefing the executive director on how the group's operations would change when parental consent laws went into effect. The internship taught her "what working at an organization under siege feels like—you have to take extra security measures like signing in and watching for suspicious packages." A nonprofit group called Asian Incorporated was the assignment of another Fellow. "Asian Inc. is dedicated to improving Asian businesses in San Francisco," he said. "I helped the group coordinate a conference of the Asian American Business Association. I handled the nuts and bolts—like contacting an assortment of Asian professional associations and arranging for state officials to speak at the conference."

The labor union internship is typically a week shorter than the other experiences, and it emphasizes observation over practical work. Assigned to the San Francisco Building and Trades Council, one intern was "virtually attached to the head of the union," with whom he attended "sensitive contract negotiations on issues relating to plumbers, carpenters, and iron workers." Another Fellow was sent to SCIU 790, a union for service workers like school cafeteria employees and groundskeepers. In addition to doing some legal research on labor contracts, he shadowed the head of the union: "At the end of the internship, I sat next to him during the contract negotiations with the city of San Francisco. It was pretty amazing to have this kind of access."

The final internship assigns Fellows to a political campaign. A Fellow from 1984 helped out at the Gary Hart for President campaign, serving as the liaison between the state office and the local campaign offices in Northern California. In 1988, another Fellow coordinated local phone bank operations for the Dukakis campaign. "I set up phone banks throughout San Francisco, soliciting volunteers and preparing scripts for them to read." A third Fellow, a self-described "diehard Democrat," was surprised to be assigned to the 1986 campaign to elect Republican Tom Heuning as San Mateo county supervisor. He recalled:

> A recent Coro class included a professional dancer, a speech and debate champion, and a third degree black belt in Chinese boxing.

"Heuning knew that we had little in common ideologically, and said something like, 'I bet I wasn't your first choice.'. . . [B]ut it worked out well—I passed out [campaign] literature for him when we walked precincts together, and I accompanied him to meetings and receptions."

In addition to completing internships, Fellows carry out two public service projects. At midyear, Fellows divide into groups of three or four and spend several weeks developing a policy-oriented project. Recent projects include a published report on the impact of Bay Area media on ethnic communities, a televised documentary on Mexican-American immigration, and a published manual on AIDS in the workplace. Said a Fellow: "It's exciting—projects typically receive some kind of formal recognition, whether they are published in a journal or shown on television."

Late in the year, Fellows complete an individual public-service project on a topic of their choice. Said a Fellow: "It's a chance to apply the skills you've learned and explore future professional interests." One Fellow did a case study analyzing the effectiveness of the California Employment Training Panel, a state organization that "sponsors businesses to retrain workers rather than lay them off." Another Fellow wrote a marketing plan for an energy information center. "I suggested ways the center could market itself better—such as through the newspaper, radio, and direct mail. . . . [T]he center heeded my recommendations, and use of the center ended up increasing dramatically."

Once a week throughout the program, Fellows meet at the Coro center for a daylong seminar. The seminar is designed to give Fellows a chance to exchange views and find out how everyone is faring in his or her internship. It also has an educational component, as Coro staff and special guests lecture on subjects like public speaking, research skills, and how to deal with the media. Past guests have included the speaker of the California State Assembly, the president of the San Francisco Planning Commission, and CEOs of Fortune 500 companies.

Interspersed throughout the nine months are several "focus weeks," designed to give Fellows intensive exposure to such areas as politics, communications, media, and entertainment. One focus week might find Fellows spending six days in Salinas Valley, learning about California's important agricultural base; another might bring Fellows to Sacramento, where they meet with state legislators, executive branch officials, and journalists covering the capital. During a focus week on negotiation, Fellows attended a workshop given by the renowned sports agent Leigh Steinberg. Said a Fellow: "Steinberg lectured on the art of negotiation and how it's so important to thoroughly research your opponent before negotiation begins. . . . Afterward, we divided into groups for mock salary negotiations. My partner and I represented a fictional athlete, and using [Steinberg's] techniques, we landed the athlete a pretty good deal."

Besides unparalleled practical and educational opportunities, the participants themselves are a glowing benefit of the Coro program. Said a Fellow: "Coro carefully selects its Fellows from a highly qualified pool of applicants—and it shows. Each of the 12 Fellows has done something special to get selected." Added another: "There was a common theme of excellence [among the Fellows]. At the same time, the Fellows bring to the program an incredible diversity of backgrounds." Indeed, a recent Coro class included a professional dancer, a speech and debate champion, a former senior class president of San Diego State University, a professional journalist, and a third degree black belt in Chinese boxing.

Nine months with Coro doesn't come cheap—tuition for the Fellows program is $3,500. But scholarships funded by outside foundations and individuals are available, as are installment plans and tuition loans administered by Coro. And as the 60 hour-a-week program precludes outside employment, grants up to $10,000 are available, based on financial need, to assist with living expenses.

SELECTION

 The program is open to anyone with a bachelor's degree. Coro stresses that Fellows "come from all academic disciplines, careers, racial and ethnic groups, and socioeconomic backgrounds." Although recent classes have ranged in age from 22 to 40, most participants are in their twenties.

APPLICATION PROCEDURE

 Applications must be submitted by January 15. Candidates must apply to only one Coro center—San Francisco, Los Angeles, St. Louis, or New York. Required materials include completed application forms and written essays. Personal interviews are conducted at a Coro office. Twenty-eight finalists per center are notified in February and invited to participate in a daylong selection process the following month. Coro sends out decision letters in April.

OVERVIEW

 When interviewed about his time as a Coro Fellow, a participant from ten years ago recalled his experiences in crystal-clear detail. Commenting on why the memory is still so vivid, he said: "It's testament to how important those nine months were to me." This attitude is shared by the vast majority of former Coro Fellows, who consider their fellowship a powerful springboard to rewarding professional careers. The Coro alumni network is among the nation's most productive and prestigious. And of Coro's more than 3,500 graduates, over 75 percent now work in the public sector. Among these alumni are Senator Dianne Feinstein, Representatives Vic Fazio and Jerry Lewis, an associate justice of the California Supreme Court, and a member of the California State Assembly.

FOR MORE INFORMATION . . .

■ The Coro Fellows Program
Northern California Center
One Ecker Street,
Suite 330
San Francisco, CA 94105
(415) 546-9690

■ The Coro Fellows Program
Southern California Center
609 South Grand Avenue
Suite 550
Los Angeles, CA 90017
(213) 623-1234

■ The Coro Fellows Program
Midwestern Center
1730 South 11th Street
St. Louis, MO 63104
(314) 621-3040

■ The Coro Fellows Program
Eastern Center
95 Madison Avenue
New York, NY 10016
(212) 683-8843

CROW CANYON
ARCHAEOLOGICAL
C E N T E R

In the late thirteenth century, the Anasazi Indians mysteriously abandoned their cliffside villages located in what is now southern Colorado. Was their departure due to the drought of 1276? Was it for religious reasons? Did warfare drive them away?

Organized in 1984, Crow Canyon Archaeological Center is dedicated to exploring the question of why the Anasazis abandoned the Mesa Verde region. A not-for-profit organization, Crow Canyon hires archaeologists and volunteers to conduct excavations in an ancient village near the town of Cortez. Although it is a place where adult volunteers pay to dig, Crow Canyon runs a serious institutional research program. With a staff of 14 professional archaeologists, the center has received grants from the National Science Foundation, the National Geographic Society, and the National Endowment for the Humanities. In 1992, it was the recipient of the President's Award for Historic Preservation, the nation's highest honor to a private organization dedicated to the preservation of America's heritage.

SELECTIVITY 🔍🔍🔍🔍

Approximate applicant pool: 40
Interns accepted: 4–6

COMPENSATION 💲💲

Room, board, and stipend (approx. $50)

QUALITY OF LIFE 🌴🌴🌴🌴

Beautiful location
Tex-Mex meals; Seminars

LOCATION(S)

Cortez, CO

FIELD

Archaeology

DURATION

11 weeks
(See dates below)

PRE-REQS

College juniors and seniors, grad students
Previous field experience for field internship

DEADLINE(S)

March 15

DESCRIPTION

Crow Canyon's excavation is performed at the Sand Canyon locality, located 12 miles west of the Crow Canyon campus. Here, researchers investigate two thirteenth-century settlements, Sand Canyon Pueblo (a 400-room settlement) and Castle Rock Pueblo (a 75-room settlement).

Assisting the professional archaeologists are field interns who work at the site in a variety of capacities. First and foremost, they excavate, using a trowel and whisk broom to remove artifacts for analysis. "It was your basic excavation process," said an intern. "After digging up a chunk of soil, we'd screen out the dirt to catch

any artifacts." Working closely with professional archaeologists, interns get the experience and guidance that help them to hone their archaeological skills. "Digging under the supervision of experienced professionals, I developed and refined my field techniques well beyond what I expected," said one intern. During a workday, field interns write narrative notes and fill out computer-coded forms indicating where each artifact was discovered. Occasionally, they take photographs and draw sketches of site areas as well.

Another responsibility of field interns is to teach lay participants archaeological techniques. Said an intern: "We supervised the paying volunteers during excavation, making sure they didn't miss any artifacts when they dug." Because a few volunteers come to the site expecting to unearth treasures of yore—the so-called Indiana Jones syndrome—interns have to remind participants that artifacts at the Sand Canyon locality are seldom glamorous. One finds mostly bones, pottery shards, and stone debris. "It's not what you find, but what you find out," as one intern put it.

Crow Canyon also hires interns to work in its laboratory. Lab interns process the archaeological specimens, samples, and records received from the field. They also maintain a small research library located in the administration building. Like field interns, lab interns work with lay participants, showing them how to wash, sort, analyze, and catalog artifacts.

A third internship area at Crow Canyon is Environmental Archeology. In this department, interns contribute to several ongoing studies designed to gain insight into the present-day vegetation of the Sand Canyon locality. "The [Environmental Archeology] projects give archaeologists a better idea of how the Anasazi altered their environment before they abandoned the Mesa Verde region," said an intern. Environmental Archeology interns work with professional archaeologists and lay participants on a range of projects, such as documenting which plants used by the Anasazi regrow after a fire, determining the seasonality of native plants, and building experimental gardens. Interns involved in the last endeavor "grow corn and beans Anasazi-style—without adding water—to recreate the type of vegetation the Anasazi consumed."

Four hundred miles southwest of Denver and ten miles from the entrance to Mesa Verde National Park, Crow Canyon is situated in one of the most pristine natural areas in America. The Crow Canyon campus is a picture of southwestern beauty. Adobe architecture is everywhere and hiking trails snake through the juniper-covered terrain.

Sweeping vistas of mountains and "incredible geological formations" are part of the area's natural beauty. Sunny weather is the norm, and uncomfortably warm temperatures are rare, even in midsummer.

Housing is intense—that is, it's *in tents.* On an embankment affectionately known as "intern hill," interns are lodged in cozy canopies of nylon. "It's not that bad," said an intern. "But it gets a little cold sometimes. More than once I woke up with frost on my body." Heat-seeking interns, rest assured: Winter-month participants are housed indoors.

Conditions are not so primitive that interns must use the bushes as a bathroom; toilets and hot shower facilities are provided in a bathhouse near the tents. Despite these rugged accommodations, most interns like their home on the hill, viewing it as a comfortable retreat from the bustle of daily work: "We'd end the day with an informal 'happy hour' on the hill. It was a good way to get away from it all."

> **Homemade salsas, luscious guacamole, gourmet tacos, and the house specialty—blue-corn chicken enchiladas—are enough to make one give up Taco Bell for life.**

Thanks to the paying volunteers, everyone eats well at Crow Canyon. The resident chef serves up three delicious Tex-Mex meals every day. Homemade salsas, luscious guacamole, gourmet tacos, and the house specialty—blue-corn chicken enchiladas—are enough to make one give up Taco Bell for life. Interns are grateful for this unexpected culinary bounty: "The food was terrific. With the adult volunteers in residence [Crow Canyon] really pulls out all the stops."

If they play their cards right, interns leave Crow Canyon with an education in southwestern culture. Every so often, the center sponsors workshops that interns are welcome to attend. Native American artisans give presentations in basketry, twill weaving, flute playing, jewelry making, and other southwestern specialties. "I attended a workshop on basketry and learned how Anasazi weavers used yucca fibers to create sandals and twine. It shed light on how the Anasazi clothed themselves."

Interns get the weekends off, and there's plenty of places for them to play. The closest city is Cortez, a rustic town with little more than a Wal-Mart, a gym, and a few bars. Durango, a lively college town, is a 45-minute drive away. Another popular destination, Telluride, can be reached by car in 90 minutes and features superb skiing in the winter and a film festival in the summer. For those interested in furthering their archaeological education, nearby Mesa Verde National Park features Anasazi cliff dwellings and spectacular prehistoric rock art.

SELECTION

 The program is looking for college juniors and seniors as well as graduate students. Students interested in the field internship must have previous field experience. Lab and Environment Archeology positions require no field experience, but some coursework in archaeology, anthropology, ethnobotany, botany, or museum studies is desirable.

APPLICATION PROCEDURE

 The application deadline is March 15. Internships are generally offered four times a year: mid-May to early August, early August to mid-October, mid-October to mid-December, and early January to mid-March; write to Crow Canyon for exact dates. Interested parties should submit a completed Crow Canyon application—a three-page questionnaire that asks about academic coursework, related work experience, reasons for wanting the job, and three references (phone numbers and addresses). A resumé is desirable but not mandatory. No interviews are conducted. After an initial screening, 15 applicants make it to a final round. Be forewarned: The intern coordinator calls the references of each finalist. She says, "We don't use interviews, so references are critical. They make the difference between two candidates who are equally qualified on paper."

OVERVIEW

 The Crow Canyon internship is an all-around winner. Interns work closely with experienced professionals excavating and recording artifacts, processing and analyzing lab samples, or conducting studies of past and present environments. Along the way interns sharpen their archaeological skills and gain teaching experience. Add to this bounty of benefits a gorgeous campus, gourmet southwestern meals, and enriching extracurricular opportunities—and you've got an experience worth getting dirty for.

FOR MORE INFORMATION . . .

■ Crow Canyon Archaeological Center
Internship Program
23390 County Road K
Cortez, CO 81321
(303) 565-8975

The Walt Disney Studios

©DISNEY

SELECTIVITY	🔍 🔍 🔍 🔍 🔍
Approximate applicant pool: 1,000 Interns accepted: 20	

COMPENSATION	💲 💲
$200 per week	

QUALITY OF LIFE	🌴 🌴 🌴
Movie-making seminars Company bicycles; Disney lot	

LOCATION(S)	
Burbank, CA	

FIELD	
Entertainment	

DURATION	
3 months Summer	

PRE-REQS	
Undergrads	

DEADLINE(S)	
March 31	

"What are you doing this summer?"
"Working at Disney."
"Well, I hope I'll be able to recognize you in a Mickey Mouse costume."

To many people, working at Disney conjures up images of a bulbous, fiberglass-and-feather mouse-head roaming around Disneyland with a sweaty teenager underneath, greeting passersby with exaggerated cheer. But there is more to Disney than most expect. A sprawling empire covering not only theme parks but also movies, toys, and records, the Walt Disney Company has become a world-famous entertainment conglomerate.

Originally a partnership of brothers Walter and Roy, the company began modestly on October 16, 1923, when the entrepreneurial Walt signed a contract to produce some cartoons. Back then, the office rent was $35 per month, and Walt and his brother worked tirelessly. Five years later, in November of 1928, Mickey and Minnie Mouse made their first screen appearance. The Walt Disney Studios, the movie and television facet of the company, have since spawned Pluto, Goofy, Donald Duck, and many others memorable characters. Operating through Disney TV, Hollywood Pictures, and Touchstone Pictures, the Walt Disney Studios has also churned out a memorable list of movies—*Beauty and the Beast*, *Aladdin*, *Dead Poets Society*, and *Pretty Woman*, to name only a few. Today, the familiar Mickey Mouse logo appears just about everywhere. Walt would certainly be proud.

DESCRIPTION

First offered in 1988, The Walt Disney Studios' internship program met with instant success, attracting nearly 300 requests for 20 positions. Interest has increased since, but the opportunities remain the same. Interns can work in Production, the department that reads scripts, determines locations, and analyzes film footage; in Marketing, the division that handles advertising, promotions, and press junkets; in Finance, the department handling budgets; and in Feature Animation, the birthplace of the cartoon characters and animated films.

No matter where interns are placed, they start at the entry level and must shoulder a good portion of the clerical responsibilities. Most days find interns hard at work photocopying, filing, taking notes, and running errands. "Seventy percent of the time," said one

BUSYWORK
MEDIUM
LOW HIGH
OLDMAN & HAMADEH
METER

intern, "we were just gofers—reorganizing people's schedules and files, delivering daily videos to the execs, distributing mail, and getting coffee."

Then why do these interns uniformly praise the internship? Why do some return for a second or even third summer for the experience? The answer lies in Disney's mystique. As one intern put it: "There's an aura to walking on the Disney lot. You can't do that unless you're an intern or an employee." Moreover, many of these interns have a strong desire to learn the creative and production side of the industry, to use that knowledge in entertainment strategy consulting or in entertainment law. Said one intern: "Working at the number one box-office movie producer in the business, I had a tremendous opportunity to see how development and production work."

It appears, however, that the experience is only as rewarding as each intern makes it. Word has it, that some interns expecting to be the center of attention have done little but complain. As expected, they sat the entire summer, merely photocopying and filing. Patient, adaptable interns who take initiative, on the other hand, have been rewarded with a memorable experience. Confirmed a Production manager: "Once interns prove themselves, we'll give them a bit of responsibility, show them how to break down a script and prepare a budget, and even let them observe high-level meetings."

A few interns rotate within the Production department, working on movie cost estimates, scene scheduling, and film editing. "In preproduction," explained one intern, "we figured out how much producing a new script would cost, and then, if we had exceeded budget, we found ways to reduce the costs without sacrificing quality." Another intern in production was charged with handling a scene in which a flaming car would fly over a cliff. "I had to secure a location, permits, remote-controlled explosives, stuntmen, a fire crew, and of course, a car. I looked in a special book to find out what all these people and devices would cost." Accordingly, interns in preproduction might spend some of their time at the Disney and Hollywood libraries, scouting out

potential hot spots for the scenes; or they might sit in front of a Macintosh, inputting scene information into Movie Magic, a program that organizes the scenes to create the shoot schedule.

Similarly, a go-getter in Feature Animation found herself deluged with work. In this department, animators sketch furiously to meet tight deadlines. Interns observe head animators "roughing" every ten frames, other animators roughing the ones in the middle, followed by "keys" and "in-betweeners," the clean-up artists, sprucing up the frames. "In the later stages of production, I used this computerized camera to shoot frame by frame some of the scenes from *Beauty and the Beast*. I also hosted screenings for public relations firms, ad agencies, and distributing companies."

Now imagine doing all this in an "absolutely incredible miniature city," as one described it, where roads are named Mickey Mouse Lane and Goofy Drive and where one can ride company-owned bicycles to perform functions required elsewhere on the massive lot. In the backlot, one finds the sound stages and the one-story buildings housing the production executives. Then there's the large cafeteria with its moderately priced deli, grill, and salad bar. And in the front sits the Team Disney building, with its Seven Dwarfs standing, arms overhead, as massive columns supporting the roof. One cannot find the Feature Animation unit on the lot, however. Located about five minutes away in Glendale, it was described by one admirer as "a huge maze of cubicles, decorated in Art Deco, with movie posters and artwork everywhere."

During the first week, interns are treated to an orientation luncheon. In other weeks, interns can participate in seminars with senior-level people from Labor Relations, Music, Production, or Costuming. Interns may also enjoy additional perks if they seek them out. One intern read screenplays on weekends and wrote two-page critiques, including synopses, analyses, and recommendations. "I read 20 or 30 that summer," said an intern. "It was an immensely enjoyable learning experience."

> Imagine doing all this in the "absolutely incredible miniature city" . . . where roads are named Mickey Mouse Lane and Goofy Drive and where one can ride company-owned bicycles . . .

Not all dimensions of the internship are so well regarded. Living arrangements and social activities, many interns said, can suffer because of the low pay, though interns rave about the multitude of things to do in sundrenched Los Angeles. Interns also agree that not everyone is friendly or accessible: "In Hollywood, pretentious people abound." But as one intern pointed out: "This is a people business, so you have to make it a point to introduce yourself, act like an employee, and ask the key people in the department for their opinions. They don't have time to go out of their way to meet you."

In three months, interns receive only a taste of the inner workings of movie making. Nevertheless, most are exhilarated by the training. "You may do a lot of mundane things, but this is the front-row seat to the game. Even while you're delivering mail or filing contracts, you hear deals being cut. You just can't learn this stuff from a book."

SELECTION

 All college students are eligible to apply. Although many applicants attend schools in Los Angeles, Disney strives to create a balanced representation and accepts students from around the country. No particular major is required, but a relevant background is helpful. "Being in radio, film, or TV gives you a slight edge for production positions," says the coordinator. "In a similar way, marketing and economics majors with experience fare better in marketing and finance positions, respectively." Warning: The feature animation position is purely administrative and "not for would-be animators."

APPLICATION PROCEDURE

 Students can begin sending in the required materials to the above address as soon as January 1, but in no case should the material be postmarked after March 31. Prospective interns may include a transcript, if they wish, but must submit a resumé and a cover letter conveying their interest in the program. "The cover letter is especially crucial," says the program administrator, "because it expresses your qualifications, goals, and what you hope to gain from the experience." After the administrator gives the applications a first glance and sorts them by department, department heads interview top candidates over the phone. Requests for on-site interviews are not granted.

OVERVIEW

 For people with a deep interest in entertainment, especially in movie administration, development, and production, a summer as a Walt Disney Studios intern can lead to many opportunities. After getting their foot in the door, interns can meet executives and make potential connections for future work. "The key to internships is meeting people," reflected one intern. "You may just drop off a tape to an office, but you can meet the exec, say hello, ask him or her how they got into the business—make a contact." During his first two weeks, one intern made such a favorable impression that the studio hired him on the spot as a permanent employee for Touchstone Pictures, where he has worked for nearly two years. Another, still in college, returned for a third summer. Still another combined previous Wall Street experience with the Disney stint to land a job at MTV's Strategic Planning and Business Development unit upon graduation. "Dream and do," taught Walt Disney. This internship allows students to do just that.

FOR MORE INFORMATION . . .

■ The Walt Disney Studios
    Internship Program Administrator
    500 South Buena Vista Street
    Burbank, CA 91521-0880
    (818) 560-6335

John Casablancas

The face of Cindy Crawford graces the covers of *Vogue* and *Cosmopolitan*. Iman dances in husband David Bowie's new MTV video. Paulina Porizkova's face promotes the new line of makeup at the local department store's Estée Lauder counter. Naomi Campbell poses in a bathing suit for *Sports Illustrated*'s swimsuit issue. The first few pages of *GQ* find voluptuous Anna Nicole smiling sensually for Guess Jeans. What do all these women have in common? Are they the 5'10" Society? Do they have an exercise videotape on the shelves of the local video store or an ability to mesmerize most of male America? Perhaps they share all of these things but the one very important common denominator among them is that they all have relied on Elite to catapult them to supermodel status.

Why Elite? In 1971, a young European man named John Casablancas opened his first Elite in Paris. Back then, top American agencies like New York's Ford and Wilhelmina sent him their hot new prospects. Under his guidance, the fledgling models became Europe's stars. Once world-famous, the models returned to the United States and posed for the country's top fashion magazines. They rarely returned to Europe. Frustrated by an inability to retain the women whose fame he fostered, Casablancas resolved to open an agency in the United States, and in 1977, Elite set up shop in the Big Apple. Focusing on editorial and up-scale catalog clientele, today Elite continues to attract the industry's crème de la crème. No fewer than six of the world's top ten models, featured on the cover of *Vogue*'s April 1992 "100th Anniversary Special," worked for Elite.

DESCRIPTION

Since 1985, Elite has allowed college students to observe first-hand the inner workings of one of the most prestigious modeling agencies in the world. Interns work out of the New York, Chicago, Los Angeles, Atlanta and Miami offices, in the Scouting, Model Management, New Faces, and Elite divisions, assisting employees in every capacity, from the clerical duties to the actual work of the booking agents. While the New York office takes on 5 to 10 interns per year, the others hire only 2 each.

Naturally, interns don't assume the responsibilities of Elite booking agents until well into the internship. During the first few weeks interns answer phones and open mail, sifting through unsolicited photographs and

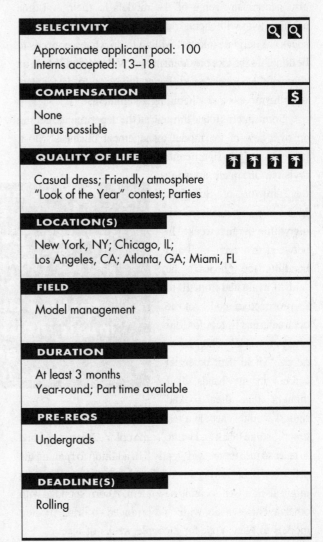

SELECTIVITY

Approximate applicant pool: 100
Interns accepted: 13–18

COMPENSATION

None
Bonus possible

QUALITY OF LIFE

Casual dress; Friendly atmosphere
"Look of the Year" contest; Parties

LOCATION(S)

New York, NY; Chicago, IL;
Los Angeles, CA; Atlanta, GA; Miami, FL

FIELD

Model management

DURATION

At least 3 months
Year-round; Part time available

PRE-REQS

Undergrads

DEADLINE(S)

Rolling

BUSYWORK
LOW MEDIUM HIGH
OLDMAN & HAMADEH
METER

creating Yes and No piles for the scout to peruse later. Interns also accompany some of the models to their first-time appointments with clients (referred to as "go-sees" in model-speak). Energetic interns "willing to do whatever needs to be done," as the vice president put it, "will eventually take on some of the bookers' tasks, maintaining day-to-day contact with the models and scheduling assignments."

Some interns rotate through all the departments, getting an overview of the model management business. Most, however, spend a significant portion of their time in just one division. One intern, assisting the director of Scouting, found herself actually scouting within the first week. "In between answering mail and handling the phones," she said, "I evaluated from 10 to 25 prospective models at the open calls that Elite holds four times a week." She elaborated: "I held their potential careers in my hands. If I thought that they looked right, I would schedule a test shoot—simple, clean photographs, some black and white, some color. Otherwise, I had to learn to turn them away gently." In addition to running the office and interviewing potential models, interns in Scouting might also assist in locating new talent. "I corresponded with other agencies nationwide and arranged to bring in their models to New York for a couple weeks of testing," explained another intern. "I would also acquaint the girls to the city once they arrived, as well as field telephone calls from concerned parents."

An intern in Model Management spent the initial part of his summer sorting mail, pulling models' cards, and photocopying "futures" (models' schedules) for the accounting department's use. While such work might sound monotonous, the intern pointed out: "Those activities helped me to learn models' names and faces and to understand the way business is done." Interns in this department also put together composite cards for new faces and make "go-see" appointments for Elite's models. One diligent, enthusiastic intern eventually worked his way up to a spot at the spirited octagonal bookers' table—equipped with a phone, drawers,

and all the models' calendars spread out before him. "It's like sitting at a lively Thanksgiving dinner with six or seven of your family members," he said. There, he learned how to book work for the models. "Eventually," he said, "I even recommended certain models for our clients. It got to the point where clients thought that I was just another booker."

Most Elite interns also work on the agency's annual "Look of the Year" contest, a highly touted nationwide search for new models. Cindy Crawford was a finalist in 1988's contest. According to the organization, in the most recent contest, over 300,000 women sent in their pictures, with the hope of becoming one of 10 to 15 finalists. One of the interns sifted through thousands of applications, helping to determine which would be retained. Another served as a gofer at the actual Look of the Year show. "I just stood there and whenever someone asked me to do something, like find a participant for her photo shoot, I took care of it," he said. "I didn't do anything specific, but to be [at the show] was amazing. . . . Over 60 models from around the world were there, and Fox filmed it."

Two floors of a converted five-story townhouse in Manhattan house Elite's headquarters. Adorning the walls of the reception area, dozens of magazine covers flaunt Elite models. Beyond, one finds sleek, modern hallways and rooms, as well as an intense yet friendly atmosphere, where "most everyone gets along," several interns said. Employees work together in "a laid-back environment, not a suit-and-tie place," as one described it. But another conceded that "while the atmosphere is often spirited, it's sometimes also stressful—phones are ringing off the hook, models are coming in and out, and people are running around trying to get everything done."

Interns, especially those in New York, enjoy a panoply of perks. For example, they occasionally accompany the director of Scouting to client dinners. Interns are also invited to join Elite employees, models, and their families at weekly parties and promotional events put on by fashion designers,

> Interns are invited to join Elite at weekly parties and promotional events put on by fashion designers, music industry gurus, movie big-wigs, or Elite itself.

music industry gurus, movie bigwigs, or Elite itself. "I went to a big party at the Banana Café for all the Elite models appearing in the spring fashion-show," said one New York intern. "About 100 people attended, and I mixed with agents, models, and photographers. I made many contacts that night." Those who intern for two or more terms might find themselves traveling to scout at an upstate New York convention or at the nearby Waldorf Astoria Hotel. Anyone looking to sidle up to the office's superstars, be forewarned: These women are very busy and they don't stop in often.

To be sure, most interns do a fair share of the grunt-work. But they appreciate the opportunity to work at an epicenter of the modeling business. "Reading the faxes and files was fascinating," one intern said. "Plus, I learned how to talk to models, to clients, and to photographers." Interns do complain about the lack of pay, however: "You can't live that way in New York." Still, interns are expected to work at least five half-days or three full days per week. The reward for hard work? Possibly a farewell party and a bonus check of a few hundred dollars at the conclusion of the internship.

SELECTION

 Undergraduates of any level are eligible to apply. No area of study is excluded; past interns have majored in political science, women's studies, fashion merchandising, business, and advertising.

APPLICATION PROCEDURE

 Internships are available year-round, and materials may be submitted at any time to the desired office. Send a resumé and cover letter, but be personal. The vice president is quick to point out that "your personality must come out in these typically bland documents." Applicants who reach the final round participate in telephone interviews.

OVERVIEW

 Elite arguably occupies the premier position among the world's modeling agencies. There might not be a better internship for those who wish to work permanently in modeling or who simply want impressive material for cocktail party conversation. Claimed one intern: "Elite is the most influential

agency in the business, representing the most famous models." Compared to competitor Ford's five agencies, Elite manages nearly 50 modeling centers and operates out of 16 agencies worldwide. Following a summer stint, one former intern took a permanent position with Elite. Another went to work for Ford. One was named director of model relations at a prestigious scouting firm. Still others have moved into related fields—entertainment or fashion merchandising. But all are quick to say that they will never forget the experience. "I would love to be an Elite intern forever," concluded one.

FOR MORE INFORMATION . . .

- Elite Model Management
  111 East 22nd Street
  New York, NY 10010
  (212) 529-9700

- Elite Model Management
  345 North Maple Drive #397
  Beverly Hills, CA 90210
  (310) 274-9395

- Elite Model Management
  212 West Superior St.
  Suite 406
  Chicago, IL 60610
  (312) 943-3226

- Elite Model Management
  One Buckhead Plaza
  3060 Peach Tree Road, NW
  Suite 1465
  Atlanta, GA 30305
  (404) 674-9500

- Elite Model Management
  1200 Collins Avenue
  Miami Beach, FL 33139
  (305) 674-9500

A decade or so ago, in a section of Chicago known as the South Side, newspapers, cardboard, and junk mail would pile up like so many leaves on an autumn day. If they didn't litter the roadsides, they'd pack the nearby landfill.

In came Michael Finn, a 1981 graduate of Northern Illinois University. In 1982, he did an internship with Chicago's Neighborhood Institute, working on a South Side recycling program to demonstrate that recycling efforts could promote economic development. Seeing an opportunity to make recycling a career, he and his supervisor left the Neighborhood Institute in 1984 to found Recycling Services, Inc. Now a $4 million company, Recycling Services collects, sorts, and bales wastepaper for paper mills.

But who provided Finn with the internship that gave him the experience necessary to embark upon such an environmental endeavor? A nonprofit group called the Environmental Careers Organization (ECO). Its story begins in 1972, with a recent college graduate named John Cook. Realizing that the environmental movement was gaining steam and that few people were adequately prepared to tackle environmental problems, Cook founded ECO to "protect and enhance the environment through the development of professionals, the promotion of careers, and the inspiration of individual action." Though it sponsors an annual environmental conference, publishes books on environmental careers, and maintains environmental-career libraries, its main business is finding and creating environmental internships. Twenty-odd years later, ECO has nearly 5,000 alumni.

DESCRIPTION

ECO (pronounced "EE-ko") places over 450 students annually in two programs—approximately 325 students year-round in the Environmental Placement Services (EPS) program and 140 minority students, primarily during the summer, through its Diversity Initiative program (DI). Forty percent of all interns are graduate students; 40 percent are recent graduates; and the remaining 20 percent are undergraduates. Projects last six months on average and are available in a majority of states.

Approximately 175 organizations sponsor ECO interns. Many of the internships, according to ECO, aren't established programs open

---

SELECTIVITY 🔍 🔍 🔍

Approximate applicant pool: 3,000
Interns accepted: 450

COMPENSATION 💲 💲 💲 💲

$200–$800/week
Average Salary: $425–$450/week

QUALITY OF LIFE

N/A

LOCATION(S)

Nationwide — see Index

FIELD

Environment

DURATION

12 weeks–1 year
Year-round

PRE-REQS

DI—minority undergrads, recent grads, grad students
EPS—college juniors and seniors, grad students,
college grads of any age

DEADLINE(S)

DI .... May 14
EPS .... Rolling

to the general public but are specially arranged; in other words, by soliciting environmental professionals whose projects could use interns, ECO creates environmental internships. "We're specialized, and we understand the environmental language," says ECO president John Cook. "We can place a student who wants to work in wetlands ecology with a position in wetlands ecology." Almost every type of environmental career is covered, as both EPS and DI place students within corporations, environmental consulting firms, governmental agencies, and nonprofit organizations like the Natural Resources Defense Council, Environmental Defense Fund, and the Nature Conservancy. According to Cook, 10 to 20 percent of the placements are with the U.S. Environmental Protection Agency.

Corporations sponsoring interns include IBM, Ford, Boeing, and Polaroid. Placed in departments like Environmental Health & Safety, interns often help their sponsors compile reports that satisfy local, state, and national regulatory or compliance boards. An intern for Pacific Gas & Electric (PG&E) in San Francisco was placed in Qualifying Facilities Contracts, a PG&E department in charge of evaluating the power produced by alternative-energy sources such as solar facilities and wind farms. According to a law dating back to the Carter administration, she explained, PG&E was required to purchase alternative power from sources that qualified under the Carter program. "I updated contracts," she said, "checking to see if our contracted facilities were fulfilling their reporting requirements." She also determined what type of energy each of the producers was creating and what percentage of the total energy distributed by PG&E was alternative energy. "By the end of the summer, I had a greater understanding of the private side of energy issues and the economics of power producers," she said.

Approximately 15 percent of interns are placed with environmental consulting firms, companies that recommend and implement solutions to environmental problems for clients—usually corporations, government agencies, and cities. Assigned to CH2M Hill in Deerfield Beach,

Florida, an intern spent approximately one third of his time collecting water and soil samples in the field. "Sometimes I dipped a jar in the water or soil and capped it," he said. "Other times, I set up the automatic sampling machine, which takes a weighted average of measurements made every half hour [or so]." After samples were analyzed by CH2M Hill's laboratories, he wrote reports, using charts to present the data—information on water levels, chemical composition of the samples, and extent of contamination. "By the end of the internship," he said, "I definitely had gained a good sense of how science and technology are used in practice to solve environmental problems." Another intern, this one at Environmental Research and Technology, Inc. in Boston, tracked energy regulations for the Department of Energy and studied circulation patterns of people in a local park. "I made so many contacts [at ERT]," he concluded, "that my job hunting a few months later was significantly easier."

Over half of all interns work for local, state, and federal agencies. Past interns have studied how a local government can better regulate air pollution from automobiles, investigated undersea corals for the U.S. Geological Survey, monitored salmon and bald eagles for the city of San Francisco, assessed the level of metals contamination at the site of a former treatment plant in Seattle, and developed solid-waste management and recycling programs for an Ohio sewer district. An intern with the EPA in Washington, D.C., during the summer of 1993 was assigned to the EPA's Energy Star Computers project, an effort to encourage computer companies to create energy-saving computers. "Because a large percentage of people leave their computers on 24-hours a day, seven days a week," she elaborated, "the EPA wants computer makers to manufacture energy-conscious computers—[for example, ones that] automatically turn off if left idle for 30 minutes." Working on a campaign to sign up as many computer companies as possible, she sent out agreements to interested executives, whose companies became part of the project once the completed forms were returned. "I helped sign up nearly 100 companies," she said.

> As members of ECO, past and present interns can count on ECO for guidance and career advice.

She also attended a press conference led by EPA administrator Carol Browner and Vice President Al Gore, which was attended by representatives of 24 major computer companies. "[The summer] certainly proved to me that [America] can grow economically while . . . conserving energy," she concluded.

Though ECO's primary function is to provide students with internships, it's more than a clearinghouse. It also maintains contact with interns throughout their experience, intercedes on their behalf should problems arise, and organizes a social event or two. At the beginning of the internship, the program director and staff at ECO's five offices—in Boston, Cleveland, Seattle, San Francisco, and Tampa—contact their interns to welcome them to the program. After that initial call, ECO officials attempt to make on-site visits to meet interns over lunch. Each ECO office occasionally hosts an informal reception, dinner, or picnic where interns meet one another, ECO sponsors, and ECO alumni and hear about other ECO projects. "The networking opportunities [at these functions] are prime," said an intern. Throughout the summer, interns receive additional phone calls from ECO staff checking on interns' progress. "It's great that ECO takes time out to keep communication lines open," said an intern. "That way, sponsors and interns know what to expect."

As members of ECO, past and present interns can count on ECO for guidance and career advice. Alumni get *Connections* magazine, ECO's newsletter to keep alumni informed of ECO's programs. "It keeps me tied into the organization," says an intern from 1973. "Reading about other experiences gives me a benchmark against which to compare an internship program that I run [as president of the Quebec-Labrador Foundation and its Atlantic Center for the Environment]." At each of ECO's offices, interns are welcome to use the career library to search current job listings. They can also attend the organization's annual Environmental Career Conference. Typically held in the fall, the conference provides an overview of job opportunities in the environmental industry and features a keynote address—in 1992, Paul Hawken, of the upscale garden-shop chain Smith & Hawken, spoke on the impact of environmental problems on the economy. To participate in the conference, interested alumni and interns must pay an admission fee (approximately $50) as well as travel and lodging expenses. But for the price, attendees get two days' worth of workshops, career advice, a career fair, and panel discussions on topics such as forestry, parks, law careers, and graduate schools. The conference also offers special sessions for minorities looking for employment in the environmental industry.

SELECTION

 ECO's EPS program seeks college juniors, seniors, and graduate students as well as career-changers and those who have recently completed their B.S., M.S., or Ph.D. degrees as applicants. DI targets minority undergraduates of any level, recent graduates, and graduate students—primarily those of African-American, Hispanic, Asian/Pacific Islander, and Native American descent. Any major is acceptable—approximately two thirds of interns have science and technology backgrounds, one third are concentrating in liberal arts.

APPLICATION PROCEDURE

 The deadline is rolling for EPS applications, May 14 for DI applications. Applicants to the EPS program are encouraged to apply at least three months before they are available to intern. Regardless of where they wish to work, students need submit only one application. Both programs require a completed application form (there's a different one for each program), which asks for two recommendations (one for DI), writing sample, resumé, list of relevant courses, and application fee of $15 if applying to one region or $25 if applying to two or more regions (there is no application fee for DI, and EPS applicants with financial hardship may request a fee waiver). Applications are kept active for 12 months after receipt. After ECO screens the applications, it recommends to each sponsoring organization approximately five applicants per position to interview.

OVERVIEW

According to research done by San Diego's Environmental Business International Inc. in 1992, nearly 500,000 new jobs will have been created by the environmental industry between 1992 and 1995—that's a world of opportunity for those interested in the environment. Students who want to explore these positions should check out the Environmental Careers Organization. Providing career advice, networking opportunities, and oftentimes internships inaccessible to the general public, the Environmental Careers Organization prepares students to become the next generation of environmental scientists and engineers, chemists and biologists, teachers, recycling coordinators, eco managers, and environmental lawyers.

FOR MORE INFORMATION . . .

■ The Environmental Careers Organization
286 Congress Street
Boston, MA 02210-1009
(617) 426-4375

SELECTIVITY		🔍 🔍 🔍
Approximate applicant pool: 450 Interns accepted: 75–100		

COMPENSATION		💲 💲 💲
$4,000–$6,500 grant		

QUALITY OF LIFE
N/A

LOCATION(S)
Nationwide—see Description

FIELD
Environmental policy, management and science

DURATION
10–14 weeks: Fall, Spring, Summer Part time available

PRE-REQS
Undergrads: minimum 3.0 GPA, at least 4 courses in environmental studies Grad students: minimum of one semester completed

DEADLINE(S)
December 20

A grim specter has crept upon us almost unnoticed . . .

So wrote marine biologist Rachel Carson in 1962 in the now-classic *Silent Spring.* Her book, says Vice President Al Gore in his *Earth in the Balance,* "eloquently warned America and the world . . . of the dangers posed to migratory birds and other elements of the natural environment by pesticide runoff." It was her admonishment that touched off a series of national protests and government actions, from a 1962 special panel investigation of pesticides by President Kennedy's Science Advisory Committee to the first Earth Day held in 1969. By the time President Nixon signed the 1970 National Environmental Policy Act, which mandated that federal agencies submit Environmental Impact Statements whenever projects might affect their surroundings, the 1970s had been heralded as "the decade of the environment."

But no environmental decade could be complete in Nixon's eyes without a powerful body to enforce government environmental mandates. So on July 9, 1970, he created the U.S. Environmental Protection Agency (EPA), with an initial budget of $900 million. Today, the EPA's budget has ballooned to over $6 billion, and its enforcement arm—capable of implementing a host of penalties, from fines to criminal lawsuits—extends to 14 major laws, including the Clean Air Act, the Clean Water Act, and Superfund.

DESCRIPTION

 In 1987, the EPA created the National Network for Environmental Management Studies (NNEMS) program—pronounced "nemz" —in order to give students exposure to environmental professions. Three years later, the 1990 National Environmental

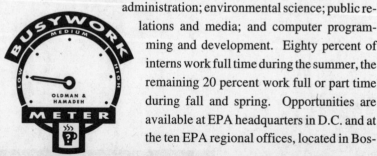

Education Act created the Office of Environmental Education (OEE) to foster environmental education, and in 1991 the OEE took over the NNEMS program. Work is available in the following areas: environmental policy, regulations, and law; environmental management and administration; environmental science; public relations and media; and computer programming and development. Eighty percent of interns work full time during the summer, the remaining 20 percent work full or part time during fall and spring. Opportunities are available at EPA headquarters in D.C. and at the ten EPA regional offices, located in Boston, New York, Philadelphia, Atlanta, Chicago, Dallas, Kansas City, Denver, San Francisco, and Seattle. The EPA also offers positions in its Office of Research and Development, at research laboratories in Research Triangle Park, North Carolina; Duluth, Minnesota; Ann Arbor, Michigan; Las Vegas, Nevada; Ada, Oklahoma; Corvallis, Oregon; Gulf Breeze, Florida; and Athens, Georgia.

The EPA's Region 3 office in Philadelphia sponsors several students every year. One undergraduate was placed in the office's Water Management Division to investigate farm pollution regulations in relation to animal wastes. "When farmers' animals make waste in tributaries that traverse farms, the wastes pollute the drinking and recreational water sources downstream. We were trying to figure out what should be the EPA's role, versus state and city roles, in remedying those waters polluted by animal wastes." Because it's difficult to determine who is responsible for the pollution, she explained, the EPA currently helps fund farmers who use best management practices (BMPs)—such as manure holding tanks, which prevent cow dung from getting into waterways. "But I didn't think that was enough," she said. "A report I wrote at the end of the summer also called for a joint effort of the federal, state, and local governments to educate farmers on acceptable water uses."

Sometimes a sponsoring agency allows its NNEMS intern to work out of his or her home. That's what happened in the case of a New York student who received a project from the EPA's Boston office on nitrogen loading in Long Island Sound. "I went to Boston for three days in the beginning to get briefed on the project. The critical question was—will BMPs such as wetlands, detention ponds, and infiltration ditches reduce the Sound's high nitrogen levels?" To find an answer, she read articles and EPA reports on the effectiveness of such BMPs. "I solicited the opinions of several experts and asked them to send me relevant maps and models." Four months later, she attended a meeting of the Long Island Sound Study Group to present her findings to members of the EPA, New York City officials, professors,

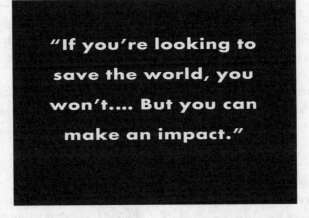

"If you're looking to save the world, you won't.... But you can make an impact."

and concerned citizens. "I concluded that the nitrogen buildup is so huge, we might have to put BMPs in residential areas. Now imagine asking some residents in Stamford, Connecticut, to move out so that we can dig a detention pond where their homes are."

Another intern, assigned to the Boston office's Indoor Air section researched residential air quality. "Most indoor air studies focus on the office and known hazardous materials. I felt that the home harbors a number of potentially hazardous substances as well . . . cleaners and paint thinners, for example." After researching various household products, she realized that the EPA should "work cooperatively with industry to label products that contain possibly carcinogenic materials."

Interns often travel in order to better investigate the regions involved in their research. The intern working on animal waste pollution, for example, visited a nearby lake. "Six EPA employees, a water quality expert, and I went out on a boat to the middle of Lake Nockamixon. We ran water quality tests, lowering various equipment into the water in order to determine how much pollution there was." Back on land, she visited some farmers near the lake. "We interviewed them about the steps they were taking to prevent animal waste pollution. I was in charge of filming the interviews on our video camera."

Because environmental issues are often contested and solutions not readily available, interns' final reports often generate disagreements. The intern who did the animal waste study, for example, was convinced that waste could potentially be a major source of pollution. Others didn't share her opinion. "The USDA issued an animal waste report that contradicted mine—they concluded that the animal waste problem was confined only to a few 'hot spots' [i.e., concentrated areas of pollution]—and they asserted that the contribution of animal waste is minor when compared with other sources of pollution."

Despite differing opinions about environmental issues, intern reports are often praised as fresh and interesting. "As a student, you come in with an open mind and are potentially more critical than EPA employees because you aren't biased by any politics," explained an intern. "The people working in my office appreciated such candor." The intern who worked on the indoor air report, for example, discovered that while many EPA employees were wary of her proposal, at least one person extolled her tenacity. "I attended an EPA meeting half a year later to answer questions about my paper, which by this time had been widely distributed around the agency. After I finished, one person came up to thank me for getting the ball rolling."

Because NNEMS projects aren't designed to be accomplished by team effort, interns must tackle research completely on their own. Nevertheless, those who "fight to the finish" can make an impact. "After all, the EPA has us working on projects it needs answers to," explained an intern. Word has it, however, that graduate students, given their greater experience and educational training, often leave a more lasting imprint than the undergraduates. The aforementioned Long Island Sound report, for example, written by a graduate student, has now become an official EPA document.

Pay at the EPA is average—close to $4,000 for undergraduates and as high as $6,500 for graduate students, depending on the complexity and duration of the project as well as a student's academic level. But some interns complain that the stipend is on the low side. Spread out over the life of the work, the money (after taxes) doesn't go a long way. "Most of these projects end up growing into something bigger than you initially envision," said an intern. "In the end, the money is just not enough to cover the time you must spend to solve the problem."

SELECTION

The internship is open to undergraduates of any level and graduate students. While graduate students must only have completed at least one semester of graduate studies, undergraduates must have taken at least four courses in environmental studies—hard sciences, engineering, or resource management—and must have at least a 3.0 GPA. Any major is eligible, but students must show a strong interest in environmental issues.

APPLICATION PROCEDURE

The deadline is December 20 for receipt of materials. The NNEMS program catalog explains that students may apply for agency-sponsored projects or for EPA office positions. Students must specify the project and/or position they are seeking, as described in the NNEMS catalog. For each project, the application requires the NNEMS research proposal page, the five-page application for federal employment (called an SF-171), and an official transcript. For each position, the application consists of the NNEMS position page (statement of objectives), the SF-171, an official transcript, and a letter of recommendation from a professor or academic adviser. Although projects are geared toward graduate students and positions are geared toward undergraduates, students may apply to either category. Students may also submit more than one application, though each application submitted must include a photocopy of itself. In 1993, 104 colleges and universities' career centers received NNEMS brochures and program catalogs. Students attending universities that do not receive the materials should ask their school's career center to request them by writing to the address below.

OVERVIEW

The EPA is one of America's greatest allies in the fight to improve the environment. Fortunately for college students, a congressional law mandates educational programs in environmental studies. Called NNEMS, the EPA's program affords students the opportunity to analyze real environmental problems. Circulated among EPA personnel, interns' final reports often become important EPA documents. But to get there, interns must invest long hours researching their topics. And their reports sometimes generate disagreement and succumb to bureaucratic foot-dragging. "If you're looking to save the world, you won't," concluded an intern. "But you can make an impact."

FOR MORE INFORMATION . . .

■ Environmental Protection Agency
NNEMS National Program Manager
US EPA (1707)
401 M Street SW
Washington, DC 20460
(202) 260-4965

In 1971, accountant John Emil List murdered his mother, wife, and three children at their Westfield, NJ home. Despite an international search, he disappeared. Eighteen years later, the case was still unsolved; so the FBI Special Projects Unit used advanced technology to create a clay bust depicting what List, now probably bald and wrinkled, would look like. Within hours of the bust's appearance on the TV show *America's Most Wanted*, List was apprehended. He is now serving five consecutive life sentences.

Since its founding in 1908, the FBI has been responsible for tracking down and arresting criminals like List. Its efforts have helped immortalize some of history's most notorious criminals including—Al Capone, Pretty Boy Floyd, Baby Face Nelson, and Machine Gun Kelly. Currently, the FBI enforces over 260 federal statutes—organized and white-collar crime, bribery, copyright matters, bank robbery, kidnapping, terrorism, civil rights violence, and drug trafficking. About 10,000 Special Agents and 13,000 personnel contribute to this enforcement effort. These men and women have a computerized network of crime information, DNA profiling techniques, millions of fingerprint cards, and the lofty ideals emblazoned on the FBI seal—Fidelity, Bravery, Integrity—to lead them in their mission.

DESCRIPTION

The FBI Honors Internship Program was started in 1985 to familiarize college students with the bureau and its mission. Interns are placed in Washington, DC at headquarters or in Quantico, VA, at the Academy, the Engineering Research Facility, or the Forensic Science Research and

SELECTIVITY	
Approximate applicant pool: 2,000 Interns accepted: 50–70	🔍🔍🔍🔍🔍

COMPENSATION	
$390/week	💲💲💲

QUALITY OF LIFE	
Lunch with FBI director Firearms training; Field trips	🌴🌴🌴

LOCATION(S)
Washington, DC; Quantico, VA

FIELD
Domestic intelligence and criminal investigation

DURATION
10 weeks
Summer June 1–August 20

PRE-REQS
College seniors, grad students
U.S. citizenship; Background check

DEADLINE(S)
November 15

Training Center. They work in units such as Personnel Resources, Behavioral Science Services, Criminal Informant, Accounting and Budget Analysis, Legal Forfeiture, European/Asian/Money Laundering, Undercover and Sensitive Operations, and Audit. Unfortunately, interns cannot designate preferences for unit or location. Assignments are based on academic major and bureau need.

The internship starts with a two-day orientation during which interns listen to an overview of the FBI, tour headquarters, receive summer assignments, learn about employee benefits, and discuss security. The FBI director makes a brief speech, and interns are officially sworn in. They get a notebook containing interns' names and phone numbers, maps of D.C., and information on public transportation. Introductions to division supervisors mark the end of the orientation.

Prospective interns should realize that they do not play Agent Clarice Starling, the gun-toting girl-wonder from the movie *Silence of the Lambs*. "Interns aren't here to make arrests or do surveillance," explained the coordinator. "Besides being terribly dangerous, it would be inconvenient; eventually, they might have to give testimony in court." So in lieu of danger and glamour, interns do important research for investigations.

The sensitive nature of most FBI work precludes interns from giving anything but vague descriptions of their projects. One intern, placed in the Mexican Traffickers Unit, compared Mexican and American criminal justice systems. "My research took me to the Library of Congress, the Department of Justice, and the Mexican Embassy," she said. "In the end, my project furnished agents with an understanding of Mexican law enforcement."

Another intern worked in Civil RICO (Racketeering Influenced Corrupt Organizations). The unit investigates Mafia corruption of labor unions. "I researched complaints filed with the bureau," she said. "Then I analyzed a complaint's validity, based on the amount of information available in FBI files. The files were restricted, so a supervisor had to be with me when I checked them out from the library. At the end of the summer, I compiled the researched complaints into a booklet that the unit could use for further investigation and possible litigation."

There are as many intern projects at the FBI as there are confiscated guns. An intern in Behavioral Science Services researched the usefulness of hypnosis on witnesses. One in Forensic Science Research used electrophoresis techniques to separate pieces of DNA. A Language Services intern worked with translation experts to translate foreign documents. An intern in Audit traveled to Houston, Texas, to assist in a weeklong audit of the local field office.

Several graduate students intern at the organization. One law student found himself in Legal Forfeiture, the unit in charge of seizing money and property of suspected drug dealers. "I researched the Eighth Amendment to see if these seizures jibed with the provision against cruel and unusual punishment," said the soon-to-be lawyer. "I also wrote a lot of legal briefs. Overall, my internship was similar to a clerkship with a judge, because the unit's Special Agents often made administrative law rulings on FBI promotion, transfer, or disciplinary policies."

The majority of interns works at the D.C. headquarters, called the J. Edgar Hoover Building. A sprawling, 11-story structure, Hoover's namesake stands as a testament to law and order. In addition to housing most of the units, the building holds the Special Operations Center which is on alert 24 hours a day in case of a national crisis. Most interns work out of their own cubicle, equipped with "modular furniture" and often a computer. Linoleum-floored, white-walled corridors, "drab" carpets, and "gender-neutral office colors" are sure to offer little distraction from the work going on.

Occasionally throughout the summer, interns meet with senior management. An assistant director from one of the ten divisions like Laboratory, Identification, or Criminal Intelligence may lecture on his division's mission, or agents may speak on career opportunities within the bureau. Interns also meet as often as possible after-hours with their mentor—an FBI field agent, whom they share with four other interns.

Approximately once every two weeks, interns make an organized trip. The Baltimore field office is a typical destination. The secluded Quantico Academy—30 buildings on over 400 acres—is another. A training ground for new agents, the academy features Hogan's Alley, a simulated town with a bank, pool hall, and hotel. Here, agents-in-training shoot blanks at actors pretending to be criminals.

> **Interns whose hearts are set on brandishing a gun receive a half-day of firearms training.**

Though interns rarely see the alley in action, they do learn about FBI training techniques. Interns also visit the academy's Engineering department to see classified equipment: "These gadgets looked like Q's inventions from the James Bond movies." The interns hear the Behavioral Sciences "spook squad," a group of world-class homicide experts speak on serial killer cases, and watch a demonstration on how to free hostages from terrorists. This show is put on by the Hostage Rescue Team, considered by some to be the best SWAT team in America.

The FBI Housing Office helps interns find apartments in D.C. It is able to arrange accommodations at the Oakwood Apartments for $350 to $400 per month. To those Oakwood-bound, be wary: Many describe the apartments as "badly in need of repairs."

Several perks keep interns happy. Accrued sick and annual leave entitle them to one paid vacation during the summer. They have access to the FBI gym, where they are likely to encounter agents shaping up for annual physical fitness tests. They may also purchase T-shirts, mugs, and caps from the employee store and gift shop, both of which are inaccessible to the public.

Like other employees, interns may prearrange a guided tour of headquarters for visiting family members. Displayed on the tour are antique toys—fake handcuffs, FBI agent badges, pistols, and uniforms from the 1920s and 1930s. Back then, these toys suggest, kids loved to dress up like G-men and apprehend "criminals." Not surprisingly, many FBI interns wouldn't mind playing cops and robbers, too. But the closest they'll get is a Ride-Along with D.C.'s metro police. "At least then they can feel what it's like to wear a bulletproof vest," said the coordinator. For those whose hearts are set on brandishing a gun, though, there is hope: Interns receive a half day of firearms training. "They fire the .38 Smith & Wesson revolver, the semiautomatic 9 mm Sig-Sauer model P226 pistol used by our agents, and the fully automatic H & K MP5 assault weapon, used by SWAT teams," said the coordinator. "A firearms instructor monitors them, and they leave with a videotape, a photograph, and their bullet-ridden target."

Not all shooting is directed at paper targets; interns also take a few shots at the program. Some interns were frustrated that their writing was found unacceptable: "We were not taught how to write in 'bureau-ese'." A few others bemoan the occasional wimpy project. "My year, two interns were given mostly secretarial assignments," one said. She blamed the situation on poor placement and charged the bureau with indifference: "A request for transfer was shrugged off without the FBI's batting an eyelash." To discuss such concerns, interns meet formally with management once or twice during the summer. But these formal meetings usually occur too late to make any immediate impact.

During the final week of the program, the FBI director hosts a closing lunch. After answering interns' questions, he pauses for a group photograph. This photograph, combined with a yearbook and the occasional "Honors Intern Alumni Newsletter," provide certified proof that the student was, however briefly, part of the FBI's shadowy world.

SELECTION

 The FBI seeks undergraduates with three years of college under their belt and a few graduate students (J.D., M.B.A., master's, and Ph.D. candidates), who will be returning to school after the internship. A minimum 3.0 GPA and U.S. citizenship are required, but all majors are eligible. Thoroughness in completing the application, academic achievement, work experience, and academic major are all important "but you must show a strong interest in law enforcement." Extensive arrest records or use of cocaine is a no-no. Use of marijuana, however, does not always bar an applicant from employment.

APPLICATION PROCEDURE

 The deadline falls on November 15 every year to allow time for the FBI's thorough background investigation. Submit an official academic transcript, a resumé, one letter of recommendation from a dean or department head, a recent photograph, a 500-word essay explaining reasons for applying to the program, and the one-page FBI Preliminary Application. All materials must be turned in to the nearest FBI field office. Applications are initially screened by these field offices, who nominate up to four candidates. Headquarters makes final selections, but the ordeal doesn't end there. Selected applicants must complete the bureau's Application for Employment (an 11-page monster), a background investigation, a physical examination, a drug test, and an interview at their sponsoring field office. Be advised: If the FBI questions an applicant's truthfulness, or if an applicant has traveled overseas, then he or she must submit to a polygraph (lie detector) test. Out of formality, the director approves the final list of interns.

OVERVIEW

 Scotland Yard, Japanese National Police, Royal Canadian Mounted Police, and Interpol are among the world's top criminal investigation organizations. But the king of them all is the FBI. Luckily for America's students, this leader of law enforcement takes on interns. Internship participants work on projects related to ongoing investigations. They have access to Special Agents. They take tours of field offices, DNA labs, and the Quantico Academy. The internship also improves their chances of later becoming FBI agents or technical specialists; former Honors interns are heavily recruited to serve as technical support personnel after graduation or as agents after three years of work experience. Aside from setting the nearest town ablaze and fleeing the country, there's no easier way to make it on the FBI's Most Wanted list.

FOR MORE INFORMATION . . .

■ Federal Bureau of Investigation
Honors Internship Program
Personnel Resources Unit
FBI HQ
Room 6329
10th and Pennsylvania Avenue NW
Washington, DC 20535
(202) 324-4991

THE FUND FOR THE
FEMINIST MAJORITY

The scene is the back room of a local church. The time is early morning. Several dozen community members speak in hushed tones, organizing to blockade the area's abortion clinic. They are members of Operation Rescue, and they uphold the rights of the unborn fetus. One of them notices the time and the group moves toward the door. What they don't notice is the plain-looking woman who has already headed for her car, who now calmly calls out from her car phone. Who is she? Impersonating a right-to-lifer, she's a pro-choice advocate working with the Feminist Majority's Clinic Defense Project to mobilize readied forces throughout the city. When Operation Rescue gets to the clinic, it finds several hundred demonstrators—a veritable human shield—blocking its path. People are pushed, punched, and kicked, but women can still walk in. Chalk up another victory for the Feminist Majority.

Founded by TV producer and philanthropist Peg Yorkin and former National Organization for Women (NOW) president Eleanor "Ellie" Smeal in 1987, the Feminist Majority wasn't always so controversial. The organization initially set out to encourage more women to run for public office. In its first year, two dozen women traveled the country, setting up campaign rallies in twelve major cities, much like Republicans and Democrats do every four years. The plan succeeded, inspiring dozens of feminists nationwide to run for local and national office. Today, the Feminist Majority still espouses its more-women-in-public-office philosophy. But it has added to its agenda an Empowering Women campaign, a Rock for Choice project, abortion clinic defense, lobbying, and women's rights research.

SELECTIVITY

Approximate applicant pool: 120
Interns accepted: 20

COMPENSATION

None
Limited stipends available

QUALITY OF LIFE

Substantive projects
Travel opportunities; Lobbying on Capitol Hill (DC)

LOCATION(S)

Los Angeles, CA and Washington, DC

FIELD

Women's rights/think tank

DURATION

Two months minimum
Year-round; part time available

PRE-REQS

High school students, undergrads, grad students

DEADLINE(S)

Rolling

BUSYWORK
MEDIUM
LOW HIGH
OLDMAN & HAMADEH
METER

DESCRIPTION

Since 1987, the Feminist Majority has given students the opportunity to tackle feminist issues on a national level. One of the women touring the country for those first campaign rallies, in fact, was a junior from a New Jersey state college. One morning she got a call from a woman she had met during an ERA campaign a year earlier. "How would you like to join Ellie Smeal's Feminist Majority?" Six days later, the college student was on a plane heading to Los Angeles. Fortunately, today's prospective interns get a little more time to think about it. Before starting, interns sit down with the coordinator to figure out which Feminist Majority research project best matches their interests.

Students may intern part or full time, for a period of eight weeks to a year. In any case, interns monitor press conferences and congressional hearings and analyze policy. They also work on current campaigns such as Feminization of Power, which strives to place feminists in public office or college-campus leadership positions, and Empowering Women, which encourages women to seek top positions in their professions. Interns also write position papers and engage in research, exploring such areas as abortion, sexual harassment, gender balance, and RU 486 (the French abortion pill that may be taken up to nine weeks after conception).

One intern analyzed the legislative processes in 23 states. "We wanted to know how to get issues on the ballot," she said. "In order to bring such issues to a vote, we needed to understand how the law is structured in each state." The intern also researched reapportionment—the federal distribution of boundaries for use as congressional districts. "[The Feminist Majority] wanted to influence the reapportionment process in order to form a 'woman's district,' which could then elect a female candidate." Though she found several areas with a majority of women, the organization could not influence the government to redraw the boundaries. However, her research was not conducted in vain: "My work showed us that we need to focus our energies on recruiting women candidates."

As part of the Feminization of Power campaign, another intern compiled demographic statistics on New York, using Excel to record the political parties to which the state's residents belonged. "It's tedious to sit in front of the computer and punch in what seems like useless data, but such information helps us put more women in elected office," said

> The organization is so intimate that regular contact with the top brass is commonplace.

the intern. "It allows us to figure out whom we need to target in each district in order to win." She also created a press book for the Rock for Choice project, a series of rock concerts (Red Hot Chili Peppers, Pearl Jam, etc.) that raise money for the Feminist Majority's abortion rights campaigns.

As one would expect, most interns are women. But men are welcome, and a few have served as interns. One male intern, in addition to becoming involved in the Feminization of Power campaign during the 1992 elections, oversaw part-time interns. "I had to make sure that they were making good progress in whatever they were doing— be it arranging fund-raising walkathons, researching government funding of abortions, or compiling information on female candidates." He also served as the administrative liaison to the Women's Advisory Council to the police commission. "I wrote letters, coordinated presentations, put together phone lists, and created memos. . . . [A]nd I did research on gender balance in the police force, looking at recruitment policies and hiring strategies." He made such a thorough examination, that back at school, he "consulted the [local] police force, which was revamping hiring practices."

The Feminist Majority applies pressure to antiabortion movements in major cities like New York, Atlanta, Chicago, and Houston. Occasionally, interns participate in these efforts. Bankrolled by the Feminist Majority, they travel to the sites to organize clinic defenses: "I mobilized local abortion rights groups and arranged advertising to inform more people about our cause." Back at home, staff and interns sometimes stage their own protests. In D.C., the interns occasionally organize intern lobby days and, depending on the piece of legislation pending at the time, spend an entire day lobbying congresspeople.

Some interns are frustrated by the Feminist Majority's nonprofit status, which makes it difficult for the organization to do sophisticated research. "One of my projects was stonewalled because of low funding." Limited funding also prevents interns from receiving any sort of compensation (save a few who get small stipends) and means that the office can't afford secretaries. So interns sometimes photocopy, file, and stuff envelopes. They also put together press packets and make phone calls. "In order to compile state-wide election results one season," an intern said, "I called [the office of] each state's secretary of state until I was blue in the face."

Interns are encouraged to seek the help of staff and to speak their minds on research projects and campaigns. "Besides including us in regular strategy sessions, people here want us to tell them what we think," said an intern. "They want to hear the student perspective." Said another: "It's such a small group that you can always knock on someone's door and make suggestions." The organization is so intimate, in fact, that regular contact with the top brass is commonplace. "The executive director and the chair of the board were always available if I had questions or needed advice," said an intern.

SELECTION

 The Feminist Majority welcomes applications from high school, undergraduate, and graduate students who display strong interest in women's issues. Students of any educational background are eligible; past interns have pursued degrees in journalism, women's studies, public policy, government, and history.

APPLICATION PROCEDURE

 The deadline to submit materials is rolling. Applicants must send a resumé, cover letter, and writing sample of two to ten pages (an academic paper is sufficient) to either the LA or DC office. Finalists are given phone interviews.

OVERVIEW

 In 1987, in a large theater off Los Angeles' Wilshire Boulevard, California state senator Diane Watson and actor Ed Asner were among the keynote speakers who had gathered at the Feminist Majority's first event—a Feminization of Power rally. "We are working too hard to convince legislators to adopt our positions," they said. "Let's just put ourselves in public offices nationwide." The audience erupted in applause. Today, the Feminist Majority is one of the few feminist organizations embracing a national perspective. Grooming interns as the feminist movement's future leaders, it exposes them to abortion laws, RU 486, sexual harassment issues, and women's rights. It allows them to mingle with dedicated staffers and feminist greats like Ellie Smeal. It even sends some of them to cities around the country to organize defenses of abortion clinics. "What a fantastic experience," said an intern. "It prepared me for a lifelong career in feminism."

FOR MORE INFORMATION . . .

- The Feminist Majority
  8105 West Third Street,
  Suite 1
  Los Angeles, CA 90048
  (213) 651-0495

- The Feminist Majority
  1600 Wilson Boulevard,
  Suite 801
  Arlington, VA 22209
  (703) 522-2214

After Southern plantations were confiscated at the end of the Civil War, there was talk that the Union would make reparations to the millions of former slaves. General William T. Sherman, in a special field order of 1865, is thought to have promised every black family "forty acres and a mule." But history proves that no such restitution was made.

When Spike Lee needed a name for his film company, Forty Acres and a Mule seemed like the logical choice. It was Spike's way of underscoring his intention to reclaim, through film, the power that has been denied African-Americans. Since the release of *She's Gotta Have It* in 1986, Forty Acres has done much to advance Spike's goal. Movies such as *Do the Right Thing*, *Mo' Better Blues*, and *Malcom X* have changed the face of American cinematography, garnering mainstream interest in movies both by and about blacks. The success of Spike's films has ushered in a generation of black filmmakers, including John Singleton (*Boyz N the Hood*) and the Hudlin Brothers (*House Party*), for whom blacks are the main characters and no longer just bit players in the white story.

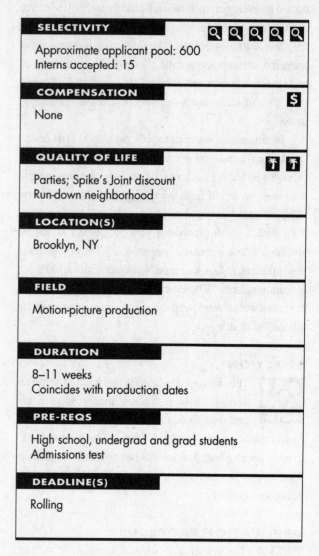

SELECTIVITY

Approximate applicant pool: 600
Interns accepted: 15

COMPENSATION

None

QUALITY OF LIFE

Parties; Spike's Joint discount
Run-down neighborhood

LOCATION(S)

Brooklyn, NY

FIELD

Motion-picture production

DURATION

8–11 weeks
Coincides with production dates

PRE-REQS

High school, undergrad and grad students
Admissions test

DEADLINE(S)

Rolling

DESCRIPTION

Interns work for Forty Acres when the company is shooting a film. Positions are available in Wardrobe, Props, Extras Casting, Accounting, Director's Assistant, Production, and Editing.

In Production, interns perform variations on the gofer theme: phoning and faxing, writing letters to lawyers and agents, and running messages to staff on the set. But they are also responsible for putting together the daily production reports and call sheets which provide basic information to the crew and actors, everything from "makeup schedules to the day's weather report." Interns are also in charge of purchasing supplies for the office and the set. If the bulk of the work seems mundane, interns are quick to point out the silver lining: "Spike wanted the script for *Malcolm X* to be 'closed' [read only by actors and high-level staff], but Production interns, who often photocopy and deliver pieces of the script, got to see the whole document."

An intern in Props had exposure to all sorts of work related to stage property. She was constantly on the phone tracking down props that would add realism to *Malcolm X*. "I located great soul food at Sylvia's [restaurant] in Harlem. I found flowers for Billie Holiday's hair. I even worked on finding old license plates." Occasionally she visited stores devoted to selling props (so-called prop houses) and combed the "supermarket-style" aisles in search of material suitable for a particular scene. But as *Malcolm X*'s time frame spans several decades, the movie sometimes required antique props that were impossible to purchase. Improvisation was necessary: "We'd spend a lot of time photocopying the original labels of old-time products and pasting the color copies onto boxes and cans. We'd do this with cigarettes, candy bars, milk cartons, cereal boxes— you name it." Improvisation was also required with props involving alcohol and tobacco: "I made sure certain props on the set looked accurate, even though they weren't always the real thing. We'd use a glass of cola to pass for brandy, for example. [In another instance] the character who played West Indian Archie didn't smoke, so we had special clove cigars made for him."

In Extras Casting, an intern "basically acted as a casting director," soliciting and supervising extras for the movie. The easiest to way to round up extras is to pick them from the composite cards that actors routinely send in. But hundreds more had to be found, prompting her to hit the pavement: "With clipboard in hand, I'd go to clubs in New York City and ask people if they wanted to be extras. If they agreed, I'd give them a form telling them a call time and location." The work was exciting, but she learned (the hard way) that picking extras requires a keen eye when she unwittingly "asked a well-known director to be an extra." No harm was done, though: "He laughed it off and ended up hiring me to cast music videos for him." After casting the extras, she'd make sure they showed up at the right place at the right time, and when necessary, she'd arrange for them to be fitted by the wardrobe department.

Located in the Fort Greene section of Brooklyn, a borough of New York described as "run-down" and "well

past its prime," Forty Acres is housed in a remodeled firehouse. With metal firehouse gates in front, and a mélange of wood and metal trim inside, one is reminded of the firehouse-cum-office in *Ghostbusters*. Some interns work here, some are in a casting office in Manhattan, and others are placed on location at various points in the New York area.

A number of perks accompanies life at Forty Acres. Interns receive a 10 percent employee discount on merchandise (the ubiquitous *X* baseball caps, T-shirts, etc.) at the Spike's Joint shop in Brooklyn. Although crew jackets were given out free of charge on other films, *Malcolm X* crew jackets cost interns $100 each, which is about a 75 percent discount off of the jackets' retail price. If they play their cards right, interns may be used as extras; a few, for example, were placed in the background of a dance scene in *Malcolm X*.

> **If they play their cards right, interns may be used as extras; a few were placed in the background of a dance scene in *Malcolm X*.**

Interns often get to see (and occasionally talk with) celebrities. One intern had a chance to meet Malcolm X's wife, whom she described as "pleasant and serene."

A string of parties occurs during the months of production. Shindigs are held to commemorate the beginning, midpoint, and end of filming and there's a premier party, too. "The parties are pretty elaborate," said an intern. "They're held in great sites around New York, like [the club] Muse and the Brooklyn Academy of Music. At one, the DJ was Kid Capri [host of HBO's Def Jam Comedy Special]. At another, there was a huge cake in the shape of an *X*. And all the big names are there—from Denzel Washington to Spike himself." According to the intern coordinator, all interns are invited to these parties.

Although most consider the internship "extremely valuable," "one-of-a-kind," and "a ticket to film-biz prestige," past interns brought up a few problems. The lack of pay was uniformly denounced—"we did full-time work, so we should have received some semblance of a salary." Unsalaried work, however, is typical of the vast majority of internships in film. Others warned that having a college background is not always respected: "A lot of the people in the film industry, and indeed some at Forty Acres, are not college educated. But practically all of the interns are. It bred resentment among a few members of the crew."

SELECTION

 The internship is open to undergraduate and graduate students and a few high school students may be accepted, too. As Forty Acres is an Afro-centric organization, the majority of applicants (and thus interns) is African-American. Even so, the program welcomes applications from students of all races and ethnicities. In addition to considering academic background and film experience, the intern coordinator factors in how well an applicant performs on a half-hour "admissions test." Questions cover everything from African-American history to film trivia. One intern said "The test I took asked things like 'What's a best boy?' 'What is the movie *Cooley High* about?' and 'Who is the only black sound-mixer to win an Academy Award?'"

APPLICATION PROCEDURE

 Applicants should submit their materials a few months before the filming of Spike Lee's next movie; trade magazines such as *Variety* and *Hollywood Reporter* will list his next production. Applicants must send a cover letter and resumé to the internship coordinator. After screening the initial applicant pool, the coordinator invites about 100 applicants to Long Island University, where they sit for the admissions test. Be on time for this test if you are choosen. In the past, latecomers have not been allowed to participate. Applicants who make the final cut are called with the news a few weeks later.

OVERVIEW

 Spike Lee's movies consistently generate the three C's: commendation, controversy, and cash. The Forty Acres internship transports students to the heart of this world where they experience both the nitty-gritty and a bit of the glamor of filmmaking. Interns must endure a level of gofering that maxes out the busywork meter, but for some, it all pays off when they see their name in the film's closing credits. Moreover, the Forty Acres experience is a powerful springboard to other jobs in the movie business: "There are a lot of filmmakers out there who will be impressed that you worked for Spike, no matter what you did." But the internship can lull you into a false sense of job security. "Working on a Spike Lee film makes you feel like you're in the [motion picture] business. But when the movie production ends, so does the internship. Before you know it, you hand back your ID badge, and it's all just a memory."

FOR MORE INFORMATION . . .

■ Forty Acres and a Mule Filmworks, Inc.
Internship Program
124 Dekalb Avenue
Brooklyn, NY 11217
(718) 624-3703

SELECTIVITY	🔍 🔍 🔍 🔍
Approximate applicant pool: 300–400 Interns accepted: 25	

COMPENSATION	💲💲💲💲💲
$460–$600/wk for undgds; $540–$820/wk for grads $500 relocation stipend; $1,000 bonus	

QUALITY OF LIFE	⊼ ⊼ ⊼
3–day intern conference Team of mentors; Chip heaven	

LOCATION(S)	
Plano, TX; Dallas, TX; Atlanta, GA; Pleasanton, CA; Princeton, CA; and other cities—see Description	

FIELD	
Snack food	

DURATION	
12 weeks Summer	

PRE-REQS	
Minority student; minimum 3.0 GPA College sophomores, juniors and seniors, grad students	

DEADLINE(S)	
April 15	

Crunch, scranch, craunch, scrunch, wunch, chomp, munch.

Such were the savory sounds of success for Elmer Doolin. That first bag of Mexican corn snacks he tasted in a San Antonio cafe in 1932 spurred him to close his floundering ice cream business and start making corn chips. At night, he'd produce ten pounds an hour out of his mother's kitchen and in the daytime, he'd peddle chips from his car. This was the humble start of the Frito Company.

That same year, a Nashville man named Herman Lay discovered potato snacks and, like Doolin, he set up shop in an old touring car and the H.W. Lay & Company was born.

Each creating its own particular kind of chip, the two companies became regional giants over the next three decades, Frito in the Southwest and H.W. Lay in the Southeast. Ascribing to the addage "two heads are better than one," the companies merged in 1961, setting up Frito-Lay, Inc. in Dallas, TX.

Today, the synergy has made Frito-Lay the world's largest snack-food company, with yearly sales of nearly $4 billion. Using 1.6 billion pounds of potatoes and 600 million pounds of corn each year, its 27,000 employees nationwide churn out a couch potato's fantasy menu: Doritos tortilla chips, Fritos corn chips, Lay's and Ruffles potato chips, and Chee-tos snacks.

DESCRIPTION

In 1990, Frito-Lay started the Minority Intern Program to "provide outstanding students of color with significant business experiences across Frito-Lay." Interns are placed in Sales, Marketing, Finance, Manufacturing, Purchasing, Logistics, Engineering, Management Systems, Research and Development, Communications, and Human Resources at the corporate headquarters in Plano, TX and at the divisional headquarters in Texas, Georgia, and California. Other interns take field assignments in Sales, Operations, Manufacturing, and Distribution at such varied locations as Beloit and Milwaukee, WI; Los Angeles, CA; Phoenix, AZ; and Chicago, IL. About 20 percent of interns are graduate students.

Those working in technical positions develop packaging graphics, install new seasoning systems, develop hardware and software, and track seasoning-usage fluctuations (too

BUSYWORK METER
LOW MEDIUM HIGH
OLDMAN & HAMADEH

much paprika? too much salt?). Interns in nontechnical positions evaluate competitor products, and sell and produce chips and dips. They also write articles for the company's newsletters. A Communications intern, for instance, traveled to Atlanta and Orlando to interview employees. "I was there pursuing human-interest stories and stories about new products or company events. Back at headquarters, I wrote each story in its entirety, helped brainstorm new ideas, and edited pieces—talk about responsibility!"

A Field Sales intern working out of Arizona spent half the internship on the road, riding with semi-truck drivers, making the rounds with the sales force, and setting up displays with merchandisers: "These displays were just your basic end-aisle variety, the type you see in grocery stores, but setting them up was an education in marketing." At the office, he shadowed managers and attended a meeting of the Trade Development group, which works to improve the sales operation. Not surprisingly, the people at the meeting served a few bags of chips, since chips were the topic of conversation. "There are bags of chips everywhere at this company," remarked the intern, who is now a Sales employee. "We eat them at meetings, during lunch, on breaks, and for dinner. As you might imagine, I've gained a lot of weight."

In the company's Dallas R&D facility, interns test manufacturing processes at Semiworks, a small-scale version of Frito-Lay's manufacturing plants. "Before spending millions of dollars setting up an operation at one of the plants," explained an R&D intern, "the company needs to see if it will work; that's the purpose of Semiworks." Each intern at this mock-up is involved in a number of projects. One intern helped design a "swing line," a system configured to make different types of chips by the mere switching of mechanical parts. "It's obviously more economical when you make two or more chips with the same equipment. I designed a Supremos cutter, which worked on the same [machine] used to make Sun Chips. I also designed a quick-change apparatus that could replace the Sun Chips cutter

with the Supremos one within minutes. The hardest part was coming up with the concepts, but in R&D there are no wrong answers." Fabrication shops turned his designs into actual cutters that worked so well that they were implemented in operations.

The atmosphere at Frito-Lay is unusually supportive. "We want our interns to succeed," said the coordinator. "So we provide them with buddies, mentors, and supervisors that they may turn to for assistance." Buddies (fairly new employees) answer any questions interns may have. Mentors (senior managers) offer career advice. And supervisors (midlevel managers) assist interns with their projects. Yet, as available as supervisors are supposed to be, some interns claim that a few supervisors don't give their interns ample feedback: "After assigning me a project, my supervisor didn't touch base with me or track my progress until the internship was half over."

"There are chips everywhere. . . . We eat them at meetings, during lunch, on breaks, and for dinner."

A third of the interns work at the Plano, TX, headquarters, a four-story complex shaped like the letter *A*. In the eye of the *A* is a large waterfall that cascades into a stream that flows under the middle bar of the *A* into an eight-acre lake, home to geese and monster catfish. Fishing is allowed whenever the lake is overstocked, but this happens rarely. Surrounding the building and the lake are a four-mile running track, tennis courts, a volleyball court, and a softball diamond. Inside, there's a state-of-the-art gym, fully equipped with treadmills, free-weights, StairMasters, Nautilus machines, and aerobics classes; gym membership is a nominal $1 a week.

Money is not a problem for interns at Frito-Lay. Aside from a great salary and up to $500 for moving expenses, each intern who has participated in *any* previous internship gets a bonus of $1,000 (but don't get any funny ideas, the company checks all claims). At the conclusion of the internship, interns give formal presentations of their work to a group of five managers. Afterward, interns are formally evaluated on project results, demonstration of management skills, and overall performance (with ratings of outstanding, superior, acceptable, or unsatisfactory). Interns who receive ratings of outstanding or superior are eligible for $2,000 scholarships, which nearly 50 percent of the intern class receive.

At the end of July, the Plano headquarters serves as the site of the summer intern conference. Interns from all over the country are flown in to listen to presentations made by senior executives. They also attend workshops on how to solve business problems, and they tour manufacturing facilities. One of the tours exposes the interns to a potato chip plant. Said one intern: "We could barely hear each other; the clanging of conveyer belts and automatic potato slicers made conversation difficult. [But] we could see the slicers, spinning around so fast that [the centrifugal force] pushed the potatoes into sharp blades located at the edge. Within seconds, the straight blades cut Lay's chips and the rippled blades made Ruffles. Then they were cooked, seasoned, and bagged." On the third and final day of the conference, interns sit for a finale dinner, which is attended by as many as 35 senior executives, who spend up to two hours interacting with students. "The dinner clearly signifies our belief that interns are a real investment," said the coordinator.

SELECTION

 Only minority undergraduate and graduate students are eligible. To be considered, applicants must have finished their freshman year, must have at least a 3.0 GPA, and must be studying one of the following disciplines: business administration or finance, any engineering, logistics, operations research, or economics. Liberal arts majors with an interest in business careers are also eligible. "By far, the biggest things we look for are initiative and management skills," said the coordinator. "We want results-oriented leaders with business experience."

APPLICATION PROCEDURE

 What do the Frito-Lay internship application and your taxes have in common? Answer: Both are due on the same day—April 15. Students must send in a resumé (GPA included) and a cover letter indicating a preference for position and location. Alternatively, students may attend Frito-Lay's winter recruiting events at campuses nationwide and participate in on-campus interviews during March and April. Promising students are invited to the various locations for on-site interviews.

OVERVIEW

 "Imagination, ingenuity, and perseverance"—these traits were often attributed to Frito-Lay cofounder Elmer Doolin. These are also the qualities that the company searches for in its interns, who are sometimes called upon to undertake projects requiring innovative solutions. Such projects have included creating new graphics for packages, designing hardware for manufacturing plants, and setting up grocery store chip displays. In the middle of the summer, interns make use of their creative skills at a three-day conference. And at the end of the summer, interns judged to have the greatest employment potential receive $2,000 scholarships.

FOR MORE INFORMATION . . .

■ Frito–Lay, Inc.
Staffing
7701 Legacy Drive
Plano, TX 75024-4099
(214) 334-7000

The bearer of newborns is known as the "stork" to many American children.

But in Leslie County, Kentucky, when children ask where babies come from, adults say it's the "nurses on horseback."

The nurses to which they refer work for the Frontier Nursing Service (FNS), an organization founded in 1925 by a woman named Mary Breckinridge following the deaths of her four-year-old son and infant daughter. Believing that her children had been victims of the inadequate health care system of her rural town, Breckinridge traveled to Leslie County with the goal of reducing its maternal and infant mortality rates. At that time, they were among the highest in the United States. Armed with an extraordinary degree of courage and leather saddlebags bursting with medical supplies, FNS nurses would ride around Kentucky's Appalachian region to deliver babies and care for expectant mothers.

Today, the horses are no longer in use, but FNS still provides quality health care to many of Leslie County's poor, rural residents. In addition to delivering babies, FNS runs three outpost clinics; a women's health care center, the 40-bed Mary Breckinridge Hospital, and the Frontier School of Midwifery and Family Nursing, the oldest nursing midwife school in the United States. Now known the world over as an exceptional rural demonstration in family-centered health care, FNS has delivered nearly 25,000 babies since 1925 and has reduced the maternal and infant mortality rates in Leslie County to a percentage that is well below the national average.

DESCRIPTION

Buried in the heart of Kentucky is a little-known but outstanding internship program for those interested in teaching and/or health care. Known as "couriers," interns have been employed by FNS since its founding. In addition to delivering supplies, couriers assist nurses and doctors in one or more of five areas: Women's Health Care, FNS Outpost Clinics, Mary Breckinridge Hospital, Home Health Agency, and Literacy and Education.

Couriers spend approximately 25 percent of their time on busywork. From 11 AM to 2 PM at least one day each week, couriers hop into one of FNS's Toyotas to make necessary pickups and deliveries. First they stop by the

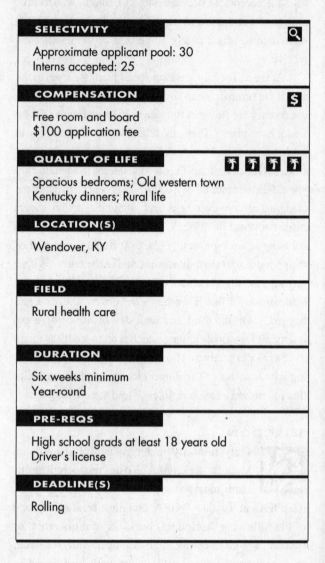

SELECTIVITY

Approximate applicant pool: 30
Interns accepted: 25

COMPENSATION

Free room and board
$100 application fee

QUALITY OF LIFE

Spacious bedrooms; Old western town
Kentucky dinners; Rural life

LOCATION(S)

Wendover, KY

FIELD

Rural health care

DURATION

Six weeks minimum
Year-round

PRE-REQS

High school grads at least 18 years old
Driver's license

DEADLINE(S)

Rolling

hospital to pick up incoming mail, medicines from the pharmacy, and supplies like gloves, blood-drawing apparatuses, and prenatal equipment. They usually spend the next three hours delivering these materials to the three outpost clinics, where they pick up outgoing mail, blood and urine samples requiring analysis, and supply orders to be delivered to the hospital. Couriers also take care of gardening, landscaping, and general office work at the FNS administrative building as well as pick up the food order from the local market.

When they're not performing these "rounds," interns help out in other capacities. At the Kate Ireland Women's Health Care Center, couriers staff the front desk and register women who have brought in their babies for checkups with midwives, physicians, and family nurse practitioners. As long as patients approve, couriers may watch midwives perform pre- and postnatal diagnoses. At the three outpost clinics, couriers help prepare exam rooms and write down patient histories and accounts of their illnesses. They also take patients' pulse, heart rate, temperature, and blood pressure and collect samples for blood, urine, and pregnancy tests.

While patients wait for their appointments, couriers at the Mary Breckinridge Hospital also jot down descriptions of patients' illnesses. Often invited into the exam rooms, couriers assist doctors and watch how exams are performed. Couriers have entertained children as the doctor checked their ears and throats, held a little child down as the doctor scrubbed coal out of the child's knee and used a stethoscope to hear a wheezing patient's lungs.

Every Wednesday, the hospital's surgeon comes in to perform various surgical procedures. Couriers may observe the doctor at work, providing they scrub up and wear a hygienic smock, white mask, and latex gloves. One courier watched the doctor insert a viewing scope into a man's colon: "I couldn't believe that I was seeing the insides of the guy's large intestine." Another courier watched the doctor perform a hysterectomy: "I felt important—[the doctor]

asked me to hold the suture [i.e., the thread] while he sewed the patient together." And a third observed a cesarean section. "We gained so much firsthand experience with the patients themselves," said a courier. "It made me want to become a doctor."

Home Health Agency couriers travel with nurses to the homes of six to ten patients a day. Taking vital signs and assisting in bathing retarded, deaf-mute, disabled, and elderly patients, couriers learn the practices of home health care. "It was a real opportunity to help people who genuinely couldn't help themselves," said a courier. After finishing their medical duties, it's not uncommon for nurse and courier to sit down and chat with a patient for as long as 20 minutes. "I'd come back from a day of Home Health glowing," said a courier. "It's the place where you probably make the most difference in people's lives."

> **Couriers may be exposed to country-western dancing, the music of bluegrass bands, and the bite of homegrown moonshine.**

Couriers also assist FNS in its Literacy and Education project. They tutor adults in English, act as teachers' aides at elementary, vocational, and high schools, and help young kids gain basic skills in reading and math. "Tutoring was rewarding because the illiteracy rate [in Leslie County] is so high," said a courier. "Getting these people interested in reading was a challenging but satisfying assignment."

FNS's offices are the only buildings located in Wendover, just four miles from Hyden, a community of 500 residents. Much like many people's vision of an old western town, Hyden is home to a supply store, two churches, a hardware store, a bank, and the Breckinridge Hospital. Throughout the county, roads are often unpaved and unmarked, making travel difficult until couriers learn the routes. With little industry, Leslie County is a poor area, most of whose residents are on welfare. Couriers looking for the conveniences of a slightly larger town—a movie theater, restaurants, and a Wal-Mart—can drive to Hazard, located 20 miles away.

All couriers live at FNS. Male couriers are housed in the renovated Barn; female couriers live in the Garden

House on the second floor just above the administrative offices. Couriers are given their own rooms, each with a bed, desk, and closet. The Big House, the two-story log cabin that served as Mary Breckinridge's home until 1965, houses visitors and serves three meals per day to staff and couriers. Lunches and dinners include typical Kentucky home cooking such as fried chicken, mashed potatoes with mounds of butter, pork chops, meat loaf, and corn bread. After eating, couriers are required to wash dishes and put away leftovers, which are always available for snacking. In keeping with a tradition dating back to FNS's early years, couriers host the "Monday Night Tea," a special dinner served on fine china. Before dinner, tea and sherry are served in the living room as couriers, staff, FNS doctors and administrators chat with each other. "Teas are a good opportunity to ask questions about medicine and hospital administration," said a courier.

Though couriers are busy most of the day, free time is available in the evenings and on weekends. Journal writing and reading are common activities. Often, couriers gather to watch television in the lounge of the Garden House which has two couches, a fireplace, a VCR, and cable TV. For recreation, couriers use the Richard Nixon Recreation Center two miles away for basketball, tennis, and swimming.

An opportunity to experience rural life up close, the FNS internship can expose couriers to country-western dancing, the music of bluegrass bands, and the bite of homegrown moonshine. Couriers have the opportunity to meet famous residents like Alabam Morgan, who is all too happy to teach young people the art of quilting. "She's 70 but full of energy," said a courier. "We'd sit around with quilting bags, and she'd feed us rhubarb and fried apple pies." Then there's the 80-year-old craftsman, Sherman Wooton, who shows couriers how to make stools. "We went into the woods and cut down a hickory tree with a two-man saw," recalled a courier. "Then we removed the bark and cut it into strips to weave the seats. They were sturdy, good-looking stools. Many of us are now using them in college."

SELECTION

 Anyone 18 years of age or older who has completed high school is eligible to apply. No particular major or interest is required. "You don't even have to be in college," says the coordinator. But experience in such areas as CPR and first aid as well as Macintosh computer proficiency are helpful. FNS seeks people who can get along with others and who wish to help those in need. Before being officially accepted as couriers, applicants must show proof that they hold a valid driver's license.

APPLICATION PROCEDURE

 The deadline is rolling, as FNS accepts couriers year-round. Applicants must submit a $100 application fee, an application form (which asks for several essays), cover letter explaining their interest in the program, and resumé. Applicants under 21 are asked to bring their own cars (mileage is reimbursed) but may request an exemption. The coordinator conducts phone interviews with finalists.

OVERVIEW

 The Frontier Nursing Service is the place to turn for students interested in medicine, nursing, midwifery, public health, or teaching. A model for rural health care, FNS provides students with a taste of Kentucky life while allowing them to observe medical procedures and assist both nurses and doctors.

FOR MORE INFORMATION . . .

■ Frontier Nursing Service
Courier Program
Wendover, KY 41775
(606) 672-2317

Genentech, Inc.
Genentech, Inc.
Genentech, Inc.
Genentech, Inc.
Genentech, Inc.

In 1976, venture capitalist Robert Swanson and biochemist Herb Boyers sat down to consider a bold new business exploring the commercial potential of biotechnology. They formulated a company called Genentech, and within a year company employees had created a human protein using recombinant DNA technology—the first demonstration of its kind. But the company didn't stop there. In 1982, it introduced human insulin as the first commercial product of the recombinant DNA technology and promptly licensed the insulin to pharmaceutical giant Eli Lilly for mass distribution.

Since then, the young company has remained in the forefront of biotechnology. In 1985, it earned accolades for being the first company of its sort to market a pharmaceutical—namely "protropin," a growth hormone. In 1987, it received widespread praise for creating TPA, a medicine for treating heart attacks. With these three FDA-approved products and more on the way, Genentech is upholding its mission "to diagnose, treat and cure serious human disease—and create a better way of life for millions of people."

SELECTIVITY	
Approximate applicant pool: 1,000 Interns accepted: 85	🔍🔍🔍🔍

COMPENSATION	
$400/week for undergrads $475/week for grad students	$ $ $ $

QUALITY OF LIFE	
Bay view; Friday Ho Ho's Daily science lectures; Social activities	🌴🌴🌴🌴

LOCATION(S)

South San Francisco, CA

FIELD

Biotechnology

DURATION

10–12 weeks
Summer

PRE-REQS

College sophomores, juniors and seniors, grad students
Must be returning to school in the fall

DEADLINE(S)

April 1

DESCRIPTION

Genentech started its Summer Internship Program for college undergraduate and graduate students in 1987. In the beginning, virtually all positions were in Research, but the program has expanded to offer a taste of biotechnology to students from all sorts of academic majors. Now, positions are also available in Manufacturing, Business, Quality Control, Medical Affairs, Marketing, and Corporate Communications. But because the majority of interns continues to work in Research, this passage will focus on interns' research experiences.

BUSYWORK METER
MEDIUM
LOW HIGH
OLDMAN & HAMADEH

Research interns work in laboratories alongside a research assistant or postdoctoral student and a head scientist. One intern worked with a hormone that moderates the immune response: "I revealed the structure of the particular receptor molecule to which the hormone binds," he recalled. "We already knew that too much hormone, however, can lead to inflammation and shock in the body." Using recombinant DNA techniques, he and his team attempted to create a soluble version of the receptor. He explained: "If administered to patients with arthritic symptoms, for example, that version could render the excess hormone harmless." Another intern tested the stability of anticoagulants under different pH, temperature, and concentration conditions. "I wanted to see if [the anticoagulants] would stay together in pill form; that is, I was trying to understand the relationship between their structure and their reactivity with certain powerful digestive enzymes in the gut."

Working vigorously to bring drugs to market, Genentech involves interns in research of all of its products under investigation. Genentech is currently researching an AIDS vaccine, an insulin-like growth factor to combat physical wasting in AIDS patients, and products to treat allergies and inflammation. Research interns do not normally choose their projects; managers assign interns to laboratories that seem to be best suited to their academic and research backgrounds.

Research interns describe their labwork as intense and imbued with a great deal of responsibility. One intern recalled: "I was the sole person responsible for implementing the project. I knew from start to finish the whole plan— the DNA sequences we'd create, the mutant forms of the proteins we'd get, and the genetic engineering techniques we'd use. In the end, the team and I had completed such substantive research that our work was published in a scientific journal." To complete such tasks, most interns are supplied with their own desk and a Macintosh or UNIX computer. Given the interns' interaction with the principal scientists, it is no wonder that words like *stimulating* and *cutting-edge* are repeatedly used to describe the experience. Said an intern: "I had access to the Ph.D.s, my boss, and even his boss. They were excited to help me even though I was an intern. This is work that people with master's and doctorate degrees do."

There is serious research going on at Genentech. But one gets the feeling that although employees are highly motivated and deeply interested in science, they know how to mix business with pleasure. Spacious buildings with large windows provide a beautiful view of San Francisco Bay. Pleasing aromas emanate from the two company-run cafeterias, where one can get a great lunch for a few dollars. Moreover, each floor contains a large lounge area equipped with an espresso machine, a lunch table, newspapers, and magazines. The labs receive money for a stereo system to "blend science and rock' n' roll," as an intern put it.

Interns can attend daily lectures given by top scientists from around the world and weekly lab meetings to discuss project progress and administrative concerns. In addition, there are departmental trips to Giants games, picnic sites, and local museums. Athletically inclined interns may also partake of the company-sponsored membership to a local health club. Every Friday afternoon, interns are treated to the weekly happy hour, affectionately known as the "Ho Ho." Though no one seems to recall how the name came into being, this gathering has metamorphosed into a giant party with bands, free food, and loads of beverages. Most weeks, the party focuses on a specific theme such as ecology or the Olympics. In the off-hours, interns delight in exploring San Francisco and nearby beaches and campgrounds.

Though competitive with the salaries of other biotech internships, Genentech's compensation falls short of what other technical internships offer. No one seems to mind terribly, however. "Genentech offers such a good experience," said an intern, "that I willingly rejected a much higher-paying offer to see how a great, perhaps the best, biotech company is run."

Commuting is sometimes cited as a negative aspect of the internship. Given Bay Area traffic and the fact that most interns live as far away as Berkeley and Palo Alto, getting to Genentech is a bit of a trek. Fortunately, interns may join one of the company's carpool groups or take CAL trains or BART into South San Francisco where Genentech's shuttle will transport them to work.

> Working vigorously to bring drugs to market, Genentech involves interns in research of all of its products under investigation.

The Genentech experience ends quickly, so interns must work diligently to make a final presentation or provide a manuscript to be considered for publication. "In my three months," concluded an intern, "I got a feel for the whole biotech industry and observed how research fits in with production. By preparing for my talk at the end of the summer, I refined the verbal skills needed to defend my work."

SELECTION

Genentech is looking for students who are at least sophomores and who will return to school after completing the internship. The company recruits primarily through campus newspaper advertisements and career center bulletins, although half of the students considered send unsolicited applications. An affirmative action program screens for excellent minority and female applicants. While 80 percent of interns have science backgrounds (e.g., biology, chemistry, and chemical engineering), there is room for students who are interested in science and technology but study liberal arts.

APPLICATION PROCEDURE

The deadline is April 1. Applicants are required to send in a resumé detailing relevant laboratory and/or business skills, a cover letter, and a copy of their academic record. The company also conducts on-campus interviews at Bay Area colleges. After an initial screening of resumés, Genentech conducts on-site or phone interviews. Program participants are required to sign an agreement of strict confidentiality.

OVERVIEW

Take scientifically oriented students, throw in cutting-edge research opportunities, world-class presentations, and a bit of San Francisco and you've got the Genentech Summer Internship Program—a unique opportunity to experience the biotechnology industry. For motivated, inquisitive, and diligent students, this program opens up many doors. One door allows interns to return a second summer. Another offers permanent employment to as many as five or ten of each summer's interns. A third clears a path to Ph.D. programs or medical schools. And a fourth attracts former interns to top biotech, environmental, and engineering firms. Concluded an intern: "As far as science training goes, it's one of the best places. You come out of Genentech and are respected for your technical skills. Academics and industry people alike know that it's a place where things get done."

FOR MORE INFORMATION . . .

■ Genentech
Human Resources
Summer Internship Program
460 Point San Bruno Boulevard.
South San Francisco, CA 94080
(415) 225-1000

Gensler and Associates Architects

SELECTIVITY	🔍 🔍 🔍 🔍
Approximate applicant pool: 150 Interns accepted: 12+	

COMPENSATION	$ $ $
$9+/hour Possible scholarship	

QUALITY OF LIFE	🌴 🌴 🌴
Educational and cultural programs Airy offices	

LOCATION(S)

New York, NY; Washington, DC; San Francisco, CA; Los Angeles, CA; Denver, CO; Houston, TX

FIELD

Architecture

DURATION

2 months to 1 year
Summer, Fall, Spring

PRE-REQS

College sophomores, juniors, seniors
grad students

DEADLINE(S)

Summer .... February 1
Fall and Spring .... Rolling

That sexy shape, those alluring, angular features, stunning muscularity, a tan exterior and bright, upbeat inside—now that's a building I'd take home to Mom. A building?

Indeed. The description refers to Columbia Pictures headquarters in Burbank—one of the examples in the rich history of architectural triumphs by Gensler and Associates/Architects. Founded in 1965, Gensler is one of the leading international architectural and interior architectural firms. Its designs are fixtures on the American landscape: GAP stores, the John Wayne Airport in Southern California, Apple Computer buildings, San Francisco's expanded Moscone Convention Center, NASA headquarters in Washington—the list goes on and on. For more than a decade, surveys conducted by *Interior Design* magazine have rated Gensler the largest, most respected, and best managed interior architecture firm in America.

DESCRIPTION

Gensler runs an internship program in each of its regional offices: New York, Washington, DC, San Francisco, Los Angeles, Denver, and Houston. The internship generally lasts two to three months, but interns have the option of extending their stay up to one year. When making job assignments, the internship coordinator tries to match students' interests with the needs of a particular office. A few positions are available in support departments such as Marketing or the library, but most interns are assigned to an architect or team of architects in one of the office's design studios.

Interns with no previous design experience perform simple assignments which develop basic architecture skills. One intern learned the ins and outs of coloring: "Coloring is quite important, because when drawings are presented to a client, you want to make them look as real as possible. I learned such coloring techniques as how to prevent markers from running and how to use pastels." She also became well versed in model making, helping to create scale models of buildings and furniture out of foam core or cardboard. "For an exhibit in the lobby of Wells Fargo Bank, I created a scale model of a banker's desk, complete with doors that opened and drawers that pulled out. If I learned anything from that project, I learned not to press too hard with an X-Acto knife and to change the blade often."

BUSYWORK
MEDIUM
LOW HIGH
OLDMAN & HAMADEH
METER
?

Those with some design ability are given more involved assignments. Prior to the design process, an intern may be asked to make field measurements of the site to be designed. Said an intern: "Occasionally I'd visit a site before the design phase began. I'd make a lot of measurements and make sure there was enough space to accommodate the architect's plans. There usually wasn't much to see at this point—just columns and a ripped-out ceiling with exposed pipes and ducts."

After a design is produced, interns may be asked to make a "construction drawing," which requires transforming the architect's design into a precise drawing for contractors to read. "It's a matter of drawing up and dimensioning a design to scale . . . and labeling where elements like the furniture and walls go," said an intern. Interns who aren't computer literate sometimes complete the drawing by hand, with the help of drafting instruments, while those proficient at CAD (computer aided design) equipment make three-dimensional computer-generated drawings. Architects realize that most interns have limited experience, so construction-drawing assignments are typically simple and limited in scope. But after a few months on the job, one talented intern was asked to make a series of sophisticated construction drawings. "It was a case of being in the right place at the right time," he said. "[An accounting firm] wanted to expand its office, so using CAD, I drew up how the new floor would look—with the partners' offices on the perimeter and the associates' cubicles in a middle area."

Once the actual construction has begun, it's up to architects to visit the job site and make sure everything is being built properly. Interns sometimes accompany architects on these so-called construction administration trips. Once they arrive at the site, the architect and intern create a "punch list," which is a list of grievances that the architect has with the construction so far. "It's a way of making sure everything is finished perfectly," said an intern. "The architect inspects the site and asks himself things like 'Is this rail the proper length?' or 'Does that wall have enough coats of paint?'" These field trips are a great opportunity for interns to witness the real-world manifestations of the firm's work. One intern visited, among other sites, a Gensler-designed finance firm notable for its "lovely, curved glasswork inscribed with [the firm's name]." Another made several trips to Apple Computer's D'Anzia 3, an R&D building described as "humane looking," with an abundance of "colors and wavy lines."

Although interns seldom have direct involvement with the design process, there have been times, especially for yearlong interns, when design opportunities have arisen. One lucky intern helped architects create the design to transform Seattle's Pier 69, a run-down pier full of dead pigeons and bird droppings, into a three-floor shopping and business complex. He was assigned the ceiling plans: "I served as the design interface between Gensler and our lighting associates. I helped specify which light fixtures would be used in the building and I helped design a custom light fixture for the lobby." The intern spoke at length about the privilege of being included in the design phase, "the most interesting step of architecture." He added: "This was Gensler at its A-plus best. . . . I really felt like I made a contribution. That's the thrill of architecture—when you feel like you're affecting the lives of people for years down the road."

Gensler makes a point of exposing its interns to a variety of educational and cultural programs. The Washington office, for example, encourages interns to attend its luncheon speaker series. Open to all employees, the weekly catered luncheons are hosted by suppliers of furniture, ceiling tile, fabric, toilets, and other items needed to construct a building's interior. Said an intern: "At the luncheons you get to see the [materials] that you never think about in architecture classes but are extremely important in real life." On the opposite coast, the San Francisco office runs an "ad-hoc art gallery" in its lobby to provide its employees with a "creative stimulus." Featuring the work of local artists, the

> "That's the thrill of architecture— when you feel like you're affecting the lives of people for years down the road."

lobby usually displays paintings, but once exhibited a series of comic books; "it was beyond cool," an intern decided. The firm typically ushers in a new exhibition with an opening party, to which interns are always invited.

As one would expect a top interior-design firm to do, Gensler takes pride in the design of its offices. All of the offices are open and airy. Described an intern in the Washington office: "There are plenty of windows and glass doors. And the walls of the workstations are low so that when seated you can see other people in the office." An intern in the San Francisco office chimed in: "The office is very open, with great views, the right amount of ambient light, and comfortable workstations." Although Gensler cherishes creativity, it does not go for "crazy, artsy-fartsy decorations"; its offices have a corporate feel that, according to one intern, is "definitely more like a law firm than a funky design shop."

Interns are paid $9 an hour, though the salary may be slightly higher for students with a strong background in design. Each Gensler office recommends one or two summer interns for the annual $500 to $1,000 Student Internship Scholarship. According to the internship bulletin, scholarships go to interns who demonstrate "a high standard of achievement, leadership skills, design skills, and versatility."

SELECTION

 The program is open to college sophomores, juniors, and seniors as well as graduate students. Although the majority of applicants have taken at least a course or two in architecture, there are no academic prerequisites. Says the intern coordinator: "We choose both experienced applicants and those with no background in architecture. [Applicants in the latter group] are more likely to be used as an office assistant or placed in a support division like Marketing." In the coordinator's opinion, the best applicants demonstrate "leadership ability, design skills, and enthusiasm."

APPLICATION PROCEDURE

 The deadline for the summer internship is February 1; for the fall and winter internships, the deadline is rolling. Required materials include a cover letter, resumé, and if possible, "a photocopy of one's best design-oriented work, such as working drawings or a design project." Application materials should be sent to Gensler's corporate headquarters in San Francisco. After screening the initial applicant pool, the coordinator passes the most promising applications on to the Gensler office closest to the applicant's hometown. The regional office conducts an interview, either in person or by phone.

OVERVIEW

 In a field with few outstanding internship programs, Gensler scores a homerun. Welcoming both the beginner and the experienced, the Gensler internship is a cornucopia of practical projects and enriching programs. Supervised by the best in the business, students would be hardpressed to find a better entrée into the field of architecture.

FOR MORE INFORMATION . . .

■ Gensler and Associates/Architects
Intern Coordinator
600 California Street
San Francisco, CA 94108
(415) 433-3700

Hallmark Cards

SELECTIVITY	
Approximate applicant pool: 400–900 Interns accepted: 30–35	🔍🔍🔍🔍🔍

COMPENSATION	
$1,300–$2,300/month for undergrads $2,400–$3,400/month for grad students	💲💲💲💲💲

QUALITY OF LIFE	
Friendly culture; Luncheon seminars Field trips; Crown Center; Fitness center	🧘🧘🧘🧘

LOCATION(S)

Kansas City, MO
Other locations in KS, NY, GA, IL and CA

FIELD

Greeting cards and related products

DURATION

12–16 weeks
Summer

PRE-REQS

Students entering the final year of their
undergrad or grad program

DEADLINE(S)

February 1

Take a deep breath, can you smell it, the weeks-old potpourri, perfumed paper, scented soaps, and heady Magic-marker fumes? Memories of birthdays, perhaps even hospital visits flood your mind. You're in a greeting card shop. There's a sea of greeting cards, in every conceivable color, for every conceivable occasion. Chances are, most have a five-pointed crown on their back flap.

That crown belongs to Hallmark, the world's largest greeting card company. From its persuasive advertising slogan, "When you care enough to send the very best," to its 665-person creative staff, Hallmark is the gold standard in greeting cards. In addition to cards, it produces an extensive line of partyware and gift products, keeping the world supplied with a large selection of giftwrap, ribbons and bows, Christmas ornaments, jigsaw puzzles, and stickers. Hallmark is also a company of legendary employee satisfaction: the majority of Hallmarkers enjoy a generous string of benefits and stay with the company the better part of their lives.

DESCRIPTION

To the disappointment of many students, interns in Hallmark's College Relations Intern Program do not write Hallmark cards. Instead, interns choose from a variety of business-oriented positions like Accounting/Finance, Business Research, Engineering, Human Resources, Business Services, International, Manufacturing, Marketing, Management Information Systems, Public Affairs, and Sales Programming.

No matter where they are placed, a lot of an intern's time is spent searching databases, gathering documents in the corporate library, meeting with managers from various divisions, and writing reports. In Sales Programming, interns work on assignments which help facilitate in-

teraction between the Business unit and the Field Sales division; they also research the effectiveness of sales tools and make recommendations on programs supervised by Sales Programming. One intern, for example, conducted field surveys on Hallmark's Adopt-a-Store program and wrote a report assessing its potential for future success.

A Public Affairs intern supervised the production of the magazines Hallmark distributes to its retailers and salespeople. Writing articles and designing the layout for such publications as *Salesworld* and *Gold Crown Journal*, he learned how Hallmark communicates with its extensive retail and sales network. He also served as the editor of *Merchandise News*, a newsletter sent out to the retail merchandisers of Hallmark's companion line, Ambassador Cards. His favorite part of the job was profiling a colorful mix of employees for the magazines: "I interviewed accountants, artists, salespeople—you name it. I got to meet workers from every cross section of the company. I even did a close-up on the sculptor who designed the hugely popular *Star Trek* shuttlecraft *Galileo* Christmas ornaments."

In Human Resources, an intern worked on a job-categorization project evaluating Hallmark's previous employment decisions and predicting its future employment trends. She also worked with a manager on developing a strategic plan for the Management Information Systems, the division in charge of computer systems and data communications.

In Manufacturing, an intern spent several weeks comparing conventional, manual artwork with computer-generated art. After studying each in terms of material cost, labor cost, and time of completion, he wrote a report asserting that computer-based art was the better method, because it is less expensive and more accurate than painting by hand. Later in the summer, he helped design a system to measure productivity among employees in the photo studio. The current system measured productivity by counting the number of photos each employee shoots per day; but it didn't take into account that some jobs take more time than others. He improved on the traditional method by creating a ranking system that assigned higher values to more laborious jobs, thereby yielding a more accurate assessment of productivity. The intern found both projects to be "very satisfying, as they were real-world situations that challenged my problem-solving skills."

Interns receive a formal performance evaluation in midsummer and at the end of their tenure. "Your manager sits down with you and goes over a one-page critique he or she has written about your performance," said an intern. "A basic battery of criteria is considered: communication and listening skills, ability to get along with supervisors, and so

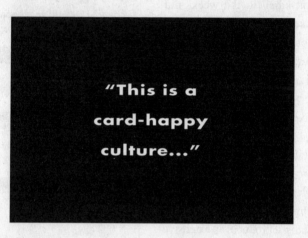

"This is a card-happy culture..."

on." Most interns appreciate these performance appraisals, viewing them as a source of constructive criticism and praise for a job well done.

In addition to the College Relations Internship Program, Hallmark runs two summer programs for minority students interested in creative positions. Selected from a portfolio competition, interns work with writers and editors (the Minority Scholarship Internship Program) or artists and illustrators (the Multicultural Artist Partnership Program). Both allow interns to work in Hallmark's creative areas.

Hallmark interns enjoy a wealth of extracurricular activities. Executives from various departments speak at luncheon seminars which are organized twice a month. Tours of Hallmark's production facilities are also arranged that give interns an insider's look at places like the Topeka Production Center, one of four production centers responsible for printing millions of cards each week. The intern coordinator plans several cultural and social activities, including a trip to a Royals game, a show at Kansas City's Starlight Theater, and an intern picnic. Interns agree that such outings are "a great way to get to know other interns, especially those in other departments," but a few complain that the activities "are scheduled so late in the summer that it isn't worth bothering to make friends."

Hallmark is proud of the perks it offers its interns. They can frequent the company store where they receive a 50 percent discount on most company products. There's also a clearance store, which sells surplus items at a 75 percent deduction. All this discounted material is too good to pass up for most interns: "I bought a truckload of greeting cards and knickknacks for every friend and family member I have." Interns have access to Hallmark's Fitness Center, a decent gym offering weights, StairMasters, Nautilus machines, and a track. Other benefits include business travel accident insurance coverage, pay for necessary absence due to a death in the family or jury duty, paid holidays, and free parking.

No description of life at Hallmark is complete without mentioning Crown Center. Located adjacent to Hallmark's headquarters, Crown Center is a "city-within-a-city." Crown Center has two hotels, 20 eating establishments, six movie theaters, a full-service bank, a parking lot that holds more than 6,000 cars, and retail stores of every kind. "It's an orgy of modern consumerism," said an intern. Happily, Hallmark employees, including interns, receive a 20 percent discount on everything sold at Crown Center.

Hallmark's Kansas City headquarters are located in a group of modern, industrial buildings that have a slew of windows, and hold an abundance of artwork, ranging from abstract paintings to sculpture. Interns are afforded the same resources given to entry-level employees which include a cubicle and their own computer equipment.

As funny as it sounds, the atmosphere at Hallmark tends to be warm and fuzzy. Employees care about their product and they care about each other. Interns are often surprised to see how seriously the company treats anniversary celebrations: "Anniversaries, particularly those commemorating 25 years with the company, are major affairs. Free cake and coffee. Dozens of well-wishers from all over the company. Sometimes top executives show up." As would be expected at the world's largest greeting card company, anniversaries find dozens of cards making their way to the honored employee. But anniversaries aren't the only events commemorated with greeting cards. Be it a holiday, birthday, illness, or job well done, greeting cards are the currency of communication at Hallmark. "This is a card-happy culture," an intern noticed. "Cards circulate at the drop of a hat."

The intern feedback on this internship is overwhelmingly positive. Said one intern, "I waited for the day I would dread coming to work and it never came. They really take care of you here." The only complaints were in reference to factors unrelated to an intern's workday. One intern groaned about the difficulty he had finding affordable, short-term housing in Kansas City: "Hallmark put me up in a hotel for three days while I was looking for housing. But I needed more time and ended up rushing into renting an overpriced, underfurnished apartment." Another said the move to Kansas City took getting used to: "Being from California, I wasn't prepared for oppressively hot weather in the summer. Also, things here are much slower. You have to adopt a Midwestern frame of mind."

SELECTION

 The Hallmark College Relations Summer Intern Program is open to students entering the final year of their undergraduate or graduate program. According to the program's brochure, which, incidentally, is designed in greeting card format, qualifications include "demonstrated academic achievement," "demonstrated leadership ability," "excellent communication skills," and "an ability to relate to a wide variety of people and disciplines." Interns stress the importance of having "skills in network and relationship building" and "the assertiveness to ask for additional projects."

APPLICATION PROCEDURE

 Although Hallmark selects some of its interns through on-campus interviews and referrals, it encourages students to send a cover letter and resumé to the College Relations department. Applications are due February 1. Applicants in the Kansas City area are interviewed at the corporate headquarters. Long-distance applicants are interviewed over the phone, and if all goes well they are then flown out to Kansas City to interview in person.

OVERVIEW

 The word *hallmark* dates back to 18th-century England when official marks were stamped on gold and silver articles to signify their purity. In all the important ways, Hallmark's internship program deserves the recognition of one of these archaic hallmarks. Challenging projects, structured feedback, group outings to Kansas City, and prime perks combined are a recipe for internship success. For students interested in spending a few months with the prime mover of the sentiment business, Hallmark's got the card.

FOR MORE INFORMATION . . .

■ Hallmark Cards
College Relations/Internship Program
Mail Drop #112
P.O. Box 419580
Kansas City, MO 64141-6580
(816) 274-5111

THE HERMITAGE
HOME OF ANDREW JACKSON

SELECTIVITY	🔍 🔍 🔍
Approximate applicant pool: 60 Interns accepted: 10	

COMPENSATION	$ $ $ $
$1,000/session Housing and $50/week food stipend	

QUALITY OF LIFE	🌴 🌴 🌴
Farmhouse residences Earthwatch meals; Sweltering weather	

LOCATION(S)	
Hermitage, TN	

FIELD	
Historical archaeology	

DURATION	
Summer; One 5–week session May 30–July 3 or July 11–August 14	

PRE-REQS	
College juniors and seniors, recent grads, grad students Previous field training	

DEADLINE(S)	
April 10	

A man of his accomplishments . . . did not belong on a farm, rusticating in Tennessee. . . . Such a man belonged in the White House.

So said the friends of Andrew Jackson in 1821, according to biographer Robert V. Remini. They were determined to see the former governor win the White House, and they got their wish seven years later when Jackson defeated John Quincy Adams to become the seventh President of the United States. But after serving two terms as president, Jackson returned to Tennessee—and "rusticate" (look it up) is exactly what he did. Can you blame him for wanting to rusticate at his sprawling Hermitage plantation and mansion?

Preserved by the Ladies' Hermitage Association, the Hermitage today differs from what it was during Jackson's time. The stately mansion still stands, as does the beautiful garden dedicated to Jackson's wife, Rachel. But there are few traces of its role as a full-scale cotton plantation left aboveground. You must dig to find.

Since 1987 archaeological fieldwork has been performed on the grounds of the Hermitage. By exploring the foundations and other subsurface artifacts adjacent to the Jackson family mansion, archaeologists and interns reconstruct what plantation life was like at the Hermitage of Jackson's time.

DESCRIPTION

Interns work at the Hermitage for one of two five-week sessions. After a brief orientation meeting and a welcoming barbecue, they begin their adventure in historical archaeology. The first few weeks of a session focus on digging test pits near the mansion and garden. Said an intern: "We dug about 175 1'x1' test pits to get an initial idea of which areas had the best collection of artifacts." After locating a few choice spots, interns spend the rest of their time opening up larger excavation units, typically 10' x 10' squares.

Trowel in hand and sweat on brow, interns are fully immersed in archaeological excavation. Such work is clearly not for everyone: "You're bending down and scraping dirt for eight hours a day. You've got to be into it." But physical discomfort is offset by the thrill of discovery. Interns unearth all sorts of artifacts including pieces of pottery, pieces of glass, animal bones, rusty nails, glass beads and coins from the 1850s.

BUSYWORK METER
LOW MEDIUM HIGH
N/A
OLDMAN & HAMADEH

One intern even came across a glass eye. "Every day brings a new discovery. It really makes you enjoy the digging," said one intern.

Each artifact helps reconstruct what life was like at the Hermitage of Jackson's day. Many objects point to the presence of slaves. "I found a blue glass bead. From what [the staff archeologist] told me, blue jewelry was worn by slaves to ward off evil and sickness," said an intern. Another found an amulet in the shape of a clenched fist—an old Islamic symbol. The Hermitage staff surmised that because the amulet was probably a necklace charm worn by slaves, it suggests that not all of Jackson's slaves were Christian, as is commonly thought by historians. Even the animal bones are useful bits of evidence, because they indicate what people were eating in a given area.

Interns also find evidence of structures that were present at the original Hermitage. One group pinpointed the location of a few slave cabins when it uncovered a series of cellar holes and postholes. Another discovered a well-like hole filled with trash from the mid-19th century. Archaeologists hypothesize that in Jackson's time the hole was filled with snow and used as an ice house. Interns working near the garden uncovered an unnaturally narrow layer of gravel thought to be a 19th century walkway.

An integral part of life as a Hermitage intern is interaction with the public. Hundreds of tourists visit the grounds every day, and inevitably they encounter interns hard at work excavating. Although a sign explains the basics of the project, it's up to interns to answer any questions visitors have about the excavation. "We got a lot of inquiries about what we were doing and about archaeology in general. And there were always a few tourists who asked if we were digging for gold." Despite a seemingly constant stream of questions, most interns find public interaction worthwhile: "It was fun talking with all those people—I felt like a spokesperson for the field of archaeology. It was also a great reason to take a break from digging."

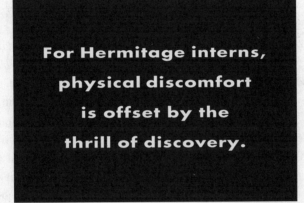

For Hermitage interns, physical discomfort is offset by the thrill of discovery.

There's no way around it: Life on the job is gritty and exhausting. Tennessee summers are oppressively humid, so interns begin their eight-hour workdays at 6:30 AM to avoid some of the afternoon heat. But, according to one intern, "It's still sometimes hot enough to melt the mercury in a thermometer." Nevertheless, if interns take frequent breaks, they'll begin to adjust to the scorching heat. The staff archaeologist said, "Although no one gets fully acclimated to outside summer work in this area, you will find after a few days of pacing yourself [that] you will more or less get used to the heat." Equally bothersome are the omnipresent insects. "This place is crawling with bugs," said an intern. "The sweat bees were the worst. They sting you in the elbow and behind the knees." Consequently, interns are advised to stock up on several cans of bug repellent.

Interns live in one of two 1930s-era farm houses located on the Hermitage property about a half mile from the mansion. Although the houses "aren't the lap of luxury," each has a bathroom, a few pieces of furniture, and a fully equipped kitchen. Six people live in each house, with two or three to a bedroom. No air-conditioning is available (gasp) but a few well-placed fans seem to keep things cool. As expected of a Southern abode, the houses come complete with comfortable front porches. Said an intern: "At the end of the day, we'd sit on the porch, pop a beer, and watch the thunderstorms roll in. Those storms were always a relief from the heat."

A unique aspect of the Hermitage experience is that interns live and work with participants from the Earthwatch program. For three two-week sessions during the summer, Earthwatch sends a crew of paying volunteers to work on the excavation site. They come from a wide range of backgrounds and ages, and add an interesting dimension to the internship. "Earthwatch people worked alongside the interns. [The staff archaeologist] went out of his way to make sure that the two groups blended together. I found the Earthwatch people friendly and fun to be with. There was definitely a team spirit going on." This sense of community extends into the dining room as well. When Earthwatch is in session everyone gathers for dinner at one of the two crew houses. Earthwatch hires its own cooking director, making meals "elaborate and satisfying." Said one intern: "Meals are a terrific dividend of having the Earthwatch people around. In their absence, we had to go to the grocery store and make our own meals."

There's plenty to do when Hermitage life becomes stale. Memphis and Knoxville are popular weekend destinations. Downtown Nashville is just a 15-minute drive away. No stay in Tennessee is complete without checking out Nashville's Country Music Row, a collection of museums chronicling the lives of country music's biggest stars. "I liked the Elvis and Randy Travis museums the best," said an intern. If live music is desired, Nashville's Summer Lights Festival offers a mélange of country and rock bands.

SELECTION

The Hermitage accepts college juniors and seniors, recent graduates, and "early-phase" graduate students. Although most have had a least one field course in archaeology, the staff archaeologist is willing to consider applicants who lack field experience but have academic backgrounds applicable to historical archaeology. In recent years, for example, the program has taken on students majoring in history and architecture. The Hermitage attracts applicants from all over the country; a student who completed two Hermitage internships says his peers hailed from Maine, California, New York, Ohio, Texas, Georgia, and Canada. According to interns, applicants should "be able to adapt easily to strangers," "enjoy working in close contact with people," and "be able to endure sweltering weather."

APPLICATION PROCEDURE

The deadline is April 10. Submit a letter summarizing education and field experience, and a statement explaining interest in the program. Specify a session preference. Applicants must also have a professor or previous employer send a letter of recommendation directly to the Hermitage. No interviews are conducted and therefore the recommendation is particularly critical. "It's important that the reference indicates whether an applicant works well with people," the staff archaeologist said. Final selections are made by April 30.

OVERVIEW

The Hermitage offers one of the best archaeological internships available. Compensation is unusually generous for an archaeology program; interns receive room, board, *and* an ample stipend for food. Supervision is unusually educational. The staff archaeologist goes out of his way to help interns perfect their excavation skills and also advises them on graduate schools and career choices in archaeology. And excavation at the Hermitage is unusually important. By digging up artifacts and other pieces of evidence, interns help archaeologists discover aspects of the workings of the original estate that would otherwise remain unknown. Excavations yield a clearer picture of the lifestyle of the Hermitage's inhabitants and the locations of its buildings. In this way, Hermitage interns help add missing pieces to a historical jigsaw puzzle.

FOR MORE INFORMATION . . .

■ The Hermitage
Internship Program
4580 Rachel's Lane
Hermitage, TN 37076-1331
(615) 889-2941

A small makeshift garage stands at 367 Addison Avenue, Palo Alto, CA.

That's where two Stanford University engineering graduates named Bill Hewlett and David Packard set up shop in 1939. Offering for sale an audio oscillator that Hewlett had invented under the tutelage of Stanford Dean of Engineering Fred Terman, the pair set out "to make a run for it." After selling eight oscillators to The Walt Disney Studios, Hewlett-Packard—the company name they came up with after tossing a coin—was well on its way.

For over a half century, Hewlett-Packard has manufactured a diverse line of products that includes everything from high-speed frequency counters and fetal-heart monitors to the world's first scientific handheld calculator (the HP-35) and the world's first desktop laser printer (the LaserJet). With over 92,000 employees and nearly $17 billion in annual revenues, HP now offers 18,000 electronic products and dominates its industry in several areas. It's number one worldwide in laser printers, test-and-measurement devices, patient-monitoring systems, gas chromatographs, and high-speed couplers. No wonder the garage where it all began is now California historical landmark No. 976 and recognized as the birthplace of Silicon Valley.

DESCRIPTION

Hewlett-Packard's Student Employment and Educational Development (SEED) program was formed in the early 1970s to replace a high school summer internship program called the Engineering Pool that had been in place since 1955. Today, SEED fosters "practical work experience[s] in a sophisticated technical environment." Interns can choose from a wide variety of areas, including Research & Development, Manufacturing, Marketing,

Field Sales, Quality, Materials, Facilities, Information Technology, Finance, and Personnel. Marketing and Finance positions are primarily open to M.B.A. students, who make up approximately 30 percent of the intern class; the remaining 70 percent, mostly undergraduates studying technical fields, work in the other areas. Only five interns work in Sales and Personnel while over 100 interns are placed in R&D and Manufacturing. Though interns are concentrated in the San Francisco Bay Area, there are positions available in Colorado, Delaware, Georgia, Idaho, Mas-

SELECTIVITY 🔍🔍🔍
Approximate applicant pool: 2,500
Interns accepted: 300–500

COMPENSATION 💲💲💲💲💲
$450–$625/wk for undergrads; $700–$950/week for grad students; round-trip travel; relocation allowance

QUALITY OF LIFE 🌴🌴🌴🌴🌴
"Management-by-objective"; Beer busts
Free HP calculator; Social activities

LOCATION(S)
CA, CO, DE, GA, ID, MA, NH, NJ, OR, WA

FIELD
Computers and electronics

DURATION
10–14 weeks
Summer

PRE-REQS
College sophomores, juniors and seniors
grad students

DEADLINE(S)
April 30

sachusetts, New Hampshire, New Jersey, Oregon, and Washington. The company runs a similar program called WEEP (Work Experience and Education Program), offering summer employment, part-time employment, and scholarship programs to high school students 16 years of age and older. For further information about this program, high school students should consult a guidance counselor or the nearest division's staffing manager.

At the Disk Mechanisms Division in Boise, Idaho, an R&D intern helped to decrease a disk-drive assembly line's "cycle time," the time it takes to go through the assembly line once. Designated head of a group of five engineers, he interviewed the line's workers and figured out the cause of bottlenecks—disk-drive tests for cleanliness. "[The tests] were taking too long," he said. "We'd connect the disk drive to a power supply so that [the drive] would spin. Then we'd put a nozzle through the slot and pump in compressed air to stir up the dust particles. Finally, we'd insert an instrument called a particle analyzer to measure the amount of dust. . . . [And] whether or not a disk drive passed inspection, employees would type the drive's ID number and the results of the test into a computer, sometimes making mistakes." It quickly became apparent to him that he had to shorten the test times and reduce the number of employee data entry errors. "I connected the compressed-air nozzle and particle analyzer to one another so that they could do their respective tasks at once. And I set up a new system, using bar codes and a scanner, to more accurately input each disk drive's ID number and status."

An intern at Sunnyvale's Personal Computer Software Division worked on developing a new release of a PC graphics product called Graphics Gallery. "It was part drawing program, part chart, so that the user could type in or import data and then graph it. I spent the first month or so learning the program by talking to its designers and going over the code. After that, I worked on fixing bugs that HP testers had discovered." Eventually, his managers became

so confident in him that they asked him to implement a "device control interface," a series of screens used to configure printers, plotters, and cameras. "All the engineers hated the previous version of the interface because its code was long and complicated. So I simplified it, rewriting sections and adding features that would support new printer configurations. At the end of the summer I pulled together the work of the 15 engineers who were developing the new version, helped administer a few tests, and then created the final disk that went to manufacturing."

At the Medical Products Group in Andover, MA, the company manufactures "transducers," devices that send out the oscillating signals in ultrasound machines. One summer intern was asked to improve the system of testing the transducers. "A transducer up for testing would be attached to a 'network analyzer,' a machine that measures the frequencies at that a tranducer vibrates. The analyzer required calibration before each and every test, about six or seven in all." But the people on the line weren't technically skilled and had to call an engineer over to do the calibrations, a process that was delaying the testing. So, the intern wrote a program in BASIC for each of the calibrations on HP's 95L calculator. "The programs allowed the line workers to do the calibrations at the push of a button, eliminating the need to bring over the engineers."

In 1957, HP wrote its Corporate Objectives, which said that "each individual at each level in the organization should make his or her own plans to achieve company objectives and goals." This "management-by-objective" policy, as HP refers to it, means that interns may approach projects with a lot of freedom. While in most cases it affords interns a great deal of responsibility, it also opens up the possibility that a few projects every summer will not be clearly defined or will be supervised inadequately. Said an intern: "Students need to ask plenty of questions of their supervisors and stay on top of things; otherwise, they'll accomplish nothing significant." Each intern also has the freedom to take HP-offered

> HP's "management-by-objective" policy means that interns may approach projects with a lot of freedom.

classes. "I took a two-day, in-house C-programming course and a class on presentation skills," said an intern. "Whatever your reason, HP will let you take any of its classes, just like that."

HP's Palo Alto headquarters consists of a few buildings spread out over nearly 12 acres. There's a jogging track that goes around the central building, whose four stories jut out in a staggered fashion to form what "looks like a staircase." Each floor has an open-sky atrium, used for meetings or one-on-one talks with supervisors. To the disappointment of health-conscious interns, there are no corporate fitness centers.

HP is described by one intern as "family oriented." Employees interact with one another on an informal basis. There is a "low-key, casual, no suit-and-tie" attire that reaches even the corporate level, and there's friendly, upbeat chatter in the offices and the cafeterias. An open-door policy encourages employees and interns alike to raise any concerns they have with management or personnel. When new products are released, divisions often throw afternoon "beer busts," employee and intern get-togethers offering beer, soft drinks, music, cheese, crackers, and fruit. It's all part of "The HP Way," which Bill Hewlett once described as "the policies and actions that flow from the belief that men and women want to do a good job, a creative job, and that if they are provided the proper environment they will do so."

This so-called proper environment includes great employee benefits, to which interns are made privy. Treated like regular employees, interns receive holiday pay and medical insurance coverage. A relocation program chaired by two administrators (one for east of the Mississippi River, the other for west) provides detailed packets of housing information to simplify interns' apartment hunts. Interns may also purchase products at employee cost. LaserJets at 40 percent off the retail price, for example, are common.

Each site offers a one-day orientation at the beginning of the summer. In Boise, interns view a video on HP, receive badges, and learn administrative procedures. At the Bay Area orientation, they are treated to a continental breakfast and buffet lunch in between speeches given by Executive Vice President William Terry and CEO Lewis Platt. "[Platt] gave a 45-minute talk on the importance of having youthful energy at the company," said an intern. He also stressed HP's commitment to hiring summer students as permanent employees."

All summer long, HP organizes social activities for interns. Boise interns go horseback riding, camping, and white-water rafting down the Snake River ("one of the wildest rides in the country") as well as attend minor league baseball games and participate in intern volleyball leagues. Bay Area interns attend the company's annual summer picnic: "My year HP rented out Great America amusement park for an entire day; we played volleyball, ate barbecue, and rode the roller coasters."

HP's intern pay is some of the highest in the industry. Undergraduates pursuing technical degrees make from $2,000 to $2,500 per month while graduate students working in technical areas receive from $3,000 to $3800 per month. Nontechnical and business students receive 10 to 15 percent lower salaries.

SELECTION

Applicants must have completed their freshman year and must be pursuing B.S., M.S., M.B.A., or Ph.D. degrees in one of the following fields: accounting, engineering (electrical, computer, mechanical, or industrial), computer science, information technology, operations research, finance, or business administration. "Ability to work in a team and problem-solving skills" are essential, according to the coordinator. While the program is open to everyone, it seeks to hire one third women and one third minorities.

APPLICATION PROCEDURE

The deadline is April 30, but students may begin submitting materials as early as January 1. Required materials include a resumé and a cover letter. Most students either send in materials to headquarters or meet HP recruiters at one of the 65 campuses the company visits nationwide. In addition to applying to headquarters, students may write directly to a specific division, each of which concentrates on a different area of the company's expertise—from desk jet components in Vancouver, WA to laser jets in Boise, ID, to workstations in the San Francisco area. Students are advised to call for the company's "Where You Can Work in HP" brochure, which describes all facility locations and functions, and/or call headquarters in March, when coordinators know which divisions need interns.

OVERVIEW

 These days, Hewlett-Packard is riding high. HP is the sixth largest manufacturer of personal computers. It is second only to Sun Microsystems in the production of computer workstations. Profits are up and orders are growing. As part of HP's SEED internship, students can get in on the action. Armed with a free HP calculator and empowered with the same resources as the rest of the HP workforce, interns are asked to manage projects involving products from disk drives and computers to calculators and laser printers. For their efforts, interns can look forward to one of the highest rehire rates of any internship—nearly 70 percent of interns receive offers of permanent employment.

FOR MORE INFORMATION . . .

■ Hewlett-Packard
SEED Program
3000 Hanover Street
Mail Stop 20-AC
Palo Alto, CA 94304-1181
(415) 857-2092

HILL AND **KNOWLTON**

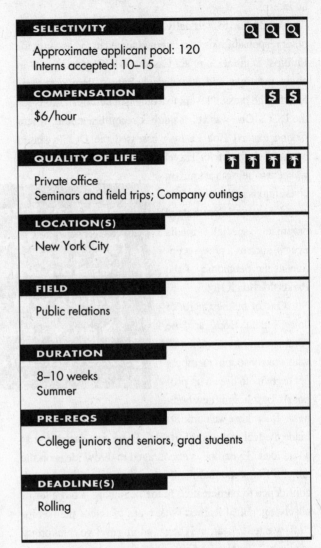

SELECTIVITY

Approximate applicant pool: 120
Interns accepted: 10–15

COMPENSATION

$6/hour

QUALITY OF LIFE

Private office
Seminars and field trips; Company outings

LOCATION(S)

New York City

FIELD

Public relations

DURATION

8–10 weeks
Summer

PRE-REQS

College juniors and seniors, grad students

DEADLINE(S)

Rolling

Which public relations firm represents six out of the top ten Fortune 500 companies and 35 percent of the entire Fortune 500 list? Hill and Knowlton does. It is the leader of the public relations jungle. Founded in 1927, Hill and Knowlton has been an agency of firsts. In the fifties, H&K became the first American public relations firm to have offices in Europe. In 1985, it was the first to expand its network to the People's Republic of China and six years later it was the first to establish a presence in Hungary. Today, in addition to its New York headquarters, H&K has 61 outposts across the country and all over the world, with offices on every continent except Africa and Antarctica. H&K's client list reads like Gordon Gekko's ideal stock portfolio, with such heavyhitters as PepsiCo, Heinz, and Procter & Gamble.

DESCRIPTION

According to the internship bulletin, Hill & Knowlton's Summer Internship Program is "designed to introduce students to the day-today business of a public relations agency and help them develop the essential written and oral communication skills required to conduct public relations activities." Interns are assigned to work with one or two supervisors. Depending on their interest and agency need, interns are matched with particular accounts like Hiram Walker and Procter & Gamble, or are placed in specific account areas like Travel and Leisure Communications.

No matter what account they work on, virtually all interns perform a standard set of publicrelations tasks. The closest they come to busywork is writing media lists, which requires one to "research the names, addresses, and phone numbers of news organizations who may be interested in your client's activities." More substantive intern work is press release writing, a one- or two-page account of a client's activities. "After researching the client in detail, I'd write up a draft of the press release which my supervisor would then edit. It took considerable effort. I would submit the press release for editing again and again until it read well." When they're not writing press releases, interns spend a lot of time composing pitch letters. Designed to convince journalists to cover a client's activities, pitch letters require more creativity than press releases, according to interns. "You need to think of fresh ways to get journalists interested in a client. Your writing has to grab the reader," said an intern.

In addition to their daily tasks, interns have a variety of other responsibilities. An intern assigned to the account for Phillips' Digitial Compact Cassette (DCC) participated in client meetings and attended equipment demonstrations held for the press. "I went to a bunch of demonstrations for the DCC. One was at Masterdisk recording studio, where [sound expert] Bob Ludwig assessed the DCC's sound quality." An intern for Travel and Leisure Communications was sent to help out at tourism conventions in the New York area. Another intern helped organize special media events, such as a press reception in the penthouse of the Parker Meridian Hotel.

One of the best parts of daily life at H&K are the "brainstorming sessions," where ten or so staff members get together to dream up proposals for soliciting new business. Interns are welcome at these meetings: "[Senior staff] made me feel really comfortable. There's no such thing as a bad idea. Everyone is encouraged to throw ideas on the table." For some interns, it takes time to muster enough confidence to participate: "In the beginning, I did a lot of observing. But I learned what types of issues the [senior staff] wanted to hear, and I began adding my two cents pretty regularly." To give participants a better idea of the product being discussed, samples are often passed around the conference table and (if edible) they are consumed. Sessions involve tastings of everything from spaghetti sauce to milk. Said an intern who attended a session where shots of tequila were available: "You've got to know a product before you sell it."

The highlight of a summer at H&K is the Intern New-Business Competition. Divided into teams of three or four, interns have a month to create a new-business proposal based on a hypothetical scenario involving a fictional client. One scenario, for example, required intern teams to write a media strategy for Blockbuster Video. During the last two weeks of the competition, teams meet regularly with H&K's

worldwide creative director who gives them intense training in presentation skills. By the end of the month, the teams are ready to present their proposals to the "client," represented by a group of agency executives that includes the president of the New York office. "It's really hard-core," said an intern. "Each team has 15 minutes to describe its proposal to an audience of senior managers. We pulled out all the stops—using visuals, overheads, and video clips." After all of the presentations are given, the executives critique each performance and choose a winning team. "The winners my year proposed running a promotion where 'golden tickets' were inserted into Blockbuster boxes—similar to the golden tickets in *Willy Wonka and the Chocolate Factory*."

Beside giving interns "invaluable practical experience in creating new-business proposals," the competition serves to bond interns together. "You don't get to choose who's on your team, so you have to learn how to get along and function effectively as a team. . . . The people in my group ended up becoming not just colleagues, but buddies." But one intern complained that this bonding experience comes too late in the internship: "During the weeks preceding the group project, it felt like [the interns] were not relating to each other as well as we could. . . . It would have helped to have more social activities earlier in the summer."

In H&K's defense, there are other extracurricular events where interns can meet each other. One-hour weekly seminars are held with different senior executives to expose interns to a variety of practice specialties within the public relations profession, including financial relations, media relations, environmental affairs, and crisis communications. Field trips to the offices of publishing, advertising, radio, and television companies are also organized; a favorite destination among interns is the headquarters of *Good Housekeeping*, where they see "food testers cooking new recipes." Once or twice a summer, interns are treated to a party in their honor, such as a catered picnic in Central Park where they watch an outdoor concert.

> **Said an intern who attended a brainstorming session where shots of tequila were available: "You've got to know a product before you sell it."**

Hill and Knowlton is located in the Graybar Building, which is attached to Grand Central Station. But unlike the bustling train terminal, the atmosphere at the offices of Hill and Knowlton is sedate and understated. Most interns work on the 12th floor, which, for one intern, has the sterile feel of a hospital—"friends would visit me and joke, 'Paging Dr. So-and-So . . . please report to floor eleven.'" But what the agency lacks in aesthetics it makes up for in office space. H&K is one of the few organizations that grants interns their own offices. Said an intern: "The agency is really good about taking care of interns. I had my own office with window, phone line, nameplate, and IBM computer." When they have time, interns may dine at a cafeteria located on the eighth floor, although some are less than enthralled with its food—"I'd only go there on rainy days."

SELECTION

The program is open to college juniors and seniors as well as graduate students. While there are no set academic criteria for selection, candidates—in the words of the internship bulletin—"must demonstrate good oral and written communication skills, a genuine interest in the field of public relations, [and] the ability to assume responsibility, prioritize and organize their work, and to think creatively." Previous extracurricular and/or work experience related to the field of public relations is also helpful.

APPLICATION PROCEDURE

Although the deadline is rolling, the intern coordinator gives preference to applications submitted before April 1. Required materials include a cover letter, resumé, and writing sample ("any paper demonstrating one's proficiency in writing" says the brochure). The coordinator conducts interviews with selected applicants, preferably in person, but occasionally over the phone.

OVERVIEW

If there was ever a textbook example of an excellent internship in public relations, Hill and Knowlton's program would come pretty close. It has everything; prestige, real-world assignments, seminars and trips, and a well-organized group project. All this, *and* interns get their own office.

FOR MORE INFORMATION . . .

■ Hill and Knowlton
Internship Coordinator
420 Lexington Avenue
New York, NY 10017
(212) 697-5600

HILL, HOLLIDAY

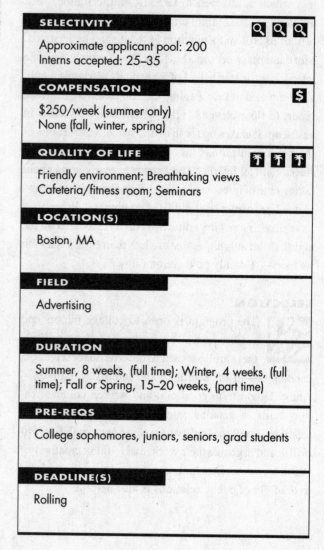

SELECTIVITY	🔍🔍🔍
Approximate applicant pool: 200 Interns accepted: 25–35	

COMPENSATION	💲
$250/week (summer only) None (fall, winter, spring)	

QUALITY OF LIFE	🌴🌴🌴
Friendly environment; Breathtaking views Cafeteria/fitness room; Seminars	

LOCATION(S)
Boston, MA

FIELD
Advertising

DURATION
Summer, 8 weeks, (full time); Winter, 4 weeks, (full time); Fall or Spring, 15–20 weeks, (part time)

PRE-REQS
College sophomores, juniors, seniors, grad students

DEADLINE(S)
Rolling

You won't find a copy of *Internal Affairs* at any library. But for a recent group of interns at Hill, Holliday, this 12-page newsletter was the highlight of their eight weeks at the Boston ad agency. As part of a group project, interns created a slick newsletter, complete with snazzy graphics, feature stories like "Green Marketing, the Ad Industry, and the Green Consumer" and tongue-in-cheek articles like "You Know You're Having a Bad Day When . . . " Few advertising agencies have the time and inclination to encourage their interns to embark on such a venture. Yet, Hill, Holliday believes its interns are capable of doing more than babysitting photocopy machines.

Founded in 1968, Hill, Holliday is one of the county's leading midsize advertising agencies. Not only does it service well-known local clients like *The Boston Globe* and the Bank of Boston but it also handles the advertising for such national companies as Gillette, Spalding Sports Worldwide, Sony Corporation of America, and Latrobe USA (makers of Rolling Rock beer). The agency has picked up its fair share of honors, including the 1992 EFFIE award for its Reebok Blacktop campaign.

DESCRIPTION

Unlike many advertising agencies, Hill, Holliday (HH) hires interns for virtually every one of its departments. Said an intern: "This policy allows students to get in-depth exposure to a particular stage of the advertising process, whether it's pitching new accounts or putting the finishing touches on an ad." Interns are placed in one of the following departments: Accounting, Account Service, Administration, Art, Broadcast, Community Relations, Copy, Corporate, Design, Direct Marketing, Human Resources, Market Research, Mechanical Art, Media, Management Information Systems, New Accounts, and Traffic.

Wherever they are assigned, interns serve as all-around assistants, helping a department with clerical work and a variety of short- and medium-term projects. Art interns shoot photostats and paste them up on foam-core boards. In Account Service, interns attend and write reports for client meetings. An intern in Traffic, the department that "mediates between the creative and business people," helped the Traffic manager prepare print ads to be sent to newspapers around the country.

One intern liked working in New Accounts because it's the "very first step of the advertising process—and you get to see what's involved in winning an ad account." Part of her job involved tracking down ads produced by competitor agencies. "I pulled competitors' ads from dozens of magazines and newspapers so that when HH made its pitch to a potential client, it could say, 'Everyone else is advertising this way . . . but this is what we can do for your business.'" She also helped type, edit, and copy the so-called leave-behinds, informational booklets that HH gives to potential clients after account executives make a live pitch. "For a pitch the agency was making to Weight Watchers in New York, I stayed up the entire night helping to get the information together for a leave-behind. Easy it wasn't, but when it was over I had a better perspective of how [ad] agencies pitch an account."

For some, the Broadcast department is the most exciting place to be. Interns there do "anything needed to get the production of television commercials off the ground." While there's plenty of classic busywork tasks like faxing, distributing schedules, and sitting at the phones, there are also substantive editing projects. "One of my jobs was to create video mock-ups that account executives would use to show a client what a commercial will look like when it is filmed. We called these 'steal-o-matics,' because they are pieced together from bits of TV shows, movies, and other random footage." To his delight, a piece of one of his steal-o-matic was actually used in the finished commercial: "Footage I found of Lee Trevino was incorporated into the final version of a Spalding golf ball commercial. I liked knowing that I made a difference."

To ensure that everyone gets a sense of what's involved in all stages of an advertising campaign, the agency divides interns into three groups for a special project to be completed during the course of the internship. In the past, groups were often asked to create an in-house newsletter, as described previously. These days, however, groups are given a hypothetical topic for which each devises its own ad campaign. A recent class of interns, for example, was asked to create a campaign to promote Hill, Holliday's 25th anniversary. Said an intern, "We acted as a mini-ad agency, with some of us planning creative executions and others overseeing business matters. We went through all the stages a real agency would—establishing a target market, deciding the best means of advertising, and developing a creative strategy. Our creative approach emphasized the idea that just because the agency is getting old doesn't mean that it has lost its innovative edge." Interns have access to the agency's resources and equipment, so when "judgment day" arrives at the end of the internship, they are able to make sophisticated presentations to a group of agency executives. For some, the moments before making the final presentation are anxiety ridden—"you could hear a few knees knocking"—but they soon find that the judges are "receptive" and "unintimidating."

> One had better like heights — Hill, Holliday is located 40 stories above Boston in the John Hancock Building, the city's tallest skyscraper.

In addition to their daily work and group project, interns have a few excellent extracurricular opportunities. Interns are welcome to accompany staff to the studio to watch a television or radio commercial being made. Said one: "I attended a recording session for a *Boston Globe* radio spot. It was fun to observe the talent and the producer run through the commercial over and over." There's also a seminar series that introduces the interns to a department head every week. "The executives gave some terrific presentations. A creative director, for example, showed us a reel of his best work and described what people in his department do to avoid creative blocks—such as throwing a tennis ball against the wall."

One had better like heights because HH is located 40 stories above Boston in the John Hancock Building, the city's tallest skyscraper. Employees have a "breathtaking" view of the Massachusetts State House and Copley Place. The agency is spread out over four floors and has an "open-door" design whereby offices are predominantly glass and doorless to promote a community spirit. The creative areas of the agency tend to have their share of wacky decorations, such as toy figures, sporting equipment, and a "sculpture of spaghetti with fork." Observed an intern: "I don't think you'd see this type of decor in any other industry." Although a few may have their own office when space permits, most interns sit in cubicles.

Interns' nutritional and fitness needs are well taken care of at Hill, Holliday. There's a subsidized cafeteria available to all employees of the building, and word has it that the chow is cheap ("you can fuel up for under $5") and satisfying ("100 times better than my school's cafeteria"). As far as fitness goes, there's a room on one of HH's floors with a few exercise bikes and showers and another room with a selection of dumbbells—a far cry from Gold's Gym, but the fact that an ad agency takes exercise into account at all is praiseworthy.

SELECTION

 The program seeks college juniors and seniors but sometimes accepts outstanding sophomores and graduate students. Candidates of any academic background are welcome.

APPLICATION PROCEDURE

 Although applications are accepted on a rolling basis, the intern coordinator urges candidates to submit their materials at least two weeks before the beginning of the internship. The summer internship runs from mid-June through mid-August, the fall internship runs from mid-September through early December, winter internship runs through the month of January, and the spring internship runs from early February through early May. Applicants should submit a resumé and a cover letter (with a list of department preferences). After screening the initial applicant pool, the coordinator conducts phone interviews with a group of finalists.

OVERVIEW

 Hill, Holliday offers interns the best of both worlds. It has the feel and energy of a small agency; people are, in the words of interns, "warm," "friendly," and "spunky." At the same time, it has the financial strength and talented people that are hallmarks of a large agency. In this rich environment, interns work alongside professionals and become familiar with a particular area of the advertising process. Assigned a group project, they also gain a sense of what it takes to see a marketing project from its inception to fruition.

FOR MORE INFORMATION . . .

■ Hill, Holliday, Connors, Cosmopulos
Advertising, Inc.
Internship Coordinator
200 Clarendon Street
Boston, MA 02116
(617) 572-3418

INROADS.

On a sweltering afternoon in August 1963, a Princeton University graduate named Frank Carr stood among more than 300,000 people at the Washington Mall. Having traveled from New York to Washington, DC, during the wee hours of the morning, he braved the heat to listen to a man dream of the day when oppressed peoples would be "free at last."

"I have a dream that one day this nation will rise up and live out the true meaning of its creed . . ." declared the impassioned Martin Luther King, Jr.

But as a white man of privilege, Carr wasn't expected to understand King's dream. He had grown up in a family famous for its work in publishing, with the founder of Pocket Books for an uncle and a cousin named Doubleday. As a boy he had attended Andover and played varsity high-school soccer with George Bush. Yet the deeply religious Carr understood that things weren't right. "I couldn't imagine, if we were all God's children, how this inequality could exist. It must be man-made, I thought, not God-made," remembers Carr, who is now a Catholic priest.

So after a few years of these troubling thoughts, he quit his job to right what he saw as a pervasive wrong. "I didn't want special treatment for minorities," he says, "only a level playing field." Carr set out to arm young minority men and women with the skills necessary to make it in corporate America. Soon he had created an organization called Inroads.

Training minorities for management positions, Inroads provides students with internships in business, engineering, and science. Founded in 1970, the organization has grown from one office, 25 students, and 17 sponsoring companies to 40 affiliates, nearly 5,000 students, and a roster of sponsors that includes most of the Fortune 1000 companies.

SELECTIVITY	🔍🔍🔍
Approximate applicant pool: 5000 Interns accepted: 800–1000	

COMPENSATION	$ $ $
$170–$750/week	

QUALITY OF LIFE	🌴🌴🌴
Business workshops; Public service projects Mentors; Academic counseling	

LOCATION(S)

Nationwide—see Description

FIELD

Business-career development

DURATION

8–14 weeks
At least 2 Summers

PRE-REQS

Minority high school and college students minimum 3.0 GPA

DEADLINE(S)

December 31

DESCRIPTION

Students may join Inroads as early as their junior year in high school or as late as their sophomore year in college. The Pre-College Component is offered at 14 locations (marked with an asterisk in the list that follows). Internships with sponsoring companies are offered nationwide, usually near Inroads' offices, which are located in Birmingham, AL; Phoenix, AZ; Los Angeles, San Diego, and San Francisco, CA; Denver, CO; Hartford and Stamford, CT; Jacksonville*, Miami and Tampa

Bay, FL; Atlanta, GA; Chicago*, IL; Indianapolis, IN; New Orleans, LA; Boston, MA; Baltimore, MD; Detroit, MI; St. Paul*, MN; Kansas City* and St. Louis*, MO; Charlotte* and Raleigh*, NC; New Brunswick and Newark*, NJ; New York City, Rochester, and Syracuse, NY; Cincinnati*, Cleveland*, Columbus, and Toledo, OH; Philadelphia and Pittsburgh, PA; Memphis and Nashville*, TN; Dallas and Houston, TX; Richmond, VA; Charleston*, WV; Beloit* and Milwaukee*, WI; and Washington, D.C.

Inroads' application process is rigorous in its requirements. Besides submitting a form that reminded one Inroader of "a college application—only a little shorter," almost all Inroads applicants have to go through Inroads's Talent Pool, a series of workshops held in January and February. To prepare applicants for their interviews with sponsoring companies, the workshops teach students how to interview, how to dress for success, how to write a resumé, and how to research a company. "Each of my on-site visits was about four hours long, consisting of interviews with several managers," said an intern. "The Talent Pool really helped to make [the interviews] seem so familiar."

Once accepted by one of the sponsoring companies, an applicant officially becomes an Inroads intern and is offered a summer job with that company until graduation (barring release from Inroads, as described below). Although companies in certain popular fields (e.g., medicine, law, and teaching) aren't represented, Inroads has internships in nearly every industry, from advertising to utilities. Organizations such as AT&T, American Express, 3M, Johnson & Johnson, Anheuser-Busch, Nestlé, the May Company, Federal Express, and the Federal Reserve Banks are all part of the Inroads team. Like other sponsoring companies, they provide interns with summer salaries, two formal evaluations, and mentors. Despite corporate downsizing, which has forced some companies to withdraw their sponsorship and reduce the number of upper-level managers who would act as interns' mentors, Inroads continues to be singularly

> Inroads' alumni include over 30 company presidents or owners.

successful. "Even though companies are downsizing, they still need talent," says Inroads President Charles Story. "And because we cover such a wide spectrum of occupations, companies can rely on us to take care of that need."

For many interns, the first summer with Inroads follows their senior year in high school. Because high school grads often aren't sufficiently skilled to tackle entry-level projects, their assignments tend to emphasize busywork. "My company didn't have much work for me to do my first two summers," said an intern who spent a virtually unheard-of six summers at Clorox. "I worked on the production line the first summer and did manual labor in the shipping department the next." But such lackluster experiences, common among freshman and sophomore Inroaders, have their purpose. They prepare interns to handle more responsibility later on. "I realized that the work I did my first two years allowed me to learn the company's culture and understand the company's mission," explained the Clorox intern. "It's important to know those things . . . [that understanding] allowed me to approach tougher problems [in later summers] from a seasoned employee's point of view." As a process operator during his third summer, for example, he managed the production line that churns out Clorox products like Tilex, 409, and Liquid Plumr. "I was the sole person in charge of opening the valves and putting the correct raw materials through the mixers. It was a significant undertaking—each day, we produced a few thousand cases [of products]." During his fourth summer spent at the Clorox Technical Center (the last for the vast majority of Inroads interns), he was asked to find the optimal dimensions and cap tightness for different Clorox bottles. "It was pretty difficult. I had to ask some of the original bottle designers for assistance, but by the end I had gained a good sense of what R&D is all about."

Students who begin Inroads in their freshman or sophomore years are still afforded the same kinds of experiences as interns who commit to Inroads before college. A student who joined Inroads in his sophomore year, for example, worked his first summer on an airflow analysis at an aluminum can manufacturing plant. Spending a total of three summers with Ball Corporation, he next helped design a heating-and-air-conditioning system for which he wrote an 80-page report complete with diagrams and charts: "I did all the steps that any company engineer would have." During his final summer, he helped overhaul Ball's system for processing scrap aluminum. "It was amazing how much responsibility I had," he said in retrospect. "I realized that [my sponsor] had grown confident in me, and that was a great feeling."

Inroads helps its students to become successful managers by offering them a substantial degree of career training. Every Saturday during the summer, interns gather for a full day of workshops in topics such as time management, assertiveness, negotiation, presentation skills, and group interaction. As an exercise in decision making, for example, interns pretend to be lost in the woods and work together to figure out what to do. "You typically don't get this type of training until you've been with a company for a few years," stressed an alumna. Because the meetings are held on a Saturday, however, many Inroaders complain that their summer vacation is infringed upon. Others say that's the price one must pay for success.

In between summer jobs, Inroads provides personal counseling and academic guidance. Counselors from the various affiliate offices visit nearby campuses and schedule appointments with their Inroads students every month during the school year. Meeting one on one, the counselor and student discuss how things are going. If the student is not doing particularly well in a course, they decide together whether the Inroader should hire a tutor, the costs of which are covered by Inroads.

Inroads places a great emphasis upon community leadership. Two Saturdays every summer, interns are required to participate in Inroads-sponsored projects—a charity volleyball tournament or a landscaping project at a homeless shelter, for example. "You can't forget your community," admonishes a Chicago Inroads board member. Indeed, the idea of "giving back" is an important facet in the Inroads philosophy and interns are encouraged to participate in such volunteer work as caring for the elderly, helping the Salvation Army, tutoring illiterate individuals, and coaching Little League baseball.

After completing two to four or more years of summer jobs, Inroaders cap off their experience with Inroads' Senior Conference. Usually held in St. Louis, the conference assembles Inroads' approximately 1,000 college seniors for three days of social and educational activities. On one hand, they enjoy a banquet, riverboat cruise with dinner and dancing, and basketball, volleyball, and softball tournaments pitting Inroads affiliates against one another. On the other hand, workshops in such topics as time management and networking reinforce the lessons interns have learned over the past few years. "It was a lot of fun . . . a terrifc way to finish Inroads," said an intern, who was honored as Inroads' 1993 National Senior of the Year. "I made a lot of contacts with people from all over the country."

Inroads is not for the uncommitted—in fact, interns who are unable to perform to expectation are released from the program. The requirements are so tough that at the end of four years, approximately twenty percent of an Inroads class will have dropped out. The reasons are varied: unsatisfactory grades (below 3.0), poor work performance, and lack of participation in workshops, for example. However, many interns leave the program because they have changed to a major not related to business or engineering or because they have received lucrative scholarships with conflicting requirements.

But students who stick it out through the recommended four years of the program find many doors open. "You've built confidence and learned skills that will help you succeed," explained an alumna, who after completing Inroads in 1979, interviewed for full-time positions with twelve companies and received eleven job offers, including one from her sponsoring company, to which she returned. Another former Inroader, who graduated from college in 1977, is still working for his Inroads sponsor—a department store chain in Denver. During his fifteen years of employment there, he has risen from intern to vice president. "Inroads prepared me for what to expect," he said. Anywhere from 70 to 90 percent of Inroads interns receive job offers from their sponsors, and over half accept. "I liken it to a courtship or marriage," says Inroads' president. "The more time you've spent with a company, the better your chances of success."

SELECTION

For its Pre-College Component, Inroads seeks high school sophomores and juniors. For the internship program (called College Component by Inroads), only high school seniors and college freshmen and sophomores are eligible, as Inroads requires a two-year minimum commitment. Inroads seeks African-American, Native American, and Hispanic-American students who meet one of the following criteria: 3.0 GPA or better, ACT composite score of 20 or better, SAT combined score of 800 or better, or top 10 percent of high school class. Some Inroads' affiliates have higher selection standards. Students must be interested in pursuing business or technical college degrees.

APPLICATION PROCEDURE

The deadline to apply is December 31. Students should apply to the Inroads affiliate nearest to them. After applications are processed and applicants are interviewed by Inroads staff, approximately 50 percent of applicants are chosen to participate in Inroads' Talent Pool. Students' performance in the Talent Pool dictates whether they receive interviews with sponsoring companies.

OVERVIEW

Minority students wishing to develop careers in the areas of business, engineering, and science would do well to turn to a career development organization appropriately called Inroads. Provided with up to four summers of top internships, year-round personal counseling, and leadership training, students leave Inroads ready to embark upon management and technology positions with Fortune 1000 companies. About to celebrate its 25th anniversary, Inroads has made a monumental impact, infusing corporate America with talented African-Americans, Hispanics, Native Americans, and other minorities. Alumni include hundreds of middle managers, nearly 20 CFOs, approximately 20 corporate vice presidents, and over 30 company presidents or owners.

FOR MORE INFORMATION . . .

■ Inroads, Inc.
1221 Locust Street
Suite 800
St. Louis, MO 63103
(314) 241-7330

SELECTIVITY	🔍 🔍 🔍
Approximate applicant pool: 4,000 Interns accepted: 750–800	

COMPENSATION	💲 💲 💲 💲 💲
$450–$750/week (U); $750–$1,000/week (G); $500–$700 relocation allowance; round-trip travel	

QUALITY OF LIFE	🌴 🌴 🌴 🌴
Intel University; Weekly brown-bags Social events; Free rental car	

LOCATION(S)
Phoenix, AZ; Folsom and Santa Clara, CA; Albuquerque, NM; Portland, OR

FIELD
Microprocessors/computers

DURATION
8–15 weeks: Summer 4–8 months: Fall, Spring

PRE-REQS
Minimum 3.0 GPA Undergrads, grad students

DEADLINE(S)
Rolling

In 1971, a fledgling company called Intel dazzled Silicon Valley by unleashing the world's first "microprocessor," a silicon chip used to process computer data. Eight years later, the company convinced IBM to use the Intel 8088 microprocessor to power the IBM PC, and the precursor to today's personal computer was born.

Since its founding in 1968 by Robert Noyce, Andrew Grove, and Gordon Moore, Intel Corporation has grown increasingly more influential. In 1987, the company ranked tenth in chip production. Five years later, it had surpassed industry giants NEC, Toshiba, and Motorola to become the world's largest manufacturer of semiconductors. Intel's computer chips are currently inside three out of every four personal computers worldwide. Intel produces other kinds of chips as well—over 10,000 of them. In fact, Intel technology powers everything from traffic lights, cash registers, and taxi meters to laptops, laser printers, and supercomputers.

DESCRIPTION

Every summer, approximately 800 students work at Intel. Nearly 500 of them are summer interns. The rest comprise 40 Minority Scholars funded by the Intel Foundation and about 250 co-op students, interning from January to August or June to December. Positions available include Design Engineer, Product Engineer, Process Engineer, Test Engineer, Quality/Reliability Engineer, Technical Sales Engineer, Application Engineer, and Equipment Engineer as well as Financial Analyst and Human Resources staff. Five sites offer internships: Phoenix, AZ; Folsom and Santa Clara, CA; Albuquerque, NM; and Portland, OR.

Intel has built its success in recent years around the 386 and 486 microprocessor families—powerful central processing units, with hundreds of thousands of transistors on each chip. In addition to these are several upgrades that were introduced in 1992, including OverDrive processors. When plugged into an existing socket on Intel486 SX and DX CPU-based systems, these processors boost PC performance by up to 70 percent. An intern in Santa Clara's End-User Components Division worked on developing a database of companies whose computers might be compatible with the OverDrive processor. "My job was to indicate whether each computer could be upgraded, and if so, to input

BUSYWORK
MEDIUM
LOW HIGH
OLDMAN & HAMADEH
METER

the requirements or process for doing so." The task required her to contact about 80 computer companies and interview several employees.

However, she said, someone had already started making the database on an Excel spreadsheet. "After trying to use it, I realized that Excel was not the right tool. The program required too much memory and wouldn't allow you to call up just a small selection of companies." So after thoroughly evaluating Paradox and Quest, two data management programs, she decided on Quest. "It's so much more suitable for this kind of database: Quest allows multiple users simultaneous access, retrieves one company's records if you want, and can search the database by indexed words—three things computer users can't do in Excel." Eventually, she became comfortable enough with Quest to write a "cheat sheet," a small manual for employees to learn the program's functions. "My project was definitely challenging," she said. "I had to design the database and the questions I asked of companies—all on my own."

A second intern was assigned to Arizona's Packaging Division. "At first I thought they were talking about cardboard and bubble wrap," said the materials science student. She soon learned, however, that the "package" actually refers to the plastic that covers a chip and protects it from humidity and dust. That plastic is formed by a process known as "transfer molding," whereby powdered plastic is heated to create a liquid that fills the mold surrounding the chip. The liquid is then "cured" (i.e., heated, then cooled) to create the solid plastic. "I was asked to test how curing parameters such as time and temperature affect package performance," she said. After creating packages from different curing conditions, various sets of times and temperatures, she subjected them to nearly 100 percent humidity for one week and finally tested them on a circuit board. "It was exhilarating to finally determine an optimal temperature and time for the curing process."

> **Interns working in Intel's clean rooms must first remove all traces of perfume, hair spray, and makeup before donning a bunny suit.**

Intel's culture is described by interns as both "intense" and "kinetic." Employees are constantly pushing to create the next line of faster, more reliable products—as if competitors were right at Intel's heels. In fact, whereas Intel used to release a new microprocessor every four years, it now plans on introducing new chip families every two years, a pace that none of its rivals can match. This rate is partly fueled by Intel's vast cash base. In 1993, for example, the company set aside $900 million (17 percent of 1992's sales) for R&D expenditures and $1.6 billion for capital expenditures, the highest spending of its kind among semiconductor and computer companies worldwide. Such drive forces employees to work a lot of overtime. But it also encourages them to be creative. "Intel employees are risk takers," observed an intern. "Even if their ideas are shot down by upper management, they keep trying."

As hard as people work, however, the atmosphere remains casual and friendly. There's essentially no dress code, so jeans, shorts, sneakers, and sandals keep people comfortable. In addition, employees are exceedingly willing to help interns—a tendency manifested in an open-door policy that calls for no room, except conference rooms, ever to be closed. "If you have a valid reason, you can always go talk to managers or VPs," said an intern. "Some upper managers even took the time to discuss what I should do with my career plans."

Each of Intel's West Coast sites is composed of a vast industrial complex that's well landscaped with small waterfalls and man-made ponds. Available to interns at each location is a technical library, a free recreation center with courts and weights, and cafeterias with cuisine comparable to that of a good delicatessen. Each site oversees different Intel products or functions. Albuquerque and Portland, for example, contain the bulk of Intel's fabrication facilities, where thin slices of silicon, called wafers, are made in "clean rooms." One thousand times cleaner than hospitals, clean rooms ensure that not a single speck of dust (disastrous to semiconductors) creeps inside the chips. To keep the environment pristine, interns working in Intel's clean rooms must first remove all traces of perfume, hair spray, and makeup before donning the typical clean-room uniform, or "bunny suit." Equipped with a helmet and a filter pack, the bunny suit filters the wearer's exhalations before releasing them into the purified space.

Intel spends $45 million a year on employee training. A portion of that funding is dedicated to the internship program. Like all employees, interns are offered courses in management, quality, and corporate values at the Intel University. Senior managers, including CEO Andrew Grove, teach the college's classes. Arizona and Santa Clara interns may take Intel Culture with COO Craig Barrett. "He talked about the company's founding and how Intel tries to maintain a small-company attitude," an intern recalled. "It was exciting to hear him, because he's a high-level person." Other classes teach resumé writing, interviewing, time management, networking, leadership, and technical topics such as hazardous chemicals, circuit analysis, and VLSI design. Interns are encouraged to take as many classes as possible.

The company also organizes developmental and social activities for interns. Weekly brown-bag lunches feature VPs and division managers sharing information about the business. "It's a way of finding out what's going on in the company," said an intern. Interns are also invited to attend at least two social events. For Arizona interns it's a bus trip to the Grand Canyon followed several weeks later by a party at a top executive's house. In between these events, business groups gather informally for water-skiing, barbecues, and dances.

The company also provides students with housing options and cars. Apartments vary from site to site, but most are completely furnished two-bedroom/two-bathroom arrangements at $800 to $1,200 per month, that comfortably house two to four students. Every two roommates share a rental car and Intel pays for everything except gas. "Because we shared the cars, it was sometimes difficult to schedule who got it when," said an intern, "but for the most part, sharing worked out fine."

Pay is commensurate with education, area of study, and experience. A freshman interning in a nontechnical area will earn approximately $1,800 per month, while a freshman in a technical area receives $2,100. Experienced seniors studying technical fields earn $3,000 per month, as do graduate students with no work experience. But Ph.D., M.S., and M.B.A. candidates with several years of experience take the cake. They earn a whopping $4,000 per month.

SELECTION

Intel seeks students of all ages, from college freshmen to Ph.D. candidates. A minimum 3.0 GPA is required. The company targets the following majors: electrical engineering (55 percent of Intel's interns), computer science (25 percent), computer engineering (10 percent), other technical degrees such as materials science, mathematics, chemical engineering, or industrial engineering (5 percent), and business, finance, accounting, education, and human resources (5 percent).

APPLICATION PROCEDURE

The deadline is rolling, but the majority of positions are filled by March 1. For co-ops, applications are due approximately two to three months before the start of the internship. While the company recruits at approximately 35 schools for most of its interns, students from other colleges are welcome to apply. Applicants should send a resumé and cover letter which Intel scans into its database for managers to search.

OVERVIEW

If the Intel internship were a computer chip, the chip's many transistors would symbolize the program's perks. They include interaction with management and organized social activities to free cars and some of the highest intern pay in the country. Working intimately with the components that make nearly every electronic device tick, interns gain a firm foundation in microprocessor engineering. That valuable training has convinced Intel to implement a new hiring strategy: by 1996 70 precent of all college graduates hired will be former Intel interns. Considering that Intel plans on hiring at least 800 new college graduates annually for the next several years, landing an internship at Intel all but ensures you a future job with the king of computer-chip makers.

FOR MORE INFORMATION . . .

■ Intel Corporation
Staffing Department
FM4-145
P.O. Box 1141
Folsom, CA 95763-1141
(916) 356-8080

The Kennedy Center

SELECTIVITY

Approximate applicant pool: 60–100
Interns accepted: 20

COMPENSATION

$500/month

QUALITY OF LIFE

Tickets to performances
Weekly seminars; Spartan workspaces

LOCATION(S)

Washington, DC

FIELD

Arts management

DURATION

12–16 weeks
Summer, Fall, Winter/Spring

PRE-REQS

Undergrads, recent grads, grad students
and teachers of the arts

DEADLINE(S)

Summer .... March 1   Fall .... June 1
Winter/Spring........ November 1

Just what is *the* Kennedy Center?

An airport in New York? A stadium in Philadelphia? A school of government in Cambridge, MA? Hundreds of elementary schools across the country? If you think about it, our whole Camelot-loving country is a Kennedy Center!

Yet, officially speaking, the Kennedy Center is one of the country's foremost performing arts institutions. Founded in 1971 as a memorial to President John F. Kennedy, the Center not only was a sorely needed addition to Washington's cultural scene, but also quickly became an arts center of national and international importance. Indeed, today the center has the drawing power to attract the country's finest music, dance, and theater companies while also providing a home to the National Symphony Orchestra, the American Film Institute, and the National Opera. It also runs an admirable array of cultural enrichment programs and competitions for students of all ages.

DESCRIPTION

If *choice* is the spice of life, then the Kennedy Center internship offers an industrial-sized spice rack of opportunity. Positions are available in a whopping 18 departments: Advertising, Alliance for Arts Education, Kennedy Center American College Theater Festival, Community Outreach, Cultural Diversity Affairs, Development, Education Administration, Events for Teachers, Government Liaison, Marketing, National Symphony Orchestra, Performance Plus, Press Office, Programming, Public Relations, Special Events, Subscriptions, and Theater for Young People.

The Press Office is a high-profile department that most interns find stimulating. In addition to performing some requisite clerical work, Press Office interns help publicize events by compiling media lists, calling television and radio contacts, and writing press releases. Best of all, they get to escort artists to interviews at news agencies around Washington. "I'd accompany an artist or director in one of the center's hired cars. Once we got to the news office, such as *The Washington Post* or a local radio station, I'd introduce the artist and make sure the interviewer had a press release." Interns have had the opportunity to escort all sorts of VIPs, from Jonathan Demme to the head of the Geoffrey Ballet.

Most positions, however, are more behind the scenes. Interns in Subscriptions, for example, help the Center with its campaign to recruit and renew members. A lot of the work is monotonous: "I performed 'batch balances,' tracking the money generated from membership dues. . . . It was very tedious." But there are also interesting assignments: "I helped organize a direct mail campaign, editing—and improving—the letters we'd send out to solicit new members."

Programming is another department where interns see both the mundane and the substantive. On one hand, interns "act as a secretary for the office, photocopying production contracts and answering phones." At the same time, they are directly involved in arranging the visits of incoming artists, scheduling their housing and booking rehearsal space. They also put together the paperwork enabling foreign artists to enter the country. "I helped write petitions to the government requesting visas for foreign artists—such as the National Ballet of Spain. I'd find reviews and articles testifying to the group's artistic worth."

> **Recent Showcases have seen interns sing, act, read poetry, play the French horn, and even tap dance.**

Some interns work for a specific program. The American College Theater Festival is a national competition, selecting a handful of college theater groups to perform at the Kennedy Center every April. It runs concurrently with another national contest, the Irene Johnson Festival, in which 16 finalists vie for distinction as best actor. Interns for these programs have their hands full making travel arrangements for the visiting groups, preparing for the arrival of festival judges, and working with the Press Office to promote the events. Said an intern: "Preparing for the festivals was a lot of work, but it was rewarding. I was in charge of distributing tickets to the events. I also met the visiting groups at the airport and escorted them—via Metro—back to the center." The position offers a unique opportunity to schmooze: "I networked with some big-name festival judges. [Among them were] the casting director from Paramount Studios and the head of daytime casting for ABC."

Because they are spread out over 18 departments, interns sometimes feel estranged from their peers. "The Kennedy Center is a big place. We were all in our separate worlds. There wasn't much chance for interns to meet each other." Responding to this criticism, the program tries to build cohesiveness by inviting interns to the weekly Executive Seminar, an hourlong presentation featuring executives of the center such as the chairman, general manager, or director of Marketing. The intern coordinator is currently expanding the seminar series to include experts from other arts institutions. Interns may get the chance to have a group lunch with center founder Roger Stevens, who likes to treat interns to a meal at the center's elegant Roof Terrace restaurant when his schedule allows it. Stevens talks at length about his myriad accomplishments, not the least of which include owning the Empire State Building and serving as the producer for *West Side Story*. But an intern warns: "Stevens is fascinating, but he is a real mumbler. Make sure to sit near him if you want to hear him clearly."

The internship has a unique feature for interns who long for the limelight. Once a session, interns may strut their stuff in the Performing Arts Intern Showcase. Held in the center's grand foyer, "the Showcase gives interns who are performers a chance to display their talent, no matter what type of act they do," said the intern coordinator. Recent Showcases have seen interns sing, act, read poetry, play the French horn, and even tap dance. Traditionally, the Showcase has been attended by center staff and local businesspeople during the lunch hour, but plans are underway to hold the Showcase in the early evening before a main show, giving patrons a chance to watch.

Despite its reputation as a highbrow arts institution, the Kennedy Center has an office atmosphere that is reportedly "down to earth" and "friendly." Explained an intern: "The people who work there are warm and outgoing. I noticed a down-home midwestern ethic."

Paces away from the infamous Watergate complex, the Kennedy Center is an impressive sight, perched proudly on the edge of the Potomac River. The center's grand Italian marble exterior is matched by a foyer "so big that the Washington Monument could lie inside," regal red carpet, and an 18-foot-high bust of JFK. But interns say that the physical plant is getting "a bit run-down" and "could use a tune-up." Offices tend to be on the spartan side—"windowless, sparsely decorated, and cramped." Interns sit at desks or cubicles, each outfitted with a phone and, if you're lucky, a computer.

Kennedy Center interns enjoy a veritable smorgasbord of entertainment. They have dibs on two tickets to any event, including previews and opening nights—"I went to as many shows as I could and returned to school an unabashed culture vulture." Interns are also welcome at special events like cast parties and the annual Open House, a free festival in September featuring performances by local artists. Star gazers will be amply satisfied. Interns observe and sometimes meet the celebrities visiting or performing at the center. One intern had "brushes with greatness" with Mikhail Baryshnikov and Kathy Bates.

SELECTION

 While the majority of applicants will be college juniors and seniors, the program welcomes undergraduates of any level, recent graduates, graduate students, and teachers of the arts. If you haven't spent the past few years studying the arias of Puccini, don't fret, the program requires no formal background in the arts. In fact, the intern coordinator says that each session sees a few interns majoring in subjects like "biology, sociology, and physical education . . . so long as they have a genuine interest in the arts."

APPLICATION PROCEDURE

 The application deadlines are as follows: summer internship, March 1; fall internship, June 1; and winter/spring internship, November 1. Submit a cover letter, resumé, three letters of recommendation, and academic transcript(s). Those interested in a position in Government Liaison, Public Relations, or the Press Office must also send in a few writing samples. After applications are received, they are reviewed by a committee. The committee then sends them to the appropriate department heads, who each conduct phone interviews with a handful of finalists.

OVERVIEW

 Internship seekers interested in performing arts opportunities in the Washington area often narrow their search to two choices: Wolf Trap and the Kennedy Center. Both are top-of-the-heap programs that expose interns to the ins and outs of arts management. But for candidates who crave a dose of glamour with their internship, the Kennedy Center is king. A cultural beacon in the nation's capital, the center exudes an aura of prestige and grandeur. A bit of this luster rubs off on interns' resumés, helping them land juicy jobs in the arts. Internship alumni include a talent coordinator for Disney World, the general manager of New York's Ice Theater, the operations manager of the Arlington Symphony, and a cultural affairs officer in San Juan, Puerto Rico.

FOR MORE INFORMATION . . .

■ The Kennedy Center
Internship Program Manager
Washington, DC 20566
(202) 416-8800

KRAFT GENERAL FOODS

Kraft Cheez Whiz fights cancer?

Perhaps, if we are to believe Dr. Michael Pariza, microbiologist at the University of Wisconsin in Madison. According to Pariza, Cheez Whiz contains rich amounts of a polyunsaturated fat called CLA, which wards off several kinds of cancer in laboratory animals.

Whether or not Cheez Whiz has healthful effects, the story is an example of how Kraft General Foods's products are in the public eye. It is no real surprise that they are since Kraft General Foods is North America's largest food company. Generating sales upwards of $29 billion annually, it churns out over 2,500 products, among them such household favorites as Oscar Mayer meats, Kool-Aid, Philadelphia Brand cream cheese, Post Grape-Nuts, Velveeta, and Jell-O. Of every dollar spent on food in the United States, 10 cents goes to one of Kraft General Foods's products.

DESCRIPTION

Kraft General Foods (KGF) places 90 percent of its interns, half of whom are graduate students, in one of five locations: Kraft USA and KGF Technical Center, both in Glenview, IL; KGF Corporate in Northfield, IL; General Foods USA in White Plains, NY; and General Foods USA Technical Center in Tarrytown, NY. At Kraft USA, interns work in Oscar Mayer, Retail Cheese, Grocery, and Specialty Products; at General Foods USA and General Foods USA Technical Center, interns are placed in Beverages, Desserts, Dinners & Enhancers, Post Cereals, and Maxwell Coffee; at KGF Technical Center, interns may conduct research on any KGF product. At KGF Corporate, as well as at all of the other locations, interns work in Corporate Affairs, Sales, Finance, and Human Resources.

SELECTIVITY	🔍🔍🔍
Approximate applicant pool: 3,000 Interns accepted: 100–150	

COMPENSATION	💲💲💲💲💲
$400–$600/week for undergraduates $800–$900/week for graduate students	

QUALITY OF LIFE	↑↑↑
STEPS class Entemann's Bakery tour; $3 lunches	

LOCATION(S)	
Glenview, IL; Northfield, IL; White Plains, NY; Tarrytown, NY	

FIELD	
Foods	

DURATION	
12 weeks Summer	

PRE-REQS	
Undergrads and grad students	

DEADLINE(S)	
March 31	

Employment at KGF gives interns a chance to work with childhood treats such as Jell-O, Oscar Mayer hot dogs, Kraft Macaroni and Cheese, and Kool-Aid. In 1991, the General Foods' Technical Center changed the formulation of Kool-Aid, and an intern in the Process Development group studied the new formula's viability. "We wanted to investigate what side effects the new ingredients would have on shelf life. I analyzed the data from several previous experiments and realized that we couldn't correlate shelf life to caking [the powder's forming into a hard mass] unless we considered some other variables. So I set up a new experiment—an accelerated pantry study—whereby Kool-Aid was subjected to six weeks of harsh conditions, equivalent to its sitting in a pantry for six months."

In the Beverage division, an intern tested the materials used in drink packaging. "Our shipping boxes are made out of corrugated cardboard. I'd compress them and also subject them to various temperatures to see how strong they are." After becoming proficient with materials, he was flown to Chino, CA, where he spent half the internship supporting a plant start-up. "The plant was being "configured to bottle a ready-to-drink beverage. During line trials, we noticed that bottles would sometimes break at the conveyor system's transfer points. So I did some troubleshooting, testing the bottles, the shrink wrap used to package six-packs, and the shipping container. What I finally came up with to solve the problem is proprietary and no less of a contribution than the principal scientist's."

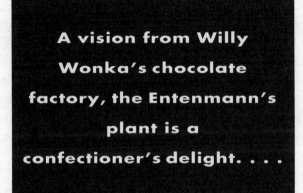

A vision from Willy Wonka's chocolate factory, the Entenmann's plant is a confectioner's delight. . . .

From a melting pot of academic backgrounds, interns take on a range of responsibilities at the company. One electrical engineering intern did a power survey of industrial distribution systems that deliver electricity to plant equipment. "You can't just plug in the machines and turn the switch," he said. "I had to draw electrical plans indicating the loads and where the electricity would come from." But first, he needed to observe plants in operation. "There are no plants in Glenview, so the company sent me to Texas and Wisconsin and put me up in hotels. I'd stay anywhere from a day to a week in order to learn the system. By the end of the summer, I was doing the same kind of work as the company's plant-consulting engineers."

So when he asked to return to Kraft a second summer, he was welcomed with open arms. "Though I was stationed in Glenview, I spent most of that summer in Tulare, CA, setting up process control equipment at a new $4 billion plant. I programmed the PLCs [programmable logic computers], which control the blenders, conveyor belts, etc. and

monitor the operation. For example, if something gets too hot, a PLC activates a cooling mechanism." He also supervised contractors to make sure that wiring designs were followed properly. "I was surprised to be given so much responsibility," he said. Nevertheless, he and a few other interns had the plant up and running by fall. "We worked 60 to 70 hours a week to get the project done, but at least the company flew me home to Chicago twice a month."

Kraft General Foods is a large, decentralized company, so some interns get lost in the corporate shuffle. Said an employee: "Every year a few interns simply sit in front of the CAD machines all summer, transferring designers' hand sketches onto the computer." Yet the company is making a concerted effort these days to assign interns challenging projects. However, interns shouldn't expect a lot of guidance. Managers are often too busy with their own projects to do anything more than sign interns' paperwork and point them in the right direction. "They don't have time to hold our hands here. The burden is on us to create value; it's a lot of responsibility."

You'll never want for social and developmental activities as a KGF intern. In the middle of the summer, interns participate in Kraft General Foods's strategic problem-solving class. Called STEPS, the full-day class held in a hotel conference room has interns reading ten-page case studies, similar to those used in business school. "They analyze real business situations, sometimes involving KGF products," says the staffing manager. "The scenario: A product's market share is plummeting, and the interns must come up with an action plan to reverse the situation." Interns also undergo a half day of diversity training, a highly interactive awareness-building session. A current employee explained: "In today's corporate world, you will be facing a multitude of cultures, and you need to learn how to work with different people."

Interns also tour nearby plants, such as Kraft's largest cheese plant, in Champaign, IL. Barbecue sauce, pasta, and macaroni and cheese, in addition to Velveeta, and Kraft Singles are all manufactured there. Upon entering the factory, interns are greeted by blenders, conveyer belts, and cookers all rattling and humming at once. "The conveyer belts deliver 3 by 3 by 3 [feet, that is] blocks of Velveeta to the processing area, where huge blenders mix 10,000 pounds [of the processed cheese] into a gooey mass. The blob then goes to giant-sized cookers, and a packaging machine spits out a continuous strand of soft Velveeta onto plastic wrapping every few seconds. Finally, slices are cut, organized into packages, and placed in boxes, ready for shipping."

The summer wouldn't be complete without a visit to one of the Entemann's Bakeries, located all over the country. A vision from Willy Wonka's chocolate factory, an Entenmann's Bakery is a confectioner's delight, complete with "huge ovens, 12-foot blenders, and doughnut makers." Machines are whirling and the sweet smells of cakes, cookies, and doughnuts entice interns' olfactory senses. After hours of touring, interns are finally allowed to sample the wares: "Sheer ecstasy!—a hot chocolate chip cookie right off the conveyer belt."

KGF locations rate high in quality of life. Employees at the three headquarters locations enjoy subsidized cafeterias with "fantastic $3 lunches" and free health clubs, with treadmills, fitness counselors, aerobics rooms, and basketball and volleyball courts. Artwork commemorates KGF's rich history. Near the entrance to the Tarrytown Technical Center cafeteria, for example, there's a Hall of Fame wall, featuring decades of General Foods products. At the Kraft USA cafeteria, the company sometimes coordinates lunchtime events, such as a speech by the company president and free Breyers ice cream on the front lawn.

The company has high expectations of its interns. Midsummer, they go through a performance review. "A supervisor determines if you're reaching your goals and objectives," explained an intern, "and your rating affects whether you later receive an offer of permanent employment [about 45 percent of interns do; 30 percent return for full-time jobs]." And at the end of the summer, each intern is required

to give a presentation to approximately five senior managers, including the department head. Don't worry if public speaking turns your knees to Jell-O, a class on presentation techniques is offered a few weeks before the oral report.

SELECTION

Sophomores, juniors, and seniors and graduate students are eligible to apply. Targeted majors include information systems, engineering (chemical, mechanical, industrial, electrical, etc.), food science, chemistry, microbiology, biology, and biochemistry as well as any liberal arts majors interested in Corporate Affairs, Sales, Finance, and Human Resources. KGF seeks leaders who have excelled in their coursework and who have participated in significant extracurricular activities. "We expect good grades, taking into account the strength of the student's college and his or her level of participation in activities," said the staffing manager. "Of course, the more relevant experience one has, the better."

APPLICATION PROCEDURE

The deadline is March 31. Send in a resumé and cover letter c/o Manager of University Relations to one of the company's addresses. "Show that you know our company and you've thought about what department you want to work in," says the staffing manager. KGF recruits at about 50 college campuses nationwide and advertises the location, time of presentations, and interviews well in advance. It also targets talented students at the national and local chapters of the National Society of Black Engineers, the National Society of Black M.B.A.s, the National Society of Hispanic M.B.A.s, and the National Society of Women Engineers. While most interns are selected through the campus recruiting process, unsolicited resumés are accepted. But the staffing manager warns: "You've got to make it stand out from the thousands that flood in."

OVERVIEW

Kraft Macaroni and Cheese is eaten by 72 percent of U.S. college students. For some, this is reason enough to want to intern at Kraft General Foods. But even if KGF weren't the king of mac and cheese, its internship program would still be a must-do. The KGF internship puts students in the center of the action where they improve manufacturing processes, enhance food ingredients, implement computer systems, and assist in plant start-ups. Their reward is the realization, as one intern put it, of "a child's dream—to see and work with goodies we've eaten all our lives."

FOR MORE INFORMATION . . .

■ Kraft USA
University Relations
One Kraft Court
Glenview, IL 60025
(708) 646-2000

■ General Foods USA
University Relations
250 North Street
White Plains, NY 10625
(914) 335-2500

■ Kraft General Foods Corporate
University Relations
Three Lakes Drive
Northfield, IL 60093
(708) 646-2000

LATE SHOW

with

David Letterman

Where would America be without Stupid Pet Tricks, Brushes with Greatness, and the Dancing Waters fountain? What if the Top Ten List, Small Town News, and the Monkey Cam never existed? Where would we be without the lovable jowls of Larry "Bud" Melman, as the rotund mystery man passes out hot towels to incoming passengers at New York's bus terminal? Life in their absence is an impossibly grim thought, indeed.

It is a new era for David Letterman. The man who started as a local TV weatherman in Indiana, moved on to become the warm-up comedian before "Barney Miller" tapings, and then spent 11 years perfecting his craft hosting NBC's "Late Night with David Letterman," now sits comfortably atop the talk-show mountain as host of CBS's "Late Show with David Letterman." His gap-toothed highness has a new studio (the old Ed Sullivan Theater), a new time slot (11:30–12:30), and—the clincher—a new salary ($14 million a year).

DESCRIPTION

Despite Letterman's defection to CBS, the main features of his talk show remain relatively unaltered. This goes for the show's internship program, too. While the interns interviewed for this passage worked for "Late Night," the internship coordinator at "Late Show" says that very little has changed for interns at the new studio. "Late Show" hires interns for Talent, Research, Production, Writing, Music, Producer's Office, and David Letterman's Assistant.

Before prospective applicants start imagining themselves booking Madonna for an upcoming appearance or penning a comedy skit for Dave himself, it must be noted that the bulk of intern work, no matter where they are, is decidedly unglamorous. Internships in television go heavy on the busywork, and "Late Show" is no exception. If answering phones, running errands, and making copies are unacceptable, then it's time to turn the page. The same goes for other mindless tasks, not the least of which is preparing Dave's lunch. Several interns reported being asked to pick up Dave's lunch ("every day it was the same: pasta primavera and vegetable soup") or whip up a snack ("Dave always had to have his fresh pineapple—cut in strips, not squares"). As one intern exhorted: "Know what you're getting into."

SELECTIVITY	🔍🔍🔍🔍🔍
Approximate applicant pool: 250 Interns accepted: 10	

COMPENSATION	$
None	

QUALITY OF LIFE	🌴🌴
Few "official" perks Hectic environment	

LOCATION(S)
New York City

FIELD
Television

DURATION
10 weeks Summer, Fall, Spring

PRE-REQS
Undergrads and grad students Must receive academic credit

DEADLINE	
Summer .... April 1	Fall .... July 1
Spring .... October 1	

BUSYWORK METER

LOW MEDIUM HIGH

OLDMAN & HAMADEH

But for many interns, interspersed between periods of gofer work are some pretty fun assignments. An intern in Talent, for example, helped the department find human-interest guests for Dave to interview. "I'd comb through newspapers and write to network affiliates. The department looked for, and I say it in the most reverential way, 'loonies' —people who collected snowballs, people who collected strings of dirt, anyone with a unique personality or terrific story to tell." He ended up finding four guests for the program, including a "manic cooking lady from Idaho" and a "barber in St. Louis who made vests from human hair." He also helped reject aspiring guests who wanted to tell their story but didn't meet the show's standards. Over the phone or by letter, he "shattered their dreams of national notoriety." On hearing the news, they would sometimes become angry or crestfallen because "where else can a person show off his potato chip collection to eight million people?"

> "In another skit, I played a woman in drag and pretended I was lost on my way to the 'Donahue' show."

Research is another department that yields the occasional memorable moment. Part of a Research intern's job is assembling packets of biographical information about "Late Show" guests. Using on-line databases, reference books, and the "Late Show's" own celebrity file, interns collect articles on upcoming guests, which they then pass on to the segment producers. The producers use the information to create entertaining questions for Dave to ask. Resourcefulness is encouraged and some interns have gone to great lengths to track down a titillating tidbit about a celebrity. One intern, for example, spent an afternoon tracking down the high school yearbooks of film critics Siskel and Ebert. "I had [Siskel and Ebert's] high schools Fed Ex me copies of their yearbooks," she said. "Their senior pictures were typically dorky and Dave ended up displaying them to the camera before he introduced the two men. But he didn't hold up the picture I found of Siskel wearing a dress."

The singular long-term benefit of interning at "Late Show" is the potential for networking. Said an intern, "Interns mostly do gofer work, it's par for the course. But the key to the internship is tapping into the great connections that can be made." Added another, "You're around some of the best minds in comedy TV. The setting is ripe for networking, but you've got to seek out mentors; they won't come to you." Because he befriended the right people, one intern secured a job as a runner for "NBC Sports" after his internship ended, "It wasn't the best job, but every day I got to deliver hot dogs to Merlin Olson and Dick Enberg." Another intern used connections to land a job assisting the publisher of a cutting-edge cult magazine in Boulder, CO. She was one of three people working on the humor magazine, whose subject matter included articles by "Saturday Night Live" writers.

Interns never forget that they are behind the scenes at a major television show. Although it is broadcast late at night, the show is taped in the early evening (5:30 to 6:30), so most interns work at least until 7:00 PM. Interns usually watch the show on monitors in their office, but they occasionally get the chance to view a live taping. "A couple of times I sneaked into the studio to watch the show. The crew didn't mind so long as I stayed out of their way. I watched the show from the hallway, the control room, and a peephole behind Dave's desk." Because celebrities are attracted to the show like honeybees to nectar, interns have their own "brushes with greatness" every now and then. "Richard Simmons was my favorite," said an intern. "When he encountered a bunch of us interns hanging out backstage, he said hello and made up a little song about each one of us. It was funny to stand there and have Richard Simmons sing to me, 'Your name is Brenda—I think I like you.'"

Students often wonder how much contact they will have with Dave himself. The answer is minimal. Most interns, however, run into him by chance and they report that Dave is "cordial" but seems "aloof" and "often sarcastic." "Once I shared an elevator with Dave," said an intern. "And I asked him how his weekend was. His response: 'I went out and bought vegetables and made vegetable soup.' It was a little awkward." Word has it that in lieu of making conversation, Dave likes to toss a football or baseball to interns he passes in the hallway. "It was kind of strange at first. You'd see Dave walking somewhere, and he'd throw you a baseball he had been carrying. It was his little way of saying hi."

There are few benefits afforded to interns on a consistent and official basis. One intern saw the internship as a source of "endless school supplies—lots of pens and paper." Others had dibs on the treats viewers mail to Dave: "So long as it looked pretty safe, I'd indulge in cookies, brownies, cake—anything edible sent in."

According to interns, additional fringe benefits can be had if an intern schmoozes the right people. While T-shirts are pretty easy to come by, resourceful interns may be able to finagle a staff jacket. If they get in good with Letterman's musical director, Paul Shaffer, interns can watch the "world's most dangerous band" warm up for a night's show. The lucky few may even find themselves tapped for a part in one of the show's skits. "[The producer] had me play the part of a drunken teenager in a polling booth. In another skit, I played a woman in drag and pretended I was lost on my way to the 'Donahue' show."

SELECTION

The internship is primarily for undergraduates, although graduate students are welcome to apply. All applicants must secure a letter from their school verifying that they will receive academic credit for the internship. The program is open to students with any major. In the estimation of past interns, the best Letterman interns are "enthusiastic" but "discrete." One intern warned that "some interns think they need to be funny all the time, [when they should] relax and be themselves."

APPLICATION PROCEDURE

The deadlines for application are as follows: summer internship, April 1; fall, July 1; spring, October 1. Candidates must submit a cover letter and a resumé. A word on cover letters: It's okay to be witty, but avoid being cutesy or clichéd. Says an intern, "Every year, dozens of applicants submit a top-ten list describing why they should be picked. Don't do it: It's worn out." After reviewing the initial applicant pool, the internship coordinator picks about 50 finalists, whom she invites to New York (at applicants' expense) for a day of interviews. At the "Late Show" offices, finalists meet with the heads of each department hiring interns. A week or two later, the department heads choose which candidates they want.

OVERVIEW

Too much busywork and too few benefits prevent the "Late Show" internship from qualifying as a top-ten internship, or a top-50 internship for that matter. But, in one intern's words, "If you go in with the right attitude—i.e., not expecting to run the show—you can leave with fun memories and powerful connections."

FOR MORE INFORMATION . . .

■ Late Show with David Letterman
Internship Coordinator
1697 Broadway
New York, NY 10019
(212) 975-5300

L|E|K| Alcar

In 1978, Boston's Bain & Company sent six of its people overseas to set up a London office. Five years later, the London concern had blossomed into a successful operation; in fact, it was so profitable that three of the six founders decided to start their own consulting firm. Understandably, the executives at Bain were unhappy. "There was a bit of a hiccup when the three of us left," recalled James Lawrence, one of the original crew, in an old brochure. Lawrence, along with partners Iain Evans and Richard Koch, took the first letters of their last names to create the name of their new firm—LEK.

Agreeing to steer clear of Bain's clients for three years, LEK had humble origins, barely scraping together enough business during its first years of operation. But steadfast resolve, savvy marketing, and a commitment to objectivity prevailed. By 1993, LEK had expanded with a total of 16 partners and over 250 professionals, and offices in such diverse locations as Los Angeles, Boston, Chicago, New York, Milan, Paris, London, Munich, and Sydney. Moreover, that first office in London has eclipsed Bain in terms of revenues, second only to McKinsey & Company. In April 1993, in order to increase the list of services it offered clients, LEK's U.S. practice merged with The Alcar Group's consulting and educational practices to create the LEK/Alcar Consulting Group.

DESCRIPTION

Since 1988, LEK/Alcar has worked on over 300 transactions worth over 200 billion dollars. The management consulting firm specializes in corporate strategy, value-based planning, mergers and acquisitions, and advice to business start-ups. As interns, students have an opportunity to work in all four of these areas.

SELECTIVITY

Approximate applicant pool: 200–225
Interns accepted: 4–6

COMPENSATION

$500–$600/week

QUALITY OF LIFE

Professional atmosphere; Mentors
Summer party; 50+ hour workweeks

LOCATION(S)

Los Angeles, CA; Boston, MA; Chicago, IL

FIELD

International management consulting

DURATION

8 weeks minimum
Summer

PRE-REQS

College seniors

DEADLINE(S)

Approximately March 1

Dozens of phone calls, Lotus number-crunching, on-line searches, Freelance graphs, and market analysis are part of the "typical" day for the four to six summer interns stationed at LEK/Alcar's Los Angeles, Boston, and Chicago offices. The workday consistently lasts approximately ten hours, and interns' work is rarely mundane. After a week of classes in accounting and finance as well as general training in the use of Lotus, WordPerfect, on-line databases, and various other equipment in the office, interns plunge into casework.

A case focuses on LEK/Alcar's recommendations to solve a problem designated by a client. Whether the case investigates new or existing product lines, competitors, new markets, or potential acquisition candidates, interns must collect and analyze a host of financial data within a wide variety of industries. Most of the time, interns conduct phone research on a potential market and followed up with strategy discussions with managers. One intern explained: "The information required was often of a very sensitive nature involving competitors' methods, materials, and profits. . . . So of course, you had to be cordial but effective on the phone. Sometimes you had to state and restate questions to elicit the answer you wanted."

In addition to casework, interns are kept busy with academically oriented projects such as developing a financial model or detailing the relationship between company "beta" (i.e., a financial parameter that indicates the risk of a company) and rate of return. Then, of course, they must learn the etiquette of the client meeting. "My heart was pounding at the client meeting," said one intern. "The client was especially focused on the numbers and kept asking the associates, including me, how we did the research. It was a really intense, yet thrilling, experience."

LEK/Alcar believes in nurturing the professional aspect of the intern. Through participation in LEK/Alcar's intern-mentor program, client-development projects, and client meetings, interns learn the ropes of strategy consulting. Treating interns to lunch and helping them solve research problems, mentors probably make the most impact on interns' summer at LEK/Alcar. One intern, fondly recalling his relationship with his mentor, said: "He was both teacher and friend. I was able to turn to him not only when I needed help with Lotus or a difficult analysis but also when I needed advice about living in LA." Moreover, LEK/Alcar provides end-of-summer evaluations so that interns can get feedback on their overall performance. When all is said and done, the conscientious intern will become eminently prepared to enter the consulting, corporate, or business worlds.

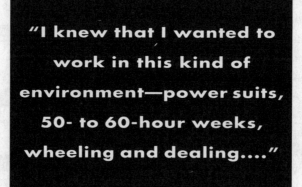

"I knew that I wanted to work in this kind of environment—power suits, 50- to 60-hour weeks, wheeling and dealing...."

All interns concur that the program requires a great deal of dedication—the workweeks are an average of sixty hours, with perhaps one weekend spent hard at work putting the finishing touches on a final report. But most interns agree that the weekly pay of approximately $500 to $600 is ample compensation. Los Angeles interns add that their offices, located above the Santa Monica Bank building on the corner of Wilshire and Bundy, are "an especially pleasant place to work." There's a spacious kitchen where interns and employees often eat lunch. Each employee, including interns, is provided with a desk and computer, as well as use of top-of-the-line laser printers, fax machines, and photocopying equipment.

During off-hours, interns rarely want for things to do. For one, they are invited to the annual summer shindig. "It was held at a posh restaurant, followed by a nighttime cruise on a yacht," recalled a Los Angeles intern. "I ate great food and danced the night away." Additionally, the company designates every Friday a Casual Day, on which interns dress informally (jeans, shorts, etc.). On Casual Day during the summer, the offices shut down at 3:00 PM, allowing interns to enjoy an early weekend. And the camaraderie that a small firm fosters—40 people in Los Angeles, 15 to 20 in Chicago, and 30 to 35 in Boston—carries over after work. One intern remembered: "I never had time to sleep. If I wasn't in the office, which was a rare event, I was working out at this great gym in Santa Monica and then going out with my officemates in Hollywood."

SELECTION

The program is open only to college seniors. Though LEK/Alcar does not limit its applicant pool to any specific majors or GPAs, it looks for people who have excelled in their classes—the majority of selected candidates have at least a 3.4 GPA. Analytic ability and computer competence are definitely a plus since interns spend much of the work day crunching numbers.

APPLICATION PROCEDURE

 The deadline is late February/early March. Though LEK/Alcar will consider applicants from all schools, it recruits heavily at about 15 colleges nationwide through campus newspaper advertisements and career-center bulletins. Applicants are required to send or fax a detailed resumé, a cover letter, and transcript (unofficial is sufficient) to the location nearest them (regardless of where they want to work) "c/o Recruiting Coordinator." Students who make it past the initial screening of resumés are interviewed in person either on campus or at the nearest LEK/Alcar office. Those who make the final round are usually flown into the offices for a full day of interviews. Insider's tip: Be prepared for questions that test analytical abilities; applicants have been asked to show, for example, how they would determine the number of checking accounts in the United States.

OVERVIEW

 Talented, strategically-minded students who participate in the LEK/Alcar internship will find a treasure trove complete with mentors, professional development, exposure to management consulting, and excellent potential for permanent employment (at least half of all interns receive LEK/Alcar permanent job offers). "Even if you don't return, you'll have great leverage in interviews with investment banks and consulting firms," reported an intern. "I knew that I wanted to work in this kind of environment—power suits, 50- to 60-hour weeks, wheeling and dealing. It rivals anything you'd experience on Wall Street."

FOR MORE INFORMATION . . .

- The LEK/Alcar Consulting Group
  12100 Wilshire Boulevard, Suite 1700
  Los Angeles, CA 90025
  (310) 442-6500
  (310) 207-4210 fax

- The LEK/Alcar Consulting Group
  101 Federal Street, 27th Floor
  Boston, MA 02110
  (617) 951-9500
  (617) 951-9392 fax

- The LEK/Alcar Consulting Group
  5215 Old Orchard Road, Suite 600
  Skokie, IL 60077-1035
  (708) 581-2200
  (708) 581-2201 fax

The rivet at the base of the fly is history, but a button front remains. Out of suspender buttons, cinch, and belt loops, only the last survives. Formerly they had one back pocket, now there are two. The red tab—once it was in all capital letters, now it's partially lowercase. The width has become gradually narrower.

They've changed over their 120-year history, but they're still Levi's 501 jeans. When German Levi Strauss came to California in 1853, he didn't plan on making pants. In fact, he didn't create the first copper-riveted jeans until 1873. It was then that he realized California's gold-seekers needed leggings that could withstand the rough surfaces in the mines. Soon "those pants of Levi's" were as hot as gold.

Dyed blue and assigned the lot number "501" in 1890 to distinguish them from his company's other denim products, Levi's 501 jeans are now an American icon. The company is run by Levi's great-great-grandnephew Robert Haas (whose family owns the Oakland A's) and produces yearly sales close to $6 billion. Privately owned, it makes 501 and other Levi's jeans, Dockers and Brittania clothing, men and women's sportswear, and youthwear.

DESCRIPTION

Since the late 1970s, Levi Strauss & Co. has employed college students in positions throughout the company. Jobs range from 20 to 40 hours per week, with the majority of interns (approximately two thirds, according to the coordinator) working full time; 40 percent are graduate students, usually M.B.A. candidates. Hourly pay is contingent upon year in school and experience. Although internship positions change every year, departments offering internships include: Merchandising, Treasury (i.e., Accounting), Operations, Design, Telemarketing, Claims Administration (for wrong or damaged shipments and overpayment claims), Retail Marketing (which runs the Levi's-owned jeans shops), Retail Relations, Consumer Affairs, LeviLink (called Information Resources at other companies), and Global Sourcing (coordinates purchase of fabrics). The company also runs a Summer Youth Program for high school students to hone their clerical skills and learn office procedures.

Levi Strauss & Co., known as LS & Co. to insiders, believes that interns will do a better job if they understand the history of the organization and the way in which it makes its jeans. Consequently, the company takes college and high school interns on a tour of its San Francisco plant on Valencia Street. Built in 1906 just after the great San Francisco earthquake, it's the oldest Levi's plant. "Huge sheets of denim sit in tall stacks on one side," described an intern. "In a matter of minutes, an electric saw cuts through each stack. And, then, as in an assembly line, the pieces are sewn and riveted, button flies and pockets put in place, and belt loops added, making about 60 jeans per stack." Off to the side of the plant is a museum featuring products, ads, and photos from the company's past. "The tour was definitely cool," said an intern. "In the factory, we saw how jeans are made, and in the museum we looked at old jeans, original patents, and letters written by Levi himself."

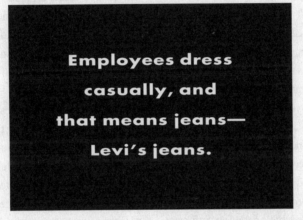

Employees dress casually, and that means jeans— Levi's jeans.

After orientation, interns tackle their assigned tasks. An intern in Consumer Affairs during the summer of 1990 first familiarized himself with the department's mission. "Our goal is twofold: to service consumers and to take what they tell us back to our quality-improvement and product-development people," he said. "Every year, our staff of about 25 product experts [receives] over 250,000 calls. People complain that a particular button keeps falling off or that they want a new feature put on the jeans but most just need the name of the nearest store that sells Levi's, Dockers, or Brittania jeans." He soon noticed that the database that keeps track of these calls could be organized more efficiently. "I came up with some new codes to categorize comments. Then I played around with the codes in order to determine consumer trends. [The new codes] made it easier later on when I helped write an LS & Co. 'Topline Report,' our name for the newsletter that goes to Bob Haas and which summarizes what customers are saying."

Since 1990, however, the Consumer Affairs department has tripled the number of reports it generates, keeping interns busier than ever. Now an employee in Consumer Affairs, the intern from 1990 explained what an intern in 1993 did. "Our intern this summer analyzed the possibility of installing an 800 number in Mexico so that our Mexican customers can call us with questions about products," he said. "She described the culture, figured out how we could subscribe to 800 service in Mexico, and tracked how the 800 numbers of companies like AT&T are faring down there."

An intern in Retail Relations worked on improving the company's compliance with retailers' requirements for packaging, labeling, and shipping. "Sometimes we weren't meeting our retailers' requests—the size of the box in which products should be shipped, the number of items that should be put in one box, or how the products are supposed to be tagged," he said. "For example, Spiegel catalog wants each individual unit put in a special plastic bag, a label indicating the Spiegel merchandise number, item number, color, and size, and all units packed solid size per carton [apparel jargon for 'one size only per box']." Gathering information on LS & Co.'s top 200 retail customers, he embarked on a mission to catalog all the requirements. "If we could meet requirements with minimal, if any, changes, fine; otherwise, we negotiated with the retailer for a different requirement."

But in order to ship the right quantities to retailers, LS & Co. must keep track of orders. Maintaining information systems that do that is the job of the LeviLink department, home to an intern or two every summer. A graduate student intern wrote a manual, teaching retailers how to use the company's orders-management systems. "They help reduce overstock and stockout [i.e., when a particular size is not in stock] by matching with sales figures the number of items placed into inventory." Studying how the systems work, she read through 25 old manuals, talked with the technical people who developed the computer programs, and interviewed users. "By the time I was finished," she said, "I had a mammoth, 75-page document."

Just like a pair of Levi's 501 jeans, the internship combines functionality with shrink-to-fit individuality. The company not only assigns projects that ultimately improve the way it does business but it also embraces what a LeviLink intern called "empowerment." She said: "LS & Co. is very big on allowing you to establish a vision and then do whatever you want to get there. For example, I thought that my department should teach sales reps about the stock-management system. I mentioned my idea, and the managers said do it, just like that. So I put a manual together from scratch." But one intern disagreed that the freedom was a good thing: "Coming up with great ideas is sometimes expected rather than encouraged—that can create tension, since most people are vying for permanent job offers."

Every week, interns meet with executives and managers to learn more about the various divisions within the company. CEO Bob Haas, the vice presidents of Women's Wear and Product Development, and the company historian usually attend. For many, the meetings are the highlight of the internship. One intern remembered: "It was interesting to hear how the speakers started out with the company and to get their perspective on the role of different divisions." Afterward, interns may schedule what's called an "informational interview" with one of the speakers in order to make a contact or ask for advice on employment.

The Levi's Plaza is made up of five red brick buildings—Levi Strauss, Stern, Saddleman, Koshland, and Ice House—parked on eight acres. The entire complex is affectionately known as "Levi's U." Poised along San Francisco Bay, the "campus" sits at the base of Telegraph Hill, on top of which stands historic Coit Tower, built in 1933 to commemorate the city's volunteer firefighters. The buildings surround a paved two-acre plaza known as "Hard Park" and a three-acre grassy area named "Soft Park." Equipped with benches, the parks are "a great place to eat lunch."

Inside the work areas, most windows afford lush views of the Bay, Coit Tower, or the business district's imposing Transamerica Building. Open spaces, conference rooms, lounges, and balconies encourage teamwork. Employees dress casually, that means jeans—Levi's jeans. "Because if you don't, you'll get teased," said an intern, "good-naturedly, of course." So interns who don't own a pair might be disappointed to hear that, unlike employees, they can't purchase new ones out of the employee discount catalog.

No piece on Levi's would be complete without a little history on the material used to make those famous jeans. The story goes like this: When the tent canvas Levi Strauss had brought to America ran out, he turned to a sturdy fabric from France called *serge de Nimes*. It had a rich, brown color and a canvaslike texture. But it was too complicated for Americans to pronounce *serge de Nimes*, so they conveniently shortened the name to "denim." Denim has been the lifeblood of the company, so LS & Co. is careful not to waste it. The scraps from its jean-making operation are now recycled to create all kinds of light blue paper products—letterhead, envelopes, memo pads, and business cards. An intern remarked: "It's neat to think that the material on which you're writing used to fit snugly around your bottom."

SELECTION

College juniors, seniors, and graduate students returning to school in the fall are eligible to apply. Graduating seniors enrolled in graduate school for the fall semester are also eligible. Students must have at least a 2.5 GPA. The most represented majors are merchandising, fashion design, marketing, accounting, and finance, but other majors are also welcome.

APPLICATION PROCEDURE

The deadline to apply was not established at the time this book went to press, but will be determined after January 1. At that time, a detailed list of job descriptions is mailed to college career centers throughout the country. If your center does not receive one, call the number below, after January 1st. Ask for the internship hotline, which explains each position's duties, pay, eligibility requirements, and code number. Students must send a resumé and a cover letter indicating area(s) of interest, describing qualifications, and specifying one of the codes listed in the job description. "It's in a student's best interests to make reference to only one or two codes," says the coordinator. "More than that shows a lack of focus." After separating applications by code, recruiters screen applicants by phone or in person (nonlocals may come visit at their own expense).

OVERVIEW

An internship with Levi Strauss & Co. is an opportunity to see how the venerable San Francisco company makes, markets, and distributes its omnipresent jeans. "It [also] teaches you that companies don't have to be uptight and suit-wearing," said an intern. And for those seeking employment after college, there's no better way to improve your chances of lending a permanent position with LS & Co. "With over 100 applications flowing in each day, it's clear that lots of people want to work here," said an employee. "But the connections you make as an intern give you a better chance of entering this little fraternity."

FOR MORE INFORMATION . . .

■ Levi Strauss & Co.
College Intern Program
P.O. Box 7215
San Francisco, CA 94120-6914
(415) 544-7000

THE LIBRARY OF CONGRESS

SELECTIVITY	🔍🔍🔍🔍
Approximate applicant pool: 300 Interns accepted: 18–20	

COMPENSATION	$ $ $
$1,200/month stipend	

QUALITY OF LIFE	↑ ↑ ↑
Hands–on contact with artifacts Twice–weekly tours; Slow computers	

LOCATION(S)
Washington, DC

FIELD
Library

DURATION
8–12 weeks Summer

PRE-REQS
College juniors and seniors, recent undergrads, grad students

DEADLINE(S)
March 1

Whose library is it anyway?

Is the Library of Congress exclusively allocated for members of Congress? You might think so, after all, when President John Adams created the library in 1800, he intended it to be a reference tool for congresspeople only. Today it is still used by legislators who make frequent visits to its Congressional Research Service (CRS) and Law Library.

But as taxpayers would have it, the Library of Congress is not the private domain of the Capitol Hill gang. Its 90-million-item collection of books, manuscripts, maps, photographs, and films is open to anyone 18 and older who is pursuing serious research. Those who can't make it to the national library may still access its collections by requesting an interlibrary loan, purchasing copies through the mail, or writing to the reference divisions.

DESCRIPTION

The Library of Congress started its Junior Fellows Program in the summer of 1991. Generously funded by Mrs. Jefferson Patterson, a 1939 CBS News broadcaster and member of the James Madison Council (the library's advisory body), the program is designed to introduce students to the art of librarianship. Composed of an equal number of undergraduates and graduate students, the intern class is divided among the following divisions: Geography and Map, Manuscript, Music, Prints and Photographs, Rare Book and Special Collections, African and Middle Eastern, Asian, European, Hispanic, Serial and Government Publications, and Motion Picture, Broadcasting, and Recorded Sound.

Students work within these divisions to meet "arrearage" reduction goals; arrearage is a library-specific term that refers to the library's piles of uncataloged works stored in warehouses throughout Washington, D.C. Each intern's work is similar to an entry-level library employee's—they prepare material for display presentation or for researchers' use. Accordingly, past projects have seen interns catalog American companies' logos, review Chinese microfilms, arrange cartoon maps, process the Copland music collection, tag the NAACP's historical photographs, and organize rare Arabic imprints.

The Prints and Photographs division, housing over 15 million works, recently employed an intern to help process a collection of 2,000 Civil War drawings. "Two catalogers and a curator had already done most of the work, except for some photos by an artist named Alfred Waud. During the war, Waud had followed the Army of the Potomac, a predominantly African-American unit on the Union side. A picture of the soldiers running into battle at St. Petersburg is one of his most famous," she said. Referring to a special thesaurus of visual art terms used by the Library, she cataloged the photos by subject heading. "I looked carefully at each picture before listing it under such categories as 'African-Americans,' 'Battle,' 'Union,' and 'War' in the library's computerized subject databases. Now these [heretofore unavailable] works can be accessed by researchers."

> "If for no other reason, work at the Library of Congress to see and touch some of the world's greatest treasures."

In the summer of 1992, nearly 50 boxes, "some partially organized, others in chaos," sat in a room at the Rare Books and Special Collections division. They contained the personal papers of 20th century typographer Bruce Rogers. An intern with an interest in printing was charged with archiving them. "In order to come up with subjects for the cataloging, I had to understand [Rogers'] life in great detail. I spent most of the summer reading everything in the boxes. I also checked to see what else the library has on the subject to get a good overview of other Rogers' cataloging schemes. Meanwhile, I numbered and described the papers, organizing them in a word-processing file for easy access by researchers."

The arrearage reduction projects often require interns to search the institution's many databases. To access the databases, they must use the institution's central workstation. "About 15 years ago, this was the most technologically advanced library in the world," said an intern. "But the library lagged in modernizing during the fast-moving computer age. The result is that there are so many commands and files that it makes our searches at times slow and torturous."

Another intern explained that the problem was compounded by frequent computer breakdowns. "Sometimes we'd sit around for one to two hours waiting for the computer to come back on." Fortunately, the library is currently upgrading its systems, installing faster disk drives and larger mainframes.

Originally housed in the U.S. Capitol, the Library of Congress now comprises three buildings on the corner of Independence Avenue and Second Street SE. These facilities are named after John Adams (who signed the bill establishing the library), James Madison ("the Father of the Constitution"), and Thomas Jefferson, who donated his private stash of nearly 6,500 books to the library in 1814, thereby making a national library possible. Underneath the library are extensive catacombs leading to the subway and congressional buildings; access is restricted to those with passes—and interns get them!

The Jefferson Building is the oldest of the three buildings and its circular Main Reading Room serves as the central point of access to the library's collections. One-hundred-sixty feet tall at its dome's apex, the Main Reading Room is a mighty display of soaring marble columns, stained-glass windows, and bronze statutes of Moses, Beethoven, Shakespeare, and Newton. Forming three concentric circles around a reference area at the center, hundreds of desks allow readers to access computer databases and 70,000 reference works.

Interns start the summer by touring the Jefferson Building and listening to a discussion on the library's history in the Main Reading Room. After that, tours of divisions are offered approximately twice a week and, by summer's end, interns will have toured all 11 divisions. At the Manuscript division, they see Jefferson's rough draft of the Declaration of Independence, Washington's first inaugural address, and Alexander Graham Bell's first drawing of the telephone. In Rare Books, interns peruse the American classics: "We thumbed through *Leaves of Grass* and *On Walden Pond*, both signed by Whitman and Thoreau as gifts to each other."

On their twice-weekly tours, interns become familiar with other parts of the library, such as the Copyright Office and the Landover, MD, storage facility ("acres and acres of books, paintings, maps, and piles of dust"). Interns also learn about the up-and-coming technologies to improve library storage and access. At the library's National Demonstration Lab, interns hear a talk on the "virtual reality" project, designed to allow a person to—via computer—"walk" into the stacks, look through materials, and review items of interest. They see the "American Memory," a Library of Congress pilot project seeking to put American images on optical disks. They are briefed on microfilming and preservation techniques by the Preservation directorate, who oversees the microfilming of 20,000 fragile books each year. They listen to curators explain how the more unusual exhibits are prepared. In the summer of 1993, interns visited an exhibit of the Dead Sea Scrolls, the oldest surviving biblical manuscripts.

The atmosphere engenders a love for exploration. Some interns "become giddy as schoolchildren" when they make an interesting find. "These moments are treasured," explained an intern, "because our job is sometimes tedious." Interns compensate for monotonous work by poking around on their own time, since supervisors are rarely willing to allow an intern to pursue personal curiosities when there is so much cataloging to be done. "I stayed an extra one or two hours every day," said one bookworm. "I figured I might not have this chance again, so I went for it." Another intern went so far as to volunteer some Saturday hours at the reference desk: "I wanted to learn how some of the best reference librarians in the world come up with all that information." In addition, interns may borrow books on their library card; only library employees, congresspeople, and congressional staffs are eligible for one.

SELECTION

College juniors and seniors, recent graduates, and graduate students are eligible for the program. While students of any major may apply, the majority of interns study history, American studies, languages, geography, and cartography. As for GPA, the coordinator says: "We put less emphasis on grades and more emphasis on coursework. . . . We want people who are excited about the divisions to which they apply and about coming to the library."

APPLICATION PROCEDURE

The deadline is March 1. Send a cover letter (highlighting your relevant background, the division or subject area of interest, and foreign language ability, if necessary for the position), either the Application for Federal Employment (SF 171) or a resumé (including Social Security number, address, telephone number, date of birth, and citizenship), a letter of recommendation from a professor or an employer, and an official transcript. "We emphasize the letter of recommendation when selecting students, but we also want to see a well-written, enthusiastic cover letter," said the coordinator. After the coordinator checks applications for completeness, the department managers match the best candidates to appropriate projects. Final selections are determined after phone interviews.

OVERVIEW

The world's largest library, the Library of Congress gives students with a penchant for history a chance to learn archiving techniques in the company of rare manuscripts, old pictures, and antique maps. But in the process, interns must put up with slow computers and a huge backlog of uncataloged work. But persevering interns help make special collections publicly available for the first time—they may even publish articles on their work in journals like the Library of Congress' *Information Bulletin* and the American Library Association's *Meridian*. By the time they make presentations of their projects to the Librarian of Congress, most have gained a good sense of what librarianship is all about. Concluded an intern: "If for no other reason, work at the Library of Congress to see and touch some of the world's greatest treasures."

FOR MORE INFORMATION . . .

■   The Library of Congress
Junior Fellows Program Coordinator
Collections Services
LM642
101 Indepedence Avenue
Washington, DC 20540-4000
(202) 707-5325

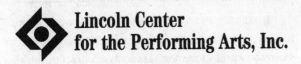

Lincoln Center for the Performing Arts, Inc.

Who celebrated a birthday with 25 army anti-aircraft lights, 18 trumpeters, and a chorus of 200 students singing Handel's "Hallelujah Chorus"? Was it the British royal family, the sultan of Brunei, or King Fahd of Saudi Arabia? Think again. It was Lincoln Center for the Performing Arts, in celebration of its 25th anniversary.

Few organizations could get away with staging such a spectacle of self-congratulation. But Lincoln Center is no run-of-the-mill institution. It is arguably the world's leading performing-arts center, home to the New York State Theater, Avery Fisher Hall, the Metropolitan Opera House, the Beaumont Theater, and the Juilliard School.

DESCRIPTION

 In 1968, Lincoln Center, Inc., created an internship program to provide hands-on training in arts administration. A nonprofit organization, Lincoln Center secured grants from the Ittleson Foundation and the Edward John Noble Foundation to fund a program offering graduate students high-level arts-management experience.

New interns are often surprised to learn that no pre-arranged project awaits their arrival at Lincoln Center. Instead, they spend their first day interviewing with key staff members, with whom they develop a few projects meeting both the needs of the organization and the interests of the intern. Emphasis is placed on creating projects that will give interns broad exposure to a range of departments, including Programming, Marketing, Finance, Operations, Planning and Development, and Education.

One intern worked on developing strategies to promote Lincoln Center's 18 month Mozart Bicentennial celebration. She put together a proposal persuading upscale retailers to publicize the Mozart Bicentennial in their

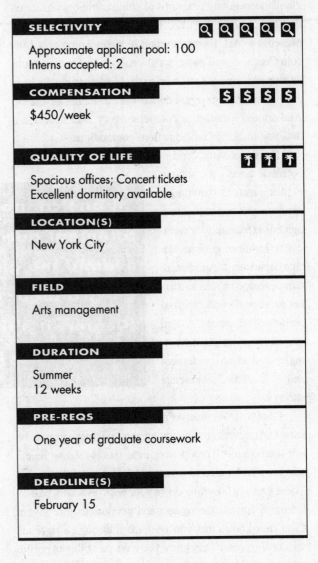

SELECTIVITY	
Approximate applicant pool: 100 Interns accepted: 2	🔍🔍🔍🔍🔍

COMPENSATION	
$450/week	$ $ $ $

QUALITY OF LIFE	
Spacious offices; Concert tickets Excellent dormitory available	🌴🌴🌴

LOCATION(S)
New York City

FIELD
Arts management

DURATION
Summer 12 weeks

PRE-REQS
One year of graduate coursework

DEADLINE(S)
February 15

stores. "It was exciting," she reported. "I went around New York soliciting support for the Bicentennial . . . talk[ing] with Godiva about making a special Bicentennial chocolate treat . . . contact[ing] Ben & Jerry's about selling a Mozart Bicentennial flavor in their New York retail stores . . . even ask[ing] the people at Rockefeller Center to play half an hour of Mozart each day at the skating rink."

Many projects focus on helping Lincoln Center in its fund-raising responsibilities. One intern helped develop a program of planned giving, whereby donors give money over time rather than straight out. "After spending weeks analyzing the planned-giving programs of comparable organizations like the New York Public Library and the Metropolitan Museum of Art, I wrote a report recommending how Lincoln Center should construct its program." Another intern examined reams of fund-raising data to determine the benefits of cultivating current donors over soliciting new ones. And another summer, a computer-savvy intern created a database tracking donations from corporations.

Promotions and fund-raising are only two of several potential areas of analysis. Figuring costs and equipment requirements, an intern investigated the feasibility of creating an in-house graphics design department. Another intern developed a plan to market the center's underutilized park-and-lock garage. A third project found an intern creating a system to implement and evaluate audience surveys.

> **If one cannot find entertainment during a summer amid the glamour and grandeur of Lincoln Center, it's time to throw in the towel.**

Although they meet periodically with the intern coordinator and relevant administrators, interns stress a need to be self-motivated. "There's very little spoon-feeding here," said one. "You receive your assignment and get to work. There's no one breathing down your neck on a daily basis." Interns appreciate the respect and freedom they're given: "The staff knows that you've made it through a rigorous selection process. They know you have the ability to get the job done." Moreover, there's virtually no busywork expected of interns; "menial tasks, like stuffing envelopes, are off-limits," said the coordinator. The closest an intern came to busywork was spending a few days conducting phone interviews of current subscribers.

The program's faith in its interns is evident in the seriousness with which senior staff evaluates completed projects. At the end of the summer, interns submit their reports to management. And management listens. According to the coordinator, "There's a great track record of implementing interns' proposals . . . More often than not, interns' work has a meaningful impact on Lincoln Center's operations." Indeed, the aforementioned garage promotion,

for example, is currently in use. "They don't just put interns through the motions here. Senior staff examines and often implements interns' recommendations," said an intern.

In addition to projects, interns spend a week working behind the scenes at the JVC Jazz Festival, considered by many the world's foremost jazz festival, attracting the likes of the late Miles Davis, Kenny G and Santana. "Basically, we shadowed the stage manager, watching him interact with everyone from artists to ushers," said an intern. They attend preproduction meetings and work at the event itself, attending to artists and the press. During the performance, interns help out any way they can. One was asked to hold the stage door open for Kenny G, who likes to scurry into the audience during his saxophone solos. Another had the opportunity to meet Ella Fitzgerald; "it was a big thrill for me," the intern said. Interns agree that helping out at the festival "gives you a good sense of what it's like to run a concert hall."

If one cannot find entertainment during a summer amid the glamour and grandeur of Lincoln Center, it's time to throw in the towel. Interns have dibs on passes to any performance produced by Lincoln Center, Inc. including such summertime shows as "Mostly Mozart," "Serious Fun!" and "Lincoln Center Out-of-Doors." Contrary to what many think before beginning the internship, free tickets aren't readily available for Lincoln Center's constituent organizations, such as the New York City Ballet and the Metropolitan Opera. Although they share the same grounds, the constituents are independent of Lincoln Center, Inc., and cooperation between the two is, according to an intern, "much less than you'd think." It's no big deal, most of the constituents don't perform during the summer, anyway.

Lucky for interns, the program recently vacated its former "cramped" quarters and relocated to a spacious office on the ninth floor of Lincoln Center's new Rose Building. Despite the Center's nonprofit status, the office has a distinctly modern "for-profit" look; it could be a "law firm or ad agency," said an intern. Interns work at carrels no different than the ones used by staff. Each comes equipped with computers and a full assortment of supplies.

For those wishing to avoid the hassles of searching for a sublet, dormitory housing is available on the upper floors of the Rose Building. Used primarily by students from Juilliard and the School of American Ballet, the dormitory floors are divided into suites, each with two singles, two doubles, and a common area. Rent is approximately $500 per month. One floor holds a common kitchen, laundry room, and recreation room. Alas, it's a dormitory, but as the coordinator puts it, "it's one of the best in America," complete with bay windows and soaring city views. *Interior Design* magazine likes it, too; the dorm received a full-page write up in a recent issue.

Interns offer a few parting words of wisdom. One stressed the fact that the substance of an intern's work depends almost entirely on the project to which he or she is assigned. "Before applying," he warned, "think long and hard about the type of project you'd like to undertake. If you're selected, you'll want to convey your interests clearly to senior management. Once you're given a project, you'll work on it for several weeks, often with little supervision." Another explained that because the internship lasts only three months, interns are occasionally unable to finish their projects. He said, "I was frustrated. By the time I really learned the ins and outs of my project, my tenure drew to a close. I needed more time to see my work to fruition."

SELECTION

The program is open only to students who've had at least one year of graduate coursework. Although recent years have seen a majority of M.B.A.s in the internship, Lincoln Center is also interested in selecting other types of grad students, such as M.A.s and M.F.A.s. While arts experience is not required, the intern coordinator would like to see a "demonstrated interest in and commitment to a career in arts management," as well as "strong verbal and analytical skills."

APPLICATION PROCEDURE

Applications are due February 15. Submit a resumé and a cover letter (describing qualifications and career goals). After making a preliminary screening, the coordinator invites 15 finalists to Lincoln Center for interviews. While many finalists find that interviews coincide with spring break, those who cannot arrange or afford a trip to New York may be able to set up a phone interview. Finalists must also submit two letters of recommendation. Applicants are notified in early April.

OVERVIEW

As an intern said, "Everyone and his brother knows Lincoln Center." It's true, the Lincoln Center internship is valuable for prestige alone. But a magnetic name is only the beginning. The program carefully chooses two interns and works with them to design challenging, real-world projects. So admired is the program that the Noble Foundation considers it a model for other arts internships the foundation is funding across the country. Alumni go on to illustrious careers, some in arts management, others not. Bill Wingate, for one, interned in the late sixties, and recently served as executive director of the New York City Ballet.

FOR MORE INFORMATION . . .

■ Lincoln Center for the Performing Arts, Inc.
Internship Coordinator
70 Lincoln Center Plaza
New York, NY 10023-6583
(212) 875-5000

Liz claiborne

SELECTIVITY	
Approximate applicant pool: 100–300 Interns accepted: 20–25	🔍 🔍 🔍

COMPENSATION	
$7/hour	💲 💲

QUALITY OF LIFE	
Nurturing environment; Garment district 35% clothing discount	🌴 🌴 🌴

LOCATION(S)
New York, NY North Bergen, NJ

FIELD
Apparel and fashion accessories

DURATION
3–6 months; Summer, Fall, Winter/Spring Part time available

PRE-REQS:
Undergrads

DEADLINE(S)
Summer .... May 15   Fall .... July 31 Winter/Spring ......Nov. 15

Everyone should wear the pants in your family.

So reads the caption in a recent Liz Claiborne, Inc. advertisement. A business woman, dressed in a jacket and pants, stands in an office, working out her next deal. The ad exemplifies the clothing giant's philosophy, stated succinctly in the notes for the 1991 spring fashion show: "Simple, straightforward fashion that's designed for women who have more important things to think about than what to wear."

But the ad's allusion to authority could just as well refer to cofounder Elisabeth Claiborne Ortenberg herself. When the company debuted in 1976, she "wore the pants," taking responsibility for all aspects of the business. She approved all clothing designs, and often enhanced them. She even designed the distinctive triangle logo.

Reaction was fast and favorable. Deemed "the envy of Seventh Avenue," "Liz" (as the company and its founder are known in the fashion world) made the Fortune 500 list only ten years after its founding. Only one other company founded by a woman has even made that honor roll. Its stock, which went public in 1981, increased in value nearly 60-fold by 1991. The fashion industry's 1980 Entrepreneurial Woman of the Year is no longer running the company, but it's doing fine without her: Liz Claiborne, Inc. is now one of the largest marketers of women's apparel in the world, selling over $2 billion worth of products every year from jewelry to dresses and menswear.

DESCRIPTION

Liz Claiborne's New York office offers internships in the Creative Resources, Marketing, Textile Design, Apparel Design, Merchandising, and Sales groups of the company's clothing divisions. Liz Claiborne's New Jersey headquarters places interns in administrative departments, such as Finance, Human Resources, Management Information Systems, and Production. Regardless of location or position, interns are assigned projects and participate in staff meetings. "But they don't sell clothes, make clothes, or handle accounts," said the coordinator. "As members of teams, though, they help make decisions."

One intern was assigned to the Textile Design group of the Elisabeth Division, which offers clothing lines for larger women. One of

BUSYWORK METER
LOW MEDIUM HIGH
OLDMAN & HAMADEH

her responsibilities was to keep track of the myriad fabrics available from suppliers. "I logged the fabrics into the books—about 80 fabrics per season; there are six seasons per year in the fashion industry." The large number of sample materials prompted her to establish a small fabric library: "I cordoned off a section of the wall and put the materials into categories like wools, cottons, etc.; it made fabrics easier to find later." After the company chooses one of these fabrics to use in clothing, she learned, it establishes a "hand standard." "Because the same kind of fabric can have different feels, the hand standard indicates the precise texture," explained the intern. "I sent the standard to the mill as a reference to maintain quality control." Acting as a liaison between Textile and Production, she also sent fabrics to employees involved in making sample products. "A particular fabric might come back as a dress or a blouse, depending on what the designer envisions."

Another student interned in the Creative Resources department. Besides helping make company posters, shopping bags, boxes, and stationery, he worked on the packaging for Liz Claiborne's new fragrance *Vivid*. "I assisted the art directors in putting together a comp of what the final product—bottle and box—would look like," he said. "The comp is a prototype used in photo shoots and market tests before the manufacturer starts making the product." His role also required that he attend marketing strategy meetings for the new product. "But I made no comments—only observations," he said.

On to the meat and potatoes of fashion—clothing design. One Apparel Design intern in the Collection division's knitwear group learned how sweaters are made. "The head designer was overwhelmed with work and sometimes sent design projects my way," she said. Taking on the role of assistant designer, she occasionally produced a layout for a sweater idea—the shape, pattern, and colors. "I first made three graphs, one for the front, one for the back, and one for the sleeves; the graphs indicate exactly where each stitch should go," she said. "I then wrote a preliminary spec sheet—neck size, width, arm length, and a sketch of what the sweater should eventually look like. Finally, I made two-dimensional, life-size, color versions of the sweater and 'sourced the trim' [i.e., found suppliers of buttons, ribbons, and any other accessories on the sweater]." After prototypes were made, the group sat down to decide which sweaters the company should include in its line: "My role involved displaying models on the wall and taking notes." In between layout assignments, she transcribed messages sent by the Hong Kong production facilities via LINCS (Liz Claiborne International Network Computer System). She also worked with tear sheets (magazine pages ripped out by the head designer). "Sometimes, I combined aspects from several of the tops or blouses pictured and created a half-dozen or so designs to show the designer."

> One intern produced a layout for a sweater idea — the shape, pattern, and colors.

New York interns work in two high-rises within a block of each other. The buildings are located in New York's famous garment district—several square blocks of clothing companies, fabric stores, and design shops. Most of Liz Claiborne's offices are "white-walled and corporate-looking," described an intern, "except for the butcher-block-like counters made out of hardwood." While the majority of interns sit behind desks outfitted with phones and computers, Apparel Design interns sit at "illuminated tables to facilitate drawing." To liven up the place, employees decorate the corridors and work spaces: "You can't walk five feet without seeing an array of magazine tear sheets, fabrics, and plants."

Perks are minimal. Interns aren't eligible for company benefits, and exposure to managers is light. However, interns do receive a 35 percent employee discount at the New Jersey outlet store, which sells inventory from past seasons. Midsemester, they convene to hear midlevel managers describe management's role in the company. At the end of the internship, an exit interview screens interns for permanent employment, about 30 percent receive full-time offers.

SELECTION

College freshmen, sophomores, juniors, and seniors are eligible for Liz Claiborne internships. All positions require computer skills, except for Design (where sketching ability is mandatory). The internship is relatively competitive, especially for the summer. "The quality of writing in the cover letter, the level of participation in extracurricular activities, and work experience in the fashion industry or an office definitely give a candidate an edge," said the coordinator.

APPLICATION PROCEDURE

The deadline for submission of materials is May 15 for the summer term, July 31 for the fall term, and November 15 for the winter/ spring term. Applicants must send in a resumé and a cover letter indicating their area of interest. Students must prove that they are part of a school program providing course credits for the work experience. Top candidates are asked to travel to New York for on-site interviews. Those who cannot arrange a trip to New York will be interviewed by phone. Students interested in working at the New Jersey office must send materials directly to One Claiborne Avenue, North Bergen, NJ 07047. "The creative positions are in New York," the New Jersey coordinator conceded, "but as a large clothing company, we still need administrative people."

OVERVIEW

"You can't love a good bag enough," states a Liz Claiborne ad for handbags. In like fashion, Claiborne employees care for their interns a great deal. From celebrating intern birthdays to providing interns with well-tailored projects, employees go out of their way, as one intern put it, "to make sure students gain connections and experience—the two most valuable commodities in the fashion industry."

FOR MORE INFORMATION . . .

■ Liz Claiborne, Inc.
Internship Coordinator
1441 Broadway
New York, NY 10018
(212) 354-4900

Los Angeles Times

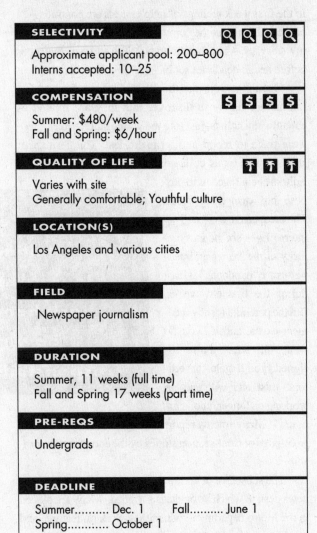

SELECTIVITY

Approximate applicant pool: 200–800
Interns accepted: 10–25

COMPENSATION

Summer: $480/week
Fall and Spring: $6/hour

QUALITY OF LIFE

Varies with site
Generally comfortable; Youthful culture

LOCATION(S)

Los Angeles and various cities

FIELD

Newspaper journalism

DURATION

Summer, 11 weeks (full time)
Fall and Spring 17 weeks (part time)

PRE-REQS

Undergrads

DEADLINE

Summer.......... Dec. 1   Fall.......... June 1
Spring............ October 1

The *Times* . . .

It brings to mind images of subways, urban grit, Mario Cuomo, Wall Street, the World Trade Center, and Howard Beach.

Hold it, hold it!

It's the West Coast—try beaches, traffic, smog, Pete Wilson, sunshine, riots, and Hollywood.

The New York Times and the *Los Angeles Times* may share a nickname, but that's where the similarities end. Whereas the former has long been internationally regarded as a leader of sophisticated journalism, the *Los Angeles Times* is an up-and-coming national newspaper, admired as much for expert journalism as it is for meticulous local coverage. Befitting a newspaper from glossy Southern California, it makes innovative use of color photography and graphics. Indeed, *Time* magazine has praised the publication for its "packages of reporting, graphics, and presentation" that offer "dramatic evidence" of how newspapers can surpass television coverage. With the largest editorial department of any newspaper in the country, the *LA Times* has won 19 Pulitzer Prizes, nine of which they've received since 1980. No wonder it was named the "Newspaper to Watch for the '90s" in the *Washington Journalism Review's* sixth annual "Best in the Business" reader poll.

DESCRIPTION

Among top newspaper internships, the *Los Angeles Times* is unique in that it disperses its interns among a wide variety of cities. Whereas most newspapers place a majority of interns in its home office, the *LA Times* retains just a few for its Los Angeles headquarters and dispatches the rest to nine satellite locations in California. Positions are available in news bureaus producing daily editions (Los Angeles, Orange County, San Diego, San Fernando Valley, and Ventura) and in suburban annexes producing semi-weekly sections (San Gabriel Valley, South Bay, Southeast, and Westside). The newspaper also hires one intern for its bureau in Washington, D.C. Most participants work as business, news, or sports reporters, although positions are also available in photojournalism, and, during summers, in copyediting and infographics (diagrams, maps, charts, etc.).

After a day of orientation, the *LA Times* internship gets under way. But, unlike other newspaper internships, which typically have participants undergo a baptism by fire, interns at the LA Times often find their workload builds gradually. In the first week feelings of helplessness are common—"I couldn't figure out the computer system or who to submit my story to"—but there's ample time to learn the ropes before hectic deadlines set in.

Once they adjust to the job and write a few stories, interns are happy to discover that they are treated as capable journalists, just like the young staffwriters. "We were there to report and write stories. The permanent staff viewed us as colleagues, not inferior underlings. Editors encouraged us to propose our own story ideas. They respected us," said an intern. Even so, the vast majority of the stories an intern writes are "handouts," at least during the first few weeks. But the potential for advancement exists, and if "you do well with what you're assigned, you'll gain the editors' trust and will end up working on longer, juicier articles." Many interns report having written five or more front-page or front-section stories by the end of their internship.

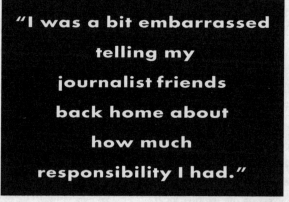

"I was a bit embarrassed telling my journalist friends back home about how much responsibility I had."

The substance of an intern's reporting depends on the news desk to which he or she is assigned. Many are placed in the Metro department, where they work on features and breaking news. Focusing primarily on crime stories, one Metro intern wrote an article about how juvenile felons convicted in Orange County have been escaping from custody at a rate of one per day; he also reported on the prevalence of home-invasion robberies whereby gangs target newly arrived immigrants who keep their valuables at home. Another Metro intern covered "softer" news, ferreting out human-interest stories about residents of the Los Angeles area. The majority of her stories had a uniquely Californian bent, such as a profile of five women who had carpooled together for 20 years, coverage of the 40th anniversary of the country's oldest surfing club, and an account of the awards ceremony for a man who had made a beach rescue 60 years ago.

Working for the Business section, an intern wrote articles on financial issues and local business news. Al-

though he had "zero business background going into the internship" and "didn't even know what a quarterly report was," he learned by doing and became comfortable writing on a wide range of business topics, from banking to state taxes and the stock market. He was also encouraged to write on more consumer-oriented topics. One week, for example, found him writing on how the unusually cool summertime weather was adversely affecting beachside businesses.

As interns wind up working in one of nine different locations, it's difficult to make definitive assessments on workplace environment. Architecture runs the gamut, from the downtown headquarters, likened to "an insurance office," to the San Fernando bureau, resembling "a white spaceship caught in the middle of an orange grove." Generally speaking, interns find their offices comfortable but not cushy. They sit in three-desk "pods," which resemble a "pie cut in three pieces." Said one intern: "It's an efficient setup. The desks are clumped together around computer terminals and interns work together in clusters." Contrary to Hollywood's depiction of the typical disheveled newsroom, the LA Times fosters a newsroom environment free from gratuitous shouting and turmoil. "A controlled calm" is how one intern described it. A few locations have cafeterias where the food is said to be "palatable, nothing more." The Orange County bureau boasts a decent gym (treadmills, StairMasters, etc.), and employees there often play hoops on a court adjacent to the parking lot.

While the LA Times offers no weekly seminar series, it does arrange a few special luncheons. Interns usually get the chance to dine with the publisher, David Laventhol, and the managing editor, Shelby Coffey. They also receive a tour of the Los Angeles printing plant, which is staffed almost entirely by robots: "It seemed right out of the Jetsons."

Students enjoy working at the LA Times because of its "young" and "dynamic" workforce. Said an intern: "The image of the Times as an impersonal corporate giant is just not true. People there are young and energetic. Staff members, many of whom were only a few years older than us, would invite us to hang out with them after work." But, interns warn, "not all bureaus are created equal," and experiences vary depending on where one works. The headquarters in downtown Los Angeles is the nerve center of the organization, but because dozens of staff reporters work there, interns are not always afforded as many reporting opportunities as those in other bureaus. The Orange County bureau garners the highest ratings among interns, who deem it "very exciting because it competes with the *Orange County Register*." Said an intern, "The Orange County market is one of the most competitive in the country. Every day, [the *LA Times* and the *Register*] cover many of the same stories. A 'beat-the-*Register*' ethic pervades the bureau and makes for a stimulating environment." Other locations, particularly the suburban annexes, which publish only twice a week, are slower paced (read: no daily deadlines) and thus less rewarding to those desiring an intense newspaper experience.

Interns offer a few pieces of criticism. One thought that before the internship begins, the editors should emphasize how much responsibility interns are afforded. "I thought they'd have me covering bake sales," he said. "Had I known the potential waiting for me, I would have begun the job with greater determination and seriousness." Another lamented the lack of a mentor system: "I would have liked to have had a mentor with whom I could consult, someone to meet with on a formal basis, if only for ten minutes a week." Other were frustrated with the newspaper's decentralized organization. "With ten bureaus, the *LA Times* is really spread out. You felt like you were only seeing a piece of the pie, not the whole dessert."

SELECTION

 To intern at the *LA Times*, one must be in college or have graduated within six months before the internship starts. No hard and fast prerequisites exist, but the intern coordinator says that successful applicants usually have had previous journalism experience at internships or college newspapers. Because Los Angeles is a city of automobiles, interns should also have access to a car in good working condition. In the opinion of past interns, those who thrive at the *LA Times* have a mixture of aggressiveness, ("the ability to vigorously go after a story and bust your butt to do it right,") and diplomacy, ("because you aren't a permanent

staff member and you'll get a lot of constructive criticism.") A "flair for writing" and an "insatiable curiosity" help, too.

APPLICATION PROCEDURE

 Students interested in the summer internship must submit their materials by December 1; fall, by June 1; and spring, by October 1. All applicants must submit a cover letter (noting which bureaus they prefer and any editorial interests, e.g., sports writing), a resumé, and three telephone references. Those interested in reporting should include up to ten newspaper clips photocopied onto sheets of 8-1/2"x 11" paper. Photographers should send in 20 to 40 slides, prints, or photocopied clips with caption information; they should also include a list of their equipment. Graphic artists need to include 10 to 20 work samples. Applicants interested in copyediting should submit up to ten newspaper clips and up to 20 headlines, both of which must be photocopied onto 8-1/2"x11" paper. A few general rules for all applicants:Clips may be reduced; use of staples, paper clips, or folders is discouraged; and the *LA Times* cannot guarantee the return of original work. Interviews are conducted in person or over the phone.

OVERVIEW

 Although it lacks the legendary prestige of a *Washington Post* or *Wall Street Jounal*, the *Los Angeles Times* offers interns a top flight indoctrination into the world of big-time reporting. Integrated fully into life at the paper, interns are given free rein to perform as capable reporters. "I was a bit embarrassed telling my journalist friends back home about how much responsibility I had," said an intern. If a major-league journalism internship in the City of Angels sounds alluring, then the *LA Times* deserves further investigation.

FOR MORE INFORMATION . . .

■ Los Angeles Times
   Editorial Internships
   Times Mirror Square
   Los Angeles, CA 90053
   (800) 283-NEWS, Ext. 74487

SELECTIVITY

Approximate applicant pool: 400–600
Interns accepted: 15–20

COMPENSATION

Summer: $4.25/hour
Fall and Spring: None

QUALITY OF LIFE

Skywalker Ranch; Bodybay gym
Seminars; Parties

LOCATION(S)

San Rafael and Nicasio, CA

FIELD

Entertainment

DURATION

9–12 weeks
Summer, Fall, Spring

PRE-REQS

College juniors and seniors
Grad Students

DEADLINE(S)

Summer .... March 30   Fall .... July 30
Spring .... November 15

Special effects in movies have come a long way since those old Buck Rogers films, the ones that show hobby-shop spaceships, pulled by supposedly invisible wire, hurtling by. The *Star Wars* trilogy revolutionized special effects, making space travel and space battle seem breathtakingly believable. *Terminator 2* upped the ante, stretching technology to startling limits; who can forget the scene where the T-1000, played by actor Robert Patrick, sustains a body-splitting Samurai blow, only to regenerate his alloy body by zipping himself together like a parka. Even a recent Miller Lite commercial displayed stunning visual effects, showing a couple as they transform magically from disco dancers to punk-rockers and then to futuristic citizens.

Today, the company responsible for all of these technical triumphs, Lucasfilm, has diversified to become one of the world's most successful entertainment companies. Founded by George Lucas, the mastermind writer and director of *Star Wars*, Lucasfilm operates a variety of cutting-edge divisions. Industrial Light and Magic, for example, is the acknowledged visual effects leader in motion pictures and commercials, creating effects for such films as *Raiders of the Lost Ark*, *E.T.*, *Cocoon*, *Who Framed Roger Rabbit?*, and *The Rocketeer*. Skywalker Sound, the postproduction division, offers a full range of sound recording, editing, and mixing services for film, video, and theme park attractions. It also includes a state-of-the-art recording studio that has attracted the likes of Mick Jagger, Linda Ronstadt, Bobbie McFerrin, and the Grateful Dead. Lucasfilm also forges new frontiers in interactive game software, educational multimedia products, and audio systems.

DESCRIPTION

A rich diversity of positions is available at Lucasfilm. Students interested in film and special effects can work in the following departments: Editorial/Visual Effects Production, Commercials, Model Making, Computer Graphics, and Art. Business-minded interns can work in Marketing, Publicity, Finance/Accounting, Merchandising/Licensing, and Human

Resources. Other departments in which students have interned include Learning, Games Art, Design, THX - Theater Operations Group, Research, and Fitness Facility. The departments that take interns vary from session to session, so it's safe to assume that not all of these positions are offered during any one session.

The work an intern performs depends entirely on the department in which he or she works. A Publicity intern, for example, worked primarily for "The Young Indiana Jones Chronicles," a weekly television show produced by Lucasfilm. To boost ratings for the show, she identified and sent press releases to special-interest groups who might be interested in a particular episode, contacting, for example, African-American groups before the episode in which young Indiana Jones travels to Africa; she also sent videotapes of the show to opinion makers such as Hillary Rodham Clinton and Katharine Hepburn. Her other responsibilities ran the gamut, from gofering on the set of a documentary about George Lucas to translating Spanish phrases for Lucas in preparation for a promo he was filming.

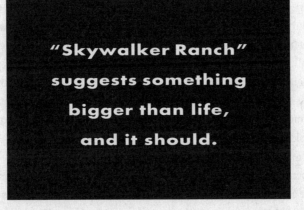

"Skywalker Ranch" suggests something bigger than life, and it should.

An intern in Marketing focused on tracking the sales of interactive games software. For bestselling games like *Indiana Jones and the Fate of Atlantis* and *The Secret of Monkey Island*, she tallied registration cards, conducted phone surveys of Super Nintendo players, arranged publicity clips, and performed market analyses.

Computer Graphics interns tend to be involved in writing the programs that produce special effects for movies. One intern did everything from animation programming to software translation for a new computer. Particularly fascinating to him were the periodic department meetings in which programmers would describe past projects. He said: "A programmer who worked on the Miller Lite commercial showed us how the ad was made. Painstaking detail went into each fraction-of-a-second frame. It was amazing to see."

Interns in the THX division carry out research and marketing projects for THX, an audio system providing unbelievably realistic sound in both movie theaters and home audio equipment. "THX is an exciting piece of technology," said an intern. "With speakers carefully situated around the theater and behind the movie screen, it makes movie-goers feel as if they are in the center of the action. It increases the believability of the images they see." One intern assembled databases tracking the licensees of the Home THX Audio System and created binders cataloging information on those licensees. While such work seems far from scintillating, he was quick to point out that "despite these relatively mundane tasks, I greatly enjoyed seeing how communications theories I learned in school applied to a real-life product. My textbooks described how TV is a passive medium, how it leaves little for the imagination. Working at Lucasfilm, I saw how THX is transforming TV and movies into more active media. It increases the imagination involved."

From day one, interns are treated to a host of activities. Orientation introduces freshly arrived students to the variety of departments at Lucasfilm and sometimes culminates in a visit to the archives; there, one can examine props from Lucasfilm movies, including everything from background paintings used in *Star Wars* to Indiana Jones's fedora. After settling into their jobs, interns are sometimes invited to "dailies," the early morning screenings of the previous day's special-effects work, open only to Lucasfilm employees. Said one intern: "The dailies were a great way of keeping up on the stunning film moments being made. At a daily for *Death Becomes Her*, for instance, we saw several takes of Meryl Streep with her head on backward and Goldie Hawn with a hole through her stomach." Interns are also free to attend advance screenings of Lucasfilm movies, held every so often in the company's main screening room. And, befitting a film company, free passes to local movies abound, and interns can find out about them via E-mail.

The best internships invite speakers to address their interns, and Lucasfilm's is no exception. Meeting every two or three weeks, interns hear words of wisdom from various department heads and executives. Past interns especially enjoyed meeting with Gordon Radley, number two in command at the company. They found him remarkably approachable and asked him a host of juicy questions, such as whether the company plans to make another *Star Wars* film. (Find out for yourself.)

Chances are interns will take in a few memorable parties during their time at Lucasfilm. Described as a "lakeside hoedown" and a "good old-fashioned western picnic," the annual Fourth-of-July bash garners high ratings. The whole company comes out for the party, as do a number of celebrities, as one intern realized when he found himself chowing down between R2D2 and the director of *Rocketeer*. Word has it that Lucasfilm puts equal effort into its Christmas and Halloween parties, sometimes renting out exotic sites, like San Francisco's Exploratorium.

Working at Lucasfilm sometimes yields a few unexpected opportunities. One student spent an afternoon assisting Robert Townsend when the actor was putting the finishing touches on his movie *Meteor Man*. Sometimes opportunities emerge on the spur of the moment. The same summer, a few interns were enlisted to make voiceovers for "The Young Indiana Jones Chronicles"; according to one, he "generated assorted noises, including applause and laughing sounds, for the show's sound track."

A large portion of a session's interns works at the Lucasfilm complex in central San Rafael, an industrial city about 20 minutes from San Francisco. Interns in film-related departments, such as Editorial/Visual Effects, Computer Graphics, Commercials, and Art, work here, as do interns working in Lucasfilm Games. Known also as ILM, short for Industrial Light and Magic, the "bustling" San Rafael complex has an industrial but modern feel. Offices are decorated with a variety of movie posters and paintings. An employee gym, called the Bodybay, is located on the premises, as is a basketball court. An array of restaurants is in walking distance of the complex.

Interns in business-minded areas like Publicity as well as those in THX work at Skywalker Ranch, a name that suggests something bigger than life, and it should. Imagine a sprawling, bucolic estate reachable by a long, sinuous road. A corral holds an assortment of horses; longhorn steer roam the mountainside. Burgundy-colored bikes dot the compound, used by employees to shuttle between buildings. Several rustic houses sit on the premises, some holding conference rooms and offices, others housing screening rooms and production equipment. A variety of artwork decorates these houses, as do fireplaces and comfortable furnishings. Arriving at the ranch, one intern asked himself: "Is this a production company or the set of *Dallas*, turbocharged?"

Like all of the rooms at the ranch, the dining areas have a handsome, personal feel. One dining room has a solarium that employees are free to use if they make reservations. The food is affordable ("a five-course meal for $5,") and highly regarded ("delicious meals prepared by able chefs, some of whom studied at the California Culinary Academy").

All interns receive a car sticker affording them access to the ranch, and even interns who do not work at the ranch are free to visit when they have free time, however rare this is.

While the ranch offers the type of edenic workplace most people only dream about, not everyone appreciates this paradise. About 45 minutes from San Francisco in a valley of West Marin, "the ranch is unbelievably beautiful," in an intern's estimation, "but it is isolated from civilization. And because the buildings are really spread out, you don't get to see a lot of what's going on. It is isolated both geographically and institutionally." Although a few prefer San Rafael's faster-paced environment, most find it hard to forsake the ranch's breathtaking beauty and low-key atmosphere.

Although the overwhelming majority of interns' comments about the internship are overwhelmingly positive, a few reveal some on-the-job frustrations. As in all film and television internships, union rules prohibit interns from undertaking tasks done by union employees, such as building sets and mixing sound. Although he found the professional staff "extremely friendly," one intern felt occasionally resented by the union workers; he said: "The stagehands would go ballistic if you lifted a box." Another intern wished there was more positive feedback from his supervisors: "People at Lucasfilm are so used to excellence that it seemed like they didn't give me enough time to learn the ropes. I could have used more encouragement." A few interns complained that they were notified about being accepted to the program too late: "I didn't hear from Lucasfilm until a week before my internship was to start. I had to cancel the alternative plans I had made."

SELECTION

 College juniors and seniors and graduate students are eligible to apply. All students must be returning to school full-time when the internship ends; thus, the program does not accept recent graduates. The program gives first consideration to students with an overall GPA of at least 3.3; it prefers that students have a 3.5 GPA in their major. In general, the internship has no hard and fast prerequisites, but students interested in technical positions (e.g., computer graphics) or creative positions (e.g., art) should have some experience in those areas. Positions in Marketing, Publicity, Finance/Accounting, Merchandise/Licensing, Human Resources, THX, and Learning have no prerequisites, but computer literacy is helpful. The intern coordinator looks favorably upon applicants with previous work experience, be it "another internship or even pumping gas." Applicants with professionalism and maturity are also highly prized: "We don't want people with pixie dust in their eyes."

APPLICATION PROCEDURE

 Deadlines for applying to the internship are as follows: summer, March 30; fall, July 30; spring, November 15. Applicants should send the following items stapled together in the order given: application form, resumé, cover letter, intern questionnaire, official transcripts, and two letters of recommendation (from college professors, guidance counselors, or employers). The intern questionnaire asks general questions about a candidate's academic background, voca-tional interests, expectations for the internship, and past accomplishments. If desired, applicants may submit copies, photographs, or slides of artwork, so long as they are no larger than 8-1/2" x 11"; except for computer animation/graphics reels, Lucasfilm does not accept film/video tapes. Applicants for the unpaid fall and spring internships must obtain a letter from their college verifying that they are receiving academic credit for the internship. After all materials have been submitted, applicants are interviewed by the intern coordinator, either over the phone or in person.

OVERVIEW

 If spending a few months exposed to the technological and creative genius of a cutting-edge entertainment company sounds appealing, Lucasfilm is the place for you. Interns carry out rewarding projects while enjoying a breathtaking array of extracurricular activities. They leave with "tremendous insight into the entertainment industry," not to mention "an incredible resumé enhancer." It's no surprise that interns often wish to repeat the program, but Lucasfilm forbids their doing so. Said an intern: "Like Cinderella at the ball, you only get one shot as a Lucasfilm intern." With less than 5 percent of the applicants accepted, landing one opportunity at the company is difficult enough. Word to the wise: Apply early, and may the Force be with you.

FOR MORE INFORMATION . . .

■ Lucasfilm
   Human Resources—Intern Department
   P.O. Box 2009
   San Rafael, CA 94912
   (415) 662-1999

The MacNeil/Lehrer
NEWSHOUR

SELECTIVITY	🔍 🔍 🔍 🔍 🔍
Approximate applicant pool: 100–150 Interns accepted: 4	

COMPENSATION	$
Interns: None Desk assistants: minimum wage	

QUALITY OF LIFE	🌴 🌴 🌴 🌴
Morning meetings Bank of information	

LOCATION(S)
New York, NY; Washington, DC; Denver, CO

FIELD
Television news

DURATION
12–16 Weeks; Summer, Fall, Spring Part-time (20 hours/week)

PRE-REQS
Interns–college juniors, seniors Desk assistants–recent grads

DEADLINE(S)
Summer .... March 31   Fall .... July 31 Spring .... October 31

"**G**ood Evening. I'm Jim Lehrer in Washington."

"And I'm Robert MacNeil in New York. Today we'll take a look at some of the day's top stories."

Since 1983, this no-frills introduction to the "NewsHour" has been broadcast over the early evening airwaves every Monday through Friday. In 1992, the show attracted some 4.6 million viewers every night and reached nearly 12.4 million viewers one or more times per week. It's certainly no surprise that the show has garnered such a devoted following. A recent *Times-Mirror*/Gallup Poll found the "NewsHour" the "most believed" news program on American television and among all journalistic sources, second only to *The Wall Street Journal* in reputation and influence. The show has won six National News Emmys and five Peabody Broadcast Awards. Congressmen, ambassadors, actors, and journalists watch it. Even Johnny Carson made reference to it in a monologue or two.

DESCRIPTION

 Since its first year, "The MacNeil/Lehrer NewsHour" has relied on unpaid News interns to assist in the production of the show. News interns' work schedules are organized around three shifts: morning, from 10:00 AM to 2:00 PM; afternoon, from 12:00 noon to 4:00 PM; and evening, from 3:00 PM to 7:00 PM. Interns manage one of these shifts each week and rotate to another shift the following week.

The morning shift usually finds News interns answering phones, running errands, and responding to viewer mail. They also attend the half-hour morning meeting, where the day's stories are discussed. Robert "Robin" MacNeil and the New York correspondents, reporters, production assistants, secretaries, and desk assistants (one level above intern) all attend. Jim Lehrer and the corresponding Washington people provide input via the speakerphone that sits at the center of the table. That interns are permitted to observe these critical conferences is a privilege granted at few other news shows.

After the meeting, interns are encouraged to make recommendations to reporters or ask producers for research work on a story of interest. Said an intern: "They were thrilled that I displayed initiative, and thus they rewarded me with great work. One time, I was allowed to help edit the day's video clips and suggest which shots should ultimately be used in a particular

BUSYWORK METER
LOW MEDIUM HIGH
OLDMAN & HAMADEH

story." Another intern "searched through old 'Wild Kingdom' episodes at the video library for some animal noises that we could use in a story."

Interns working the afternoon shifts also do some administrative tasks—answering the producers' phones or the viewer-response phones. Not all of this phone work is drudgery. "We often received phone calls from magazine writers who wanted specific questions answered," said an intern, "and we also wrote down all kinds of viewer comments, everything from criticism of a correspondent's inquisition of Barbara Bush to praise of Robin's choice of necktie." Phone work need not consume the entire shift, however. Research projects await the interns who make efficient use of their time. One researched the differing opinions as to whether there existed a religious or moral dilemma in using troops to combat hunger in Somalia. "Using NEXIS and LEXIS on-line databases, I put together a little folder containing relevant viewpoints and commentaries," she said. Another intern helped prepare an interview for Canadian Prime Minister Brian Mulroney. "I wrote some of the questions that Robin actually used on the air."

By evening, the mood of the office becomes increasingly hectic. Production assistants, desk assistants, writers, and secretaries scurry about, putting finishing touches on the day's show. Interns run the script to various people and help on phones. Once, when Robin was unavailable to check the set's lighting, one fair-complexioned intern was asked to sit in his chair on the set. "I had the same pale coloring, so the producers used me to check his makeup and its appearance under the stage lights," she said. Moreover, interns who work the evening shift occasionally greet program guests in the Green Room, the sitting area on the second floor, where PBS tapes the show. "One time, I sat there chatting with William Safire, a columnist for *The New York Times*."

The internship begins with a breakfast orientation, featuring Robin or the executive producer, followed by a tour of the workplace. A few times during the semester, interns attend informal brown-bag luncheons, where they are free to ask staff members questions about their jobs. On other days, interns are able to eat at the building's cafeteria, though many describe its food as "poor, unable to compete with the cafes nearby." Interns may also purchase mugs and T-shirts at employee prices. And to immortalize the internship for their grandchildren, interns pose with Robin for 8"x10" glossies at the end of each semester.

Located near New York's Columbus Circle, the "NewsHour" occupies the fourth and fifth floors of the Public Broadcasting Service (PBS) Building. Photographs of the anchors and correspondents adorn the walls of the hallway. At the end of the hallway is the receptionist, on whose desk interns find copies of several major newspapers, which they may have for free. Interns conduct research at the seventh-floor library or at the "morgue," a room containing two months' worth of virtually every national newspaper. And all day long, news flows into the office via the AP wire, phone calls, and daily shoots. A nerve center of information, dubbed "The Bat Cave" by one intern, the "NewsHour" office can really inspire an intern to work overtime.

> To immortalize the internship for their grandchildren, interns pose with Robin for 8"x10" glossies at the end of each semester.

One ambitious intern worked indefatigably, impressing the producers and reporters, so he was allowed to work on projects rarely undertaken by interns. For example, he attended several shoots for a series on race relations. He also set up the computer system at the "MacNeil/Lehrer" 1992 Democratic National Convention command post, which he then oversaw. "For one week, I managed the crews, made sure guests received advance copies of the script, and distributed access passes," he said. Though all the interns, including those in Washington, attended the convention that summer, his experience serves as an example of what self-motivated, perservering interns can accomplish.

"The MacNeil/Lehrer NewsHour" also takes on one intern per semester in Public Affairs, the department concerned with "keeping our name in the news," as the coordinator put it. By maintaining close contacts with the networks and the major dailies, the Public Affairs department keeps journalists abreast of stories and guests appearing on the program. Interns assist in this work, alternately spending time behind the news desk at the 58th Street office and in the show's production room on 1775 Broadway. But that's not all. Besides attending the morning meetings, the Public Affairs intern helps make editing decisions, much like an assistant producer. He or she writes the daily advance copy (DAC) summary, a "radio announcer's summary of the news" distributed to all the PBS radio and television stations nationwide, and greets the show's guests in the Green Room. The Public Affairs intern also helps with the triannual "MacNeil/Lehrer" newsletter, occasionally writing a story or two. "You get a taste of everything as a Public Affairs intern," said the coordinator, "from writing to politics to public relations strategy."

SELECTION

 Applicants interested in becoming News interns must have at least completed their sophomore year by the start of the internship; graduate students are eligible. No particular major is required; "MacNeil/Lehrer" seeks generalists. Working knowledge of domestic and foreign policy issues will prove helpful, however. Good writing, organization, and verbal skills are also a plus. In addition to News interns (and interns in Graphics), the "NewsHour" hires four recent college graduates twice per year to be entry-level Desk Assistants. Applicants interested in the Desk Assistant position must be able to commit full-time for up to six months.

APPLICATION PROCEDURE

 Students must submit materials by July 31 for fall, by October 31 for spring, and by March 31 for summer. Applicants must send in a resumé, a letter indicating that their school will grant college credit for the internship, and a completed questionnaire form. After screening resumés, the internship coordinator grants phone interviews to qualified candidates.

The *NewsHour* also has a production center in Washington and a smaller outpost in Denver. Applicants to the internship programs in Washington and Denver must apply to those offices directly.

OVERVIEW

 A small organization serving under the auspices of public television, "The MacNeil/Lehrer NewsHour" offers students a personalized look at broadcast journalism. Although it is largely structured around clerical tasks, the "MacNeil/Lehrer" experience is potentially among the best in TV news internships. Go-getter interns can do everything from working on stories and greeting guests to accompanying camera people on assignments and attending newsworthy events. As one explained: "If you have the motivation, you can learn a hell of a lot. All the interns are well chosen and capable, so the trick is to be hungry." It seems that the hungriest interns have fared well. Two reporters, an editorial assistant, and one senior producer all started as interns. One former intern now works at "20/20," another at CNN. The appetite for excellent broadcasting is what distinguishes "MacNeil/Lehrer" among news shows . . . and what distinguishes "MacNeil/Lehrer" interns among their peers.

FOR MORE INFORMATION . . .

■ The MacNeil/Leher NewsHour
Internship Coordinator
356 West 58th Street
New York, NY 10019
(212) 560-3113

SELECTIVITY	🔍
Approximate applicant pool: 50	
Interns accepted: 30	

COMPENSATION	💲
None	

QUALITY OF LIFE	🌴 🌴 🌴
Casual atmosphere	
Freebies galore	

LOCATION(S)	
New York, NY	

FIELD	
Comic books	

DURATION	
3 to 4 months	
Summer, Fall, Spring	

PRE-REQS	
College juniors and seniors; must receive academic credit	
High school program (see Application Procedure)	

DEADLINE(S)	
Rolling	

According to Marvel Comics, 76 percent of American children between the ages of 6 and 17 have read Marvel comic books. What makes these stories so compelling to young people? Vivid colors, maybe; the exciting content, perhaps; characters of superhuman strength and ability, sure. But Marvel cites an additional reason for the success of its comic books: Marvel characters, who are bastions of unearthly brawn, suffer also from human concerns and conflicts. Originally an ostracized high school student, Spider-Man, for example, is a crime fighter troubled by money, guilt, and an unappreciative public. The Incredible Hulk has extraordinary strength, but such power is driven by rage and he struggles perpetually to keep his passion in check. Living not in a fictitious city but in New York, the Fantastic Four see no need to conceal their identities and together they fight crime, but not without occasionally arguing among themselves. The Marvel formula is clear: One part supernatural ability plus one part earthly vulnerability equals compelling Super Heroes who are understood and appreciated by children of all backgrounds.

DESCRIPTION

The Marvel College Internship program hires about 30 interns per session, each of whom is assigned to one of the company's 30 editors. No matter where an intern ends up, there is a lot of gofer work to be done. "You basically assist an editor with any tasks that need to be done," reports an intern. Photocopying, retrieving mail, sending out complimentary comic books, filing, typing fan mail responses, and answering fan inquiries over the phone—all fall under Marvel interns' jurisdiction. When editors write new plots for a superhero, they rely on interns to ferret out the names of past characters and settings that may have relevance to the new stories. Interns, in search of these past issues make countless trips to the archives room. To some all this is plain gruntwork; to others, particularly those who have grown up collecting comics, it is a "labor of love."

"When an editor begins to trust you, you receive better assignments," explains an intern. Some get to put editing and writing skills to use. Interns are sometimes asked to read and critique scripts sent in by comic book writers. A few interns have the chance to write comic

BUSYWORK METER
MEDIUM
LOW HIGH
OLDMAN & HAMADEH

books' "letters pages," where fans' questions are answered in a "Dear Editor" format. Other interns work with layout and design materials. One intern worked with film negatives to enlarge the pages in the *Marvel Masterworks*, a compendium of early issues of Marvel comics. Others are asked to make various paste-ups, such as pasting thought-balloons onto comic strips. On an informal basis, editors consult with interns, asking their opinions on design decisions: "My editor asked my input on logos and cover designs. I liked being in the loop on such matters."

Marvel attempts to expose its interns to every stage of comic book production. Between tasks, interns are free to visit the various departments responsible for creating the comic books. Some attend plot lunches, where editors and writers meet to discuss how they want their stories to unfold. Interns receive demonstrations on the other stages of production, including penciling, whereby an artist sketches pictures based on what the plot describes; lettering, performed by an artist who hand-letters the dialog and narration; inking, which involves going over the penciled art in black india ink; and finally, coloring, in which each page receives a selection of Dr. Martin's watercolor dyes. Seeing the whole production process, interns can't help but be impressed: "I grew up thinking that comics were put together by magical elves. It was terrific to see the nuts and bolts of how the books are really made."

Part of the attraction of working at Marvel is its casual atmosphere. The editorial office looks like a cross between a law firm and an eighth grader's bedroom. Inside the modern, recently remodeled rooms one finds a smattering of Super Hero posters; desks sport Spider Man and Incredible Hulk action figures; and a rubber chicken that hangs from the ceiling. "This is not your typical New York office space," says a Marvel editor. "It's a jeans and T-shirt office. It's a little offbeat. Creative people need comfortable surroundings." Most interns work on the tenth floor, which is considered the main editorial area. A few work in the ninth-floor editorial annex, affectionately known as "the dungeon," because it seems isolated in comparison to the bustling floor above.

Marvel has loads of freebies. Interns receive free copies of each month's comic books, averaging out to about 20 books a week. If bundles of comics aren't enough, a healthy amount of superhero buttons, T-shirts, and toy figures come interns' way.

For interns interested in a career in comic books, interning at Marvel is clearly a stepping stone to permanent employment. A long line of assistants, artists, and editors currently at the company began their careers as Marvel interns. The intern coordinator estimates that at least 60 percent of the editorial department passed through the internship program.

The most common complaint about the internship is its lack of pay. "I had to commute from New Jersey," gripes an intern, "and factoring in transportation costs, I lost money working at Marvel." Another downside to the program is the disproportionately large share of men. Although Marvel would like to see an equal proportion of male and female interns, far fewer women apply for the internship. Each session usually has only two or three female interns. On top of that, only 6 of Marvel's 30 editors are women. These ratios make for a distinctly male culture. "The internship needs more female interns . . . a woman's perspective would balance out the overwhelming macho attitude here," said an intern.

> At Marvel, one finds a smattering of Super Hero posters; desks sport Spider Man and Incredible Hulk action figures; and a rubber chicken that hangs from the ceiling.

SELECTION

 The Marvel College Internship selects college juniors and seniors for internships. Those who get the most out of the internship have initiative and the ability to interact well with others. "Interns able to adapt to a wide variety of personalities do well at Marvel," says a past intern. Many interns have previous experience in drawing comics, but artistic skills are by no means required. Marvel gets its fair share of

English and business majors and even a few engineering majors on occasion. Above all, in the words of the program's information sheet, interns should "be familiar with the Marvel universe of characters." Knowledge of stories and characters is no small deal at Marvel. Says the coordinator: "While a general familiarity with Marvel Super Heroes is fine, some of our best interns have known comic book histories as they would the Bible, able to quote chapter and verse." Marvel-savvy interns prove valuable in helping editors do research for new stories, recalling on command arcane aspects of a superhero's history, but there can be too much of a good thing. "A few of the interns were so intense about Marvel comics that nothing else seemed to matter. If their favorite characters failed, they mourned for days. We called these interns 'fan geeks.'"

APPLICATION PROCEDURE

 The Marvel College Internship runs throughout the year and interns are hired for the summer, fall, and spring on a rolling basis. Applicants should send the intern coordinator a resumé and a letter from their college stating that they will receive credit for the internship. The coordinator then interviews applicants, preferably in person but also by phone, to find out which Marvel comic books interest them. With this information, the coordinator attempts to have editors of similar interests interview applicants. Before this interview, editors prefer applicants to have brought or sent in some sort of creative sample, be it drawings or writing samples. Interns are chosen a few days later.

There's also a high school internship, open to high school juniors and seniors. High school interns sort and answer fan mail, help conduct the weekly Marvel tour, photocopy comics in the pencil and ink stages, and assist in other stages of comic production.

OVERVIEW

 Just as Marvel characters display both super-human powers and earthly vulnerability, the Marvel College Internship offers an experience marked by duality. Interns experience the thrill of observing America's top comic book maker in action but in doing so, undertake a large share of mundane assignments. Factor in the inimitably casual atmosphere, the ability to hone writing and drawing skills, and the opportunities for permanent employment—and the internship could be a terrific way to spend a few months. Even if you don't want to make comics your life, interning at Marvel will add a lifelong conversation piece to your resumé.

FOR MORE INFORMATION . . .

■ Marvel Comics
Internship Program
387 Park Avenue South
New York, NY 10016
(212) 696-0808

When Egypt resolved to build its high dam at Aswan in 1960, it was faced with a troubling situation. Its celebrated Temple at Dendur, built in 15 B.C. and located in the path of the future dam, would be buried underwater forever. The solution: Find the huge limestone monument a new home. In 1965, the Egyptian government sent the temple to America, stone by painstaking stone. Where did it go? New York's Metropolitan Museum of Art, which houses the largest collection of Egyptian works outside of Cairo, was the logical recipient.

The Met—its abbreviated sobriquet—is the largest and most diverse museum in the Western Hemisphere, containing two million pieces that cover nearly 5,000 years of history. Unlike the majority of the world's museums, which tend to limit their scope to particular styles and periods, the Met satisfies the tastes of everyone, from the aficionado of Impressionist paintings to the pop-culture junkie. Among the Rembrandts, Sumerian stone sculptures, and classical Greek statues, one could find a 1694 Stradivarius violin, a 1973 electric guitar, a 1910 Honus Wagner baseball card reputed to be worth $500,000, and even the pointy-coned corset worn by Madonna during her "Blond Ambition" tour.

SELECTIVITY	🔍 🔍 🔍 🔍 🔍
Approximate applicant pool: 600 Und, 125 Grd Interns accepted: 22 Und, 10 Grd	
COMPENSATION	💲 💲
$2,000 for Cloister undergrads $2,200 for Met undergrads; $2,500 for grad students	
QUALITY OF LIFE	↑ ↑ ↑
Monday field trips Exploratory environment	
LOCATION(S)	
New York, NY	
FIELD	
Art museum	
DURATION	
9–10 weeks Summer	
PRE-REQS	
See Application Procedure	
DEADLINE(S)	
Met undergrads........ Jan. 21 Cloisters ....Feb. 4 Met grad students .... Jan. 28	

DESCRIPTION

In 1973, the Metropolitan Museum of Art first offered summer positions to college students. Twenty years later, the museum's internship program is still going strong. The ten-week summer internship places 10 graduate students and 14 undergraduates in Administration, Conservation, Library, and Education, and 19 curatorial departments including the Arts of Africa, Oceania, and the Americas; American Art; Ancient Near Eastern Art; Arms and Armor; Asian Art; the Costume Institute; European Paintings; Greek and Roman Art; Islamic Art; Musical Instruments; Photographs; Prints and Illustrated Books; and Twentieth Century Art. In 1986, the Met's Medieval Arts branch—The Cloisters—decided to offer a formal internship program as well. Every summer, eight students participate in the branch's nine-week internship in European art of the Middle Ages.

The Met internship program begins with a two-week orientation that introduces the interns to collections and staff members and

BUSYWORK
MEDIUM
LOW HIGH
OLDMAN & HAMADEH
METER

teaches interns how a world-class museum operates. Over the two-week period, interns visit all 19 curatorial departments, including The Cloisters. "It was a wonderful overview," said an intern. "Each curator or assistant curator would give a one-hour gallery talk, explaining the collection and its history while referring to specific pieces." In between curatorial department tours, interns visit the museum's Design department, Legal department, and reproduction studio (where reproductions are prepared for sale). They also meet with Met Director Philippe de Montebello and Met President William Luers, both well known figures in the international art world. "We discussed the possible direction the museum will take in the future, especially after the controversy surrounding certain exhibits such as the [sexually explicit] Mapplethorpe photographs," said an intern. Graduate students attend selected portions of their younger classmates' tours and afterward return to their assigned curatorial departments, where they spend the entire summer doing in-depth research and writing papers on specific collections or exhibits.

Where is the *Mona Lisa*? You had better catch the next plane to Paris.

The whirlwind orientation prepares interns for the Visitor Information Center. Staffing the desk two half days a week, the Met undergraduates answer visitors' questions that sometimes are not about art at all. "One day we amused ourselves by trying to figure out the most frequently posed question. Unfortunately, it turned out to be 'Where is the bathroom?'" But people ask art-related questions as well, from the very specific ("How much did Mr. Annenberg pay for van Gogh's *Wheat Field with Cypresses*?") to the ingenuous. "We had people ask us to direct them to the *Mona Lisa* [actually found in the Musée du Louvre, Paris] and the dinosaurs [on display at the American Museum of Natural History, New York]. Boy, were they disappointed."

Next to the Information Center is the Tour Kiosk, the starting point of the Met's one-hour highlights tours, led by the interns. Back in the 1970s, the Met was considerably smaller and more conducive to a tour that started at one end

of the museum and ended at the other. "Today, it's impossible," said an intern. Indeed, the Met's two-million-piece collection sits on 1.5 million square feet of floor space. Interns have only enough time to discuss a dozen or so specific works. "But you're given leeway to devise your own tour and choose the pieces that you feel best exemplify the entire collection."

Met interns also spend two full days each week in their respective departments. An intern in Ancient Near Eastern Art helped in the preparation of a 200-object exhibit entitled "The Royal City of Susa: Ancient Near Eastern Treasures in the Louvre." "Sometimes I watched the exhibit being built, occasionally offering my opinion as to the placement of objects. But mostly, I proofread galleys [i.e., drafts] of the exhibit brochure and assigned object numbers to photographs of the pieces, partly to catalog the exhibit and also to prepare pictures to sell out of our gift shop. I also touched up a drawing of a statue; I did a pretty good job and it ended up being published in the brochure."

Now what about The Cloisters, which resembles a 12th-century monastery? It got its name from the sections of four medieval "cloisters"—covered walkways enclosing courtyards and leading to monastic buildings—that are part of the modern architecture of the museum, opened in 1939. Named Cuxa, St.-Guilhem, Bonnefont, and Trie, the four cloisters provide, according to a Cloisters brochure, an "inviting . . . place for rest and contemplation"—the same purpose they served during medieval times. Located several miles north of the Met at Fort Tryon Park, The Cloisters is famous for its Unicorn Tapestries, stained-glass windows, a herb garden containing more than 250 species of medieval plants, and the oldest known complete set of playing cards (circa 1475).

Cloisters interns spend even more time training than their Met counterparts—three weeks. Meeting with curators at the Met and with New York art experts (dealers, curators, etc.), the interns focus on acquiring knowledge of medieval times. They visit a stained glass workshop downtown and learn how stained glass is made and restored; they listen to a lecture on reliquaries, containers in which sacred relics, sometimes skulls, are stored; and they meet with Met Director Phillipe de Montebello to hear about museum management.

The three-week orientation readies Cloisters interns for their next task—conducting five weeks of daily tours for groups of young campers, 4- to 12-years-old. Limited to two general medieval themes, each intern chooses a few objects to talk about. "My year, the tour topic was 'walls'; I had the kids sit under one of the museum's arches and build a small arch out of wooden blocks. It was a great demonstration of how medieval people created arches without cement."

But there's more to the Met and Cloisters internships than giving tours or helping out in departments. On Mondays, the Met and the Cloisters are closed to the public, so undergraduates at both locations spend the day visiting other museums and attending lectures. Met interns peruse New York's Museum of Modern Art and Museum of African Art, observe how works of art are priced for auction at Sotheby's, and visit a private artist's studio to observe art in the making. Cloisters interns listen to William Voelkle (curator at New York's Pierpont Morgan Library) speak on the history of Pierpont's manuscript collection, travel to Philadelphia's Glencairn Museum (the former mansion of a couple who collected medieval art), and meet with medieval art dealer Michael Ward, who "allowed us to touch objects without gloves and . . . even let us put a sixth- or seventh-century Byzantine ring on our fingers."

On top of all this, Cloisters and Met undergraduates spend a couple afternoons a week researching art-history topics of interest, which they eventually convert into public tours. Some interns really get into their research. One intern who prepared a talk on Images of Power in African Art said, "I contrasted court art from the Kingdom of Benin to the Minkisi figures popular among 19th-century Congo peoples—royal art symbolic of power versus popular art believed to be powerful."

Whereas Met interns give these tours from mid-summer until the end of the internship, Cloisters interns present their work only once, during the last week, to a group of visitors, the staff, and the Cloisters director. Advertised in a flyer that reads "Gallery Talks by College Interns," the talks embrace a variety of medieval subjects. One intern, for example, demonstrated the art of medieval dye making. "I used plants and flowers from the herb garden, mashing chamomile, woad, and madder to make ancient dyes as described in medieval and modern books. I even boiled and crushed hundreds of tiny cochineal insects to make a special red dye. Then I applied the dyes to unspun wool to create a rainbow of colors."

The Met is sometimes described as conservative, probably due to what one intern explains as "the drive to obtain funding from wealthy, conservative donors." The museum is also occasionally labeled as bureaucratic—not hard to believe given its size. "There are thousands of people [2,000 full-time staff and 600 volunteers, to be exact] working on a variety of collections; it's like a small university with many departments, so you might have to go several places to get the historical information you need."

SELECTION

 The Met internship for graduate students requires at least one year of graduate work in art history or a similar field (e.g., education). The Met internship for undergraduates is open to juniors, seniors, and recent graduates who have yet to attend graduate school. A strong background in art history (8 to 12 courses) is preferred. The Cloisters internship, on the other hand, is open to all undergraduates, but preference is given to freshmen and sophomores. "Applicants to our program must work well with kids," said The Cloisters' coordinator. "They also need to have an affinity for art, even if they have yet to take an art course." In both programs, the coordinators emphasize the importance of "well-thought-out, creative" essays and strong letters of recommendation. In the case of The Cloisters, a glowing letter of recommendation will give even a science student a fair shot at being admitted.

APPLICATION PROCEDURE

 Materials must be received by the third Friday in January for the Met's undergraduate program, the last Friday in January for the Met's graduate-student program, and the first Friday in February for The Cloisters' program. All candidates must submit two academic recommendations and official college transcripts. Each Met applicant must also send a resumé, a separate list of foreign language ability and art-history courses completed, and an essay of no more than 500 words indicating career goals, interest in museum work, and reasons for applying to the internship program. Each Cloisters applicant must also send a page indicating field of interest, academic major, year in class, special honors, and work experience (volunteer or paid) and submit a 500-word essay indicating reasons for applying to the internship program. Except for graduate students, all finalists are required to visit New York (at their own expense) for interviews in March. "Because undergraduate interns must give gallery talks, we want to make sure they articulate themselves well," explained The Cloisters coordinator.

OVERVIEW

 There's a rich history behind every work at New York's Metropolitan Museum of Art, even behind the museum's logo—it's called the "Leonardo (da Vinci) M." But scholars dispute its origins. Is it from Leonardo, whose style resembles that of the *M* or from Luca Pacioli, a well-known mathematician and Leonardo's contemporary and close friend, in whose book a woodcut version of the *M* appears? No one knows for sure.

This is just a sampling of the type of art history issues in store for students who intern at the internationally prestigious museum. But the Met's well-structured internship programs expose students to more than history. Interns also learn all facets of curatorship—handling art objects, setting up exhibits, meeting art dealers, and interacting with the public.

FOR MORE INFORMATION . . .

■ The Metropolitan Museum of Art
1000 Fifth Avenue
New York, NY 10028-0198
Attn: Education Dept., Internship Program
(212) 570-3710

■ The Cloisters
College Internship Program
Fort Tryon Park
New York, NY 10040
(212) 923-3700

Microsoft®

SELECTIVITY	🔍 🔍 🔍
Approximate applicant pool: 2,000 Interns accepted: 350	

COMPENSATION	$ $ $ $ $
Est. $320–$480/week; round-trip travel Subsidized housing; rental car	

QUALITY OF LIFE	🌴 🌴 🌴 🌴 🌴
Beautiful campus; Prime gym Flexible hours; Casual dress	

LOCATION(S)
Redmond, WA

FIELD
Computer software

DURATION
12–16 weeks Summer

PRE-REQS
College sophomores through seniors Computer background for most positions

DEADLINE(S)
Rolling

You saw them in high school. Pants a little too short. Glasses a little too thick. Hair unkempt and shaggy. You used to laugh at them and call them names like "dweeb," "dork," and "wonk." Well, laugh no more. Chances are, some of them are interning at Microsoft, the computer software empire built by the biggest nerd of them all, Bill Gates. That's right, $8 billion Bill Gates. You guessed it, the Bill Gates responsible for the world's most powerful software packages, including Microsoft Windows, Windows NT, Microsoft Word, Microsoft Excel, and Microsoft PowerPoint. Bill likes to invite the boy- and girl-wonders of the computer world to his sprawling corporate headquarters and give them a piece of the action. For about three months, interns assist professional programmers and managers in creating innovative computer products while enjoying one of the highest standards of on-the-job living found anywhere.

So while you slept during Introduction to Computers, some of your peers were gaining the skills that would prepare them to tackle the Microsoft Internship. For many Microsoft interns, relaxing with a beer in a warm Jacuzzi after a rewarding day of code writing or debugging, this must be the ultimate revenge of the nerds.

DESCRIPTION

Although Microsoft hires interns year-round, the majority of interns work during the summertime. In June, some 350 interns descend upon the company's wooded campus, ready to start work in a variety of divisions. Most are assigned to positions in the areas of Software Testing, Program Management, Program Development, Product Marketing, and Finance.

Software Testing interns systematically put a product through its paces, with the aim of removing all bugs before the product ships. Interns simulate all the ways a user would manipulate a program and enter any resulting deficiencies into a "bug database" that professional programmers examine. After a product ships, interns record users' complaints about the program and run tests to determine whether those complaints are bonafide bugs or just user mistakes. Most Testing interns interviewed liked their job but conceded that testing for bugs can be tedious.

BUSYWORK METER — MEDIUM — LOW — HIGH — OLDMAN & HAMADEH

Nevertheless, some find ways of making their mark, like the interns who wrote the entire configuration script for Microsoft Golf.

Interns in Program Management undertake a variety of tasks related to getting a product out the door. One wrote a help file for an in-house program, Windows Help. After completing this low-profile task, she entreated her supervisor for a better assignment and ended up participating in a design session for another product. In her words: "It was really high-powered. In the design session, we tried to achieve an overview perspective for a product, determining what we want to do, what we want the software to look like, and what it needs to do." Another Management intern spent weeks doing research to determine whether Microsoft should continue making CO-BOL software.

Program Development interns help design the features and write the code that turns the specification for a product into the finished product. But as one intern pointed out, "supervisors sometimes give interns tasks that, if fouled up, won't jeopardize the shipping of a product." This "don't touch the good stuff, you might break it" policy is particularly common when an intern works on a product that is near completion. Even so, Development interns often have rewarding work, such as writing a small piece of code. One wrote the code for the button functions in Visual Basic. Another wrote the movable ruler code for Microsoft Publisher. And one able group of interns wrote part of the code that ended up in the shipped version of the Microsoft Sound System Product.

Whatever they do, interns are treated like professional staff. "The permanent employees saw us as equals," said an intern. Upon arrival, interns are assigned both a manager and a mentor. The latter is responsible for overseeing an intern's daily progress and is available to answer any questions. Although the mentor system is generally liked by interns, a few wish mentors were better organized in their supervisory role: "It's hard for [mentors] to have enough time and free-thought to supervise us. They need a way of offering us more structured feedback."

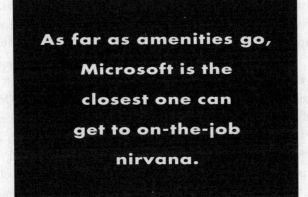

As far as amenities go, Microsoft is the closest one can get to on-the-job nirvana.

Microsoft puts an extraordinary amount of energy into its internship program. While the pay is good—most interns make around $9 an hour, though it varies with experience—the extracurricular opportunities are unparalleled. Interns take part in an orientation day, a career fair, and lunch seminars with senior-level management speakers. At the seminars, interns learn about the company's business and technical strategies from such key players as the senior program manager and the vice president of the World Product Group. To keep interns abreast of upcoming events both at Microsoft and in the Seattle area, the intern coordinator has developed intern information pieces such as a handbook, mail alias (i.e., code name), newsletter, and for 1994, a relocation guide to Redmond. Interns can create their own aliases such as "soc intern volleyball games" or "soc intern softball games," or they can simply join one of the 150 social aliases at Microsoft from flyfishing to out-on-the-town news. Interns plan trips such as white-water rafting, parachuting, and weekends at the Washington and Oregon coasts.

The Microsoft complex is located in Redmond, a sleepy suburb 15 minutes outside Seattle. Situated in a forestlike setting, with running trails, soccer fields, and fountains, the 20-building compound could be mistaken for a college campus. There are usually two interns to an office. The atmosphere is indisputably casual, with a fair number of employees sporting J. Crew dress, others in Birkenstocks and tie-dye. Toys adorn many desks, with the handy Supershooter water gun currently the rage. High-quality, affordably priced cafeterias abound. Some, like the Burger Cafe, specialize in a specific cuisine while others offer a bit of everything. As one intern pointed out: "It's hard to believe you're not at summer camp."

As far as amenities go, Microsoft is the closest one can get to on-the-job nirvana. The coddling begins when applicants are flown to Redmond for final-round interviews and put up in fully furnished apartments. Those selected for the internship are then in for a cornucopia of creature comforts. Microsoft picks up the tab for travel to Redmond, reimbursing interns for a roundtrip airline ticket or lodging, gas, and meal expenses incurred on a car trip. Microsoft also subsidizes use of apartments located within easy walking distance of the campus. Interns may elect to rent from Microsoft at $450 per month for a private one-bedroom apartment, and $350 per month for a private bedroom in a two- or three-bedroom apartment. Maid service comes every two weeks, at no extra charge. Furthermore, Microsoft will supply up to $200 for shipping personal items and it will completely cover the cost of transporting a bike. Itching to drive but have no car? Microsoft will pay portions towards the fee of a leased compact vehicle through Avis Rent A Car. The company reimburses interns for health insurance premiums up to $250 per month during the length of their work terms.

The perks continue once interns settle into work at Microsoft. At the company store, students may purchase up to $250 worth of software at a discounted price; one intern reports buying five or six pieces of software this way. All Microsoft workers receive a free membership to the PRO Club, an immense, state-of-the-art health club just two blocks up the road. "This was the nicest club I've seen," gushed an intern. "You name it, they had it—basketball, tennis, and racquetball courts, Jacuzzis, dozens of StairMasters, and even free shampoo in the shower." Interns are free to break up their workdays by visiting the PRO Club during the daytime. "Microsoft trusts you to set your own hours. Your work hours are wonderfully flexible here. I would go to the gym from 2:00 to 3:00 PM and return to work energized." Microsoft's policy on work time is indeed flexible, allowing interns to work the eight hours they want to, even if it's from 4:00 PM to midnight. The company believes that a comfortable worker is an effective worker. It's no surprise, then, that each cluster of offices has its own kitchen, fully stocked with complimentary beverages and soup.

SELECTION

 The internship is limited to college sophomores, juniors, and seniors. Most interns have a solid background in computer science, and some, particularly those working in Software Develop-

ment, are accomplished programmers. Nevertheless, liberal arts majors with a love for problem solving and a lot of enthusiasm should not be discouraged from applying. Divisions like Product Marketing and Finance often hire interns who lack in-depth computer experience. Microsoft looks for candidates who are "hungry to prove themselves," eager to immerse themselves in a project and confront challenges. According to the coordinator: "Those who thrive at Microsoft are a bit driven: They are smart, hardworking, and able to get things done."

APPLICATION PROCEDURE

 For the majority of interns, the application process begins when Microsoft conducts interviews on their college campuses. Applicants at a school Microsoft does not visit should send a cover letter and resumé to Microsoft's recruiting department. It accepts this material on a rolling basis, but applicants for the summer should get an early start the winter before. Microsoft's campus recruiting department visits over 140 schools and interviews over 1,900 students on campus. About 700 finalists are flown to Redmond for final interviews. Be advised that the final-round interview is no cakewalk. Recruiters spend a few minutes on pleasantries then launch into a battery of questions testing a student's problem-solving skills. They tend to ask brain-teasers, such as how many gas stations there are in the United States? or how would one design a remote-control for a combination TV/VCR? "There's not necessarily a correct answer. The recruiters want to see the quality of your thinking; they want to see how clever you are," said an intern.

OVERVIEW

 If computers are in your future, Microsoft is the place to be. Interns at Microsoft carry out substantive projects at a company riding the vanguard of computer technology. Program participants have the opportunity to observe and learn from the top minds in the computer industry. After all, as one intern put it, "How often do you have the chance to meet the people who wrote Microsoft Windows or DOS?" In terms of perks, Microsoft offers an embarrassment of riches. Dozens of top-quality recreational opportunities at the Redmond campus await the energetic intern, and the soaring beauty and tourist delights of the Pacific Northwest are never more than a car trip away.

FOR MORE INFORMATION . . .

- Microsoft
  Attn: Recruiting Dept. CA 171-0693
  One Microsoft Way
  Redmond, WA 98052-6399
  (206) 882-8080

R O B E R T   M O N D A V I   W I N E R Y

To utter the name Robert Mondavi in wine circles is akin to invoking Sigmund Freud at a convention of psychiatrists or Elvis at a Nashville truckstop. The most famous figure in American wine, Robert Mondavi is a major reason California wine is now among the world's finest. Established in 1966, the winery he founded has been a leading innovator in the industry, pioneering the use of computer-run fermentation, fermentation-tank rotation (which makes more flavorful wine), and fermentation at low temperatures (which leads to fresher-tasting wine). In the process, the Robert Mondavi Winery has produced a renowned line of Chardonnay, Cabernet Sauvignon, Pinot Noir, and Sauvignon Blanc (labeled "Fumé Blanc," a name created by Mondavi, which popularized the wine among Americans as never before). Committed to making fine wine accessible to mainstream consumers, the winery also produces a line of wines labeled *Woodbridge*, known for delivering high quality at moderate prices.

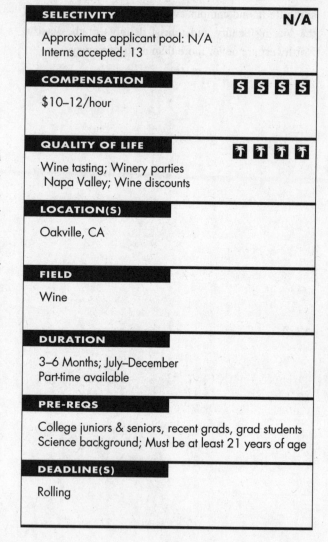

SELECTIVITY	N/A
Approximate applicant pool: N/A
Interns accepted: 13	
COMPENSATION	$ $ $ $
$10–12/hour	
QUALITY OF LIFE	🌴 🌴 🌴 🌴
Wine tasting; Winery parties
Napa Valley; Wine discounts	
LOCATION(S)	
Oakville, CA	
FIELD	
Wine	
DURATION	
3–6 Months; July–December
Part-time available	
PRE-REQS	
College juniors & seniors, recent grads, grad students
Science background; Must be at least 21 years of age	
DEADLINE(S)	
Rolling	

DESCRIPTION

The Mondavi Internship Program selects students with science backgrounds and puts them to work in various stages of wine production and research. The duration of each position varies. Ten or so Lab Technician interns work from July to December. A Research intern works from August to mid-December. A Research Enology intern is hired from August to November. The job with the shortest duration is the Enology intern, who works from October to December.

Of all the positions, Lab Technician deserves the most attention because it constitutes the most interns (10 out of the total 13), the longest duration (six months), and the fewest

restrictions (it's open to any student who has taken biology, chemistry, or food/fermentation classes). Lab Tech interns spend the first half of their internship monitoring the chemical composition of grapes ripening in the vineyard. Explained an intern, "Maturing grapes have to be watched carefully to make sure they have desirable levels of acid and sugar. These two components play a big role in what the finished wine will taste like. If either one is out of proportion in the grape, the fermented grape juice—that is, the wine—could taste too harsh, too bland, or negative in some other way." To check the grapes' progress, interns take sample bunches of grapes from the vineyard and crush them in a colander-like machine. They then analyze the resulting grape juice for pH (acidity) and Brix (sugar content). Such analysis can be crucial to grape growing, because, as one intern explained, "if, [for example], we found that there were deficient levels of sugar in a certain block of grapes, the winemaker might want to expose the appropriate vines to more sunlight so the grapes would become more sugary."

When harvest arrives in August, the focus of Lab Tech interns' work shifts to checking the grape juice during and after fermentation, the chemical process that transforms grapejuice into wine. During the ten or so days of fermentation, interns visit the huge, stainless steel fermentation tanks, open the valves at the bottom of the tanks, and take samples of the fermenting juice. As before, they scrutinize the juice's sugar and acid levels, as well as monitor other compounds such as sulfur dioxide, which is added to the juice to prevent certain undesirable chemical processes from taking place. After fermentation ends, the wine is transferred to oak barrels, where it is stored for weeks, or in the case of oak-friendly wine varieties (e.g., cabernet sauvignon), several months. To ensure that the wine is maturing properly, interns again analyze its basic chemical components, this time obtaining samples with a long, glass "wine thief," which sucks out wine from the wine barrel.

Besides performing chemical analyses, Lab Tech interns set up daily wine tastings for the winemakers. Explained an intern, "The winemakers get together every morning to taste different samples of wine. Sometimes they taste wine made from grapes in each of Mondavi's five vineyards, because the finished wine will be a blend of some or all of these vineyards' wine. They mix and taste the different samples of wine to decide what proportion of each vineyard's wine should be in the final blend." It's not hard to see how interns would find handling hundreds of wine glasses and doing endless amounts of labeling "somewhat of

> **Grapes aren't the only things that prosper amid the Napa Valley's sun-dappled hills and royal blue skies.**

a drag." But the silver lining is that once the tasting is over, interns (as well as all employees) have an opportunity to taste the wine samples. "Any time during the afternoon you were welcome to go through the day's samples," said an intern. "Some were from different vineyards. Others were finished wines. And sometimes there'd be wines from other wineries—so you could compare Mondavi wines with the competition."

As previously indicated, the other intern positions involve only one intern each and require wine-related coursework. The Research intern is primarily concerned with conducting experiments to improve grape quality and fermentation techniques. "Much of my work involved small scale, in-lab winemaking where we'd see what happens to the wine when factors like temperature, yeast type, and quantity of sulfur dioxide are varied," said an intern in this area. The third type of intern, Research Enology, does everything from crushing and fermenting grapes to bottling and analyzing experimental wine. The position also requires some work in the vineyard, where the intern helps pick small lots of grapes and learns grape-growing techniques such as canopy management and trellis systems. The final position, Enology intern, has an intern participate in the planning and implementation of winemaking activities. "The Enology intern does mostly production work, getting involved in logistical concerns like, how long this wine should sit in oak barrels, or what tank that wine should go in," said an intern.

Interns have a few wonderful benefits during their tenure at Mondavi. In addition to the daily winemaker tastings, interns are welcome at evening staff tastings held every week or two; recalled an intern, "Sometimes you'd taste a new release . . . other times there'd be a 'vertical tasting,' where you sampled several vintages of a particular wine. Verticals were great because you got to see how the same wine differs in taste from year to year." If a particular wine strikes interns' fancy, they can find it at the Mondavi shop, where employees receive a 30 to 50 percent discount on wine and wine accessories. Interns are also invited to winery parties, which occur every few months. These include the "let-loose" Crush Party, commemorating the end of harvest and the crushing of grapes into wine. "All the employees gather on the front lawn, and Robert Mondavi speaks about how good the harvest was. There's usually a band, buffet, group pictures, and free T-shirts."

As in all internships, some of the most rewarding experiences occur when participants take the bull by the horns. One intern was able to spend a week rotating through different departments. She explained: "I got to see what goes on in Marketing and Public Relations . . . and I spent a day in the cellar watching workers drag hoses, clean equipment, and shovel pomace out of huge wine tanks. [Shoveling pomace] is something to watch because the high levels of carbon dioxide inside the tank make working there extremely dangerous. [Shovelers] can die instantly if they're not careful, so they wear a face mask and an emergency harness." The same intern mustered the courage to arrange a visit with Robert Mondavi, which required nothing more than making an appointment with his secretary. "It was super. We spoke about his involvement in planning the Napa Valley Cultural Center, a first-of-its-kind educational center on wine history and consumption. . . . Mondavi is so charismatic and inspirational—it was a thrill to meet him."

Nestled in the heart of Napa Valley, Mondavi's main winery is a stunning display of California mission architecture with white stucco walls, sweeping archways, and red-tile roofs. Located in the tourist-friendly town of Oakville, the winery is a valley landmark, so every day hundreds of wine lovers can be found buzzing around the slope-roofed visitor's center (pictured in the Mondavi logo). Other buildings contain fermentation rooms ("huge metal vats and a lot of electronic equipment"), the cellar ("hundreds of oak barrels, which produce an intense, cedary smell"), offices, and various labs and tasting rooms. Interns spend most of their time in the labs or in the Production Tasting Room adjacent to the labs. While most interns are based at the Oakville winery, the Research Enology intern and a few Lab Tech interns work at the Woodbridge winery, which is located near the town of Stockton, a two-and-a-half hour drive from San Francisco.

Grapes aren't the only things that prosper amid Napa Valley's sun-dappled hills and royal blue skies—interns who enjoy bicycling, picnicking, hiking, and star gazing do as well. "On weekends, some friends and I would rent mountain bikes and ride over the most amazing countryside," recalled an intern. "Looking out over different vineyards and their colorful autumn foliage, I felt like I was in God's country." But the valley's chief attractions are the nearly 250 wineries, many of which offer free wine tasting to the public. Said an intern: "There's nothing like this place anywhere. Dozens of wineries line [the main thoroughfare] highway 29 and you can spend an entire day working your way up the highway, sampling wine at every stop." Napa is also famous for its gourmet delights: "The other interns and I would sometimes splurge and go to one of the valley's terrific restaurants. I liked Mustard's Grill, an upscale (but casual) roadhouse with the world's best mashed potatoes." If this bacchic wonderland ever grows tiresome, the city of Berkeley is about an hour's drive and San Francisco is about a 90 minute trip.

SELECTION

The program is open to college juniors and seniors (at least 21 years old), recent graduates, and graduate students. Lab Technician applicants must have taken some coursework in biology, chemistry, or food/fermentation sciences. The other three positions—Enology intern, Research intern, and Research Enology intern—require a background in viticulture or enology. A sizable proportion of applicants have traditionally been students at University of California at Davis, Fresno State University, Cornell, and other schools famous for wine-education programs. Students who do not attend these "feeder" schools should make a special effort to demonstrate a strong interest in wine.

APPLICATION PROCEDURE

Although the deadline to submit application materials is rolling, the coordinator advises candidates to apply at least four to eight weeks before the start date of the internship. Required materials consist of a cover letter and a resumé. Finalists must visit the winery for a personal interview.

OVERVIEW

 The same inspiration that once prompted the poet Keats to write, "O for a draught of vintage!, that hath been cool'd a long age in the deep delvèd earth," awaits interns at Robert Mondavi Winery. Behind the scenes at America's preeminent premium-wine winery, Mondavi interns gain an appreciation and understanding of wine that will last a lifetime. But unlike Keats, Mondavi interns experience no flights of fancy; rather, their work is grounded in the laboratory where they conduct chemical analysis and experiments on developing wine. Carrying out research of integral importance to the winery, interns contribute to Mondavi's ongoing American success story.

FOR MORE INFORMATION . . .

■ Robert Mondavi Winery
Internship Program
P.O. Box 106
Oakville, CA 94562
(707) 963-9611

JPMorgan

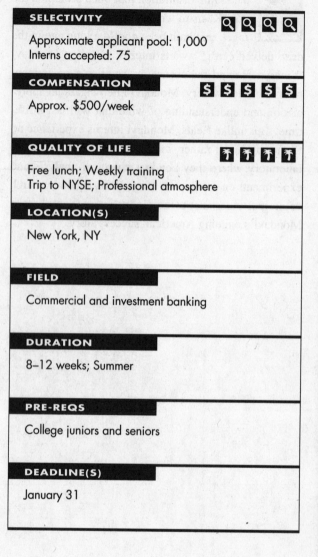

SELECTIVITY	
Approximate applicant pool: 1,000 Interns accepted: 75	🔍 🔍 🔍 🔍

COMPENSATION	
Approx. $500/week	$ $ $ $

QUALITY OF LIFE	
Free lunch; Weekly training Trip to NYSE; Professional atmosphere	🌴 🌴 🌴 🌴

LOCATION(S)

New York, NY

FIELD

Commercial and investment banking

DURATION

8–12 weeks; Summer

PRE-REQS

College juniors and seniors

DEADLINE(S)

January 31

As with any other commercial bank, you can just stroll into JP Morgan and open a checking account with little complication. But there's a catch—you must be able to maintain a minimum balance of $5 million!

Morgan's balance requirement may be a bit steep for most people, but that hasn't prevented it from operating as a traditional commercial bank. In addition to receiving deposits, Morgan issues municipal bonds and makes loans to companies and governments, including an unprecedented £10 million loan to France in 1870 to a $5.5 billion loan to Kuwait in 1992 (both loans were made to help those countries repair war damages).

In 1989, the U.S. Federal Reserve Board allowed JP Morgan to underwrite securities as well as conduct its regular business—just as it had done before the Banking Act of 1933, which forced Morgan to choose one type of banking over another. Now the nation's fourth largest bank, JP Morgan is considered a veritable "superbank," with commercial and investment banking capabilities that render it the envy of Wall Street. In addition to advancing loans and accepting deposits, JP Morgan offers corporate finance advice, underwrites and trades securities, and manages investment funds for new companies as well as established corporate giants like McDonald's, Sony, Procter & Gamble, PepsiCo, and United Airlines.

DESCRIPTION

JP Morgan hires approximately 75 interns every summer for positions in Management Services (where interns act as consultants, analyzing internal business practices throughout the firm), Audit and Financial Management, Global Technology and Operations, and Global Markets. Another 20 or so interns work in these departments as part of Inroads and SEO.

Interns in Audit and Financial Management are placed in either the Audit department or the Financial Group. Acting like public accountants, Audit interns evaluate Morgan's business practices. One Audit intern reviewed the Securities Operations department's process for handling trading records and credit tickets. "I interviewed employees to figure out how the records and tickets are handled, created a flow chart of the process, checked the chart against what the department actually does, and then wrote a one-page report on how well I thought the process worked."

Engaged in the work of traditional accounting, interns in the Financial Group prepare financial statements and budget plans for senior management, stockholders, the IRS, and regulatory agencies like the Securities and Exchange Commission (SEC). One Financial intern helped prepare a "10Q," the SEC name for a company's quarterly report. "I picked up the financial numbers on a Friday, while they were still confidential," she explained, "and was instructed that under no circumstances could I tell anyone about the information before Monday's public announcement." After contacting the chairman's office to request that he write an introduction to the report and then securing the signatures of several managing directors, she proofread the report and forwarded it to the printers. "I remember being amazed at the amount of responsibility I had," she said.

In Global Technology and Operations (GTO), an intern worked on a "pricing model," a computer program that generates prices and other key statistics for such financial instruments as swaps, swap options, caps, and floors based on interest rates. Running back and forth between JP Morgan's securities trading floor, where traders checked the pricing model's output, and his department's system designers, who modified the program in accordance with traders' intuitive "feel for what the numbers should look like," he eventually developed a pricing model that worked. "I certainly felt important," he said. "At the end of the day, the traders didn't go home until I issued my final report and the systems people didn't leave until I came back from the traders." Another GTO intern worked on a budget-forecasting program that determined how much money JP Morgan should allocate for office equipment. "[My managers] gave me free rein to create the program," he said. "So I suggested using Paradox [i.e., a data-management computer program] and interviewed employees and managers to find out what features I should incorporate." Spending the entire summer documenting the computer code and preparing a user manual, he finally

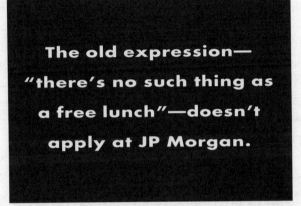

The old expression— "there's no such thing as a free lunch"—doesn't apply at JP Morgan.

finished the assignment on his second-to-last day. "The program was very helpful," he said, "because it gave employees a better handle on how to prepare the budgets."

To the disappointment of many Gordon Gekko wannabes, there isn't a formal undergraduate internship at Morgan in the investment-banking division known as corporate finance, reponsible for financing mergers and acquisitions and underwriting securities and debt issues for bank clients. However, another investment-banking component of JP Morgan—Global Markets, comprising the Sales, Trading, and Research departments—does offer an internship program. Interns in Research assist researchers in evaluating the economy and the various financial markets. In Trading, interns help traders buy and sell stocks, bonds, and other financial instruments. Interns in Sales help salespeople sell stocks for clients. One Trading intern helped Morgan's British pound-sterling trader by "keeping the position"—that is, keeping track of the running dollar total of all the traders' transactions. After the intern gained the department's confidence, the chief trader allowed him to help make trades. "When you first start, it's really nerve-racking," he said. "At the press of a button [on the computer], you can lose thousands of dollars. . . . But if you're thick skinned and savvy, you'll eventually be successful."

JP Morgan's downtown New York offices consist of four buildings in the heart of Wall Street. With mahogany-wood desks and plush banker chairs adorning the main room, a three-tiered chandelier hanging overhead, and a copper box containing founder J. Pierpont Morgan's original will, the building at 23 Wall evokes a solid sense of tradition. While a few interns work at 23 Wall, most are situated at headquarters, at 60 Wall Street and known by Morgan people as the "Taj Mahal" because it towers above nearby buildings. After flashing a Morgan ID, interns may head up to their workstations—sometimes cubicles, other times old oak desks formerly used in executive offices.

Work areas are kept open, reflecting Morgan's philosophy that teamwork is the cornerstone of the bank's success. The distinct lack of walls, however, makes chatter from employees easily perceptible. "I'd never talk on the phone about anything personal," said an intern. "There's little privacy here."

Morgan devotes a significant amount of time and resources to educating interns. "We don't have a short-term outlook here," said an employee and former intern. "We train interns in order to make them Morgan material." For nearly two hours each week, interns gather at 60 Wall's top-floor conference room to listen to vice presidents and managing directors speak on such topics as changes in the industry, bank strategy, and banking regulations. "They go the whole nine yards, showing slides and distributing handouts," said an intern. "If you intend on developing a career in this industry, it's in your best interest to take notes."

Morgan also arranges various social events and field trips for interns. Three receptions, complete with hors d'oeuvres and beverages, allow interns to meet recruiters and managers in a casual, friendly setting after work. Morgan also subsidizes for tickets to Broadway shows and Yankees games. But the highlights of the summer are said to be two afternoon field trips, one to the New York Stock Exchange and the other to the Federal Reserve Bank. At the NYSE, interns attend a lecture on the history of the Exchange and then take to a balcony to observe the trading floor. "It was somewhat crazy," said an intern. "People were yelling at each other, paper was flying, and everywhere you looked, 'floor traders' were flashing their own special sets of hand signals, sometimes a fist for 'sell' or an open hand for 'buy.'" During their visit to the Federal Reserve Bank, interns descend into the bank's vault, which holds much of the world's gold deposits. Buried 30 feet below a network of subway tunnels, the vault sports a 90-ton solid-steel door, 18-foot-thick walls forged from concrete and reinforced steel, and seemingly endless stacks of solid gold bars. "We saw a historical display of all the denominations of money ever printed in the United States, including the $10,000 and $100,000 bills," explained an intern, "And at the end, we were given a [small bag] of freshly shredded money."

The old expression—"there's no such thing as a free lunch"—doesn't apply at JP Morgan. The bank spends millions of dollars a year to ensure that all employees, interns included, eat for free at the company's main cafeteria. Found inside the 15 Broad building, the cafeteria offers everything from nonfat yogurt to fried chicken. Although "there's a lot of variety," the fare doesn't compare to the country club cuisine served in the executive dining room located on the 47th floor of the 60 Wall building. Twice during the summer, interns are invited to dine with a few of Morgan's 400 or so managing directors to discuss bank careers. With New York's breathtaking skyline visible from the room's tall windows, formally attired waiters serve three-course meals, from shrimp cocktail to broiled sirloin to chocolate mousse. "It was really intimate—just a few interns and one director, casually discussing the various areas of the bank," said an intern.

SELECTION

 Applicants to the four programs—Management Services Summer Internship Program, Global Technology and Operations Summer Internship Program, Audit and Financial Management Summer Internship Program, and Global Markets Summer Internship Program— must be juniors or seniors who are returning to school in the fall. While no specific major is required for Management Services, GTO, or Global Markets, Audit and Financial Management seeks business or related majors. In addition to strong quantitative, analytical, and communications skills, all applicants must have "a strong interest in the financial services industry."

APPLICATION PROCEDURE

 The deadline is January 31. Students should submit a resumé, cover letter, and transcript to only one program. After internship coordinators screen resumés, top candidates are interviewed at their college campuses, or at JP Morgan's New York offices at applicants' expense.

OVERVIEW

Students interested in both commercial and investment banking have a friend in JP Morgan—it's probably the only Wall Street investment firm to offer a structured internship program for undergraduates. With its assortment of receptions, lectures on banking, and projects involving finance as well as trips to the New York Stock Exchange and Federal Reserve Bank, the internship program at JP Morgan exposes students to all that is quintessentially Wall Street.

FOR MORE INFORMATION . . .

■ JP Morgan & Co., Incorporated
60 Wall Street
New York, NY 10260
(212) 648-9909

The date: August 1, 1981. The time: 12:01 AM. The video: "Video Killed the Radio Star" by the Buggles.

A characteristically iconoclastic beginning for a cable-television network whose groundbreaking impact cannot be overestimated. Over the past 13 years, MTV's ongoing tapestry of music videos has not only defined how the young consume music, but how they talk, dress, and watch television. MTV's willingness to experiment continues to stretch the possibilities of television, giving us shows like "Yo! MTV Raps," which has helped bring rap music to the mainstream, and "The Real World," which has satisfied voyeurs by capturing the unrehearsed activities of seven housemates. Despite those who blame MTV for corrupting the American mind, the network has attracted over 60 million subscribers and has even gained the respect of President Clinton, who participated in its "Choose or Lose" forum as a presidential candidate.

DESCRIPTION

MTV has been accepting interns since it hit the airwaves in the early eighties. But up until a few years ago, the internship program wasn't much of a "program"—it was disorganized, decentralized, and inconsistent from department to department. Things haven't gotten a whole lot better, but efforts have been made to improve it with the addition of a full-time intern coordinator, speaker luncheons, and a field trip. Depending on departmental need and intern preference, interns may be placed in a "business" department such as Marketing, Press and Public Relations, Programming, International Programming, and Advertising; a "creative" department such as Art Promotions, Talents Relations, Graphics, On-Air Talent, and Video Library; or a particular MTV program such as "MTV News," "Beevis and Butthead," or "MTV Jams."

Although responsibilities vary from department to department, a few tasks are common to all. Said an intern: "Working the phones, making photocopies, sending faxes, making more photocopies, running messages, making even more photocopies—these are common denominators for every intern." In addition, few interns leave MTV without becoming an expert in dubbing tapes: "Every day, I was asked to dub beta tapes to 3/4" tapes. It's a simple—and totally boring job."

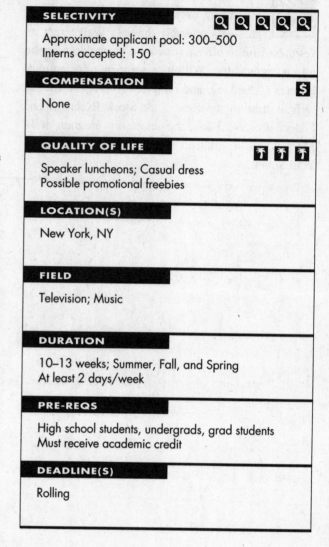

SELECTIVITY

Approximate applicant pool: 300–500
Interns accepted: 150

COMPENSATION

None

QUALITY OF LIFE

Speaker luncheons; Casual dress
Possible promotional freebies

LOCATION(S)

New York, NY

FIELD

Television; Music

DURATION

10–13 weeks; Summer, Fall, and Spring
At least 2 days/week

PRE-REQS

High school students, undergrads, grad students
Must receive academic credit

DEADLINE(S)

Rolling

Besides enduring "mega amounts" of busywork, interns have assignments unique to their department. Working for "Yo! MTV Raps," an intern solicited audience members for the show's live performances. "Before a band like Lords of the Underground or M.C. Lyte played live in the studio, I'd round up an audience by calling contacts at other departments. I'd also invite my friends." Another intern, this one in Talent Relations, organized and prepared videos for the weekly "acquisition meeting," where department heads pick which videos will be played on MTV. To her delight, she was invited to observe one of the acquisition meetings: "The meeting was pretty informal. A bunch of executives and department heads watch about 30 videos and make comments about which ones should be shown on the channel. If a video is too violent or sexually explicit, or if it's just not good enough for MTV, the group rejects it."

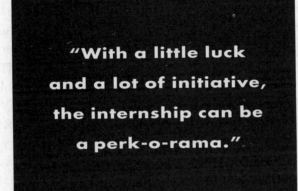

"With a little luck and a lot of initiative, the internship can be a perk-o-rama."

One of the most popular departments among interns is MTV News. Interns here start the day clipping newspaper articles for the "MTV Daily Digest," a packet of newspaper articles distributed to forty or so producers and writers. "Sifting through newspapers isn't exactly a thrill a minute. And photocopying 40 sets of articles can be maddening," said an intern. "But [the 'Daily Digest'] is really important as it's often a source of story ideas for the newswriters." News interns also do a lot of "logging tapes," which requires them to watch a particular segment and mark down the time code at various points in the action. For some it's sheer busywork, but for others "it's the rare opportunity to see raw outtakes— stuff that's never aired, like pieces of an interview with Madonna on her 'Blond Ambition Tour.'"

MTV has never been known for offering interns a comprehensive array of extracurriculars—at least not on an official basis. To be sure, recent years have seen a few speaker luncheons, featuring bigwigs like the CEO of Viacom (MTV's parent company), the CEO of MTV, and the MTV creative director. Administrators say there is the "possibility" of a field trip to the Network Operations Center on Long Island—"it's where our signal is sent to the satellite, where MTV technically becomes a TV network."

But the golden opportunities are those that are unsanctioned. Interns might catch the occasional impromptu performance, which some groups are fond of staging when they visit the MTV offices. "It was pretty cool," said an intern. "I'd be dubbing some tapes and find out that the Wildflowers or Blind Melon was downstairs doing an acoustic jam. Needless to say, I bolted down there in a hurry." When they find the time, interns sometimes steal away to the MTV studio on 42nd Street and watch veejays film their segments. Said an intern: "I'd watch the action from the control room or the sound stage. Everything is a lot smaller than it looks on TV." Interns who make the right friends might accompany a producer on a shoot. "I went with the crew to Webster Hall, where I watched [MTV News anchor] Kurt Loder interview Mick Jagger about his new solo album. . . I got to shake Mick's hand. . .[a]nd I stood by as a photographer from *The New York Times* did a photo shoot of Mick playing the harmonica."

As the previous examples suggest, being at MTV offers a smorgasbord of star-scoping. MTV veejays and news anchors are easy game: "You'd see regulars like Kurt Loder, John Norris, Kennedy, and Daisy Fuentes pretty often—it was no big deal." Appearances by other MTV personalities are less frequent but no less memorable: "Cindy Crawford came in once a month to host 'House of Style,' and I declare—she is twice as beautiful in person." But nothing compares to the bevy of artists who visit the offices. Said an intern: "MTV is a magnet for the hottest acts. They'll come by to say hi to executives or discuss a project with producers. One day Aerosmith walked by me in the hall. A week later I shared an elevator with the B-52's." Explaining the proper celebrity-watching etiquette, another intern advised: "You can't act starstruck—you've got to be cool and contain your bliss."

It's not hard to believe the intern who said that "with a little luck and a lot of initiative, the internship can be a perk-o-rama." Promotional CDs, concert tickets, and party invitations adorn the desk of virtually every high-level employee, and interns who work hard may be rewarded with a few of these spoils. Said an intern: "I got to see some great concerts during my time at MTV—[such as] Keith Richards at the Paramount and Pete Townsend at the Beacon." Added another, "My boss let me have his invitation to a Rick James listening party at the club M.K. It was a funky affair—to get inside, you had to rub a purple butterfly tattoo on your arm." There's also a variety of MTV paraphernalia to be had—if one is "at the right place at the right time." "I picked up an MTV coffee mug, tote bag, and watch," said an intern. "But I was lucky—I became friends with the right people."

Smack dab in the center of New York's honky-tonk Times Square district, MTV commandeers seven floors of a 53-floor skyscraper. The offices are decked out in "Art Deco fashion—sleek, black, and kind of 80s." The decor is suitably funky, with a reception desk "built into a huge rock," a fish tank in the shape of an *M*, and "black rubber floors." Interns are spread out throughout the offices, some with their own desks, others making do with an empty desk or conference table. A few departments devote a common office to interns, MTV News, for example, has an "intern room" described as "small, cramped, windowless, and messy." But what MTV lacks in workspace it makes up for in casualness. It's acceptable for interns to wear jeans, and those in creative departments are given even more sartorial license: "The more you dress like a rock star, the more you fit in."

SELECTION

The internship is open to undergraduates of any level and graduate students; a few exceptionally qualified high school students are also accepted. Applicants must arrange to receive academic credit for the internship. The intern coordinator says that selection is based on an applicant's "previous experience, academic record, proven responsibility, eagerness, and willingness to learn." Past interns advise applicants to "emphasize the personal qualities that make you stand out from the rest of the pack."

APPLICATION PROCEDURE

The application deadline is rolling. Required materials include a cover letter, resumé, and written verification of academic credit. The coordinator conducts a mandatory personal interview with the most promising candidates.

OVERVIEW

How many internships can boast a write-up in *Seventeen*?

The article "I Was an Intern at MTV" appeared in the magazine's August 1990 issue and described the experiences of a former intern, who said she "learned more about television [at MTV] than [she] could have in any course or from any book." A worthy point, but one in need of elaboration. The MTV internship *can* be a terrific learning experience, but perhaps more so than any other program, interns must have the gumption to ensure they don't stagnate in busywork purgatory. Said an intern: "Those who aren't afraid to ask for better assignments can shape their time at MTV into something great."

FOR MORE INFORMATION . . .

■ MTV: Music Television
Intern Coordinator
1515 Broadway
22nd Floor
New York, NY 11036
(212) 258-8000

SELECTIVITY	N/A
Approximate applicant pool: N/A Interns accepted: Est. 1,000	

COMPENSATION	$ $ $
$100–$400/week for undergrads $400–$700/week for grad students	

QUALITY OF LIFE	N/A
N/A	

LOCATION(S)
AL, CA, FL, MD, MS, OH, TX, VA

FIELD
Aerospace and aeronautics

DURATION
6 weeks–4 months Summer

PRE-REQS
Varies with program–see Selection

DEADLINE(S)
Varies with program–see Application Procedure

What do you need to become a NASA astronaut?

An ability to identify all 88 constellations, the strength to bench-press 250 pounds, and a promise to abstain from any sexual activity for two years.

Just kidding.

To qualify for NASA's Astronaut Candidate Program, you need to be between 58.5 and 76 inches in height, pass a thorough physical examination, hold a bachelor's degree in science or engineering, and have at least three years of related work experience.

But don't assume joining NASA's elite is an easy task—since 1959, only 214 individuals have been selected to become astronauts. In that time, NASA has done much to advance America's mission "to plan, direct, and conduct aeronautical and space activities." Despite its share of setbacks, NASA has landed Americans on the moon, mapped the surfaces of every planet in the solar system except Pluto, and implemented the world's first reusable system of space shuttles. With an eye toward the 21st century, NASA is making progress on a permanently manned space station, a lunar colony, and a manned Mars expedition.

DESCRIPTION

There are at least 200 different NASA programs, ranging from high school summer jobs to undergraduate and graduate internships to graduate fellowships. The multitude of programs allows students to work at NASA's nine facilities (listed below), and within its dozens of university research labs. The federal agency responsible for all of America's aeronautical and space programs, NASA has much to offer students who are interested in airplane design and outer space technology. Areas of research include robotics, earth sciences (biology, geology, environmental science, etc.), aerodynamics, biomedicine and biotechnology, materials processing, space propulsion, space structures, and satellite communications.

Most NASA programs are specific to each center and managed by the centers' University Affairs Offices. The Goddard site (infamous for helping to develop the Hubble space telescope, whose lenses were warped), for example, offers a Summer Institute on Atmospheric and Hydrospheric Sciences, where interns spend the first two weeks of the summer learning about available research projects from Goddard scientists. Afterward, one intern studied atmospheric gravity waves. "They're one of many kinds of gravity waves, all of which induce density and temperature fluctuations in the atmosphere," he explained. "It's important that we understand gravity waves completely because they adversely affect space travel, satellite communications, and radio transmissions."

Because Johnson Space Center designs the manned spacecrafts, acts as "mission control" for all piloted space-flights, and trains astronauts, it's a favorite place among interns. A graduate student intern in the Biotechnology group worked to create an "automated bioreactor" (i.e., a vat used to grow cells) that is able to function in space. "The main problem on Earth," he explained, "is that gravity creates a high shear stress environment for the cells. On Earth, these cells end up against the sides or bottom [of the vat], where they can't grow or differentiate very easily, but in space, they're free-floating." That low shear-stress environment, he explained, will allow scientists to grow whole corneas for use in eye transplants or to generate breast cancer tumors for testing anticancer drugs.

Another intern at Johnson, this one an undergraduate, worked in the Anthropometrics and Biomechanics Laboratory, where he helped redesign a shuttle treadmill that astronauts use in space to keep their bodies active. "Because there's zero gravity in space," he explained, "we attach the astronauts to the treadmill with bungee cords." But the lab figured that if the tension on the cords was made adjustable, astronauts could simulate their exact body weight. Video-taping several of the astronauts while they ran the treadmill, he helped his lab group create an adjustable model. "It was definitely exciting to work with the astronauts," he concluded. "I learned a lot from them about how the body reacts in space."

> Of the approximately 100 active NASA astronauts, as many as five are former NASA interns.

Some NASA programs are handled by universities but all are open to students nationwide. Managed by Florida A&M University, the Kennedy Space Center's Space Life Sciences Training program (SLST), for example, provides undergraduates with a six-week education in space life sciences. Rotating among departments, SLST interns study how to grow crops in space, how to keep bacteria out of the shuttle's water supply, and how to break down human wastes in space. "For a future space station, lunar colony, or manned mission to Mars (an estimated three years round trip), we'd need to recycle everything from water to food to fecal matter," explained an intern. But because such research requires that experiments be run in space, where oxygen is nonexistent and gravity's effects are not felt, interns help prepare the experiments for astronauts to perform during shuttle missions. One intern was assigned to a team that worked with sea urchin gametes (i.e., sperm and eggs). "[NASA] wanted to know how zero gravity affects embryonic development," he said, "and our job was to come up with the specifics of the tests. We created customized plastic bags to hold the gametes, determined how the astronauts were to do the experiments, and ran vibration tests to discover what percentage [of gametes] could survive a launch." Because Kennedy is situated on a 140,000-acre wildlife refuge, SLST interns also monitor endangered species, like the indigo snake, to see what impact shuttle launchings have on the animals that inhabit the center's grounds. "What made this program so great overall is that you got to see how engineering and biology come together," concluded an intern.

Administered by San Jose State University, the NASA-Ames Research and Development (R&D) program allows students to participate in Ames' projects in computer science, aerodynamics, flight simulation, and infrared astronomy, among others. As part of the Computational Fluid Dynamics branch, an undergraduate intern in the R&D Program modeled a small region of an F-16 fighter plane's wing on the computer. "We were studying airflow over the wing," he said, "and we wanted to see if the solutions we got on the computer agreed with those in wind tunnel tests." Spending some of his time in an Ames' wind tunnel, he also watched researchers collect airflow data. "Once [NASA] validates that the computer model works as well as the wind tunnel tests, [it] can test different plane designs much more efficiently," he said. Combined with information accrued from actual flight experiments, he explained, the computer model could potentially lead to more sophisticated designs for future planes.

NASA also has a contract with the Jet Propulsion Laboratory (JPL), located in Pasadena, CA. JPL designs and explores the solar system with automated spacecrafts, like *Voyager* and *Galileo* as well as the ill-fated *Mars Observer*. As part of JPL's Summer Employment Program, interns work in business administration and assist with experiments, designs, and tests. An intern in the Digital Receiver group, for example, analyzed the new generation of digital receivers, designed to replace the analog ones currently utilized at sites in Madrid, Spain, Canberra, Australia, and Goldstone, CA. By collecting incoming data from spacecrafts, receivers allow researchers to see space images and determine such facts as planet temperatures. Because the new receiver has yet to be built, the intern helped test its design by writing computer simulations. "[My work] wasn't too difficult," she said, "but everything you do at JPL has some bearing on NASA's overall mission."

Most NASA locations offer seminars and field trips in addition to social activities. The Space Life Sciences Training Program at Kennedy, for example, has students attend lectures every morning on such topics as "exobiology" (i.e., the search for extraterrestrial life) and the future Mars mission. At Ames, students can log-on to their E-mail to find a schedule of the week's lectures, from talks on algorithm theory to Cray computers. At other centers, interns may attend speeches on space medicine, fluid-flow analysis, and the affect of cosmic dust on space structures, engines, and suits. Probably one of the most compelling discussions is on the KC-135, a NASA jet flown out of Johnson to simulate zero gravity. Called the "vomit comet" in NASA circles for its ability to nauseate up to 90 percent of its passengers, the plane alternately shoots up toward the heavens and then nosedives, giving a 20-second period of

near weightlessness in which NASA may test experiments. But the highlight of any intern's summer is meeting the astronauts, who occasionally stop by the centers to recall the fascinating details of their former missions. "I think that after hearing [astronaut Charles Bolden], we all wanted to become astronauts ourselves," said an intern at Lewis.

Away from their workstations, interns certainly see some "cool stuff." Interns at Ames, for example, may tour the center's 80-by-120-foot wind tunnel, the largest of its kind. At JPL one summer, interns took a trip to Goldstone, approximately three hours northeast of Pasadena by car, to see NASA's 70-meter spacecraft-tracking antenna. "When [the antenna] wasn't transmitting," recalled an intern, "we climbed into the dish and roamed around its smooth vastness." Interns at Johnson may see a mock-up of the astronauts' sleeping quarters on the space station. "Because there's zero gravity [in space], they can sleep upright, downright, or whichever way," said an intern. "[At the mock-up], the beds were against the walls . . . and so the astronauts don't bounce around while they sleep, they Velcro themselves to the bed." At Kennedy, interns tour Space Port USA, a building housing old rockets, astronaut uniforms, and a memorial for the *Challenger* crew. Kennedy interns also see Kennedy's Vehicle Assembly Building (VAB), used to put together rockets and shuttles. "Because [VAB is] hundreds of feet tall," explained an intern, "sometimes rain clouds form in there." What would a summer be without seeing a shuttle launching or landing? At Kennedy, the mother of all shuttle launchings, interns have an opportunity to see shuttles shoot up into the sky. When it comes to landings, however, the shuttle can touch down at Kennedy or at Edwards Air Force Base near JPL. "We got up really early and boarded a bus to the base," remembered a JPL intern from 1991. "We sat on some bleachers and waited and waited. We weren't too close to the landing strip, but we saw [the shuttle] come in. The whole scene was inspiring—even better than on TV."

With often up to 300 interns at any one center, planned social activities are a real unifying factor. As part of the Ames Alliance, Ames interns meet one another to organize trips to San Francisco, biking expeditions, and Saturday broomball. At JPL, interns can join JPL's hunting, fishing, and sailing clubs, among others. Goddard occasionally holds evening receptions for interns—casual gatherings at which hors d'oeuvres, fruits, and vegetables are served. For the fitness-minded, most NASA facilities house fitness centers offering aerobics, StairMasters, stationary bikes, and free-weights. In addition, NASA sites often contain volleyball courts, running tracks, and softball diamonds.

Financial compensation for interns varies considerably. Some NASA summer internships for undergrads pay as little as $1,000 for a ten-week period, while other undergraduate summer internships compensate students with as much as $4,000. Graduate students in summer internships earn from $1,600 to nearly $3,000 a month. Pay depends on major, class level, and experience. Some interns are also provided with travel stipends and free housing. In the case of Goddard's Summer Institute, a few government cars are also at interns' disposal.

SELECTION

 Each NASA program has its own set of criteria. The Space Life Sciences Training Program, for example, is for undergraduates only (at least sophomore) studying life sciences, premedicine, bioengineering, or related fields. But NASA has an internship for virtually everyone, from high school students at least 16 years of age to college undergraduates to graduate students (including those studying medicine, business, or law) to faculty members. There are also specific programs for minority undergraduates and graduate students, like the nationwide Graduate and Undergraduate Student Researchers Programs for Minorities, in addition to minority programs at the field centers. Some programs require a minimum 3.0 GPA. Fields applicable include almost every area of science, mathematics, and engineering. For liberal arts students, there are few internships at the field centers; the largest is a nationwide cooperative-education program in NASA's budgeting, accounting, and procurement departments. Any major is eligible for this program, but business experience is preferred.

APPLICATION PROCEDURE

 NASA deadlines vary, from as early as December 31 for some summer undergraduate programs at the field offices to April 1 for some fellowships. Contact the Higher Education Branch at NASA Headquarters, c/o Editor, "University Guide to NASA" for a copy of "University Guide to NASA," a brochure outlining NASA programs for college students, graduate students, faculty members, and minorities; the brochure also provides information on such internships as the Space Life Sciences Training Program. Students may also write to the Higher Education Branch for a booklet explaining an internship called the Graduate Student Researchers Program. To receive information on programs specific to particular NASA centers, including part-time and summer work for high school students, as well as the NASA Cooperative Education Program for high school students and college undergraduates contact the offices at the addresses and phone numbers on the next page.

OVERVIEW

 In the words of NASA's head of staffing policy, an experience at NASA is "a chance to work with cutting-edge technology and leading scientific experts." That's right on the mark. Students at NASA can design space shuttle parts, study airplane wings, write computer programs for satellites, investigate the environmental impact of space programs, and research robotics and lasers. Since its creation by Congress in 1958, NASA has hired interns to make a substantial impact in aeronautics and space-related science and technology. Former interns who went on to become NASA employees are currently helping to design a space station, have helped construct *Galileo*, and have even flown in some of America's historic space missions. Of the approximately 100 active NASA astronauts, according to Johnson's Astronaut Selection Office, as many as five are former NASA interns.

FOR MORE INFORMATION . . .

■ NASA Headquarters
Higher Education Branch
Mail Code FEH
Washington, DC 20546
(202) 358-0000

■ NASA Ames Research Center
University Affairs Office
Code 241-3
Moffett Field, CA 94035
(415) 604-5802

■ NASA Goddard Space Flight Center
University Programs
Mail Stop 160
Greenbelt Road
Greenbelt, MD 20771
(301) 286-9690

■ Jet Propulsion Laboratory 183-900
Educational Affairs Office
4800 Oak Grove Drive
Pasadena, CA 91109-8099
(818) 354-8251

■ NASA Johnson Space Center
University Programs
Mail Stop AHU
Houston, TX 77058
(713) 483-4724

■ NASA Kennedy Space Center
University Liason Office
Mail Code HM-CIU
KSC, FL 32899
(407) 867-2512

■ NASA Langley Research Center
Office of Education
Mail Stop 400
Hampton, VA 23681-0001
(804) 864-4000

■ NASA Lewis Research Center
Educational Programs
Mail Stop 7-4
21000 Brookpark Road
Cleveland, OH 44135
(216) 433-2957

■ NASA Marshall Space Flight Center
University Affairs
Mail Stop DS01
MSFC, AL 35812
(205) 544-0997

■ NASA Stennis Space Center
Management Operations
University Affairs Office
Mail Code MA00
SSC, MS 39529
(601) 688-3830

National
Audubon
Society

At a recent rally in Washington, D.C. a young man in a wolf costume performed a rap before a crowd of nearly 100 people. With a boom box busting the beat, he declared: "For 50 years he's been under attack. Now it's time to bring the wolf back."

Was this a wannabe musician, a wolf lover, or an intern with the National Audubon Society? Actually, it was all of the above. As a representative of the Audubon Society, he staged the performance to encourage the U.S. Fish and Wildlife Service to place the endangered gray wolf in Yellowstone National Park.

Fighting for the rights of endangered species is only part of the National Audubon Society's mission. Founded in 1886 as an organization to protect the lives of birds, Audubon now also defends wetlands, water sources, and ancient forests. Managing more than 100 sanctuaries nationwide, the society works to restore natural ecosystems "for the benefit of humanity and the Earth's biological diversity." With 516 chapters and over 600,000 members, the nonprofit National Audubon Society has made a significant impact, helping to establish parks, halt the building of environmentally damaging infrastructures, and create various refuges and preserves.

SELECTIVITY	🔍 🔍 🔍 🔍
Approximate applicant pool: 100–200 Interns accepted: 15 (Summer), 3–8 (Fall, Winter)	

COMPENSATION	$
None	

QUALITY OF LIFE	🌴 🌴 🌴
Lobbying on Capitol Hill (DC); Weekly brown-bags Intern Alley; "Free and easy" atmosphere	

LOCATION(S)
Washington, DC and other cities (see Description)

FIELD
Environmental policy

DURATION
12 weeks: Summer 12–20 weeks: Fall, Winter

PRE-REQS
College juniors and seniors, recent grads, grad students

DEADLINE(S)
Summer .... April 1   Fall ..... August 1 Winter .... January 1

DESCRIPTION

In the early 1980s, Audubon established an internship program in environmental policy. The Government Affairs Internship Program exposes students to environmental policy-making, grassroots organizing, and lobbying in one of the following departments: Wildlife, Wetlands, Population, International, Public Lands, and Water Resources.

Like most internships, Audubon's Government Affairs Internship Program requires interns to do some busywork. In addition to performing clerical tasks, interns respond to the dozens of letters that flow into Audubon's offices every day. "Most were from [Audubon] members or kids asking for information on what they could do [to help out]," explained an intern. "We'd mail them some Audubon pamphlets, which describe the various issues." Interns also update Audubon's various computer databases. Tracking Audubon's staunch supporters of national wildlife refuges, one intern input activists' addresses and phone numbers. "These were people Audubon could count on to go above and beyond the call of duty—get on the phones, write letters, and the like."

There's ample busywork for interns to do outside the office as well. Either alone or as a pack, interns occasionally make "Hill drops," distributing Audubon literature to representatives' and senators' offices. "[Hill drops are] an important part of what we do," explained an intern. "We're here to influence Congress, and one way to do that is by getting materials into the right hands."

When they're not shuffling papers and gofering, interns draft fact sheets and reports that affect congressional legislation. One intern assembled a fact sheet on the California Desert Protection Act. "It was a one-page summary of California's current efforts, dating back to 1976, to create the Mojave National Park," he said. "I described the legislative history, the congressmen and senators who introduced the bill, and what the bill was intended to accomplish." Distributed to members of Congress and other interested parties, fact sheets are used by environmental groups to teach legislators and the public about environmental issues. Another intern wrote a report describing the effect the Endangered Species Act has had on industry. Phoning timber, oil, and chemical companies, he asked senior biologists and public relations officers for examples that showed how their companies had complied with the act. "In one case, a business had set aside a substantial plot of land for endangered animals." The report would come in handy, he explained, because the act is up for reauthorization in 1994. "[The report] showed that business development and protection of endangered animals aren't necessarily mutually exclusive."

Interns who gain the confidence of their supervisors are rewarded with "exposure to the front line," where they participate in lobbying efforts. The most effective form of lobbying, according to an Audubon lobbyist, is the grassroots kind, where congressional constituents call and write congress to suggest to their senators and representatives how to vote. On behalf of grassroots campaigns, interns spend a few hours each week on the phone with Audubon members asking them to contact their congresspeople (by phone or letter) and express their opinions on important environmental legislation. Like Audubon members, interns also write and phone congressional offices. One intern drafted a letter concerning the closing of a military base in Virginia. "I sent the letter to two senators asking them to support converting the base's land to a wildlife refuge."

Interns undoubtedly make the most substantial contributions by lobbying in person. Having secured appointments with legislative assistants (LAs), interns head for the Hill. One intern attempted to convince an LA of the benefits of reauthorizing the Endangered Species Act. "His rep was completely against it for various reasons," he said. "So trying to convince that LA was like talking to a brick wall." Other lobbying efforts are more successful. "I worked very carefully with [Senator] Feinstein's staff . . . [Feinstein] was sponsoring the California Desert Protection Act," said an intern. "Because she and her staff wanted the bill to pass, my role was easy. I provided them with pamphlets and lobbied other senators to support the bill." In rare cases, interns will actually have the opportunity to meet with a senator or representative: "I was talking to the LA, when suddenly the representative came in and asked what we were doing. So I explained the bill's focus on creating a national wildlife refuge system. Surprisingly, he agreed within a few minutes to cosponsor it."

To keep Audubon abreast of the latest developments concerning environmental legislation, interns attend congressional and agency hearings, seminars, and briefings. Taking notes for his supervisor, who was unable to attend, one intern went to a White House briefing on President Clinton's forest plan. Led by executives from the Departments of Agriculture and the Interior, this meeting featured Clinton's commission of scientists who were working to establish a logging plan acceptable to both timbermen and environmentalists. "Most hearings are extremely educational," explained the intern, "because you learn how lawmakers create bills."

> Part of an office culture that's "free and easy," interns frequently wear jeans and are even known to traipse around the office barefoot.

Approximately 35 people are employed by Audubon's D.C. office, located in southeast Washington, D.C., six blocks or so from Capitol Hill. Occupying the second and third floors of a four-story building, Audubon sits directly above a gourmet cafe, florist, and a coffee shop. The office is decorated with framed stills of Audubon-sponsored TV specials, featuring spokespersons like Meryl Streep and Robert Redford. Occupying two rows of cubicles in an area known as "intern alley," interns have their own phones and share five computers. Part of an office culture that's described by a current Audubon lobbyist as "free and easy," interns frequently wear jeans and are even known to traipse around the office barefoot.

To provide interns with an idea of what each department does, Audubon schedules weekly brown-bag luncheons specifically for interns. During most brown-bags, a vice president advises interns on such matters as how to find a job in the environmental field. At one brown-bag in particular, Audubon President Peter Berle visited from New York to lunch with the interns. A former lawyer, New York state assemblyman, and New York state environmental commissioner, Berle understands the politics of environmentalism. During this particular visit, he attempts to listen to interns' recommendations for improving the internship program. "He was genuinely grateful that we were interning at Audubon," recalled an intern. "He told us that our work was important in Audubon's fight to protect the environment."

Involved in wildlife management as well as environmental policy, Audubon also runs camps and sanctuaries, some of which offer internship programs. These programs allow students to become natural history instructors or student assistants at Audubon camps in Connecticut, Maine, and Wyoming. Students may also do field research and give public tours at Audubon's centers in Milwaukee, Wisconsin and Sante Fe, New Mexico or at its sanctuaries in Elgin, Arizona; Trabuco Canyon, California; Sharon, Connecticut; Naples, Florida; Frankfort, Kentucky; Monson, Maine; Garrison and Ithaca, New York; and Harleyville, South Carolina. Interns have the opportunity to do everything from build displays to lead nature walks to collect field data. Positions are generally available year-round.

SELECTION

 Audubon seeks college juniors, seniors, recent graduates, and graduate students. Any major is eligible; no environmental experience whatsoever is necessary, although an interest in the environment is appreciated. Students must possess good verbal and written communication skills.

APPLICATION PROCEDURE

 The deadline for the Government Affairs Internship Program is April 1 for summer, August 1 for fall, and January 1 for winter. Students must submit a cover letter indicating an environmental issue of interest and a writing sample of fewer than ten pages on any subject. After the coordinator screens applications, they're passed along to department managers, who interview top candidates over the phone. Students interested in the wildlife management internship programs should contact the Audubon headquarters office in New York (Attn: Human Resource Department; 700 Broadway; New York, NY 10003; (212) 979-3000) and request material on positions at Audubon camps, centers, and sanctuaries.

OVERVIEW

 If disappearing habitats and endangered species trouble you and you want to do something about it, then the National Audubon Society's Government Affairs internship is for you. Open to undergraduates, recent graduates, and graduate students —even those with no environmental experience— Audubon's program is an excellent education in resource conservation and wildlife management. Afforded an inside look at how Congress makes laws, interns become versed in the ways of Capitol Hill and the politics of environmentalism—a movement critical to the preservation of the planet.

FOR MORE INFORMATION . . .

■ National Audubon Society
Government Affairs Internship Program
666 Pennsylvania Avenue SE
Washington, DC 20003
(202) 547-9009

W ho would have imagined that two wooden peach baskets nailed to a gymnasium balcony in 1891 would beget the game that is currently the most played sport in the United States?

Not James Naismith, the Springfield, Massachusetts, divinity professor who asked his school's custodian to put up the baskets. He just wanted to give his pupils something to do indoors during those cold East Coast winters.

But without Naismith, we wouldn't have basketball or the National Basketball Association (NBA), America's professional basketball league. And without the NBA, we wouldn't have Kareem Abdul-Jabbar's goggles, Pat Riley's slicked-back hair, or Michael Jordan's wagging tongue. From Dr. J and the Big Dipper to Air and Magic, NBA players have established the NBA as the world's preeminent basketball league. Nowhere was its dominance in international basketball more recognizable than at the 1992 Barcelona Olympics, where the Dream Team defeated opponents by an average of 43 points per game to win the Gold Medal.

SELECTIVITY

Approximate applicant pool: 150
Interns accepted: 8–12

COMPENSATION

$200/week stipend

QUALITY OF LIFE

Lunches with NBA execs
Travel opportunities; Basketball mania

LOCATION(S)

New York, NY
Secaucus, NJ

FIELD

Sports management

DURATION

13–18 weeks
Summer, Fall, Spring

PRE-REQS

College sophomores, juniors and seniors
Must receive academic credit

DEADLINE(S)

Summer .... April 15   Fall .... August 15
Spring .... December 15

DESCRIPTION

At the time that the NBA was founded in 1946 as the Basketball Association of America, it had only 11 teams. Today, the organization has grown to include 27 teams, and worldwide retail sales of NBA-licensed merchandise have reached $2 billion annually, a testament to the NBA's drawing power. In 1982, with its workload burgeoning, the NBA employed one intern in Public Relations, but the next two interns didn't appear until 1984 and 1986. The NBA's internship program was off to a slow start, similar to the evolving history of the NBA itself, which saw so many teams come and go in its first five years that the future of professional basketball seemed in jeopardy. But in 1988, the NBA organized the current internship program, which assigns about ten students three times a year to NBA Entertainment in Secaucus, NJ and the following New York departments: Broadcasting, Consumer Products, Team Services (Marketing), and Public Relations.

Busywork is par for the course with sports internships, and the NBA's is no exception—it's a full-court press of unglamorous tasks. In Broadcasting, interns set up the department's eight VCRs, all attached to one television, to record NBA-related programs such as ESPN's "Sports Center" and during the season, "every single game played on TNT, MSG, TBS, and NBC." NBA Entertainment interns, placed in either the video or photo departments, retrieve videotape footage or photographs of games and players from the department's libraries. Video interns watch programs and commercials come to life in the editing rooms as employees match the selected shots with appropriate music off compact discs. Photo interns assist magazines who call in with requests for photographs. "When SI did the cover story on Reggie Lewis [the late Boston Celtic], I found nearly 30 slides for the magazine to use," explained an intern.

As part of the department's effort to keep track of the manufacturers that are licensed to use the NBA name, Consumer Products interns "open all the mail and set aside product sketches and prototypes for review by the department." They also order NBA caps and shirts for the stock room and make sure that the display room is neatly kept.

Interns in Team Services help conduct marketing surveys. "We send each team a 250-page survey asking for information on their PR and Marketing departments, game schedules . . . even how they pick their cheerleaders," said an intern. "I'd get on the phone and make sure the surveys were being completed and sent back to us in a timely manner."

Most NBA interns (four or five per session) are placed in the Public Relations department. A big part of their job is "the circ," the daily distribution of articles from major newspapers in NBA-affiliated cities. Interns scan the papers and cut out articles on NBA players, sponsor companies, as well as articles on teams and on the other major sports leagues, such as the NFL, NHL, and major league Baseball. "Every article gets filed," explained an intern, "but only the most important articles are included in the circ, which gets sent to top management." PR interns also assemble press kits and speak with fans on the phone. "Fans asked various questions—who's the shortest player? . . . the tallest player? Others wanted game schedules or player files," recalled an intern. The PR department receives its fair share of fan requests, which keeps interns busy mailing stickers, and researching trivia questions.

One would expect interns engaged in this much busywork to cry foul, but they are surprisingly accepting, realizing that it's a great way to bone up on the sport. "[Newspaper clipping is] tedious and your fingers get covered in ink," said an intern, "but by reading the articles and talking to people as you deliver the copies, you learn the NBA—its teams and players." Photo interns are equally satisfied: "I don't feel like it's gruntwork at all; I still learn the players, see exciting shots, and learn the various angles for taking pictures."

In exchange for their efforts, New York interns convene over several lunches with NBA executives, such as Senior Vice President of Legal and Business Affairs Jeffrey Mishkin, Deputy Commissioner Russ Granik, and even Commissioner David Stern, described by one intern as a "down-to-earth man who's interested in hearing what we have to say about the internship." Overall, interns find the talk at these lunches eye-opening: "Until you listen to these guys, you don't realize the extent to which basketball is a huge business."

Interns stationed in New Jersey miss out on these lunches, but they enjoy a perk that is perhaps even better than the New York meetings: During the summer, they assist older NBA players who come in to create highlight tapes with one of the editors. Said an intern: "I found pictures for Rolando Blackman and Kurt Rambis. . . . It was exciting to help them."

Interns are likely to have other stimulating opportunities. A Broadcasting intern "got to work a Knicks game with NBC out of [the network's] production truck." In Photos, an intern attended several shoots and learned how to use

> **Lace up your high-tops, grab your wrist bands, and head for New York —it's a great time to intern at the NBA.**

different kinds of cameras: "I took pictures of Ahmad Rashad and Toni Kukoc." A Team Services intern did the layout and some editing for the NBA's marketing newsletter, *Team Talk*. While autumn interns in Public Relations wrote "intensive" team previews and player profiles for the preseason, a winter PR intern helped track when and by whom the NBA's one millionth point was scored: "We had two games going at once. Points were going back and forth, but finally we credited the Utah Jazz's Darrell Griffith with the honor."

Occasionally, interns have the opportunity to attend out-of-town NBA events. Consumer Products interns, for example, sometimes attend a sporting-goods industry trade show—either February's Super Show in Atlanta or August's National Sporting Goods Association trade show in Chicago—to help set up display booths that show off NBA-licensed products. Interns in Team Services often attend league-wide marketing meetings, held in March and September in locales such as Palm Springs, California. Public Relations interns get the chance to help run various press conferences. Interns employed during the spring of 1993, for example, attended a New York press conference honoring five players' induction into the Basketball Hall of Fame. Various big names were inducted, so interns met the likes of Julius Erving, Bill Walton, Dick McGuire, Calvin Murphy, and Ann Meyers, arguably the best women's basketball player of all time. At the press conference, each intern was assigned one inductee to escort to eight press stations. "It was kind of funny to see a relatively short intern leading around [the 6' 11"] Walton," recalled an intern.

Mirroring the increasing popularity of NBA basketball, the number of NBA employees has escalated from 70 in 1988 to over 400 today. "We're a hot commodity right now," says an employee, "so we have a tremendous image to uphold. After all, we're trying to make basketball the world's number one sport, and we need as many people as possible behind the effort." This mission breeds an "intense working environment," especially around the time of major events such as the NBA Finals, All-Star Weekend, and McDonald's Open, an annual round-robin tournament featuring international teams. "The phones were ringing off the hook with reporters looking for press passes," recalled a Public Relations intern. "I took down requests, had the director of special events verify them, and then called the reporters back with his response."

The NBA's New York headquarters occupies four floors of the 21-story Olympic Towers, located on the corner of Fifth Avenue and 51st Street. Decorating the walls are framed photographs of NBA players and displayed in the showroom are NBA-licensed products, from clothing to basketballs. At the end of the summer, the coordinator goes through the showroom to create the intern "going-away gift"—the contents of which are a surprise.

SELECTION

 The NBA seeks undergraduates who have a minimum of two semesters left to complete after the internship. Freshmen aren't eligible. While about 60 percent of the NBA's past interns have been sports management majors—a veritable dynasty that rivals that of the Boston Celtics—the rest study communications, journalism, broadcasting, and marketing. In fact, according to the coordinator, any liberal arts major is eligible so long as he or she has "excellent communication skills" and is "enthusiastic about sports."

APPLICATION PROCEDURE

 The deadline for applications is April 15 for the summer, August 15 for the fall, and December 15 for the spring. Applicants should submit a resumé, a cover letter outlining their relevant background and indicating the department to which they're applying, and a letter from their college or university explaining that they will receive at least six semester credits for the NBA internship. Candidates who are granted interviews must fly to New York (at their own expense) for an on-site visit.

OVERVIEW

 The NBA's popularity is at an all-time high. Attendance at games is soaring and more Americans are playing basketball than any other sport. So lace up your high-tops, grab your wrist bands, and head for New York—it's a great time to intern at the NBA. Unlike interning with a particular NBA team, working at the NBA exposes sports lovers to the entire roster of NBA teams and also to king-size events—the McDonald's Open, the All-Star Weekend, and the NBA Finals. "Once you're on the inside," said an intern, "you can learn all the juice that fans are dying to know. And if you want to get into the sports business, this place teaches it all—licensing, sponsorship, community relations, management, and broadcasting."

FOR MORE INFORMATION . . .

■ National Basketball Association
Intern Coordinator
645 Fifth Avenue
New York, NY 10022
(212) 826-7000

 **National Institutes Of Health**

In 1935, Congress appropriated $100,000 for what was then called the National Institute of Health for a farm to house research animals. The problem was, the NIH had no land. Then along came retired clothing manufacturer Luke Ingalls Wilson, who saved the day by offering half of his Bethesda estate to the United States government.

In the Bible, Bethesda is the name of an ancient pool, where "whoever got in enjoyed healing, no matter what ailment he suffered" (John 5:4). Is it divine intervention or simply coincidence that the federal government's disease-fighting research center, the National Institutes of Health, is located in the city whose name is synonymous with healing?

Either way, the NIH has been instrumental in disease control. From its humble beginnings as a one-person, one-laboratory operation in 1887 to its current status as the world's largest biomedical research institution, the NIH has made critical medical breakthroughs. It was the first to unravel the genetic code, to develop a vaccine against rubella, and to launch human gene therapy.

DESCRIPTION

 Students have been doing summer internships at the NIH for nearly 20 years, but in 1990 the NIH established the Office of Education to coordinate postdoctoral research and other educational programs, including a summer internship program. What resulted is a structured opportunity for students to pursue biomedical research in the area of their choice. Every summer over 800 students participate in one of more than 3,000 ongoing research projects within 16 institutes including Aging; Alcohol Abuse and Alcoholism; Allergy and Infectious Diseases; Arthritis and Musculoskeletal and Skin Diseases; Child Health and Human Development; Deafness and Other Communication Disorders; Dental Research; Diabetes and Digestive and Kidney Diseases; Eye; Heart, Lung, and Blood; Mental Health; and Neurological Disorders and Strokes as well as the Office of the Director/Office of Intramural Research, the Warren Grant Magnuson Clinical Center, the Division of Computer Research and Technology, and the National Center for Research Resources.

The breadth of interns' activities at the NIH is enormous. Interns may undertake such tasks as preparing animals for experiments,

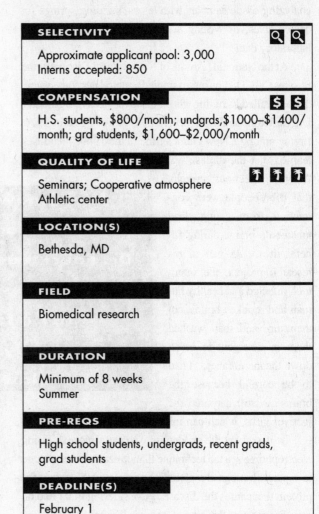

SELECTIVITY

Approximate applicant pool: 3,000
Interns accepted: 850

COMPENSATION

H.S. students, $800/month; undgrds, $1000–$1400/month; grd students, $1,600–$2,000/month

QUALITY OF LIFE

Seminars; Cooperative atmosphere
Athletic center

LOCATION(S)

Bethesda, MD

FIELD

Biomedical research

DURATION

Minimum of 8 weeks
Summer

PRE-REQS

High school students, undergrads, recent grads, grad students

DEADLINE(S)

February 1

sequencing proteins, growing cells in incubator rooms, analyzing tissue samples with lasers, building springs for heart valves, or writing computer programs to analyze laboratory data.

At the National Institute of Neurological Disorders and Strokes (NINDS), an intern studied a central nervous system disease called kuru, for whose discovery NINDS scientist Dr. Carleton Gajdusek received the Nobel Prize in 1976. Living among a New Guinea tribe in the 1960s, Gajdusek learned that the disease was due to the slow work of a "latent" infectious protein, that tribespeople were contracting from eating dead kinsmen's brains during funeral rites. As part of his research project, the intern took infected and healthy human and monkey brains, cut them up, and then washed them in detergent to break down the membranes. "I had to be careful because the brains . . . still harbored the [active] virus, which can infect you through an open cut . . . or if you get the sudden urge to eat a piece." Using electrophoresis, a lab technique that utilizes electric charge to separate biological materials, he extracted the part of the protein that causes the disease. "Considering that I had no experience doing this kind of research," he said, "it was cool that [the lab director] gave me that much responsibility."

An intern assigned to the National Heart, Lung, and Blood Institute investigated the mechanism of signal transduction—the process by which cells respond to hormones, neurotransmitters, and toxins. Her project focused on human interleukin-2 receptor, which activates the human immune response during infection. After introducing the human genes for a novel version of the receptor into mouse B-cells, she grew the cells in an incubation room. "As the cells grow, the genes create the new receptor, which eventually incorporates into the cell surface," she explained. Using certain lab techniques—"fluorescent antibody tags" and Western Blotting—she then searched cell surfaces for the altered receptors. Her work also included proofreading and revising the project's research paper, which was even-

tually published. "I feel that I made a significant contribution to an important research effort," she said. "When I apply to medical school, [this experience] will certainly give me an edge."

Like other institutes at the NIH, the National Cancer Institute (NCI) offers internships in its research specialities. But NCI is not a part of the Office of Education, so students interested in working at NCI should apply directly to its offices. An intern at NCI did research on a human protein called transforming growth factor-beta, abbreviated as TGF-Beta. "My mentor and I showed that TGF-Beta can stimulate as well as inhibit [calf heart] cell growth . . . [and that] some forms of TGF-Beta are more powerful than others at inhibiting growth." Because such an inhibitor could prove useful against cancer, in which malignant cells grow out of control, the intern embarked on a mission to "figure out the nuts and bolts of how [TGF-Beta] works." Using a microscope, a radioisotope counter, and a technique called polymerase chain reaction, she discovered that the way she conducted science at the NIH contrasted sharply with the "cookbook labwork" she completed at school.

But not all of NIH's research is about test tubes and incubation chambers, the Institutes also study patients first hand. At the National Institute of Mental Health (NIMH), an intern worked on a "protocol"—the plan of a scientific experiment or treatment—to determine if penicillin can alleviate the symptoms associated with obsessive-compulsive disorder in children. In order to recruit patients, she placed ads in The Washington Post and screened potential patients over the phone. At doctor-patient interviews, she noted patients' [medical] histories. "The patient interaction got me especially excited," she said. "Now I truly understand how research may be applied to help people."

All of these research projects are conducted in a setting that resembles a college campus with approximately 50 buildings scattered over 300 acres and with thousands of faculty and postdoctoral fellows, it's not hard to see why.

> **Well known for his appearances on "Nightline," Dr. Fauci teaches interns the process by which HIV infection eventually becomes full-blown AIDS.**

The NIH fosters a friendly, cooperative atmosphere—researchers often stop one other in the hallways to exchange research anecdotes. "In general, scientists are eager to teach people, including interns, about their research," said an intern. Available for interns' use are the NIH athletic center, NIH Library, National Library of Medicine, and four NIH cafeterias, "set up like eateries in a mall, with lots of good, medium-priced food." Because parking is described as a "nightmare," most students elect to use the Metro, which stops directly on NIH grounds. Twenty minutes south by subway is downtown Washington, D.C. and only a few minutes west is Great Falls Park, a favorite destination among hikers, canoers, and rock climbers.

For most interns, the NIH experience is the first real research they have done and they make mistakes any rookie would. To learn proper research techniques, each intern is assigned a mentor who oversees their experiments. "Whenever I mixed up the tubes or cooled when I should have heated, my mentor would say jokingly, 'You've just killed your parents.' I'd get embarrassed, but then he'd show me how to do it right." Mentors frequently alleviate interns' frustrations. "She'd tell me that when you get a different result than expected, it might not be wrong; instead, you may have stumbled on to something," an intern recalled.

Researchers are extremely busy at the NIH and often are reluctant to entrust students with much responsibility. As with most internships, interns must prove their worth. "You'd better read all the recent articles that your lab has published and ask lots of pertinent questions," advised an intern. Students would also do well to attend the weekly lab meetings. "You're certainly not needed, but your presence is appreciated," said an intern. "If you ask a question or two and occasionally put in your intelligent 50 cents, then all the better." If they arrive armed with knowledge and determination, students are often able to convince the head scientist to provide them with challenging work.

While laboratory research is a large part of the program, students don't have to stay holed up in their labs all day long. Interns may attend high-powered lectures on NIH research from studies of current cancer treatments to investigations of obscure genes in frogs. Interns can choose from about ten lectures daily. Interns are also encouraged to attend the Summer Seminar Series, which consists of weekly lectures, at a level comprehensible to high school students and college undergraduates, by senior NIH investigators. Past speakers have included Dr. Francis Collins, Director of the National Center of Human Genome Research, and obsessive-compulsive disorders expert Dr. Judith Rapoport, author of *The Boy Who Couldn't Stop Washing*. Probably the most well-received speaker has been Dr. Anthony Fauci, considered the country's premier AIDS researcher. Well known for his appearances on "Nightline," Fauci teaches interns the process by which HIV infection may eventually become full-blown AIDS. In addition to these lectures, students may attend a multitude of workshops on such topics as how to prepare for medical school and how to win fellowships to become M.D./Ph.D. students. "It's like a 'what you wish your mother told you but never did' series," explains Dr. Michael Fordis, the director of the Office of Education.

At the end of the summer, students are encouraged to participate in the NIH's two-hour Poster Day, a science meeting featuring interns' work, exhibited on 4' x 4' poster boards. While most interns are unable to make major research advances in only eight weeks' time, their contributions are nevertheless important and well received by the scientific community. Subjected to two hours of questioning, which probes the nature of their research, interns learn the shortcomings in their work. "Without Poster Day, I wouldn't have gotten a good grip on my issues," concluded an intern. "You gain confidence in explaining what you've learned to scientists."

SELECTION

 The NIH accepts applications from high school students at least 16 years of age (100 interns in 1993), college undergraduates and recent graduates (550 interns), and graduate students (200 interns, which included 125 medical and dental school students). Acceptable majors include: biology, biochemistry, chemistry, computer science, engineering, mathematics, psychology, and physics, liberal arts majors with considerable coursework in one of the aforementioned disciplines are also eligible. According to Dr. Fordis, applicants should be motivated students with good grades and demonstrated academic promise.

APPLICATION PROCEDURE

 The deadline is February 1. Students should submit the following in one large envelope: (1) resumé; (2) cover letter that describes academic plans for the upcoming fall, interest in biomedical sciences, and reasons for wanting a summer research internship; (3) official transcript; (4) letter stating that they are in good academic standing and enrolled in school full time—in a sealed envelope and signed by the registrar's office on back; (5) two confidential letters of recommendation from science professors; (6) completed Summer Internship Program Code Sheet (in brochure); and (7) self-addressed postcard. Students under 18 must turn in a parental consent form and a work permit upon acceptance into the program; spring graduates (high school or college) must submit proof that they have been accepted to an accredited institution at the next educational level. Because research areas (i.e., biochemistry, physiology, etc.) are broad, students may list up to three. Since research topics overlap among institutes (e.g., immunology is studied in seven institutes), students may apply to up to three institutes. Research projects are described in the NIH summer internship brochure and medical and dental school students' projects are described in the NIH Summer Fellowship Program catalog. All applications are tabulated and distributed to the institutes, who select the interns. No interviews are conducted.

OVERVIEW

 At the National Institutes of Health, interns contribute in the fight to cure the world's debilitating ailments. Working alongside influential scientists, NIH interns gain in-depth knowledge of an area of health while learning innovative laboratory techniques. When time permits, interns attend lectures by some of America's top researchers on AIDS, the Human Genome Project, and other timely topics. And at an end-of-summer Poster Day, they learn how to present scientific work. Whether interns stay in research or go on to medical school, an NIH experience is a valuable prelude.

FOR MORE INFORMATION . . .

- ■ Coordinator, NIH Summer Internship Program
  Office of Education
  Building 10, Room 1C129
  9000 Rockville Pike
  Bethesda, MD 20892
  (301) 402-2176

- ■ Coordinator, Summer Research Fellowship
  Program for Medical and Dental Students
  Office of Education
  Building 10, Room 1C129
  9000 Rockville Pike
  Bethesda, MD 20892
  (301) 402-2176

NATIONAL PUBLIC RADIO®

In this time of satellite dishes, "virtual reality," and handheld whatchamacallits, the medium of radio is in danger of being cast aside as a quaint holdover from generations past. But National Public Radio (NPR) is still out to prove that radio can be an exciting, provocative, and unpredictable source of information. Crackling to life in 1971, NPR is a radio network dedicated to providing its 13 million weekly listeners with lively news coverage and alternative cultural programming. Distributing its programs through some 450 member stations, NPR is famous for intellectually rich newsmagazines like "All Things Considered," "Morning Edition," and "Talk of the Nation," as well as offbeat cultural programs like "NPR Playhouse," "Car Talk," and "Rhythm Revue." It's home to a group of legendary radio personalities, including Linda Wertheimer and Robert Siegal, longtime hosts of "All Things Considered," and Nina Totenberg, the legal correspondent who broke the Anita Hill story.

SELECTIVITY	🔍🔍🔍
Approximate applicant pool: 200 Interns accepted: 20–30	

COMPENSATION	💲💲
$5/hour—first 15 interns chosen None—remainder of interns	

QUALITY OF LIFE	🌴🌴🌴
Creative environment Workshops and Evert lectures; Sketchy neighborhood	

LOCATION(S)
Washington, DC

FIELD
Radio

DURATION
8–12 weeks; Summer, Fall, Winter/Spring 16–40 hours per week

PRE-REQS
College juniors and seniors Grad students

DEADLINE(S)
Summer .... March 30   Fall ..... August 15 Winter/Spring ...... Dec. 15

DESCRIPTION

Interns are placed either in a particular department such as News and Information, Events Unit, Cultural Programming, Promotion and Public Affairs, Development, Personnel, Representation, Legal, Marketing, Engineering and Operations, or Audio Engineering or with one of NPR's programs—such as "All Things Considered," "Talk of the Nation," or "Performance Today."

The substance of an intern's work differs widely by position. An intern in News and Information spent much of her time checking facts for the NPR news desks and various programs. "When I'd get a fact-check request from, say, the national news desk or 'Morning

Edition,' I'd go to the library, log on to LEXIS/NEXIS, and double-check the facts against the relevant articles in the database." The relatively mundane nature of this job was offset by the occasional opportunity to accompany a reporter "into the field." Once, she visited the Pentagon to attend a news conference on the issue of homosexuals in the military. "We were there to get some sound bites from [General] Colin Powell after the conference. The reporter I was with ran to the bathroom, but she had told me—'If he comes out, grab him.' Powell did come out, and I ran over and asked him if any advancement was made on the issue. He didn't give me much of answer, but it was still exciting to ask a question around a group of professional reporters."

Some interns gain experience in dubbing and editing tape. In the Events Unit, an intern put together the tape of programs that NPR sends to a radio station in Budapest, Hungary. "With guidance from my boss, I picked out which NPR programs to include on the tape. The [Hungarians] particularly like shows on free trade and Eastern Europe, so I made sure to dub plenty of these." She also worked on preparing two BBC radio programs for broadcast, editing out glitches and adding the funding credits. "There was one credit that always made me laugh," she recalled. "With seventies porno music in the background, it said, 'This NPR program is brought to you by Labeled Vacuum Products—we not only produce products, we produce performance.'"

> "Going barefoot is no big deal—one of the executive producers did it all the time."

Sources say that the best position at NPR is with "All Things Considered." On the air from 5:00 to 6:30 PM, the show offers a mixture of headline news, special features, interviews, and alternative music. For those who haven't heard "All Things Considered," an intern described it as an "attempt to capture the energy and alternativeness of a college radio station, but with a larger budget and higher quality." To many, the show is the "quintessential NPR experience" because it combines "informed journalism with a high degree of creativity." One never knows what to expect: One day the show may feature a hard-hitting news feature, the next it may conduct an interview with the punk-rock band Fugazi.

It's no surprise, then, that "All Things Considered" offers interns an environment of "perpetual variety and innovation." Interns are asked to perform a mix of tasks, the most basic of which is arranging interviews for the show's hosts. "I'd make frantic phone calls all over the country to find people to interview. . . . [O]nce, I took a taxi to the Capitol, where I begged Marshall Harris for an interview—he had just finished a press conference explaining why he

quit the Bosnia desk at the State Department." Interns also "do whatever it takes to put the show together," such as finding "obscure bits of sound" for a particular segment. One intern, for example, had to track down the theme from "Mission Impossible" as well as find an "example of [President] Clinton pronouncing [FBI director] Louis Freeh's first name."

"All Things Considered," like most NPR programs, starts the day with a strategy meeting. Not only are interns free to attend these conferences they are also welcome to contribute story ideas. At one meeting, an intern proposed doing a story on how "Australia came out with dollar bills that are made partially of plastic." The show's producers liked the idea and developed it into a lighthearted story. Said the intern: "We decided to see how the plastic money would hold up under a few 'consumer tests.' With the recorders going, we ran the bill through a laundry machine, ran over it with a truck, and threw it to a bunch of puppies who tried to tear it up. . . . [I]t made for a fun segment." During NPR's coverage of the floods of '93, the intern also suggested doing a story on the survivors of the Mississippi flood of '27. After the producers gave her the green light, she set about tracking down the flood's survivors. "I called up historical societies to get the names and phone numbers of people who experienced the flood back in 1927. Then I called the survivors and arranged for them to be interviewed by the show's host," she explained.

A variety of events keep NPR interns busy. The intern coordinator arranges an in-house workshop with a series of NPR legends. In recent workshops Robert Siegal has spoken on writing for radio, J. Smokey Baer has discussed tape editing, Linda Wertheimer has covered interviewing techniques, and Daniel Schorr has lectured on analysis vs. commentary. One intern found the workshops "a little too formal" and wished "there was more opportunity for a relaxed group discussion." Interns also have access to lectures sponsored by the Evert Foundation, a Washington program sponsoring public policy internships. NPR and Evert interns join forces to welcome such speakers as Donna Shalala, U.S. secretary of Health and Human Services, and Coleman McCarthy, a columnist for *The Washington Post*. Other events include an intern scavenger hunt—"good for intern-bonding,"—and a "good-bye lunch" for interns and their supervisors

The atmosphere at NPR is uniquely casual and energetic. "There are so many cool people at NPR. You walk around the office and there's talk of new books, new films. The mood is progressive and artsy," said an intern. Some interns marvel at their bosses' creativity: "The producer I worked with was a genius—it was hard to follow the track of his mind," according one intern. "Watching the director [of "All Things Considered"] at work was like watching a maestro conduct his orchestra," said another. This creative environment touches all aspects of the job, even dress. For those wondering how to dress for success at NPR, it's time to mothball the Brooks Brothers suits and Laura Ashley dresses. NPR is about as casual as an (indoor) internship can get. "No one would blink if you wore cut-offs," said an intern, "And going barefoot is no big deal, either—one of the executive producers did it all the time."

As this book went to press, NPR was in the process of relocating to a building near Union Station. Interns report that the move is for the better in terms of space and for the worse with regard to location: "The building is triangular like [New York's] Flatiron Building and should be a lot roomier than NPR's old headquarters. But the location isn't the best, it's a run-down neighborhood between Union Station and Chinatown." If intern accommodations are anything like they were at the old location, interns should be prepared to make do with sharing computers and using the desks of vacationing reporters.

SELECTION

 NPR seeks college juniors and seniors as well as graduate students. Candidates from any academic background are welcome. According to an NPR producer, the best interns are "aggressive," "inquisitive," and "know how to [diplomatically] refuse a crappy assignment."

APPLICATION PROCEDURE

 The application deadline for the summer internship is March 30; for the fall internship, August 15; and for the winter/spring internship, December 15. Send in a resumé, cover letter, completed application form, and two letters of reference (professional or academic).

OVERVIEW

 An internship at NPR puts students at the heart of a radio network famous for innovative news and cultural programming. Offering hands-on projects, special intern events, and a singularly casual environment, the NPR internship is terrific exposure to the spirit of radio, at its intellectual and inventive best.

FOR MORE INFORMATION . . .

■ National Public Radio
   Internship Coordinator
   2025 M Street NW
   Washington, DC 20036
   (202) 822-2000

■ (Address after Feb. 1, 1994)
   National Public Radio
   Internship Coordinator
   635 Massachusetts Avenue
   Washington, DC 20001-3753
   (202) 414-2000

SELECTIVITY	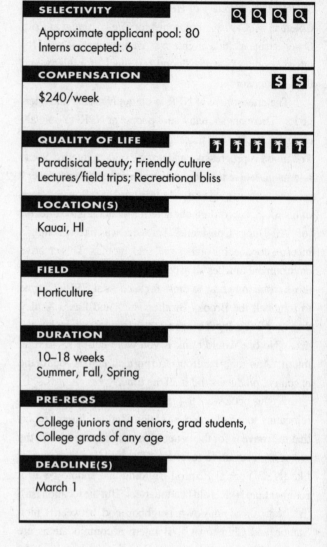
Approximate applicant pool: 80	
Interns accepted: 6	

COMPENSATION

$240/week

QUALITY OF LIFE

Paradisical beauty; Friendly culture
Lectures/field trips; Recreational bliss

LOCATION(S)

Kauai, HI

FIELD

Horticulture

DURATION

10–18 weeks
Summer, Fall, Spring

PRE-REQS

College juniors and seniors, grad students,
College grads of any age

DEADLINE(S)

March 1

A toast to my guests. . .Welcome to Fantasy Island.

No, it's not the tuxedoed Mr. Rourke ushering in yet another episode of "Fantasy Island."

Rather, it's a greeting that should meet every visitor to Kauai's National Tropical Botanical Garden (NTBG). Chartered by the U.S. Congress in 1964, NTBG is a non-profit organization overseeing six gardens on the islands of Hawaii. The showpiece of these gardens, as well as the headquarters of NTBG, is Lawai Gardens, a 186-acre expanse of Eden on southern Kauai. A must-see for tourists interested in viewing a world-class botanical garden, Lawai Gardens is also a full-fledged educational and scientific center, specializing in the collection and cultivation of tropical plant species, and the study of rare plant varieties.

DESCRIPTION

NTBG believes that the best way to educate interns is to have them rotate through a variety of departments at Lawai Gardens. Working in a different division each week, interns gain exposure to every facet of public horticulture. By the end of their stay, interns will have worked in Living Collections, Research, Administration, the Visitor's Center, and the Hawaii Plant Conservation Center.

Interns spend the majority of their time working in Living Collections. Every day they are expected to perform the "ground operations," tasks needed to maintain the garden's sea of tropical plants and trees. It's a down-and-dirty job requiring weeding, pruning, watering, fertilizing, and the like. But it's good exercise and there's something about laboring in the dirt that bonds interns together like nothing else could. "In addition to our regular chores, we'd unearth and replant Mondo grass,

which is a great ground cover. We'd dig up a patch, pull the plants apart, and replant the pieces in a new area. It was routine work, but it enabled [the interns] to really get to know each other," recalled an intern. In addition to working in the main garden, interns spend a week tending to the sculpted plant-life of nearby Allerton Gardens, a 100-acre estate managed by NTBG.

Interns find aspects of their work in Living Collections inimitably edifying. The arborist at NTBG, for example, gives them lessons in tree climbing and pruning. "I learned how to use the harness and tie the ropes. Before

I knew it, I was dangling 30 feet off the ground. It was great knowing that I pulled myself up there." Interns also learn how to operate a chain saw, which comes in handy clearing brush and removing "junk trees." Another opportunity in Living Collections is the nursery, where interns tend to the plants that will be transplanted to the garden. "You're exposed to hundreds of plants. New cuttings come in all the time. You get to see the collection in its infancy," said an intern.

When they work for the Visitor's Center, interns conduct three-hour tours of Lawai Gardens. Briefed beforehand by staff, interns teach visitors about the history and purpose of NTBG. Each tour group has approximately 15 visitors. Most are tourists, some well versed in botany, others "sightseeing grandmothers from Ohio."

In the Research department interns work in the garden's herbarium (aka, the "dead collection"), where NTBG keeps its collection of dried plant specimens. Interns spend time mounting specimens on acid-free museum paper and filing them away. Said an intern: "[It's] a tremendous education in botany. In the herbarium you get to see specimens from all over the world. . . . Sometimes you're handling specimens of plants that no longer exist in nature."

A favorite department among interns is the Hawaii Plant Conservation Center (HPCC). Funded by the MacArthur Foundation, the HPCC is a program designed to conserve and study native Hawaiian plants, particularly those that are rare or endangered. At the request of HPCC staff, interns go into the field and collect specimens. They also assist HPCC in carrying out its special science curriculum for local elementary schools. Interns visit classes to teach students about indigenous Hawaiian plants. One intern said, "It was a blast. We'd teach eager fifth graders all about plants native to the island, such as Lau' hala and Peli grass, and we'd have them grow their own personal plant. I showed my class how to grow Wili-Wili plants."

Wherever they work, interns are likely to feel the repercussions of Hurricane Iniki. The hurricane struck Kauai in September, 1992, wreaking havoc on plantlife, roadways, buildings, and irrigation systems. In the months that followed, NTBG was forced to put its internship program on hold and undertake a herculean cleanup effort. After months of reconstruction, facilities are returning to normal, but one is likely to see repairs continue for years to come.

Lawai Gardens owes its speedy recovery in part to the cooperative spirit of its employees. Interns describe the atmosphere as "friendly," "supportive," and "tinged with humor." When a stream became clogged with aquatic weeds, for example, the NTBG administration could have easily assigned the messy cleanup job to interns. Instead, everyone on the staff, from the director to the interns, spent a few hours a week wading into the murky water to dig up the weeds. "It was the worst work. We felt like prisoners on a chain gang," said an intern. "But we had the best time. The whole staff would get together and pull out those damn weeds."

Education is an integral part of life at Lawai Gardens. During their first week, interns are briefed on Hawaiian history, geography, and botany. During the course of the internship, Wednesday afternoons are devoted to instructional lectures or field trips. NTBG invites various experts in botany and horticulture to teach interns about such subjects as plant propagation, tropical plant identification, and ethnobotany. Staff members also take interns on field trips to examine plantlife on various parts of the island. One of the most cherished destinations is the Alicai swamp, a remote, high elevation area rarely disturbed by humans. Its untrodden land gives one a "sense of what Hawaiian flora was like when the Polynesians lived there." The memory of beautiful native plants, cedar trees and fragrant air prompted one intern to call Alicai "pure magic."

NTBG also arranges for interns to visit at least one of its satellite gardens. Interns are flown to Maui, where they visit Kahanu Gardens, a spectacular 126-acre site that's home to

> **At Lawai Gardens, interns get their shoes muddy and their thumbs green.**

the largest ancient Hawaiian archaeological site as well as outstanding collections of plants and fruit. On Maui, interns sometimes stay at the mountain estate of one of NTBG's trustees. On the premises is a garden surrounded by a wall of Japanese cedar trees, a sight so beautiful that one intern "thought [he] was in Shangri-la." Depending on NTBG's budget, interns may also be flown to other sites, including the Kaupulehu Preserve, a forest area in south Hawaii, and the Aweni Preserve, a mid-elevation rainforest in northern Hawaii.

The living situation at Lawai Gardens has to be seen to be believed. Interns are housed in "rustic" bungalows situated near the Visitor's Center. Each cabin has two beds, a bathroom, and a kitchen. The rent is $50 a month. Best of all, connecting the cabins is a deck with "an incredible, panoramic ocean view." For food, interns buy staples at a local grocery store, that are reported to be expensive. Interns also sample the island's exotic fare, indulging in such treats as litchis, breadfruit (a "wrinkly fruit famous in Polynesia"), papayas, and red bananas. While interns on the mainland congregate around their office's water cooler, interns at Lawai Gardens find a shady spot and crack open one of the island's endless supply of coconuts. "The unripe coconuts were the best. . . . Cool, watery milk. Pudding like meat that we'd scoop up. That gelatinous goop must have been sent from the gods. What a pick-me-up!" said an intern.

No need to airlift in the Subaru, NTBG keeps a few cars on hand for interns to borrow at $25 a month. But Range Rovers they're not. Descriptions of the cars range from the euphemistic—"they have a lot of character"—to the forthright—"fresh from the junkyard." True, these so-called Garden vehicles are "filthy," "trunkless," and "built with fenders that can be pushed off." But any means of motorized transportation is a boon, Since Kauai has yet to implement a widespread public transportation system.

Interns make good use of their jalopies. Trips to the beach are about as common as beautiful sunsets. Sun worshiping, swimming, snorkeling, and scuba diving are the activities of choice. Interns rave about the hiking and camping opportunities on Kauai. On the Na Pali coastline in northwest Kauai, there's a "glorious" 11-mile hiking trail leading to the "pristine" Kalalau beach. Campers love

Waimea Canyon, a beautiful camping area often called the "little Grand Canyon."

Never forget, however, that a summer at Lawai Gardens is a summer "in the remotest corner of the world." To the delight of many, Kauai sports no triple-decker shopping complexes, no Wal-Marts, and no Mickey D's. The closest towns are Poipu and Kalaheo, where one finds little more than a post office, a grocery store, and a few casual restaurants. Poipu also has a small health club. The largest town on Kauai is Lihue, but the best it can offer is a mall with a movie theater and battery of stores. As far as nightlife goes, "there really isn't any," according to an intern. Although the hotels in Poipu have "nightclubs," interns rarely bother to frequent these expensive tourist traps.

SELECTION

 The program is open to college juniors and seniors, graduate students, and college graduates of any age. Although most participants are in their twenties, word has it that a retired pharmacist interested in medicinal plants completed the internship a few years ago. Interns come from all over the United States. Many have backgrounds in botany and horticulture, but the program does not require academic training in these subjects. Most important, the coordinator says, an applicant should manifest a "serious interest in plants" in the cover letter.

APPLICATION PROCEDURE

 The deadline is March 1. Required materials include two or more recommendations from teachers or employers (sent directly to NTBG's education assistant), official transcripts, a note from a physician testifying that one is physically fit to do outdoor landscaping, and a cover letter describing future goals and the reasons for wanting to participate in the program. NTBG conducts no interviews, so the last document is particularly critical. Says the coordinator: "We carefully examine the cover letters to determine who would benefit most from the resources and training at NTBG."

OVERVIEW

 Break out the sunscreen and roll up your sleeves, the National Tropical Botanical Garden's program is about as hands-on as any internship can be. At Lawai Gardens, interns get their shoes muddy and their thumbs green. It's all in the name of learning everything there is to know about tropical plantlife. Some are so smitten with the work that they pursue it as a lifelong vocation. Internship alumni include the horticultural curator at Honolulu Botanical Gardens and an assistant curator at the prestigious Longwood Botanical Gardens in Pennsylvania. But even those who have no curatorial aspirations leave Lawai Gardens with an unmatched education in tropical botany and a tan that would make the Coppertone girl envious.

FOR MORE INFORMATION . . .

- National Tropical Botanical Garden
  Internship Program
  P.O. Box 340
  Lawai, Kauai, HI 96765
  (805) 332-7361

SELECTIVITY	
Approximate applicant pool: 300–400
Interns accepted: 12

COMPENSATION $ $

$270/week plus health insurance

QUALITY OF LIFE   🌴 🌴 🌴

Lobbying on Capitol Hill; Brown-bags
Environmentally-conscious office

LOCATION(S)

Washington, DC

FIELD

Environmental policy

DURATION

24 weeks
January to June; July to December

PRE-REQS

College grads, grad students

DEADLINE(S)

Jan. internship .... October 1
July internship .... April 1

Do you know who provides those dark green recycling bins marked "newspapers," "bottles," "cans" on your campus, or those special shower heads with trickling water, or your campus tree-planting projects? You probably think they're the work of local earth lovers, but chances are those projects are sponsored by the National Wildlife Federation's Campus Outreach Program, which funded conservation projects at over 150 colleges and universities nationwide during the 1992–93 school year.

Since its founding in 1936, the National Wildlife Federation (NWF) has been a powerful force in the protection of natural resources and wildlife. With 46 affiliates and over one million members nationwide, NWF is the nation's largest not-for-profit, private conservation group. As an organization composed of hunters and conservationists alike, NWF has given its two cents on nearly every major environmentally related piece of congressional legislation, from the Federal Aid in Wildlife Restoration Act of 1937 to current bills proposed to strengthen and reauthorize the Endangered Species Act. Also in the business of conservation education, NWF publishes *National Wildlife* and *Ranger Rick*, which together reach over one million readers annually. It also manages the Corporate Conservation Council, a cooperative effort between industry executives and environmental leaders to save the environment, and sponsors an annual Wildlife Week, a celebration founded in 1938 to promote nature issues.

DESCRIPTION

Since 1980, NWF has employed interns to work in its Biodiversity Conservation, Environmental Quality, and International departments. By researching existing legislation, lobbying for new legislation, and litigating when nec-

essary, these departments make sure that federal agencies comply with environmental laws and regulations. Positions are also available in the Office of Grassroots Action, the Corporate Conservation Council, and Affiliate and Regional Programs.

Interns are responsible for answering the dozens of letters and phone calls that pour in to NWF's national office every day. Most inquiries are from members requesting literature or an explanation of NWF's current position on such topics as wetlands, hunting, or whales. In order to keep legislators abreast of NWF's agenda, interns also distribute literature to congresspeople and senators. During these "Hill drops," conducted twice a week, interns walk from one Capitol Hill office to another to hand out such items as reports on wetlands protection or letters urging legislators to vote for various bills.

Assigned to teams that often consist of a scientist, a lawyer, and a lobbyist, interns perform more than administrative work. Because of NWF's broad-based agenda, interns have an opportunity to make an impact on several environmental issues at once. In Biodiversity Conservation, interns may concentrate on wetlands, endangered species, public lands, national forests, and regulation of coal, oil, gas, and mineral development. Interns in Environmental Quality focus on global warming, air pollution, acid rain, drinking water, groundwater pollution, oil spills, pesticides, and biotechnology. In International, topics include tropical deforestation and environmental aspects of free trade. Interns may also help NWF in its efforts at grassroots mobilization in the Office of Grassroots Action or push for business accountability as part of the Corporate Conservation Council. For journalism students interested in environmental issues, there's NWF's *EnviroAction*, for which interns write articles.

A must-read among environmentalists is the "fact sheet," a one-page report that establishes the facts behind a specific issue and often makes a case for supporting or rejecting it. Targeting congressional staffers and state government officials, fact sheets help NWF publicize its views on current environmental topics such as the spotted owl, clear-cutting, and grazing fees. One intern analyzed the proposed CAFE bill (Corporate Average Fuel Economy)— legislation slated to improve the nation's automobile fuel-efficiency standards. On a fact sheet, he outlined the main reasons congresspeople should pass the bill. "It will reduce global warming, air pollution, and U.S. dependence on foreign oil," he explained. "Moreover, [improved fuel economy] will save consumers money on gas." Another

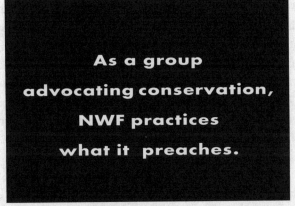

As a group advocating conservation, NWF practices what it preaches.

intern composed a fact sheet that emphasized the importance of saving the ancient forests of the Pacific Northwest. "They're America's last virgin forests," she said. "If we lose them, we lose some of the tallest and oldest trees on the planet."

As part of NWF's environmental lobbying efforts, interns sometimes participate in grassroots phone campaigns and write letters to senators and congresspeople. On one occasion, interns sectioned off regions of the country and called NWF members. "We asked them to call their senators and representatives," said an intern. "[Members'] input can often make a difference in how [legislators] vote." On another occasion, an intern wrote a three-page letter highlighting the benefits of fuel efficiency on air pollution. "I got all kinds of environmental groups to sign the letter and then had it distributed to every member of the Senate."

Interns who manage to learn an issue inside and out and impress their supervisor will have an opportunity to do some lobbying in person on the Hill. They meet with legislative aides, hand out literature and talk through the issues. "Sometimes, people aren't interested, and you have to twist their arms," said an intern. "But other times, you talk to someone who wants more information or who gives you assurances of support. Of course, the offices of congressmen [who are] aligned with NWF are easier to deal with."

Interns attend hearings, briefings, and seminars in order to take background notes for supervisors and draft secondary documents and testimony for NWF executives. An intern in the International department, for example, worked on an effort to convince two House committees to influence reform of the World Bank's International Development Association (IDA). "IDA funds Third World development projects such as the building of hydroelectric power plants," she said. "But it does so without taking into account the environmental impact of such projects. Typically, devastation to habitats isn't properly considered." After reading recent papers from governmental and nongovernmental agencies, she and her supervisor came up with a 14-page document that later became part of the committee record. "It was really satisfying to be able to make that kind of contribution," she said. Another intern drafted testimony against a bill that would provide ranchers with federal compensation every time a disease called brucellosis killed their cattle. "I had to write several drafts and get approval at many stages in the process," he said, "but it was well worth it—the testimony was included in the record."

Environmental groups often work together by forming coalitions and holding meetings, which interns may attend. One intern helped organize and attended meetings among D.C. environmental groups who wanted to provide the Clinton transition team with a list of qualified candidates for environmentally related federal positions. "To my surprise, I learned that the transition team relied on environmental groups to float possible names," she said. But often relegated to handing out documents, interns rarely are informed enough to make comments. "Just sit and observe," advised an intern. "You'll still learn plenty on how environmental strategy is formulated."

To familiarize interns with the environmental work outside of their departments, NWF arranges periodic brown-bag luncheons, featuring NWF staffers who speak on their projects. At one luncheon, NWF's peripatetic president, Jay Hair, takes time out from his busy travel schedule to meet the interns. An avid hunter and syndicated environmental columnist with a Ph.D. in zoology, Hair is a renowned conservationist, who is eager to educate interns. "We talked casually about the importance of saving the environment and NWF's role in that effort," said an intern.

Located near Dupont Circle, NWF is about a 15 minute Metro trip from Capitol Hill. The group's offices occupy three floors of a seven-story building that was unveiled in a 1961 dedication ceremony featuring President Kennedy. "By mobilizing private effort through your organization, you are helping not only to develop our wildlife resources," said Kennedy, "but you are helping to create the kind of America that is our common goal—an America of open spaces, fresh water, and green country." Though NWF is a not-for-profit group, it doesn't operate with the informality of most nonprofits. Staffers wear suits and interns receive their own desks, telephones, and a computer, to share

between every two interns. "It has a corporate feel," observed an intern. "It's a fancy building with fancy furniture," said another.

As a group advocating conservation, NWF practices what it preaches. The environmentally conscious organization has solar film on its windows to reduce incoming sunlight and thus retain cool air during the summer and warm air during the winter. In the cafeteria, NWF uses glasses only since paper cups simply increase America's paper use, the coordinator explained. Lights are regulated by motion sensors, and an innovative air-conditioning system keeps the place cool without relying on Freon, one of the dreaded chlorofluorocarbons that destroy the ozone layer; the system uses electricity in off-peak hours to freeze water and then pumps air over the ice during the day. NWF also recycles paper, bottles, and cardboard and makes two-sided copies and faxes. "As you can imagine, we get a lot of mileage out of our office supplies," said an intern.

SELECTION

NWF seeks college graduates and graduate students with extensive coursework and/or experience in economics, political science, journalism, wildlife biology, fisheries science, ecology, environmental biology, environmental science, biology, chemistry, toxicology, natural resource management, land management, forestry, geology, energy, hydrology, water resources, international environmental issues, and civil engineering. Master's degrees and previous work experience on environmental issues are helpful.

APPLICATION PROCEDURE

The deadline is October 1 for the January to June internship and April 1 for the July to December internship. Applicants should submit a cover letter indicating their areas of interest, a resumé, names and telephone numbers of three to five academic or professional references, and a two- to four-page sample of nontechnical academic or professional writing. Aspiring journalism interns must submit four writing samples, or clips, of any length instead of the two- to four- page sample. After the coordinator screens for the best candidates, department directors make final selections. No interviews are conducted.

OVERVIEW

 As an organization committed to a bevy of environmental issues, from acid rain to energy to wetlands, the National Wildlife Federation is an ideal place for college graduates to launch an environmental career. One of the few nonprofit environmental groups with a salaried program, NWF offers interns a well-structured six months in which to experience the life of the environmental policymaker. Whether mobilizing members for phone campaigns or lobbying legislators, NWF interns make vital contacts with influential nature lovers. After an NWF internship, a graduate's chance of landing full-time employment with D.C.'s prominent environmental groups has vastly improved.

FOR MORE INFORMATION . . .

■ National Wildlife Federation
Resources Conservation Internship Program
1400 Sixteenth Street NW
Washington, DC 20036-2266
(202) 797-6800

"'**N**ightline' has grown so powerful that it's assumed that any top-shelf newsmaker will do Ted first," wrote the *The Dallas Morning Star*.

The world's movers and shakers do gravitate to ABC's "Nightline" like barnacles to a hull. Oliver North, Ariel Sharon, Corazon Aquino, Rajiv Gandhi, Nelson Mandela, Mikhail Gorbachev, and Desmond Tutu are just a few of the world-famous guests who've faced the rigors of Koppel's probing questions.

Evolving in 1979 from the ABC News special broadcasts, "The Iran Crisis: America Held Hostage," "Nightline" has become an American institution. Broadcast each weekday evening from 11:30 PM to midnight, the show covers a major story in the news through a combination of live interviews with newsmakers and reports from "Nightline" correspondents in the field. The show is consistently lauded by critics as the best in daily television journalism. Its long history of journalistic coups includes the first report from Baghdad following Iraq's invasion of Kuwait, the first live television interview of former Chief Justice Warren Burger, and television's first "town meeting" (1987's "A National Town Meeting on AIDS").

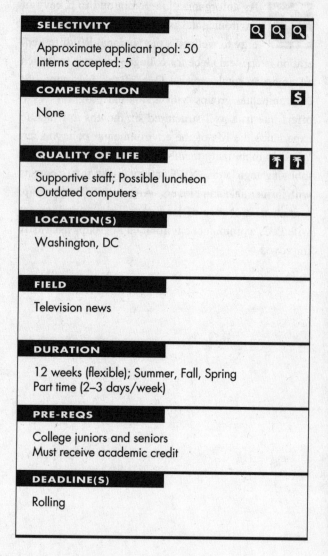

SELECTIVITY 🔍🔍🔍

Approximate applicant pool: 50
Interns accepted: 5

COMPENSATION 💲

None

QUALITY OF LIFE ⬆⬆

Supportive staff; Possible luncheon
Outdated computers

LOCATION(S)

Washington, DC

FIELD

Television news

DURATION

12 weeks (flexible); Summer, Fall, Spring
Part time (2–3 days/week)

PRE-REQS

College juniors and seniors
Must receive academic credit

DEADLINE(S)

Rolling

DESCRIPTION

Flexibility is king at the "Nightline" internship. Interns generally work 12-week sessions, which coincide with fall, spring, and summer semesters but may adjust the length of their stay by a few weeks, if necessary. They work part time, usually no more than two or three days a week. Each day they may work either the day shift (10:00 AM to 4:00 PM) or the night shift (6:00 PM to midnight). A few weeks before the internship, interns set a weekly schedule with the program's coordinator.

Of the day and night work periods, the day shift is generally considered the less desirable period to work. According to one intern, "The majority of the producers and writers aren't in the office yet, so things are pretty slow." Interns find themselves sending faxes, making photocopies, and scanning newspapers for relevant articles to clip. Answering phones is another part of the "daily grind," as interns field all types of calls, from the legitimate to "the laughable." "Most of the calls were related to the night's show," said an intern, "but sometimes people called up and rambled on and on about story ideas for the show. Dealing with these types was a lesson in diplomacy."

Interns also get a taste of the public when they open viewer mail. Some of the mail is well meaning. "I'd come across requests for information, and I'd try to research an answer. A high school student, [for example], saw a "Nightline" show on abortion and wanted more information for a report she was writing. I sent her a transcript of the show and some suggestions for further research," one intern recalled. But there are also other letters from the Twilight Zone, according to another intern who said "Every day, some guy would send Koppel a letter written in Russian. . . . [T]he office also got its fair share of love letters for Koppel—women writing to profess their love and offer snapshots of themselves."

But the day shift is not without its rewards. Every morning the producers and writers get together to brainstorm ideas for the night's show. A conference call connects them to executives from the New York bureau and reporters on the road and Koppel either attends or phones in. Interns are free to watch the morning meeting or listen to it on a speakerphone. "It's amazing to watch how the show gets put together so quickly. The topic is usually chosen the day of the show." If they're lucky, interns also have a few chances to accompany the "Nightline" crew on assignment. One intern went with ABC correspondent Brit Hume to the White House, where they attended a press conference with Treasury Secretary Lloyd Bentsen in the Press Room. Another accompanied the crew to a county jail, where Koppel interviewed Chinese inmates for a show on Chinese immigration. A third intern shadowed Koppel and the crew as they interviewed the public at several Washington locations during Clinton's inaugural ceremonies.

Interns report that the night shift is the key time to be at "Nightline." "By six o'clock, things start heating up. All the producers and writers are in the building. Everyone is going full throttle to prepare for the show," explained an intern. Busywork is still prevalent, but most find that at night even that's more exciting. "There's not as much phone work and

practically all of the calls that come in are directly related to the show," reported an intern. Sometimes interns assist staff researchers in last-minute fact checking: "I searched the LEXIS/NEXIS databases for articles on Hillary Rodham Clinton to double-check certain details." Interns also play the gofer, running messages and scripts down to the control room.

Above all, the night shift is a time to observe. The staff of "Nightline" is unusually receptive to letting interns watch preparations for the show. Said an intern, "I'd visit the editing room a lot. Everyone there was really great about explaining exactly what they were doing. Once they let me look through a series of pictures and pick out the best one for use as the show's backdrop." The Graphics department is also popular among interns. "It's great just to sit there and watch the artists play with pictures and text," said one.

> "It amazed me to see Koppel looking half asleep before the show, and then at 11:35 — boom — he comes alive and kicks butt."

But nothing beats the main attraction—live tapings. The show airs at 11:35 PM, and interns may watch from the control room or behind the TelePrompter on the set. "I'd go early and watch [the staff] check the microphones and prep Koppel," said one intern. "[I]t amazed me to see Koppel looking half asleep before the show, and then at 11:35—boom—he comes alive and kicks butt." During the interview segment of the show, guests are beamed in by satellite or are filmed in the studio. Interns report that before the show Koppel avoids getting too chummy with in-studio guests: "Koppel greets them but keeps his professional distance. There's minimal contact." Even more interesting is how in-studio guests are interviewed: "They're placed in a room adjacent to the studio where Koppel sits. Koppel can see them on the monitor, but they can't see him. Some claim this is just the way the studio is set up, but I think it's done to give [Koppel] an advantage."

There are not a whole lot of fringe benefits and extracurriculars at "Nightline." ABC News often, but not always, holds an intern luncheon for all ABC News interns where executives and producers talk about their jobs.

Speaking of food, "Nightline" orders a selection of "finger sandwiches and fruit plates" for guests to enjoy before they go on the air. When a particular show has no in-studio guests, the staff (interns included) has dibs on this "yummy" catered food. Moreover, for those concerned about traveling home after a night shift, interns are reimbursed for taxi-fare home. Finally, celebrity hounds will be happy (but not surprised) to learn that "Nightline" offers many stargazing opportunities. Observant interns regularly see such ABC personalities as Peter Jennings, Barbara Walters, Chris Wallace, Cokie Roberts, and Sam Donaldson, as well as an endless stream of politicians, government officials, and academics.

Located on the third floor of the seven-floor ABC News center, "Nightline" shares its building with the offices of "Good Morning America," "World News Tonight," and "Weekend Report with David Brinkley." With decor that offers little more than a few framed pictures of Ted Koppel, the "Nightline" office consists of a large open area surrounded by executive offices. Interns typically work in the open area at one of two large tables. They have access to a computer, but "be forewarned—it is woefully outdated." No cafeteria exists, but if they have the time, interns can grab a bite at one of the many eateries on nearby Connecticut Avenue.

A key reason "Nightline" stands out from the majority of television internships is its supportive and warm-spirited staff. From Ted Koppel down to the secretaries, interns feel welcome and appreciated on the job. Said an intern: "Koppel is a genuine guy. On my first day he walked up to me and introduced himself. I was really impressed." Kudos go to "Nightline" Executive Producer Tom Bettag, too: "[Bettag] was a great inspiration. He sat down with all the interns to answer questions and explain what makes a story newsworthy. . . . And [Bettag] has a great ability to make everyone work as a team—which differs markedly from what I've seen at other TV programs, even other ones in this building."

SELECTION

 The internship is open to college juniors and seniors. No particular majors are required. All interns, however, must receive academic credit from their colleges.

APPLICATION PROCEDURE

 The application deadline is rolling. Send in a cover letter, resumé, and writing sample. Applicants must also submit a list of references (both academic and employment) or a few recommendation letters. The intern coordinator conducts interviews (by telephone or in person) with a group of finalists. Successful applicants are usually notified within a month of their start date.

OVERVIEW

 Those looking to write news stories or operate video equipment would be well advised to steer clear of the 'Nightline' internship or any other big-name internship in broadcast journalism. While "Nightline" provides little in the way of hands-on experience, it has much to offer in other areas. Says an intern: "The potential for networking is phenomenal at 'Nightline.' If you make a good effort and earn people's respect, they'll be there with valuable job recommendations later. It's a major foot in the door." For those not necessarily planning a future in TV news, however, the internship is still a rare window on what *Time* called "the most indispensable news broadcast on television." Says Executive Producer Tom Bettag: "The 'Nightline' internship is like auditing a course. It's a chance to pick up the ambience, the rhythm of the place. . . . [Y]ou get to see experts in their field and what makes them tick."

FOR MORE INFORMATION . . .

■ Nightline
Intern Coordinator
1717 Desales Street, NW
3rd Floor
Washington, DC 20036
(202) 887-7360

SELECTIVITY	
Approximate applicant pool: 600 Interns accepted: 15	🔍🔍🔍🔍🔍

COMPENSATION	
$320/week	💲💲💲

QUALITY OF LIFE	
Awesome campus; Immense gym Thirst Thursdays; Weekly speakers	🌴🌴🌴🌴🌴

LOCATION(S)

Beaverton, OR

FIELD

Athletic shoes and apparel

DURATION

10 weeks
Summer

PRE-REQS

Minority college seniors, grad students

DEADLINE(S)

March 1

Take a track star with an M.B.A. and combine that star with a top track coach, preferably one who designs running shoes. Then add a series of innovative running-shoe designs, including the Waffle Trainer, Tailwind, Air Jordan, Air Pegasus, and Cross Trainer. Mix in dozens of Olympic champions and sprinkle with endorsements by John McEnroe, Bo Jackson, Michael Jordan, and Joan Benoit and garnish it all with a snazzy "swoosh" strip. What do you get? The recipe for a multibillion-dollar athletic-shoe empire named after the Greek goddess of victory, Nike.

Bill Bowerman and Phil Knight joined forces in 1964, and together they parlayed a basement-based sneaker company into the world's first sports and fitness company to surpass $3 billion in annual total revenues. A savvy sense of marketing and an unflagging commitment to quality have helped Bowerman and Knight make Nike synonymous with the best aspects of athletics—vigorous competition, effective teamwork, and uncompromising performance.

DESCRIPTION

 Nike strives to match a student's academic background and vocational interest with a particular area of the company. The following divisions have accepted interns: Marketing, Finance/Accounting, Records Management, International Division, Customer Service, Retail Resources, Human Resources, Research Design and Development, and Film/Video. Not surprisingly, an intern's experience at Nike varies considerably, depending on the department and supervisor to which he or she is assigned.

Finance interns, for example, spend much of their time crunching numbers and solving business problems. One Finance intern under-

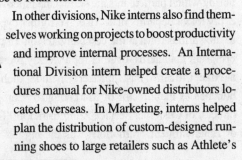

took such projects as determining why warehouse costs increased and whether hiring more full-time employees would be beneficial financially. Another helped develop a system to monitor how effectively Nike distributes its merchandise to retail stores.

In other divisions, Nike interns also find themselves working on projects to boost productivity and improve internal processes. An International Division intern helped create a procedures manual for Nike-owned distributors located overseas. In Marketing, interns helped plan the distribution of custom-designed running shoes to large retailers such as Athlete's

Foot and Footlocker. Retail Resources interns spent several weeks evaluating the success of the Gift-with-Purchase program, whereby Nike sells its products with some sort of freebie, such as a T-shirt, a pair of sunglasses, or a baseball cap. One of the most interesting jobs was assigned to a Records Management intern, who was asked to help organize and catalog Nike's gargantuan archive system. He ended up sifting through hundreds of shoes, pieces of apparel, watches, cups, mugs—anything that ever came out of the Nike factory. "It really gave me a product-by-product sense of Nike's history," he said.

Some interns work with Nike fabrics and designs. A Research Design intern worked in the apparel lab, determining the extent to which various fabrics were tearable, shrinkable, colorfast, waterproof, and breathable. "There was no busywork in my job," reported the textile major. "They threw me right into it—having me conduct all sorts of experiments on fabrics submitted by different vendors." Other Research Design interns assist in apparel and footwear design. Consulting with professional designers, they brainstorm new ideas and prepare sketches. Sometimes they create for the design team a "presentation board," in which they describe a new design concept and the external influences (logos, cars, animals, etc.) that inspired it. Design interns usually have previous experience in garment construction and drawing.

The wide variety of intern positions means that interns are dispersed throughout several buildings, prompting some to call the program "too spread out" and "not centralized enough." But efforts are made to create unity among interns. The summer begins with a two-day orientation program, during which participants are shown the inner workings of every major department at Nike. To further expose interns to the various roles at the company, the intern coordinator brings all the interns together for a weekly presentation by a Nike officer. Past speakers include such corporate honchos as the director of Marketing for Europe and the director of Customer Service Administration. The director of Entertainment Promotions was the biggest hit among interns, captivating them with stories of how she oversees the use of Nike products in movies, arranging for gifts of Nike products to everyone from Michael J. Fox to Jerry Seinfeld. The final meeting usually finds CEO Philip Knight talking to and mingling with program participants.

Nike employees do not work at a complex, corporate headquarters, or industrial park; they work at the "Nike World Campus." An ambitious name, but one Nike remarkably lives up to. Ten minutes from downtown Portland, Nike's physical plant is located in the suburban town of Beaverton and resembles a sprawling, tree-lined college campus. Seven buildings sit on the 74-acre compound, each named after a famous Nike endorser; when visitors tour Nike, they find not "Building A" and "Building B," but the "Michael Jordan Building" and the "Mike Schmidt Building." The Nike campus boasts everything an intern could want: a high-quality cafeteria, dry cleaning, film developing, an employee store selling Nike products, and even a hair salon. Subsidized by Nike, goods and services are priced reasonably for employees. The employee store, for example, sells all footwear at cost or lower. One intern reports buying a fine pair of Nike running shoes for $10.

The Nike World Campus redefines the quality-of-life concept. "This place is like a little city—no—this place is better than a little city," says an intern. For a small monthly fee, interns have full use of the Bo Jackson Sports Center, a state-of-the-art athletic facility offering aerobics, weights, weight trainers, squash, tennis courts, martial arts, Jacuzzis, massage, big-screen TV, an indoor running track, and a day care center. A summertime tradition at Nike is Thirst Thursdays, a late-afternoon party held every Thursday. At these gatherings employees and interns from all areas of the company congregate on a patio near Nike's man-made lake to listen to music and enjoy soda, wine, and beer. If Thirst Thursdays fail to quench one's thirst, the Sports Pub, a Cheers-style sports bar on the Nike campus, is the place to go for after-hours revelry.

> **The Nike campus boasts everything an intern could want . . . an intern reports buying a fine pair of running shoes for $10.**

SELECTION

Nike seeks college seniors and graduate students, all of whom must be a "racial or ethnic minority." According to the intern coordinator, targeted minorities include African-Americans, Hispanics, Asian-Americans, and Native Americans. Desired qualities in applicants include "flexibility," "passion to be the best," "a willingness to ask for additional work," and an "appreciation for sports and fitness."

APPLICATION PROCEDURE

The application deadline is March 1. Interested parties should request an application from Nike between December 1 and February 15. In addition to the application form, send three references, including phone numbers and addresses, and a resumé. Nike also requests a cover letter of two pages or less, describing an applicant's (1) career interest and academic goals; (2) contributions to an ethnic community; (3) academic accomplishments (GPA, coursework, awards, scholarships, special projects); and (4) reasons he or she would be a strong addition to the internship program.

OVERVIEW

"Love who you are . . . protect your dreams . . . and develop your talents to their fullest extent." "Play to win." "Don't allow anyone to tell you what you can and cannot do." "Tell the truth." "Live off the land." Nike likes to propagate these maxims among its employees and the values they refer to reflect a mindset that interns will encounter at the company. The Nike internship exposes its participants to the machinery of sportswear production and manufacturing, while also immersing them in a uniquely progressive, athletically minded environment. The Nike culture is at once dynamic and casual. It is a place where employees bring both an industrious ethic and a duffel bag to work. For those looking for this kind of experience, the answer is clear: Just Do It!

FOR MORE INFORMATION . . .

■ Nike
Internship Program
One Bowerman Drive
Beaverton, OR 97005
(503) 671-6453

Summer school. Few phrases cause more grief to the adolescent heart. Visions of dark, steamy classrooms, redolent of crayons and floor detergent. A wizened disciplinarian, droning on and on, propagating coffee breath and a thousand lessons better left untaught. The world outside—laughter and blue sky—passing you by.

But at the Phillips Academy, summer school doesn't have to be scholastic hell. Every summer, the prestigious Massachusetts boarding school runs innovative academic programs for high school students. The Summer Session Program enrolls over 800 students in a wide range of enriching classes designed to accelerate students' secondary education. In addition, the (MS)[2] Program offers promising African-American, Hispanic, and Native-American students rigorous coursework in mathematics and science, to prepare them for careers in the medical, engineering, and scientific professions. Students of both programs take advantage of the academy's college-caliber facilities and stunning Colonial beauty.

DESCRIPTION

Phillips Academy (or "Andover," as it is commonly called) hires Teaching Assistants for both the Summer Session and (MS)[2] Programs. Those in the Summer Session assist in teaching courses related to their major field of study, from anthropology to zoology. Those in the (MS)[2] Program help teach classes in biology, chemistry, physics, and mathematics as well as English. Both groups of TAs work six days a week for the six-week session. They assist in two different classes, each meeting three days a week from 8:00 AM to 12:30 PM.

All TAs share a basic set of classroom responsibilities. Paired with a master teacher (an adult with several years teaching experience), each assists the teacher in completing administrative work, organizing lesson plans, and grading papers and tests. With regard to the last task, TAs typically share grading responsibilities with the teacher. A TA in English reported, "I had a lot of input in terms of grading. Before assigning a grade, [the teacher] and I would sit down and discuss a student's paper in considerable depth." An-

BUSYWORK
LOW MEDIUM HIGH
OLDMAN & HAMADEH
METER

other TA was a bit uncomfortable with the Phillips Academy grading system: "All the classes use the official grading system, which ranges from six to zero, six being high honors and zero a failing grade. Unfortunately, this system doesn't necessarily correspond to the [letter system] students are used to. It made for some confusion, both on my part and with my students."

TAs in the (MS)^2 Program are also required to lead nightly help and tutorial sessions. In help sessions TAs review the day's concepts and answer beneficial questions from students. They also con-duct tutorials, which provide a chance for students to meet one on one with the TA. "Tu-torials allow students to ask questions and work through problems fully. It was always neat to see the shyer students open up. The individual at-tention was really good for them," said a TA. Another TA found tutorials personally enlightening: "You really get to know your students [in tutorials]. You appreciate how many of them have faced powerful socioeconomic obstacles at home."

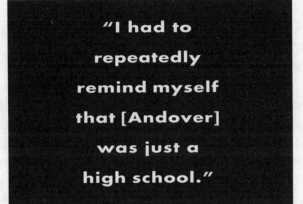

"I had to repeatedly remind myself that [Andover] was just a high school."

Beyond their support duties, TAs are often given op-portunities to teach. "How much you teach depends on the teacher," said a TA. "Most will let you teach at least a few classes alone; others are less willing to give you free rein." Indeed, one TA "got to take over a class for two weeks, teaching an entire novel" while another "worked with a teacher so set in her ways that there never was a chance to address the class alone." As for TAs who do "fly solo," it's an exhilarating and educational experience. "It's pretty amazing," said a TA. "You learn so much in front of a class—how to pace the discussion, how to get everyone to contribute, how to throw out a question and then bring the discussion back to a unifying theme." For many TAs, any initial public speaking anxiety soon gives way to a newfound confidence. "Although I was a bit apprehensive at first, teaching eventually felt no different than explaining something at the dinner table," said one intern.

TAs play an integral role in students' extracurricular activities. First of all, TAs serve as coaches or supervisors for a variety of afternoon activities, such as volleyball, martial arts, and aerobics. Afternoon supervisory positions are mandatory for Summer Session TAs and optional for (MS)^2 TAs. All TAs are also required to chaperon four of the students' weekend activities. Some TAs accompany students on Sunday outings to the movies or the beach. Said a TA: "I went with a group [of students] to the Rockingham Park Mall in New Hampshire. It was pretty mellow. I just made sure they were all accounted for and didn't get into trouble." Other TAs serve as chaperons at the Saturday night dances. "The dances are a big social scene for the kids and are always packed," said a TA. "Most are attended by students from both programs, but (MS)^2 students, many [of whom] prefer more urban music, sometimes hold their own." Like in the other activi-ties, TAs play a low-key role: "You're not holding a ruler between couples to make sure the kids aren't dancing too close. It's really casual—you just need to be there, not much else."

Andover administration makes sure TAs are well pre-pared to do their jobs. Before classes begin, TAs participate in a few days of intensive orientation. "[Administration] made a huge effort. The directors of both programs gave us a pep talk, as did past teachers, TAs, and students. Then they had seminars on TA strategies and how to work effectively with teachers. There was also a panel discussion on how to help students adjust to racial diversity on campus," said a TA.

The Andover campus is beautiful. Descriptions range from "big and gracious" to "lovely sweeping lawns" to "stately and brick, like the University of Virginia." With a library of more than 100,000 volumes, an arts and commu-nications center, an archaeological museum, and a gallery of American art, Andover definitely has a big-time collegiate feel. One TA said, "I had to repeatedly remind myself that it was just a high school." A 20-minute train ride from Boston, the town of Andover is of the "sleepy New England" sort, with a "little Main Street," "Colonial-style houses," and "quaint shops." TAs make the ten-minute walk to town several times a week, whether it's to visit the 24-hour CVS pharmacy (for some, "a late-night place to be") or to kick back at Justin's, a popular bar.

All TAs live on campus. Summer session TAs are required to live in an Andover dormitory, where they have their own room but share bathroom facilities with students. TAs in the (MS)^2 Program reside in faculty-only cottages, which also have single-occupancy bedrooms and common bathrooms. (MS)^2 TAs often relish their time apart from the high schoolers. "To be honest, it was really nice to have a retreat away from the students. At night I went home and had peace of mind," said one (MS)^2 TA. TAs and students eat in one of four dining halls, each with "high ceilings, arched windows, and wooden tables." The food is "good for institutional grub," but one carnivore sniffed: "There were too many things like turkey burgers, tofu, and frozen yogurt and not enough stuff for us meat eaters." To work off their cafeteria visits, TAs take advantage of the athletic center, a state-of-the art facility that "rivals any college gym." There's also a huge forest adjacent to campus with running trails and shady areas where "students go to break rules."

SELECTION

The Summer Session and (MS)^2 Programs seek college seniors, recent graduates, and graduate students. No other prerequisites exist, except that students should have "a strong academic background in their field and a generosity of spirit." Students of color are strongly urged to apply.

APPLICATION PROCEDURE

The application deadline for TA positions with the Summer Session is January 7; for the (MS)^2 Program, it is January 15. Applications received after the deadlines are still valid, but the applicant's chance for a position is greatly reduced.

Candidates should apply directly to either program. Both programs require a completed application and an official undergraduate transcript. The Summer Session also asks for two recent photographs and a personal essay describing one's (1) most memorable intellectual experience and (2) most challenging personal experience at college. After applications have been read, a number of candidates are invited to Andover (at their own expense) for personal interviews with the director of the program to which they are applying. In rare instances, long-distance applicants may be able to substitute a phone interview for the personal interview. Final decisions are made in late February or early March.

OVERVIEW

Is teaching for you? A summer spent at the Phillips Academy may provide the answer. Teaching Assistants in the Summer Session and (MS)^2 Programs spend six weeks teaching, tutoring, and tending to students. The pace is hectic, the demands are many, but TAs receive a wonderful taste of both teaching and boarding-school life.

FOR MORE INFORMATION . . .

- Phillips Academy
  Director, Summer Session
  Andover, MA 01810

- Phillips Academy
  Director, (MS)^2: Math and Science for
    Minority Students
  Andover, MA 01810

- Phone: (508) 749-4000

In 1879, chemist James N. Gamble invented Ivory soap. A few years later, the first ads for the white soap boasted that it was—"99 44/100% pure." Did you ever wonder just what's in that other 56/100%? Well, according to an independent analysis conducted by the company in 1882, Ivory is 0.11% uncombined alkali, 0.28% carbonates, and 0.17% mineral matter. Nothing scandalous to be certain, this is just an interesting fact about a famous Procter & Gamble product.

Founded in 1837 by brothers-in-law William Procter and James Gamble (father of James N.) as a soap and candle business, Procter & Gamble has since grown by leaps and bounds. It's now a $30-billion-a-year household-products empire, with 100,000 employees worldwide who produce 100 U.S. products. Its top-selling brands include Tide, Cheer, Clearasil, Cover Girl, Pampers, Charmin, Crest, Folgers, Hawaiian Punch, Jif, Pringles, and Crisco.

DESCRIPTION

Procter & Gamble recruits an army of interns for the following departments and locations: Brand Management (primarily M.B.A. students) at the headquarters in Cincinnati, at the Pharmaceuticals division in Norwich, NY, and at the Cosmetics and Fragrances division in Baltimore; Product Supply/ Engineering and Research and Product Development at one of the four technical centers in Cincinnati; Product Supply (Customer Services or Purchases), Financial Management, Market Research, and Management Systems in Cincinnati; Sales Management (primarily undergraduates) in field sites throughout the country; and Product Supply/Manufacturing, with positions at 49 manufacturing sites nationwide. Overall, two thirds of the intern class is based in Cincinnati.

In 1879, Harley Procter convinced his partners that P&G should pour money into advertising Ivory as the "99 44/100% pure" soap that floats. That ad campaign marked P&G as one of the first companies in American business history to advertise its products. Over 100 years later, it's said that P&G, widely recognized as the world's best marketer of products, spends more on advertising than any other U.S. company. Consequently, interns in Brand Management (i.e., Advertising) are in for a real education. Acting as assistant brand managers, they design and execute national promotional events, develop marketing strategies for new products, improve package designs, and identify consumer habits.

A Research and Product Development intern in P&G's Bar Soap and Household Cleaning Products division worked on a project that analyzed how cleaners are distributed on fabric surfaces. "We use an image analyzer—a computer attached to a video camera, which we focus on a piece of fabric with detergent spread on it," he said. "The computer records the level of intensity per pixel, from zero for black to 256 for pure white. [The pixel intensities] are statistically analyzed to determine the distribution of soap on the fabric. It was my job to put together the image analyzer and write computer software for it. Assembling it was relatively easy, but composing the software was more difficult. I bounced ideas off P&G's computer scientists, image experts, and the other members of the project team to determine exactly what was needed."

At the Winton Hill Technical Center, a Supply/Engineering intern learned how Charmin and Bounty are made. "Pre-bleached fiber containing water is injected onto a moving wire mesh, which creates a thin, long sheet of fiber. . . . [G]ravity, vacuum, and P&G's proprietary 'predryer process' get rid of most of the water. However, to remove the last traces, the sheet is put on a 'Yankee dryer,' a tube about 20 feet long and 18 feet in diameter. The dry paper is then subjected to 'creping'—the act of scraping it off the Yankee to create two ten-ton rolls about ten feet wide apiece [each called a half-Yankee]."

After learning the paper-making process, he was asked to develop a mathematical model for the predryer. "I made about 80 prototype Bounty and Charmin samples . . . wet them down, and ran them through small-scale machinery at the pilot plant. [The experiments eventually] led us to a simple equation in three variables. It was definitely a good starting point." At the end of the summer, he presented his results, just as all P&G interns do, to a group of about 20 scientists, who posed many challenging questions. "When I couldn't defend myself, my mentor interjected and answered [the scientists'] concerns."

P&G's Product Supply/Purchases department manages the supply of materials and services needed to produce the company's products. A Purchases intern was asked to figure out how much sulfuric acid P&G needed in the next year to meet its laundry detergent output. "I flew out to San Francisco to learn how sulfuric acid is made, and then I researched the raw materials markets. I found out that the price of sulfur was declining, so I asked our five suppliers to fly to headquarters for a meeting, where I suggested that they lower their price and improve delivery and billing services. . . . After appraising each supplier's pros and cons, I redistributed [the volume] of sulfuric acid that each supplier would make. This shuffling saved us $800,000."

Sales interns each sell products to approximately one million dollars' worth of major accounts. As part of the regular sales force, interns get full use of a company car in which to make their rounds and for transportation on weekends. One Sales intern, stationed in Boston with 15 other interns, was responsible for accounts at 14 grocery stores. "You walk in and make sure our products are in stock and are being displayed properly. Afterward, you meet with the manager in order to sell him more inventory or discuss problems with presentation. But sometimes the store manager doesn't want to talk to you because you're a college kid. You have to be pretty persistent." Described as "very demanding" and "intense," the Sales position is more than just a casual visit to grocery stores. One intern worked on convincing a grocery store chain to carry a display for a new 16-ounce version of Sunny Delight juice. "I merged data from City Hall and P&G's own database to determine the demographics of our customers and created graphs representing changing market trends. My manager and I made a presentation to the chain's board members, who liked the

> As part of the regular sales force, each Sales intern gets full use of a company car in which to make his or her rounds.

idea. Two days later, they approved the display and required that all their stores use it."

P&G's internship program is well structured. An apartment-locater service arranges housing for Cincinnati interns at nearby Xavier University apartments. About 200 interns live in the apartments every summer. The program also organizes many social activities including dinners, a cruise on the Ohio River, trips to Cincinnati Reds games, and an outing to the Cincinnati Zoo. Some years, interns are invited to visit King's Island amusement park (paid for by P&G) or a downtown jazz festival. "The company bought each of us a $25 ticket; I got to listen to six hours of Chaka Khan and Jeffrey Osbourne," recalled one intern.

Early in the summer, P&G hosts two orientations, one for interns stationed at headquarters and one for Sales interns. Headquarters interns attend a half day of business presentations by vice presidents followed by a reception and dinner given by the chairman and president. Sales Management interns are flown to Cincinnati to attend the headquarters orientation and also to participate in their own week of seminars. Starting with a 7:30 AM breakfast and lasting until 6:00 PM, these seminars teach Sales interns business ethics, company history, and selling strategies. Sales interns are put up in hotels and often spend the evenings at Cincinnati Reds baseball games or the local amusement park, all of which is paid for by the company. "I hadn't had that much fun or eaten that well in a long time," said one Sales intern.

P&G's Cincinnati headquarters is a sprawling corporate compound. Rippling proudly are the flags of ten countries displayed to remind visitors that P&G is an international company (P&G actually does business with 140 countries and rotates the flags every few weeks). Buildings are spread out over a ten-mile radius, and include the General Offices Complex and four R&D facilities. Each location offers a cafeteria with a convenient payment method—simply slide your ID card through the magnetic card reader and the meal will be deducted automatically from your paycheck. Interns may join the General Offices' Lifestyle Center that is equipped with Lifecycles, treadmills, Nautilus and free-weights, for a mere $11 per month.

One-hour seminars and training sessions, which feature employees or outside consultants, are scheduled occasionally at P&G. Interns attend such seminars as an R&D lecture on mass spectroscopy and a Purchases workshop on how to analyze consumer trends and forecast prices. They may also take work-related classes like "Seven Habits of an Effective Manager," "Memo Writing," and "Total Quality," which range from a half day to a few days in length and are held at P&G's training center. "There are so many activities going on," said an intern. "If you attend a lot of them, you might not have enough time to do your work."

SELECTION

 College sophomores, juniors, seniors, and first-year graduate students are eligible to apply. Required fields of study depend on the department to which application is being made. Targeted technical majors include engineering (computer, chemical, electrical, mechanical, and industrial), computer science, information systems, math, statistics, and operations research. Applicants to Sales must demonstrate a clear interest in business, hold a valid driver's license, and pass a pre-employment physical. A brochure lists "leadership qualities, problem-solving abilities, creativity, interpersonal skills, and a strong record of personal achievement" as key selection criteria.

APPLICATION PROCEDURE

 The deadline is February 1. While P&G does almost all of its internship recruiting at approximately 100 campuses nationwide, unsolicited applications from students at other campuses will be considered. Send a cover letter and resumé as follows: applications to Brand Management, Sales Management, Market Research, Financial Management, and Management Systems internships go to the first address listed c/o (Name of Division) Internship Program Recruiting Manager; applications to Product Supply internships in Customer Services, Engineering, Manufacturing, and Purchases go to the second address c/o Product Supply Internship Program Recruiting Manager; and Research and Product Development internship applications go to the third address listed c/o R&PD BS/MS Internship Program Recruiting Manager. Final selections are made after the company conducts on-campus and on-site interviews.

OVERVIEW

 Ever heard of Chipso or Handy Soap? They're discontinued P&G brands. But that doesn't mean that Chipso and Handy Soap failed. Rather, their phase-out illustrates P&G's commitment to constantly improving its already high-quality products. To further that commitment, the company brings college students on board. Working to improve, manufacture, and sell products, they help ensure that Americans will continue to get the Tide out, squeeze the Charmin, choose Jif, and keep Zestfully clean.

FOR MORE INFORMATION . . .

■ Procter & Gamble
P.O. Box 599
Cincinnati, OH 45201-0599

■ Procter & Gamble
5299 Spring Grove Avenue
Cincinnati, OH 45217-1087

■ Procter & Gamble
6090 Center Hill Avenue
Cincinnati, OH 45224-1792

■ Phone: (513) 983-1100

History has given us many famous "houses"—the House of Parliament . . . the House of Usher . . . the House that Babe Ruth built.

In 1927, few would suppose that the new house being contemplated could gain similar recognition. But pals Bennett Cerf and Donald Klopfer, who had acquired a classic-books line called the Modern Library in 1925, were convinced that a publishing house printing original books "on the side at random" was the way to go. "I've got it— Random House," Cerf said, inventing a name that would stand the test of time. An artist present in the room at the time immediately drew a trademark—a three-story house with clouds in the back. His five-minute sketch has been the company's emblem ever since.

Random House, Inc. is now the world's largest general-trade publisher, and its "house" has published authors like John Updike, Toni Morrison, James Joyce, Albert Camus, William Faulkner, Eugene O'Neill and—last, but not least—Dr. Seuss. Owned by publishing magnate Si Newhouse (another famous "house"), Random House, Inc. issues books under approximately 25 imprints, including Alfred A. Knopf, Random House, Crown, Villard, Pantheon, Times Books, and Ballantine.

SELECTIVITY	🔍 🔍 🔍 🔍 🔍
Approximate applicant pool: 300 Interns accepted: 7	

COMPENSATION	$ $
$250/week	

QUALITY OF LIFE	🌴 🌴 🌴
Youthful staff; Free books Weekly seminars	

LOCATION(S)	
New York, NY	

FIELD	
Publishing	

DURATION	
10 weeks Summer	

PRE-REQS	
College juniors and seniors, grad students	

DEADLINE(S)	
April 15	

DESCRIPTION

The Random House Internship Program was established in the summer of 1990 to train college students interested in the field of publishing and thereby increase the company's pool of potential employees. In the begining, some interns worked strictly in editorial positions while others juggled publicity and marketing posts. But in response to interns who wanted to experience both sides of the business, Random House modified the program. Interns are still placed in one of the company's five major publishing groups—Crown, Ballantine, Knopf, Random House, or Juvenile Merchandise—but to get an in-depth look at publishing, they now rotate through Publicity, Marketing, Production, and Editorial.

"It's a crash course in the business of book publishing," said the coordinator.

One morning during the first week of the program, interns convene in a small conference room. Robert Bernstein, president of Random House, Inc., sits at the head of the table. At his sides are the CFO, COO, vice president of Personnel, and the internship coordinator. After introductions, Mr. Bernstein sifts through the interns' resumés that are stacked in front of him. "He asked specific questions about our backgrounds," said an intern. "Actually, we were impressed that he was even there, so when he said he wanted us to tell him how to improve the program at the end-of-summer meeting, we knew he meant it." The meeting makes an indelible mark, and interns realize that they are considered important, even though they are temporary employees.

By the time orientation takes place, interns have already started their tour of duty in one of the publishing groups. At Crown, for example, interns spend equal time with Crown's Harmony, Clarkson N. Potter, Orion, and Crown imprints. Over ten weeks, each intern's experience touches on everything from reading manuscripts to sitting in on book cover meetings. One intern read approximately ten manuscripts in a two-week period and composed a two-page summary for each one. Her analysis included a synopsis and her reasons for rejecting or recommending the manuscript. "My first manuscript was a book already under Crown contract," she said, "but I didn't know it. . . . I guess [my editor] was testing me, and fortunately I recommended that we publish it." Approximately two years after a book hits the shelves, Random House creates what are called "postmortem" profit-and-loss statements. "They reveal how well the book sold compared with our prediction," explained an intern who completed nearly 30 of them during her time at Harmony. "By doing P-and-Ls, I learned what goes into making a book. During the process, I visited almost all the departments to determine each book's design fees, printing costs, legal payments, publicity expenses, advance, sales, royalties—there's a lot to include."

To generate demand for new books, Random House has interns help crank the company's publicity machine. An intern in Publicity worked on the radio giveaway of a sports book. "I researched in which cities we could best promote the book, looking for strong sports stations. I sent off about 15 packets, including a picture of the cover and a descriptive page from the catalog, to about five cities." Another intern worked on a promotion for Peter Benchley's *Beast*. He drove to the beach and handed out baseball caps and copies of the book to sunbathers, while planes overhead dragged banners advertising the book.

Random House's departments are notified from the start that under no circumstances are interns to be given only clerical work. This is not to say that interns won't be photocopying the occasional manuscript. "This is a very labor-intensive business," said the coordinator. "They get some busywork just like everyone else." But it does mean that interns won't be engaged in mindless errands at the behest of an editor. Moreover, interns may turn to the coordinator should they find themselves in an awkward situation. "My editor asked me to pick up her laundry and that's not right. I was too intimidated to say anything, so I told [the coordinator] about it," said an intern. By the next day, the coordinator had moved her to a new editor.

The internship is well structured but not rigid. "We create the blueprint," said the coordinator, "but it's loosely defined so that interns with initiative can explore areas of interest." Indeed, some interns observe editors in the later stages of editing, while others work on finance department projects. Interns in editorial positions write "flap copy" (the synopsis on the inside of a hardcover's jacket) and "bound-galley copy" (the description appearing on the back cover of the uncorrected proof given to reviewers for the first critical reading). One editorial intern even wrote a cookbook's "fact sheet," a marketing tool used by publishers to describe a book to booksellers. "It includes information like title, trim size [i.e., the book's dimensions], publishing date, and author's previous works and sales, if any. It also provides a few descriptive selling points and a 'handle,' the one-sentence punch line on why you should buy the book."

About the only thing Random House interns don't do is visit the company's main distribution center in Westminster, MD. In fact, in one intern's estimation, her

> About the only thing Random House interns don't do is visit the main distribution center in Westminster, MD.

work was more stimulating and challenging than that of her current position as entry-level editorial assistant: "[The editorial assistants] are more like secretaries, answering the phones at the reception desk two hours each day, dealing with paperwork, and only occasionally reading manuscripts." But for interns, piles of manuscripts sit waiting to be read during those occasional moments when there's a lull in the day. "Even when they're bad," said an intern, "it's an interesting way to spend two hours."

No two interns ever work in the same department at the same time. "We want them to learn on their own," explained the coordinator, "and we don't want them competing with one another." One might expect that the isolation prevents them from getting to know each another, but that's not so at low-key Random House. There's a friendliness that transcends the separation. Interns quickly bond, frequenting restaurants, attending Shakespeare in Central Park, and going clubbing on weekends.

Interns also convene once a week at noon to hear various employees speak about their positions within the company. Served a free lunch from a nearby deli, they listen to production managers, editors, people from finance, and Random House's legal counsel. "In one talk, a guy from production taught us about the art of typesetting—two people each key a whole manuscript into a computer and then a special program compares the two typeset works for discrepancies. . . . In another talk, Crown's legal counsel [discussed] legal issues in entertainment and then told us how the company decides which books should be scanned for libelous content."

Random House, Inc. occupies over 30 floors of a 40-story building in midtown Manhattan. The 12th-floor conference room, outfitted with a deck, has a great view of the East River and Long Island beyond. Walking about are "predominantly young" employees in casual clothes. The informal dress befits what the coordinator says is "far from a stuffy corporate environment"—piles of manuscripts clutter desks, and of course all sorts of books occupy every inch of shelf space.

Strolling through the offices gives one a feeling that the book publishing industry is dominated by women. That's confirmed by Personnel, which estimates that 65 percent of the nearly 1,100 Random House employees in New York are female. The female makeup among interns is even greater: 23 of the 28 former interns, as of the end of 1993, are coeds.

SELECTION

 Students of all majors are eligible to apply "because we publish books on every subject," said the coordinator. The program is open to college juniors, seniors, and graduate students who have at least one year of school left upon completion of the internship. Excellent communications skills and a "can-do, make-it-happen attitude" are essential, according to the coordinator.

APPLICATION PROCEDURE

 The deadline to submit materials is April 15, but students may begin applying as soon as January 1. Applicants must send in a resumé demonstrating an interest in publishing, and a cover letter indicating what they want out of a book publishing internship and why. "The cover letter gives us a sense of who you are and how well you write," said the coordinator, "and is especially important for people who have no prior publishing-related experience." Top prospects must travel at their own expense to New York for a personal interview.

OVERVIEW

 A First-Rate Publishing Internship by Random House. The selling points? Good pay by publishing industry standards; rotation through imprints and departments, a feature allowing interns to see most facets of the business; meetings with editors-in-chief and senior executives; and a plethora of books available for free or at a 50 percent discount. The handle? The world's largest book publisher, Random House, Inc., provides students with an excellent training-ground in publishing and offers a whopping 50 percent of the program's interns permanent positions.

FOR MORE INFORMATION . . .

■ Random House, Inc.
Internship Program
201 East 50th Street
New York, NY 10022
(212) 572-2610

Raychem

SELECTIVITY	🔍 🔍 🔍 🔍 🔍
Approximate applicant pool: 2,000 Interns accepted: 40	

COMPENSATION	$ $ $ $
$400–$500/week for undergrads $700–$1,000/week for grad students; RT travel	

QUALITY OF LIFE	✈ ✈ ✈
Plant tours; Intramurals Dedicated employees	

LOCATION(S)	
Menlo Park, CA	

FIELD	
Materials science/high-tech	

DURATION	
10–12 weeks Summer	

PRE-REQS	
College sophomores, juniors and seniors, grad students; Minimum 3.0 GPA	

DEADLINE(S)	
March 1	

What would you call a computer screen that responds to touch? How about a cord that is used on rooftops to automatically melt excess ice and turns off automatically when enough ice has been removed?

What would you call a self-resetting fuse that prevents batteries that short-circuit from starting fires or ruining electronic devices?

Some would say it's magic, but Raychem simply calls them modern technology. Manufacturer extraordinaire of materials-science products, Raychem Corporation is on the cutting edge of scientific discovery. In addition to the aforementioned touch-screen technology, IceStop cord, and PolySwitch fuse, Raychem has invented more than 10,000 high-performance products, from fiber-optic cables and computer touchscreens to cable TV coaxial-cable connectors and gel sealants. These products bring this Fortune 300 company nearly $1.5 billion in sales every year.

DESCRIPTION

Raychem's Intern Program dates back to the mid-1970s. Opportunities are available in the areas of Engineering, Research & Development (R&D), Product Design, Manufacturing, Marketing, Finance, Human Resources, and Accounting. Three quarters of all interns are undergraduates.

Every year Raychem's managers submit approximately 150 requests for interns, a number significantly higher than the number of interns Raychem eventually employs. So, the company pares down the requests to the 40 most challenging jobs by adhering to a principle articulated by Raychem's president and CEO, Robert Saldich: "The key to a successful internship program rests on who [interns are] working for and what they're working on. If they get a good mentor and an important project, they'll have an excellent experience."

Raychem's R&D division is the company's "primary engine for growth." Spending 11 percent of sales on R&D in 1992 alone, Raychem ranks among the top 100 corporations for R&D expenditures. With that much money pumped in to the department in which they are placed, interns in R&D have an opportunity to do research on products with excellent commercial potential. An intern assigned to the Gels group, for example, worked on a project to replace the silicone polymers usually used in gels with ethylene-propylene co-polymers.

"The ethylene-propylene co-polymer is roughly $10 per unit less in cost, so if we could make the same gels using the ethylene-propylene co-polymers, we'd get a substantial savings." But first, he had to make sure that the company could get these new kinds of polymers to "cross-link" with one another. "Cross-linking" refers to the process in which high-energy electron beams are focused on a polymer to get the polymers' molecular chains to bond together at random points. The cross-linking results in an elastic yet structurally stable gel that can both adhere well and be easily removed from the surfaces on which it is placed. "Using IR, NMR, and GC techniques, I proved not only that the ethylene-propylene co-polymers cross-link, but also that we could control the reaction to make gels of varying hardness."

The hit-or-miss nature of R&D means that some projects will fail. For example, an intern in R&D worked on creating polymer-based electrodes that could "pull ions out of wastewater." Using a thin piece of metal surrounded by a polymer backing, the electrodes attracted copper and other ions. "We were trying to market it to the photography industry, but the electrode wasn't designed well, and it wasn't sucking up enough ions." Beside learning that "not every project is successful," this intern also realized that R&D work requires "lots of tedious testing; you've got to be willing to try all possibilities and keep plugging away until a solution presents itself."

To support R&D and Manufacturing, the Product Design department builds prototypes, designs assembly tools, and improves manufacturing processes. One intern worked on the company's new surge arresters, those foot-long successions of metal disks attached at the ends of electric lines that protect the lines from overvoltages caused by lightning. "Raychem's hybrid insulator is made out of a ceramic rod wrapped by a silicone cover called a shed. I designed a mold to make the shed, a die to make the rod, and special tools needed to put the surge arrester together. It was a lot of responsibility."

Rigorous projects aren't the only activities in which interns at Raychem participate. Interns are taken on plant tours to gain an overview of the company's ten divisions. Interns also have lunch with CEO Bob Saldich, "a down-to-earth, likable guy—at the meeting, he [articulated] his vision to make Raychem a premier materials company." Raychem also recruits university professors to speak on innovation in the field of science (e.g., nonlinear properties of polymers or relaxation times in liquid crystals). And occasionally, managers challenge interns to a softball game or take them to Gordon Biersch microbrewery, where they "toast a few beers."

Raychem's financial package is exemplary. The company covers round-trip airfare or gasoline expenses, if interns drive to Menlo Park. It also pays interns' first week of room and board while they search for an apartment. Weekly pay depends on experience and age. Freshmen typically make $400 per week while seniors receive $500. Master's and Ph.D.-level students, on the other hand, earn $700 to $800 per week, while M.B.A. candidates get a whopping $1,000 per week. One would think that after investing so much money on interns, Raychem would consistently offer most of them permanent jobs. But hire rates vary from year to year. Some years only one intern is hired while in other years it's ten.

Headquartered in Menlo Park, CA, about 30 minutes from San Francisco, Raychem's main campus consists of 26 buildings that sit on an 82-acre site. Another 26 Raychem buildings are within a four-mile radius. On the grounds, easily accessible basketball and volleyball courts mean that summer intramurals are a big part of company athletic life. "If you can handle a challenging bunch of players, the intramurals are a great way to meet employees and other interns," said an intern.

Indoors, student office accommodations are mixed, ranging from cubicles to private offices. Spending most of their time in the laboratory, interns notice that "there's a high degree of dedication." Said an intern: "[Employees] love

> **Easily-accessible basketball and volleyball courts mean that summer intramurals are a big part of company athletic life.**

science and technology; it's a positive atmosphere that emphasizes teamwork and communication." One intern found it amazing that "we got to work alongside some top-notch, well-published patent holders. . . . It's like being a batboy in the big leagues."

At the end of the summer, these "batboys" come up to the plate at the Summer Intern Presentation. Like a science fair, the presentation is a forum for students to exhibit their project in the form of posters, photographs, and product samples. After answering employees' questions, interns and managers make a trek to the Farewell Reception, held at Palo Alto's Gatehouse restaurant.

SELECTION

 Applicants should have finished their freshman year in college and should have at least a 3.0 GPA. The company seeks the following majors: engineering (electrical, mechanical, industrial, chemical), materials science, physics, chemistry, computer science, marketing, finance, and accounting. The internship flyer indicates that "academic record [and] extracurricular activities as well as interpersonal and leadership skills are the basis for selection."

APPLICATION PROCEDURE

 The deadline is March 1. Students should submit a resumé and cover letter discussing their work experience (including any other internships completed), leadership activities, and area of interest. After resumés undergo a preliminary screening by College Relations, managers conduct phone interviews to match top candidates to available projects.

OVERVIEW

 Since 1957, Raychem has been making magical products—products that keep pipes from freezing, protect computers from short-circuiting, and seal telephone splices from water and dirt. "The operative word is pioneering technologies," says CEO Saldich. "We don't copy products and try to make them better. We try to be the first to invent products that solve customer problems." This policy means that interns, whom Raychem intentionally places "in the guts of [the company's] businesses," work with cutting-edge materials-science products. "I was studying chemical engineering back when the only elements were earth, air, fire, and water," says the 60-year-old Saldich. Fortunately for Raychem's interns, science has come a long way.

FOR MORE INFORMATION . . .

■ Raychem
College Relations Manager
M/S 111/8201
300 Constitution Drive
Menlo Park, CA 94025-1164
(415) 361-4999

The Rhebok is a small South African gazelle. It is extraordinarily aggressive, agile, and fleet-footed. The image of this animal well-serves the Reebok company, whose humble beginnings go back to 1895. That year, Englishman Joseph William Foster, member of the Bolton Primrose Harriers running club, made himself the world's first pair of spiked running shoes. Though he had sewn the left shoe and nailed the right, his fellow club members all demanded a pair. What started as a curious enterprise soon became J.W. Foster & Sons, hand-crafter of shoes for the world's top sprinters, long-distance runners, soccer players, ruggers, and "footballers." Around 1950, J.W.'s grandsons Joseph and Jeffrey Foster apprenticed at the family business. The experience convinced them to build J.W. Foster & Sons into a new sportswear company, so in 1958, Reebok was born.

Twenty-one years later, an outdoor sporting goods distributor named Paul Fireman spied Reebok's shoes at an international trade show and acquired the North American distribution license. In ten years, Reebok grew from a $1 million- to a $1 billion-per year sporting goods company. Now Reebok International, Ltd. comprises Reebok, Rockport, AVIA, Weebok, and BOKS brands and holds 25 percent of the U.S. market, second only to Nike. Manufacturer of the world's first aerobic dance shoe, developer of a new exercise movement called Step Reebok, and inventor of the PUMP, Reebok is now a $3 billion-per-year operation.

DESCRIPTION

In the summer of 1990, Reebok started the College Relations Internship Program to identify potential employees and to give students experience in the athletic sportswear industry. Every summer, seven undergraduates and

SELECTIVITY	🔍 🔍 🔍 🔍 🔍
Approximate applicant pool: 2,500 Interns accepted: 10	

COMPENSATION	$ $ $ $
$460/week for undergraduates $625–$690/week for graduates, NFL players	

QUALITY OF LIFE	🌴 🌴 🌴 🌴
Independence; 40% discount on shoes Lunchtime basketball games; $5 massage	

LOCATION(S)
Stoughton, MA; Irvine, CA; Atlanta, GA; Chicago, IL

FIELD
Athletic shoes and apparel

DURATION
10–12 weeks Summer

PRE-REQS
College juniors and seniors, recent grads, grad students; Minimum 3.0 GPA

DEADLINE(S)
May 15

three graduate students are chosen to participate in the program. Placed in the company's Stoughton, Irvine, Atlanta, and Chicago offices, undergraduates work in the company's Reebok division in areas such as Promotions, Human Resources, Retail, Management Information Systems (MIS), Finance, and Sales. Graduate students, usually M.B.A.'s, receive assignments within the Reebok division's Marketing unit.

An undergraduate intern in the Sales division's field service group acted as a liaison between Reebok's fitness shoes groups

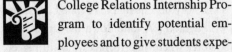

(aerobics, cross training, walking, etc.) and the field representatives. He collected data on each of the new lines being introduced. That summer, for example, Reebok released about ten lines, each featuring two to four shoes. "One such line was the Preseason cross-trainer series featuring the PUMP Paydirt, the Scrimmage Mid, and the Scrimmage Low," he said. "I compiled information on this and every other new line—what sport or activity the shoe targeted, what professional athletes used the shoe, and the shoe's materials." In order to put together such a list of characteristics, the intern had to become well versed in "shoe-ology." "I described what materials made up the upper [visible part of the shoe], the tongue [the flap under the laces], the midsole, and the outsole," he said, "and I learned that Reebok has access to three kinds of leathers and an ingredient called hexalite." Hexalite, a honeycomb-like material, is used in space shuttles to absorb the shock a craft experiences upon hitting the earth's atmosphere. Reebok sometimes puts hexalite in a shoe's heel to reduce the shock on an athlete's knees and ankles.

The gym features
—joy!—
a fifteen-minute
massage for $5.

But College Relations interns aren't the only students sniffing around the company. Since 1990, Reebok has hosted a design competition, entitled Designovation, which targets design students at five American schools: Parsons School of Design (New York), Rhode Island School of Design, Art Center College of Design (Pasadena), Syracuse University, and University of Michigan. The top five candidates from each school are flown to New York where their work is judged by top designers such as Niels Diffrient and Nicole Miller. Nine finalists are christened Designovation interns and placed in the Design groups of Reebok, Rockport, AVIA, Weeboks, and BOKS. Round-trip airfare, housing, a $3,400 stipend, a mentor, daily transportation to and from work, and plant tours are all provided. But first there's an awards ceremony, featuring "all the glitter usually reserved for the Oscars." For 12 weeks during the summer, interns play designer. A

Rockport intern, for example, was told to design a progressive shoe for the women's active lifestyle line. She came up with 12 prototypes and at the final presentation, Reebok's CEO "was duly impressed." While the Designovation program is currently limited to a few colleges, other design schools may be eligible. Interested students should contact the company for further information.

Reebok sponsors a third internship program as well. The company places professional football players in summer account-executive internships at field offices around the country and also at Reebok's headquarters in Stoughton, MA. Past participants include Buford McGee, Jimmy Johnson, Keith Neubert, and Stanford Jennings. Though the NFL internship ends one week after the College Relations program begins, exposure to the players is possible. "One time, I shared an elevator with six huge players in slick suits," said a Designovation intern. Another intern found a reason to call Stanford Jennings: "I needed a figure from his department."

Reebok's definition of internship uses words and phrases such as *structured*, *meaningful*, and *impact upon the business group*. Few interns dispute the value of their contributions, but none calls the internship structured. In fact, interns point out that it affords them quite a bit of independence. "I came up with some crazy shoe designs," said an intern. "It seemed like I was free-falling at 100 miles a minute—you do a lot of unplanned projects," said another. One undergraduate collected information from field representatives' surveys of shoe store outlets. "I ranked shoe sales, summarized Reebok's representation at displays, and noted what customers are looking for," he said. "The report went out to management, and I was told that the president of Reebok USA looked at it during strategy sessions."

Reebok's six-story headquarters is located in "suburban, woodsy" Stoughton. A mile down the street is the Reebok outlet store, where interns receive a 40 percent discount on blemished shoes and overstocked clothing. The headquarters' six floors are home to the divisions (except for Rockport and AVIA, which are located in Marlboro, MA and Portland, OR, respectively), a computer center, two cafeterias (which serve an all-you-can-eat special every Friday during the summer), and an atmosphere described by several interns as "informal," "laid-back," and "family-like." On the last night of the company's summer sales meeting, interns join several hundred "Reebok-ites" as they embark on a cruise of Boston harbor.

As expected, most employees at the company love sports. At lunchtime employees gather at the company's basketball court—Reebok shoes only, of course. "I played basketball every day with vice presidents, other interns, and company employees. Even guys from the warehouse would come over," said an intern. Interns with no flair for hoops may play Rollerblade hockey and tennis on nearby courts or work out at the company gym. The gym (membership: $2 per week) features weights, aerobics, StairMasters, treadmills, bikes, fitness experts, and—joy!— a 15-minute massage for $5.

Interns at headquarters attend a two-hour orientation in the third week of the internship. They are introduced to the structure, culture, and mission of the company. "But we were already baptized by then. The introduction should come sooner," complained an intern. Orientation also breaks the ice between interns. "We encourage them to get together socially," said the coordinator, who hands out a list of all interns' names and phone numbers. One year, interns hosted after-hours cookouts that were subsidized by Reebok. Another year, the intern class sponsored a road race for charity.

SELECTION

 Undergraduates must have completed their sophomore or junior year by the start of the internship. Recent graduates starting master's-level work in the fall and first-year master's students (including M.B.A. candidates) are eligible for the graduate internship. Applicants must be enrolled in school on a full-time basis at the time of application.

Reebok targets liberal arts, business, economics, management information systems, and accounting majors. A minimum 3.0 GPA and excellent communication skills are required. The company looks for well-rounded people: "We want students who have not just excelled in the classroom but also participated in extracurricular activities and held leadership positions." Work experience (volunteer or paid) related to one's academic major or intended profession will also provide an edge.

APPLICATION PROCEDURE

 The final deadline is May 15, but decisions are made on a rolling basis months before. Applicants must send in a resumé, cover letter, and two professional references (letters of recommendation or addresses and phone numbers). Finalists are determined via phone or on-campus interviews followed by on-site interviews with managers and potential supervisors.

OVERVIEW

 For nearly a hundred years, Reebok has been a purveyor of top-notch athletic footwear. For the last few of these years, Reebok has provided college students with practical training in the footwear business in a youthful environment that "allows you to run with the ball." Armed with Macintoshes and the freedom to dream, interns attempt to improve Reebok operations. For their efforts, they receive good pay and at least one free pair of shoes. If you love sports and sportswear, then take a lap around the Reebok track. Just remember to give it your heart and sole.

FOR MORE INFORMATION . . .

■ Reebok
c/o College Relations Program
100 Technology Center Drive
Stoughton, MA 02072
(617) 341-5000

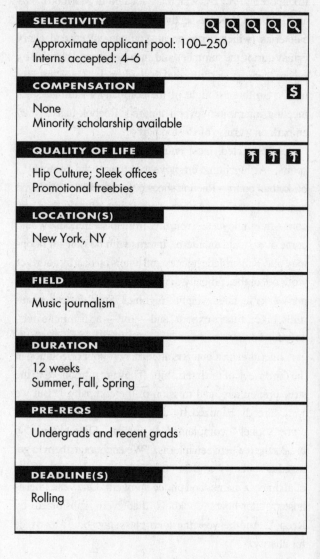

SELECTIVITY	
Approximate applicant pool: 100–250 Interns accepted: 4–6	🔍🔍🔍🔍🔍

COMPENSATION	
None Minority scholarship available	$

QUALITY OF LIFE	
Hip Culture; Sleek offices Promotional freebies	🌴🌴🌴

LOCATION(S)	
New York, NY	

FIELD	
Music journalism	

DURATION	
12 weeks Summer, Fall, Spring	

PRE-REQS	
Undergrads and recent grads	

DEADLINE(S)	
Rolling	

Okay music-trivia buffs—Who coined the phrase "rolling stone?" The Rolling Stones, that venerable supergroup headed by weather-beaten showman Mick Jagger, or *Rolling Stone*, that venerable magazine featuring musicians, music reviews, and political commentary? The answer is neither. In 1965, Bob Dylan churned out the rock-and-roll classic, "Like a Rolling Stone." The blues-great Muddy Waters' "I'm a Rollin' Stone" put the phrase in the public's consciousness a few years earlier. And, eh, don't forget the age-old maxim: "A rolling stone gathers no moss."

It may not be the original namesake, but *Rolling Stone* magazine has made a huge contribution to music journalism. Beginning in 1967 as a grassroots publication distributed mostly in Northern California, *Rolling Stone* has become the world's premier music magazine, grossing more than $110 million annually and reaching upwards of 1.2 million readers per issue. Published biweekly, and issued 24 times a year, it features incisive interviews and photographs of the music world's hottest performers.

DESCRIPTION

The staff at *Rolling Stone* minces no words about an intern's role at the magazine. Part gofers and part research assistants, interns are not entrusted with the job of writing articles: they receive no bylines, no feature stories, and no literary glory. Participants do, however, gain exposure to all aspects of magazine publishing, from photography to editing. Hundreds of interns have passed through *Rolling Stone* since the program began in the mid-seventies and most give their experience high marks.

While positions are available in a variety of departments, such as Advertising and Publicity, word has it that the best place to work is the Editorial department. "It's the nerve center of the place. It's where the action is," remarked one intern.

As with most entertainment internships, the Editorial internship at *Rolling Stone* includes a good deal of filing, faxing, photocopying, and phone work. But, as an employee pointed out, unlike phone work at a law firm, phone work at the magazine can be fun. "We deal with a number of 'crazies'—people looking to speak to Mick Jagger, tell us stories about playing guitar with Jimi Hendrix, and offer ideas about why rock-'n'-roll died with Chuck Berry [he's still alive]," said one intern. Busywork is busywork, though, and interns must accept that gofering is an integral part of their experience.

Rolling Stone strives to answer every legitimate letter it receives and most of the burden of this admirable task falls on interns' shoulders. Interns separate the letters for the editor from the letters requesting information. For the former, interns record whether the letters are positive or negative and pick the best ones to submit to an editor. For the latter, interns do their best to answer queries, be they requests for information on rock stars or requests about the magazine itself. Interns often find themselves sending out rejection letters to writers hoping to interview a particular band, cover the Grammys, or write record reviews. After Rolling Stone polled its readers about their favorite albums, one intern sifted through the hundreds of letters and helped pick the ones that would be published in the magazine's 25th Anniversary Issue. She also designed a reader-response chart, which was published in the magazine and for which she was credited at the bottom of the page as a researcher.

Interns undertake a host of other short-term projects. One spent a few days tracking down the publicists of celebrities the magazine wanted to interview. Cold-calling hundreds of agents and production companies, she gained exposure to "the crazy world of celebrities and their agents." Another was asked to call major magazine associations and create a complete list of the awards Rolling Stone had won over the years.

Typing and basic computer skills are essential for Rolling Stone interns. Interns are responsible for updating the computer index system by entering the titles and dates of recently published articles into the in-house computer files.

> "If you can't be a member of the Rolling Stones, you might as well be an Editorial intern at Rolling Stone."

Helping writers research facts for stories, interns spend a lot of time logging on to databases like NEXIS. They do this at the library, a narrow chamber with two computers, hundreds of music-related books, and a plethora of record albums. Believe it or not, a seasoned librarian works there, ready to guide the hapless intern in his or her research.

Many intern assignments relate to Rolling Stone's "Campus Issue," a special edition dedicated to college news and trends that is published twice yearly. "I was asked to sift through a variety of college newspapers and find anything offbeat or outrageous that might be of interest to the editors," said an intern. Aware that "interns are in touch with the college scene," editors often consult them for suggestions about stories being written for the college issue. They also encourage interns to call college contacts to find anyone with an interesting story or unusual part-time job.

A few interns remarked that they wished the internship allowed an intern to work closely with a writer on a particular story. Said one: "I would have loved to stay with a particular story for a period of time—brainstorming ideas, doing research, and accompanying a writer on interviews. Instead, it seemed like every few days brought another task, preventing me from getting too involved with any one story." Despite this system, writers and editors try to be accessible to interns, and most are willing to take time out to offer interns words of wisdom. One editor, for example, would occasionally advise interns on the ins and outs of music journalism and even invite them to submit sample stories that he would critique.

An undeniable boon of being at Rolling Stone is the perks that come with working at a music magazine. Concert tickets, promotional T-shirts, advance movie screenings, and promotional compact discs all float an intern's way. They aren't doled out in a formal manner, rather, when an editor has no need for them, he or she usually passes them along to interns, especially those who have done a good job. Some editors allow interns to borrow their CDs, and interns often have the opportunity to hear new records weeks before they are released to record stores. "I got to put my hot little hands on advance CDs that even radio stations didn't have," gloated an intern. As would be expected, interns also have dibs on free copies of current or past issues.

Although interns attend the occasional in-house birthday or good-bye party, many are disappointed that they aren't invited to magazine or music-industry parties. "Interns are out of the loop on the party scene. It would have been nice to attend a few, especially since we work for free," said an intern. Some were crestfallen at not receiving invites to *Rolling Stone*'s 25th anniversary party, a once-in-a-lifetime blowout attended by every rock-'n'-roll star imaginable. But the employees who attended were not even permitted to bring dates, so it's understandable that invitations were distributed sparingly.

Occupying an entire floor of a midtown skyscraper, *Rolling Stone* shares its space with sister-magazines *US, Men's Journal*, and *Family Life*. The office is sleek, with an abundance of natural wood and glass. Some windows overlook the famous neon marquee of Radio City Music Hall. A variety of artwork decorates the walls of the spacious office, including an assortment of distorted rock-star illustrations by Philip Burke, whose sketches normally appear on the contents page of the magazine. Nearby on display is the paint-splotched suit Steve Martin wore on a 1981 *Rolling Stone* cover. Line sketches by John Lennon adorn an adjacent wall, and an entire alcove is devoted to displaying, in chronological sequence, every *Rolling Stone* cover since the magazine's inception.

Interns like their workspace. Each occupies a fully equipped cubicle, similar to those used by the editorial staff. All of the cubicles are situated near each other and not far from the cushy office of Jann Wenner, the magazine's editor and publisher. "Our location was choice. We had a good view of Jann's office and scoped out the celebs who came in to visit him," an intern said. Interns also enjoy the music that often fills their workspace, as several members of the editorial staff have boom boxes, which they play when the mood strikes them. One intern's "productivity increased threefold with reggae jamming in the background." If on-the-job visual and auditory stimulation aren't enough, free coffee and tea are a short walk away.

Interns grin and bear their lack of pay, most realizing that the majority of entertainment-related internships offer no salary. In 1993, however, *Rolling Stone* introduced a minority scholarship for two positions in the Editorial department and one in Advertising. The scholarship is only available for the 12-week summer session and awards a $3,000 stipend to each participant. Interested minority students should write to the *Rolling Stone* Summer Scholarship Program for an application.

SELECTION

 Although the program looks for college juniors, seniors, and recent graduates, a few of the interns surveyed worked at *Rolling Stone* as college freshmen or sophomores. No prereqs apply, but past interns stress the importance of being outgoing and self-motivated. An avid interest in rock-and-roll helps, too. According to the intern coordinator, the best interns "want to learn every aspect of magazine publishing" and are "inquisitive and enthusiastic, even when carrying out clerical work."

APPLICATION PROCEDURE

 Applicants should submit their applications at least one month prior to the beginning of the session they wish to work. A complete application includes a resumé, a transcript, a letter of recommendation from a professor or professional, and a cover letter stating the session to which the student is applying and the reasons for wanting to work at *Rolling Stone*. Local applicants are requested to interview in person, but phone interviews are also conducted.

OVERVIEW

 Abandon all (editorial) hope ye who enter here. Although *Rolling Stone* interns rarely, if ever, do any actual writing for the magazine, they rave about just being *at* a place like *Rolling Stone*. "If I did the same work at a drier magazine, the internship would have been completely different. Being at a hip, progressive place like *Rolling Stone* made it all worthwhile," said an intern. Several former interns have made their mark in the publishing world, including one who's an editor of *Sassy* magazine and another who's the music editor at *Vibe*. For music fans who wish to spend a semester on the cutting edge of the music industry, an intern advised, "If you can't be a member of the Rolling Stones, you might as well be an Editorial intern at *Rolling Stone*."

FOR MORE INFORMATION . . .

■ Rolling Stone
Editorial Department
1290 Avenue of the Americas
New York, NY 10104
(212) 484-1616

It swims with hooked jaw. It swims in cold, clear waters. But most important, as far as Rosenbluth is concerned, it swims against the stream.

Rosenbluth International chose a salmon as its mascot to reflect the company's willingness to buck tradition. CEO Hal Rosenbluth outlined the company's unconventional "customer comes second" policy in an article he wrote for the *Harvard Business Review*. In it, he said, "What we have is a hierarchy of concerns: people, service, profits. We focus on our people, our people focus on service, and profits result —a by-product, you might say, of putting our associates [Rosenbluth-talk for "employees"] ahead of our customers." Whether it is training its workforce with games like Rosenopoly and Travel Jeopardy, employing managers (called "leaders") who go out of their way to encourage associates, or planning festive events like Hawaiian Shirt Gonzo Friday to boost morale, Rosenbluth leads the corporate pack in employee satisfaction. Its motivated workforce has helped make it the nation's fourth largest travel agency. But the term "travel agency" doesn't do this company justice. Rosenbluth is a worldwide travel management empire, arranging the travel for over 1,500 corporate clients, including Oracle, Eastman Kodak, Compaq Computer, GE, and Westinghouse.

SELECTIVITY

Approximate applicant pool: 100
Interns accepted: 5

COMPENSATION

None

QUALITY OF LIFE

Friendly, upbeat culture; Unique orientation
Associate of the Day program; Knickknacks

LOCATION(S)

Philadelphia, PA

FIELD

Travel management

DURATION

10 weeks
Summer, Fall, Spring

PRE-REQS

Undergrads, recent grads, grad students

DEADLINE(S)

Rolling

DESCRIPTION

 Although positions are available in a variety of areas, including Industry Relations, M.Power (corporate meetings and events), and Human Resources, sources say that the Corporate Communications department offers the juiciest work. Corporate Communications coordinates the activities related to Rosenbluth's corporate identity— advertising, public relations, internal communications, and sports marketing. As the company does not rely on outside ad agencies or PR firms, there's extensive marketing work to be done.

Corporate Communications interns are entrusted with a wide range of marketing projects. Some research or write articles for *Executive Traveller* magazine, a publication Rosenbluth sends to its corporate clients. Said one: "I wrote the CEOs of top travel companies, asking them to submit to *Executive Traveller* a brief article about the travel industry. I found about six executives willing to write articles, including the CEOs of Marriott

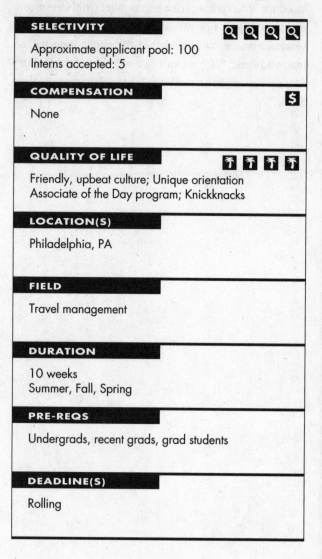

and USAir." Chances are that interns will also write press releases, work one on one with suppliers (printers, designers, etc.), and attend client meetings. One intern designed a "Rosenbluth Rolodex card" to give the company better exposure among local businesses. "I put together a special Rolodex card, figuring out everything from a color scheme to a catchy slogan."

Every so often, Corporate Communications interns plan and execute a promotional event for a professional sports team. Because Rosenbluth makes the travel arrangements for the Philadelphia Eagles, the Philadelphia Phillies, and the Pittsburgh Pirates, it often sponsors game-time promotions with these teams. Interns are an integral part of such events, writing the messages that announce the contest over Diamond Vision, picking contest winners, and escorting winners to the field. A perennial favorite is the Rosenbluth field goal contest, that involves random fans who try to kick a field goal during halftime; successful kickers win a free trip. "At every Eagles home game, I'd go up into the stands and escort preselected fans to the field. Some fans got so excited; one older man stood paralyzed, mouth [agape]—I thought he was going to have a heart attack," said an intern. When they are not busy with contest work, interns are welcome to join the "Rosenbluth cheerleaders" on the field, where they dance around wearing Rosenbluth's "Richie Cunningham-style" sweaters.

The internship, however, is not always a day at the ballpark. A modest amount of administrative work awaits the Rosenbluth intern. "Sure, there was some monkey work," said an intern. "But it wasn't all-consuming." Interns may be asked to fax press releases to the media, drop off media kits to locations around Philadelphia, update the media list in the company's database, fill out Fed Ex forms, and stuff envelopes with the *K.I.T.* "Keep in Touch" internal newsletter. Even so, Rosenbluth has a support staff that keeps clerical work to a minimum for interns.

> **Interns are welcome to join the "Rosenbluth cheerleaders" on the field, where they dance around wearing Rosenbluth's "Richie Cunningham-style" sweaters.**

If anything makes Rosenbluth stand out, it's the company's remarkably warm-spirited atmosphere, one that brings to mind the REM song, "Shiny Happy People." Hal Rosenbluth said as much in an October, 1990, interview in *Inc.* magazine: "A company has an obligation to the people it employs to make that part of life pleasant and happy." The 42-year-old Rosenbluth sets the tone with his power-of-positive-thinking attitude. Once, for example, he sent crayons to 100 employees and asked them to draw a picture of what the company meant to them. This touchy-feely spirit trickles down to interns. "The attitude at Rosenbluth is very tolerant and upbeat. People here care about each other," said an intern. Birthdays are celebrated with "miniparties" in a conference room—"expect lots of bagels and doughnuts." At the end of the internship, interns are given a surprise (shhh) going-away party, where one should (again) "expect lots of bagels and doughnuts."

The end of the internship may be enjoyable, but the beginning is even better. New interns don't just experience a few hours of orientation, they participate in the two-day, no-holds-barred New Associate Orientation Program. Designed for all new employees, from interns to new vice presidents, the program steeps them in the Rosenbluth mindset. "[Orientation leaders speak about] one of the most important facets of quality customer service, one that is rarely emphasized: listening. We talk about teamwork, or more specifically, barriers to successful teamwork . . . [like] stubbornness, lack of a clear goal, and preconceived notions," an associate reported in *Travel Weekly* magazine. Not content with conveying their message by lecture alone, orientation organizers ask new associates to dream up and act out a bad-service scenario, such as a careless barber giving a client a botched haircut. Orientation culminates in a visit to the executive offices where new associates chat with Hal Rosenbluth. "Mr. Rosenbluth took off his jacket and served us tea in expensive china," said an intern. "I had to ask myself, 'Is the president of the company really serving us tea?' I was blown away by his willingness to take time out to talk to us."

Access to the boss doesn't have to end after the first week. Rosenbluth's Associate of the Day program enables interns who've done an exceptional job to spend a day shadowing any employee, even the president. "It's a great opportunity," said an intern. "You pick anyone who intrigues you—a reservation agent, the vice president of marketing, or Hal Rosenbluth himself—and you observe that person for an entire day. It's the ultimate behind-the-scenes experience."

While the logical fringe benefit, travel packages, are reserved for permanent employees, interns have their fill of smaller perks, namely Rosenbluth knickknacks. As one intern put it, "They're big on corporate culture here." A few months at Rosenbluth will yield a fine wardrobe of salmon-emblazoned merchandise, not the least of which includes Rosenbluth T-shirts, golf caps, key chains, sweatshirts, and windbreakers. If interns want more items, they can always order from the aptly named "Upstreamer" catalog.

SELECTION

While Rosenbluth relies on Inroads and the Great Lakes College Association to find many of its interns, unsolicited applications are also welcome. Undergraduates of any level, recent graduates, and graduate students are eligible to apply. The program looks for students "with excellent writing skills, poise, maturity, and the ability to handle pressure, responsibility, and meet deadlines," according to the coordinator.

APPLICATION PROCEDURE

Applications are accepted on a rolling basis. Interested parties should submit a cover letter, resumé, writing samples, and any other creative samples (clips from campus newspapers, flyers, brochures, etc.). After an initial screening of applications, the intern coordinator invites a group of finalists to interview at Rosenbluth. The company does not pay for travel expenses and in-person interviews are mandatory.

OVERVIEW

Haven't heard of Rosenbluth before? Don't worry if you haven't; virtually all of its clients are corporations. While Rosenbluth may not be a household name, there's more to a top internship than immediate name recognition. Not only does Rosenbluth expose students to the nuts and bolts of travel management, it also offers one-of-a-kind opportunities in marketing communications, such as planning promotional events and writing articles for publication. Rosenbluth staff seem sincerely committed to having interns squeeze as much as possible out of their jobs; some associates even assist interns in creating a portfolio of their work. Only the most cynical curmudgeon could resist the company's warm and fuzzy culture. Hal Rosenbluth said it best in *Inc.* magazine: "We look at human resources the way others look at financial assets."

FOR MORE INFORMATION . . .

■ Rosenbluth International
Internship Program
1911 Arch Street
Philadelphia, PA 19103
(215) 557-8700

RUDER·FINN

As the saying goes, "In the modern world, propaganda is as important as ammunition." No one understands this principle better than Ruder-Finn, the New York public relations firm that has handled publicity for the breakaway republics of Croatia and Bosnia. For the past few years, Ruder-Finn has been instrumental in drawing international media attention to the human rights violations in former Yugoslavia. With Ruder-Finn communicating the message, the world has become aware of Serbian attempts at ethnic cleansing, prompting everyone from the Clinton administration to Jewish lobby groups to condemn the Serbs.

But representing foreign governments is only one of Ruder-Finn's specialties. Since 1948, the privately held, family-owned firm has excelled in corporate communications, science and health-based campaigns, marketing support, environmental marketing, and corporate support of the arts. As New York's third largest public relations agency, Ruder-Finn handles such clients as Citibank, Johnson & Johnson, House of Seagram, L.L. Bean, and Stouffer Foods.

SELECTIVITY

Approximate applicant pool: 200
Interns accepted: 8

COMPENSATION

$300/week

QUALITY OF LIFE

Educational curriculum; Office meetings
"The Playpen"

LOCATION(S)

New York, NY

FIELD

Public relations

DURATION

12–16 weeks
Summer, Fall/Winter, Winter/Spring

PRE-REQS

College grads of any age

DEADLINE(S)

Summer .... April 15   Fall/Winter .... April 15
Winter/Spring ...... November 15

DESCRIPTION

The 16-year-old internship program at Ruder-Finn assigns interns to one or two account groups or has them serve as "floaters" to assist groups throughout the firm. Account groups include Marketing Communications, Investor Relations, Healthcare, Lifestyle, Public Affairs, High-Tech, Arts, Research, Visual Technology, Media, Japan Desk, and Financial Services.

All interns have a basic set of responsibilities, no matter where they work. Creating and updating media lists are interns' least favorite chore, but "it's elemental to the public relations process, so it has to be done." While one intern warned that spending hours on media lists can "make one cross-eyed with boredom," another emphasized a benefit of such work: "By making the dozens of calls needed to assemble a media list, you learn not to fear talking on the phone. . . . [I]t teaches you professional savvy." Interns also spend a lot of time writing pitch letters in hopes of convincing journalists to cover a particular client. "I'd pull my hair out trying to be creative," said an intern. After writing a pitch letter, interns typically submit them to a supervisor for editing and reediting. A corollary to pitch letters are pitch calls, for which interns dial up news organizations and ask them to "run a client's public service announcement or cover a client's activities."

Other responsibilities vary from department to department. An intern in Visual Technology was asked to conduct on-the-street interviews to test public opinion of a local hospital. "Microphone in hand, I approached passersby and asked if they knew about the hospital. Not everyone was willing to be interviewed—it sometimes took some coaxing and joking around to warm them up." Working for the Glad Bag-a-thon promotion, an intern in Marketing Communications traveled to Newport News, VA, where he solicited news coverage for the town's massive cleanup effort. "I drove to a series of newspapers and TV stations and tried to generate interest in the final day of the Bag-a-thon." An intern in the same department helped out at a press conference for a Citibank/Visa Card promotion. "When reporters arrived, I told them where to sit and answered their questions. . . . [M]ost questions were pretty basic, but occasionally a reporter threw me a curve like 'How will all this impact the Dow Jones?'"

A telltale sign of how an organization views its interns is its willingness to include interns in office meetings. Ruder-Finn comes through with flying colors in this regard. Interns are not only encouraged to attend creative sessions but also are encouraged to participate. "At creative sessions, executives would sit around and think of innovative publicity ideas for a client," said an intern. "These meetings always had an open, unintimidating feel. Intern input was enthusiastically encouraged." One session was held to brainstorm ways of spicing up Mr. World's American Tour, a geography program, sponsored by Citibank and the National Geographic Society, that traveled the country visiting elementary schools. An intern thought up a way to increase student involvement by having students at every school draw a "map" of the important elements in their lives. Management liked the proposal so much that they imple-

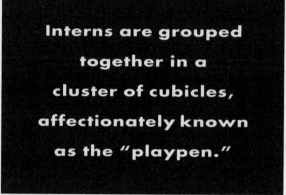

Interns are grouped together in a cluster of cubicles, affectionately known as the "playpen."

mented it, and according to the intern, "Young students across the country sent in maps of their lives, drawing their bus stops, families, pets, and so forth. . . . [W]e attached these maps to the back pages of a 6'x4' book, which went on tour with Mr. World."

A unique feature of this internship is the educational curriculum. During the first week of the program, interns attend all-day classes on the public relations profession; thereafter, interns have class once a week. Classes feature lectures by staff experts and group discussions emphasizing journalistic writing skills and various practical components of the profession. The curriculum covers such topics as "Strategic Thinking in Public Relations," "Basic Newswriting," "Introduction to Major National Broadcast Press," and "Ethical Issues in Public Relations." Every week, interns are given a homework assignment relating to the week's topic. They might be asked to write a press release, draft an article announcing an employee promotion, or think up possible headlines for a hypothetical story. Assignments are critiqued by the week's speaker or the intern coordinator, but "no grades are given—it's a low-key, constructive process."

Ruder-Finn is located on three floors of an office building in midtown New York. The decor is described by interns as "unimpressive" and "nothing to write home about," except for the abundance of photographs taken by president David Finn, about which one intern said, "Finn is a big photography buff, so he hangs his work all over the agency. The photos are of people, street scenes, statues—things like that. I think they make neat decorations—they add a common thread to the agency." Interns are grouped together in a cluster of cubicles, affectionately known as "the playpen" by executives because it tends to be lively and social. "The intern area is isolated from the rest of the agency," said an executive. "So it gives interns a chance to discuss projects and gossip. Because they all work for different departments, together they have the scoop on everything going on."

SELECTION

Applicants must be college graduates at the time the session for which they are applying begins. The program accepts candidates from any academic background, including those with graduate degrees.

APPLICATION PROCEDURE

The deadline for the summer internship (mid-June to mid-September) is April 15; for the fall/winter internship (mid-September to mid-January), April 15; and for the winter/spring internship (mid-January to mid-May), November 15. Required materials include: an application form, resumé, writing sample, names and addresses of two references, and, for those who have graduated within the past six months, an unofficial transcript. Do not use staples or folders. Applicants must also submit responses to a writing test, which typically requires a few 300-word essays on hypothetical public relations situations.

Approximately two weeks after the deadline, the Intern Committee arranges interviews with selected applicants. The interview period runs the fifth and fourth weeks before the beginning of the internship. Interviews are conducted with two Ruder-Finn executives—a senior interviewer and a recent graduate of the program—either in person or by phone. Candidates selected for interviews are notified in

writing and receive a case history to analyze prior to the interview. A good part of the interview session is devoted to discussion of the case study. Those selected to participate in the internship program are notified three weeks before the start of the program.

OVERVIEW

For the lucky few, Ruder-Finn offers a one-of-a-kind introduction to the public relations profession: practical experience combined with a structured training program. Although an average of 50 percent of participants are hired as permanent employees, interns warn against going into the internship expecting permanent employment: "It's a gamble. You can work your tail off as an intern and still be passed over for a job." But even if it fails to lead to a job offer with Ruder-Finn, the program shines because—in an intern's words—"it's so respected in the profession that it will open several other doors."

FOR MORE INFORMATION . . .

- Ruder-Finn
  Intern Coordinator
  301 East 57th Street
  New York, NY 10022
  (212) 593-6400

For a painting, a sculpture, a musical instrument, a coin or even a locomotive, there's no greater honor than to be accepted into the Smithsonian Institution. To become part of the Smithsonian, an artifact is judged for its physical condition, exhibit potential, size, and "readability" (whether a visitor can understand the artifact by looking at it). Pieces that pass muster are incorporated into the world's largest museum complex, the Smithsonian Institution, composed of 16 museums, the National Zoo, and several research facilities. With upwards of 25 million visitors each year, the Smithsonian is a wonderland of things valuable and collectable.

DESCRIPTION

The Smithsonian Internship places interns among 40 museums, administrative offices, and research programs. "There's truly something for everyone," as the internship brochure points out, and it's no overstatement. Animal lovers may work for Friends of the National Zoo, and art aficionados have the National Portrait Gallery, National Museum of American Art, and Hirshhorn Museum, among others. *Jurassic Park* groupies can get their ya-yas out at the National Museum of Natural History and the Smithsonian Environmental Research Center is a natural choice for environmentalists. Budding librarians may hit the books at the Smithsonian Institution Libraries—the list goes on and on.

One of the most popular museums in which to intern is the National Museum of American History (NMAH), where the majority of interns help prepare for upcoming exhibitions. An intern in the African-American Cultures department, for instance, worked with a curator to acquire materials for Wade in the Water, an exhibition to be presented in 1995 on the African-American sacred-music tradition of the 19th and 20th centuries. On one of her assignments she visited the National Archives and Library of Congress, where, among other relevant artifacts, she "found pictures of fugitive slaves [for whom] music was a means of survival." She arranged for the Smithsonian to purchase prints of these photographs and expects them to be incorporated into the upcoming exhibition.

But not all interns at NMAH work directly on exhibitions. In the Department of Social and Cultural History, an intern worked with inner-city high school students on a theatrical presentation relating to one of the museum's exhibitions. To augment an exhibition on the African-American migration to the North between 1840 and 1940, the intern and her group of students staged *A Man of Letters*, a play that dealt with the issue of "passing" (i.e., light-skinned African-Americans who tried to "pass" for white). Involved in all aspects of the production, she oversaw the students, designed costumes, and even played three roles in the performance. Another intern, this one in NMAH'S Division of Public Programs, conducted research for the museum's concert series. "Part of my job [entailed] calling agents to find music groups who would amplify the themes of the exhibitions," she explained. "The museum looks for a wide variety of top-notch but lesser-known musicians, from Native American bands to singing cowboys from Texas." Conducting this research and dubbing tapes of past concerts, she learned that a culture's musical traditions often transcend those stereotypically attributed to it: "There's so much [musical] diversity [within a culture] that most people aren't aware of. Native Americans [for example] not only have the traditional drum and chant, but also songwriters and guitar-and-harmonica groups."

For those seeking experience in artifact conservation or those enrolled in a graduate conservation training program, the Smithsonian offers intern positions in its Conservation Analytical Laboratory (CAL). Interns at CAL help preserve a variety of paintings, textiles, furniture, and other objects. An intern assigned to the "objects lab," for example, participated in an ongoing project to excavate and restore a group of 8,500-year-old Jordanian statues. "Jordan doesn't have the facilities to recover the statues . . . so the Jordanian government asked the Smithsonian to help," she explained. The statues were in pieces and buried in the original block of dirt in which they were found, so she documented the exact location of the fragments as she removed them. "You had to be very careful and photograph where each piece was being taken from. The process was very tedious." After excavating the fragments, the intern strengthened the pieces with a resin and set about reassembling them into statues. "It was really neat to see the figures regain their original shape. . . . [One particular statute] was very strange—it turned out to have two heads."

With its awesome collection of historic airplanes hanging overhead, the National Air and Space Museum is a perennial favorite of the public. Interns here have done everything from photographing the ongoing restoration of airplanes to assisting in the creation of new curriculum packages to writing the museum's first intern handbook. Assigned to the Library, one intern found herself organizing a collection of rare books on aviation. "I went through and recorded the bibliographic data for dozens of fascinating books—some on ballooning, others on the Wright brothers, and even one autographed by Amelia Earhart, which displayed a miniature American flag she carried with her in flight." The intern was also asked to look over another collection of books and make recommendations as to which should be included in the museum's rare-book collection. "I rated each book in terms of its age, exhibition potential, rarity, and uniqueness (e.g., if it's autographed by a famous aviator)."

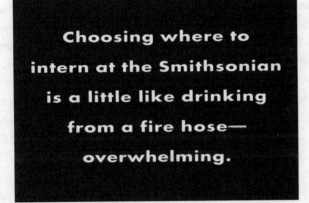

Choosing where to intern at the Smithsonian is a little like drinking from a fire hose—overwhelming.

No intern leaves the Smithsonian without the chance to attend a variety of seminars. Most museums have their own program for interns. The National Air and Space Museum, for example, holds luncheons where each intern makes a presentation on his or her project. Alternatively, the National Museum of American History runs a weekly brown-bag luncheon with one of the museum's curators. Said an intern about the luncheons: "They were top-notch. One week we had Lonnie Bunch, a well-known curator who spoke about being commissioned by Japanese companies to create an American history exhibition in Japan. [Another week] we listened to a curator who put together the First

Lady exhibition and how he went about [procuring] Hillary Rodham Clinton's briefcase and headband for it." Beyond events unique to each museum, there's a workshop on museum careers that is open to all Smithsonian interns. Gathering four times during the summer and once during the fall and spring, interns hear presentations by museum directors, curators, and education staff. They also attend a workshop on resumé building and meet with representatives from graduate programs in museum studies.

As for other perks, the most useful is a 20 percent discount at museum gift shops. Interns take full advantage of this privilege, buying oodles of postcards, posters, ceramics, and for one intern at the Air and Space Museum, "*Star Trek* paraphernalia, especially punch-out paper models of the new *Enterprise*." Interns may apply for a full tuition scholarship to take a Smithsonian Institution summer course. Taught by local professors and museum experts, courses are open to the public and cover topics in areas such as art history, music history and American history.

The museums of the Smithsonian Institution line the perimeter of The Mall, a rectangular expanse of grass bordered by the Washington Monument at one end and the U.S. Capitol at the other. Tourists are everywhere, which for one intern presented the opportunity to make new friends. "It was easy to meet visitors from all over the world during lunch breaks and after work." Intern accommodations vary with each museum and each office therein, ranging from "a conference table but not much else" to "my own cubicle—including a desk, IBM computer, and voice mail." A cafeteria exists in every museum, but some eating facilities receive higher marks than others: "Having done several Smithsonian internships, I think the best food is at [the] Air and Space [Museum]. There are just better cooks over there. . . . The lasagna was *really* good." For those looking to get physical, the Interstate Commerce Building (a ten-minute walk) has a weight room and aerobics classes open to federal employees (including Smithsonian interns).

SELECTION

 Just about anyone is welcome to apply to the Smithsonian Internship including high school seniors, undergraduates of any level, recent graduates, graduate students, and career changers. Prerequisites vary with each position. Interested parties

may write to the Office of Museum Programs (OMP) for "Internships and Fellowships," a free brochure listing museum addresses and position descriptions, or send the OMP a $5.00 check for *Internship Opportunities at the Smithsonian Institution,* a book providing detailed information on each museum's internship.

APPLICATION PROCEDURE

 The application deadlines are as follows: summer internship, February 15; fall internship, June 15; and spring internship, October 15. Candidates who wish to apply to one particular Smithsonian office/museum should send their materials directly there. Those interested in applying to more than one office should send their materials (one set of materials for each office) to the Office of Museum Programs, who will then submit the materials to the appropriate offices.

Required materials consist of a completed Internship Application Packet (which may be obtained from the Office of Museum Programs), a two-page essay on reasons for seeking the internship, two letters of recommendation, undergraduate transcripts, and graduate transcripts (if applicable). No interviews are conducted.

OVERVIEW

 Choosing where to intern at the Smithsonian is a little like drinking from a firehose—overwhelming. But once the choice is made, interns can count on an internship filled with rewarding projects and edifying seminars. Whether or not they go on to pursue a museum-related career, interns leave the Smithsonian with a "quantum-leap increase in cultural awareness" and a name "you put in boldface on your resumé."

FOR MORE INFORMATION . . .

■ Smithsonian Institution
Internship Coordinator
Office of Museum Programs
Arts & Industries Building
Suite 2235, MRC 427
Washington, DC 20560
(202) 357-3102

Sony Music

SELECTIVITY	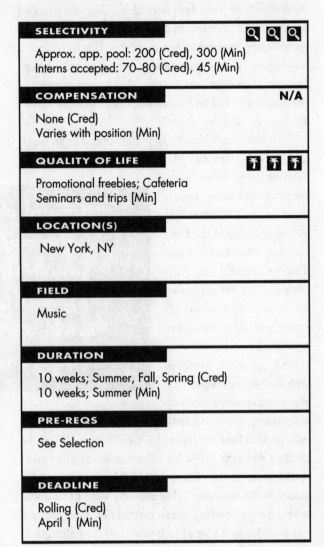
Approx. app. pool: 200 (Cred), 300 (Min) Interns accepted: 70–80 (Cred), 45 (Min)	

COMPENSATION	N/A
None (Cred) Varies with position (Min)	

QUALITY OF LIFE	
Promotional freebies; Cafeteria Seminars and trips [Min]	

LOCATION(S)	
New York, NY	

FIELD	
Music	

DURATION	
10 weeks; Summer, Fall, Spring (Cred) 10 weeks; Summer (Min)	

PRE-REQS	
See Selection	

DEADLINE	
Rolling (Cred) April 1 (Min)	

If Martians were to visit America and take a good look around, what would they think was important to the human race—Love, honesty, trust? Perhaps, but if they judged our values by the labels appearing most often in our households, they might think our most prized ideal was "Sony." After all, it's rare to find a household without a few televisions, stereos, and radios emblazoned with the distinctive Sony logo.

But Sony is much more than electronics. In 1988, the company acquired CBS Records, arguably the world's most successful record empire. The resulting division, Sony Music Entertainment, Inc. (SMEI), took over CBS Records Columbia and Epic record labels and also established new labels such as Chaos Recordings and TriStar Music Group. The upshot for SMEI has been an impossibly rich roster of artists, including the likes of Michael Jackson, Bruce Springsteen, Sade, Mary-Chapin Carpenter, Harry Connick, Jr., Mariah Carey, Michael Bolton, Pearl Jam, and Spin Doctors.

DESCRIPTION

 Sony Music Entertainment, Inc. runs two internships. The Credited Internship is open to undergraduate and graduate students who are able to secure academic credit for their work. The Minority Internship is a paid experience for minority undergraduate and graduate students that is augmented by a number of seminars, trips, and training sessions. Both internships place students in a full range of SMEI departments, including Promotions, Publicity, Retail Marketing, Artists and Repertoire (A&R), A&R Administration, and Business Affairs.

Interns in Publicity help keep artists in the public eye. Assigned to Epic Records's Black

Music division, a Publicity intern spent much of her time putting together press kits. "The basic way we publicize an artist is through press kits," she said. "They consist of a brief biography of the artist, an 8x10 glossy, and a CD or tape of the artist's new album. I was in charge of assembling these kits and sending them to various publications." Her most exciting job involved assisting with the department's "press day," a "mini news conference" where an artist would answer questions from a group of reporters and magazine editors. Whether creating a special booklet to brief the press on a particular artist or calling journalists to invite them to the conference, she had a finger in all aspects of press-day preparations. She also attended the event, and even escorted journalists to the conference room before the meeting began. "Press-days were a great way to hype a band, to create a buzz. We had them for groups like Patra, Hoodratz, and Shakim. And a good showing of publications would be represented, ones like *USA Today*, *Ebony*, *Vibe*, and *Rap Sheet*."

An intern in Video Production worked as an assistant on video shoots. "On a Sony soundstage or on location around New York, the producers in my department created artist-profile videos with established artists like Tony Bennett and Tom Chapin," she explained. "I accompanied the production team on shoots and did a little of everything—running errands, setting up props, working with the lighting people . . ." Happy to volunteer for any assignment, she once found herself driving downtown to pick up soul food for rapper LL Cool J, who "loved the chicken and grits." For her efforts, she was allowed to spend hours in the edit room watching editors put together video footage. "[The editors] were great about letting me see how they transform the clips into a finished video—I learned a lot of technical stuff . . . I also got to see all sorts of outtakes and raw footage. They really give you insight into the personality of an artist."

Not all interns work in creative departments. An intern in A&R Administration, for example, worked with record contracts. Despite having "no previous experience with contracts," she was asked to read several contracts, glean their essential points, and enter the information into a computer database. She described: "It was not easy. I had to cut through the confusing language and determine an artist's rights in terms of things like royalties, artwork, and budgets for music videos." She eventually became a pro at reading record contracts, learning the nuts and bolts of legal jargon like "override royalties" and "leaving-member options." She also got to read the confidential deals worked out with various artists. "I wasn't given the really big-name contracts, but I did get to see the details in contracts for [Bruce Springsteen's wife] Patti Scialfa and [the group] Bad Brains."

Participants in the Minority Internship Program participate in several special events. Every Thursday they attend a brown-bag luncheon featuring a senior-level executive. One week they may meet with the director of A&R at the luncheon, the next week it may be a senior VP from Columbia or Epic Records. The coordinator also likes to plan a get-together with interns and Minority Internship alumni currently working at Sony Music; says the coordinator, "It's the chance for interns to meet people who've been in their positions . . . and it's the ideal time for networking." The coordinator then takes interns' education a step further by spending an afternoon watching and discussing a video adaptation of Steven Covey's bestseller "Seven Habits of Highly Effective People." No summer would be complete without a field trip to Sony Music Studio ("a veritable shrine of high-tech equipment") and a Sony CD-manufacturing plant in Pitman, NJ.

Although interns receive no official perks, working at a thriving record company is bound to yield a few unexpected rewards. A few interns, for example, were asked to help pick the winners of the *Poetic Justice* competition, a poetry and rap contest publicizing the soundtrack of Janet Jackson's *Poetic Justice* movie. "We reviewed all of the poetry and rap submissions and picked three finalists for each category," said one of the interns. "The rap songs were especially fun to screen. We looked for originality (the fewer samples, the better) and professionalism (a clean-cut sound that was good enough for radio)." In addition to the possibility of receiving a "cool assignment," interns can usually get their mitts on some promotional goodies. Past interns have tapped into free CDs ("although you can't go shopping and clean out the whole place"), T-shirts, concert tickets ("I saw Billy Joel and Terence Trent

> "Among my friends who applied to [music industry] internships, Sony was everybody's first choice."

D'Arby"), and free movie passes to Sony Pictures films. Invitations to listening parties are also a possibility, one intern reports attending listening parties for Columbia Records stars Kris Kross and Baby Face.

Located in a skyscraper whose roof is "curved like a scoop," Sony headquarters has the "extremely modern," black-and-white decor one would expect of a Japanese electronics company. Everything in the building is sleek and streamlined, from the fifth-floor "sky lobby" to the omnipresent modular furniture. The offices of Sony Music Entertainment are decorated with gold and platinum albums, posters of different artists, and various plaques. The majority of desks have a stereo, all of which, of course, sport the Sony logo. Intern accommodations vary from "a cubicle equipped with voice mail and a typewriter" to "my own desk in a secretarial bay" to "a chair on the side of my supervisor's desk." The sky lobby has a cafeteria with a variety of pasta, grilled foods, pizzas, and salad bar offerings.

SELECTION

The Credited Internship is open to undergraduates and graduate students who will be entering or returning to school after their internship. Participants in this program must receive academic credit for their work. The Minority Internship targets undergraduates and graduate students who are African-American, Latino, Asian-American, and American Indian. Minority Interns must have at least a 3.0 GPA in their majors and be entering or returning to school after the internship. Both programs accept students from any academic background, but in the brochure's words, "an interest in the music business is an asset."

APPLICATION PROCEDURE

The deadline to submit materials for the Minority Internship is April 1; the Credited Internship has a rolling application deadline. Applicants should submit a cover letter and resumé to the appropriate address. Finalists are invited to Sony for personal interviews with the Recruiting and Placement Department and, in exceptional cases, long distance applicants may substitute a phone interview for an on-site visit.

OVERVIEW

What has the Sony Music Entertainment internship got that the others don't? A well-organized program in which it's possible to be something other than a copy room beast of burden, a record company flush with big-name artists (and the cash to make sure they remain big-name artists), and a minority internship that goes out of its way to acclimate students to an industry traditionally underrepresented by minorities. The word is out that Sony has a top-notch program, as one intern reports: "Among my friends who applied to [music industry] internships, Sony was everybody's first choice."

FOR MORE INFORMATION . . .

■ Sony Music Entertainment, Inc.
Credited Internship
550 Madison Avenue,
2nd Floor
New York, NY 10022-3211

■ Sony Music Entertainment, Inc.
Minority Internship
550 Madison Avenue,
13th Floor
New York, NY 10022-3211
Attn: Department 13-5

SOTHEBY'S
FOUNDED 1744

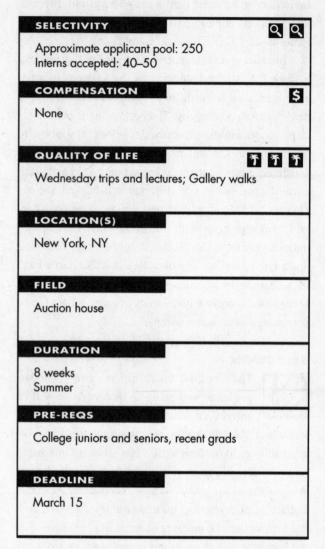

SELECTIVITY

Approximate applicant pool: 250
Interns accepted: 40–50

COMPENSATION

None

QUALITY OF LIFE

Wednesday trips and lectures; Gallery walks

LOCATION(S)

New York, NY

FIELD

Auction house

DURATION

8 weeks
Summer

PRE-REQS

College juniors and seniors, recent grads

DEADLINE

March 15

Winking and nodding. Glasses on, glasses off. Pencil in pocket, pencil in hand. Tugging the earlobe . . .

What's happening here? Is someone having a nervous fit, or in desperate need of a bathroom? No, these are just a few of the signals bidders use when they wish to remain anonymous at a Sotheby's auction. Explains Sotheby's auctioneer (and former intern, '78) Bill Ruprecht: "Some people like to participate discreetly, so they prearrange with me a certain signal."

"Mystery bidding" is just one factor in the mystique that pervades the hallowed halls of Sotheby's, arguably the world's most famous and respected auction house. Founded in 1744 so British citizens could exchange property without the burden of face-to-face bargaining, Sotheby's today is known the world over as *the* place to sell property of great value and interest. Recent Sotheby's auctions have featured the Duchess of Windsor's jewelry collection, Andy Warhol's art collection, paintings by Georgia O'Keefe, Vincent van Gogh's *Irises* (sold for $53.9 million, making it one of the most expensive paintings in history), and even Elton John's collection of jewelry and clothes (read: enormous sunglasses, Doc Martens boots, and sequined stage-suits).

DESCRIPTION

You better not blink or you might miss the Sotheby's internship—it lasts only a scant eight weeks. Interns don't seem to mind, though: "It's enough time to decide if the auction business is for you." Interns are placed either in a client-service department like the Press Office, Graphics, or Marketing, or in one of 33 expert departments like American Paintings or Chinese Works of Art.

The advantage of working in a client-service department is that it provides exposure to all areas of the organization. Interns in Marketing, for example, help put together newspaper and magazine advertisements for upcoming sales, and in doing so, work with expert departments to highlight their pieces. Explained a Marketing Intern: "When a department—say, Watches and Clocks—was running a sale, I'd collect the vital information—date, viewing time, the pieces being sold, and any photographs. The Graphics department would design the actual ad, but I'd arrange for the ad to run in an appropriate publication, such as *Watch and Clock Review* or the *The New York Times*." Similarly, interns in the Press Office assist the expert departments in notifying the press about past and future auctions. "I did the legwork for press releases, researching how a certain piece sold or was predicted to sell at an upcoming auction. The best part was that I got to deal with all of the other departments—which gave me a broad view of the auction business," said a Press Office intern.

The benefit of being in an expert department is that it familiarizes interns with a particular period of art or type of antique. Virtually everything interns do increases their knowledge about an area of art, whether they tag pieces for identification purposes, record how much was paid for an item, or file pictures of the art in the department's archives. In addition to these tasks, an intern in American Paintings was asked to run paintings over to the offices of art dealers, who would verify the paintings' authenticity. Although this assignment was essentially gofer work, it was still edifying: "After interacting with these [art dealers], I really got a sense of how experts judge whether a painting is genuine. Sometimes it's a matter of what corner of the painting the artist signs his name or whether the artist signs his full name or just his initials."

Paintings are but one specialty interns are exposed to at Sotheby's. Interns work in a remarkable variety of departments, including Animation Art, Books and Manuscripts, Jewelry, Musical Instruments, Rugs and Carpets, Silver, and Vintage Cars. If weaponry fires your interest, there's the Modern Sporting Guns or Arms and Armor departments. Said an intern who worked in both areas: "In addition to compiling data on potential consignors [people who sell the property through Sotheby's], I unpacked and organized an endless stream of guns. I learned all about the art of gunsmithing . . . [such as] how to read the marks of authenticity on 19-century British guns."

The internship brochure's warning that "most departments require a minimum typing speed of 40 to 50 wpm" is cause to put the busywork meter on red alert. While this is no false alarm—interns typically spend a major portion of their time typing, phoning, and faxing—most see gruntwork as a necessary evil in order to "get a foot in the door at one of the world's most prestigious auction houses."

Interns participate in an excellent orientation day during the first week of the program. A few hours are spent taking care of business—"you learn the corporate structure and the phone system, and you get an ID card," reported an intern. Interns are then welcomed by Sotheby's president, Diana D. Brooks, described by an intern as "a truly remarkable person, and one of the few female top executives in the auction business." There's also a movie that traces for interns the auction process, from "appraisals to the postauction follow-up." Best of all, interns have ample opportunity to meet each other. "It was obvious that [the intern coordinator] wanted us to build a sense of community." Not only are interns asked to introduce themselves to the group, but the coordinator pairs them off and sends them to lunch on Sotheby's tab. "It was a great way of making a friend right off the bat," said an intern.

One intern spied Madonna looking at old European paintings of madonnas.

Every Wednesday at Sotheby's is devoted to educating interns about the art world. In the morning, interns receive guided tours of New York art museums and galleries. Recent summers have found interns visiting museums like The Cloisters, the Whitney, the Cooper Hewitt, and the Brooklyn Museum, as well as more unusual sites like the sculpture garden at the headquarters of PepsiCo. Said an intern of the trips: "It was a chance to glimpse eight widely differing art worlds in New York. And it was interesting to contrast galleries and museums with the much faster-paced auction world." In the afternoon, interns return to the office, where they attend a lecture by a Sotheby's executive or art expert. The speaker, who could be anyone from the president to the head of Decorative Arts to an auctioneer, talks about his or her background in the arts and how it led to Sotheby's. Sometimes the presentations get the interns involved, like the expert who challenged interns to appraise various objects he displayed. "Great fun! We'd inspect and attempt to put a dollar value on a variety of pieces," an intern recalled. "The only catch was that some of the pieces were fake. We found out later, for example, that an Asian porcelain bowl was actually a soup bowl someone swiped from a Chinese restaurant!"

In the week prior to a sale, Sotheby's holds exhibitions at which the public can inspect the items up for auction. Whenever possible, interns are taken on a "gallery walk" through the exhibitions. A department specialist responsible for the exhibit leads them through the exhibition room and highlights important pieces. Said an intern: "The gallery walks were a great way to learn about another type of art. The specialists are very thorough and easy to understand." When they have the chance, interns are also welcome to check out the exhibitions without a guide. Some go just to spy on visiting celebrities. One intern reported seeing Nancy Reagan, Bruce Willis, John McEnroe, and Madonna ("who [appropriately enough] was looking at old European paintings of madonnas").

A wise philosopher once said that there's nothing like watching a baseball game to learn the ropes of baseball. In a similar vein, there's nothing like watching a Sotheby's auction to learn the art of the auction. Although summer is "off-season," with far fewer auctions than in the spring and fall, interns are still able take in a few auctions when they have the time. Items sold at a Sotheby's auction, are (1) rare, (2) historic, or (3) owned by someone who habitually bathes in Dom Perignon. Although the majority of auctions do not cause a sensation, every now and then there's an adrenaline-charger. A former intern who was hired on as a permanent employee witnessed the sale of one of 16 copies of the Declaration of Independence. (How much is freedom worth? A cool $2.4 million). Another intern was around when a gold and enamel reproduction of a Fabergé egg went for $2.3 million.

But auctions need not involve millions of dollars to be enjoyable. One intern dropped by auctions for sheer people watching. "It's fun to check out the type of people each kind of auction attracts. French furniture auctions bring in a very well-heeled, predominantly female group. On the other hand, sales of watches attract a mostly male audience of watch dealers." Sometimes it's not the audience but the auction itself that's entertaining. Comic book and cartoon companies, for example, sometimes send costumed representatives of their characters to promote a sale. An auction of a vintage Marvel comic book featured a Spider-Man who "got up on the stage and struck spiderlike poses." At a reception after the sale of *Beauty and the Beast* cartoon cells, Disney had a decked-out Beauty and Beast "greet guests and generate excitement."

Despite its Upper East Side address, Sotheby's isn't the bastion of opulence one might expect. Its exterior has a modern, corporate feel to it, with unassuming glass doors and an awning made of metal latticework. Inside, the utilitarian decor is predominantly beige, creating an environment suggesting (at best) neutrality and (at worst) drabness. There are several auction rooms, each with gray partitions to subdivide the room into smaller sections when necessary. The expert departments are nothing special to look at, save for the fact that some (e.g., American Paintings) have hallways decorated with soon-to-be auctioned artwork. Interns get their own desks, and in some departments, their own computer.

SELECTION

 The internship is open to college juniors and seniors as well as recent graduates who receive their degree in the spring before the internship. Unlike most internships in the auction business, (e.g., Christie's), Sotheby's accepts students of any major, not just those studying art history or fine arts. According to the coordinator, successful interns have "a genuine interest in some area of art" and are "outgoing," "polite," and accepting of all assignments, no matter how mundane.

APPLICATION PROCEDURE

 Interested candidates should send an introductory letter and resumé to Sotheby's Personnel Department between January 15 and March 15. Sotheby's sends back an application form in March. The application asks for department preferences and reasons the applicant wants to work at Sotheby's. The strongest applicants are interviewed by the individual departments in April and May. Phone interviews are acceptable for most departments, but the Press Office requires an in-person interview (at applicant's expense).

OVERVIEW

Sotheby's interns get a taste of what's it's like to be knee-deep in the excitement and the workaday details of a top auction house. Despite being served a generous helping of busywork, interns end up learning a great deal about the auction business, be it through projects or a wonderful array of field trips and in-house speakers. In the hand-signals of an auctioneer, the Sotheby's internship gets two thumbs up.

FOR MORE INFORMATION . . .

■ Sotheby's
Internship Program
1334 York Avenue
New York, NY 10021
(212) 606-7000

It's a long-standing dilemma: Corporate recruiters want talented minorities, but talented minorities have difficulty breaking into the established channels at law firms, investment banks, consulting companies, and accounting firms. Is there any hope?

Call in Sponsors for Educational Opportunity (SEO), founded in 1963 to help "motivated, but underserved" minority elementary and high school students get into college and in doing so improve their chances of landing corporate jobs. Thirty years later, approximately 85 percent of the 4,000 New York City minority youths who have gone through SEO's programs have received college degrees.

In 1980, SEO decided to tackle the lack of minorities on New York's Wall Street. Over ten years later, SEO has made a tremendous impact. In addition to two Fulbright and four Rhodes Scholars, SEO counts among its alumni one of the "25 Hottest Blacks on Wall Street" (*Black Enterprise*, 1992), the CEO and president of the former Cisneros Asset Management firm, and the 24-year old mayor of Baldwin Park, CA.

SELECTIVITY	🔍 🔍 🔍
Approximate applicant pool: 800–1,000 Interns accepted: 125–175	

COMPENSATION	$ $ $ $
$400–$500/week	

QUALITY OF LIFE	🌴 🌴 🌴 🌴
Weekly seminars; Mentors Travel opportunities; Professional atmosphere	

LOCATION(S)
New York, NY

FIELDS
Investment banking, asset management, management consulting, corporate law, and accounting

10 weeks minimum Summer

PRE-REQS
Minority undergrads

DEADLINE(S)
Inv. Banking, Consulting, & Asset Mgmt ...... Feb. 15 Corporate Law and Accounting .... March 1

DESCRIPTION

In 1980, 11 minority college students gathered at SEO's now-former office, a renovated brownstone on East 31st Street in New York City. Before them stood an opportunity to explode an invidious myth: There are few talented minorities capable of working on Wall Street. As the first interns in SEO's newly formed investment banking program, they were each about to spend the summer at a Wall Street investment bank. Thirteen years later, SEO targets additional business fields in need of minority talent, offering internships in five programs: Investment Banking (approximately 100 to 125 interns), Corporate Law (30), Management Consulting (5 to 10), Accounting (6), and Asset Management (5 to 10). In total, 41 firms participate in these career programs (contact SEO for a complete listing).

Since the emphasis in the eighties upon *Wall Street* (the movie), junk bonds, and huge takeover deals, Wall Street has generated a lot of press. "The awareness of the financial services industry was low in the early eighties," says a current SEO board member who interned with SEO in 1981. "But by 1985, Wall Street came of age in popular culture. Consequently, students are interested in becoming the next great financier." In keeping with this demand, SEO's Investment Banking program is by far the organization's largest internship, with over 530 alumni. Placed in 16 heavy-hitter firms like Goldman Sachs, Morgan Stanley, Salomon Brothers, Merrill Lynch, JP Morgan, and First Boston, interns work in such areas as corporate or public finance, sales and trading, and research. Besides compiling financial figures or building financial models on computers, interns may travel nationwide to interview employees of companies targeted for acquisition. In a rare move, one intern flew to London with his supervisor to an insurance conference to gather information for a research report analyzing the impact of AIDS on insurance companies. Another intern read business plans as part of his firm's venture-capital group and spent time on his firm's hectic trading floor. After attending a "condom conference" in Chicago, a third intern analyzed trends in the condom market and wrote a report on how those trends affect the stock prices of such companies as Carter-Wallace, the manufacturer of Trojans.

Management Consulting interns work at firms like Booz Allen & Hamilton and McKinsey & Company. Creating financial models on spreadsheets and interacting with clients "just as a full-time analyst would," interns help consultants come up with recommendations to solve client business problems. One Consulting intern helped improve the distribution channels for a toy manufacturing company. For an appliance-leasing company, he assessed the market potential for an expansion into Mexico, traveling to New Jersey and to Mexico City to speak with department store managers about the company's products. "It was especially neat to speak Spanish with the Mexican credit managers," he said, "and it was really challenging to pull together all the information I had gathered and come up with the recommendation."

In Accounting, interns are divided among a few firms, including Big Six accountants Price Waterhouse and KPMG Peat Marwick. Starting off with one to two weeks of training, interns learn the nature of "auditing," the process of formally reviewing an organization's financial books. "My firm placed all of its interns in one room for a week of self-study followed by a week of instruction from managers and [senior accountants]," recalled an Accounting intern. Afterward, interns are assigned to various work areas. There they "sit waiting like relief pitchers in a bullpen for managers to call with assignments." Most assignments take interns off-site to help with audits. One intern spent two weeks at a New York publishing house auditing cash and fixed assets. "It was typical staff work . . . what you'd expect to do as a first year," he said. "But on top of that, you learn how to interact with a client's employees and how to confidently approach CFOs and VPs of Finance for financial information."

Corporate Law interns are placed in some of the biggest law firms in New York—Skadden, Arps, Slate, Meagher & Flom; Baker & McKenzie; Sullivan & Cromwell, and Paul, Weiss, Rifkind, Wharton & Garrison, to name a few. Because undergraduates have had no legal training, however, interns must immerse themselves in a great deal of clerical work. Assisting attorneys with whatever tasks need to be done, interns copy cases out of the library or type documents, occasionally putting in 12- or 13-hour days. For their efforts, interns are invited to client meetings, where they witness partners and clients discuss the legalities of such transactions as stock issues or asset acquisitions. Concluded an intern: "I didn't learn much about the law per se, but by the end, I understood the role of litigation in corporate law and I learned that the law is incredibly diverse—there's room for specialization."

Providing minorities with coveted Wall Street, corporate law, accounting, and management consulting jobs is not enough for SEO. To give minorities a leg-up during their job hunts later on, each program also runs a weekly seminar series, hosted by a different firm in the field. Seminar speakers are investment bank chairmen and presidents, law

> "Whether you're black, white, yellow, or red... [t]here's only one color on Wall Street, and that's green."

firm and accounting firm senior partners, and managers of recruiting. Following a discussion of issues in the field—such as real estate, bankruptcy, and the legal issues of mergers and acquisitions for Law interns—interns and hosts mingle. With the 20 to 30 high-level people present, the seminars provide an ideal opportunity to make a contact: "When you're interviewing for jobs later, you'll not only have a connection at each firm but you'll also already have a feel for the type of personalities working there."

All interns are assigned mentors at their firms to assist in career planning and to provide a perspective on the industry. "Your mentor can show you how to negotiate a more reasonable project deadline or how to approach your bosses for more work," explained an intern. "It's the kind of guidance you want when you're a college grad coming to the firm for the first time," said an SEO board member and alumnus. Many mentors not only provide guidance but also help interns create their own personal network of contacts inside and outside the firm. "My mentor introduced me to a director at [one of the other banks]," said an intern. Over a dozen years later, he still turns to that director for advice.

So SEO teaches interns the unwritten rules of corporate America at an early June orientation. Beside listening to former SEO interns and board members speak about their experiences, interns learn proper business etiquette and behavior. SEO also stresses the significance of the seminars: "They told us that VPs are there to meet us and that we should be aggressive, but not forcefully so, when approaching them." Emphasizing the importance of setting goals, the orientation conveys that as minorities, interns must work harder to prove themselves. "Some people were intimidated," said an intern.

In addition to the orientation, Investment Banking interns experience a week-long series of training seminars, where they obtain knowledge of the basic framework of investment banking. Besides teaching stocks and bonds, currency trades, and LBOs (leveraged buy-outs), the workshop instructors reiterate the message from the orientation: "Be palatably aggressive, strive for excellence, exhibit a superhuman work ethic, and have unimpeachable integ-

rity." The SEO graduate who started the training program in 1986 explains that, although this philosophy is directed at minorities, it really applies to everyone on Wall Street. "It doesn't matter if you're black, white, yellow, or red," he says. "Wall Street is color blind. There's only one color on Wall Street, and that's green."

SELECTION

 Applicants must be minority students and should have at least a 3.0 GPA. Though the Investment Banking, Management Consulting, and Asset Management programs are open to college sophomores, juniors, and seniors, it is rare for sophomores to be accepted. And while the Corporate Law program accepts juniors and seniors, the vast majority of Law interns are spring graduates who will be attending law school in the fall. The Accounting Program is open only to students who have completed a minimum of 3 accounting courses. The four other programs require no particular major. SEO cites leadership, professionalism, academic excellence, and maturity as important qualifications.

APPLICATION PROCEDURE

 The deadline is February 15 for the Investment Banking, Management Consulting, and Asset Management Programs. The deadline is March 1 for the Corporate Law and Accounting Programs. Students should submit a resumé, a one-page typed essay explaining their interest in the SEO program, a completed application form (available at many college career centers), two recommendations from professors, official transcript, two self-addressed labels, and a passport-sized photo. After SEO reviews application materials, top candidates are either invited to New York for on-site interviews, interviewed on campus by SEO representatives, or interviewed at designated locations throughout the country by SEO alumni. Note: Students must apply to one program only and cannot indicate a preference for a specific firm.

OVERVIEW

 Landing an internship on Wall Street or with a corporate law firm as an undergraduate is next to impossible. "Unless your dad is a partner or a major client," said an intern, "you can't easily get one." But if you're a minority college student, you can call on a guiding light named SEO. A "new-boy network for people who have been denied access to the old-boy network," SEO offers structured internships in corporate law and all areas of investment banking as well as internships in management consulting and accounting. Through weekly seminars with the movers and shakers in their fields, interns make valuable connections for the future. Such connections help nearly 75 percent of Investment Banking interns secure full-time job offers upon graduation from college.

FOR MORE INFORMATION . . .

■ Sponsors for Educational Opportunity
23 Gramercy Park South
New York, NY 10003
(212) 979-2040

SELECTIVITY				
Approximate applicant pool: 75 Interns accepted: 4				🔍🔍🔍🔍

COMPENSATION	
$50/week	$

QUALITY OF LIFE	
Unhierarchical atmosphere Fun neighborhood; Closing dinners	⚲⚲⚲

LOCATION(S)

New York, NY

FIELD

Humor magazine

DURATION

12–24 weeks
Summer, Fall, Spring

PRE-REQS

College juniors and seniors,
recent grads and grad students

DEADLINE(S)

Rolling

One glance at *Spy*'s masthead reveals the magazine's propensity for bucking tradition. There, underneath the names of various editors and managers, lies a listing of *Spy*'s interns. Whereas most publications wouldn't dream of acknowledging their college-age workers in print, *Spy* credits its interns alongside its permanent employees.

The maverick role is nothing new to *Spy*. The magazine was founded in 1986, when Kurt Anderson and E. Graydon Carter, writers for *Time* and *Life*, respectively, saw the need for a magazine that would take a satirical look at celebrities. Rejecting the typical Robin Leach–style of fawning over famous personalities, Anderson and Carter envisioned a publication that focused on deflating fat-cat celebrities. After receiving financial backing from venture capitalist Thomas Phillips, Jr., *Spy* became a reality, hitting the magazine racks with a feature article titled "Jerks: The Ten Most Embarrassing New Yorkers." Since then, *Spy* has let its engines of satire roar. The magazine has churned out such memorably iconoclastic pieces as "1000 Reasons Not to Vote for George Bush," "Let's Panic!—The High Strung Fun of New York Fear," and "Was JFK a Drag Queen? The U.S. Navy's Dirty Little Secrets."

DESCRIPTION

Despite *Spy*'s irreverent reputation, life at the magazine is not all fun and games. Interns must shoulder a fair share of mundane assignments such as errand running and photocopying. Some interns, for example, are asked to compile the "Gossip Pack," a daily packet of gossip articles clipped from New York newspapers. But the bulk of interns' work revolves around research assignments.

Interns often travel to the New York Public Library and Mid-Manhattan Library to gather articles and fact check stories. The latter task is taken quite seriously at the magazine; says a *Spy* editor: "A satirical magazine like ours must have airtight accuracy." Summer interns are introduced to the art of fact checking, as they are called upon to verify the accuracy of the "Spy 100," the magazine's annual compendium of the "most annoying, alarming and appalling people, places, and things."

BUSYWORK
MEDIUM
LOW
HIGH
OLDMAN & HAMADEH
METER

Every issue of *Spy* includes a number of pranks, some are ingenious, and some are downright silly. Interns happily find themselves called upon to help carry them out. Many interns, for example, embark on missions of surveillance, shuttling around New York to spy on unsuspecting victims. Do cops really eat doughnuts? An intern executed a 5:00 AM stakeout of a few doughnut shops to find out. How tight is security on Wall Street? Ask the intern who dressed in a banker's outfit and infiltrated a supposedly well-guarded investment bank. There is virtually no limit to where a *Spy* intern may be dispatched. Past stakeouts have taken interns to the Met Life heliport, society balls, a lingerie show at A&S, and a press conference for Cher's new perfume just to name a few.

Pranks often require more than mere surveillance. One involved calling various congressional offices to ask what America should do about the ethnic cleansing in "Fredonia"; several officials gave serious answers, not realizing that Fredonia is a fictitious country taken from a Marx Brothers movie. Another prank satirized the lengths to which marketers will go in order to sell a product. An intrepid intern found himself dressed in a pink bunny suit, test-marketing "Bunny Burgers" to disgusted shoppers at a New Jersey shopping mall.

A distinguishing feature of the *Spy* internship is, according to one intern, the "delightfully unhierarchical atmosphere." Editors are often unexpectedly receptive to interns' ideas. "We were hired because they thought we were bright and had something to contribute," said an intern. A true meritocracy, *Spy* rewards talented, self-directed interns with editorial responsibility. Several past interns have penned entries in the "Spy 100." Others have had the chance to write a feature story for the magazine. Two former interns wrote the first draft for *Spy High*, a tongue-in-cheek yearbook of the rich and famous. Importantly, respect for interns does not end after-hours. Interns, for example, are routinely invited to each "closing dinner," a morale-boosting meal

held at a local restaurant to celebrate an issue's completion. In a past intern's words, such dinners have "a charming lack of snobbery—an intern can wind up sitting next to a senior editor."

Interns are pleased with the setup at *Spy*. The office has an airy feeling and is filled with a lot of blond wood and glass partitions. Interns sit at desks in the main room but are never far from the editors' cubicles. The Spy Building is located in Union Square, a vibrant neighborhood known for its publishing houses, trendy restaurants, and record stores. Interns often live in nearby Greenwich Village, one of the most colorful and exciting neighborhoods in New York.

SELECTION

 College juniors and seniors, recent graduates, and graduate students are eligible for the internship. As *Spy* is first and foremost a humor magazine, its prospective interns should have a penchant for dry wit and humorous writing. But the magazine cares less for comedy writers and more for talented journalists who also happen to be funny. Indeed, while journalism experience is not explicitly required, most interns have gained writing experience working for a college publication. The ideal *Spy* intern is also, in the words of an intern, a "pop-culture junkie," someone who loves to keep up with the maneuverings of high-profile politicos and glitterati.

APPLICATION PROCEDURE

 Spy accepts applications on a rolling basis. Applicants should specify in a cover letter whether they are interested in the summer internship (generally three months, starting in early June) or the full-time internship (generally six months, at various times during the year). Both internships require a commitment of 40 hours a week, although summer interns have sometimes worked slightly less. Applicants

> An intrepid intern found himself dressed in a pink bunny suit, test-marketing "Bunny Burgers" to disgusted shoppers at a New Jersey shopping mall.

should also send *Spy* a resumé and a few writing samples. Writing samples may embrace anything from essays written for school to tear sheets from work in a publication. In any case, an applicant's submission should be "concise and cogent." Finalists are invited to visit the office to interview with an editor. In special cases, a phone interview will substitute for an on-site meeting.

OVERVIEW

 Spy's three founding partners have gone on to pursue other projects, prompting some insiders to predict that the magazine will eventually lose its cutting-edge reputation. Critics notwithstanding, most *Spy* aficionados still appreciate the magazine's unique mix of witty journalism and biting satire. Working at a magazine of this character makes for an intense internship. For the energetic, witty, and journalistically minded individual, it could be an ideal experience. The dozen or so internship alumni holding prestigious editorial positions—at places like *Vanity Fair*, *GQ*, *Variety*, and *Mirabella*—would surely agree.

FOR MORE INFORMATION . . .

■ Spy Internship Program
The SPY Building
5 Union Square West
New York, NY 10003
(212) 633-6550

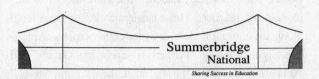

Summerbridge
National

Sharing Success in Education

To teach or not to teach?

That is the question that many college students face. The established route requires a degree in education, state certification, and a long-term commitment.

College graduates can sidestep these requirements by joining Teach for America, a corps of nearly 2,000 noncertified teachers from various academic backgrounds, each working a minimum of two years in underresourced urban or rural public schools.

But what about undergraduates who are interested in teaching but who want to find out before they graduate if teaching is for them?

Summerbridge National helps many of these students make up their minds about teaching. Founded in 1978 at San Francisco University High School, Summerbridge allows high school students and college undergraduates to spend eight weeks in the summer teaching a group of predominantly underprivileged kids. With nearly 20 outposts nationwide, Summerbridge has rapidly become a national institution. Given that the high schoolers and college undergraduates not only teach the classes but also manage the entire program, it's as much teaching responsibility as a student could hope for.

DESCRIPTION

Summerbridge is a two- to three-year "Workshop in Education" for "talented, often at-risk" students in the fourth through eighth grades. Nationwide, approximately 1,400 students participate in Summerbridge's two- to three-year program of six-week summer sessions, school-year tutorials, and year-round counseling. Having older students teach courses that prepare middle-school students for high school is not

Summerbridge's only innovation—the school is also tuition-free.

From 1978 to 1990, the Summerbridge program was run in conjunction with San Francisco University High School only. Its success in preparing often economically and academically disadvantaged students for the rigors of high school was so widely acclaimed that 18 new programs were established in the early 1990s, at schools in San Francisco, San Diego, and Ross, CA; New Haven, CT; Miami, FL; Louisville, KY; New Orleans, LA (2 schools); Cambridge and Concord, MA; Kan-

SELECTIVITY	
Approximate applicant pool: 1,500 Interns accepted: 450–500	

COMPENSATION	
$750 stipend & up to $1,500 aid available for undergrads; $500 stipend for H.S. students	

QUALITY OF LIFE	
Independence; Creative environment Workshops on teaching; Long workdays	

LOCATION(S)	
Nationwide (See Description)	

FIELD	
Education	

DURATION	
8 weeks Summer	

PRE-REQS	
High school sophomores, juniors and seniors Undergrads	

DEADLINE(S)	
March 1	

sas City, MO; Manchester, NH; Bronx, NY; Cincinnati, OH; Portland, OR; Lehigh Valley, PA; Providence, RI; and Hong Kong. The 19 schools hire nearly 500 teachers every summer, employing an equal number of high school and college students.

Summerbridge's mission was acknowledged in a recent *Newsweek* article on "alternative training programs." "[Summerbridge] attack[s] the lack of minority educators on a more local level . . . " explained the piece, "[and] is designed to get the younger kids into learning and the older kids into teaching." It does so by putting only four to ten students in each class and by giving the young teachers, half of whom are minorities, free rein over the entire program, from creating their own classes to chairing the academic departments. Teachers are assigned to three academic classes related to their interests from a list of over 40 titles in literature, math, science, foreign language, and social studies. Teachers also design one elective course. But there's more to the teachers' work than developing unique lesson plans. Teachers also advise students, take care of administrative matters, and organize field trips.

From 8:30 to 3:30, students take seven classes—five academic courses such as Speech and Debate, Geography, and Spanish as well as two electives in arts, sports, or drama. Uninspired methods of teaching are tossed out the window in favor of more interactive and creative styles. Drawing a baseball diamond on the blackboard, a teacher instructs her students to come forward one at a time to respond to various math questions. With every correct response, the students get closer to "home plate," eventually earning a run for their team. In a Writing Through Literature class, students play a game of "Jeopardy!" Hitting their desks in lieu of pressing the buttons used on the game show, students respond to the clues provided with a question—in this case, "What is proofreading?" is the correct answer to "The act of marking corrections in writing." When students read college-level plays such as Lorraine Hansberry's *A Raisin in the Sun* or

Shakespeare's *A Midsummer Night's Dream*, they act out scenes on a nearby grassy area or the cafeteria stage. "Acting out the plays increases students' understanding of them," explained a teacher. These academic classes are offered alongside unusual student-designed courses such as American Sign Language, Fantasy Role-Playing Games, and Animation. Taught in the afternoon, these "mini-courses," are educational but focused on fun. A teacher at the San Francisco school, for example, designed a Cooking class: "I brought in recipes and had the students try them out. Everything we made—wontons, pizzas, cakes—we naturally got to eat afterward."

Teachers also organize field trips, workshops, clubs, and school dances. Designed to teach students about real life, they take trips to meet local businesspeople, participate in scavenger hunts, or go to City Hall. Back at school, a business workshop teaches resumé writing, business dress, and the art of the handshake. For socializing, groups of students and teachers form clubs with imaginative titles such as Purple Smurf Cult, Dennis the Menace to Society, and the Hyperactive Hysterics. Every other Friday, students may tango at the school dance. The summer culminates with the "Olympics," a day of mental as well as physical challenges. In one of many competitions, a 50-yard dash requires students to stop every 10 yards and answer questions such as "What is the name of the president's daughter?"

The young teachers, committed to increasing the knowledge of their impressionable pupils, have high expectations for themselves and their students. Teachers often ride "an emotional roller coaster," feeling more elated certain days about their work than others. "Some days the kids just don't get it," said a teacher. But such frustration is often swept away by a sense of accomplishment. "When the students seem to be catching on, it's wonderful." And teachers' hard work does not go unnoticed by the students. For example, because a Spanish teacher consistently brought in props, prepared special lessons, and tutored

> **Teachers work from 7:30 AM to 6:00 PM on campus and then well into the evening to correct homework assignments.**

her pupils after school, her students presented her with a bouquet of flowers and a certificate of appreciation.

Summerbridge teachers are more than classroom lecturers they are also role models. Admirably, many have overcome difficult circumstances, such as having grown up in dangerous neighborhoods or having been raised by non-English-speaking parents. Usually only a few years older than their students, teachers are in the unique position of being able to relate to the students. "We feel that we can talk to them," said a student. That's important in a school where many of the students contend with problems at home or violence in the neighborhood. "We give them hope and direction and excite them about the possibility of going to college," said a teacher.

Teachers accomplish all of these tasks after ample training and with continuing guidance. The week before the program begins, Master Teachers (professional adult teachers) spend hours conducting workshops on lesson planning and diversity. Once the program gets under way, teachers attend additional workshops on managing classrooms, grading and commenting on students' work, and writing formal evaluations. There are also weekly staff meetings for interns and one-on-one consultations with the program director. The faculty lounge is also open throughout the day for teachers to meet and go over teaching strategies. Fortunately, problem kids are few. "These students want to be here," said a teacher, "so motivating them is not too difficult."

If it sounds like teachers are deluged with responsibilities, you've heard right. Most teachers report working from 7:30 AM to 6:00 PM on campus and then well into the evening, as late as 9:00 PM, to correct homework assignments. Teachers also make themselves available to answer students' questions by phone. "We want them to call us if they need any sort of clarification about what we've done in class," explained a teacher, "because it's important that they understand the material."

Teachers must be willing to accept what is described by many as "really low pay." Fortunately, Summerbridge offers ways to alleviate this problem. Many teachers win grants from third parties such as the Ford Foundation and the J.W. Saxe Memorial Fund. Summerbridge itself awards a few college students already on financial aid with additional stipends of up to $1,500. For teachers from out-of-town, Summerbridge can arrange free room and board with families of the program's students.

The "workshop" is so short-lived that before they know it, teachers are evaluating final exams (there are no grades at Summerbridge) and it's time to say good-bye. Sprawled out on a floor in a lounge, the teachers are amazed at the impact they've made in just six weeks. A few students have picked up a whole new language. Some are more outgoing while others are more motivated to learn. "But it's not long enough," said a disappointed teacher. "You just start to see changes, and then the program is over." On the last day, it's common to find an outpouring of emotion, often resulting in a free flow of tears. "I look back now and smile," said a teacher, "because I know that we helped those kids make it."

SELECTION

 High school applicants must be sophomores, juniors, or seniors. College applicants must be undergraduates returning to school in the fall to complete their undergraduate education. While there is neither a minimum GPA nor a particular major required, all applicants must have the "heart and desire to teach." Summerbridge seeks students who have done well academically and who "want to work with young motivated students."

APPLICATION PROCEDURE

 The application must be postmarked by March 1. Students must submit the written application and a resumé or list of skills and previous experience. Send away early for the application because it is extensive: ten pages asking for Summerbridge location(s) desired, general information, short essays, a personal statement, and sample lesson plans. "Some of our teachers say that [the application] is more difficult than a final exam," says the coordinator. High school students are required to sit for "station interviews" (where they must spontaneously come up with solutions to hypothetical staff situations) and give a 15-minute teaching presentation to a group of adult teachers. College students, on the other hand, receive less formal yet challenging in-person or phone interviews by program directors.

OVERVIEW

 How would you like to spend the summer teaching chemistry, English, geography, or Chinese to 9- to 14-year-olds? Throw in some "extra-cool" classes, too, such as The History of Rap or Jogging for Fun. Did we mention that you'll also help run the entire school? Now add school dances, an "Olympics," parent-teacher conferences, and field trips. You're hooked? That's Summerbridge—utter immersion in the teaching experience. Playing role model, confidant, and—yes—educator, Summerbridge's student-teachers are making an impact on America's declining public-education system.

FOR MORE INFORMATION . . .

■ Summerbridge National
3101 Washington Street
San Francisco, CA 94115
(415) 749-2037

SELECTIVITY 🔍🔍🔍🔍

Approximate applicant pool: 40
Interns accepted: 2

COMPENSATION $

None
$1,000 scholarship may be available

QUALITY OF LIFE 🌴🌴🌴

Law-clerk luncheons
Cafeteria/gym; Rigid bureaucracy

LOCATION(S)

Washington, DC

FIELD

Government

DURATION

3–4 months
Summer, Fall, Winter

PRE-REQS

College juniors and seniors, recent grads
Constitutional law coursework

DEADLINE(S)

Summer .... March 10	Fall ..... June 1
Winter .... October 10	

Corinthian columns. Marble halls. The aura of history and of great thinkers of years past. No, it is not a mausoleum, far from it. The Supreme Court of the United States sits like a Greek temple atop Capitol Hill in Washington, D.C., and its stately grandeur never fails to impress passersby. This architectural magnificence provides a fitting home to America's highest judicial body. The nine justices of the Supreme Court meet to discuss and issue decisions on our nation's most important jurisprudential issues. The Supreme Court is the solemn interpreter of the Constitution, the source of controversial policy decisions, the eleventh-hour provider of stays of execution, and home to immensely powerful but publicly invisible jurists.

DESCRIPTION

In 1972, the Office of the Administrative Assistant to the Chief Justice established the Judicial Internship Program, enabling college students to work under the auspices of the administrative assistant, who serves as the chief justice's right-hand man or woman. While each session's two Judicial interns answer ultimately to the administrative assistant, they work primarily with the Judicial Fellow, typically a lawyer or professor serving the year-long Judicial Fellowship at the Court. The Judicial Fellow oversees the interns' daily activities and long-term projects.

A typical day for the Judicial intern includes mundane and substantive tasks. The least appealing daily task requires interns to clip, categorize, and file articles from about eight newspapers and magazines, adding to the office's extensive archives of law-related news articles. While article-clipping keeps interns abreast of current events, it can be time-consuming and monotonous: "There were always more news-

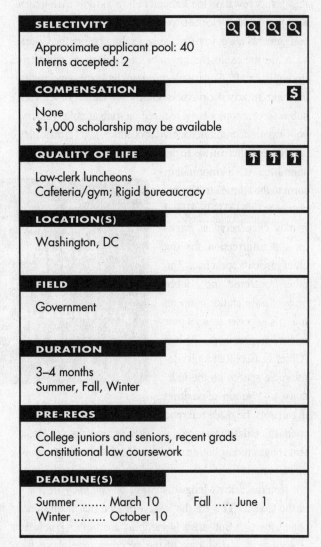

papers to clip. We'd spend entire mornings cutting out and filing articles. Real brainy stuff—not!" But the Judicial Internship brochure warns applicants that interns must have a "willingness to shoulder one's share of less glamorous tasks." Even so, there are interns who become frustrated when their jobs are not the apprentice justiceships they were expecting: "I was insulted to spend an afternoon stuffing information booklets into envelopes." On the whole, however, most interns willingly accept the requisite busywork in exchange for the opportunity to work at America's most prestigious legal institutions.

Other facets of the Judicial Internship are more exciting. Every few days the Judicial Fellow assigns each intern a project. Contrary to the expectations of many interns, these assignments never involve cases pending before the Court; such are the exclusive province of the justices and their immediate staff. Nevertheless, interns have the opportunity to research and write memorandums on a variety of relevant subjects; past topics have focused on such areas as judicial confirmation, problems of civil procedure, legal ethics, jury reform, and alternatives to litigation. An intern's research is submitted in memorandum form to the administrative assistant or Judicial Fellow, and it may even serve as background information for the chief justice's speeches. The latter outcome no doubt brings exhilaration to an intern's experience; as a past intern emphasized: "When [Chief Justice] Rehnquist delivered a speech on the judiciary to a group of visiting dignitaries, he made reference to a congressional bill I had spent three days researching . . . it was gratifying to know that I made a contribution to the chief's speech, albeit a small contribution!"

Interns acknowledge the rigid bureaucracy in place at the Court: "You are the lowest link on the institutional food chain." But strict hierarchies are nothing new in government, and alumni of the program rave about the advantages of being one of only two interns, as opposed to one of hundreds of congressional interns. "You may be a small fish, but you are one of two small fish in a prestigious, marble-lined pond," said an intern. "With a little luck, you'll gain great insight into the inner workings of the judiciary." Indeed, Judicial interns are exposed to a wealth of experiences. They receive special tours of the Court's internal offices, observing the outer reaches of places like the clerk's office and the commodious, chandelier-filled library. During days when oral arguments are heard (typically Monday through Wednesday, from October to April) interns are encouraged to observe the hourlong exchanges between justices and lawyers. Interns are also invited to several "law-

> "You may be a small fish, but you are one of two small fish in a prestigious, marble-lined pond . . . "

clerk luncheons," where they dine with the 30-odd law clerks and hear a distinguished speaker, such as the chief justice, an associate or retired justice, or a government honcho like the attorney general. As one alumnus puts it, "This is heady stuff for an undergrad."

Interns give respectable ratings to quality of life. The Court's cafeteria serves up an array of hot and cold meals, as well as a salad bar, and is frequented by tourists, staff, and occasionally even a hungry justice. For those athletically inclined, the Court's top floor features a modest weight room, allegedly the site of Justice O'Connor's aerobics class and a full-size basketball court, affectionately referred to as the "highest court in the land." Playing hoops is an ideal way to get to know a broad mix of Court personnel such as law clerks, policemen, and various staff members. On the Court's first floor there's a collection of fascinating exhibits on Supreme Court history, arranged with loving care by the curator's office for those seeking a bit of culture.

Judicial Internships are held three times a year. While summer is often the easiest time for students to complete the internship, interns reveal that a fall or winter tenure allows students to experience the Court in session, with its oral arguments and daily influx of lawyers and reporters. One intern warned that the summer internship is like "working at a football stadium during off-season!" Whichever term interns work, however, the Judicial intern workweek leaves little room for other employment, as interns work eight-hour days, five days a week.

Until 1991, the Judicial Internship program offered students no financial compensation. But recently it seems to have loosened the purse strings a bit, as program coordinators report the possibility of granting a $1,000 scholarship to interns who successfully complete the internship and return to academic studies. The program also helps students receive academic credit through work-study programs affiliated with their universities.

SELECTION

 The Judicial Internship Program is open to college juniors and seniors as well as recent graduates. While students from any academic major are welcome, program coordinators say applicants should have taken some coursework on constitutional law or the Supreme Court. After an initial screening, the Judicial Fellow winnows the pool to a handful of applicants, each of whom are then given a phone interview. You may want to keep in mind that the fall and winter internships occur during the academic year, and therefore usually have fewer applicants than the summer internship and thus are slightly less competitive.

APPLICATION PROCEDURE

 Application deadlines are as follows: summer, March 10; fall, June 1; winter, October 10. The application procedure is nothing short of laborious. Required materials include: a resumé, an official transcript, a statement explaining the applicant's reasons for seeking the internship, a short writing sample, three letters of recommendation, and a two-page essay on the American constitutional system. Past interns stress the importance of the applicant's personal statement: "Use it to explain why you can offer the Supreme Court something extraordinary. Cite examples. Don't exaggerate."

OVERVIEW

 The Judicial Internship Program offers an unmatched opportunity to become immersed in the inner workings of the U.S. Supreme Court. Limited to only two interns, the program offers an intimate working environment of substantial responsibility, learning, and collegiality. Students who enjoy the program are able to accept their low-profile role within the Court's rigid bureaucracy, while taking advantage of enriching research projects and luncheons. The sheer luster of the Supreme Court attracts top-notch interns who tend to end up in prestigious jobs and graduate schools. A recent reunion of Judicial interns included several graduates of top law and business schools, an award-winning journalist, a White House Fellow, a Marshall Scholar, and four Rhodes Scholars.

FOR MORE INFORMATION . . .

■ Supreme Court of the United States
Judicial Internship Program
Office of the Administrative Assistant
to the Chief Justice
Room 5
Washington, DC 20543
(202) 479-3374

A group of surfers dedicated to environmental activism? Whoaaa. *Bitchin'!* What do they do, wax their boards with organic paste?

The Surfrider Foundation blows away the misconception that all surfers care about is shredding waves. Fed up with Southern California's increasingly polluted waters, a circle of surfers banded together in 1984 to create a group dedicated to the preservation of coastal waters and beaches. Today, Surfrider is an international organization with over 25,000 members. Its track record as a coastal watchdog is impressive: It helped divert storm drain waters from Santa Monica Bay to the city's sewage treatment system, settled the second largest Clean Water Act enforcement lawsuit in U.S. history, and it stopped the California Coastal Commission from building a $200 million beach-destroying breakwater at Bolsa Chica State Beach in Southern California. These are just a few of its triumphs. Surfrider also spends time educating local students and lifeguard associations about ocean pollution and coastal ecology.

DESCRIPTION

Surfrider believes in making good use of its interns' capabilities. Sure, there's a lot of busywork to be done—phone work, faxing, stuffing envelopes, and the like—but that's par for the course at a nonprofit group. Over the past few years, Surfrider has made a concerted effort to have interns carry out important projects.

One intern's project involved analyzing the effectiveness of Surfrider's Blue Water Task Force, a program encouraging people across the country to test samples of ocean water for pollution and send in the results to Surfrider. Using the data these testers submit, the organization keeps track of pollution patterns and attempts to pinpoint where the pollution originates. Another intern was involved in a project that assessed the environmental impact of tollways on the land and waterways they disturb. Describing the damage that automobiles on one tollway have caused to the surrounding environment, an intern wrote a 20-page report, which she presented to Surfrider's executive director, Jake Grubb.

Another intern researched the "coastal reserves" section of California's Proposition 132. Designed to set aside areas for scientific research, the coastal reserves policy bans recreational use of four ocean sites. He investigated the implications of this prohibition, weighing the state's need for research sites against the public's right to access the ocean. He said: "After weeks of research, I concluded that although the idea of coastal reserves is good, the way it's worded in Prop 132 is ambiguous. It's open to interpretation in a way that may unfairly restrict ocean use from the public." Excerpts of his report were published in *Longboarder* magazine and the Surfrider newsletter.

Surfrider Foundation is based in San Clemente, a beach community known for its health food stores and trinket shops. Located in a three-story office building, Surfrider headquarters is up the street from the San Clemente pier but about a mile from the ocean. The office has a beachy feel to it; the walls are decorated with framed surfing posters and paintings by famous surf artists. Conch shells and an abundance of plants and windows complete the laid-back decor. "It's a comfortable place to work," said an intern. "But since it's nonprofit, expect to share computers and make do with few amenities."

Interns love the office environment at Surfrider. "People here are positive and, for the most part, relaxed," said an intern. "There's not a profit-driven ethic here. People come to Surfrider because they have a love for the California coastline." Interns say that the positive energy at Surfrider is directed their way: "The staff bends over backward to show that they think interns are important. Working hours, for example, are flexible. If you come in late because you're working on your project at the library, no problem. . . . They trust you."

One is not likely to forget that Surfrider is an organization founded by surfers. Although the Jeff Spicoli surfer-dude persona is "an exaggeration," Surfrider employees definitely do surf. One intern estimates that at least 80 percent of the employees at Surfrider actually "ride the surf." In fact, when the surf is unusually good, it's acceptable for staff to take time out to hit the waves. "It doesn't happen a

> When the surf is unusually good, it's acceptable for staff to take time out to hit the waves.

lot, but occasionally you'll see people grabbing their boards and heading out to the ocean," said an intern. For those who have never had the chance to hang ten, a veteran Surfrider is usually willing to offer an early morning lesson.

Interns are encouraged to help out at the informational booths Surfrider sets up at events throughout Southern California. In return, they get to enjoy the events for free. Interns work the booth at surfing competitions, environmental-awareness expositions, and even the Lollapalooza concert. They also participate in cleanup days held at Bolsa Chica and other nearby beaches. Parties are another extracurricular option, to interns who help out at such soirées as the Surfing Industry Manufacturers Association Ball. Said one intern about the SIMA Ball: "In exchange for selling drink tickets part of the time, I enjoyed an elaborate ball in a beautiful sculpture garden. Celebrities like Ted Danson were milling around. It was pretty cool."

SELECTION

Surfrider welcomes applications from high schoolers, college students, graduate students, and recent graduates. According to the intern coordinator, the program looks for applicants who are "outgoing" and "environmentally aware." Knowledge of the surf industry and computer proficiency help, too.

APPLICATION PROCEDURE

Although applications are accepted on a rolling basis, applicants are advised to submit their materials at least three weeks before the date in which they wish to start. Send in a cover letter explaining the reasons for wanting to work at Surfrider; also enclose a resumé or listing of relevant skills. The intern coordinator prefers to conduct in-person interviews but is willing to use phone interviews for long-distance applicants.

OVERVIEW

 Ponytails, goatees, and easygoing attitudes may be the standard at the Surfrider Foundation, but get one thing straight—Surfrider is an effective lobby that's here to stay. Combining a passion for surfing with an inclination for environmental activism, Surfrider is committed to protecting the coastal environment. Whether carrying out badly needed administrative work or completing projects central to Surfrider's mission, interns are key players in the organization's success. For diehard surfers or mere ocean enthusiasts, interning at Surfrider is a means of ensuring that the endless summer lives on.

FOR MORE INFORMATION . . .

- Surfrider Foundation
  Internship Program
  122 South El Camino Real
  Number 67
  San Clemente, CA 92672
  (800) 743-SURF

TBWA

SELECTIVITY	🔍🔍🔍
Approximate applicant pool: 75 Interns accepted: 8–12	

COMPENSATION	💲💲
$225/week	

QUALITY OF LIFE	⬆⬆⬆⬆
Hip atmosphere; Luncheon seminars International flavor; Parties/picinic	

LOCATION(S)
New York, NY

FIELD
Advertising

DURATION
10 weeks Summer

PRE-REQS
Undergrads

DEADLINE(S)
April 1

Every month it seems there's a new one. As a ski slope. A swimming pool in L.A. An Art Deco building in Miami. Carved out of a wheat field. A peeled lemon. Painted by Andy Warhol. Keith Haring. Configured in gold, steel, stone, and light bulbs. As a Christmas tree. Twice.

The mighty Absolut Vodka bottle has been etched into the minds of millions of consumers, thanks to an ingenious advertising campaign featuring the sleek Absolut bottle in over 300 different ads. The mastermind behind this campaign is TBWA, a high-quality, medium-sized advertising house in New York. With $1.2 billion in billings, TBWA is ranked among the world's top 20 advertising agencies. It has executed ad campaigns for an impressive roster of clients. Eagle Snacks, for example, benefited from a series of TBWA television commercials that reunited America's favorite odd couple, Tony Randall and Jack Klugman. Other TBWA clients include: Nissan Europe (automobiles), Philip Morris (cigarettes), Evian (mineral water), Nivea (skin cream), Barilla (pasta), and Henkel (detergent).

DESCRIPTION

At TBWA each intern is assigned a job in one of three work areas: Market Research, Account Management, or Media. Market Research interns spend their days investigating potential clients and figuring out what the agency can do for them. "An agency can't rest on its current accounts," said one intern. "It must progress and find new clients. As interns, we help it do so." Interns examine all sorts of markets and companies. Baby products, Swiss-army knives, the U.S. Army, an Italian import company—all are fair game for an intern's research. Sometimes interns in Market Research carry out projects suggesting new directions for a current client. One intern, for example, spent three weeks studying and writing about how companies like Nissan can become more socially responsible. To carry out their research, interns do everything from searching computer databases to combing the AAAA Library, a midtown library that is exclusively used by ad agencies.

In Account Management, interns contact clients, attend client meetings, and help out with the agency's billing and budgeting. "I have no creative ability," said an intern in response to why Account Management was the best department for her. "As an Account Management intern, I carried out side projects for account executives, doing research and writing reports . . . I wrote a binder full." Among other papers, she wrote a detailed report exploring whether outdoor advertising would be beneficial for Carvel ice cream.

Like Market Research and Account Management, the Media department assigns its interns a host of research projects. These projects often focus on determining the best medium (TV, newspaper, magazines, etc.) for TBWA's clients. While carrying out research for Evian, one intern, for example, investigated whether *Vanity Fair* readers have a higher propensity to drink mineral water than readers of other magazines. Computer databases prove immensely helpful in this kind of research, and by the end of the summer interns have a great deal of experience searching them to find appropriate statistics.

While interns generally find their daily work rewarding, they rave about their other main task during the internship—the marketing project. At the beginning of the summer, interns are divided into teams of five or six and are asked to develop complete marketing and communications plans for a TBWA client. With guidance from an assigned mentor, each team must create specific marketing, advertising, and media plans for a real product or service that is complete with creative examples. One group was asked to reposition the advertising for Air France's Concorde. Another worked on a stain pump for Woolite. The year before, a group of interns created a Club Med campaign targeting Hispanic communities. Still another developed an advertising plan to sell Carvel ice cream in Texas.

The marketing project requires a concerted effort throughout the term of internship. Meeting after work and on the weekends, the teams research the market for their particular product. The Concorde team, for example, called airlines and market-research firms to determine what type of person flies the New York-to-Paris route. The team then developed strategies to attract these targeted flyers, such as lowering the ticket price while retaining the plane's elite image. Also discussed were ways to convey new positioning strategies, such as emphasizing the Concorde's time-saving speed and the idea of Paris as a gateway to Europe. All along, interns have access to the agency's editorial and art resources, and they use them to write detailed reports and construct creative supplements like storyboards and sketches.

The marketing project culminates in a final exam of sorts at the end of the summer. Each team presents its work to the senior management of TBWA and then shows it to representatives of the actual client. "We, a bunch of college students, had the full attention of a group of Air France managers. It was something!" said one team member. After three months of preparation, interns are ready to strut their stuff, making use of overhead projections, storyboards, on-the-street interviews, and sample products. The Woolite group even worked music into its presentation, jamming Aretha Franklin's "Respect" while it unveiled its stain pump's motto: "Stains need no respect, but your clothes do." The client representatives are often duly impressed and many take the groups' projects to heart, carrying the information back to the home office for further consideration. Interns cannot say enough good things about the experience: "We acted as a bona fide advertising unit, doing everything real advertising professionals would. And [TBWA's senior management] trusted us to present our plan to real clients. I'll never forget it."

Every week or two, interns attend special two-hour luncheon seminars designed to teach them about advertising subjects (media, creative, production, research) and other areas like promotion, public relations, and presentation techniques. Past speakers include the creative director, copywriters, art directors, client representatives, and even the president. The last, Bill Tragos, got stellar reviews. "In one sense, it was really humbling. After all, he is the

> **The Woolite group jamm[ed] Aretha Franklin's "Respect" while it unveiled its stain pump's motto: "Stains need no respect, but your clothes do."**

president of the fifth largest privately-held advertising agency in the world," an intern said. "But he was totally unpretentious and direct. He answered all our questions."

TBWA is located on Madison Avenue, a street synonymous with advertising the world over. The agency occupies four floors of its building, and every floor has a different feel, though all are modern and inviting. The executive floor, for example, has a handsome, Japanese look, while the creative floor is less chic, with everything from basketball hoops to advertising awards affixed to the walls. Interns sit in cubicles decked out with all the office supplies one could want —"a real professional setup," in one intern's estimation. A lucky few have their own offices, though such good fortune shouldn't be expected.

The office atmosphere at TBWA gets high ratings. "Even more hip than I imagined," said an intern. "It's youthful, energetic, and stimulating." Another attributes the mood to the agency's president, saying, "Mr. Tragos is very charismatic and friendly. His attitude filters down to everyone, even the interns." Interns enjoy hanging around together and they learn a lot from each other's different cultural backgrounds. TBWA has outposts in every major capital in Europe, so it's no surprise that its internship attracts international students. American interns are often surprised (and pleased) to find that several of the interns are foreign students: "Our group looked like a meeting of a mini-United Nations." Recent years have attracted students from England, France, Italy, Germany, Japan, Korea, Sweden, Austria, and Tahiti.

Interns are satisfied with the fringe benefits that come their way at TBWA. Parties are an occasional treat, periodically thrown and hosted by clients like Absolut. The agency annually sponsors a midsummer picnic at a New Jersey park, and, at the end of the internship, the executive vice-president holds a lunch at which an intern is chosen as the "Intern of the Year." This honor is presented to the intern who has made the best impression on TBWA management. In addition to the in-house announcement, the executive vice president takes the Intern of the Year out to a celebratory lunch at a posh restaurant.

In most respects, TBWA is an intern's dream. "This is a full-fledged, knock-'em-dead internship program. Big commitment, bigger reward," an intern concluded. But there are a few gripes. Workdays are long, especially when interns stay late to work on their marketing projects. Some wished their supervisors were around more often to offer guidance with daily tasks. Others groaned that the lunchtime seminars were postponed too often.

SELECTION

 College students of any level may apply for the internship, though most participants are between their junior and senior years. No particular majors are favored, but the program brochure states that successful applicants often demonstrate "a consuming interest in the advertising business" and "have a point of view about it." The brochure adds that "extracurricular activities, work experience, and personal interests are also taken into account since all of these provide insight into the candidate's leadership qualities and overall personality. According to past interns, those who thrive in the program have "high self-esteem, as advertising is a business of big egos," "positive attitudes, because you're not working in a funeral home," and "good public speaking skills—you'll need them when presenting your final project."

APPLICATION PROCEDURE

 Applicants should submit their materials by April 1. The procedure is relatively simple: Send in a resumé and cover letter explaining your reasons for seeking the job. Live interviews are mandatory for all but overseas students, who can interview at one of TBWA's European outposts. TBWA selects its interns in late April.

OVERVIEW

 If you're looking for a career in advertising, TBWA's internship is hard to beat with its substantive work, stimulating environment, and a "real-world" marketing project. TBWA believes strongly in its internship program, and it shows. In the program's brochure, the agency even enumerates its reasons for hiring interns, not the least of which is the desire to offer "participants a hands-on work experience that generates a real understanding of what agency 'life' is really about." Another dividend of the internship is the opportunity to work closely with a highly talented and delightfully international group of interns. Chances are an intern will leave TBWA with a network of friends from around the world. A summer at TBWA is (Absolut)ly worthwhile.

FOR MORE INFORMATION . . .

■ TBWA
Internship Program
TBWA House
292 Madison Avenue
New York, NY 10017
(212) 725-1150

3M

SELECTIVITY	
Approximate applicant pool: 4,000 Interns accepted: 200	

COMPENSATION	
$425–$500/week for undergraduates $550–$650/week for graduate students	

QUALITY OF LIFE	
Employee camaraderie; Social activities 3M Center	

LOCATION(S)	
St. Paul, MN; Austin, TX; and 80 plants nationwide–see Index	

FIELD	
Consumer, health care, commercial, and industrial goods	

DURATION	
14 weeks Summer	

PRE-REQS	
College sophomores, juniors and seniors, grad students; Minimum 3.0 GPA	

DEADLINE	
December 31	

Don't you hate it when your bookmark falls out and you've lost the page you were on? Back in 1974 so did Art Fry, a Division Scientist at 3M. A member of his church choir, he would mark his hymnal with bookmarks, but the bookmarks would often fall out, leaving him unable to keep his place. Taking advantage of 3M's "15 % policy" (whereby the company's engineers and scientists may spend up to 15 percent of their time on projects of their choice), Fry worked to create a sticky bookmark. He sought out a semisticky adhesive invented by a 3M employee four years earlier and started applying it to various types of paper. "At first, the adhesive left some residue on the hymnal ... [but] I finally figured it out ... and started making [sticky paper] for other employees, who used it as notepaper. After about ten sheets, they were all addicts." The invention? 3M Post-it Notes. Introduced nationally in 1980, they were an instant success.

Besides Post-it Notes, 3M's 15 percent policy has spawned a host of classics, including masking tape and Scotch Brand transparent tape. These innovative products have made 3M, which stands for Minnesota Mining & Manufacturing, a world-recognized company with yearly sales of nearly $14 billion and an employee base of nearly 90,000 people. Founded in 1902 as a maker of sandpaper, 3M now manufactures nearly 60,000 office, household, and industrial goods from sponges, videotapes, and computer disks to overhead projectors, medical laser imagers, and surgical masks.

DESCRIPTION

3M started its summer program in 1951, making it one of the oldest internship programs in corporate America. Today, over 200 college undergraduate and graduate-student interns from around the country participate in a variety of programs, including minority-only programs which target students nationwide. The Summer Intern Program places 140 to 160 students in laboratory, engineering, and manufacturing positions, where they help improve old products and create new ones. Approximately 80 interns are also placed in finance, marketing, and administrative positions. About 70 percent of the students work in St. Paul, the rest in Austin, TX, or one of the 80 plants throughout the country. Ninety percent of 3M interns are undergraduates.

Each intern starts the summer by going through a small-group training session, administered to all new 3M hires. In Corporate Accounting, the session educates interns on profit-and-loss statements and teaches them how to read production summaries. After the session, one Accounting intern was placed in the Specialty Adhesives and Chemicals Division. She worked on two projects, one analyzing the cost of incinerating 3M's toxic wastes and another involving 3M's Distributive Unit Cost System (referred to as DUCS, pronounced "ducks"). "DUCS is an in-house computer system we use to determine the unit cost for each chemical produced in our division. It takes into account the labor, the material, the packaging, and many other variables. Some of the numbers generated seemed too high and others too low, so I was charged with going through it." Scour it she did, finding that some of the data were old, that other data were incorrectly input, and that a third problem was so complex that "even after talking to 3M's best programmers, I could not solve it in the short time I was there."

But making products is what 3M is all about. "You could work on diaper tape and sandpaper during the same summer," said the coordinator. "Hopefully, you don't get the two mixed up!" One intern worked on a color digital-imager, a machine that transforms electronic data from X rays and CAT scans, for example, into photograph-quality pictures. "3M had already figured out how to produce the images in color. I was there to help figure out the mechanics." Accordingly, he broke the task down into discrete projects with workable deadlines. He tinkered with an old black-and-white imager to determine if any of the parts or processes could be improved. "We realized that the circuit board would need a protective cover to prevent certain components from touching each other. But the cover also had to cool the components. I sat down with design engineers to figure out how we could do that. By the time I left, I had designed a fan and specified its location and air flow."

Another intern worked in Dental Products on dental clay, that plasterlike guck orthodontists use to make impressions of your teeth. Assigned to the product development group, she worked on a new and improved version to address dentists' concerns. "I used a Brookfield viscometer to measure the viscosity of [the clay] and make sure that it was within the range specified by the engineers who designed it. Once a statistical test confirmed that the [new clay] met the specifications, I worked with labeling and marketing to get it into dentists' hands."

Interns cannot choose which products they want to work on. If they could, "[they'd] all ask to work on Post-it Notes and wouldn't learn anything about other products," said an intern who ended up testing adhesives for medical dressings, and in the end optimized the hold and release properties of a particular 3M medical adhesive. "I mixed the chemicals together to create new formulations, spread them onto dressings, and then did the initial tests, which consisted of putting two dressings against one another and recording how well they stuck." Once he found a few formulations that adhered well and were also easily removable, it was time for the human trials. "At 3M, employees are willing to test your products so long as you test theirs. My test was unfortunately a little painful; some of the dressings tended to pull off arm and leg hair!"

Interns report that 3M's projects are "challenging" and come with "very little supervision." The combination frustrates some interns at first. "My supervisor didn't know how to help a student—he wasn't able to respond adequately to questions I had on my project." But most interns find that their frustration eventually gives way to a sense of accomplishment: "It forced me to go through the project on my own, and it was rewarding because I actually solved a 3M problem." Tackling a project alone also prepares them for the presentations they must give at a two-day affair in front of managers and employees at the end of the summer. "I was so nervous at the time," remarked an intern, "but in hindsight, I am happy that 3M made me give one. I learned that I could stand in front of a group and defend my work."

> "You could work on diaper tape and sandpaper during the same summer. . . . Hopefully, you don't get the two mixed up!"

3 M

3M works with an apartment locator service to help students find housing for the summer. Within a mile and a half of work, two apartment buildings house nearly three quarters of the summer interns. Some students are pleased with their assignments: "It was fairly cheap and much like living in a big dorm—lots of parties." Others are disappointed: "My apartment was located in East St. Paul right off the highway. I also didn't hit it off with my two roommates, both 3M interns."

Most interns work at the 3M Center, the company's headquarters in St. Paul, MN, described by the College Relations Manager as "a marvelous place to live, a cultural center with everything from sports to theater." With 25 buildings on over 400 acres, the 3M Center is "an easy place to get lost." In front of the complex are several office buildings and behind are orange-brick R&D facilities. On-site are also a barber, bakery, convenience store, and discount gift shop, all for 3M employees. With fountains, a well-manicured lawn, and lots of shady trees, it's like a minicommunity, nicknamed "the campus" for its university-like setting. The only thing missing is an on-site gym, a fact one intern deemed "a big disadvantage." But there are subsidized cafeterias, where interns and employees rarely stop talking about 3M products. "We are continuously improving things and developing ideas. You can't help but get excited. When you see your friends in the 'caf,' you feel like telling them what you've been up to."

The camaraderie usually continues off-hours as well. Departments frequently organize picnics at a nearby park, also the site of the company-wide welcome and farewell intern picnics. Staffing also plans trips to Twins games, dinners with management, and a riverboat cruise. For athletes, there are company intramural leagues in volleyball, softball, tennis, and golf—played on the 3M-owned golf course.

But the company can't arrange every social and recreational event, so interns take it upon themselves to make their own fun. They keep each other abreast of activities by advertising various functions like trips to the horse track, dog track, zoo, and Valley Fair amusement park in the weekly newsletter. For those who love the outdoors, St. Paul is full of biking and running trails. Roller Blading is popular among residents, and tubing down the calm Apple River, 40 minutes away, is a popular 3M intern event, described by one as "an inexpensive day in the sun."

SELECTION

For the Summer Intern Program, although the majority of positions require interns to be seniors, there are a few opportunities for sophomores and juniors. Eligible majors include chemistry, engineering (chemical, electrical, mechanical, industrial, and ceramic), computer science, materials science, biology, and physics. For finance positions, applicants must be seniors in accounting or business, though a few sophomores, juniors, and M.B.A. candidates have been accepted in the past. For marketing positions, applicants must be seniors pursuing marketing-related degrees, including communications, journalism, or advertising; M.B.A. candidates are also eligible. All applicants must have at least a 3.0 GPA.

APPLICATION PROCEDURE

The deadline is December 31. Students must submit a resumé and cover letter. Interviews with Staffing or specific departments, by phone or on-site, are arranged as needed.

OVERVIEW

Life without 3M products would be life in the Dark Ages—no Post-it Notes, no Scotch Brite sponges, and no Scotch Brand transparent tape. But there's no need to entertain such a thought, since the scientists and engineers at 3M continue to churn out products that make modern life easier. As 3M interns, students get to contribute to the mission and carry out projects of significance. Some interns improve processes, while others help to create new products. Either way, every year the program launches a good 50 percent of graduating interns into permanent employment with 3M. It did so with Art Fry, the Post-it Notes inventor, who completed his 3M internship in 1955.

FOR MORE INFORMATION . . .

■ 3M
Staffing & College Relations
224-1W-02
3M Center
St. Paul, MN 55144-1000
(800) 328-1343

Students interested in gaining exposure to the United Nations are faced with a bewildering array of options. UN headquarters used to offer the Ad Hoc Internship Program and now has the Headquarters Programme administered through its Human Resources department. Once eligible for these programs, undergraduates are no longer accepted. Furthermore, American citizens comprise only about one third of the graduate students accepted. Added to the morass is the fact that UN-affiliated organizations have their own internship programs, each independent of the others—UNICEF, UNIFEM, UNIDO—what a UNI-*pain!*

The United Nations Association of the United States of America (UNA) stands as a beacon in this dark night of internship confusion. A private, nonprofit organization, the UNA dedicates itself to enhancing U.S. participation in the UN system through programs in public outreach, policy analysis, and international dialogue. Though not officially a part of the UN, it is a bastion of information about and analysis on the UN, disseminating its work through 175 UNA chapters, 133 affiliated organizations, 130 Model UN Conferences, and a wide variety of publications. Most importantly, the UNA offers an internship that gives motivated students the opportunity to gain a comprehensive understanding of the United Nations.

DESCRIPTION

Internships are available in Communications, Congressional and Corporate Programs, the Field Department, the Model UN and Youth Department, Multilateral Studies, and Public Studies. The UNA internship bulletin describes the role of each department and interns' responsibilities therein. Nevertheless, a few positions are worth elaborating on here.

SELECTIVITY	🔍 🔍
Approximate applicant pool: 100 Interns accepted: 20	

COMPENSATION	$
None	

QUALITY OF LIFE	🏃 🏃 🏃
Access to UN; Brown-bags Free books/posters	

LOCATION(S)	
New York, NY	

FIELD	
International affairs	

DURATION	
10–12 weeks; Summer, Fall, Spring Part time available	

PRE-REQS	
High school students; undergrads, recent grads, grad students	

DEADLINE	
Summer .... before April 1 Fall .... before Aug 1 Spring .... before Jan 15	

Interns in Communications research, fact check, and write small articles for UNA publications. Some interns are assigned to the *InterDependent*, an eight-page, bimonthly newsletter distributed to UNA members, the international affairs community, and journalists. Interns research and analyze such UN-related issues as arms control, international trade, human rights, and environmental protection. Writing assignments aren't always as dry as one might expect; one intern wrote a short piece for the *InterDependent* on the "hairy potato," a fuzzy, insect-trapping spud that needs no insecticide. Other interns do research or proofreading for *A Global Agenda:*

BUSYWORK METER
LOW MEDIUM HIGH
OLDMAN & HAMADEH

Issues Before the General Assembly of the United Nations, an annual volume that offers an overview of global political issues (e.g., disarmament) and the complex UN agenda.

The Model UN and Youth Department oversees the 130 Model United Nations conferences held throughout the country. Thousands of high school and college students attend these conferences to participate in simulated UN Security Council meetings. Interns research and write chapters for UNA's *Guide to Delegate Preparation*, a book that briefs conference participants on the delegates who comprise the Security Council, the international conflict under consideration, the countries involved, and suggestions as to how to resolve the conflict. Combing the stacks of the UN's Dag Hammarskjöld Library and the New York Public Library, interns research a particular country or group of countries, digging up statistics and analyzing governments. They also try to interview a representative of the appropriate country's "mission" (i.e., embassy) to the UN. Most interviews take place by phone, but sometimes diplomats are willing to meet with interns in person. One intern, for instance, arranged a luncheon interview with a press officer from the British mission. She elaborated: "[The *Guide to Delegate Preparation*] circulates throughout the UN. Diplomats care about what we say about their country. They want interns to get it right. Every so often, they'll grant you a live interview."

The Policy Studies department assigns interns to one of its Parallel Studies Programs. In the Asian Security program, for example, interns study such topics as North Korea's nuclear potential, the growing tension in Indian-Pakistani relations, and the establishment of a new political and economic order in the Asia-Pacific region. Alternatively, the East and Central Europe program finds interns analyzing the region's integration into the international economy, the implementation of human rights standards, and the management of security issues.

Approximately one fifth of an intern's work is administrative. Interns must deal with the daily "three *ph*'s": photocopying, phone work, and (ph)axing. "It was never as boring as it could have been," said an intern. "We made the best of it. . . . We played a radio in the background." Interns may also be asked to pick up and deliver documents to UN headquarters, a chore that isn't as dull as it may seem: "It taught you the ins and outs of headquarters—which is valuable when you need to do research there later on."

A brief orientation program marks the beginning of the internship. Interns receive a special handbook that goes over the mechanics of their jobs and lists a series of do's and don'ts ("don't make long-distance personal calls," "don't stay in the office after-hours," etc.). They also get together to plan which speakers they want to invite for the weekly brown-bag luncheons. Past interns have arranged luncheons with such big shots as the president of the UNA and UN delegates from the Netherlands and Malta.

The UNA experience is at once formal and flexible. Interns must adhere to a conservative dress code—suit and tie for men, dresses for women; "sloppy jeans don't go over well here," says the intern coordinator. On the other hand, interns are afforded a lot of freedom. "There's no strict nine-to-five law at the UNA. They let you do your own thing." No one minds if an intern occasionally takes time out for a personal matter or takes a break to get some fresh air.

Located across the street from the marble lions of the New York Public Library, UNA occupies the second floor of a midtown office building. The elevator opens up to an attractive waiting room, decked out with glass walls and official flags. Inside are several offices, a full kitchen, and a conference room resembling "an anteroom to the Oval Office." Interns work together, often three to an office, where they make do with a minimum of office equipment. "The UNA's nonprofit status really shows itself in its lack of equipment," said an intern. "There was no computer terminal expressly for interns and every day we'd have to borrow a computer that wasn't being used by the regular staff."

When life grows tiresome at the UNA office, interns are free to make the 15-minute walk to UN headquarters.

> The Delegate's Lounge "crackled with energy—you didn't actually hear anything, but you knew by people's faces that important discussions were going on."

Armed with a prized UN pass, they have easy access to UN territory. As one intern commented, "although it's in New York, UN headquarters feels like a world unto itself." Indeed it should, for the compound is an international zone, complete with its own laws, flag, and postage stamps. Interns are free to roam through the 39-story glass-and-marble Secretariat tower and the low-domed General Assembly Building. At the latter, they may observe the General Assembly, which is the primary meeting of UN member countries that is held for several months in autumn. Interns may also dine at the Delegate's Lounge, a private, red-carpeted dining room overlooking the East River. A hotbed of "behind-the-scenes diplomatic discussion," the Delegate's Lounge, "crackled with energy—you didn't actually hear anything, but you knew by people's faces that important discussions were going on," said one intern.

Don't count on leaving the internship with a bag full of UNA key chains and windbreakers (if they existed). But there are a few excellent souvenirs to be had. Free copies of books and pamphlets circulate through the office. "I took home all sorts of literature on the UN and international affairs. These reports—especially one on the UN and disarmament—would have come in handy for my senior thesis," said one intern. The Non-Governmental Organization (NGO) office at UN headquarters is another treasure trove of UN literature. But if a sea of UN pamphlets isn't enough, NGO also stocks an assortment of posters, all free for the asking. "Among others, I snagged a sharp-looking poster commemorating the Year of the Indigenous Person," said an intern. By virtue of their internship, interns also receive free membership in the UNA Network, which distributes a bimonthly newsletter and sponsors conferences on international affairs.

SELECTION

The UNA welcomes applications from undergraduates of any level, recent graduates, and graduate students. There are two exceptions; Communications accepts only college seniors and older, and Policy Studies prefers graduate students. Also, the UNA occasionally takes on a few high school students who are, as the coordinator put it, "really sharp." Ideal applicants have strong backgrounds in international affairs as well as good writing and research skills. Although most departments have no hard-and-fast prerequisites, Policy Studies requires foreign language skill and familiarity with a particular country's foreign policy; Congressional and Corporate Programs requires proficiency with computers. Before applying, check the UNA internship bulletin for more details.

APPLICATION PROCEDURE

Final selections for summer internships are made on April 1; for fall internships, August 19; and for spring internships, January 15. The earlier applicants apply, the better their chances of securing the position they desire. Submit a resumé, a writing sample (any brief academic paper), and a UNA application. In addition to asking applicants to name the dates they are available and the program they prefer, the UNA application requires three brief essays explaining one's (1) background in international affairs, (2) special qualifications for the internship (fluency in a foreign language, etc.), and (3) impressions of the UN and its effectiveness in the international system. Application materials are circulated to the director of the programs in which applicants indicate interest. All interviews are held by phone. Selections are often made within a few days of submission of materials.

OVERVIEW

If interning at UN headquarters is like being in the dugout during a baseball game, then interning at the UNA is like having a seat behind home plate. The former may get one closer to the players, but the latter yields a better view of the game. By virtue of the UNA's nonpartisan commitment to education and analysis on the UN, interns leave the UNA with a broad understanding of how the UN works and the issues it faces. Besides important research and writing assignments, UNA interns are given a coveted UN pass with which they may observe UN meetings and briefings. They also have the unique opportunity of selecting their own speakers for a weekly luncheon seminar. In all the right ways, the UNA internship is designed with its interns' education in mind.

FOR MORE INFORMATION . . .

■ United Nations Association of the USA
Intern Coordinator
485 Fifth Avenue
New York, NY 10017
(212) 697-3232

SELECTIVITY	
Approx. applicant pool: 250–300 (Fall,Spr), 500–600 (Sum); Interns accepted: 25–30	

COMPENSATION	$
$45/week, plus room & board	

QUALITY OF LIFE	
Intern seminars; Stunning recreational facilities Excellent food; Freebies; Travel opportunities	

LOCATION(S)
Colorado Springs, CO; Lake Placid, NY; and Marquette, MI

FIELD
Sports Administration

DURATION
Winter/Spring: 21 weeks
Summer: 13 weeks   Fall: 15 weeks

PRE-REQS
College juniors and seniors, recent grads Grad students

DEADLINE
Spring .... October 1   Summer February 15
Fall .... June 1

Johnny Weissmuller snares an amazing five golds in swimming and one bronze in water polo at the 1924 and 1928 Olympics and then plays Tarzan in the 1932 Hollywood classic *Tarzan, the Ape Man*. American Jesse Owens battles racial stereotypes and baffles Adolf Hitler by winning four track-and-field gold medals at the 1936 Olympic Games in Berlin. Prancing pugilist Cassius Clay, later boxing as Muhammad Ali, dazzles the crowds with his punching might and strikes gold at the 1960 Olympics in Rome. A little-known 1980 U.S. ice hockey team upsets the Soviet titans in an inspiring semifinal round match-up at Lake Placid and then defeats Finland to win the gold. A virtual unknown and teenage underdog, Mary Lou Retton captures an all-around gymnastics gold, in addition to two silver and two bronze medals, at 1984's contests in Los Angeles. Since 1896, the modern-day Olympic Games have represented the ultimate athletic contest, testing the strength and will of its participants. Initially a meeting of 13 nations, the Olympic Games now hosts over 180 countries' premier athletes, each intent on returning home, with a medal swinging proudly around his or her neck.

DESCRIPTION

Founded in 1896 by James E. Sullivan as an informal association, the United States Olympic Committee (USOC), as it became known in 1961, served as the major promoter of amateur athletics in America. As the United States' sole coordinating body for the Olympic and Pan American Games competitions, the USOC quickly rose to prominence and attracted such presidents as Major General Douglas MacArthur and sporting goods manufacturer A. G. Spalding. In 1977, the committee unveiled the first-of-its-kind Olympic Training Center in Colorado Springs. One year later, it named the Colorado Springs facility its headquarters as well and hosted the U.S. Olympic Festival, which it now holds every summer between Olympic Games to give American athletes the chance to compete at an Olympic-caliber event.

Today, the USOC has 17 divisions, including Broadcasting, Accounting, Journalism, Computer Science, Sports Administration, Public Relations/Marketing/Fundraising, and Athlete Performance (Weightroom)—and houses the national governing bodies (NGBs) of 25 sports associations. Internships have been available in most of these areas since the early 1980s. While nearly every intern works out of Colorado Springs, there are a few positions in Lake Placid, NY, and Marquette, MI.

Because of the unique nature of each division and NGB, interns' experiences vary considerably. One former intern, working for Coaching Development, became heavily involved in writing for the quarterly magazine *Olympic Coach*. "I wrote research articles, mostly for coaches and physiologists," said the intern. "The stories were usually technical, on subjects like altitude training, banned substances, or time management." He also worked on a special project analyzing whether old military bases could be used as training facilities for future athletes, and attended the annual coaching symposium, hosted by the USOC for coaches from around the world. "I helped out in every way," he said. "I even drove to the airport to pick up the symposium speaker, Digger Phelps, the television sports analyst and former Notre Dame basketball head coach."

Another intern, assigned to Information Services within the U.S. Swimming NGB, sat down with the director her first day to discuss the long- and short-term goals of her public relations internship. For the next three months, she not only answered phones and wrote correspondence but also created a central database of swimming information. "I downloaded facts from the USOC main computer and arranged them in a way that was accessible to the media," she explained. "And I went down into the Archives, a huge vault in the USOC basement, to find old articles and handwritten notes and diaries that described, often in foreign languages, the environment surrounding various swimming meets." She also wrote press releases and articles for *U.S. Swimming*. "I interviewed [famous swimmers such as] Jeff Rouse, Matt Biondi, and Janet Evans," she said. "I was hooked in to the national team."

An intern with the Olympic Job Opportunities Program, which arranges job interviews and employment for the athletes, studied athletes' job training and job transition and went on to develop a career-transition workshop. "I administered self-exploration and career-exploration tests to many of the athletes," he said. "I would match these up to find suitable jobs for them and also provide help with resumés and cover letters." An intern for the U.S. Volleyball Association helped run the association-sponsored volleyball camps. "I scheduled gym and training times, provided keys, arranged transportation, and collected money," she said. Beyond administrative tasks, this intern wrote a manual and worked with sports scientists to design exercise programs for high school and college volleyball players.

Through the gates of the USOC compound, an athlete's paradise awaits. Gymnasiums, weight room, pool, and recreational facilities—this place has it all. A former Air Force base, the center houses athletes and interns, each in their own dormitories. Rent is deducted directly from interns' paychecks. Though no phone jacks are found in the rooms, AT&T sponsors a booth that E.T. would die for that offers free and unlimited five-minute long-distance calls for all interns, athletes, and staff. Gluttons, rejoice, for the USOC provides copious amounts of quality food at the on-site cafeteria. "The dining hall was open from 7:00 AM to 8:00 PM every day," said an intern. "Some of the food was donated by sponsors and we could eat all we wanted." In recent years interns have received free bottles of Evian water at an Evian stand and free haircuts from a Supercuts booth.

The USOC holds biweekly intern seminars, featuring the USOC president, sports psychologists, or career personnel, for example. The intern coordinator also plans events like Broomball Night, trips to Denver Nuggets or Colorado Rockies games, and an end-of-term intern dinner followed by a show at the local theater.

Depending on the office and time of year, interns may also travel. Some interns have worked at the Olympic Festival in various cities around the country and

> "[It's] America; it's red, white, and blue, an opportunity to meet sports figures from around the world."

others have attended an NGB's annual meeting. Interns at the Wrestling NGB once went to North Dakota for the Nationals. The Swimming NGB once flew its intern to Minneapolis for a two-week international swimming competition. Another intern at U.S. Swimming was sent to Olympic Trials in Indianapolis to run the press office: "Here I was, 21 years old, telling people from ABC, CBS, and NBC camera crews where to go and what to do." In a rare fit of adventurousness, the USOC, after listening to a business proposal, sent a Spanish-speaking intern to Barcelona for the '92 Games, where she hired interpreters and set up the hospitality program for corporate sponsors.

But not all is gold in Olympic country. Some interns complain that there is too much secretarial work: "It's frustrating to answer so many phone calls and do so much filing." Others groan about the low pay. And a few complain about the delays inherent in the bureaucracy: "People are always traveling, so if a person whose approval you need is out of town, a project can be put on hold for weeks."

Overall, though, former interns glow about the 12- to 21-week experience. "What you do at the USOC is important and relevant," said an intern. "And the recreational opportunities are terrific." Indeed, in winter months interns ski in Vail. They also attend rock concerts, hike up Pike's Peak, and ride bikes through the nearby Garden of the Gods. Less outdoorsy interns, like the one who described Colorado Springs as "the cultural black hole of America," will find metropolitan Denver a mere 45 minute drive away.

SELECTION

 Undergraduate and graduate students currently working on a degree are eligible to apply. The former must have finished at least two years of college by the start of the program. Recent college graduates will not be considered unless they have been accepted into a graduate program. Moreover, applicants to the International Relations division must be fluent in French or Spanish. Applicants interested in the Legal Affairs division must have completed at least two

years of an accredited law school's program. Because all of the USOC groups utilize computers in their work, familiarity with IBM and/or Macintosh computers and WordPerfect, Paradox, and/or Lotus 1-2-3 is highly desirable. Good writing skills as well as a GPA of 3.0 or better give one an edge. After the intern coordinator screens the applications, "to see how well the applicant followed directions," the materials get passed on to specific departments for review. Interns must have personal accident/health insurance or purchase a short-term policy from the USOC's broker representative.

APPLICATION PROCEDURE

 Applicants must submit the necessary materials by June 1 for the fall semester, February 15 for the summer term, and October 1 for the winter/spring semester. Write for the Student Intern Program Application, which must be included. The form requires the applicant to name three faculty references. A resumé and transcript must also accompany the completed application form. Students may also enclose up to three letters of recommendation and other information that might be relevant, so long as none of it is placed in page protectors or binders. Note: Applicants to the Journalism program must submit six recent writing samples as well. The samples must be on 8-1/2" x 11" paper; newspaper, magazine, booklet, or brochure pieces must be photocopied. The USOC does not return submitted materials.

OVERVIEW

 Representing the major continents, five interlocked rings—blue, black, red, yellow, and green—have stood for nearly 100 years as a symbol of the meeting of world athletes. For over a decade, the USOC's internship program has stood as a symbol of student involvement in the Olympic movement and spirit. Indeed, the coordinator boasts: "The environment here is America; it's red, white, and blue, an opportunity to meet sports figures from around the world." Indeed, this one-of-a-kind program's alumni hold all sorts of positions: University of Miami Athletic

Department administrator, editor for *Cleveland Health* magazine, communications director with the Birmingham Chamber of Commerce, head swimming coach at Colorado College, and marketing employee at Kellogg's Corn Flakes. All in the tradition of *"Citius, Altius, Fortius,"* the Olympic motto meaning "Swifter, Higher, Stronger."

FOR MORE INFORMATION . . .

■ United States Olympic Committee
  Intern Coordinator
  One Olympic Plaza
  Colorado Springs, CO 80909-5760
  (719) 632-5551
  Fax: (719) 578-4817

The City of New York

John Williams is 35 years old, has a prison record, is a possible substance abuser, perhaps mentally ill and is living on the streets.

By one New York City agency's estimate, there are thousands of people like John Williams walking the city's streets every day. Until recently, the City's Department of Social Services was responsible for providing housing and income support to such individuals. But this approach hadn't yielded sufficient results. That's why in February of 1992, the Cuomo Commission recommended that the city create an autonomous agency to focus upon the city's homelessness problem. One of several people in charge of implementing the recommendation was a 22-year-old city employee and a recent college graduate. Working out of the Mayor's Office of Operations, she drafted parts of the implementation plan, organized meetings with the Department of Social Services, and analyzed the new agency's request for vehicles to transport homeless individuals, food, and clothing. She was part of the city's quarter-century-old Urban Fellows Program, a nine-month internship in city management.

SELECTIVITY	🔍 🔍 🔍 🔍
Approximate applicant pool: 350 (UF), 350 (GS) Interns accepted: 24–30 (UF), 24–30 (GS)	

COMPENSATION	$ $ $
Government Scholars – $250/week Urban Fellows – $460/week	

QUALITY OF LIFE	♟ ♟ ♟
High-powered atmosphere; Weekly seminars Government bureaucracy	

LOCATION(S)
New York, NY

FIELD
City government

DURATION
GS: 10 weeks, Summer UF: 9 months, Academic Year

PRE-REQS
GS: College sophomores, juniors and seniors, recent grads   UF: Recent grads

DEADLINE
GS .... January 27 UF .... January 20

DESCRIPTION

In 1968, an administrator at the office of Mayor John Lindsay made a proposal: "Why don't we give 20 students the opportunity to work full-time in city management?" The city agreed; the Alfred P. Sloan Foundation donated two years' worth of stipends, and the Urban Fellows Program was born. It soon evolved into a nationwide competition for the country's brightest college students. "This was the late 1960s," said founder Sigmund Ginsburg, now vice president of New York's Barnard College. "It was a period of hope, and the charisma of Mayor Lindsay attracted the best students. We placed them in his office back then—as assistants to the commissioner, budget director, superintendent, and the like."

But the desire for direct contact with citizens became greater and greater. "Not every student wanted to sit behind a desk all day long. Some wanted 'street work,'" explained Ginsburg. "So we made available up to 100 meaningful jobs from which the Fellows could choose—jobs affording daily contact with people." The Fellows were also exposed to various big-shots at weekly off-the-record seminars, featuring such guests as the police

BUSYWORK METER
LOW MEDIUM HIGH
OLDMAN & HAMADEH

commissioner, the mayor, political commentator William F. Buckley, and columnist Jimmy Breslin.

Little has changed since that promising beginning. The Urban Fellows Program still starts with an orientation, though the original two weeks have been expanded to nearly four. Fellows spend a week exploring a borough and then make presentations on their findings. They attend lectures. They take tours of the city, to observe how city policy affects the city's residents and sometimes ride along in patrol cars with on-duty police officers. "Over four or five hours, we ran across vandalism . . . and even the scene of a shooting," said a ride-along participant. Other interns have toured Rikers Island, a state maximum-security penitentiary. "I talked to some inmates and learned how complex our whole penal system is," said one. "It was a chilling experience. To this day, I can still hear the checkpoint gates slamming behind me as we left."

After orientation, Fellows explore as many as two hundred placement possibilities within the mayor's office and its agencies. On the basis of a dozen to several dozen interviews, Fellows select positions best suiting their interests and needs. "You get to decide where you want to go—a sleepy old office or the firing line," said an Urban Fellow. Once Fellows are placed, their tasks run the gamut. Working on short- and long-term projects, they do everything from policy consultation and planning to administrative problem solving and delivery of services.

One Fellow, working as an assistant commissioner to Personnel, helped to reshape the entire 3,000-member Human Resources department. "I evaluated the goals of the department, changed the way performance evaluations are conducted, added recognition awards, established training and development programs, and set up an internship program," he said. Twelve years later, many of the programs he implemented are still in place.

A Fellow with the Economic Policy and Marketing group worked on several research projects with the chief economist. One project dealt with recycling. "I tried to develop a strategy to dispose of the large volume of waste collected," he said. "We figured out ways to entice businesses to come into the city and create jobs in waste management." Another project analyzed Business Improvement Districts (BID), areas in which property owners have agreed to pay additional fees in exchange for extra security and sanitation services. "I reworked the 24 different formulas that determine how much each BID should pay," he said.

Like the two previous examples, most Fellows occupy bureaucratic positions. Some Fellows, however, get involved with the public. A Fellow at the Center for Collaborative Education co-taught an elective course at a local high school. Titled *Power New York City*, the class provided an insider's view of the history and politics of the city. The experience was particularly relevant to a Board of Education project upon which he worked—the construction of 12 new high schools. "I helped find space, teachers, and funds," he said.

Committed to providing the Fellows with a broad overview of city management, program administrators arrange weekly seminars with high-level city officials. Since Mayor Lindsay's administration, officials from a host of departments like the Department of Corrections, the Police department, the Center for Collaborative Education, and the Board of Education, have made appearances. In unofficial one- to three-hour meetings, Fellows comment on city policies. "I'd go for the guts and ask politically challenging questions, putting the speaker on the defensive," said one Fellow.

Urban Fellows make two formal out-of-town visits—one to the state capital in Albany, the other to the nation's capital in Washington. In Albany, Urban Fellows tour government buildings and meet legislators and state officials. In Washington, Fellows evaluate the federal government's obligations to America's cities, particularly

> "You get to decide where you want to go—a sleepy old office or the firing line. . . ."

New York City. In 1993, Fellows met with senators and representatives, observed Mayor Dinkins give testimony to a committee on urban policy, talked with officials from HUD, Labor, and Commerce, and met with Attorney General Janet Reno.

Because the goal of the program is to promote learning and to offer a beneficial experience, unhappy Urban Fellows may request a transfer to another city department. Though rare, these transfers have occurred. One Fellow felt that he was spending too much time transcribing notes, so he switched departments to relocate to the New York City Transit Authority, which runs the city's subways and bus lines. "I worked in the Special Events unit and helped arrange the filming of subways for movies like *Ghost*," he said. "Sometimes I staffed the night filmings, making sure that the producers adhered to safety considerations as laid out in the contracts." Transferring doesn't guarantee happiness, however. "Because the Transit Authority is such a huge organization, I did almost as much memo writing and paper pushing as before," he said.

In 1980, then-Deputy Mayor Ronay Menschel decided that college undergraduates would benefit from a full-time introduction to city management as well. Modeled after the Urban Fellows Program, the Government Scholars Program began placing students that year.

Government Scholars participate in a shorter orientation than in the Urban Fellows Program. During this time, they interview with potential supervisors in order to best match their interests and needs. Like Urban Fellows, they work on short- and long-term projects in such areas as human services, criminal justice, health, housing, transportation, and economic development. They also analyze and review policy and do fieldwork.

One Government Scholar worked for the deputy chancellor of New York City public schools. "I wrote a lot of letters explaining school-wide policy to parents and matched corporate resources to school programs," he said. "But I benefited most by watching rather than doing— observing task force briefings and participating in seminars." Another researched AIDS-discrimination cases, writing reports and making recommendations. "Some of my work even got incorporated into policy," she said.

Focusing on homeless shelters, a Scholar in Social Services found that the city's transitional housing was not being allocated efficiently. "I would visit the three shelters in our charge and talk to homeless people so I could understand their point of view," she stated. Out of these first-hand glimpses, she developed a guide for case workers, which is still used today.

Government Scholars have the opportunity to attend weekly seminars. Though these seminars "do not provide as in-depth a look at the issues as the Urban Fellow seminars," explains the program director, Government Scholars speak well of them. "We met many high-powered commissioners, usually politically astute people we'd read about in the papers," said a former Scholar.

Government Scholars and Urban Fellows work throughout the city, in buildings described mostly as needing major renovation. Interns are often afforded their own cubicle space, equipped with a computer and a phone. They have access to municipal libraries and New York University research facilities.

Government Scholars work ten weeks while Urban Fellows serve nine-month tenures. "[We] can't get very involved in that short amount of time," commented one Scholar. "Urban Fellows' yearlong commitment and direct contact with the mayor, on the other hand, elevate them to a whole new level." Affirmed another: "If the Urban Fellows Program is the main course, then the Government Scholars Program is the appetizer." Nevertheless, the Government Scholars experience heightens many participants' awareness to sensitive urban issues. "It got me addicted to city government," one scholar said.

Many Government Scholars go back to school optimistic about their ability to make a difference. But many Urban Fellows finish the program frustrated at their difficulty in breaking through an entrenched bureaucracy. "Agencies are too slow to respond," said one. "City administration is neither effective nor efficient," added another. "Moreover, the inflexible nine-to-five work schedule often makes our job routine." However, many fight back in creative ways. "My year, the 24 Urban Fellows created a network," said one of them. "We finished projects faster by collaborating and by sidestepping formal channels."

SELECTION

 By the start of the internship in September, Urban Fellows must be college graduates but must not have been out of college for more than two years. Government Scholars must be sophomores, juniors, or seniors. College graduates less than a year out of college by the start of the Government Scholars Program may apply as well. So long as they are interested in pursuing public service careers, students of any academic major are eligible. Applicants must display demonstrated leadership, whether as elected campus officials or as heads of organizations. The director mentions "intellectual ability and flexibility," "scholastic aptitude," and "willingness to look at issues with an open mind" as additional helpful traits.

APPLICATION PROCEDURE

 Deadlines are as follows: January 20 postmark for Urban Fellows; January 27 postmark for Government Scholars. Applicants must submit a completed original application form, a resumé, an official transcript, three (two for Government Scholars) letters of recommendation from academic or professional sources, and two essays—a description of goals and an autobiographical statement. A panel of readers, consisting of Urban Fellow and Government Scholar alumni, and city managers, scores all applications. While Government Scholars are selected solely on the highest scores, Urban Fellows are selected on the highest scorers' completion of a half day of interviews in New York. The interview process includes three one-on-one interviews and one panel interview. Insider's tip: The panel interview consists of a public policy exercise in which the applicant recommends some solution to a social problem.

The Department of Personnel manages three other internship programs as well—the Urban Corps, the Summer Graduate and Undergraduate Internship, and the Public Service Corps. The Urban Corps, the first public service internship established in America, places up to 2,500 undergraduate and graduate students in paid or academic credit/volunteer positions throughout the city. The next program provides salaried employment to graduate students in city agencies. The last internship places high school students, undergraduates, and graduates in health and human services jobs. Write or call to get more information (Urban Corps [212] 487-5669, Public Service Corps [212] 487-5655, Summer Graduate and Undergraduate Internship [212] 487-5698).

OVERVIEW

 New York, New York—city of possibility and opportunity. "If I can make it there, I'll make it anywhere," as the song goes. That city, in fact, is the only city in the United States to offer a comprehensive government internship to young people. If interns can make a dent in the problems ravaging America's largest city, then there's hope for cities nationwide. Challenging officials at weekly meetings, these college students and graduates—Government Scholars and Urban Fellows—help the impoverished, analyze AIDS policies, and tackle problems in recycling, education, transportation, and many other areas. Now many of them are making it in the Big Apple and elsewhere as assemblymen, vice presidents on Wall Street, and directors of public service organizations. Most of the former Urban Fellows are also part of the Urban Fellows Alumni Association, which volunteers time at homeless shelters, drug rehab clinics, and the like. "We made an impact then," said an alumnus, "We feel that we should make an impact now, too." Now that sounds like the determination and optimism characteristic of someone who has lived in the "city that never sleeps."

FOR MORE INFORMATION . . .

■ City of New York
Department of Personnel
(Name of Program)
2 Washington Street, 15th Floor
New York, NY 10004
(212) 487-5698

It is 1969, and Disney Studios wants to feature a car in its upcoming movie. After filling the parking lot with suitable candidates, Disney employees examine each automobile, scrutinizing the frame, fondling the upholstery, beeping the horn, and kicking the tires. But when they come to one car—a Volkswagen Beetle—they simply pat it. They don't have to subject the Beetle to any tests—they've found their star. That Beetle would eventually play Herbie, the hero of 1969's *The Love Bug* and its sequel, *Herbie Rides Again*. A few years later, on reflection, producer Bill Walsh (not the football coach) would say: "The VW had a personality of its own, which reached out and embraced people."

Interestingly enough, that's just what the Beetle's inventor intended back in the 1930s when he dreamed up his peculiar-looking auto, calling it Volkswagen—"people's car" in German. But the first Beetles built, in 1935, were used solely by the German military for World War II. Dr. Ferdinand Porsche (the first "modern" Porsche sports car was his brainchild) had to wait until 1945 to make his first commercial Beetle. Nevertheless, it was a hit; within two years his factory had built more than 10,000 Beetles and had also introduced the Microbus, aka, the VW Bus. By the end of the 1960s, Volkswagen was selling nearly 500,000 Beetles per year in the United States alone, and their owners were in love with their car. This prompted *Life* to write: "A VW is a member of the family that just happens to live in the garage." Volkswagen has now sold over 21 million Beetles (a world record for a single model) and millions of Audis, Golfs, Rabbits, Cabriolets, Sciroccos, Jettas, Passats, Corrados, Vanagons, and EuroVans too, making it the world's fourth largest car maker.

SELECTIVITY

Approximate applicant pool: 100
Interns accepted: 13

COMPENSATION

None

QUALITY OF LIFE

Monthly intern meetings
International flavor

LOCATION(S)

Auburn Hills, MI

FIELD

Automobiles

DURATION

1–6 months
Year-round

PRE-REQS

Undergrads

DEADLINE

Rolling

BUSYWORK MEDIUM
LOW HIGH
OLDMAN & HAMADEH
METER

DESCRIPTION

Volkswagen's internship program differs from those of other large corporations in one important respect: VW's doesn't pay. But that doesn't mean that interns are second-class citizens, says the coordinator. "We may not provide them with an hourly wage like we used to, but we still carefully screen for candidates who would qualify for our full-time College-Grad-In-Training (CGIT) positions after college." Unfortunately, the auto-industry slump, which prevents VW from paying interns, has also slowed the flow of new hires to a trickle.

Yet no pay and no guarantee of permanent employment doesn't keep VW from assigning interns the work of its regular full-time employees. It also doesn't stop the company from placing interns in every division—Volkswagen United States, Audi of America Sales & Marketing, Public Affairs, Human Resources, Finance, VW Credit Inc., Parts and Information Organization, and Corporate Staffing. "This is a real job with real responsibilities," confirmed an intern. "There's no coddling going on here."

An intern in Audi Marketing worked on a project stemming from Audi's European golf tournament. "Audi wanted to start a tourney somewhere in the United States, perhaps Chicago or Dallas," he said. "I went over rules and regulations and analyzed the advantages and disadvantages of making it pro or amateur." In another project he analyzed Audi's auto show budgets. "In 1992, over ten million people attended the United States' 24 auto shows. . . . [W]e wanted to make an impact on that many people, but our costs were too high relative to returns." Breaking down last year's figures into costs for transportation, setup, take-down, warehousing, and space, he helped determine where cuts should be made. "I worked side by side with VW's special promotions manager," he said.

A Public Relations intern wrote articles for VW and Audi newsletters. Sometimes he searched for auto industry news in major newspapers. Other times, he wrote serious stories on management changes, new technologies, and new services. "Of course, some pieces were more fun to do than others," he said, "like the one about all the special effort that went into delivering Michael Keaton's customized van to his Montana home, or another about my two-day trip to Oklahoma City to cover Auto Cross, a road race pitting two VW Corrados against each other."

Like employees, interns are encouraged to offer suggestions to management. "Maybe because we aren't paid,

managers feel obligated to include us as much as possible," said an intern. "They make us feel like part of the team." The vice president of Audi, for example, makes it a point to know all interns on a first-name basis. He is often seen walking up to interns and asking them how their projects are going. "When he asks, he means it," said an intern. "VW wants everyone, including interns, to help improve operations."

In order to streamline business operations, the company frequently asks interns to transform their ideas into action. For example, an Audi Marketing intern attended a meeting of district operations managers and sales consultants from around the country. "They pointed out that all of VW's incentive and advertising programs are described in separate booklets, perhaps twenty in all," said the intern. "Many expressed how inefficient that was and said that they were often missing information, especially since they didn't always get every booklet. I thought to myself, this is a situation ripe for consolidation." After the meeting, he went up to the division head and proposed putting together a guide. "The guide would provide a reference for VW's zone and district managers and consultants. Impressed, his boss gave him the go-ahead. "I interviewed people and pored through booklets to find out what information should be included," he said. "Now the company has a guide that shows managers what kinds of ads are acceptable for local campaigns, tells them how to do a direct mailing, and describes in detail all of VW's dealer incentive programs." The intern pointed out that VW's outside consultant would have charged $50,000 to undertake such a project. "My bid—free of charge—obviously saved the company a lot of money."

Interns work out of fully furnished, Macintosh equipped cubicles in a four-story building shaped like an *L*. "It looks like a boomerang or like a Pac-Man getting ready to chomp down on some dots," said an intern. On sunny days, interns can often be found eating their lunch on the company picnic tables in the backyard, amidst a spouting fountain, a river, a walking path, and a man-made pond "containing six families of geese."

> On sunny days, interns can often be found eating their lunch on the company picnic tables in the backyard, amidst a spouting fountain and a man-made pond.

Interns are treated no differently than VW employees. Both groups get security cards (for access into the building), security clearances to use computers, and computer files for E-mail, spreadsheets, and word processing. When employees listen to a sports medicine doctor speak on the health benefits of walking or to a vice president discuss company policies, interns are often in attendance as well. At the company picnic, interns chow chicken and flick Frisbees with the best of them.

About once a month, interns get together on their own. "These occasional meetings are the only things that distinguish us from regular employees," said an intern. Interns tour a Detroit VW dealership and visit a Mazda manufacturing plant in order to witness the intricacies of auto manufacturing. "We would have loved to see VW cars being manufactured," said one disappointed intern, "but unfortunately, the nearest VW plant is in Mexico." Other gatherings introduce new products or discuss how to handle VW's German employees calling from overseas with questions: "We were reminded to take our conversations slowly and not get frustrated by the broken English."

International interns, mostly German and usually selected by the company's international headquarters in Wolfsburg, Germany, often join their American counterparts in these activities. Engaged in the same type of work as American interns, overseas students are also assigned housing by VW, either with an employee's family or in an apartment with several other interns. Fortunately, American interns may also tap VW for these housing arrangements. But the similarities stop there. Unlike Americans, international students are provided with funds for housing, living, and transportation expenses. One might think that this salary policy is as acceptable to Volkswagen's American interns as Wiener schnitzel in a burger joint. Maybe so, were the two kinds of students working under the same program. However, overseas students situated in Detroit work under the auspices of the German parent's more rigorous trainee program. Administered out of Wolfsburg, the program places an overwhelming majority of them in permanent positions upon completion of the internship. No matter, the Americans say, because the Germans infuse the company with that famous Bavarian work ethic and teach interns about another culture.

During the summer, interns convene in the board room for a reception with the president and other top management. A total of about 20 people discuss the effectiveness of the internship program. "I told them that I had felt cramped, that VW didn't give me enough opportunities to explore the other departments," said an intern. Added another, "At the orientation, they should have given us a reference guide explaining how to use the voice mail, phone, and computer systems; I finally settled in, but it took some time." Add to these comments the supervisor and intern evaluations, which are written at the conclusion of students' internships, and VW gets its fill of feedback that is sure to improve the program.

SELECTION

 All undergraduates are eligible to apply, although "older, experienced students" are more likely to be accepted. No particular major is required. While the company does not adhere to a minimum GPA, the coordinator says that successful applicants tend to have at least a 3.0 GPA. "Applicants must show something in their backgrounds—a focus or some experience relevant to a VW department," she adds. "That helps us to make a good match."

APPLICATION PROCEDURE

 The deadline is rolling. Applicants should submit a resumé and cover letter several months before the anticipated starting date. Candidates making it past the initial round will receive a letter that reiterates that the internship is nonpaid and asks them to call the internship coordinator should they still want the internship. Those whose interest hasn't waned receive phone or on-site interviews with the department in which they have been placed. In some cases, interns can arrange to receive academic credit by taking the VW internship as an independent study class. If so, VW will reimburse students' tuition fees for up to four semester units, so long as they turn in the Tuition Refund Application Form and supporting documentation prior to the start of the internship.

OVERVIEW

 The needs of the people—this was VW's driving concern when it designed the Beetle. After nearly 50 years, the company still focuses on the common consumer. VW also realizes that self-motivated employees are critical to its success. Because interns are a potential source of such employees, the company creates an atmosphere that allows the ablest interns to have an impact upon the business. They're regular employees, working on team projects, under the eyes of managers who hold high expectations. "If you think about it, I'm just an everyday student," said an intern. "But VW treated my ideas with the utmost seriousness." No doubt a policy Dr. Porsche, "people's car" inventor, would have endorsed.

FOR MORE INFORMATION . . .

■ Volkswagen of America, Inc.
Staffing Department
3800 Hamlin Road
Auburn Hills, MI 48326
(313) 340-5000

THE WALL STREET JOURNAL.

What do Spam and the Pulitzer Prize have in common? If you ask Tom Knudson, he might tell you that if you write about the former, you may eventually win the latter. A tenuous connection at best, but Knudson got his journalistic feet wet as an intern with *The Wall Street Journal*, where he wrote, among other stories, a witty piece on the history of that lunch-box favorite, Spam. In the 12 years that followed, Knudson reported for the *Des Moines Register*, *The New York Times*, and the *Sacramento Bee*, and won two Pulitzer Prizes in the process.

Interning at *The Wall Street Journal* does not destine a person to win the Pulitzer Prize, even if that person has an abiding interest in canned pork shoulder. It does, however, expose one to the inner workings of what many deem America's most influential newspaper. Founded in 1889 as a four-page bulletin pledging to offer "a faithful picture of the rapidly shifting panorama of [Wall] Street," the *Journal* has grown into an international daily with a circulation larger than that of any other U.S. newspaper. Despite this stature, it strives to adhere to old values, namely "accuracy, independence, and fairness." If the independent surveys that consistently show the *Journal* to be America's most trusted publication are any indication, it is doing an admirable job.

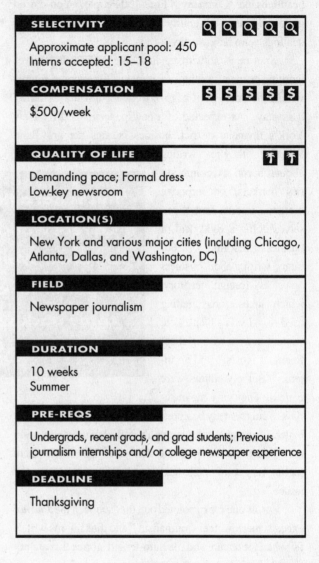

SELECTIVITY

Approximate applicant pool: 450
Interns accepted: 15–18

COMPENSATION

$500/week

QUALITY OF LIFE

Demanding pace; Formal dress
Low-key newsroom

LOCATION(S)

New York and various major cities (including Chicago, Atlanta, Dallas, and Washington, DC)

FIELD

Newspaper journalism

DURATION

10 weeks
Summer

PRE-REQS

Undergrads, recent grads, and grad students; Previous journalism internships and/or college newspaper experience

DEADLINE

Thanksgiving

DESCRIPTION

The Wall Street Journal interns concur: The internship begins fast and furious. "A story was assigned to me at noon on my first day. It was panic city! But I made it through relatively unscathed," said an intern. His experience sums up a distinctive feature of the *Journal* internship: An intern's work is completely substantive and demanding, particularly in the sense that interns are not coddled through it. "You do the kind of work a regular reporter does," stated an intern. "The editors give you direction, but there isn't much hand holding. They throw you into the fire, expecting you to write from day one."

Interns spend a good deal of time working on "spot news," meaning they man phones and watch news wires for the latest news on companies. Fielding press releases as soon as the news comes in, interns determine which pieces are appropriate as small stories for the paper. Spot news also provides information for the Dow Jones News Wire, a financial news service used by investment banks, brokerage houses, and private investors. "I'd constantly call the New York office to report headlines like 'Company X Fires 100 People.' You'd need good judgment—an ability to evaluate whether business dealings were newsworthy."

Spot news notwithstanding, interns find themselves working on meaty writing assignments. On average, interns write about three front-page or front-section stories during their stay. As expected of a newspaper named for New York's financial district, business stories are prevalent. Whether they're writing about tobacco tax, commodities markets, or corporate mergers, interns find themselves doing a good deal of business reporting. For many, writing about business news is foreign territory, which takes some getting used to. "I was a blank slate when it came to writing about financial issues," said an intern. "But my editors were patient. They gave me materials to augment my business background. Gradually, I got better." In general, interns rave about the business education they receive working at the *Journal*: "You leave there feeling very comfortable talking and writing about financial issues."

But, as one intern pointed out, the "scope of the *Journal* exceeds mere business journalism," and thus interns write a fair share of feature and medium-length stories that are not directly business related. One intern wrote a feature story analyzing whether 900-number legal help services provide valuable advice. Another wrote about men who have chosen the priesthood as a second career, his story focusing on how the traditionalists of one seminary viewed these second-career clergymen. Stories are many and varied: "At the *Journal* I wrote on a different topic every few days . . . things stayed fresh and involving." One intern remembers reporting on the decline in Chicago's housing market one week and the perils of pig farming another.

Many interns have ample opportunity to work on so-called softer news. Some write "orphans," the small, offbeat stories appearing in the lower left-hand corner on page-one of the paper's Marketplace section. "I had a lot of fun writing

an orphan about a white-water rafting trip executives take in West Virginia," recalled an intern. Others write "a-heds," the quirky stories found on the middle of the front page. A-hed topics run the gamut and have covered everything from old-fashioned sporting goods stores to Memphis barbecue stands to a man who spends his life retrieving and reselling used golf balls. One enterprising intern convinced an editor that he should write an a-hed about rock musicians who engage in social activism; he ended up being flown to Philadelphia, where, armed with a press pass, he covered the historic Live Aid concert. "It was a kick," he said. "I mingled backstage with rock stars, talked with all sorts of music industry bigwigs, and was invited back to Jackson Browne's house, where I interviewed him over lunch."

> "This is not a fluff internship—it's a real working experience. You are a *Wall Street Journal* reporter for a summer . . . come back with a story or fall flat on your face."

While the Live Aid piece demonstrates the editors' receptivity to self-generated stories, the majority of stories are assigned by the editors. After writing a story, an intern submits it to an editor, who critiques it and often allows the intern to make revisions. "After an editor read your story, you'd get to do your own editing, which differs from other newspapers I've worked on, where once you wrote the first draft, it was out of your hands," recalled an intern. Reworking their stories, interns hone their writing skills, learning journalism under the guidance of some of the best newswriters in the business. Interns also learn the inimitable style of the *Journal*, which, some say, is sharp, punchy, and more analytical than most newspapers. Said one intern: "Unlike the vast majority of papers, which tell what happened and little more, the *Journal* strives to provide analysis of what happened. Its reporters try to link situations together and draw conclusions."

Just as the perspective of the *Journal* differs from most newspapers, so does its office environment. At the New York office, one finds not a frenetic Lou Grant-style sweatshop, but a relatively low-key newsroom, more reminiscent of an insurance office than a major newspaper. One intern likened the feel of the New York office to that of a university, populated by reporters who debate issues and write books in their spare time. Most of the staff in New York dress formally; "jackets and ties were commonplace among men," observed an intern. Situated on New York Harbor, *Journal* headquarters stands across from the World Trade Center, with a view of the Statue of Liberty. Interns get their own desks, although in recent years a lack of space has necessitated that some use the desks of vacationing reporters.

In addition to the seven or so interns who work in the New York office, interns are placed in bureaus across the country. *Journal* outposts in such cities as Washington, D.C., Chicago, Atlanta, and Dallas accept interns, with usually one intern per bureau, although the bureaus hiring interns vary from year to year. Bureaus are considerably smaller than the New York office, and are thus more conducive to meeting people. They also tend to be roomier, as most are located in cities where space is not such a scarce commodity. Happily, the dress code is usually looser in the bureaus, too.

The *Journal* has no special programs for interns. It's a no-frills experience: no orientation, no weekly speaker series, and no parkside picnics. Perhaps the intern coordinator said it best: "This is not a fluff internship—it's a real working experience. You are a *Wall Street Journal* reporter for a summer. Come back with a story or fall flat on your face." Interns generally appreciate the *Journal*'s no-nonsense attitude, seeing it as an opportunity for responsibility and freedom: "The permanent staff respected [the interns]. They didn't need to indulge us with a lot of extra activities because there was so much meaningful work to do. They wanted us to learn to be better reporters." Even so, the *Journal*'s relatively unstructured program does not garner unanimous praise. "Some interns during my tenure at the *Journal* felt lost," remarked an intern. "They weren't getting much to do and they didn't have gumption to demand more action." Another intern echoed the same problem: "It's a fast-paced place. Some interns floundered when they did not receive enough guidance." On the whole, however, interns are more than satisfied with their work and the way in which it was assigned.

This satisfaction is evident in the large number of interns who seek permanent positions at the *Journal*, although openings are scarce. According to the coordinator, in one year 5 former interns were hired out of an intern class of 15; in other years, none were hired. On the average, the *Journal* taps one former intern about every other year.

SELECTION

 The internship is open to undergraduates, recent graduates, and graduate students. About half of the internships go to minority applicants. The application bulletin states that "in-depth reporting and writing experience on campus papers and previous internships at other newspapers are essential." While the majority of interns surveyed had solid journalistic backgrounds before applying, a few had relatively little experience; said one intern: "It varies; most interns my summer were well-credentialed journalists, but I knew a few without much experience, especially when it came to reporting on business. There's a sense that the *Journal* will take a chance on a few applicants who lack a lot of experience but demonstrate great enthusiasm." Besides having a passion for their work, interns should be "adaptable," "assertive," and "enterprising." Said one intern: "This job is 90 percent attitude. You've got to soak up everything you can from the permanent reporters. You must be open to their guidance."

APPLICATION PROCEDURE

 Procrastinators, take note: Application materials must be submitted before Thanksgiving. Applicants should send a cover letter, resumé, and clips of journalistic work to Richard Martin, the *Journal*'s assistant managing editor and longtime intern coordinator. He and a few other staff members comprise a committee that whittles the applicant pool down to a final group of about 40 applicants. Finalists are interviewed in person or over the phone. The bureau chiefs in various cities then choose whom they want as interns, selecting a total of about 15 applicants.

OVERVIEW

 Interning at *The Wall Street Journal* is no toe-dip in a bubble bath, it's a full-body plunge into a chilly sea of journalistic responsibility and prestige. Although coddling is about as likely as a "Dear Abby" column's appearing in the *Journal*, interns receive an unmatched initiation into the world of big-time reporting. With a *Journal* internship under one's belt, there's no limit to what one can do professionally. Just ask Derek Dingle. After interning in the *Journal*'s Chicago bureau, he eventually became managing editor of *Black Enterprise* magazine. He now runs a company that makes comic books featuring black superheroes, and when recently the *Journal* described his venture in its Business and Race section, he remarked: "In ten years, I went from writing *for* the *Journal* to being written about *by* the *Journal*."

FOR MORE INFORMATION . . .

■ The Wall Street Journal
Internship Program
c/o Richard Martin, Assistant Managing Editor
200 Liberty Street
New York, NY 10281

Washington Internships for Students of Engineering

At many colleges, students are divided into two camps—"techies" and "fuzzies," the former are number-crunching, formula-figuring, laboratory-dwelling science lovers, while the latter are politically minded, java-drinking, essay-writing, liberal arts students. But have you ever run across a "fuzzy techy"? They're a rare breed, particularly when it comes to engineering students who have a solid grasp of government. Yet, in our increasingly technological society, the need for people conversant in both science and policy cannot be overemphasized: The Washington Internships for Students of Engineering (WISE), was created to address this necessity.

DESCRIPTION

In 1973, University of Washington Engineering Professor Barry Hyman served a one-year tenure as a congressional Fellow. Through this experience, he realized that undergraduate engineering students would benefit from a similar experience and founded WISE in 1978. Supported by a generous National Science Foundation grant and funds from private engineering societies, the program welcomed its first class of interns in 1980. Now entirely self-supporting, the program is "one of the few things in Washington operating with no government funding," said Director Michael Devine. About ten professional engineering societies sponsor one or two students each, providing WISE with around $6,000 per student. A portion of this money goes to the faculty-in-residence, an engineering professor chosen each year to oversee the interns and their work.

WISE introduces students to Washington and the technical public policy issues debated

SELECTIVITY	🔍 🔍 🔍
Approximate applicant pool: 100 Interns accepted: 15	

COMPENSATION	$ $ $
$2,700 stipend plus travel allowance	

QUALITY OF LIFE	⬆ ⬆ ⬆ ⬆
Independence; Meetings with political big-wigs Dorm housing; Faculty-in-residence	

LOCATION(S)
Washington, DC

FIELD
Technological policy research

DURATION
10 weeks Summer

PRE-REQS
College seniors in engineering

DEADLINE
December 20

there. Students attend 20 to 30 meetings organized by their faculty-in-residence. One to two hours in length, the meetings begin with a presentation followed by a question and answer period. One year, for example, saw sessions with Senators David Pryor (D-Ark.) and John Glenn (D-Ohio) as well as the heads of the Office of Technology Assessment, the House Committee on Science, Space, and Technology, the National Academy of Sciences, and the Office of Science and Technology Policy. The same year, interns were treated to a meeting with President Bush's science adviser. "We took a

tour of the Executive Office Building and then discussed Bush's science policy," said one intern. "Although we had heard a rumor that the adviser disapproved of Bush's science policy, none of us dared to bring it up."

But discussions with government officials do not constitute the entire experience. The primary objective of the program obligates each student to write a research paper "that analyzes specific engineering public policy issues of concern to the sponsoring society," as the brochure explains. Papers explore topics like global environmental governance, free-trade policy, U.S. industrial competitiveness, and defense downsizing. One student, who analyzed the Nuclear Regulatory Commission's response to the Three Mile Island disaster, read briefs and interviewed several of the people involved. "In Washington, the most valuable information comes from the people currently wrestling with the issues," he said. "So I talked to decision makers at NASA and the Department of Defense, and to lobbyists and technical assistants. By the end of the summer, I understood nuclear policy better than I ever thought I could."

Another intern, exploring the government's control of unclassified information, combed through books and journals in an attempt to familiarize herself with current policies. She soon learned that the timeliness of the issues demanded an investigation of the committees and legislators themselves. "This was no ordinary research paper," she said. "Because my topic was current, I needed to interview those people helping to shape policy, particularly aides to the top brass at the Defense Department."

Aware that the average college student has little access to high-level officials, the full-time faculty-in-residence often helps track down important policymakers. When an intern needed to speak with the person in charge of nuclear plant licensing but couldn't arrange an interview, so he turned to the faculty-in-residence. "The professor knew some important people at the Nuclear Regulatory Commission," he said. "His connections helped me land several meetings."

Sponsored by the American Institute of Chemical Engineers, an intern researched hazardous waste minimization in the United States. Starting at the Georgetown library, he read many articles on his topic to gain insight into the issue. "Once I had done that," he said, "I talked extensively to staff members in all three branches of government in order to understand the government's policy toward hazardous waste." By the end, interns often amass so much material that a gargantuan task awaits. Some feel rushed to complete the write-up on time. Even so, one ambitious intern wrote 100 pages on his topic. While few interns go to such extreme lengths, final papers average 40 pages and are comparable in scope, the director says, to an undergraduate thesis.

Housed together in a George Washington University dormitory, interns can't help but interact with each other daily. Though the faculty-in-residence does not live in the dorm, interns are able to discuss research issues and paper ideas with the professor at daily morning meetings. "The faculty-in-residence," said one, "is an integral part of the program." Besides the in-house professor, students take advantage of Washington resources like the Library of Congress and the Congressional Research Service. Interns typically analyze the information derived from these sources in the privacy of their communal office, which is equipped with computers and a laser printer.

In addition to the meetings organized by the faculty-in-residence, WISE arranges a few special luncheons and dinners. Interns congregate on The Mall for a picnic. They also travel to various points beyond the Beltway. One year, for example, interns toured the infamous Three Mile Island nuclear power plant. Occasionally, a sponsoring society sends an intern to its annual convention, where the intern presents his or her summer paper.

Some interns are unhappy with the stipend, especially since they must earmark half of it for rent. "The pay may be sufficient to live on," said one intern, "but it's still not enough." WISE eases some of the financial burden by

> "If you are an engineer interested in the broader implications of engineering, in understanding how technology plays a role in public policy, then WISE up—this program is for you."

covering round-trip travel, whether students fly or drive. At the end of the summer, interns receive an overall grade and three units of credit from Florida State University, which they can transfer to their respective institutions, offsetting graduating requirements in some cases.

SELECTION

 The internship is for undergraduate engineering students only. Applicants must have at least completed their junior year by the start of the internship and must be returning to school the following academic year for at least one semester. While applicants should have good grades, they must also demonstrate leadership in campus activities and be interested in public policy.

APPLICATION PROCEDURE

 The deadline is December 20. Students must turn in a completed application form, a short essay, resumé, transcript, and letters of recommendation to the address below. WISE administrators screen the initial pool of applicants. Finalists are then chosen by the sponsoring engineering societies, who assist the interns in choosing research paper topics before the program begins.

OVERVIEW

 Engineering students, think big. Abandon the classroom and spend a summer discovering how science can contribute to public policy decisions. WISE invites a troop of talented techies to the nation's capital and brings them face-to-face with top policymakers. Factor in the required research paper, and interns have one heck of a learning experience. At the very least, a summer with WISE will heighten students' overall interest in politics. And some may even be inspired to incorporate government into their technical careers. One WISE intern went on to assist President Bush's domestic policy adviser. Another was inspired to augment his engineering background with a law degree, and he ended up clerking for Supreme Court Justice Sandra Day O'Connor. As a WISE alumnus puts it: "If you are an engineer interested in the broader implications of engineering, in understanding how technology plays a role in public policy, then WISE up—this program is for you."

FOR MORE INFORMATION . . .

■ Washington Internships for Students of Engineering
1899 L Street NW, Suite 500
Washington, DC 20036
(202) 466-8744

The Washington Post

SELECTIVITY	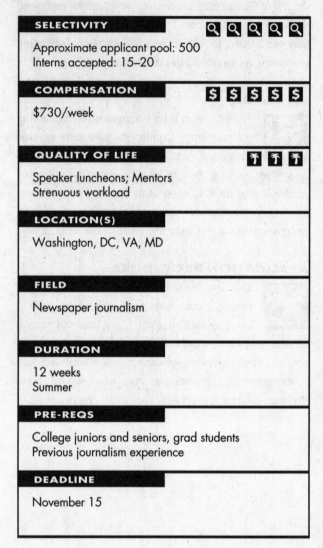
Approximate applicant pool: 500 Interns accepted: 15–20	
COMPENSATION	
$730/week	
QUALITY OF LIFE	
Speaker luncheons; Mentors Strenuous workload	
LOCATION(S)	
Washington, DC, VA, MD	
FIELD	
Newspaper journalism	
DURATION	
12 weeks Summer	
PRE-REQS	
College juniors and seniors, grad students Previous journalism experience	
DEADLINE	
November 15	

Take a walk in the history section of your local bookstore. Chances are you'll come across *All the President's Men*, perhaps the greatest political detective story of the century. It reveals how two newspaper reporters, Carl Bernstein and Bob Woodward, blew open the Watergate scandal, delivering revelations that led to Richard Nixon's political demise. Where did these men do this Pulitzer Prize–winning reporting? *The Washington Post*, of course. You might also encounter another work in your bookstore—*Power, Privilege, and the Post*, the story of Katherine Graham, a woman who helped build a spectacularly profitable, internationally renowned newspaper empire. What paper did she command? You guessed it: *The Washington Post*. One of the world's most respected newspapers, the *Post* is a locus of power in the United States, reporting on, and in some instances shaping, the course of American history.

DESCRIPTION

The Washington Post assigns its interns to either the National, Metro, Business, Sports, or Style departments. Wherever they go, one constant holds true in every department: There's no busywork. "[The *Post*] assumes you are there to be a reporter—photocopying, answering phones, and the like are unheard of," a former intern reported. Indeed, the closest a *Post* intern gets to busywork is occasionally doing the legwork for a staff reporter's story.

Mostly, interns are expected to report and write their own stories. Responsibility is the operative word and *Post* interns get a lot of it, so much so that newly arrived interns sometimes underestimate the amount of responsibility they are afforded from day one.

"On my first day on the job my supervising editor had me travel the then unfamiliar streets of Washington and report a story on a lawyer who had been censured by a judge for wearing a West African shawl in the courtroom. After scrambling for courtroom interviews and searching computer databases for background information, I wrote the story—and it ended up on the front page of the paper! If that wasn't heady enough, John Chancellor [of NBC News] called me the next day to ask a few other details about my story."

The above experience is obviously not representative of every intern's first day, but it indicates the potential for adventurous and substantive work at the *Post*. Interns usually write at least one story a week. Most see at least one of their stories appear on the front page of the newspaper or the front page of a section and some pen as many as five or six front-page stories during the internship. Story ideas come from one of the editors or reporters with whom an intern works and from an intern's own ability to brainstorm new ideas. "We would report and write about a tremendous variety of people and events," said an intern.

Indeed, the scope of topics interns cover is breathtaking. Metro interns report on everything from local crime stories to Washington politics to plane crashes. One even covered a Boy Scout jamboree in Virginia, where she was one of a few women among 40,000 Boy Scouts. Sports interns find themselves in the locker-rooms and press boxes of such professional sports teams as the Washington Redskins and Baltimore Orioles. A Style intern spent a night with a group of LSD-using high school students and wrote a story about it which went on to win the D.C. Press Association's Best Feature Story Award. But the rewarding stories are not always the splashy ones. A Metro intern spent an afternoon interviewing random people on the streets of D.C. about the abundance of rain the city was receiving. "This assignment helped me get over my fear of working a crowd," he recalled, "and tackling a deceptively simple subject like rain taught me how to appreciate the subtle, finer points of a story."

While the wealth of reporting opportunities makes the *Post* an intensely educational and enriching internship, such work carries certain pressures. "This is a high-octane place," warns an intern. "It is strenuous, definitely not for someone who wants a relaxing job between tough semesters." Long days and strict deadlines surprise new interns who underestimate the extent to which they will be treated

as capable reporters. Said one: "When I started, I was a bit unnerved at the demanding routine reporters follow at the *Post*. No matter how early I arrived for work, it seemed like my supervisor came earlier." The newspaper's fast pace and ability to attract overachieving interns gives it an environment of competition that some even describe as cutthroat. "You feel a little envious when your fellow intern gets assigned a better story," reported an intern. "Sometimes it seems as if some interns jockey for power, striving to impress their editors in hopes as being invited back for permanent employment." As only an average of one or two interns are asked back each year, some interns can't help but feel pangs of competition. A few conclude that this environment stifles camaraderie among interns. But, as one intern pointed out, "Every class of interns has a different complexion, and intern unity varies from summer to summer."

> For those willing to follow a hectic, demanding schedule, a treasure trove of journalistic opportunity awaits.

The majority of interns work at the *Post*'s 15th Street headquarters, located in the heart of downtown Washington. Comments on the office's appearance range from "spacious" to "grungy" to "just what you'd expect—a sea of desks, right out of *All the President's Men*." The *Post* assigns a few Metro interns to its bureaus in Virginia and Maryland, which for some is "a bit isolated, especially because you are usually the only intern there" and for others is "less competitive and just as substantive as working in downtown Washington."

Perks abound at the *Post*. Pay is terrific, commensurate with the salary of a beginning-level reporter; in recent summers, interns were paid around $730 a week. Interns enjoy a daylong orientation program including a bus tour of D.C. and a lunchtime picnic. Virtually every week the newspaper holds a special intern luncheon, at which interns hobnob with a *Post* editor or reporter, often a "mythical figure in the world of journalism"; past lunch guests have included Bob Woodward, executive editor Len Downey, former editor Ben Bradley, and syndicated columnists David Broder and Richard Cohen. The *Post* also conducts an informal mentor program in which each intern is paired with a staff member; in one intern's estimation, "this buddy system is a great way of learning about the newspaper business on a more personal level."

SELECTION

The program accepts college juniors and seniors as well as graduate students. Although the application states that previous journalism work is "preferred," a survey of past interns suggests that previous internships or college newspaper experience is virtually required. Said a former intern: "It seemed like all of my fellow interns had strong journalism backgrounds—everything from part-time work with local newspapers to previous internships with *Time*, *The Wall Street Journal*, and *Newsday* to editorial experience on college papers." Besides experience, the *Post* looks for individuals with initiative and self-confidence, able to vigorously pursue a story and see it through to fruition; "relentless" is how one former intern described the desired ethic.

APPLICATION PROCEDURE

The application deadline is November 15. This date is earlier than most other prestigious newspaper internships, in part, according to a past intern, to give the *Post* first dibs on the best applicants. Applicants should write for an application well in advance of the deadline. Besides returning a completed application, applicants must send two letters of recommendation, a 500-word typewritten autobiography, half a dozen clips of journalistic work (e.g., clips from a college paper), and a college transcript. Finalists are either flown to Washington to interview at the *Post* or are interviewed by *Post* representatives in major cities around the country.

OVERVIEW

Interning at *The Washington Post* is not merely a three-month observer's post at a pinnacle of American journalism. It is a chance to learn the art of reporting and writing under the supervision of professional journalists in one of the world's most powerful and newsworthy cities. For those willing to follow a hectic, demanding schedule, a treasure trove of journalistic opportunity awaits. The internship program has been in existence for more than a quarter of a century and it has produced a star-spangled array of alumni. In fact, the newspaper's executive and managing editors both launched their careers as *Post* interns—now that's scaling the journalistic ladder.

FOR MORE INFORMATION . . .

■ The Washington Post
Internship Program
1150 15th Street NW
Washington, DC 20071-5508
(202) 334-6000

Weyerhaeuser

SELECTIVITY		🔍 🔍 🔍
Approximate applicant pool: 200 IT, 5000 Co-wide Interns accepted: 35–40 IT, 210 Co-wide		

COMPENSATION		💲 💲 💲 💲
$280–400/week for undergrads; $440–560/week for grad students; round-trip travel		

QUALITY OF LIFE		🌴 🌴 🌴 🌴
Mentors Seminars/tours; Parties		

LOCATION(S)	
Tacoma, WA and several of the 250 offices and plants nationwide–see Index	

FIELD	
Forest products	

DURATION	
IT: 6 months; Summer/Fall; Winter/Spring Company wide: 3 months; mostly summer	

PRE-REQS	
Varies with position – see Selection	

DEADLINE	
IT:Wtr/Spr .... October 1 Sum/Fall ...... January 10 Company wide ....Rolling	

In 1935, an obituary discussing the Weyerhaeuser family fortune appeared in a Tacoma newspaper. Shortly thereafter, three kidnappers snatched nine-year-old George H. Weyerhaeuser as he was walking home from school. A week and a large ransom later, he was released alone in a nearby forest.

In retrospect, it seems fitting that Weyerhaeuser was liberated among trees, because 31 years later he was elected to lead the world's premier forest products company as its president and CEO. By then, the company known as Weyerhaeuser had become a household name, with a history that dates as far back as 1858. In that year, George's great-grandfather Frederick Weyerhaeuser set his sights on timber and purchased a lumberyard. By the turn of the century, the 65-year-old Frederick had gained a sterling reputation as a leader in the American lumber industry. So when he met with Midwestern lumbermen in 1900 to form a timber company, the investors decided to call their creation Weyerhaeuser. Acquiring 900,000 acres of Pacific Northwest timber at $6 per acre, the company adopted a unique policy for that era—the practice of growing timber as a crop. Weyerhaeuser's foresight has most certainly paid off. Today, the company has virtually an unlimited source of trees; it plants three to four for every one harvested. Currently the owner of nearly six million acres of timber, Weyerhaeuser is one of the world's largest producers of forest products such as lumber, pulp, wood chips, paper, and cardboard.

DESCRIPTION

In 1975, Weyerhaeuser's Information Technology (IT) unit established its own internship program for about a half-dozen students. Now, having grown in size and popularity, the program attracts a group of 35 to 40 IT interns yearly. These interns are dispersed throughout the company's headquarters to further IT's mission: deliver quality computer service to the company's business units. Assigned to teams, interns program computers, install and test hardware and software, provide computer support, and analyze and design systems. But according to the coordinator, the internship requires "as much use of soft skills and teamwork as knowledge of computers."

An intern in Containerboard Packaging worked on developing a database to track the company's huge PC (personal computer) in-

BUSYWORK METER
MEDIUM
LOW / HIGH
OLDMAN & HAMADEH

ventory. "Company PCs move around a lot," she explained. "Cataloging them decreases the chance of misplacing them." Using a commercial program, she created the database. "I set up fields for the serial number, type of computer, make, and model," she said. "And I also wrote some code so that people working with the database could delete, add, or print information."

Another intern worked with the Customer Support Team. "As an intern with this group," he said, "I helped IT keep tabs on all of its capital projects, much like Capital Management does for the corporate offices." He helped create a computer system to consolidate project information. "Each business unit had a project that it wanted to do," he explained. "We input each project's duration, total cost, benefits—nearly 100 elements for about 300 projects. It was a lot information to track. I was in charge of maintaining the system, by creating new functions and removing bugs."

Just as Weyerhaeuser nurtures its trees, so it nurtures its interns. Each week, interns congregate for development programs, the same as those given to entry-level associates. IT puts a lot of thought and effort into these activities. In fact, the entire year's activities—workshops, videos, and tours— are scheduled before interns even arrive. One to five hours in length, the programs teach interns how to become Weyerhaeuser professionals. Considering that about half of all IT interns return for permanent employment, it's no surprise that the company spends a considerable amount of time training them.

Workshops address such topics as project estimating, software testing, total quality, project management, and uses of technology. One workshop administered a version of the Myers-Briggs personality test. "The exam indicated whether we were introverted, extroverted, or split personality," said an intern.

Videos teach interpersonal, telephone, and presentation skills. With flicks like *If Looks Could Kill* (a half-hour British mystery) and *In Search of Excellence* (a one-and-one-half-hour film based on the best-seller by Tom Peters and Robert Waterman, Jr.), interns rarely become bored. Other videos, like *The Trees Go On Forever*, discuss Weyerhaeuser's vision and values.

Videos on Weyerhaeuser probably don't provide as much insight into the company as tours, conducted every month or two. Interns visit The Weyerhaeuser Technology Center, which houses the engineers, scientists, and their research and development projects. They also see the Bonsai Gardens, a collection of Oriental trees honoring Weyerhaeuser's good trade relations with the Pacific Rim. "Interns get an overview of our manufacturing processes and learn the company's role as environmental steward," said the coordinator.

At the end of the internship, interns are required to show off what they have learned to a group of Weyerhaeuser employees. In front of supervisors, mentors, and IT management—50 to 60 people in all—each intern makes a five-minute presentation of his or her work.

Weyerhaeuser's corporate headquarters is spread between Tacoma and Federal Way, separated by a 20-minute drive. The five-story corporate building in Federal Way is flanked on one side by a meadow and on the other by a lake that is home to ducks, geese, and swans. Employees and interns are often seen jogging on the area's snakelike running trails or pumping iron at one of the corporate fitness centers, where membership is $16 per month.

The headquarter's grounds also serve as the setting for the Welcome Intern Party, where former and new interns gather for conversation and barbecued drumsticks. This isn't the last of the parties, either. Whether it's the Bring Your Boss and Mentor picnic, the Lake Tapps water ski party or the Former Intern party, interns enjoy several organized social activities.

The IT program, however, is not as old as the company-wide internship also available at Weyerhaeuser. In the

> **Employees and interns are often seen jogging on the area's snakelike running trails or pumping iron at one of the corporate fitness centers.**

1950s, the company provided Forestry internships to students interested in agriculture. Decades and scores of alumni later, the company offers experiences not only in Forestry but also in Accounting and Finance, Engineering, Human Resources, Marketing and Sales, and Production Management—approximately 60 spots at corporate headquarters and nearly 150 positions with many of the 250 offices and plants around the country.

Company-wide interns work with mentors to develop projects related to the wood industry. Engineering interns build log-infeed decks for sawmills, work in pulp-testing labs, and develop total quality processes. Forestry interns work in the field, helping to plant, grow, and harvest trees; they manage contract crews and keep timber inventory. After going through a three-day orientation in Tacoma, Audit interns return to their field offices to assist audit teams of senior-level employees.

Interns at headquarters take organized field tours of company facilities such as a tree farm, a tree regeneration nursery, a log exporting facility, and a recycling plant. Although there are fewer development programs, corporate interns are still considered an important part of the company. At the end of the summer, an Intern Recognition Day acknowledges that all interns, IT included, are valued contributors. An array of speakers, including a senior VP, addresses them, and then interns hop on a bus for a tour of Weyerhauser facilities. Said one: "We spent a whole day traveling from one mill site to another, where boards, paper, and pulp are manufactured. We watched paper get turned into corrugated boxes at the box plant and observed employees caring for seedlings at the nursery. And we saw that every part of the tree is used to make something, from fuel for the boilers to fine printing paper."

SELECTION

 The IT program targets college juniors and seniors (as well as a few graduate students) studying computer science, management information systems, or computer information systems. Industrial engineering, electrical engineering, and physics majors with some experience and interest in these areas are also eligible. Freshmen and sophomores (affectionately called "rookies" by the division) may apply for summer-only positions supporting and troubleshooting PCs, modifying inventory tracking systems, or setting up computer hardware. The brochure cites "business and computer skills," "initiative and self-motivation," and "academic strength" as some of the "key selection criteria."

The company-wide program selects students of all levels, from freshmen to graduate students, for positions nationwide. Bachelor's and master's candidates in engineering (mechanical, chemical, electrical, and industrial), pulp and paper science, accounting, forestry, environmental science, and communications are eligible. Human Resources interns must be master's students. The company also hires high school students for clerical work.

APPLICATION PROCEDURE

 The IT deadline falls on January 10 for the June to December internship and on October 1 for the January to June internship. The latter internship may be extended to August. Applicants must submit a cover letter, resumé, transcript, and IT application form to the IT Intern Program Manager at the address below. Well-qualified candidates receive on-campus or phone interviews. Those garnering highest marks in the interviews are brought to headquarters for more interviewing. Selections are made a few days later. Offers are contingent upon successful drug testing.

The deadline for the company-wide program is rolling, though most of the internships are for summer. A resumé stating a one-line objective and a cover letter expanding on that objective may be submitted to Weyerhaeuser recruiters at one of the 70 campuses that Weyerhaeuser visits. Otherwise, applicants may submit the resumé and cover letter directly to the desired company location. Call or write Recruiting and Staffing (next-page) for a brochure of addresses and phone numbers.

OVERVIEW

 In the early 1800s, daring pioneers ventured west to claim their fortunes in the American forests. Legend has it that Paul Bunyan, a mythical lumberjack, hovered closely above in spirit while they axed trees and sawed lumber. Students who venture into Weyerhaeuser territory will find a Paul Bunyan watching over them, too. Caring mentors and supervisors ensure that interns work on projects of value to the company. Videos, workshops, and tours help interns develop professional skills. Coordinators make sure interns balance hard work with recreational and social activities. Just as Bunyan, patron saint of the American lumber industry, protected early loggers, so Weyerhaeuser grooms its interns for roles as future wood-industry professionals.

FOR MORE INFORMATION . . .

■ Weyerhaeuser
Recruiting and Staffing
CH1 J26
Tacoma, WA 98477
(206) 924-2602

■ Weyerhaeuser
IT Intern Program
PC2-18
Tacoma, WA 98477
(206) 924-4403

THE WHITE HOUSE
WASHINGTON

SELECTIVITY	🔍
Approximate applicant pool: 600 Interns accepted: 200	

COMPENSATION	💲
None	

QUALITY OF LIFE	🌴 🌴 🌴
Brown-bags, Farewell reception Athletic and service opportunities	

LOCATION(S)	
Washington, DC	

FIELD	
Government	

DURATION	
Summer: two 6–week sessions Fall and Spring: 12 weeks	

PRE-REQS	
Undergrads, recent grads, grad students	

DEADLINE	
Summer .... April 15 Fall......June 1 Spring .... November 15	

Since I came to the White House I got two hearing aids, a colon operation, skin cancer, a prostate operation, and I was shot. The damn thing is I've never felt better in my life.

—President Ronald Reagan, 1987

Take it from the Gipper, the White House is a tough place. Impossible deadlines, predatory reporters, a dizzyingly busy schedule—it drives even the hardiest souls to daily doses of Grecian Formula and Metamucil.

But, hey, life at the world's most powerful address isn't all bad. The president has a shiny 747 and a battery of helicopters at his disposal. There's also plenty of room for a First Cat or First Dog. A gastronomic predilection can always be indulged—whether it's pork rinds or Big Macs.

DESCRIPTION

With the new presidential administration in 1993 came a new White House Intern Program. The program is more substantive and better organized than in previous administrations, according to those who've been there. Students may apply for the fall, spring, or summer internship. Applicants for the summer internship must choose either session I (early June to early July) or session II (mid-July to late August). Twenty-two White House offices take on interns, including Advance, Cabinet Affairs, Chief of Staff, Communications, Correspondence, Domestic Policy, Office of the Executive Clerk, First Lady's Office, General Counsel, Intergovernmental Affairs, Legislative Affairs, Management/Administration/Operations, National Economic Council, Office of National Service, Photography Office, Political Affairs, Presidential Personnel, Public Liaison, Scheduling, Staff Secretary, Vice President's Office, and Visitor's Office.

The substance of interns' work varies greatly from office to office. Some positions, for example, consist of assignments relating to a specific issue. An intern in Domestic Policy collected background material on health care reform and incorporated it into a briefing book for senior adviser Ira Magaziner; he also drafted letters to citizens who had written Magaziner about health care issues. Other positions are a bit of a grind. Correspondence interns, for example, spend most of their

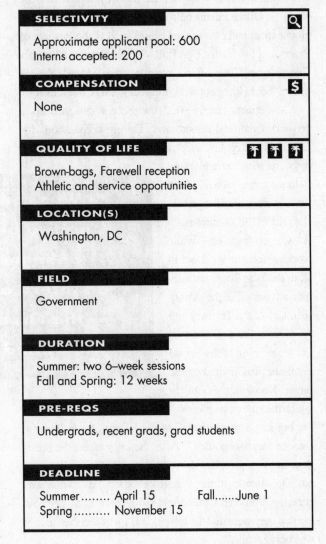

time responding to the president's huge volume of mail, phone calls, and faxes. Some positions are just plain old fun. Visitor's Office interns help coordinate requests for White House tours and plan special events such as the Pageant of Peace and the Easter Egg Roll. Helping out at Clinton's Georgetown Class of '68 reunion, one Visitor's Office intern "got to hang out with [musical guest] Chuck Berry."

Sometimes interns find themselves assigned to a project of national importance. During preparations for Clinton's budget bill, a Communications intern spent long days running errands and fielding calls. Asked about the high degree of busywork, she said: "I didn't mind at all. It was a trade-off—while working the phones, I got to sit in the War Room with senior advisers like the deputy secretary of the Treasury and Al Gore's press secretary." On the evening of the Senate vote, she was invited to the plush Roosevelt Room to watch the vote on television: "I felt like I was in a dream. All the big names were there—Mac McLarty, Leon Panetta, George Stephanopoulos." After the bill passed, the president and vice president dropped by the Roosevelt Room to pay their thanks to the War Room staff: "Everyone was cheering, and then Clinton and Gore came in to say how excited they were that the bill passed. I was there as history was being made."

As in many internships, the best departments to work in are not always the ones with the sexiest names. One intern, for example, had a terrific experience in the Office of the Executive Clerk, the office charged with handling and cataloging official presidential documents. Part of his time was spent on the phone fielding inquiries about bills and nominations signed by the president. He also filed documents in the office's archives—a rewarding task "if only because you got to see valuable presidential papers dating back to 1890." But nothing could compare to his other responsibility: hand-delivering presidential messages and nominations to Congress. Twenty or so times during the summer he went to Capitol Hill to deliver presidential papers, each document in a special envelope sealed with an official wax stamp. The highlight of this job was delivering the Supreme Court nomination of Ruth Bader Ginsburg: "A military car took me up to Capitol Hill, where I was escorted to the Senate floor and was introduced to the Senate as one of the president's secretaries. I bowed, then handed over the envelope and said, 'I am directed by the President of the United States to deliver a message in writing.'" The delivery was filmed on C-SPAN and immortalized on the pages of the *Congressional Record*.

> "I was convinced it had to be a first of some sort— an intern allergic to the First Pet of the United States."

While some experiences are simply awesome, others are delightfully silly. An intern in the Visitor's Office, for example, once had the rare opportunity to meet Socks the cat. "Socks' caretaker came by and dropped him off for an hour. Everyone in the office played with him. I even had my picture taken with the cat." But events soon took a turn for the worse: "About ten minutes later, I had an allergic reaction. I started sneezing and itching. My supervisor had to take me to the White House's doctor." Laughing all the way to the doctor's office, he contemplated his crazy luck: "I was convinced it had to be a first of some sort—an intern allergic to the First Pet of the United States."

The internship kicks off with a daylong orientation. The early part of the day is spent with representatives of the Secret Service, who brief interns on security issues. Said an intern: "They basically scare you out of doing what you're not supposed to do." Afterward, interns receive an official welcome and "major pep talk" from a VIP (Tipper Gore did the honors in 1993). Following the VIP's welcome, the director of the Office of National Service takes to the podium and speaks on the importance of public service.

The focus of interns' extracurricular life is a weekly series of brown-bag luncheons with presidential assistants, Cabinet secretaries, and congressional leaders. The luncheons are held in the Old Executive Office's Indian Treaty Room, a marble-and-tile chamber with an intricately decorated balcony overhead. Recent speakers have comprised a constellation of Washington stars: Dee Dee Myers (White House press secretary), David Wilhelm (Democratic party chairman), Janet Reno (U.S. attorney general), Joan Baggett (White House political director), and George Stephanopoulos (White House senior adviser). One of interns' favorite speakers was political consultant James Carville, who peppered his remarks with "genuinely funny" jokes and finished to a standing ovation.

A variety of other activities keep interns busy. Intern-jocks run the bases in an intern softball league. Service-oriented interns participate in DC Cares, a program that pairs students with underprivileged children. Curious interns may arrange to watch a presidential helicopter arrival or departure on the White House's South Lawn. The South Lawn is also the site of the White House's Fourth of July party, where interns may watch fireworks with White House staff and their families. (Paparazzi, take note: one recent party-goer spied Chelsea Clinton hanging out on the roof with her friends.) Last but certainly not least, interns get to meet Bubba himself, when Bill, Hillary, and Al Gore host a good-bye reception at the end of the internship. Described an intern: "[Bill] gave us a two-minute thank-you speech. We each then got to shake his hand, and we all posed together for a group picture."

Contrary to common expectations, few interns actually work in the White House itself. With the exception of East and West Wing offices such as Staff Secretary, Chief of Staff, and Legislative Affairs, most interns are situated in the Old Executive Office Building. Next door to the White House, the Old Executive Office Building has four floors of handsome, scrubbed-clean corridors and black-and-white diamond tiles. Interns' accommodations vary—some interns have their own desks; others make do with "floating between open desks." In the coordinator's words, "facilities and equipment are well shared."

SELECTION

The program is open to undergraduates of any level, recent graduates, and graduate students. Students of any major are welcome, as are conservatives. Says the intern coordinator: "As this is a nonpartisan White House, the program is open to everyone, even those of the opposite political persuasion."

APPLICATION PROCEDURE

The application deadline for the summer internship is April 15; for the fall internship, June 1; and for the spring internship, November 15. Submit a resumé, two letters of recommendation (preferably one from a college professor and one from a political/professional source), writing sample (two to three pages), and unofficial transcript. In a cover letter, applicants may describe any interesting, unusual, or significant information about their family, upbringing, or heritage. Applicants must also fill out and submit the one-page White House Internship Application, which asks for personal and academic data as well as three department preferences. No interviews are given. Applicants should hear a decision from the coordinator at least a month before the start date of the internship.

OVERVIEW

If this book had a "prestige meter," the White House internship would shatter its limit. But the program offers more than mere resumé radiance; it is the rare chance to experience life on the doorstep of the world's power center. Some offices are more substantive and exciting than others, but all interns should expect some busywork, some projects, and a whole lot of exposure, both formal and informal, to Washington's movers and shakers. An intern who had previously served three other government internships said it best: "The White House—there is no substitute."

FOR MORE INFORMATION . . .

■ The White House
Intern Program
Office of Presidential Personnel
Old Executive Office Building
Room 151
Washington, DC 20500
(202) 456-6676

Whitney Museum of American Art

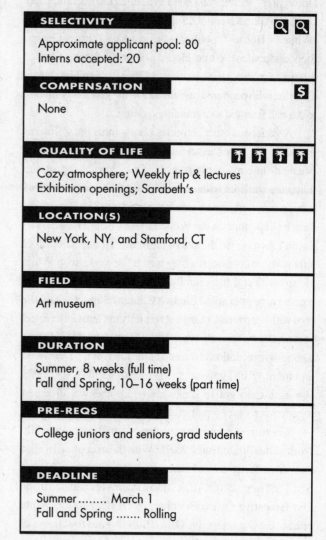

SELECTIVITY				🔍 🔍
Approximate applicant pool: 80 Interns accepted: 20				

COMPENSATION	$
None	

QUALITY OF LIFE	🌴 🌴 🌴 🌴
Cozy atmosphere; Weekly trip & lectures Exhibition openings; Sarabeth's	

LOCATION(S)

New York, NY, and Stamford, CT

FIELD

Art museum

DURATION

Summer, 8 weeks (full time)
Fall and Spring, 10–16 weeks (part time)

PRE-REQS

College juniors and seniors, grad students

DEADLINE

Summer .... March 1
Fall and Spring .... Rolling

"**C**ultural War at the Whitney," declared the headline of a March 1993, issue of *U.S. News & World Report.*

This was not the first time the Whitney was lambasted for its Biennial exhibition and it was certainly not the last. Since 1932, the museum's Biennials have showcased the work of living American artists, providing a forum for unconventional art that is often displayed provocatively. Biennials of years past have been criticized for transgressions like underrepresenting female artists, combining paintings and sculpture, and overdosing on political correctness. But no matter how feisty or radical or infuriating they are, Biennials fulfill founder Gertrude Vanderbilt Whitney's desire to support American artists, regardless of whether their art is accepted at the time of exhibition.

But judging the Whitney by its Biennials is like judging a bookstore by its unconventional book festival. With all the hoopla generated by the Biennials, it's easy to lose sight of the fact that the Whitney is arguably the world's most comprehensive museum of 20th century American art. Its permanent collection of over 10,000 works reads like a who's who of modern American artists, including the likes of Joseph Stella, Georgia O'Keefe, Charles Demuth, Edward Hopper, Max Weber, and George Bellows.

DESCRIPTION

Interns are placed in the following departments: Curatorial, Development, Education, Film and Video, Library, Operations, Public Relations, Publications, and Registrar. Positions are also available in the two Whitney branches, located at the Philip Morris building in Manhattan and the Champion International Corporation in Stamford, Connecticut.

Those who desire exposure to new exhibitions should head for the Curatorial Department. Interns here spend their time helping the curator track down paintings for upcoming exhibitions. Said an intern: "Locating paintings is detective's work. I was constantly on the phone with other museums, galleries, auction houses, and private owners. . . . Sometimes it was necessary to consult the archives of art magazines to determine the artists and locations of lesser-known paintings." Exhibition preparation also requires interns to do extensive bibliographic research on the featured artist or group of artists. "The curator wanted me to find out what everyone else had said on a particular artist, so I searched [the curator's] archives for every article that had been written about the artist," one intern said. "It was the type of thorough research that one does for a paper in graduate school."

Interns in the Education department perform research for a variety of seminars, symposiums, gallery tours, and films. One intern, for instance, put together material that prepared docents for talks they give to the public. "I spent a lot of time in the Whitney's library gathering background material on artists that the docents would lecture on. [It] gave me a great background in American and contemporary art." Later in her internship, she was asked to create a collection of news articles on the then-raging Robert Mapplethorpe controversy. "After searching dozens of magazines and newspapers, I put together a substantial collection of articles. They were later used for a Whitney symposium on censorship."

Publications is a small department (only five staff members) with the big responsibility of editing and producing all of the Whitney publications including catalogs, brochures, posters, and calenders of events. Interns here work on a mixed bag of projects—one day they're creating wall labels, the next they're helping with brochures. Working on the production of a postcard book, one intern did everything from organizing the captions to helping select which prints to make into postcards. She also assisted in the publication of an Edward Hopper poster, a Charles Demuth catalog, and program notes for the Film and Video department. "I had no background in creating brochures and catalogs," she said. "But my summer at Whitney was incredibly productive. I left with a good grasp of what publishing is all about."

Housed in an angular building that looks like an "upside-down wedding cake," the Whitney has four floors of galleries and a fifth floor devoted to administration. Interns work on the fifth floor or next door in a brownstone that houses several of the museum's departments, including Education. Although the working environment is "cramped" and "often windowless," it is also described as "homey" and "relaxed." This casual atmosphere is largely due to the museum's relatively small staff of 160, as compared with "Pentagon-size" museums in New York like the Metropolitan Museum of Art, which has two thousand employees. Said one intern: "At other museums, people talk in whispers and are uptight. At the Whitney, the mood is relatively relaxed. Its small size makes for a cozy atmosphere where making friends is easy."

Nothing enhances an internship like seminars and field trips—and fortunately for interns, the Whitney agrees. Every week the Personnel department arranges a half-day presentation to provide interns with an overview of the museum and career possibilities. Past seminars have featured lectures from department heads as well as films and panel discussions about art. Observed an intern: "The seminars really gave you a sense of the different pieces that work together to make the museum run."

In addition to attending the seminars, interns embark on several afternoon field trips. One week it might be to Sotheby's. The next, a foray to the Studio Museum of Harlem. Next on the agenda is a tour of the Whitney's Permanent Collection storage facility. One of the most influential trips is to the Whitney's Independent Study Program in lower Manhattan, where interns meet with the artists and curatorial fellows who are completing this prestigious fellowship. A number of interns have applied to and completed the Independent Study Program after having been introduced to it during their internship. Said one: "I would never have heard of the Independent Study Program if I hadn't been an intern. I saw how great it could be."

Whenever the Whitney launches a new exhibition, it holds a private "opening" to introduce the artists and their work to selected guests. There's plenty of schmoozing, wine, and hors d'oeuvres—and best of all, interns are invited.

It's a heady experience for some: "Openings are definitely a scene—artists and critics abound. It's exciting to know that you're seeing an exhibition before virtually everyone else in the city does." Others see openings through a more cynical lens: "There's a good bit of pretension ... sometimes it seems that few guests are there to actually look at the artwork." Interns typically get to go to a wide assortment of openings during the internship; one intern, for example, attended openings for exhibitions featuring Jasper Johns and Agnes Martin as well as a Biennial opening.

Membership in Whitney's Internship Program has its privileges. A Whitney Intern ID card is good for free admission to most New York museums; says an intern, "I loved not having to pay the $7.50 admission fee to the Museum of Modern Art." Interns receive a 33 percent discount at the museum sales desk where they may purchase Whitney-produced items like posters, books, T-shirts, and postcards. They also get 20 percent off on merchandise in the Store Next Door, which stocks hand-crafted items designed by American artists (e.g., ceramics, jewelry, quilts, and watches). Food-seeking interns will be satiated at Sarabeth's at the Whitney, an in-house gourmet restaurant offering a 10 percent discount to museum employees. Best of all, interns receive free admission to museum talks held for the public in the fall and spring. The talks are given by an artist or art critic and have featured such notables as Elizabeth Murray, Yoko Ono, Ross Bleckner, Laurie Anderson, and Barbara Kruger.

SELECTION

The program primarily looks for college juniors and seniors, though graduate students are selected on occasion. While there are no other pre-reqs save for having "a strong background and interest in American art and/or museum studies," the Curatorial department gives preference to art history majors.

APPLICATION PROCEDURE

The deadline for the summer internship is March 1; the fall and spring internships have rolling application deadlines. An eight-part application procedure awaits: (1) a resumé, (2) a letter of recommendation from a college professor or employer, (3) college transcripts, (4) a list of three museum departments, in order of work preference, (5) proposed beginning and ending dates of internship, (6) housing arrangements, (7) availability for an in-person interview (give dates), and (8) a one-page statement of purpose stating one's reasons for requesting the internship and what one hopes to gain from and contribute to the experience. After reviewing applications, the Personnel office calls selected applicants for personal interviews; in rare cases, phone interviews may be substituted for live interviews. Since last-minute openings sometimes occur, those not selected for an initial interview, or who are interviewed but not initially accepted, are placed on a waiting list.

OVERVIEW

In an admirable display of initiative, a recent group of Whitney interns designed and wrote their own four-page "Whitney Interns Newsletter," because—in their words—they "wished to create something that was truly by, for, and interesting to the interns as a group." Things like this happen at the Whitney because by and large interns are happy and staff members are supportive. The Whitney offers interns a unique environment in which to learn the ropes of the museum world—it is a place of ferment, a place unafraid of experimentation. It is also a place where interns are well appreciated. Said an intern: "To the Whitney, interns aren't temporary observers—they're the future. Staff treat interns like protégés and try to get as much knowledge into them as possible. Why? They know some of the interns will return as permanent staff."

FOR MORE INFORMATION . . .

■ Whitney Museum of American Art
  Internship Program
  Personnel Office
  945 Madison Avenue
  New York, NY 10021
  (212) 570-3600

THE WIDMEYER
GROUP, INC.

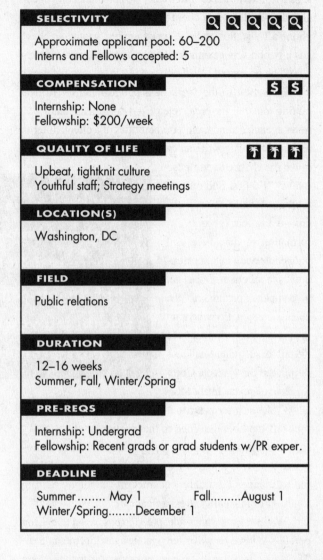

SELECTIVITY

Approximate applicant pool: 60–200
Interns and Fellows accepted: 5

COMPENSATION

Internship: None
Fellowship: $200/week

QUALITY OF LIFE

Upbeat, tightknit culture
Youthful staff; Strategy meetings

LOCATION(S)

Washington, DC

FIELD

Public relations

DURATION

12–16 weeks
Summer, Fall, Winter/Spring

PRE-REQS

Internship: Undergrad
Fellowship: Recent grads or grad students w/PR exper.

DEADLINE

Summer .... May 1   Fall.........August 1
Winter/Spring........December 1

Sometimes slang words capture the essence of meaning in a way conventional words never could. So it is with "spin doctor," a fashionable term defined by the *Random House Webster's Dictionary* as a "press agent skilled at spin control," which is the "attempt to give bias to news coverage, especially a political event."

The Widmeyer Group is a spin doctor extraordinaire. As Washington's fastest-growing independent public relations agency, Widmeyer creates media strategies for leading corporations, foundations, and nonprofit advocacy groups. The realm of public policy and government is one of Widmeyer's specialties. It has written speeches for political candidates and members of Congress, organized national forums for everyone from Ronald Reagan to Bill Clinton, and conducted research for groups like the Rockefeller Foundation and the Secretary of Labor's Commission on Achieving Necessary Skills.

DESCRIPTION

Political scientist or poet, engineer or English major—the Widmeyer internship wants you. The only requirement is an enthusiastic interest in the public relations profession. And for older candidates with previous PR experience, there's a Fellowship program. Fellows do the same type of work as interns but receive a stipend for their efforts.

An internship in public relations is almost sure to include some busywork, and Widmeyer's does. Interns may find themselves photocopying a 400-page report, faxing dozens of press releases, and covering the phones for the receptionist. Every day interns spend the morning clipping and photocopying newspaper articles to keep senior staff abreast of events relevant to Widmeyer's clients. A definite no-brainer, but

one that offers some reward: "It kept me clued in to the daily news. Where else do you get to read newspapers as part of your job?"

After their daily two to three hours of mundane work, interns dive into assignments directly related to public relations. Common to all interns is the making of media lists and pitch calls. The former requires one to compile a list of news organizations who may be interested in a client's activities. Consulting news industry resource books, interns update the vital statistics (contact person, address, and phone numbers) of various magazines, TV stations, and radio stations. After putting a list together, interns make "pitch calls" to persuade news agencies that Widmeyer's client is worth covering. "I'd telephone a TV station and say, for example, 'So-and-so client has a public service announcement in which your viewers would be interested. Will you use it?'"

Elemental to the work of a public relations firm is putting together the press release—a document sent out to news agencies announcing the activities of a client. Interns are taught how to write an effective press release and then given the chance to compose a few. "I'd first find out everything I could about a client—using background information in the office and phone interviewing representatives of the client. Once I got a complete picture of the client's mission, I'd write it up in press release format. . . . I did this for such clients as Trans Africa and the National Commission to Prevent Infant Mortality." After interns write a press release, it is edited by the staff member assigned to that particular client. "My supervisor made excellent suggestions on how to improve the press releases I wrote," said an intern. "With his guidance, I quickly became proficient at putting together high-quality press releases."

When clients want widespread exposure on television or radio, Widmeyer will often arrange a satellite media-tour. This tactic involves having a spokesperson for the client answer questions via satellite transmission from reporters around the country. It's a complicated production—one that definitely benefits from the help of interns. Spending hours on the phone, interns make pitch calls to get news organizations to participate. They also help out at the video studio where the actual satellite interviews take place. "At one [satellite media tour], I'd call the reporters who were scheduled to participate and let them know they were on. And I'd sometimes hold up cue-cards for the client if he needed to be reminded of a fact or statistic."

Sometimes interns' work is as simple as distributing press passes at an event. As humdrum as it seems, this task puts interns in some exciting settings. One intern attended a few press conferences, where in addition to signing in members of the press, he handed out press kits and background bulletins about the client sponsoring the conference. "Checking in the reporters as they arrived, I stood in the doorway and tried to look important. Playing the gatekeeper was fun." Another intern was asked to distribute press passes at the HFStival, a rock concert sponsored by Widmeyer's client, Washington radio station WHFS. "Over a few hours, I handed out [the passes] to reporters from MTV, ABC, and the like. But for the most part, I watched a great concert—which featured such bands as INXS and the Posies—and roamed around backstage, where there was plenty of free food and free compact discs."

The Widmeyer experience is augmented by a few extracurricular opportunities. Interns are welcome to sit in on company strategy meetings, where account executives discuss how they should approach a client's publicity needs. "I mostly watched," said an intern. "But I made a few suggestions—which were warmly received. The permanent staff was excited that I wanted to make a contribution." And on rare occasions, interns get to travel, like the two who were sent on a four-day trip to Pittsburgh to help out at a convention of the American Federation of Teachers.

Widmeyer has the dubious distinction of being situated only paces away from the Washington Hilton, the hotel where President Ronald Reagan was shot. Infamy aside, the neighborhood—Dupont Circle—happens to be one of Washington's liveliest, with a plethora of cafes, ethnic restaurants, and movie theaters. The Widmeyer office is located in a modern, ten-floor office building. Senior staff have their own offices, but interns and young associates work at six-person pods, where each worker has his or her own desk space, phone, and computer. The office keeps a refrigerator stocked with free soda and mineral water. There's also a concierge in the lobby of the building with whom employees can leave their dry cleaning.

> **Widmeyer is a positive, forward-moving place. There is delightfully little of the office politics and backbiting you see at larger, mass-production firms.**

A definite advantage to working at Widmeyer is the agency's small size. Said an intern, "There are only about 25 employees, including the interns. It makes for a homey atmosphere. Everyone seems happy working here." Relative to other public relation firms, Widmeyer is young—with regard to both the age of its employees and its corporate philosophy. "It's a youthful, social place," said an intern. "Many of the executives I worked with weren't much older than me." Added another: "Widmeyer is a positive, forward-moving place. There is delightfully little of the office politics and backbiting you see at larger, mass-production firms." Office morale is sustained in part by opportunities to loosen up. Every Friday is a "casual day," where employees dress in comfortable clothes (no jeans, though). Some Friday afternoons find the office holding a happy hour—"Around five or so, we'd kick back with a beer. It was a great way to start the weekend."

The one recurrent complaint among Widmeyer interns involves the long days they work. Said one intern: "You work from 9:00 to 5:30—technically. In reality, you sometimes stay as late as seven o'clock. That's a long day to be putting in without being paid any salary." Added another: "It was assumed that we'd stay as late as it took to get a project done. At times staying late became tiring."

SELECTION

 The internship program is open to undergraduates of any level; no previous experience in public relations is required. The Fellowship program is geared toward recent graduates with prior public relations experience or graduate students in journalism, media relations, political science, marketing, or communications.

APPLICATION PROCEDURE

 The application deadline for summer internships is May 1; for fall internships, August 1; and for winter/spring internships, December 1. A word to the tardy: The internship coordinator may accept applications a few days after the deadline; call for details. The application process is relatively simple: Send in a cover letter, resumé, and a few brief writing samples. Interviews are conducted in person or over the phone.

OVERVIEW

 Scott Widmeyer, the 39-year-old president of the Widmeyer Group, is no stranger to internships. Before founding the agency that bears his name, he worked for both President Carter's re-election campaign, which hired "a lot of excellent interns," and the American Federation of Teachers, where he started its internship program. Widmeyer was even once an intern himself, beginning his career interning for a Maryland newspaper. There he "gain[ed] valuable practical experience" and realized how "internships can raise a person's level of understanding about an industry."

Widmeyer's appreciation for interns comes through in his agency's program. Interns are made to feel part of the Widmeyer family, whether working directly on public-relations projects or taking care of clerical work. Said an intern: "The fact that Widmeyer is not a multicity public relations giant is clearly a virtue. Interns get to break in to the field of public relations in an intimate, progressive setting."

FOR MORE INFORMATION . . .

■ The Widmeyer Group
1875 Connecticut Avenue NW
Suite 640
Washington, DC 20009
(202) 667-0901

WILEY

I t's three AM and you're cramming for your calculus midterm. The clock is ticking, your stomach is kicking, and none of your lessons are sticking. Nothing left to do but bite your lip and curse the makers of your calculus textbook.

Chances are your cursing is directed at John Wiley & Sons, the oldest independent publishing company in North America. Founded in 1807, Wiley has spent the past two centuries establishing itself as a leading publisher of college textbooks. Wiley textbooks are found in lecture halls, seminar rooms, and backpacks across the world. Specializing in mathematics, engineering, and the sciences, Wiley churns out such classroom classics as Halliday and Resnick's *Fundamentals of Physics*, Anton's *Calculus*, Weygandt's *Accounting Principles*, and Solomon's *Organic Chemistry*. Wiley is also a major publisher of professional reference and trade books, including bestsellers like *The Ernst & Young Tax Guide*, *Hard Drive: Bill Gates and the Making of the Microsoft Empire*, and *A Consumer's Guide to Home Improvement, Renovation, and Repair*.

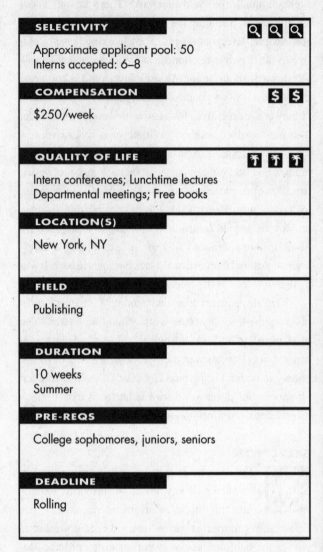

SELECTIVITY 🔍 🔍 🔍

Approximate applicant pool: 50
Interns accepted: 6–8

COMPENSATION 💲 💲

$250/week

QUALITY OF LIFE 🌴 🌴 🌴

Intern conferences; Lunchtime lectures
Departmental meetings; Free books

LOCATION(S)

New York, NY

FIELD

Publishing

DURATION

10 weeks
Summer

PRE-REQS

College sophomores, juniors, seniors

DEADLINE

Rolling

DESCRIPTION

The Wiley Internship assigns interns to its Editorial, Marketing, Finance, or Production departments. Every department requires some busywork, but the amount depends on the requirements of an intern's supervisor. "The editor I worked with wanted five copies of everything I did—it was a real drag," said an intern. "But other supervisors were far less demanding about making copies." In any case, interns should expect to "become a pro at the Minolta copier" by the end of their stay.

Interns assigned to the Editorial department assist a particular editor in a range of tasks. Phonework is prevalent, as interns are asked to check up on authors and remind them of deadlines. Interns also spend time on the phone finding professors willing to critique chapters of a book being written: "It really helps to have a professor read over a manuscript and give suggestions. For a book on, say, the geography of China, I'd call geography departments at different colleges in hopes of locating a professor to read the initial chapters. If all goes well, we keep the professor on board as a consultant for the whole project." Every so often, interns also add their own commentary: "I reviewed a few chapters of a 'physics-for-poets'-type book. I'd go through it, making spelling corrections and noting where a paragraph was too difficult to understand. I was happy to find out later that the author used several of my suggestions."

An intern in Production spent a few weeks rotating through each of the the department's divisions—Main Production, Design, Illustration, and Photo Research. In the first, she focused on "comparing drafts of manuscripts to make sure corrections transferred accurately to revised drafts." Because she had "absolutely no background in art," she spent the better part of her time in the Design division "looking over a lot of shoulders" and trying her hand at designing a sample book cover. The Illustration division found her sifting through manuscripts and marking the locations of photographs and artwork. In Photo Research, she arranged the acquisition and return of photographs with various photography agencies. "Depending on the textbook, I might be handling a photo of Indonesian rice fields one minute and a photo of an erotic costume [for a psychology textbook] the next."

> **The fact that Wiley specializes in publishing textbooks can be a blessing or a bane.**

Marketing interns work on a variety of promotional and advertising projects. One intern designed a series of flyers for display at a convention of the American Statistical Association. "I was in charge of creating flyers that would generate interest in a line of statistics books." In order to write the text for the flyers, she had to first figure out what the books were about: "These books were pretty advanced—deciphering them was no small feat. A few times I called the authors to double-check that what I had written was accurate." But the best part of the project was the chance to be creative in designing the layout: "I had figure out ways to make the flyers eye-catching. I played around with a variety of typefaces, colors, and illustrations until I came up with something that would stand out."

Interns are welcome to attend various departmental meetings. A Marketing intern sat in on a conference where new books were introduced to representatives of Wiley's sales force. "The meeting gave me an overview of the different factors that make a given book sell well—[such as] price, audience, and packaging." Alternatively, an Editorial intern was a regular attendee at his department's biweekly progress meetings. "Everyone involved in the production process was there—marketing, design, and product managers as well as the editor. They'd discuss how a book's production was going and what changes in schedule needed to be made." These meetings are a good place to learn various bits of production lingo. By the end of the internship, I had picked up all sorts of words of the trade—[such as] *signature*, *page openers*, and *sub-chapter headings*."

Depending on how one looks at it, the fact that Wiley specializes in publishing textbooks can be a blessing or a bane. Said an intern: "If you're interested solely in fiction publishing, then working at Wiley will seem like a dead end." But another says: "I wasn't particularly passionate about textbook publishing before [working at Wiley], but it grew on me as my internship wore on." Some enjoy working with textbooks for sheer intellectual stimulation: "Believe it or not, it was fun to read the biology textbooks around the office—especially because I knew I didn't have to be tested on what I read." Others see their job as a rare opportunity to learn what goes into publishing a textbook: "Working here really pertains to my life. Several of [Wiley's] books— *Abnormal Psychology*, for example—I used in school. It's fascinating to see how a book you've spent a semester with is actually put together."

Unlike most internships in publishing, Wiley's program is structured to include a selection of extracurriculars. Every other Friday the Human Resources department brings interns together to discuss how their work is going. Said an intern: "Since everyone is working in different departments, the intern meetings are a good time to find out what goes on in departments other than your own." The intern coordinator also organizes a few lunchtime lectures with various department heads. "A lecture given by the head of Marketing was great. He spoke about a variety of promotional gimmicks to get professors interested in using a particular textbook. For a textbook on stress, for example, he showed us an electronic ball that screamed when you pressed it."

A smattering of fringe benefits awaits the Wiley intern. As would be expected of a publishing house, interns may request a free copy of any book. Although most Wiley textbooks are a far cry from pleasure reading, they're good to have if only to "remind you of the internship" or to "pass on to younger siblings who can use the books for their classes." Wiley paraphernalia also finds its way into interns' hands, including such items as water bottles, mugs, tote bags, and "really cool T-shirts picturing a surfer and the words—A GROOVY HAPPENING KIND OF PLACE." Moreover, the company holds a picnic every summer that interns may attend. Said an intern: "The picnic is for everyone in the New York and New Jersey offices. It's held in a park in New Jersey, and a good time is had by all—there's barbecuing, softball games, and bumper boats."

Occupying seven floors of a midtown skyscraper, Wiley is located in a "bustling business-oriented neighborhood close to Grand Central Station." The office is decorated with framed covers of Wiley books and "a sea of blue carpet." Interns typically work at cubicles, but in rare cases they may have their own offices. There's a small cafeteria on the seventh floor that's open to the public but has a "special Wiley employees section." The cafeteria gets mixed reviews—one intern says it's "only good for rainy days"; another reports its worth a visit if only for "terrific Otis Spunkmeyer cookies and Columbo yogurt."

SELECTION

Officially, the program is open only to college juniors, but sophomores and seniors are considered in exceptional cases. While the majority of applicants are English majors, Wiley welcomes applicants from all academic disciplines. The intern coordinator looks for applicants who "demonstrate a real interest in publishing" and "have basic computer skills."

APPLICATION PROCEDURE

The application deadline is rolling, but the coordinator suggests students apply for the internship after February 1. Applicants need only submit a cover letter and resumé. After the coordinator screens the initial applicant pool, she conducts personal interviews with finalists. In rare cases, a telephone interview may be substituted for a live appearance.

OVERVIEW

Although structured internships in publishing are about as scarce as water fountains in the Sahara, John Wiley & Sons sees the value in introducing interns to nonfiction publishing through an organized program of projects, discussion meetings, and luncheon seminars. For students willing to work in a publishing house whose primary focus is textbooks and tradebooks, Wiley is a valuable three-month introduction to the art of the printed page.

FOR MORE INFORMATION . . .

■ John Wiley & Sons, Inc.
Internship Program
605 Third Avenue
New York, NY 10158
(212) 850-6000

WOLF TRAP FOUNDATION
FOR THE PERFORMING ARTS

The Wolf Trap Foundation for the Performing Arts does things a little differently. Whereas major performance centers are typically found wedged in the canyons of an urban landscape, Wolf Trap is situated on an expanse of Virginia farmland. While most prestigious arts organizations stage their performances in stuffy, chandelier-lined theaters, Wolf Trap has an open-air amphitheater with thousands of lawn seats. Despite the fact that the majority of performance centers focus primarily, if not entirely, on programming events, Wolf Trap performs public service through a variety of educational programs for children.

But just because Wolf Trap prefers moonlight to chandeliers and retains a social conscience doesn't mean it's minor league. Since its founding in 1968, the organization has attracted performers of every kind, including Bob Dylan, James Brown, Leonard Bernstein, Beverly Sills, Sammy Davis, Jr., Johnny Cash, and Dolly Parton. It is also home to the Wolf Trap Opera Company, one of America's outstanding career-entry programs for young singers.

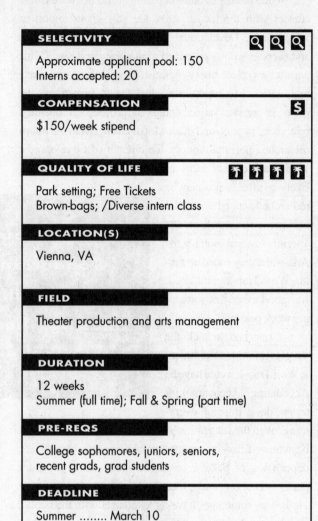

SELECTIVITY

Approximate applicant pool: 150
Interns accepted: 20

COMPENSATION

$150/week stipend

QUALITY OF LIFE

Park setting; Free Tickets
Brown-bags; /Diverse intern class

LOCATION(S)

Vienna, VA

FIELD

Theater production and arts management

DURATION

12 weeks
Summer (full time); Fall & Spring (part time)

PRE-REQS

College sophomores, juniors, seniors,
recent grads, grad students

DEADLINE

Summer .... March 10
Fall & Spring .... Rolling

DESCRIPTION

While Wolf Trap offers a few part-time intern positions in the fall and spring, the vast majority of students complete the full-time summer internship. During the summer, the organization places a few interns in each of the following departments: the Wolf Trap Opera Company, Opera Administration, Institute for Education (Early Learning Through the Arts), Development and Special Projects, Accounting, Public Affairs, Human Resources, and Public Affairs —Photography.

Only one department gives interns hands-on experience in theater production—the Wolf Trap Opera Company. In season from June to August, the company assigns interns tasks in stage management, carpentry, scenic painting, lighting, props, costuming, wigs, and makeup. Those who lack experience in technical theater but still yearn for close contact with the opera may intern in Opera Administration. Here, interns perform jobs that help keep the opera running, such as assisting in the development and distribution of promotional materials, coordinating housing and transportation arrangements for singers and staff, updating repertoire lists, and assisting in the procurement and distribution of orchestra music.

While interns in other departments do not have direct contact with the theater, they are still given important assignments. Development interns, for example, research and prepare reports on potential donors. Said one: "This wasn't the typical empty-the-trash internship—I had to use real skills. My supervisor asked me to investigate the giving histories of various donors and prospects. I consulted reference materials and made a lot of calls." After the intern researched potential donors, the director of Development would call some of them and make a formal solicitation. Every so often, a prospect he researched panned out: "I did background research on the Virginia Commission for the Arts—and they ended up giving Wolf Trap a grant. . . . It was good to see that some of my work paid off."

If one had to pick the least glamorous department at Wolf Trap, it would have be Accounting. Accounting interns "do a little of everything" with the foundation's financial activities, whether it be writing financial reports, maintaining a computerized deposit log of ticket receipts, or—for lack of a jazzier phrase—counting cash. Despite these dry tasks, Accounting interns sometimes have direct contact with the public, which may add a little zest to an otherwise monotonous day. One intern was asked to call ticket buyers who had used bad checks or credit cards. "It was kind of fun. A few people would come up with the darndest stories as to why their payment didn't go through. One guy practically gave me his life's story, complete with the details of how his ex-girlfriend was responsible for his lack of funds."

A unique aspect of Wolf Trap is its Institute for Education. Established in 1981 under a grant from the federal government's Head Start program, the Institute trains teachers in the use of performing arts techniques that help young children learn basic academic concepts (e.g., shapes and colors) as well as life skills (e.g., hand washing, sharing, and problem solving). Interns in this department assist the professional actors, musicians, and storytellers who run such innovative workshops as "Singable Songs for Non-Singers," "Using Gestures and Drama for Language Development," and "Songs and Stories about Science and Nature." They also help plan special performances attended by preschool students from the Washington, D.C., area.

Interns are often struck by the academic and geographic diversity of their peers. As there are no academic prerequisites (except for positions with the Opera Company), the program attracts students from all disciplines, some with a vocational interest in arts management, others just curious about what makes an arts center tick. Because Wolf Trap is nationally known, students come from all over the country to complete the internship. In recent years students have come from a majority of states, including Wisconsin, Iowa, Alabama, Maine, and New Mexico.

There's plenty of entertainment when interns want it. First and foremost, they receive two complimentary tickets to every performance and they're sure to be pleased with at least one, as Wolf Trap "endeavors to schedule something for everyone." Past interns not only have had access to first-rate operas but they also took in a range of shows, from Bill Cosby to symphonies. If pre- or post-performance discussions are held in conjunction with the show, interns are welcome to attend. They may also view dress rehearsals of the Wolf Trap Opera Company, where the company "performs without stops—unless a major problem arises." About three times during the summer, the intern coordinator schedules brown-bag lunches, where interns may cross-examine a department head about his or her role in the organization.

If skyscrapers, subways, and concrete are requisite surroundings, then read no farther. But if a "glorious" wooded wonderland stocked with wildlife sounds alluring, then Wolf Trap hits the target. Wolf Trap doesn't just seem like a park—it is one. A half-hour's drive from Washington, D.C., the organization is nestled among the flora and fauna of the Wolf Trap Farm Park, the country's only national park for the performing arts. On the park's 168 acres are the Filene Center, a cedar-wood amphitheater seating over

> If a "glorious" wooded wonderland stocked with wildlife sounds alluring, then Wolf Trap hits the target.

7,000, and the Barns of Wolf Trap, a performance facility that houses the Wolf Trap Opera Company during the summer months. Joining the theaters is a motley assortment of farm houses that have been converted into administration buildings. Interns are spread out among these "kooky little houses," some of which are log cabins. The setting has a distinct *Green Acres* feel to it: "From a window in my office I'd see all sorts of wildlife . . . deer, rabbits, groundhogs. Once I even saw a stray goat."

SELECTION

 The Wolf Trap internship is for college sophomores, juniors, and seniors, as well as recent graduates and graduate students. Most departments have no pre-requisites save for strong writing skills and familiarity with computers. The Wolf Trap Opera Company, however, requires prior experience in technical theater, and Public Affairs—Photography expects its interns to have access to basic camera equipment. Consult the internship brochure for more details.

APPLICATION PROCEDURE

 The application deadline for the summer internship is March 10; and for the fall and spring internships, it's rolling. Submit a cover letter (including a brief personal statement and outline of career goals), resumé, two references (academic or professional), and two contrasting samples of writing. After the coordinator screens the initial applicant pool, each department head chooses a handful of interns to interview. The majority of interviews take place over the phone, but in-person meetings can be arranged.

OVERVIEW

 Wolf Trap is the type of venue that encourages its patrons to kick off their shoes, quaff a few glasses of wine, and enjoy first-rate performances in a parklike setting. Similarly, interns at Wolf Trap gain valuable theater-operations experience in a hassle-free and uniquely pastoral environment. Unlike the plethora of performing arts organizations who've suffered in these uneven economic times, Wolf Trap remains robust financially, so its interns can be sure that the organization has the resources to ensure students a rewarding internship. For aspiring arts administrators or those who just want a taste of the footlights, the Wolf Trap internship is a worthy backstage pass to the world of arts management.

FOR MORE INFORMATION . . .

■ Wolf Trap Foundation for the Performing Arts
Intern Coordinator
1624 Trap Road
Vienna, VA 22182
(703) 255-1900

AMERICA'S TOP 10 INTERNSHIPS

Abbott Laboratories
Apple Computer
Boeing
The Coro Foundation
Intel
Lucasfilm
Microsoft
National Tropical Botanical Garden
TBWA
The Washington Post

HIGHEST COMPENSATION

Abbott Laboratories
Apple Computer
Arthur Andersen
Boeing
Citibank
Frito-Lay
Hallmark Cards
Hewlett-Packard
Inroads
Intel
Kraft General Foods
The LEK/Alcar Consulting Group
Microsoft
JP Morgan & Co.
Procter & Gamble
The Wall Street Journal
The Washington Post

MOST SELECTIVE

Academy of Television Arts & Sciences
Apple Computer
Boeing
Coors Brewing Company
Federal Bureau of Investigation
Forty Acres and a Mule Filmworks
Hallmark Cards
Kraft General Foods
Late Show with David Letterman

The LEK/Alcar Consulting Group
Levi Strauss & Co.
Lincoln Center for the Performing Arts
Lucasfilm
The MacNeil/Lehrer NewsHour
The Metropolitan Museum of Art
MTV: Music Television
National Wildlife Federation
Nike
Random House
Raychem
Reebok
Rolling Stone
Ruder-Finn
The Wall Street Journal
The Washington Post
The Widmeyer Group

HIGHEST QUALITY OF LIFE

Abbott Laboratories
Boeing
Hewlett-Packard
Microsoft
National Tropical Botanical Garden
Nike
United States Olympic Committee

DEADLINES BEFORE JANUARY 1 (FOR SUMMER)

AT&T Bell Laboratories (December 1 — SRP only)
Central Intelligence Agency (September 30)
Environmental Protection Agency (December 20)
Federal Bureau of Investigation (November 15)
Inroads (December 31)
Los Angeles Times (December 1)
National Aeronautics and Space Administration
    (December 31 — a few programs only)
3M (December 31)
The Wall Street Journal (Thanksgiving)
Washington Internships for Students of Engineering
    (December 20)
The Washington Post (November 15)

DEADLINES AFTER MARCH 1 (FOR SUMMER)

Abbott Laboratories (March 31)
Academy of Television Arts & Sciences (March 31)
American Conservatory Theater (May 15)
American Enterprise Institute (April 30)
American Heart Association
    (March 11 — Louisiana only)
The Brookings Institution (April 15)
Butterfield & Butterfield (March 15)
The Carter Center (March 15)
Center for Investigative Reporting (May 1)
Citibank (April 1)
Crow Canyon Archaeological Center (March 15 —
    same for the two fall and one winter programs)
The Walt Disney Studios (March 31)
The Environmental Careers Organization
    (May 14 — DIP only)
Frito-Lay (April 15)
Genentech (April 1)
The Hermitage (April 10)
Hewlett-Packard (April 30)
Kraft General Foods (March 31)
Late Show with David Letterman (April 1)
Liz Claiborne (May 15)
Lucasfilm (March 30)
The MacNeil/Lehrer NewsHour (March 31)
National Aeronautics and Space Administration
    (April 1 — a few programs only)
National Audubon Society (April 1)
National Basketball Association (April 15)
National Public Radio (March 30)
National Wildlife Federation (April 1 — July to
    December internship)
Random House (April 15)
Reebok (May 15)
Ruder-Finn (April 15)
Sony Music Entertainment (April 1 — Minority
    Internship only)
Sotheby's (March 15)
Supreme Court of the United States (March 10)
TBWA (April 1)
United Nations Association of the United States of
    America (April 1)
The White House (April 15)
The Widmeyer Group (May 1)
Wolf Trap Foundation for the Performing Arts
    (March 10)
See also Rolling Deadlines

ROLLING DEADLINES

Association of Trial Lawyers of America
Backer Spielvogel Bates
Bertelsmann Music Group
Elite Model Management
The Environmental Careers Organization (EPS only)
The Feminist Majority
Forty Acres and a Mule Filmworks
Frontier Nursing Service
Gensler and Associates/Architects (Fall and
    Spring only)
Hill and Knowlton
Hill, Holliday, Connors, Cosmopulos Advertising
Intel
Marvel Comics
Microsoft
Robert Mondavi Winery
MTV: Music Television
Nightline
Rolling Stone
Rosenbluth International
Sony Music Entertainment (Credited Internship only)
Spy
Surfrider Foundation
Volkswagen of America
Weyerhaeuser (Company-wide program only)
Whitney Museum of American Art (Fall and Spring
    only)
John Wiley & Sons

INTERNSHIPS OPEN TO HIGH SCHOOL STUDENTS

American Heart Association
AT&T Bell Laboratories
Association of Trial Lawyers of America
Center for Investigative Reporting
The Feminist Majority
Forty Acres and a Mule Filmworks
Hewlett-Packard
Inroads
Levi Strauss & Co.
Marvel Comics
MTV: Music Television
National Aeronautics and Space Administration
National Institutes of Health
Smithsonian Institution
Summerbridge National
Surfrider Foundation
United Nations Association of the United States of
    America
Weyerhaeuser

INTERNSHIPS OPEN TO COLLEGE FRESHMEN

American Enterprise Institute
American Heart Association
Association of Trial Lawyers of America
Bertelsmann Music Group
Center for Investigative Reporting
Center for Talented Youth
Elite Model Management
The Environmental Careers Organization (DIP only)
Environmental Protection Agency
The Feminist Majority
Forty Acres and a Mule Filmworks
Frontier Nursing Service
Inroads
Intel
The Kennedy Center
Late Show with David Letterman
Liz Claiborne
Los Angeles Times
The Metropolitan Museum of Art (The Cloisters only)
MTV: Music Television
National Aeronautics and Space Administration
National Institutes of Health
Rolling Stone
Rosenbluth International
Smithsonian Institution
Sony Music Entertainment
Summerbridge National
Surfrider Foundation
United Nations Association of the United States of
     America
Volkswagen of America
Weyerhaeuser
The White House
The Widmeyer Group

INTERNSHIPS OPEN TO COLLEGE SOPHOMORES

Academy of Television Arts & Sciences
American Conservatory Theater
American Enterprise Institute
American Heart Association
AT&T Bell Laboratories (SRP only)
Apple Computer
Association of Trial Lawyers of America
Bertelsmann Music Group
Center for Investigative Reporting
Center for Talented Youth

Coors Brewing Company (Public Relations only)
The Walt Disney Studios
Elite Model Management
The Environmental Careers Organization (DIP only)
Environmental Protection Agency
The Feminist Majority
Forty Acres and a Mule Filmworks
Frito-Lay
Frontier Nursing Service
Genentech
Gensler and Associates/Architects
Hewlett-Packard
Hill, Holliday, Connors, Cosmopulos Advertising
Inroads
Intel
The Kennedy Center
Kraft General Foods
Late Show with David Letterman
Liz Claiborne
Los Angeles Times
The Metropolitan Museum of Art (The Cloisters only)
Microsoft
MTV: Music Television
National Aeronautics and Space Administration
National Basketball Association
National Institutes of Health
Procter & Gamble
Raychem
Rolling Stone
Rosenbluth International
Smithsonian Institution
Sony Music Entertainment
Sponsors for Educational Opportunity
Summerbridge National
Surfrider Foundation
TBWA
3M
United Nations Association of the United States of
     America
Urban Fellows/Government Scholars Programs
Volkswagen of America
The Wall Street Journal
Weyerhaeuser
The White House
The Widmeyer Group
John Wiley & Sons
Wolf Trap Foundation for the Performing Arts

INTERNSHIPS OPEN TO COLLEGE JUNIORS

Every program, except:
Citibank
The Coro Foundation
Federal Bureau of Investigation
Hallmark Cards
The LEK/Alcar Consulting Group
Lincoln Center for the Performing Arts
National Wildlife Federation
Nike
Phillips Academy
Ruder-Finn
Washington Internships for Students of Engineering

INTERNSHIPS OPEN TO COLLEGE SENIORS

Every program, except:
The Coro Foundation
Inroads
Lincoln Center for the Performing Arts
National Wildlife Federation
Ruder-Finn

INTERNSHIPS OPEN TO RECENT COLLEGE GRADUATES

Academy of Television Arts & Sciences
American Conservatory Theater
American Enterprise Institute
Aspen Center for Environmental Studies
Association of Trial Lawyers of America
Brookfield Zoo
Butterfield & Butterfield
Center for Investigative Reporting
The Coro Foundation
The Environmental Careers Organization
Frontier Nursing Service
The Hermitage
The Kennedy Center
Levi Strauss & Co.
The Library of Congress
Los Angeles Times
The MacNeil/Lehrer NewsHour
The Metropolitan Museum of Art
Robert Mondavi Winery
National Audubon Society
National Institutes of Health
National Tropical Botanical Garden
National Wildlife Federation
Phillips Academy
Reebok
Rolling Stone
Rosenbluth International

Ruder-Finn
Smithsonian Institution
Sotheby's
Sponsors for Educational Opportunity (Corporate
    Law program only)
Spy
Supreme Court of the United States
Surfrider Foundation
United Nations Association of the United States of
    America
United States Olympic Committee
Urban Fellows/Government Scholars Programs
The Wall Street Journal
The White House
The Widmeyer Group
Wolf Trap Foundation for the Performing Arts

INTERNSHIPS OPEN TO GRADUATE STUDENTS

Abbott Laboratories
American Enterprise Institute
American Foundation for AIDS Research
American Heart Association
AT&T Bell Laboratories (UR only)
Apple Computer
Aspen Center for Environmental Studies
Association of Trial Lawyers of America
Backer Spielvogel Bates
Bertelsmann Music Group
Brookfield Zoo
Butterfield & Butterfield
The Carter Center
Center for Investigative Reporting
Center for Talented Youth
Central Intelligence Agency
Citibank
Coors Brewing Company
Crow Canyon Archaeological Center
The Environmental Careers Organization
Environmental Protection Agency
Federal Bureau of Investigation
The Feminist Majority
Forty Acres and a Mule Filmworks
Frito-Lay
Frontier Nursing Service
Genentech
Gensler and Associates/Architects
Hallmark Cards
The Hermitage
Hewlett-Packard
Hill and Knowlton
Hill, Holliday, Connors, Cosmopulos Advertising

Intel
The Kennedy Center
Kraft General Foods
Late Show with David Letterman
Levi Strauss & Co.
The Library of Congress
Lincoln Center for the Performing Arts
Lucasfilm
The MacNeil/Lehrer NewsHour
The Metropolitan Museum of Art
Robert Mondavi Winery
MTV: Music Television
National Aeronautics and Space Administration
National Audubon Society
National Institutes of Health
National Public Radio
National Tropical Botanical Garden
National Wildlife Federation
Nike
Phillips Academy
Procter & Gamble
Random House
Raychem
Reebok
Rosenbluth International
Smithsonian Institution
Sony Music Entertainment
Spy
Surfrider Foundation
3M
United Nations Association of the United States of
    America
United States Olympic Committee
The Wall Street Journal
The Washington Post
Weyerhaeuser
The White House
Whitney Museum of American Art
The Widmeyer Group
Wolf Trap Foundation for the Performing Arts

INTERNSHIPS OPEN TO COLLEGE GRADUATES OF ANY AGE

American Conservatory Theater
Brookfield Zoo
Butterfield & Butterfield
Center for Investigative Reporting
The Coro Foundation
The Environmental Careers Organization
Frontier Nursing Service (high school graduates of
    any age)
National Tropical Botanical Garden
Smithsonian Institution

INTERNSHIPS WITH MINORITY PROGRAMS

(M = Minority Internship is the only program available)
AT&T Bell Laboratories
Central Intelligence Agency
The Environmental Careers Organization
Frito-Lay (M)
Hallmark Cards
Inroads (M)
Intel
National Aeronautics and Space Administration
Nike (M)
Rolling Stone
Sony Music Entertainment
Sponsors for Educational Opportunity (M)
3M

INTERNSHIPS AVAILABLE DURING THE SUMMER

Every program, except:
American Conservatory Theater
The Coro Foundation
Robert Mondavi Winery

INTERNSHIPS AVAILABLE DURING THE ACADEMIC YEAR

American Conservatory Theater
American Enterprise Institute
American Heart Association
Arthur Andersen
Backer Spielvogel Bates
Bertelsmann Music Group
Boeing
Brookfield Zoo
The Brookings Institution
Butterfield & Butterfield
The Carter Center
Center for Investigative Reporting
Central Intelligence Agency
Coors Brewing Company
The Coro Foundation
Crow Canyon Archaeological Center
Elite Model Management
The Environmental Careers Organization
Environmental Protection Agency
The Feminist Majority
Forty Acres and a Mule Filmworks
Frontier Nursing Service
Gensler and Associates/Architects
Hill, Holliday, Connors, Cosmopulos Advertising
Intel
The Kennedy Center
Late Show with David Letterman
Liz Claiborne
Los Angeles Times
Lucasfilm
The MacNeil/Lehrer NewsHour
Marvel Comics
Microsoft
Robert Mondavi Winery
MTV: Music Television
National Audubon Society
National Basketball Association
National Public Radio
National Tropical Botanical Garden
National Wildlife Federation
Nightline
Rolling Stone
Rosenbluth International
Ruder-Finn
Smithsonian Institution
Sony Music Entertainment (Credited Internship only)
Spy
Supreme Court of the United States
Surfrider Foundation

United Nations Association of the United States of
   America
United States Olympic Committee
Urban Fellows/Government Scholars Programs
   (Urban Fellows Program only)
Volkswagen of America
Weyerhaeuser
The White House
Whitney Museum of American Art
The Widmeyer Group
Wolf Trap Foundation for the Performing Arts

FREE HOUSING

Abbott Laboratories
Aspen Center for Environmental Studies
Center for Talented Youth
Crow Canyon Archaeological Center
Frontier Nursing Service
The Hermitage
Microsoft (first two weeks only)
National Aeronautics and Space Administration
   (some programs only)
Phillips Academy
Summerbridge National
United States Olympic Committee

HOUSING ARRANGEMENTS AVAILABLE

AT&T Bell Laboratories
Boeing
Central Intelligence Agency
Federal Bureau of Investigation
Intel
Lincoln Center for the Performing Arts
Microsoft
National Tropical Botanical Garden
Procter & Gamble
3M
Volkswagen of America
Washington Internships for Students of Engineering

FREE MEALS

Aspen Center for Environmental Studies
Center for Talented Youth
Crow Canyon Archaeological Center
Frontier Nursing Service
The Hermitage
JP Morgan & Co.
Phillips Academy
Summerbridge National
United States Olympic Committee

CARS PROVIDED

Frontier Nursing Service
Intel
Microsoft
National Aeronautics and Space Administration
(Goddard's Summer Institute)
National Tropical Botanical Garden
Procter & Gamble (Sales interns only)

ROUND-TRIP TRAVEL COVERED

Abbott Laboratories
Academy of Television Arts and Sciences
AT&T Bell Laboratories
Apple Computer
Boeing
Frito-Lay
Hewlett-Packard
Intel
Microsoft
National Aeronautics and Space Administration
(some programs only)
Procter & Gamble
Raychem
Weyerhaeuser
Washington Internships for Students of Engineering

SCHOLARSHIPS AVAILABLE

AT&T Bell Laboratories
The Coro Foundation
Frito-Lay
Gensler and Associates/Architects
Hewlett-Packard (high school students only)
Smithsonian Institution
Summerbridge National
Supreme Court of the United States

FITNESS FACILITIES AVAILABLE

Abbott Laboratories
AT&T Bell Laboratories
Association of Trial Lawyers of America
Boeing
Center for Talented Youth
Central Intelligence Agency
Citibank
Coors Brewing Company
Federal Bureau of Investigation
Frito-Lay
Frontier Nursing Service
Hallmark Cards
Hill, Holliday, Connors, Cosmopulos Advertising
Genentech
Intel
Kraft General Foods
Los Angeles Times
Lucasfilm
Microsoft
National Aeronautics and Space Administration
National Institutes of Health
National Tropical Botanical Garden
Nike
Phillips Academy
Procter & Gamble
Reebok
Smithsonian Institution
Supreme Court of the United States
United States Olympic Committee
Weyerhaeuser

SCHOOL CREDIT REQUIRED

Late Show with David Letterman
Liz Claiborne
Lucasfilm (Fall and Spring only)
The MacNeil/Lehrer NewsHour
MTV: Music Television
National Basketball Association
Nightline
Sony Music Entertainment (Credited Internship only)

PART-TIME AVAILABLE

American Foundation for AIDS Research
American Heart Association
Backer Spielvogel Bates
Bertelsmann Music Group
Brookfield Zoo
The Brookings Institution
Butterfield & Butterfield
The Carter Center
Center for Investigative Reporting
Elite Model Management
Environmental Protection Agency
The Feminist Majority
Hill, Holliday, Connors, Cosmopulos Advertising
Liz Claiborne
The MacNeil/Lehrer NewsHour
Robert Mondavi Winery
MTV: Music Television
National Public Radio
Nightline
Smithsonian Institution
United Nations Association of the United States of
    America
Wolf Trap Foundation for the Performing Arts

CASUAL DRESS ALLOWED

Apple Computer
Aspen Center for Environmental Studies
Brookfield Zoo
Crow Canyon Archaeological Center
The Walt Disney Studios
Elite Model Management
Frontier Nursing Service
Genentech
The Hermitage
Hewlett-Packard
Intel
Levi Strauss & Co.
The Library of Congress
Marvel Comics
The Metropolitan Museum of Art
Microsoft
Robert Mondavi Winery
MTV: Music Television
National Audubon Society
National Institutes of Health
National Public Radio
National Tropical Botanical Garden
Nike
Procter & Gamble
Random House
Raychem
Reebok
Rolling Stone
Spy
Summerbridge National
Surfrider Foundation
Washington Internships for Students of Engineering

HIGH PROPORTION OF MALES OR FEMALES

The Feminist Majority (female)
Marvel Comics (male)
The Metropolitan Museum of Art (female)
Random House (female)
Sotheby's (female)
Whitney Museum of American Art (female)

OPPORTUNITIES FOR STAR-GAZING

American Conservatory Theater
American Enterprise Institute
American Foundation for AIDS Research
Aspen Center for Environmental Studies
Academy of Television Arts & Sciences
The Brookings Institution
Butterfield & Butterfield
Forty Acres and a Mule Filmworks
The Kennedy Center
Late Show with David Letterman
Lincoln Center for the Performing Arts
Lucasfilm
The MacNeil/Lehrer NewsHour
MTV: Music Television
National Basketball Association
Nightline
Sotheby's
United States Olympic Committee
The White House

GOOD PROSPECTS FOR PERMANENT EMPLOYMENT

(Approx. 50%+ Former Interns Offered Jobs)
Academy of Television Arts & Sciences
Bertelsmann Music Group
Frito-Lay
Hewlett-Packard
Inroads
Intel
Kraft General Foods
The LEK/Alcar Consulting Group
Marvel Comics
Procter & Gamble
Random House
Reebok
Ruder-Finn
Sponsors for Educational Opportunity
3M
Weyerhaeuser

ACCOUNTING

Abbott Laboratories
Arthur Andersen
Boeing
Coors Brewing Company
Federal Bureau of Investigation
Forty Acres and a Mule Filmworks
Hallmark Cards
Hewlett-Packard
Hill, Holliday, Connors, Cosmopulos Advertising
Inroads
Intel
Levi Strauss & Co.
Lucasfilm
JP Morgan & Co.
National Aeronautics and Space Administration
Nike
Procter & Gamble
Raychem
Reebok
Sponsors for Educational Opportunity
United States Olympic Committee
Weyerhaeuser
Wolf Trap Foundation for the Performing Arts

ADVERTISING

Backer Spielvogel Bates
Hill, Holliday, Connors, Cosmopulos Advertising
The Kennedy Center
MTV: Music Television
Procter & Gamble
Rolling Stone
Rosenbluth International
TBWA

AEROSPACE

Boeing
Inroads
National Aeronautics and Space Administration
Smithsonian Institution

AIDS

Abbott Laboratories (science research)
American Foundation for AIDS Research (policy)
Genentech (science research)
National Institutes of Health (science research)
Urban Fellows/Government Scholars Programs
    (policy)

ARCHITECTURE

Gensler & Associates/Architects

ARCHAEOLOGY

Crow Canyon Archaeological Center
The Hermitage

ART

See Museums/Auction Houses

AUCTION HOUSES

See Museums/Auction Houses

AUTOMOBILES

Volkswagen/Audi

BANKING/MANAGEMENT
CONSULTING/ECONOMICS/FINANCE

Abbott Laboratories
Apple Computer
Arthur Andersen
Central Intelligence Agency
Citibank
The Walt Disney Studios
Frito-Lay
Genentech
Hallmark Cards
Hewlett-Packard
Inroads
Intel
Kraft General Foods
The LEK/Alcar Consulting Group
Lincoln Center for the Performing Arts
Liz Claiborne
Los Angeles Times
Lucasfilm
Microsoft
JP Morgan & Co.
National Aeronautics and Space Administration
Nike
Procter & Gamble
Raychem
Reebok
Sony Music Entertainment
Sponsors for Educational Opportunity
3M
Urban Fellows/Government Scholars Programs
Volkswagen of America
The Wall Street Journal
The Washington Post

Weyerhaeuser
The White House
John Wiley & Sons

BIOTECHNOLOGY
Genentech
Inroads
National Aeronautics and Space Administration
Washington Internships for Students of Engineering
(policy)

CAREER DEVELOPMENT
The Coro Foundation
The Environmental Careers Organization
Inroads
Sponsors for Educational Opportunity

CHEMICALS/PHARMACEUTICALS
Abbott Laboratories
Genentech
Inroads

CLOTHING
Inroads
Levi Strauss & Co.
Liz Claiborne
Nike
Reebok

COMPUTERS/INFORMATION SYSTEMS/
ELECTRONICS
Abbott Laboratories
Apple Computer
AT&T Bell Laboratories
Boeing
Central Intelligence Agency
Environmental Protection Agency
Frito-Lay
Hallmark Cards
Hewlett-Packard
Inroads
Intel
Kraft General Foods
Levi Strauss & Co.
Liz Claiborne
Lucasfilm
Microsoft
National Aeronautics and Space Administration

National Institutes of Health
Procter & Gamble
Raychem
Reebok
3M
United States Olympic Committee
Washington Internships for Students of Engineering
(policy)
Weyerhaeuser

CONSUMER GOODS
Coors Brewing Company
Frito-Lay
Hallmark Cards
Inroads
Kraft General Foods
Procter & Gamble
3M

DESIGN (ART, GRAPHIC, AND/OR
TEXTILE)
Apple Computer
Brookfield Zoo
Central Intelligence Agency
Gensler and Associates/Architects
Hallmark Cards (minority programs only)
Hill, Holliday, Connors, Cosmopulos Advertising
Levi Strauss & Co.
Liz Claiborne
Los Angeles Times
Lucasfilm
The MacNeil/Lehrer NewsHour
Marvel Comics
MTV: Music Television
Nike
Reebok
Sotheby's

ECONOMICS
See Banking/Management Consulting/Economics/
Finance

EDUCATION
See Teaching/Education

ELECTRONICS
See Computers/Information Systems/Electronics

ENGINEERING/HIGH TECHNOLOGY/ MANUFACTURING
Abbott Laboratories
Apple Computer
AT&T Bell Laboratories
Boeing
Central Intelligence Agency
Coors Brewing Company
The Environmental Careers Organization
Federal Bureau of Investigation
Frito-Lay
Genentech
Hallmark Cards
Hewlett-Packard
Inroads
Intel
Kraft General Foods
Microsoft
National Aeronautics and Space Administration
National Institutes of Health
National Public Radio
Procter & Gamble
Raychem
3M
Washington Internships for Students in Engineering
Weyerhaeuser

ENTERTAINMENT/FILM/TELEVISION
Academy of Television Arts & Sciences
Bertelsmann Music Group
The Walt Disney Studios
Forty Acres and a Mule Filmworks
Late Show with David Letterman
Lucasfilm
The MacNeil/Lehrer NewsHour
Marvel Comics
MTV: Music Television
National Basketball Association
National Public Radio
Nightline
Rolling Stone
Sony Music Entertainment
Spy
United States Olympic Committee

ENVIRONMENT/NATURE
Aspen Center for Environmental Studies
Brookfield Zoo
The Environmental Careers Organization
Environmental Protection Agency
National Audubon Society
National Tropical Botanical Garden
National Wildlife Federation
Ruder-Finn
Smithsonian Institution
Surfrider Foundation
Urban Fellows/Government Scholars Programs
Washington Internships for Students of Engineering
Weyerhaeuser

FILM
See Entertainment/Film/Television

FINANCE
See Banking/Management Consulting/Finance

FOREIGN AFFAIRS
The Brookings Institution
Carter Center
Central Intelligence Agency
United Nations Association of the United States of America

GOVERNMENT
Central Intelligence Agency
The Coro Foundation
The Environmental Careers Organization
Federal Bureau of Investigation
The Library of Congress
National Aeronautics and Space Administration
National Institutes of Health
Supreme Court of the United States
Urban Fellows/Government Scholars Programs
Washington Internships for Students of Engineering
The White House

HEALTH CARE/MEDICINE
Abbott Laboratories
American Heart Association
Frontier Nursing Service
Genentech
National Aeronautics and Space Administration
National Institutes of Health
Ruder-Finn
3M
Urban Fellows/Government Scholars Programs
The White House

HIGH TECHNOLOGY
See Engineering/High Technology/Manufacturing

INFORMATION SYSTEMS
See Computers/Information Systems/Electronics

JOURNALISM
American Enterprise Institute
Association of Trial Lawyers of America
Center for Investigative Reporting
Central Intelligence Agency
Coors Brewing Company
Los Angeles Times
The MacNeil/Lehrer NewsHour
MTV: Music Television
National Public Radio
National Wildlife Federation
Nightline
Rolling Stone
Rosenbluth International
Spy
United Nations Association of the United States of
     America
United States Olympic Committee
The Wall Street Journal
The Washington Post

LAW
American Foundation for AIDS Research
Association of Trial Lawyers of America
Central Intelligence Agency
The Coro Foundation
The Environmental Careers Organization

Environmental Protection Agency
Federal Bureau of Investigation
National Aeronautics and Space Administration
National Audubon Society
National Public Radio
National Wildlife Federation
Sony Music Entertainment
Sponsors for Educational Opportunity
Supreme Court of the United States
Surfrider Foundation
United Nations Association of the United States
     of America
United States Olympic Committee
Urban Fellows/Government Scholars Programs
Washington Internships for Students in Engineering
The White House

LIBRARIES
Gensler and Associates/Architects
The Library of Congress
The Metropolitan Museum of Art
MTV: Music Television
Smithsonian Institution
Whitney Museum of American Art

MAGAZINES
See Newspapers/Magazines

MANAGEMENT CONSULTING
See Banking/Management Consulting/Finance

MANUFACTURING
See Engineering/High Technology/Manufacturing

MARKETING
See Advertising
See Public Relations/Marketing

MEDICINE
See Health Care/Medicine

MODEL MANAGEMENT
Elite Model Management

MUSEUMS/AUCTION HOUSES
Butterfield & Butterfield
The Metropolitan Museum of Art
Smithsonian Institution
Sotheby's
Whitney Museum of American Art

MUSIC
See Entertainment/Film/Television

NATURE
See Environment/Nature

NEWSPAPERS/MAGAZINES
Los Angeles Times
Rolling Stone
Spy
The Wall Street Journal
The Washington Post

PERFORMING ARTS/THEATER
American Conservatory Theater
The Kennedy Center
Lincoln Center for the Performing Arts
Wolf Trap Foundation for the Performing Arts

PHOTOGRAPHY
Butterfield & Butterfield
Central Intelligence Agency
The Library of Congress
Los Angeles Times
National Basketball Association
Smithsonian Institution
Sotheby's
The White House
Wolf Trap Foundation for the Performing Arts

PUBLIC POLICY
American Enterprise Institute
American Foundation for AIDS Research
Association of Trial Lawyers of America
The Brookings Institution
The Carter Center
The Coro Foundation
The Environmental Careers Organization
Environmental Protection Agency
The Feminist Majority

National Audubon Society
National Wildlife Federation
Surfrider Foundation
United Nations Association of the United States of America
Urban Fellows/Government Scholars Programs
Washington Internships for Students in Engineering
The White House

PUBLIC RELATIONS/MARKETING
Academy of Television Arts & Sciences
American Enterprise Institute
Apple Computer
Association of Trial Lawyers of America
Bertelsmann Music Group
Boeing
Brookfield Zoo
Butterfield & Butterfield
The Carter Center
Coors Brewing Company
The Walt Disney Studios
Environmental Protection Agency
Frito-Lay
Genentech
Gensler and Associates/Architects
Hallmark Cards
Hewlett-Packard
Hill and Knowlton
Hill, Holliday, Connors, Cosmopulos Advertising
The Kennedy Center
Kraft General Foods
Levi Strauss & Co.
Lucasfilm
The MacNeil/Lehrer NewsHour
Microsoft
MTV: Music Television
National Basketball Association
National Public Radio
Nike
Procter & Gamble
Raychem
Reebok
Rolling Stone
Rosenbluth International
Ruder-Finn
Sony Music Entertainment
Sotheby's
3M

United States Olympic Committee
Volkswagen of America
Weyerhaeuser
The White House
Whitney Museum of American Art
The Widmeyer Group
John Wiley & Sons
Wolf Trap Foundation for the Performing Arts

PUBLIC SERVICE
The Carter Center
The Coro Foundation
Inroads
Urban Fellows/Government Scholars Programs
The White House

PUBLISHING
Random House
John Wiley & Sons

RADIO
See Entertainment/Film/Television

SALES
Abbott Laboratories
Apple Computer
Frito-Lay
Hallmark Cards
Hewlett-Packard
Kraft General Foods
Liz Claiborne

Procter & Gamble
Reebok
Volkswagen of America
Weyerhaeuser
Whitney Museum of American Art

SCIENCE
Abbott Laboratories
American Heart Association
AT&T Bell Laboratories
Center for Talented Youth
Central Intelligence Agency
Coors Brewing Company
The Environmental Careers Organization
Environmental Protection Agency
Federal Bureau of Investigation
Genentech
Inroads
Kraft General Foods
Robert Mondavi Winery
National Aeronautics and Space Administration
National Institutes of Health
National Tropical Botanical Garden
Raychem
3M
Weyerhaeuser

SPORTS
Coors Brewing Company (Wellness Center/
    Recreation)
Los Angeles Times
National Basketball Association
Nike
Reebok
Rosenbluth International
United States Olympic Committee
The Washington Post

TEACHING/EDUCATION
Association of Trial Lawyers of America
Aspen Center for Environmental Studies
Brookfield Zoo
Center for Talented Youth
Crow Canyon
Frontier Nursing Service
The Kennedy Center
Lincoln Center for the Performing Arts
The Metropolitan Museum of Art
Phillips Academy
Smithsonian Institution
Summerbridge National
Urban Fellows/Government Scholars Programs
Whitney Museum of American Art
Wolf Trap Foundation for the Performing Arts

TELEVISION
See Entertainment/Film/Television

THEATER
See Performing Arts/Theater

TRAVEL MANAGEMENT
Rosenbluth International

WINE
Robert Mondavi Winery

ZOOKEEPING
Brookfield Zoo
Smithsonian Institution

INTERNSHIPS BY LOCATION

ALABAMA
Boeing
Environmental Careers Organization
Inroads
National Aeronautics and Space Administration
Procter & Gamble
3M
Weyerhaeuser

ALASKA
Environmental Careers Organization

ARIZONA
Frito-Lay
Inroads
Intel
National Audubon Society
Procter & Gamble
3M

ARKANSAS
American Heart Association
Environmental Careers Organization
Procter & Gamble
3M
Weyerhaeuser

CALIFORNIA
Academy of Television Arts & Sciences
American Conservatory Theater
American Heart Association
Apple Computer
Arthur Andersen
Bertelsmann Music Group
Butterfield & Butterfield
Center for Investigative Reporting
Center for Talented Youth
Citibank
The Coro Foundation
The Walt Disney Studios
Elite Model Management
Environmental Careers Organization
Environmental Protection Agency
The Feminist Majority

Frito-Lay
Genentech
Gensler and Associates/Architects
Hallmark Cards
Hewlett-Packard
Inroads
Intel
The LEK/Alcar Consulting Group
Levi Strauss & Co.
Los Angeles Times
Lucasfilm
Robert Mondavi Winery
National Aeronautics and Space Administration
National Audubon Society
Procter & Gamble
Raychem
Reebok
Summerbridge National
Surfrider Foundation
3M
Weyerhaeuser

COLORADO
Arthur Andersen
Aspen Center for Environmental Studies
Bertelsmann Music Group
Coors Brewing Company
Crow Canyon Archaeological Center
Environmental Protection Agency
Gensler and Associates/Architects
Hewlett-Packard
Inroads
The MacNeil/Lehrer NewsHour
Procter & Gamble
3M
United States Olympic Committee

CONNECTICUT
American Heart Association
Arthur Andersen
Environmental Careers Organization
Inroads
National Audubon Society
Summerbridge National
Whitney Museum of American Art

DELAWARE
American Heart Association
Environmental Careers Organization
Hewlett-Packard

FLORIDA
American Heart Association
Arthur Andersen
Bertelsmann Music Group
Elite Model Management
Environmental Careers Organization
Environmental Protection Agency
Inroads
National Aeronautics and Space Administration
National Audubon Society
Procter & Gamble
Summerbridge National

GEORGIA
American Heart Association
Arthur Andersen
Bertelsmann Music Group
The Carter Center
Citibank
Elite Model Management
Environmental Careers Organization
Environmental Protection Agency
Frito-Lay
Hallmark Cards
Hewlett-Packard
Inroads
Procter & Gamble
Reebok
3M
The Wall Street Journal

HAWAII
Environmental Careers Organization
National Tropical Botanical Garden
Procter & Gamble

IDAHO
Environmental Careers Organization
Hewlett-Packard

ILLINOIS
Abbott Laboratories
American Heart Association
Arthur Andersen
Bertelsmann Music Group
Brookfield Zoo
Citibank
Elite Model Management
Environmental Careers Organization
Environmental Protection Agency
Frito-Lay
Hallmark Cards
Inroads
Kraft General Foods
The LEK/Alcar Consulting Group
Procter & Gamble
Reebok
3M
The Wall Street Journal

INDIANA
American Heart Association
Arthur Andersen
Environmental Careers Organization
Inroads
Procter & Gamble
3M

IOWA
American Heart Association
Procter & Gamble
3M

KANSAS
Boeing
Environmental Protection Agency
Hallmark Cards
Procter & Gamble

KENTUCKY
Environmental Careers Organization
Frontier Nursing Service
National Audubon Society
Procter & Gamble
Summerbridge National
3M

LOUISIANA
American Heart Association
Arthur Andersen
Environmental Careers Organization
Inroads
Procter & Gamble
Summerbridge National

MAINE
Environmental Careers Organization
National Audubon Society

MARYLAND
Center for Talented Youth
Environmental Careers Organization
Inroads
National Aeronautics and Space Administration
National Institutes of Health
Procter & Gamble
3M
The Washington Post

MASSACHUSETTS
Arthur Andersen
Bertelsmann Music Group
Center for Talented Youth
Environmental Careers Organization
Environmental Protection Agency
Hewlett-Packard
Hill, Holliday, Connors, Cosmopulos Advertising
Inroads
The LEK/Alcar Consulting Group
Phillips Academy
Procter & Gamble
Reebok
Summerbridge National
3M

MICHIGAN
Arthur Andersen
Bertelsmann Music Group
Environmental Careers Organization
Environmental Protection Agency
Inroads
Procter & Gamble
3M
United States Olympic Committee
Volkswagen of America
Weyerhaeuser

MINNESOTA
Arthur Andersen
Bertelsmann Music Group
Environmental Protection Agency
Inroads
Procter & Gamble
3M

MISSISSIPPI
National Aeronautics and Space Administration

MISSOURI
American Heart Association
Arthur Andersen
Bertelsmann Music Group
The Coro Foundation
Hallmark Cards
Inroads
Summerbridge National
3M

NEBRASKA
American Heart Association
Arthur Andersen
3M

NEVADA
Environmental Protection Agency

NEW HAMPSHIRE
American Heart Association
Environmental Careers Organization
Hewlett-Packard
Summerbridge National

NEW JERSEY
American Heart Association
Arthur Andersen
AT&T Bell Laboratories
Environmental Careers Organization
Hewlett-Packard
Inroads
Liz Claiborne
National Basketball Association
Procter & Gamble
3M

NEW MEXICO
Intel
National Audubon Society

NEW YORK
American Heart Association
Arthur Andersen
Bertelsmann Music Group
Backer Spielvogel Bates
Center for Talented Youth
Citibank
The Coro Foundation
Elite Model Management
Environmental Careers Organization
Environmental Protection Agency
Forty Acres and a Mule Filmworks
Gensler and Associates/Architects
Hallmark Cards
Hill and Knowlton
Inroads
Kraft General Foods
Late Show with David Letterman
Lincoln Center for the Performing Arts
Liz Claiborne
The MacNeil/Lehrer NewsHour
Marvel Comics
The Metropolitan Museum of Art
JP Morgan & Co.
MTV: Music Television
National Audubon Society
National Basketball Association
Procter & Gamble
Random House
Rolling Stone
Ruder-Finn
Sony Music Entertainment
Sotheby's
Sponsors for Educational Opportunity
Spy
Summerbridge National
TBWA
3M
United Nations Association of the United States of
America
United States Olympic Committee
Urban Fellows/Government Scholars Programs
The Wall Street Journal
Whitney Museum of American Art
John Wiley & Sons

NORTH CAROLINA

American Heart Association
Arthur Andersen
Bertelsmann Music Group
Environmental Careers Organization
Environmental Protection Agency
Inroads
Procter & Gamble
3M
Weyerhaeuser

NORTH DAKOTA

American Heart Association
3M

OHIO

American Heart Association
Arthur Andersen
Environmental Careers Organization
Inroads
National Aeronautics and Space Administration
Procter & Gamble
Summerbridge National
3M

OKLAHOMA

American Heart Association
Environmental Careers Organization
Environmental Protection Agency
3M
Weyerhaeuser

OREGON

American Heart Association
Bertelsmann Music Group
Environmental Careers Organization
Environmental Protection Agency
Hewlett-Packard
Intel
Nike
Procter & Gamble
Summerbridge National
3M
Weyerhaeuser

PENNSYLVANIA

American Heart Association
AT&T Bell Laboratories
Arthur Andersen
Bertelsmann Music Group
Boeing
Center for Talented Youth
Environmental Careers Organization
Environmental Protection Agency
Inroads
Procter & Gamble
Rosenbluth International
Summerbridge National

RHODE ISLAND

Environmental Careers Organization
Summerbridge National

SOUTH CAROLINA

National Audubon Society
Procter & Gamble
3M

SOUTH DAKOTA

3M

TENNESSEE

Arthur Andersen
Environmental Careers Organization
The Hermitage
Inroads
Procter & Gamble

TEXAS

American Heart Association
Arthur Andersen
Bertelsmann Music Group
Citibank
Environmental Careers Organization
Environmental Protection Agency
Frito-Lay
Gensler and Associates/Architects
Inroads
National Aeronautics and Space Administration
Procter & Gamble
3M
The Wall Street Journal

UTAH
3M

VERMONT
Environmental Careers Organization

VIRGINIA
American Heart Association
Central Intelligence Agency
Federal Bureau of Investigation
Inroads
National Aeronautics and Space Administration
Procter & Gamble
The Washington Post
Wolf Trap Foundation for the Performing Arts

WASHINGTON
American Heart Association
Arthur Andersen
Bertelsmann Music Group
Boeing
Environmental Careers Organization
Environmental Protection Agency
Hewlett-Packard
Microsoft
Procter & Gamble
3M
Weyerhaeuser

WEST VIRGINIA
Inroads
3M

WASHINGTON, D.C.
American Enterprise Institute
Arthur Andersen
Association of Trial Lawyers of America
Bertelsmann Music Group
The Brookings Institution
Central Intelligence Agency
Environmental Careers Organization
Environmental Protection Agency
Federal Bureau of Investigation
The Feminist Majority
Gensler and Associates/Architects
Inroads
The Kennedy Center
The Library of Congress
Los Angeles Times
The MacNeil/Lehrer NewsHour
National Audubon Society
National Public Radio
National Wildlife Federation
Nightline
Smithsonian Institution
Supreme Court of the United States
The Wall Street Journal
Washington Internships for Students of Engineering
The Washington Post
The White House
The Widmeyer Group

WISCONSIN
American Heart Association
Arthur Andersen
Frito-Lay
Inroads
National Audubon Society
Procter & Gamble
3M
Weyerhaeuser

WYOMING
National Audubon Society

WE WANT TO HEAR FROM YOU!

Please tell us about your internship experience. If you've participated in one of the programs listed in *America's Top 100 Internships*, tell us how it compares with our description. If your program's not in the book, tell us why it deserves to be a "Top 100 Internship." Then mail this form (feel free to attach additional sheets if necessary) to the address listed below. Thanks!

Name of organization: _____

City in which internship is located: _____

Phone number and contact person (if available): _____
_____

What did you do?:_____
_____
_____
_____

Describe any extracurricular activities (seminars, field trips, etc.) and perks: _____
_____
_____
_____

Your name: _____

Phone: _____

School: _____

Year in school during internship: _____

■ **America's Top 100 Internships**
Ansonia Station
P.O. Box 463
New York, N.Y. 10023

Mark Oldman graduated in 1992 with a B.A. and M.A. in English from Stanford University. At Stanford, he taught an undergraduate seminar on the U.S. Supreme Court, ran the Stanford Wine Circle, and spent a term at Oxford University. He has completed internships in government, law, television, music, and advertising.

Samer Hamadeh graduated in 1992 with a B.S. in Chemistry and an M.S. in Chemical Engineering from Stanford University. At Stanford, he managed his own printing company, played rugby, and served a teaching assistantship in the Chemistry Department. He has served internships in engineering, management consulting, and public policy.